Pro Web 2.0 Mashups
Remixing Data and Web Services

Raymond Yee

Apress®

Pro Web 2.0 Mashups: Remixing Data and Web Services

Copyright © 2008 by Raymond Yee

ISBN-13 (pbk): 978-1-59059-858-0

ISBN-10 (pbk): 1-59059-858-X

ISBN-13 (electronic): 978-1-4302-0286-8

ISBN-10 (electronic): 1-4302-0286-6

Printed and bound in the United States of America 9 8 7 6 5 4 3 2 1

Trademarked names may appear in this book. Rather than use a trademark symbol with every occurrence of a trademarked name, we use the names only in an editorial fashion and to the benefit of the trademark owner, with no intention of infringement of the trademark.

Lead Editor: Matthew Moodie
Technical Reviewer: John Watson
Editorial Board: Clay Andres, Steve Anglin, Ewan Buckingham, Tony Campbell, Gary Cornell,
    Jonathan Gennick, Kevin Goff, Matthew Moodie, Joseph Ottinger, Jeffrey Pepper, Frank Pohlmann,
    Ben Renow-Clarke, Dominic Shakeshaft, Matt Wade, Tom Welsh
Project Manager: Richard Dal Porto
Copy Editor: Kim Wimpsett
Associate Production Director: Kari Brooks-Copony
Production Editors: Laura Esterman, Lori Bring
Compositor: Kinetic Publishing Service, LLC
Proofreader: Liz Welch
Indexer: Broccoli Information Management
Cover Designer: Kurt Krames
Manufacturing Director: Tom Debolski

Distributed to the book trade worldwide by Springer-Verlag New York, Inc., 233 Spring Street, 6th Floor, New York, NY 10013. Phone 1-800-SPRINGER, fax 201-348-4505, e-mail orders-ny@springer-sbm.com, or visit http://www.springeronline.com.

For information on translations, please contact Apress directly at 2855 Telegraph Avenue, Suite 600, Berkeley, CA 94705. Phone 510-549-5930, fax 510-549-5939, e-mail info@apress.com, or visit http://www.apress.com.

Apress and friends of ED books may be purchased in bulk for academic, corporate, or promotional use. eBook versions and licenses are also available for most titles. For more information, reference our Special Bulk Sales–eBook Licensing web page at http://www.apress.com/info/bulksales.

The information in this book is distributed on an "as is" basis, without warranty. Although every precaution has been taken in the preparation of this work, neither the author(s) nor Apress shall have any liability to any person or entity with respect to any loss or damage caused or alleged to be caused directly or indirectly by the information contained in this work.

The source code for this book is available to readers at http://www.apress.com. You may need to answer questions pertaining to this book in order to successfully download the code.

For Laura, the love of my life

Contents at a Glance

PART 1 ■■■ Remixing Information Without Programming

PART 2 ■■■ Remixing a Single Web Application Using Its API

PART 3 ■■■ Making Mashups

PART 4 ■■■ Exploring Other Mashup Topics

Contents

PART 1 ■■■ Remixing Information Without Programming

PART 2 ■ ■ ■ Remixing a Single Web Application Using Its API

PART 3 ■ ■ ■ Making Mashups

PART 4 ■■■ Exploring Other Mashup Topics

About the Author

 **RAYMOND YEE** is a data architect, consultant, and trainer. He is currently a lecturer at the School of Information, UC Berkeley, where he teaches the course "Mixing and Remixing Information." While earning a PhD in biophysics, he taught computer science, philosophy, and personal development to K–11 students in the Academic Talent Development Program on the Berkeley campus. He is the primary architect of the Scholar's Box, software that enables users to gather digital content from multiple sources to create personal collections that can be shared with others. As a software architect and developer, he focuses on developing software to support learning, teaching, scholarship, and research.

Raymond is an erstwhile tubaist, admirer of J. S. Bach, Presbyterian elder, aspiring essayist, son of industrious Chinese-Canadian restaurateurs, and devoted husband of the incomparable Laura.

About the Technical Reviewer

JOHN WATSON is a professional freelance software developer and has been creating web-based software since 1994. He is best known on Flickr for fd's Flickr Toys (Bighugelabs.com), a popular collection of free photo manipulation utilities that use various APIs from Flickr, Google, and Yahoo! John is married and living happily in southern California with his wife and two young children. You can find out more about John and his recent projects at http://watson-net.com.

Acknowledgments

I'm deeply thankful to those who provided detailed feedback to parts of my manuscript: Jason Cooper, Andres Ferrate, Michael Kaply, John Musser, Paul Rademacher, Jon Udell, and C. K. Yuan. John Musser graciously provided access to some data from Programmableweb.com.

I would never have written this book without the inspiration I drew from my former colleagues at UC Berkeley. I want to particularly thank Chris Ashley, Isaac Mankita, and Susan Stone, who helped me persevere by listening patiently to my exuberant book talk over lunch or tea. Thom King and Tom Schirmer generously shared their knowledge of data architecture and software development. Shifra Gaman and Rich Meyer provided tons of technical and moral support. Thanks to David Greenbaum for his supportive attitude toward my teaching work and to Rick Jaffe, a colleague who took my class and who has been tirelessly championing my teaching to others. Sara Leavitt and Aron Roberts generously helped me learn about iCalendar and the Berkeley Events Calendar.

The School of Information at UC Berkeley has been an important intellectual home for the past several years. I'm grateful for the opportunity to teach my course "Mixing and Remixing Information" and the collegiality of the faculty and staff. Most of all, I want to thank my students, who gave me their attention and created wonderful projects and in turn inspired me. Thanks also to my teenage summer students for creating their mashup projects in a six-week sprint and teaching me about music mashups.

Thanks to the many people at Apress who made this book a much better product than what I alone could have written. In addition to consistently savvy editorial judgment, Matt Moodie provided me with just the right amount of encouragement in the last months of writing. Richard Dal Parto provided able project management, while Grace Wong pinch-hit in that capacity. Thanks also to production editors Laura Esterman and Lori Bring, senior production editor Kelly Winquist, and copy editor Kim Wimpsett for their work in turning code and text into a publishable form. I'm grateful to Tina Nielsen who was one of the first people I dealt with at Apress. A special thanks goes to Chris Mills, who, as my first editor, got me off to a solid start in the writing process with his enthusiasm and detailed feedback.

I learned much from the insightful comments of John Watson, who served as technical reviewer, as well as from his very cool Flickr mashups!

I would like to thank my friends, who were excited for me and cheered me on. My family, as always, was there for me; thank you so much for loving me and believing in me as I took on this huge project.

And finally, I thank my wife, Laura, for everything she did for me while I wrote this book: her love, encouraging words, and wise counsel; her listening to my ideas-in-process; her editing; and her sacrificial willingness to free up time for me to write. It's time for us to take that long-postponed vacation!

Introduction

How many times have you seen a web site and said, "This would be exactly what I wanted—if only . . ." If only you could combine the statistics here with data from your company's earnings projections. If only you could take the addresses for those restaurants and plot them on one map. How often have you entered the date of a concert into your calendar with a single click instead of retyping? How often do you wish that you could make all the different parts of your digital world—your e-mail, your word processor documents, your photos, your search results, your maps, your presentations—work together more seamlessly? After all, it's all digital and malleable information—shouldn't it all just fit together?

In fact, below the surface, all the data, web sites, and applications you use could fit together. This book teaches you how to forge those latent connections—to make the Web your own—by remixing information to create your own mashups. A *mashup*, in the words of the Wikipedia, is a web site or web application "that seamlessly combines content from more than one source into an integrated experience."[1] Learning how to draw content from the Web together into new integrated interfaces and applications, whether for yourself or for other others, is the central concern of this book.

Let's look at a few examples to see how people are remixing data and services to make something new and useful:

- Housingmaps.com brings together Google Maps and the housing and rental listings from Craigslist.com. Note that it was invented by neither Google nor Craigslist but by an individual programmer, Paul Radamacher. Housingmaps.com adds to the functionality of Craigslist, which will show you on a map where a specific listing is located but not all the rentals or houses in an area.[2]

- Google Maps in Flickr (GMiF) brings together Flickr pictures, Google Maps, Google Earth, and the Firefox browser via Greasemonkey.[3]

- The Library Lookup bookmark is a JavaScript bookmarklet that connects Amazon.com and your local library catalog.[4]

---

1. http://en.wikipedia.org/wiki/Mashup_(web_application_hybrid), accessed as
   http://en.wikipedia.org/w/index.php?title=Mashup_%28web_application_hybrid%29&oldid=98002063

2. http://housingmaps.com/

3. http://webdev.yuan.cc/gmif/

4. http://weblog.infoworld.com/udell/stories/2002/12/11/librarylookup.html

To create your own mashups and customize the Web, you will look at these examples in greater detail, in addition to many other examples large and small, in this book. You can solve countless specific problems by remixing information. Here are some examples of techniques you will learn in this book:

- Taking a book you found on Amazon.com and instantly locating it in your local library

- Synthesizing a single news feed from many news sources through Yahoo! Pipes

- Posting Flickr photos to blogs with a click of a button

- Displaying your photos in Google Maps and Google Earth

- Using special extensions to Firefox to learn how to program Google Maps

- Inserting extra information into web pages with Greasemonkey

- Plotting stories from your favorite news source (such as the *New York Times*) on a map

- Making your own web site remixable so that others can create mashups from your content

- Creating Google calendars from your event calendars from the Web

- Storing and retrieving your files from online storage (S3)

- Creating an online spreadsheet from your Amazon.com wishlist

- Recognizing and manipulating data embedded in web pages

- Adding an event listed on the Web to your calendar and e-mailing it to other people with one mouse click

- Building web search functionality into your own web applications

- Republishing word documents that are custom-formatted for your web site

Mashups are certainly hot right now, which is interesting because it makes you part of a shared undertaking, a movement. Mashups are fun and often educational. There's delight in seeing familiar things brought together to create something new that is greater than the sum of its parts. Some mashups don't necessarily ask to be taken that seriously. And yet mashups are also powerful—you can get a lot of functionality without a lot of effort. They might not be built to last forever, but you often can get what you need from them without having to invest more effort than you want to in the first place.

The Web 2.0 Movement

The Web 2.0 bandwagon is an important reason why mashups are popular now. Mashups have been identified explicitly (under the phrases "remixable data source" and "the right to remix") by Tim O'Reilly in "What is Web 2.0?"[5] Added to this, we have the development of what might be accurately thought of as "Web 2.0 technologies/mind-sets" to remix/reuse data, web services,

---

5. http://www.oreillynet.com/pub/a/oreilly/tim/news/2005/09/30/what-is-web-20.html

and micro-applications to create hybrid applications. Recent developments bring us closer to enabling users to recombine digital content and services:

- Increasing availability of XML data sources and data formats in business, personal, and consumer applications (including office suites)

- Wide deployment of XML web services

- Widespread current interest in data remixing or mashups

- Ajax and the availability of JavaScript-based widgets and micro-applications

- Evolution of web browsers to enable greater extensibility (for example, Firefox extensions and Greasemonkey scripts)

- Explosive growth in "user-generated content" or "lead-user innovation"

- Wider conceptualization of the Internet as a platform ("Web 2.0")

- Increased broadband access

These developments have transformed creating mashups from being technically challenging to nearly mainstream. It is not that difficult to get going, but you need to know a bit about a fair number of things, and you need to be playful and somewhat adventurous.

Will mashups remain cutting-edge forever? Undoubtedly, no, but not because they will prove to be an irrelevant fad but because the functionality we see in mashups will eventually be subsumed into the ordinary "what-we-expect-and-think-has-always-been-there" functionality of our electronic society.

Moreover, mashups reflect deeper trends, even the deepest trends of human desire. As the quality, quantity, and diversity of information grow, users long for tools to access and manage this bewildering array of information. Many users will ultimately be satisfied by nothing less than an information environment that gives them seamless access to any digital content source, handles any content type, and applies any software service to this content. Consider, for example, what a collection of bloggers expressed as their desires for next-generation blogging tools:[6]

> *Bloggers want tools that are utterly simple and allow them to blog everything that they can think, in any format, from any tool, from anywhere. Text is just the beginning: Bloggers want to branch out to multiple media types including rich and intelligent use of audio, photos, and video. With input, having a dialog box is also seen as just a starting place for some bloggers: everything from a visual tool to easy capture of things a blogger sees, hears, or reads point to desirable future user interfaces for new generations of blogging tools.*

Mashups are starting to forge this sought-after access and integration of data and tools—not only in the context of blogging but also to any point of interaction between users and content.

---

6. http://www.cadence90.com/blogs/2004_03_01_nixon_archives.html#107902918872392913

Overall Flow of the Book

A central question of this book is, how can both nontechnical end users and developers recombine data and Internet services to create something new for their own use for and for others? Although this book focuses primarily on XML, web services, and the wide variety of web applications, I'll also cover the role played by desktop applications and operating systems.

The Book's Structure

The following is a breakdown of the parts and chapters in this book:

- **Part 1**, "Remixing Information Without Programming," introduces mashups without demanding programming skills from you and teaches skills for deconstructing applications for their remix potential.

  - Chapter 1, "Learning from Specific Mashups," analyzes in detail a selection of mashups/remixes (specifically, Housingmaps.com, Google Maps in Flickr, and the LibraryLookup bookmarklet) to get you oriented to mashups in general and to some general themes we will continually revisit throughout the book.

  - Chapter 2, "Uncovering the Mashup Potential of Web Sites," analyzes Flickr (as our primary extended example) for what makes it the remix platform *par excellence* for learning how to remix a specific application and exploit features that make it so remixable. We compare and contrast Flickr with other remixable platforms such as del.icio.us, Google Maps, and Amazon.com.

  - Chapter 3, "Understanding Tagging and Folksonomies," covers tagging. Tagging, which allows users to attach words to pictures, and websites—almost anything on the Web—is the glue that holds many things together, both within and across websites. This chapter illustrates how tags are used in Flickr, del.icio.us, and Technorati and discusses how to create interesting tag-centric mashups, how people are "hacking" the tagging system to create ad hoc databases, and how tags relate to other classification systems.

  - Chapter 4, "Working with Feeds, RSS, and Atom," presents RSS and Atom, perhaps the most widespread dialects of XML, as both a potent technology for remixing in its own right and also as a specific way to learn about XML more generally. Not to be missed are the sections on the various RSS/Atom-related formats and their significance for information remix. The chapter includes a tutorial on using Yahoo! Pipes to filter and synthesize feeds.

  - Chapter 5, "Integrating with Blogs," uses Flickr's integration with weblogs as a jumping-off point for an exploration of weblogs and wikis and their programmability. Integration with blogging is an important topic since blogs represent a type of remixing in a narrative, as opposed to data-oriented remixing via tags and the straight RSS so far discussed. A brief discussion of integration with wikis concludes the chapter.

- **Part 2**, "Remixing a Single Web Application Using Its API," concentrates on teaching the broad classes of web-based APIs by studying exemplars of each class.

  - Chapter 6, "Learning Web Services APIs Through Flickr," studies Flickr in detail. In addition to be an exemplar for a range of nonprogramming remixing techniques in Part 1, Flickr is also an excellent playground for learning XML web services. This chapter will show you how to use the Flickr API, looking first at how to make a simple call to the API, next looking at how to make sense of the entire variety of calls available, and then generalizing to handle authentication.

  - Chapter 7, "Exploring Other Web APIs," explains commonalities and contrasts among various API providers, specifically those between Flickr and other systems, and surveys the types of services available and how to think about the sheer range of APIs. You will learn how to call REST, XML-RPC, and SOAP-based services. This chapter looks at sites, such as Programmableweb.com, that document these various APIs and the challenges faced in doing so.

  - Chapter 8, "Learning Ajax/JavaScript Widgets and Their APIs," describes the other large class of web application remixability: those of JavaScript-based widgets, many of which are Ajax applications. This chapter contrasts old-style web applications with Ajax approaches through specific examples in Flickr and other applications and introduces the Yahoo! UI Library, a specific JavaScript widget library to demonstrate how to program widgets. You will also learn how to use the Firebug Firefox extension and the JavaScript Shell to learn about JavaScript. The chapter concludes with an introduction to using Greasemonkey.

- **Part 3**, "Making Mashups," is the heart of the book; it's a discussion of how to use what you learned in Parts 1 and 2 to create mashups.

  - Chapter 9, "Moving from APIs and Remixable Elements to Mashups," analyzes mashups and their relationship to APIs through studying a series of specific problems for which mashups can provide useful solutions. The chapter looks at how you can track books, real estate, airfare, and current events by combining various APIs. You will learn how to use Programmableweb.com to analyze these problems.

  - Chapter 10, "Creating Mashups of Several Services," teaches you how to write mashups by providing a detailed example that you'll build from the ground up: a mashup of geotagged Flickr photos and Google Maps using first the Google Maps API and then the Google Mapplets API.

  - Chapter 11, "Using Tools to Create Mashups," discusses tools that have been developed to make creating mashups easier than by using traditional web programming techniques. This chapter walks you through using one of these tools—the Google Mashup Editor—and briefly surveys other tools.

  - Chapter 12, "Making Your Web Site Mashable," shifts the focus of the book briefly from the consumption to the production of data and APIs. This chapter is a guide to content producers who want to make their web sites friendly to mashups. That is, this chapter answers the question, how would you as a content producer make your digital content most effectively remixable and mashable to users and developers?

- **Part 4**, "Exploring Other Mashup Topics," covers how to remix and integrate specific classes of applications, using the core conceptual framework of Parts 1 to 3 to guide the discussion.

  - Chapter 13, "Remixing Online Maps and 3D Digital Globes," covers popular online maps and virtual globes, offering examples of map-based mashups. You'll learn about making maps without programming and data exchange formats (GeoRSS and KML), and then you'll turn to the various APIs: Google Maps, Yahoo! Maps, and Microsoft Maps. I'll also cover geocoding American and non-American addresses. The chapter closes with a discussion of Google Earth, its relationship to KML, and how to display Flickr photos via KML.

  - Chapter 14, "Exploring Social Bookmarking and Bibliographic Systems," covers how social bookmarking responds to a fundamental challenge—the job of keeping found things found on the Web, which, at a basic level, is done through URLs, but you'll learn about other digital content such as images and data sets. Social bookmarking is interesting not only for the extensibility/remixability being built into these systems but also for the insight it offers into other systems. This chapter walks you through a select set of social bookmarking systems and their APIs, as well as discusses interoperability challenges among these systems. The chapter shows how to create a mashup of Flickr and del.icio.us.

  - Chapter 15, "Accessing Online Calendars and Event Aggregators," shows what data you can get in and out of calendars without programming (using iCalendar and XML feeds), how to program individual calendars (using Google Calendar and 30boxes), and how to program individual event aggregator APIs (using Upcoming.yahoo.com and Eventful.com). The chapter concludes with a mashup of a public events calendar with Google Calendar.

  - Chapter 16, "Using Online Storage Services," surveys the potentially important and growing area of online storage solutions and shows the basics of using Amazon S3.

  - Chapter 17, "Mashing Up Desktop and Web-Based Office Suites," shows how to do some simple parsing in ODF and OpenXML, demonstrates how to create a simple document in both ODF and OpenXML, explains some simple scripting of Microsoft Office and OO.o, and concludes with a mashup of Google Spreadsheets and Amazon.com web services.

  - Chapter 18, "Using Microformats and RDFa As Embeddable Data Formats," studies two answers to the problem of how to embed information in web pages that is easy to understand by both humans and computer programs: microformats and RDFa. You will learn how to use and program the Operator Firefox extension to recognize and manipulate microformats.

  - Chapter 19, "Integrating Search," shows how to use the Google Ajax Search API, Yahoo! Search APIs, and Microsoft Live.com search; the chapter also introduces OpenSearch and the Google Desktop HTTP/XML gateway.

Intended Audience

This book is accessible to a wide range of readers, including those who are curious about Web 2.0 applications and those who want to know more about the technical underpinnings of it. The technical perquisites are a good understanding of HTML, basic CSS, and basic JavaScript. References to appropriate background materials will be provided. In this book, most of the server-side code is presented in PHP. Some code is in Python.

At the same time, experienced developers will also be able to learn much from the book. Although there will be a breadth of coverage, I will strive to state deep, essential facts about the technologies in question (with respect to their applicability to remix)—aspects that might not be obvious at first glance.

Information remixing can easily come across as a confusing grab bag of techniques. Beginners have a hard time understanding the significance of XML, web services, Ajax, COM, and metadata for remixing data. It is not that difficult to get going, but you need to know a bit about a fair number of different topics, and you need to be playful and somewhat adventurous. Usually these topics are found scattered throughout a large selection of books; this book is the guide to show you where to begin.

Updates

Please go to http://mashupguide.net to find updates and supplementary materials for this book.

PART 1

■■■

Remixing Information Without Programming

In Part 1 of this book, we look at how to recombine information without resorting to formal programming techniques. There is much that can be done by carefully examining various web applications from the perspective of an end user looking for integrative opportunities. In Chapter 1, we'll study in detail several specific mashups to get you oriented to mashups and to some general themes that we will continually revisit throughout the book. In Chapter 2, we'll analyze Flickr, a remix platform *par excellence* that we'll study throughout the book, comparing and contrasting it with other remixable platforms, including del.icio.us, Google Maps, and Amazon.com. Chapter 3 shows how user-generated tags are used in Flickr, del.icio.us, and Technorati and discusses how to create interesting tag-centric mashups. Chapter 4 discusses RSS and Atom feeds, perhaps the most widespread dialect of XML, as both a potent technology for sharing information across the Web and as a specific way to learn about XML. Finally, Chapter 5 uses Flickr's integration with weblogs as a jumping-off point for exploring weblogs and wikis and their programmability. Part 1 lays the foundation for the rest of the book, which teaches you how to programmatically create mashups.

■ ■ ■

## CHAPTER 1

Learning from Specific Mashups

Before you set out to build your own mashups, you'll study some specific examples in this chapter. Mashups combine content from more than one source into a new integrated whole. You can understand a specific mashup by answering a number of basic questions:

- What is being combined?

- Why are these elements being combined?

- Where is the remixing or recombination happening?

- How are various elements being combined (that is, first in the interface but also behind the scenes in the technical machinery)?

- How can the mashup be extended?

This chapter will explore three major examples:

- Housingmaps.com

- The Google Maps in Flickr Greasemonkey script

- Jon Udell's LibraryLookup bookmarklet

In this chapter, I will analyze these three examples using the previous questions loosely as a framework. A close study of each of these mashups will be amply rewarded when you start creating your own mashups.

Looking for Patterns in Mashups

One pattern you will see repeated among mashups that link two web sites is the combination of three actions:

1. Data is extracted from a source web site.

2. This data is translated into a form meaningful to the destination web site.

3. The repackaged data is sent to the destination site.

Of course, the details differ among the mashups, but this general pattern holds true, as you will see in the three mashups presented in detail in this chapter. *Where* the remixing actually happens differs in the three mashups you'll see in this chapter: in a separate application as in Housingmaps.com, in Flickr for the Google Maps in Flickr script, and in the browser without a change of interface as in the LibraryLookup bookmarklet.

Although you'll see this pattern of data extraction, translation, and redirection in the mashups covered in this chapter, you'll find other patterns in mashups as well. Chapter 9 will explore those other patterns in detail.

UNDERSTANDING THE TERMINOLOGY

Throughout the book, I use a number of related terms (*mashup*, *remix*, *recombine*, *data*, and *services*) to describe differing aspects of reusing intellectual and creative work to build derivative works. Of course, reuse—whether in the form of artistic appropriation, scholarly attribution, literary quotation and allusion, parody, or satire—has a long history throughout human intellectual, creative, and commercial endeavors. Some terms, such as *reuse* (as in *software reuse* or *code reuse*), have been in popular usage for a while. Others, such as *remix* and *mashup*, have more recently arisen in the context of discussions around Web 2.0 to apply to the combination of data from disparate sources, often via the use of XML and XML web services. In some ways, *mashups* has won out as the term to refer to web interfaces and applications that combine content into something new, whereas the term *remix* is generally about reusing media while still having broader usage (as in *remix culture*).

The boundary between *mashup* and *remix* is a bit fuzzy, though. *Mashup* and *remix* are terms that have their origins in popular music.[1] Roughly speaking, a *remix* is an alternate version of a song, while a *mashup* brings together elements of two or more songs. The term *mashup* has expanded recently to describe the combination of video from multiple sources in a new video.[2] At this point, I will say that if I wanted to make the parallels from popular music hold up for digital applications, I would use *remix* to describe scenarios that are about reusing or repackaging data without combining it with other content (for example, using the Flickr API to make a web page that has only Flickr images), and I would reserve *mashups* to refer to combinations of data from a variety of sources (for example, combining Flickr photos with photos from Picasa). But the lines are fuzzy and, in my opinion, not worth the effort to draw too carefully.

Broadly speaking, I focus in this book on software mashups, mostly but not exclusively on web mashups that are remixing data and services. By *data*, I mean any digital content, whether it is on a computer network, on your computer, or on any other device. By *services*, I roughly mean services as in service-oriented architecture and software as a service, meaning web services and any applications that can be reused.

Whereas mashups are strongly associated with Web 2.0, parallel developments going under such names as *composite applications* are occurring in enterprise computing and service-oriented architectures. Composite applications are also concerned with weaving together data and services, though they usually integrate corporate data and supply chains sitting behind firewalls instead of public APIs from Google and Amazon. Although mashups and composite applications share common techniques, they are driven by vastly different cultural factors.

This book focuses on personal information instead of information reuse from an enterprise perspective. Personal information is distinct for its heterogeneity, its connection to personal information management, the need for mass customizability, and the many permutations of hardware, software, and data derived from the unique needs of individuals. Nonetheless, if there are opportunities to draw upon synergies with enterprise Web 2.0 without going far afield, I will do so here.

---

1. http://en.wikipedia.org/wiki/Mashup_%28music%29 and http://en.wikipedia.org/wiki/Remix
2. http://en.wikipedia.org/wiki/Mashup_%28video%29

Housingmaps.com

When I explain mashups to others, I typically use the example of the web site Housingmaps.com, a mashup of Craigslist and Google Maps. Housingmaps.com is useful in ways that are quick and easy to understand, which invites repeated usage. It also requires no software beyond a modern web browser. Moreover, Housingmaps.com takes two already well-known web applications to create something new.

Figure 1-1 shows Housingmaps.com displaying a specific rental listing. Note the photos of the apartment and the links to Craigslist. All the data is drawn from Craigslist and then displayed in a Google map.

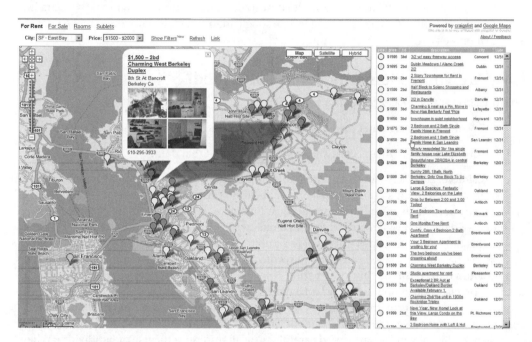

Figure 1-1. *Housingmaps.com*

What Is Being Combined?

Housingmaps.com takes the list of houses, apartments, and rooms that are for sale or rent from Craigslist and displays them on a Google map. Note that it was invented by neither Google nor Craigslist but by an individual programmer, Paul Rademacher, who, at the time of its invention, was working for neither Google nor Craigslist but who was later hired by Google.

Why Are the Constituent Elements Being Combined? What's the Problem Being Solved?

Craigslist provides links to Google Maps and Yahoo! Maps for any individual real estate listing, but it does not map the listings collectively. The single listing per map on the Craigslist interface makes it a challenge to mentally track the location of all the properties. Moreover, when looking for real estate, you often want to look at a narrowly defined neighborhood or find houses with good access to transit. With Craigslist, you have to click many links and manually piece together a lot of maps to focus your search geographically.

Housingmaps.com addresses these challenge by letting you see on a Google map all the Craigslist apartments or houses in a specific area, not just an individual item. At Housingmaps.com, geographical location becomes the primary lens for looking for real estate, with a map as the central element of the user interface.

Where Is the Remixing Happening?

The remixing occurs on the server side on a web site (Housingmaps.com) that is distinct from both the source web site (Craigslist) and the destination application (Google Maps). Data is drawn from the source and transformed into a Google map, which is embedded in web pages at Housingmaps.com.

How Are These Elements Being Combined?

This question really breaks down into two questions:

- How does Housingmaps.com obtain the housing and rental data from Craigslist?

- How does Housingmaps.com create a Google map of that data?

A desirable, and increasingly common, method for mashups to obtain data from a web site is through a web site's publicly available application programming interface (API). An API is designed specifically to facilitate communication between programs, often including the exchange of data. (You will be introduced in detail to APIs in Chapters 6 and 7.)

At this time, Craigslist does not provide a public API but does provide RSS feeds. As I will discuss in Chapter 4, RSS feeds are used to *syndicate*, or transport, information from a web site to a program that *consumes* this information. The RSS feeds, however, do not provide enough detail to precisely position the listings on a map.

Consequently, Housingmaps.com *screen-scrapes* (or *crawls*) Craigslist; that is, Housingmaps.com retrieves and parses the HTML pages of Craigslist to obtain detailed information about each listing. The crawling is performed carefully so as to minimize the use of bandwidth. When you access Housingmaps.com, you are accessing not real-time data from Craigslist but rather the data that has been screen-scraped by Housingmaps.com.

■**Note** Public APIs and RSS feeds are generally preferable to screen-scraping web sites. Screen-scraping, when poorly implemented, can overtax the data source. Always check that you are complying with the terms of service of the data source in how you use the data.

To display the real estate information on a Google map, the current version of Housingmaps.com uses the Google Maps API,[3] which is the official Google-sanctioned way of embedding Google maps in a non-Google-owned web page. (You will look in detail at the Google Maps API in various other places, particularly in Chapter 13.)

---

3. http://www.google.com/apis/maps/

It's interesting to go into a bit of history here to understand the emergence of the mashup phenomenon. When Housingmaps.com first showed up in April 2005, Rademacher was using Google Maps before it had any real API. He deciphered the original JavaScript of Google Maps and figured out how to incorporate Google Maps into Housingmaps.com. During the period between the release of Google Maps on February 8, 2005, and the publication of version 1 of the Google Maps API (on approximately June 29, 2005[4]), there was a period of intense "hacking" of Google Maps, described in the following way by members of the Google Maps team:[5]

> For this and other reasons we were thrilled to see "hackers" have a go at Google Maps almost immediately after we launched the site back in early February. Literally within days, their blogs described the inner workings of our maps more accurately than our own design documents did, and soon the most amazing "hacks" started to appear: Philip Lindsay's Google Maps "stand-alone" mode, Paul Rademacher's [Housingmaps.com], and Chris Smoak's Busmonster, to mention a few.

Comparable Mashups

Since the debut of Housingmaps.com, many other mashups—in fact, tens of thousands—have followed this pattern set of recasting data to make geographical location the organizing principle. These mashups cover an incredible range of topics and interests.[6]

Many other mashups involve extracting geocoded data (location information, often latitude and longitude) from one source to then place it on an online map (such as a Google map or Yahoo! map). I name two prominent examples here:

- Adrian Holovaty's Chicago crime map (`http://chicagocrime.org`), which is a database of crimes reported in Chicago fronted by a Google Map interface

- Weather Bonk, which is a mashup of weather data on a Google map (`http://www.weatherbonk.com/weather/about.jsp`)

Google Maps in Flickr

In the earlier days of Flickr (before August 2006), there was no built-in feature that allowed a user to show pictures on a map. The Google Maps in Flickr (GMiF) script was created to fill in that gap by letting you see a Flickr photo on a Google map. Today, even with Flickr's built-in map of geotagged photos, which uses Yahoo! Maps technology, GMiF remains a valuable mashup. GMiF allows users to use a Google map, which many prefer over Yahoo! Maps, to display their photos. Moreover, GMiF also integrates Google Earth, a feature not currently built into Flickr. GMiF provides an excellent case study of how you can extend an application such as Flickr to fit user preferences.

---

4. `http://benmetcalfe.com/blog/index.php/2005/06/29/google-make-map-api-available-finally/`

5. *Google Maps Hacks* by Rich Gibson and Erle Schuyler (O'Reilly Media, 2006)

6. See `http://googlemapsmania.blogspot.com/` for many new mashups based on Google Maps that appear every day.

What Is Being Combined?

GMiF (http://webdev.yuan.cc/gmif/) brings together Flickr pictures, Google Maps, and Google Earth within the Firefox browser via a Greasemonkey script. I'll break this down for you:

- Flickr (http://flickr.com) is a popular photo-sharing site.

- Google Maps (http://maps.google.com/) is an online mapping system.

- Google Earth (http://earth.google.com/) is a desktop "magic-carpet" interface that lets you pan and zoom around the globe.

- The Firefox web browser (http://www.mozilla.com/firefox/) is an open source web browser. Notable among its features is its extension/add-on architecture, which allows developers to add functionality to the browser.

- The Greasemonkey extension (http://www.greasespot.net/) is a Firefox extension that "allows users to install scripts that make on-the-fly changes to specific web pages. As the Greasemonkey scripts are persistent, the changes made to the web pages are executed every time the page is opened, making them effectively permanent for the user running the script."[7] Greasemonkey scripts allow you—as the user of that web site and not as the author of the web site—to make customizations, all within the web browser.

HOW TO INSTALL THE GMIF SCRIPT

To run the GMiF Greasemonkey script, you must use the Firefox web browser in conjunction with the Greasemonkey add-on and the GMiF script.

Here's how you install GMiF:

1. If you do not already have Firefox installed on your computer, go to http://getfirefox.com, hit the Download Firefox button, and follow the instructions to install it.

2. Now you need to install the Greasemonkey add-on for Firefox, so go to the following URL: https://addons.mozilla.org/en-US/firefox/addon/748.

3. Click the Install Now button. Restart the browser to activate the Greasemonkey add-on.

4. Now you need to install the GMiF Greasemonkey script, so go to the following URL: http://webdev.yuan.cc/gmif/.

5. Click the "Download GM user script: flickr.gmap.user.js (latest version)" link. Click Install when you are asked whether to install the script.

Why Are the Constituent Elements Being Combined? What's the Problem Being Solved?

GMiF is a Greasemonkey script that allows you as a user to display a Flickr picture on a Google map or in Google Earth at the geographic location associated with that picture. GMiF was written

---

7. http://en.wikipedia.org/wiki/Greasemonkey, accessed on January 1, 2007, as http://en.wikipedia.org/w/index.php?title=Greasemonkey&oldid=97588087

to support geotagging in Flickr. *Geotagging*, in the context of Flickr, is the process of associating a location with a given photo, which is typically but not necessarily the location where the photo was taken.

Until geotagging was officially integrated into Flickr with the use of Yahoo! Maps in August 2006,[8] there was no direct way to associate geocoding (location information) with any given picture. Rev Dan Catt catalyzed the mass-geotagging phenomenon by suggesting that Flickr users shoehorn the latitude and longitude information into the tags associated with a photo. Many people took up the practice. The GMiF Greasemonkey script uses that geocoding for a photo.

Let's take a look at how GMiF works. Consider one of my own photos, shown in Figure 1-2 (also available at `http://flickr.com/photos/raymondyee/18389540/`). Notice two things:

- This photo has associated geotagging information (for example, `geo:lat=37.8721`, `geo:lon=-122.257704`, and the tag `geotagged`).

- Note the presence of the rightmost GMap button above the photo. This button is the result of the GMiF script, which inserts the GMap button. In other words, if you do not have the GMiF Greasemonkey script installed, you won't see this button.

Figure 1-2. *The Flickr photo "Campanile in fog" (*`http://flickr.com/photos/raymondyee/18389540/`*) with associated geocoding embedded in the tags. (Reproduced with permission of Yahoo! Inc. ® 2007 by Yahoo! Inc. YAHOO! and the YAHOO! logo are trademarks of Yahoo! Inc.)*

---

8. `http://blog.flickr.com/flickrblog/2006/08/great_shot_wher.html` and `http://blog.flickr.com/flickrblog/2006/08/geotagging_one_.html`

Clicking the GMap button opens a Google map embedded in the Flickr web page, with a pin indicating the location of the picture in question (as shown in Figure 1-3). Note the red pin indicating the location of the photo. The blue pins correlate to other geotagged photos. The map also has a thumbnail of the photo in the upper-right corner.

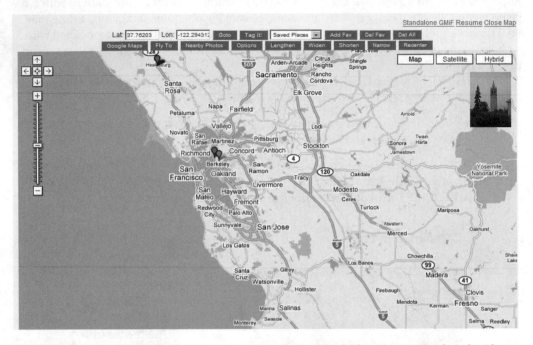

Figure 1-3. *Clicking the GMap button opens a Google map in the browser. (Reproduced with permission of Yahoo! Inc. ® 2007 by Yahoo! Inc. YAHOO! and the YAHOO! logo are trademarks of Yahoo! Inc.)*

Clicking the pin opens a callout with a picture and options of other things to do with the picture. Note how the latitude and longitude listed correspond to the information in the geo:lat and geo:lon tags, respectively (as shown in Figure 1-4).

Figure 1-4. *Clicking the red pin opens a balloon containing the photo and further geotagging functionality offered by GMiF. (Reproduced with permission of Yahoo! Inc. ® 2007 by Yahoo! Inc. YAHOO! and the YAHOO! logo are trademarks of Yahoo! Inc.)*

Among the GMiF functions is integration with Google Earth. If you hit the Fly To button, you will be presented with a file to download. If you have Google Earth installed and it is configured in the default fashion, downloading the file launches Google Earth, and you will be "flown" to the location of the Flickr photo (as shown in Figure 1-5).

Figure 1-5. *Clicking the GMiF Fly To button launches Google Earth, which then displays the photo at the latitude and longitude associated with the photo.*

How Are These Elements Being Combined?

The GMiF Greasemonkey script rewrites the HTML of the Flickr page to insert the GMap button (this rewriting of the HTML DOM is akin to looking in the HTML source for where the Flickr buttons are and inserting HTML code for the button). Furthermore, JavaScript code is added to embed a Google map in the Flickr page, when you (as the user) click the GMap button.

Integration happens in the context of Flickr web page, loaded in the user's browser. Note how powerful this is: you don't have to go to another application to see the picture on a Google map because you get to use a slightly modified version of Flickr. These modifications do not require the intervention of Flickr itself. Hence, there is room for a lot of customization.

■**Note** Of course, there are potential pitfalls with GMiF. GMiF, as with all Greasemonkey scripts, can cease to function if the HTML and JavaScript source of the underlying web page the script operates on changes. Also, with enough Greasemonkey scripts at play, instead of having a strong communal experience of Flickr, users have many different fragmented understandings of the interface. I think these benefits of being able to radically customize your interaction with a web site by actually changing your own version of the interface are worth dealing with these risks.

How is the integration of GMiF with Google Earth created? The downloaded file is a KML file. KML is a dialect of XML, which is the closest thing we have to a *lingua franca* for exchanging data. The KML file contains the latitude and longitude associated with the picture and a URL of the picture. KML is used to exchange geographic type data that is understood by Google Earth. In other words, GMiF takes information from one source (the URL of the picture and the latitude and longitude of the picture embedded in tags from Flickr) and translates that information into a form that is understood by the destination application, namely, KML for Google Earth. Once you translate that information, you still need to get the information to the destination; in this case, the transport happens through the formation and downloading of the KML file.

Admittedly, GMiF is a bit "hackerish," requiring the installation of the Firefox web browser (which does not come by default on Windows or Mac OS X), the Greasemonkey extension, and the GMiF script. But I bring this up here to talk about the lengths to which people are willing to go to experiment with their tools to combine technologies.

Comparable Mashups

Mappr (http://www.mappr.com/), "an interactive environment for exploring place based on the photos people take," is a mashup of Flickr and a Flash-based map.

FORMAL VS. INFORMAL APIS AND INTEGRATION MECHANISMS

I mentioned in previous sections how the proliferation of formal integration mechanisms in the form of APIs and XML feeds, for instance, are giving rise to many more mashups and remixed possibilities. It's important to note that you want to depend on not only these formal mechanisms but also on informal mechanisms. Hence in this book, I'll teach you how to look for both formal and informal mechanisms. The example mashups I describe here use both. I hope to convey to you how to look for those Informal hooks.

LibraryLookup Bookmarklet

Let's say you find a book at an online bookstore (for example, Amazon), but instead of buying the book, you want to borrow it from your local library.

Jon Udell's LibraryLookup bookmarklet[9] makes it easy to jump from the Amazon page to the corresponding catalog entry in your local library catalog—via the simple click of a button. To accomplish the same task without LibraryLookup, you might instead manually re-enter your search in your local library catalog, which is a tedious task if you have to do it for many books.

LibraryLookup is a *bookmarklet*, which is "a small JavaScript program that can be stored as a URL within a bookmark in most popular web browsers or within hyperlinks on a web page."[10] A bookmarklet does not require the Greasemonkey extension in Firefox and works in web browsers other than Firefox. LibraryLookup is, in a manner of speaking, a mashup of online bookstores and library catalogs.

---

9. http://weblog.infoworld.com/udell/stories/2002/12/11/librarylookup.html

10. http://en.wikipedia.org/wiki/Bookmarklets, accessed as http://en.wikipedia.org/w/
    index.php?title=Bookmarklet&oldid=96304211

LibraryLookup is less flashy than previous examples; it's also not server side, like Housingmaps.com. It is client side like the GMiF script, but not in exactly the same way. But it shows another way to create browser-based integration.

Let's look at how LibraryLookup works from the user's point of view. To use the LibraryLookup bookmarklet, you need to do the following:

1. Configure a bookmarklet for the library of your choice.

2. Invoke that bookmarklet when you arrive on a web page for the book you want to look up in your library.

Configuring a LibraryLookup Bookmarklet

Go to the LibraryLookup Bookmarklet Generator at the following URL:

```
http://weblog.infoworld.com/udell/stories/2002/12/11/librarylookupGenerator.html
```

Now enter the base URL and library name, and select the catalog vendor corresponding to your library. Consider, for example, the Berkeley Public Library (BPL). In comparing the BPL OPAC to the examples of vendor online public access catalogs (OPACs) provided by Udell, you can determine that the BPL OPAC is an instance of an Innovative system. When you type in the base URL for the BPL OPAC (`http://www.berkeley-public.org`) and the name of the library (Berkeley Public Library), select Innovative for the vendor (as shown in Figure 1-6), and then hit Submit, you get a bookmarklet that you can then drag to your browser toolbar. The source of the bookmarklet is as follows:

```
javascript:var%20re=/([\/-]|is[bs]n=)(\d{7,9}[\dX])/i;
if(re.test(location.href)==true){var%20isbn=RegExp.$2;
void(win=window.open('http://www.berkeley-public.org'+'/search/i='+isbn,
'LibraryLookup','scrollbars=1,resizable=1,location=1,width=575,height=500'))}
```

■**Note** If your library is not one of the vendors listed by Udell, it is not difficult to take these templates and make them work for libraries with slightly changed systems.

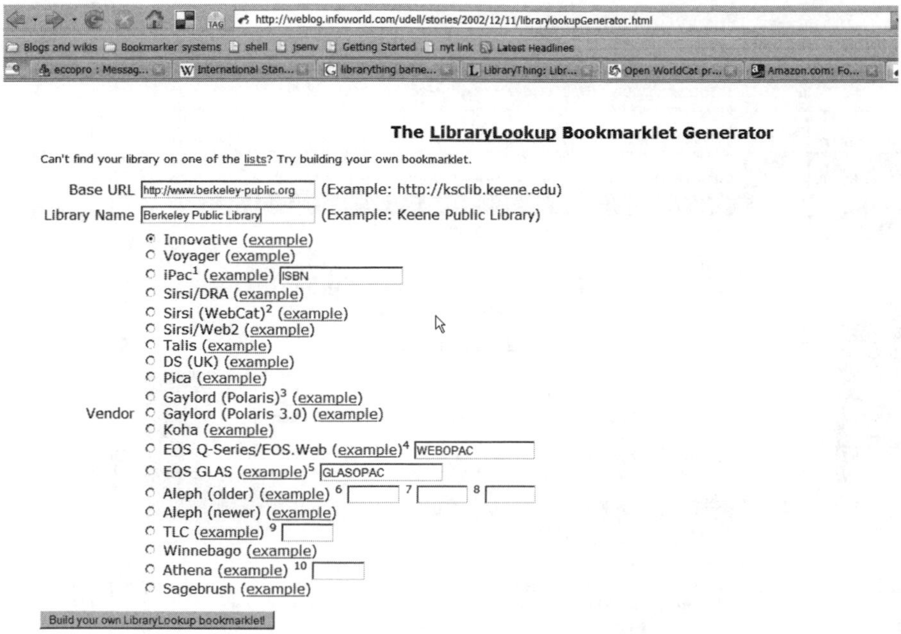

Figure 1-6. *The LibraryLookup Bookmarklet Generator with parameters for the BPL*

Invoking the LibraryLookup Bookmarklet

Let's see this bookmarklet in action. Here I use the LibraryLookup bookmarklet for the BPL, applied to the book *Foundations of Ajax*, which is published by Apress with an ISBN-10 of 1590595823. If you go to the corresponding Amazon page (`http://www.amazon.com/Foundations-Ajax-Foundation-Ryan-Asleson/dp/1590595823/`) and hit the BPL Library-Lookup bookmarklet, you would see a window pop up showing the book in the BPL (see Figure 1-7).

Figure 1-7. *Invoking the LibraryLookup bookmarklet to look up* Foundations of Ajax *at the BPL. (Software copyright Innovative Interfaces, Inc. All rights reserved.)*

How Does This Mashup Work?

The LibraryLookup bookmarklet looks for an ISBN (or ISSN) in the URL of the book-related site to identify the book you want to find. The bookmarklet does the following:

1. It extracts an ISBN from the URL of the library catalog.

2. It repackages the ISBN in a new URL to look up that book in your library catalog.

How Can This Mashup Be Extended?

This bookmarklet has some limitations. If you want to query multiple libraries in your area, you might find it tedious to create the bookmarklet for each of these libraries. One approach is to modify the bookmarklet to send ISBNs to the OCLC Open WorldCat catalog. Here's the corresponding bookmarklet:

```
javascript:var%20re=/([\/-]|is[bs]n=)(\d{7,9}[\dX])/i;
if(re.test(location.href)==true){var%20isbn=RegExp.$2;
void(win=window.open('http://worldcatlibraries.org/wcpa'+'/isbn/'+isbn,
'LibraryLookup','scrollbars=1,resizable=1,width=575,height=500'))}
```

There is a deeper limitation of the LibraryLookup bookmarklet, which you can see through the following example. If you use the BPL bookmarklet to see whether Czesław Miłosz's *New and Collected Poems: 1931–2001* is in the library by first looking it up at Amazon and finding a paperback version at http://www.amazon.com/exec/obidos/ASIN/0060514485 and then invoking the bookmarklet to arrive at http://library.berkeley-public.org/search/i=0060514485, you might be surprised to not turn up the book in question, especially since the Nobel Prize winning poet spent the last 40 years of his life in Berkeley. It turns out that there are indeed copies of Miłosz's book in the BPL, but they are a different edition with a different ISBN (006019667X). See the following URL:

http://library.berkeley-public.org/search/i=006019667X

Different editions of a work have different ISBNs. Furthermore, it's not obvious how to derive the ISBN of related editions.

In recognizing that the LibraryLookup bookmarklet, by using an ISBN to uniquely identify a work, is not able to recognize various editions of a book, Udell has taken a number of different approaches to overcome this limitation, all of which use the OCLC xISBN service, a web service that returns a list of ISBNs that are associated with a submitted ISBN:[11]

- The first is a Greasemonkey script that works on an Amazon page for a book. The script first checks whether Udell's local library has a book with the same ISBN as the Amazon book in question. If not, the script then queries the local library for any of the ISBNs associated with the book, a listed generated by the xISBN service.[12]

- The second extension is a port of the Greasemonkey script (which is tied to Firefox) to something that works in Internet Explorer.[13]

Udell has also worked on another type of mashup between Amazon and a local library: a service that checks your Amazon wish list in order to receive notifications about availability in a Keene, NH library (Udell's local libraries).[14] This service awaits generalizations for multiple OPACs and multiple libraries.

---

11. http://www.worldcat.org/affiliate/webservices/xisbn/app.jsp

12. http://weblog.infoworld.com/udell/2006/01/30.html

13. http://blog.jonudell.net/2007/04/23/greasemonkeying-with-ie/

14. http://elmcity.info/services

Comparable Mashups

BookBurro, in the form of either a Firefox extension or a Greasemonkey script, displays the price of a corresponding book as a pop-up window.[15]

LibraryThing is "an online service to help people catalog their books easily."[16] It is much more than a typical mashup but has elements that are mashup-like—including the thingISBN API[17] described in the following way:

> Today I'm releasing thingISBN, LibraryThing's "answer" to xISBN. Under the hood, xISBN is a test of FRBR, a highly developed, well-thought-out way for librarians to model bibliographic relationships. By contrast, thingISBN is based on LibraryThing's "everyone a librarian" idea of bibliographic modeling. Users "combine" works as they see fit. If they make a mistake, other users can "separate" them. It's a less nuanced and more chaotic way of doing things but can yield some useful results.

William Denton has been experimenting with both xISBN and thingISBN, showing that it might be better to use both services rather than just one.[18]

Tracking Other Mashups

Of course, many mashups exist other than the ones I have highlighted in this chapter. You can always learn more by studying other examples of mashups.

In studying mashups, you will find one web site that is a particularly useful resource: `http://programmableweb.com`. This site is created and managed by John Musser.

I will be referring to Programmableweb.com throughout the book but want to highlight some specific parts here that will help you keep up with mashups:

- The Programmableweb.com blog is a narrative of the latest developments in the world of mashups and APIs.[19]

- The Mashup Dashboard provides an overview of the mashups in the Programmableweb.com database, which as of August 2007, covers more than 2,220 mashups.[20]

Summary

In this chapter, you studied three major examples of mashups: Housingmaps.com, Google Maps in Flickr, and the LibraryLookup bookmarklet. I chose these examples to illustrate some commonalities and differences you will find among mashups. By posing a number of analytic

---

15. `http://bookburro.org/`

16. `http://www.librarything.com/about.php`

17. `http://www.librarything.com/thingology/2006/06/introducing-thingisbn_14.php`

18. `http://www.frbr.org/categories/librarything/`

19. `http://blog.programmableweb.com/`

20. `http://www.programmableweb.com/mashups`

questions (What is being combined? Why are these elements being combined? Where is the remixing or recombination happening? How are they being combined, in terms of the interface and behind the scenes in the technical machinery? How can the mashup be extended?), you saw a repeated pattern:

1. Data is extracted from a source web site.

2. This data is translated into a form meaningful to the destination web site.

3. The repackaged data is sent to the destination site.

There are important differences among the various mashups, specifically in where the integration happens and what is being integrated. For instance, Housingmaps.com is a server-side application, whereas the mashing up of GMiF and LibraryLookup occurs within the browser.

Now that you have a sense of how mashups are constructed and what they are used for, you'll turn now to a study of the individual services and sources of data that can be recombined.

CHAPTER 2

■ ■ ■

Uncovering the Mashup Potential of Web Sites

In the previous chapter, you studied several examples of mashups in depth. With the goal of learning how to create your own mashups, you'll turn now to the raw ingredients of mashups—individual web sites and web applications. Although the focus of this book is on public web application programming interfaces (APIs), you'll first study the human user interface (UI) of web sites for their mashup potential.

Why not jump straight to using APIs if that's what you want to use to create mashups? After all, wouldn't the APIs be the most useful place to begin with since they are especially designed for enabling access to the web site's data and services? What you learn from studying a web site's user interface is useful—even essential—to using APIs effectively. When you exercise a web site's public API, you usually need to understand the overall logic of the web site. For instance, some mashups, such as those created with Greasemonkey (like the Google Maps in Flickr [GMiF] script from Chapter 1), extend the application directly by hooking into and blending with the existing user interface. To create something like GMiF, you would need detailed knowledge of the application you plan to mash up. One of the best ways to uncover potential hooks of a web site is to use the web site as an end user, armed with a developer's sensibility.

Creating mashups doesn't always require much programming. It can be as simple as linking to the right part of an application, accessing the appropriate feed, or connecting the web site to a weblog. In this chapter, I will point out how features created for end users can enable you to create mashups with minimal or no programming.

Flickr is the central example in this chapter, one that I analyze extensively. I follow with Google Maps as an important complementary example. Flickr and Google Maps are among the most mashed up APIs on the Web. I also discuss del.icio.us, a pioneering social bookmarking site, and Amazon, which is an example of an e-commerce platform. In this chapter, I have selected highly remixable applications—as opposed to web sites that are difficult to recombine—as a way to ease into your study of creating mashups.

In this book, I focus mostly on how to use public APIs but briefly mention screen-scraping. APIs often don't do everything you might want from them. Although you can do a lot with public APIs, screen-scraping provides an important alternative or complementary approach. Nonetheless, you should use the API as the first resort. You can screen-scrape if you need to, but always use a web site's computational and network resources respectfully, being mindful of the legal ramifications of what you are doing.

What Makes Web Sites and Applications Mashable

I'll now cover the aspects of web sites and web applications that make them amenable to mashups. Some features are useful regardless of whether you are using the API or whether you are using informal mechanisms for integration. In either case, you are looking for ways to hook into an application. The following sections will help you to analyze a web site for these integration hooks.

UNIDERSTANDING THE TERMINOLOGY

You want to be careful to distinguish different uses of the term *hacking*. When I say you want a site to be *hackable*, I don't mean people should easily be able to break the security elements of the web site. Such activity isn't hacking—that's *cracking*. When you design a site to be hackable, you are designing it to be extensible, even in what you hope to be highly transformative ways. See Eric Raymond's Jargon File web site for a relevant definition of a hacker (http://www.catb.org/jargon/html/H/hacker.html), especially the following:

- "A person who enjoys exploring the details of programmable systems and how to stretch their capabilities"

- "One who enjoys the intellectual challenge of creatively overcoming or circumventing limitations"

Note the deprecated usage: "A malicious meddler who tries to discover sensitive information by poking around. Hence *password hacker*, *network hacker*. The correct term for this sense is *cracker*."

Some people are talking about "designing for hackability" (http://www.brianoberkirch.com/2007/04/03/designing-for-hackability/).

I'm using the term *reverse engineering* to refer to a careful study of a web site, its functionality, and how it's put together. I outline some techniques, but there are more to use. Reverse engineering is a long-honored tradition in this society—but you need to be aware of some of the legal and ethical issues of it. Please refer to http://www.chillingeffects.org/reverse/faq.cgi for some information. (What I write here, of course, is not legal advice on reverse engineering.)

Ascertaining the Fundamental Entities of the Web Site

The basic questions to begin with when analyzing a web site are the following: What is the web site fundamentally about? What are the key entities, or *resources* to borrow a term from W3C parlance? How are these entities or resources associated with specific URLs/URIs? A resource is anything with a URI associated with it. A formal definition of a resource comes from "Uniform Resource Identifier (URI): Generic Syntax" (RFC 3986):[1]

> This specification does not limit the scope of what might be a resource; rather, the term "resource" is used in a general sense for whatever might be identified by a URI. Familiar examples include an electronic document, an image, a source of information with a consistent purpose (e.g., "today's weather report for Los Angeles"), a service (e.g., an HTTP-to-SMS gateway), and a collection of other resources. A resource is not necessarily accessible via the Internet; e.g., human beings, corporations, and bound books in

---

1. http://tools.ietf.org/html/rfc3986#section-1.1

a library can also be resources. Likewise, abstract concepts can be resources, such as the operators and operands of a mathematical equation, the types of a relationship (e.g., "parent" or "employee"), or numeric values (e.g., zero, one, and infinity).

The question of resources and their corresponding URIs are not as abstract as they may sound. In fact, looking at resources may seem rather obvious. For example, for Flickr, which is self-described as "almost certainly the best online photo management and sharing application in the world," important entities are, not surprisingly, photos and users. As you will see later in the chapter, these entities are also resources; you can identify specific photos and users in the URLs produced by Flickr. For example, this URL:

```
http://www.flickr.com/photos/raymondyee/508341822/
```

is for photo 508341822, which belongs to user raymondyee. A Flickr photo is *addressable* via a URL; that is, a URL can lead you right to the photo in question. As experienced users of the Web, we all know the useful things we can do when there are specific URLs. You can bookmark a link, e-mail it, and use it as a reference in a web page. You don't have to tell someone to go to Flickr and type in the photo number to get to the photo.

As you will see later in this chapter, granular URLs also enable mashups. A major part of this chapter is devoted to studying web sites by analyzing their end-user functionality and how it can be seen through its URI structure (*URL language*). In the following sections, I discuss in greater detail notions of addressability, granularity, transparency, and persistence in URLs. I will present a detailed listing of entities and how you can refer to them in URIs for Flickr, as well as a brief analysis of Google Maps, Amazon, and del.icio.us for comparison.

Public APIs and Existing Mashups

Is there a public API for the web site? A web site's public API is specifically designed as the official channel of programmatic access to the data and services of the web site. It essentially lets you access and program the web site almost like a local object or database. For a slightly more formal definition of an API, consider the one by John Musser from Programmableweb.com: "a set of functions that one computer program makes available to other programs so they can talk to it directly."[2] Although there are APIs for operating system, applications, and programming toolkits, this book focuses on the APIs of web sites and web applications.

If there is a public API for a web site, how have people used the API? Looking for what others have done with the API helps you get right into the application without wading through any documentation.

What's the range of the third-party wrappers available for the API? How many are officially supported by the web site owners? Which ones were developed by the community?

Are there many people working with the API, or is there little evidence that it is being used at all? Have any mashups using the web site been developed? How sophisticated are the mashups? Are they straight-up remixes of the data or presentations of the data in a new context? Do you see some emergent and unexpected property? Surprising mashups often reveal a capacity in the formal API or some integration point that might not be obvious from a quick glance at the documentation.

---

2. http://programmableweb.com/faq#Q2

The more interesting mashups that exist for an application, the more likely it is that the application is amenable to mashups. Look for mashups that contain functionality similar to what you want to include.

Chapter 6 and Chapter 7 present an overview of how to use public web site APIs, starting with a study of the Flickr APIs and then moving on to a survey of other APIs.

Use of Ajax

Does the web site use Ajax and allied JavaScript techniques to integrate data dynamically into the user interface? As you will learn in Chapter 8, the presence of Ajax is an indicator that there is likely an API at work—either a formalized public API or a programmatic structure, though not intended for public interfacing, that might possibly be used for mashup making. (Recall from Chapter 1 how Housingmaps.com placed markers on the first generations of Google Maps by tapping into the programming logic before any public API for Google Maps was released.)

Embedded Scriptability

Can people embed plug-ins, add-ons, or extensions (as opposed to writing external applications) to extend the web site directly? Here are examples of extension frameworks for specific web sites:

- Google Gadgets (http://www.google.com/ig/directory) to extend iGoogle (http://www.google.com/ig) and Google Mapplets (http://www.google.com/apis/maps/documentation/mapplets/) to extend Google Maps (http://maps.google.com/maps/mm?mapprev=1)

- Microsoft Web Gadgets (http://gallery.live.com/) to extend Windows Live (http://live.com)

For web applications, these are some examples:

- WordPress plug-ins (http://codex.wordpress.org/Plugins)

- MediaWiki extensions (http://www.mediawiki.org/wiki/MediaWiki_extensions)

For desktop applications/OS environments, take a look at these examples:

- Microsoft Office macros and add-ins (http://msdn2.microsoft.com/en-us/office/default.aspx)

- OpenOffice.org macros, add-ins, and add-ons (http://wiki.services.openoffice.org/wiki/Extensions)

- Yahoo! Widgets (http://widgets.yahoo.com/)

- SketchUp Ruby (http://www.sketchup.com/?sid=79)

If you have the required permissions, you can install or write extensions that incorporate other services into the applications.

Browser Plug-Ins

Are there Firefox add-ons (`https://addons.mozilla.org/en-US/firefox/`) that supplement or enhance the user interface to the web site? For example:

- Better Flickr Firefox Extension (`http://lifehacker.com/software/lifehacker-code/upgrade-flickr-with-the-better-flickr-firefox-extension-263985.php`)

- The del.icio.us Firefox extension (`http://del.icio.us/help/firefox/extension`)

- S3Fox Amazon S3 Firefox Organizer (`https://addons.mozilla.org/en-US/firefox/addon/3247`)

If you see a form of communication between the add-on and the application, you know there is some form of public or private API. Other browsers have extension mechanisms,[3] but I single out Firefox add-ons because you can unzip the add-on to study the code (if it hasn't been obfuscated) to gain more insight into the hooks of the corresponding web site.

Getting Data In and Out of the Web Site

How can you import data into the application? With what protocols? What data or file formats are accepted?

How can you export data from the application? What formats are provided? What protocols are supported?

It's much easier to make mashups out of widely deployed data formats and protocols (whether they are *de jure* or *de facto* standards) than with obscure data formats and protocols.

Can you embed data from the web site elsewhere? An example of such embedding is a JavaScript badge (such as `http://www.platial.com/mapkit/faq`). What options do you have for customizing the badge? Super-flexible badges can be used themselves to access data for mashups and hint at the existence of a feature-rich API.

The Community of Users and Developers

What communities of users and developers have grown around the web site? Where can you go to participate in that community and ask questions? What are members of the community discussing? What are some of the limitations of the application that they want to be overcome? What clever solutions or workarounds—*hacks*—are being popularized in that community, not only among developers but also among nonprogramming power users in the community?

Again, seeing how the API gets used and discussed is a great way to get a handle on what is possible and interesting. And if you don't see much activity around the API, realize that you are likely to be on your own if you decide to use it.

Why do I stress looking at the community around an application and its API? A vibrant and active community makes a lot of mashup work practical. When making mashups, some things are theoretically possible to do—if you had the time, energy, and resources—but are practically impossible for you as an individual to pull off. A community of developers means there are other people to work with, lots of examples of what other people have done, and often code libraries that you can build upon.

---

3. `http://blog.mashupguide.net/2007/04/29/browser-extension-mechanisms-for-various-browsers/`

Mobile and Alternative Interfaces and the Skinnability of the Web Site

How many versions of the user interface are there for the web site? Is there a mobile interface? A mobile version is often easier to decipher than the main site and highlights what the web site's creators believe to be some core logic of the web site. A mobile version might be more easily integrated into a mashup for a phone; there is typically no JavaScript to worry about, and the HTML is easier to parse.

How difficult is it to change the look of the interface? That is, how "skinnable" is the web site? Easy customizability of the interface for end users is an indicator that the application developers have likely separated the application logic from presentation logic. And if skinnability is available to end users, that functionality might also be programmable. For example, WordPress themes typically allow the owner of a WordPress site to change the set of global styles of the site.

Documentation

Good documentation of the features, the API, the data formats, and any other aspect of the web site makes it much easier to understand and recombine its data and functionality. Are the input and output data documented? If so, are there schemas, in other words, ways to validate data? Are the formats properly versioned?

Documentation reduces the amount of guesswork involved. Moreover, it brings certainty to whether a function you uncover through reverse engineering is an official feature or an undocumented hack that has no guarantee of working for any length of time.

Is the Web Site Run on Open Source?

If the web site is powered by free or open source software, you have the option of studying the source directly should reverse engineering—or reading the relevant documentation—not give you the answers you need.

Intellectual Property, Reusability, and Creative Commons

Does the web site allow users to explicitly set the licensing of content and data, under Creative Commons, for instance? Does the web site enable users to search and browse content by license? Explicit licensing of digital content clears away important barriers to creating mashups with that content. A detailed discussion of the Creative Commons is beyond the scope of this book. To learn more, consult the following:

http://creativecommons.org

Tagging, Feeds, and Weblogging

Here I present a series of questions that will be explored at length in the chapters that immediately follow.

Does the web site use tagging? That is, can users tag items and search for items by tags in the web site? Chapter 3 covers tagging and folksonomy in detail and shows how tags provide mashups with hooks within a web site and among web sites.

Are there RSS and Atom feeds available from the site? Do they give you fine-grained access to the web site? (That is, can you get feeds for a specific search term or for a specific part of a web site?) In the absence of a formal API, syndication feeds become a source of structured, easy-to-parse data. See Chapter 4 for detailed coverage of RSS and Atom feeds.

Does the web site allow you to send content to a weblog or wiki? Studying how the web site is connected to a weblog in this manner is an excellent way to get some practice with configuring APIs without programming. See Chapter 5 for more on blogging and wiki APIs.

URL Languages of Web Sites

I will spend most of this chapter analyzing a web site's functionality by explaining the way its URLs relate to its various entities and resources. In other words, I decipher the web site's *URL language*. At the beginning of the chapter, I already made an argument for the usefulness of having URLs that give you direct access to a resource. Before analyzing Flickr, Google Maps, Amazon, and del.icio.us for their URL languages, I'll make some general comments about URL languages. Each web site has its own URL language, but URL languages vary in terms of addressability, granularity, transparency, and persistence.[4]

Leonard Richardson and Sam Ruby present a helpful definition of *addressability*: "Addressability means that every interesting aspect of your service is immediately accessible from outside. Every interesting aspect of your service has a URI: a unique identifier in a format that's familiar to every computer-literate person.... Addressability makes it possible for others to make mashups of your service: to use it in ways you never imagined."

Some URL languages are highly expressive, making resources and their associated data addressable at high *granularity*. Others expose relatively little of the functionality of the web site or only at a very course-grained level. Some URL languages are relatively *transparent*; their meaning and context are easily apparent to those who did not design the site. Other URL languages tend to the opaque, making it difficult or impossible to refer to web site's functionality in any detail. Finally, some URL languages have URLs that have high *persistence*, which means to last, while others do not, making them difficult to link to.

---

4. *Restful Web Services* by Leonard Richardson and Sam Ruby (O'Reilly Media, 2007). The idea of analyzing URIs in terms of addressability, granularity, transparency, and persistence comes from *Restful Web Services*.

UNDERSTANDING THE RELATIONSHIP AMONG URI, URL, AND URN

Universal Resource Identifier (URI) is a specific type of identifier. URIs fall into two classes: Universal Resource Locators (URLs) and Universal Resource Names (URNs). You're likely to be much more familiar with the former. An example of the latter is `urn:isbn:159059858X`, which refers to this book. Many of the things I write about URLs in this book apply to URIs in general.

RFC 3986 clarifies the relationship among URI, URL, and URN (`http://tools.ietf.org/html/rfc3986#section-1.1.3`):

A URI can be further classified as a locator, a name, or both. The term "Uniform Resource Locator" (URL) refers to the subset of URIs that, in addition to identifying a resource, provide a means of locating the resource by describing its primary access mechanism (e.g., its network "location"). The term "Uniform Resource Name" (URN) has been used historically to refer to both URIs under the "urn" scheme [RFC2141], which are required to remain globally unique and persistent even when the resource ceases to exist or becomes unavailable, and to any other URI with the properties of a name.

An individual scheme does not have to be classified as being just one of "name" or "locator." Instances of URIs from any given scheme may have the characteristics of names or locators or both, often depending on the persistence and care in the assignment of identifiers by the naming authority, rather than on any quality of the scheme. Future specifications and related documentation should use the general term "URI" rather than the more restrictive terms "URL" and "URN" [RFC3305].

Some Mashups Briefly Revisited

Let's see how the ideas and questions presented so far in this chapter (for example, studying the user interface of the applications, their URL languages, and how they exploit certain hooks such as RSS) would have come in play for the developers of the mashups in Chapter 1:

- Housingmaps.com depends on a combination of screen-scraping the web pages of Craigslist and the RSS feeds of Craigslist since Craigslist doesn't have a public API. (Chapter 9 is a fuller analysis of the logic behind Housingmaps.com.)

- The construction of Google Maps in Flickr (GMiF), a Greasemonkey script that sticks an icon into the Flickr interface, rests on understanding the UI of Flickr, how the user community geotags photos, and how to screen-scrape information that is in the HTML page—in addition to the public API of Flickr.

- Creating the LibraryLookup bookmarklet depended centrally on speaking the URL languages of both the source of book information (that is, Amazon) and the destination for the query (that is, library catalogs).

Flickr: The Fundamentally Mashup-Friendly Site

Let's start our study of highly remixable web sites with Flickr, looking for features that make this site amenable to mashups. In addition to many features for storing and sharing photos, Flickr is chock-full of features that make it easy to mash up Flickr, not least of which is its use of XML, XML web services, tagging, and Ajax. These features are blended in a surprisingly coherent, comprehensive demonstration of how to knit this new technology together. You won't be surprised then to read Flickr's own description of its goals at `http://www.flickr.com/about`:

> *To do this, we want to get photos into and out of the system in as many ways as we can: from the web, from mobile devices, from the users' home computers and from whatever software they are using to manage their photos. And we want to be able to push them out in as many ways as possible: on the Flickr web site, in RSS feeds, by e-mail, by posting to outside blogs or ways we haven't thought of yet. What else are we going to use those smart refrigerators for?*

This flexibility of functionality makes Flickr a good web site to study when learning about mashups. Flickr is made to be mashed up. You can see in one web site a great variety of mashup-enabling techniques—and actually how they can be well integrated in one web site.

■**Caution** In the following analysis of Flickr, I answer many but not necessarily all the questions listed earlier in the chapter. I'll answer some of the questions later in the book. Moreover, it's important to understand that since Flickr is a constantly evolving web site, any of the details recorded here about Flickr can become out of date. My hope is to provide you with enough ways to think about web sites so that you will be able to adapt to those changes.

Resources in Flickr

Let me now explain Flickr in terms of its URI language, detailing resources and their corresponding URIs. As you use Flickr as an end user and think about its functionality in terms of key entities, you will probably come up with a list similar to the following:

- Users (or people)
- Photos
- Tags
- Archives
- Sets (which are also called *photosets*)
- Collections
- Favorites
- Geo

- Notes
- Comments (for both photosets and photos)
- Licenses
- Prefs
- Groups
- Contacts
- Blogs

This list is meant to cover the broad range of what Flickr does, but I'm not attempting to be exhaustive. Remember that there are different ways to slice the pie, so any listing of resources won't necessarily agree. We will end up agreeing on how the URLs are structured, though.

How did I come up with this list?

- I used Flickr, looking at each piece of functionality available to me. For each function, I identified the "nouns," or entities, at work and noted the corresponding URIs and how the URLs change as the state of the application changes.

- I culled common terminology from the Flickr UI itself, from the documentation of the UI, and from the documentation for the API (`http://www.flickr.com/services/api/`). The structure of an API often points out key entities in the web site.

■**Caution** Keep in mind the warning about the opacity of unique identifiers in Flickr: "The Flickr API exposes identifiers for users, photos, photosets and other uniquely identifiable objects. These IDs should always be treated as opaque strings, rather than integers of any specific type. The format of the IDs can change over time, so relying on the current format may cause you problems in the future."[5]

Users and Photos

The host URL of the entire site is as follows:

`http://www.flickr.com/`

URLs using a host URL of `http://flickr.com` also seem to be valid, but I will use the former since the API returns URLs that use www.flickr.com as the host URL.

Since Flickr is a social photo-sharing site, let's start with the two entities you expect at the least: a Flickr user (or person) and a photo.

■**Note** I use URI Templates (`http://bitworking.org/news/URI_Templates`) to express the URL language. These are strings into which I place variables that are replaced to form the full URI. The variables to be substituted are delimited by { } (which are not part of legal URIs). Note that the URI Template is currently an IETF draft, but the convention I use here is simply denoting the embedded variable with { }. Substituted variables need to be properly URL encoded (`http://en.wikipedia.org/wiki/Percent-encoding`).

The profile page for a user, the URL that most closely represents a Flickr user, is as follows:

`http://www.flickr.com/people/{user-id}/`

---

5. `http://www.flickr.com/services/api/misc.overview.html`

The `user-id` can take one of two forms:

- An NSID (a unique identifier that contains a @ character) generated by Flickr when the user signs up for an account (for example, `48600101146@N01`)

- A custom URL handle or "permanent alias" chosen by the user, which can be set at `http://www.flickr.com/profile_url.gne` (for example, `raymondyee`)

My profile page is thus accessible as either this:

`http://www.flickr.com/people/48600101146@N01/`

or this:

`http://www.flickr.com/people/raymondyee/`

As a logged-in user, you can upload photos to your account using the following form:

`http://www.flickr.com/photos/upload/`

Photos belonging to a user are collected here:

`http://www.flickr.com/photos/{user-id}/`

Representations of a Photo

Every photo belongs to one specific user, has a unique identifier `photo-id`, and is associated with a URL:

`http://www.flickr.com/photos/{user-id}/{photo-id}/`

For example:

`http://www.flickr.com/photos/raymondyee/508341822/`

A given photo has a variety of representations, as documented here:

`http://www.flickr.com/services/api/misc.urls.html`

When you upload a photo to Flickr, Flickr retains the original image and generates versions (in different sizes) of the photo, as recorded in Table 2-1.

Table 2-1. *Representations of a Flickr Photo*

photo-type	context-type	Image Type	Sizes of Photo
s	sq	Small square	75×75
t	t	Thumbnail	100 on longest side
m	s	Small	240 on longest side
blank	m	Medium	500 on longest side
b	l	Large	1024 on longest side
o	o	Original image, either a JPG, GIF, or PNG, depending on source format	

There are two types of URLs for each size of photo:

- The context page for the photos

- The photos themselves in their various sizes

The context page is of the following form:

```
http://www.flickr.com/photo_zoom.gne?id={photo-id}&size={context-type}
```

where context-type is one of sq, t, s, m, l, or o. Not every context-type is available for any given photo. (Some photos are too small; nonpaying Flickr members cannot offer original photos for downloading.)

To understand the URLs for the photos themselves, you need to know that in addition to photo-id for every photo, there are the following parameters:

- farm-id

- server-id

- photo-secret

- original-secret

- file-suffix

The URL for the photos takes one of three slightly different forms:

- For the original photo, it is as follows where file-suffix is jpg, gif, or png:

  ```
  http://farm{farm-id}.static.flickr.com/{server-id}/{photo-id}_{o-secret}_o.
  {file-suffix}
  ```

- For all the derived sizes except the medium size, the URL is as follows:

  ```
  http://farm{farm-id}.static.flickr.com/{server-id}/{photo-id}_{photo-secret}_
  {photo-size}.jpg
  ```

- For medium images, the URL is as follows:

  ```
  http://farm{farm-id}.static.flickr.com/{server-id}/{photo-id}_{photo-secret}.jpg
  ```

Let's consider http://www.flickr.com/photos/raymondyee/508341822/ as an example. If you go to the URL and hit the All Sizes button, you'll see the various sizes that are publicly available for the photo. If you click all the different sizes and look at the URLs for the photos and the context pages, you can determine the values listed in Table 2-2, thus confirming the values of the parameters in Table 2-3.

Table 2-2. *URLs for the Various Sizes of Flickr Photo 508341822*

Image Type	Context Page URL	Image URL
Small square	http://www.flickr.com/photo_zoom. gne?id=508341822&size=sq	http://farm1.static.flickr.com/193/ 508341822_2f2bfb4796_s.jpg
Thumbnail	http://www.flickr.com/photo_zoom. gne?id=508341822&size=t	http://farm1.static.flickr.com/193/ 508341822_2f2bfb4796_t.jpg
Small	http://www.flickr.com/photo_zoom. gne?id=508341822&size=s	http://farm1.static.flickr.com/193/ 508341822_2f2bfb4796_m.jpg
Medium	http://www.flickr.com/photo_zoom. gne?id=508341822&size=m	http://farm1.static.flickr.com/193/ 508341822_2f2bfb4796.jpg
Large	http://www.flickr.com/photo_zoom. gne?id=508341822&size=l	http://farm1.static.flickr.com/193/ 508341822_2f2bfb4796_b.jpg
Original	http://www.flickr.com/photo_zoom. gne?id=508341822&size=o	http://farm1.static.flickr.com/193/ 508341822_5ab600db14_o.jpg

Table 2-3. *Parameters Associated with Photo 508341822*

Parameter	Value
photo-id	508341822
farm-id	1
server-id	193
photo-secret	2f2bfb4796
original-secret	5ab600db14
file-suffix	jpg

Tip I suggest you look at the current documentation for the Flickr URLs every so often because the URLs that Flickr produces have changed over time, and I suspect they will continue to change as Flickr scales up its operations. Don't worry about any URLs you have generated according to older schemes—Flickr tries to keep them working. (It's worthwhile to update your software to use the latest URL structures if you are able to do so.)

Data Associated with an Individual Photo

Each photo has various pieces of information associated with it, including the following:

- Title

- Description

- Tags

- Machine tags

- Dates (the time it was uploaded as well as the time it was taken, if that time is available)

- EXIF data

- Owner of the picture

- Any sets to which the photo belongs

- Any groups to which the photo belongs

- Comments

- Notes

- Its visibility

I listed these data elements associated with each picture because each of the elements is an opportunity for integration if you want to use that picture in another mashup context. Many of data elements can be addressed in the URL, which is part of the Flickr URL language.

Miscellaneous Editing of Attributes

If you have JavaScript turned on in your browser while accessing Flickr, you might not see the distinct URL for editing the tags, description, and title of the photo—beyond the URL for the photo itself:

```
http://flickr.com/photo_edit.gne?id={photo-id}
```

You can see the EXIF data of a photo here:

```
http://www.flickr.com/photo_exif.gne?id={photo-id}
```

For example:

```
http://www.flickr.com/photo_exif.gne?id=688436870
```

You can edit a photo date here:

```
http://www.flickr.com/photo_date_taken.gne?id={photo-id}
```

Tags

Tags are one of the most important ways to organize photos in Flickr. Tags are words or short phrases that the owner (or others with the proper permission) can associate with a photo. A tag typically describes the photo and ties together related photos within a user's collection of photos and sometimes between photos of different users. However, there is no requirement that tags have meaning to anyone except the tagger, or even the tagger! See Chapter 3 for an extended discussion on tagging and folksonomy.

Flickr lets users search and browse photos by tags. First, let's study how to address tags as they are used throughout Flickr to describe pictures among all users. Then, you will examine the functionality in the context of a specific user.

You can see a list of popular tags in Flickr here:

```
http://www.flickr.com/photos/tags/
```

Popular tags allow you to get a sense of the Flickr community, over the longer haul, as well as over the last 24 hours or 7 days.

The URL for the most recent photos associated with a tag is as follows:

```
http://www.flickr.com/photos/tags/{tag}/
```

For example:

```
http://www.flickr.com/photos/tags/flower/
```

You can page through the photos with this:

```
http://www.flickr.com/photos/tags/flower/?page={page-number}
```

Instead of sorting photos by the date uploaded, you can see sort them by descending "interestingness" (a quantitative measure calculated by Flickr of how interesting a photo is):

```
http://www.flickr.com/photos/tags/{tag}/interesting/
```

Finally, for some tags, Flickr identifies distinct clusters of photos, which you can access here:

```
http://www.flickr.com/photos/tags/{tag}/clusters/
```

For example:

```
http://www.flickr.com/photos/tags/flower/clusters/
```

You can display the popular tags used by a specific user here:

```
http://www.flickr.com/photos/{user-id}/tags/
```

You can list all the user's tags here:

```
http://www.flickr.com/photos/{user-id}/alltags/
```

You can show all photos with a given tag for a specific user here:

```
http://www.flickr.com/photos/{user-id}/tags/{tag}/
```

You can edit the tag for the given user, if you have permission to do so, here:

```
http://www.flickr.com/photos/{user-id}/tags/{tag}/edit/
```

You can delete a tag here:

```
http://www.flickr.com/photos/{user-id}/tags/{tag}/delete/
```

You can show a slide show of these tagged photos here:

```
http://www.flickr.com/photos/{user-id}/tags/{tag}/show/
```

User's Archive: Browsing Photos by Date

You can browse through a user's photos by date—by either the date the photo was taken or when it was uploaded. Dates are an excellent way to organize resources such as photos. Even if you leave a photo completely untagged, Flickr can at the very least place the photo in the context of other photos that were uploaded around the same time. If you are careful about generating good time stamps for your photos, you can display photos in an accurate time stream. I have found looking at a user's photos by date to be an effective way to make sense of large numbers of photos.

The main page for a user's archive is here:

```
http://www.flickr.com/photos/{user-id}/archives/
```

For example:

```
http://www.flickr.com/photos/raymondyee/archives/
```

You can sort your archive by the date taken or date posted with this:

```
http://www.flickr.com/photos/{user-id}/archives/{date-taken-or-posted}/
```

where {date-taken-or-posted} is date-taken or date-posted.

You can view the photos for a given date with a different {archive-view} here:

```
http://www.flickr.com/photos/{user-id}/archives/{date-taken-or-posted}/
{archive-view}
```

where {archive-view} is one of detail, map, or calendar.

You can also set the display option and limit photos by year, year/month, or year/month/date. The following set of URLs use the default list view:

```
http://www.flickr.com/photos/{user-id}/archives/{date-taken-or-posted}/{year}
http://www.flickr.com/photos/{user-id}/archives/{date-taken-or-posted}/
{year}/{month}
http://www.flickr.com/photos/{user-id}/archives/{date-taken-or-posted}/
{year}/{month}/{day}
```

The following URLs use the other display options where {archive-view-except-calendar} is either detail or map—but not calendar:

```
http://www.flickr.com/photos/{user-id}/archives/{date-taken-or-posted}/{year}
http://www.flickr.com/photos/{user-id}/archives/{date-taken-or-posted}/
{year}/{archive-view}
http://www.flickr.com/photos/{user-id}/archives/{date-taken-or-posted}/
{year}/{month}/{archive-view}
http://www.flickr.com/photos/{user-id}/archives/{date-taken-or-posted}/
{year}/{month}/{day}/{archive-view-except-calendar}
```

Here are some specific examples:

```
http://www.flickr.com/photos/raymondyee/archives/date-taken/2007/
http://www.flickr.com/photos/raymondyee/archives/date-taken/2007/06/22/
http://www.flickr.com/photos/raymondyee/archives/date-posted/2007/calendar/
```

Sets

Sets or *photosets* (both terms are used in the Flickr UI and documentation) are groupings created by users of their own photos. (Note that sets cannot include other users' photos.)

You can see a user's sets here:

```
http://www.flickr.com/photos/{user-id}/sets/
```

You can see a specific set with the unique ID set-id here:

```
http://www.flickr.com/photos/{user-id}/sets/{set-id}/
```

You can control the view for a given set here where set-view is one of detail, comments, or show:

```
http://www.flickr.com/photos/{user-id}/sets/{set-id}/{set-view}
```

Consider some examples of sets:

```
http://www.flickr.com/photos/raymondyee/sets/72157600434284985/
http://www.flickr.com/photos/raymondyee/sets/72157600434284985/detail/
```

To display a photo in the context of a containing set, use this:

```
http://www.flickr.com/photos/{user-id}/{photo-id}/in/set-{set-id}/
```

For example:

```
http://www.flickr.com/photos/raymondyee/591991800/in/set-72157600434284985/
```

Collections

Users can create collections to make groupings of their sets. A user's collections are found here:

```
http://www.flickr.com/photos/{user-id}/collections/
```

And you can find a specific collection here:

```
http://www.flickr.com/photos/{user-id}/collections/{collection-id}
```

For example:

```
http://www.flickr.com/photos/raymondyee/collections/72157600592620295/
```

Favorites

Users can add other users' photos to their favorites:

```
http://www.flickr.com/photos/{user-id}/favorites/
```

Note that you can't add your own photos to your favorites. There are also not many ways to organize your favorites. You can search within your favorites using this:

```
http://www.flickr.com/search/?w=faves&q={search-term}
```

Since sets and collections can contain only those photos belonging to a user, there is no built-in way in Flickr for you to group your own photos with photos belonging to others.

A User's Popular Photos

Users can track which of their photos are the most popular (by interestingness, number of views, number of times they have been added as a favorite, and number of comments) here:

```
http://www.flickr.com/photos/{user-id}/{popular-mode}/
```

where {popular-mode} is one of popular-interesting, popular-views, popular-faves, or popular-comments. Users can access popularity statistics for only their own photos.

Contacts

As a social photo-sharing site, Flickr allows users to maintain a list of contacts. From the perspective of a registered user of Flickr, there are five categories of people in Flickr: the user, the user's family, the user's friends, the user's contacts who are neither family nor friend, and everyone else. Contacts, along with their recent photos, belonging to a user are listed here:

```
http://www.flickr.com/people/{user-id}/contacts/
```

Depending on access permissions, you may be able to access more fine-grained lists of contacts for a user here where {contact-type} is one of family, friends, both, or contacts:

```
http://www.flickr.com/people/{user-id}/contacts/?see={contact-type}
```

Users can see their own list of users they are blocking here:

```
http://www.flickr.com/people/{user-id}/contacts/ignore/
```

Users can see their "reverse contacts" (users who consider them contacts) here:

```
http://www.flickr.com/people/{user-id}/contacts/rev/
```

To invite others to join Flickr, you go here:

```
http://www.flickr.com/invite.gne
```

Groups

Groups allow people to organize themselves into communities based around themes, places, and common interests. Take a look at all the groups that are in Flickr:

```
http://www.flickr.com/groups/
```

You access an individual group here:

```
http://www.flickr.com/groups/{group-id}/
```

where group-id is the NSID of the group or its friendly name, which the group owner sets here:

```
http://www.flickr.com/groups_url.gne?id={group-nsid}
```

Consider, for instance, the Flickr Central Group, which is accessed from here:

```
http://www.flickr.com/groups/34427469792@N01/
```

and from here:

```
http://www.flickr.com/groups/central/
```

You can page through the discussion in a group here:

```
http://www.flickr.com/groups/{group-id}/discuss/page{page-number}/
```

You can post a new topic here:

```
http://www.flickr.com/groups_newtopic.gne?id={group-nsid}
```

For example:

```
http://www.flickr.com/groups_newtopic.gne?id=34427469792@N01
```

You access a specific thread here:

```
http://www.flickr.com/groups/{group-id}/discuss/{thread-id}/
```

For example:

```
http://www.flickr.com/groups/central/discuss/140537/
```

You access a specific comment in the thread here:

```
http://www.flickr.com/groups/{group-id}/discuss/{thread-id}/#comment{comment-id}
```

For example:

```
http://www.flickr.com/groups/central/discuss/140537/#comment1192964
```

You can edit, delete, or lock a thread if you have the appropriate rights:

```
http://www.flickr.com/groups/{group-id}/discuss/{thread-id}/{thread-action}
```

where {thread-action} is edit, delete, or lock.

Similarly, for the comments that hang off a thread (one-deep), you can find them here:

```
http://www.flickr.com/groups/{group-id}/discuss/{thread-id}/{comment-id}/
{comment-action}/
```

where {comment-action} can be edit or delete.

Each group has a photo pool accessible here:

```
http://www.flickr.com/groups/{group-id}/pool/
```

For example:

```
http://www.flickr.com/groups/central/pool/
```

You can look at the geotagged photos from the group on a map here:

```
http://www.flickr.com/groups/{group-id}/pool/map?mode=group
```

You can look at a list of the most popular tags used for photos in a group here:

```
http://www.flickr.com/groups/{group-id}/pool/tags/
```

You can look at photos with a certain `tag` in the group here:

```
http://www.flickr.com/groups/{group-id}/pool/tags/{tag}/
```

You can look at photos that have been contributed to the pool by a specific user here:

```
http://www.flickr.com/groups/{group-id}/pool/{user-nsid}/
```

Account Management

Some URLs are used for account management functions. You need to be logged in to access them.

To access your contacts' photos, go here:

```
http://www.flickr.com/photos/friends/
```

To manage your account, go here:

```
http://www.flickr.com/account
```

You can adjust various specific options at the following URLs:

```
http://www.flickr.com/account?tab=e-mail
http://www.flickr.com/account/?tab=privacy
http://www.flickr.com/account/?tab=extend
http://www.flickr.com/account/order/history/
http://www.flickr.com/account/prefs/screenname/
http://www.flickr.com/account/prefs/layout/
```

Browsing Through Flickr

Flickr's jumping-off point for looking at the world of Flickr is this:

```
http://www.flickr.com/explore/
```

To look at what Flickr rates as the most "interesting" photos, go here:

```
http://www.flickr.com/explore/interesting/
```

The page gives some sense of how Flickr rates interestingness (even if there aren't complete details given):

There are lots of things that make a photo "interesting" (or not) in the Flickr: where the clickthroughs are coming from, who comments on it and when, who marks it as a favorite, its tags, and many more things which are constantly changing. Interestingness changes over time, as more and more fantastic photos and stories are added to Flickr.

You can look at the photos the most interesting photos for a specific period of time. A special case is a random selection of photos from the last seven days:

```
http://www.flickr.com/explore/interesting/7days/
```

You can see interesting photos for a given month or day, the latter as a calendar or slide show:

```
http://www.flickr.com/explore/interesting/{year}/{month}/
http://www.flickr.com/explore/interesting/{year}/{month}/{day}
http://www.flickr.com/explore/interesting/{year}/{month}/{day}/show/
```

For example:

```
http://www.flickr.com/explore/interesting/2007/01/04/show/
```

Search

Flickr provides interfaces for basic and advanced photo searches.

Basic Photo Search

The photo search URL is constructed as follows:

```
http://www.flickr.com/search/?w={search-scope}&q={search-term}&m={search-mode}
```

where `search-scope` is one of `all`, `faves`, or the `{user-id}` of a user and where `search-mode` is `tags` or `text`. You can use some optional parameters to qualify the search:

- `&z=t` for thumbnails (as opposed to the detail view)

- `&s=int` or `&s=rec` to sort by interestingness or by recent date

- `&page={page-number}` to page through the results

Advanced Photo Search

For the advanced photo search (`http://www.flickr.com/search/advanced`), you can figure out other ways to modify the search URL.

You can add terms to `{search-term}` by adding a hyphen (-) before the term. For instance, you can look for photos that are tagged with `flower` but not `rose` or `tulip` with this:

```
http://www.flickr.com/search/?q=flower+-rose+-tulip&m=tags&ct=0
```

You can use add `safe-search` options with this:

```
&ss={safe-search}
```

where `{safe-search}` is 0,1, or 2 corresponding to `on`, `moderate`, and `off`, respectively.

You can limit searches to a particular `content-type` by using this:

```
&ct={content-type}
```

where `{content-type}` is one of the following:

- 0 for photos

- 1 for screenshots

- 2 for other stuff (art, drawings, CGI, and so on)

- 3 for photos and screenshots

- 4 for screenshots and other stuff

- 5 for photos and other stuff

- 6 for photos and other stuff and screenshots

You can also limit photos by a date range:

```
&d={taken-or-posted}-{from-date}-{to-date}
```

where `{taken-or-posted}` is `taken` or `posted` and where `{from-date}` and `{to-date}` are of the form yyyymmdd. You can state one or both of the dates. For example:

```
&d=posted--20070702
&d=taken-20070613-20070702
```

Finally, you can search for photos with certain Creative Commons licenses by using this:

```
&l={CC-license}
```

where `{CC-license}` can be one of `cc` (for any Creative Commons license), `com` (for licenses that permit commercial reuse), or `deriv` (for licenses that permit derivative works).

■Note I do not provide a full analysis of the URL language for searching groups (`http://flickr.com/search/groups/`) and users (`http://flickr.com/search/people/`).

Geotagged Photos in Flickr

You can use the Flickr World map to plot georeferenced photos here:

```
http://www.flickr.com/map/
```

You can control the center, zoom level, and display type of the map with this:

```
http://www.flickr.com/map/?&fLat={lat}&fLon={lon}&zl={zoom-level}&
map_type={map-type}
```

where `zoom-level` is an integer ranging from 1 to 17 (17 is the most zoomed out) and `map-type` is `hyb` or `sat`. If `map-type` is not explicitly set, the map has a default (political-style) map.

You can filter photos in various ways by adding more parameters to the URL:

- By search terms with this:

  ```
  &q={search-term}
  ```

- By group with this:

  ```
  &group_id={group-nsid}
  ```

- By person with this:

  `&user_id={user-nsid}`

- By date bounds where `taken-date` is of the form `yyyy-mm-dd%20hh:mm:ss`:

  `&min_taken_date={taken-date}`
  `&max_taken_date={taken-date}`

  and with the following:

  `&min_upload_date={upload-date}`
  `&max_upload_date={upload-date}`

  where `upload-date` is a Unix timestamp (number of seconds since January 1, 1970, UTC).

- By page with this:

  `&page={page-number}`

- By interestingness with this:

  `&s=int`

For example, this address:

`http://www.flickr.com/map/?&q=flower&fLat=37.871268&fLon=-122.286414&zl=4`

produces a map of geotagged pictures around Berkeley, California, filtered on a full-text search of `flower`. A corresponding list view according to Flickr is as follows:

`http://www.flickr.com/search/?&q=flower&m=text&s=rec&b=-122.346496,37.847598,`
`-122.226333,37.894938&a=10&d=taken-19700101-`

This search uses parameters I have already presented in the "Advanced Photo Search" section in addition to this for a geographic bounding box:

`&b={lon0},{lat0}{lon1},{lat1}`
and this:

`&a={accuracy}`

where `accuracy` is presumably the same parameter as the accuracy parameter used in the Flickr API in `flickr.photo.search` to denote the "recorded accuracy level of location information."[6]

The Flickr Organizer

You can use the JavaScript-based Organizer to process your Flickr photos:

`http://www.flickr.com/photos/organize/`

---

6. `http://www.flickr.com/services/api/flickr.photos.search.html`

Most of its functionality is not addressable through URLs, but a few aspects are. You can process your recently uploaded photos here:

```
http://www.flickr.com/photos/organize/?start_batch=recent_uploads
```

You can create and organize your sets and collections here:

```
http://www.flickr.com/photos/organize/?start_tab=sets
```

Finally, you can tag your untagged photos here:

```
http://www.flickr.com/photos/organize/?start_batch=untagged&mode=together
```

Recent Activities

You can look at recent activities around your photos here:

```
http://www.flickr.com/recent_activity.gne?days={time-period}
```

where `time-period` can be any of the following:

- A natural number (up to some limit that I've not tried to determine) to indicate the number of days

- A natural number appended with `h` for number of hours

- Blank to mean "since last login"

Mailing Interfaces

Flickr has its own e-mail type interface for facilitating communication among Flickr people:

```
http://www.flickr.com/messages.gne?ok=1
```

This messaging facility allows communication by proxy to retain the anonymity of users. You can access your sent mail here:

```
http://www.flickr.com/messages_sent.gne
```

You can read a message here:

```
http://www.flickr.com/messages_read.gne?id={message-id}
```

You compose a new message here:

```
http://www.flickr.com/messages_write.gne
```

Interfacing to Weblogs

One fun thing to do with pictures is to send a picture to one's weblog along with some commentary. Flickr helps make the process easier to do. You configure weblogs here:

```
http://www.flickr.com/blogs.gne
```

You can configure the settings for a specific weblog here:

```
http://www.flickr.com/blogs_edit.gne?id={blog-id}
```

You can configure the layout here:

```
http://www.flickr.com/blogs_layout.gne?id={blog-id}&edit=1
```

In Chapter 5, I go into greater detail about how the properties used to set up a blog to work with Flickr is a reflection of the blogging APIs that you will study.

Syndication Feeds: RSS and Atom

RSS and Atom feeds are well integrated in Flickr. These feeds are an example of XML, and you will learn more about that in Chapter 4. Flickr implements RSS and other syndication feeds in an extensive manner, as documented here:

```
http://www.flickr.com/services/feeds/
```

There's a lot to cover, which I'll come back to in Chapter 4.

Mobile Access

Flickr provides a model to help you integrate your own services with mobile devices. For example, you can e-mail pictures to Flickr. This functionality is not strictly tied to mobile devices but is particularly useful on a mobile phone because e-mail is perhaps the most convenient way to upload a picture from a camera phone while away from your desk. You can configure e-mail uploading here:

```
http://www.flickr.com/account/uploadbye-mail/
```

You can also look at pictures on a mobile device through a simplified interface customized for small displays here:

```
http://m.flickr.com
```

Third-Party Flickr Apps

Flickr has an API that enables the development of third-party applications or tools. The API is at the heart of what makes Flickr such a great mashup platform. Hundreds of third-party apps have been written to use the API, and these apps have made it easier and more fun and surprising to use Flickr. The Google Maps and Flickr Greasemonkey script are examples of third-party Flickr apps.

Go to `http://www.flickr.com/services/` to see a list of such third-party Flickr apps. To get inspired about how you can use the Flickr API in fun, useful, and imaginative ways, play with John Watson's collections of Flickr Toys:

```
http://bighugelabs.com/flickr/
```

While looking at the Flickr Toys, think about what content and services from Flickr are being accessed.

I analyze various Flickr third-party applications in more detail in conjunction with my study of the Flickr API in Chapter 6.

Creative Commons Licensing

Under copyright laws in the United States, you can't reuse other people's pictures by default except under the "fair use" rule. If someone uses a Creative Commons (CC) license for a picture, the owner is saying, "Hey, you can use my picture under looser restrictions without having to ask me for permission." You can see a license attached to any given picture.

Flickr makes it easy for users to associate CC licenses with their photos. You can browse and search for photos by CC license here:

```
http://www.flickr.com/creativecommons/
```

You can look at pictures by specific license here:

```
http://www.flickr.com/creativecommons/{cc-license}/
```

where {cc-license} is currently one of the following:

- by-2.0

- by-nd-2.0

- by-nc-nd-2.0

- by-nc-2.0

- by-nc-sa-2.0

- by-sa-2.0

Consult the following to get an understanding of the various licenses:

```
http://creativecommons.org/licenses/
```

Cameras

Flickr enables users to view photos by the brand of cameras used to take them:

```
http://www.flickr.com/cameras/
```

To get at all the brands of cameras, see the following:

```
http://www.flickr.com/cameras/brands/
```

You can look at pictures by the specific camera type here:

```
http://www.flickr.com/cameras/{camera-company}/{camera-model}/
```

For example:

```
http://www.flickr.com/cameras/canon/
http://www.flickr.com/cameras/canon/powershot_sd600/
```

The Mashup-by-URL-Templating-and-Embedding Pattern

Let's now apply Flickr's URL language to make a simple mashup with Flickr. In this section, I'll show how to create a simple example of what I call the Mashup-by-URL-Templating-and-Embedding pattern. Specifically, I connect Flickr archives and a WordPress weblog by virtue of translating URLs; an HTML page takes a given year and month and displays my Flickr photos along with the entries from the weblog for this book (http://blog.mashupguide.net). The mashup works because both the Flickr archives and the entries for the weblog are addressable by year and month. For Flickr, recall the following URL template for the archives:

```
http://www.flickr.com/photos/{user-id}/archives/{date-taken-or-posted}/
{year}/{month}/{archive-view}
```

For example:

```
http://www.flickr.com/photos/raymondyee/archives/date-taken/2007/06/calendar/
```

The weblog has URLs for posts by year and month (if posts from those dates exist):

```
http://blog.mashupguide.net/{year}/{month}
```

For example:

```
http://blog.mashupguide.net/2007/06/
```

The mashup takes the year and month from the user and loads two iframes correspon-ding to the Flickr photos and Mashupguide.net entries for the month by constructing the URLs for the year and month:[7]

```
<!DOCTYPE html PUBLIC "-//W3C//DTD XHTML 1.0 Transitional//EN"
    "http://www.w3.org/TR/xhtml1/DTD/xhtml1-transitional.dtd">
<html xmlns="http://www.w3.org/1999/xhtml">
  <head>
    <meta http-equiv="Content-Type" content="text/html;charset=utf-8" />
    <title>Raymond Yee's Flickr and mashupguide weblog</title>
    <script type="text/javascript">
      //<![CDATA[
      function reloadFrames() {
        // get a handle to the iframes and the year and month in the form
        var dateForm = document.getElementById('date');
        var flickrFrame = document.getElementById('FlickrFrame');
        var wpFrame = document.getElementById('WPFrame');
        year = dateForm.year.value;
        month = dateForm.month.value;
        var year, month, dateForm;
        var flickrURL =
          "http://www.flickr.com/photos/raymondyee/archives/date-taken/" +
```

---

7. http://examples.mashupguide.net/ch02/Flickr.and.WordPress.html

```
                year + "/" + month + "/calendar";
            var wpURL = "http://blog.mashupguide.net/" + year + "/" + month + "/";
            //reset the URLs for the iframes
            flickrFrame.src = flickrURL;
            wpFrame.src = wpURL;
            return false;
        }
        //]]>
    </script>
  </head>
  <body>
    <form id="date" action="#" onsubmit="return reloadFrames();">
      Year: <input type="text" size="4" name="year" value="2007" />
      Month: <input type="text" size="4" name="month" value="06" />
      <input type="submit" value="Reload Frames" />
    </form>
    <iframe id="FlickrFrame"
            src="http://www.flickr.com/photos/raymondyee/archives/date-taken/2007/
06/calendar/"
            name="Flickr" style="width:600px; height:500px; border: 0px"></iframe>
    <iframe id="WPFrame" src="http://blog.mashupguide.net/2007/06/"
            name="WordPress"
    style="width:600px; height:500px; border: 0px"></iframe>
  </body>
</html>
```

This example may seem trivial, even accounting for its intentional simplicity as an illustration, but ask yourself, what if you wanted to add a third source, such as the posts I made to del.icio.us posts for a given month? As you will see later in this chapter, there is no delic.io.us URL corresponding to a listing of the bookmarks uploaded in a given year or month (that is, the human UI to del.icio.us is not addressable by the posting date), so I can't add del.icio.us to my mashup by adding a corresponding iframe and URI template. Addressability of resources is what makes the Mashup-by-URL-Templating-and-Embedding pattern possible.

■**Note** You can use `https://api.del.icio.us/v1/posts/dates` to get a list of the number of posts for a date and then use `https://api.del.icio.us/v1/posts/get?` to retrieve them. You can configure del.icio.us to send your daily postings to your blog (`https://secure.del.icio.us/settings/user-id/blogging/posting`).

Granular URI addressability, the ability to refer to resources through a URI in very specific terms, enables simple mashups. This is especially true if the parameters in the URI templates are ones that have the same meaning across many web sites. Such identifiers are often the point of commonality between URIs from different sites. You have seen a number of such identifiers already:

- ISBN

- Year, month, day

- Latitude and longitude

- URLs themselves; for example, `http://validator.w3.org?uri={uri-to-validate}`, where uri-to-validate is a URL to validate, such as `http://validator.w3.org/check?uri=http%3A%2F%2Fvalidator.w3.org%2F`)

These identifiers contrast with application-specific identifiers (such as NSIDs of Flickr users and groups). Somewhere between widely used identifiers and those that are confined to one application only are objects such as tags, which may or may not have meaning beyond the originating web site. I'll return to this issue in Chapter 3.

Google Maps

Now, let's turn to studying the functionality of Google Maps, located at `http://maps.google.com/`.

With the standard Google Maps site, you can do the following:

- You can search for locations on a map.

- You can search for businesses on a map.

- You can get driving directions between two points.

- You can make your own map now with the My Maps feature.

You can also embed a Google Maps "widget" into a web page via JavaScript—using the Google Maps API.[8] The focus of this chapter is on maps that are hosted directly by Google. I examine third-party embedded Google maps in Chapters 8 and 13.

Even though Google Maps is not the most highly trafficked online map site,[9] it is (according to Programmableweb.com), the application is often used in mashups.

URL Language of Google Maps

Understanding the syntax and semantics of URLs in Google Maps will help you better recombine the functionality of the standard Google Maps site. Consider an example: I have an address I want to locate—for instance, the address of the White House (1600 Pennsylvania Ave., Washington, D.C.). I go to Google Maps (`http://maps.google.com/`) and type **1600 Pennsylvania Ave, Washington, DC** into the search box to get a map. I get the URL for the map by examining the "Link to this page" link:

```
http://maps.google.com/maps?f=q&hl=en&q=1600+Pennsylvania+Ave,+Washington,+DC&
sll=36.60585,-121.858956&sspn=0.006313,0.01133&ie=UTF8&z=16&om=1&iwloc=addr
```

---

8. `http://www.google.com/apis/maps/`

9. `http://news.yahoo.com/s/ap/20070405/ap_on_hi_te/google_maps`—"Google's maps already are a big draw, with 22.2 million U.S. visitors during February, according to the most recent data available from comScore Media Metrix. That ranked Google Maps third in its category, trailing AOL's Mapquest (45.1 million visitors) and Yahoo (29.1 million visitors)."

What do the various parameters in the URL mean? Table 2-4 draws from the Google Maps Parameters page of the Mapki wiki.[10]

Table 2-4. *Dissecting Parameters for a Link to Google Maps*

Parameter	Description
f=q	The f parameter, which controls the display of the Google Maps form, can be d (for the directions form or l for the local form). Without the f parameter, the default search form is displayed.
hl=en	Google Maps supports a limited number of host languages, including en for English and fr for French.
q=1600+Pennsylvania+Ave, +Washington,+DC	The value of the q parameter is treated as though it were entered via the query box at http://maps.google.com.
sll=36.60585, -121.858956	sll contains the latitude and longitude for the center point around which a business search is performed.
spn=0.006313, 0.01133	spn is the approximate latitude/longitude span for the map.
ie=UTF8	ie is the character encoding for the map.
om=1	om determines whether to include an overview map. With om=0, the overview map is closed.
iwloc=addr	iwloc controls display options for the info window.

A good way to get a feel for how these parameters function is to change a parameter, add new ones, or drop ones in the sample URL and take a look at the resulting map. For instance, if you have only the q parameter, you would still get a map with some default behavior:

```
http://maps.google.com/maps?q=1600+Pennsylvania+Ave,+Washington,+DC
```

That is, the other parameters are not mandatory. Let's play with the z parameter to adjust the zoom factor:

```
http://maps.google.com/maps?q=1600+Pennsylvania+Ave,+Washington,+DC&z=0
```

versus the following:

```
http://maps.google.com/maps?q=1600+Pennsylvania+Ave,+Washington,+DC&z=17
```

There is a comprehensive list of Google Maps parameters[11] to help you figure out the common and uncommon parameters. Since the wiki page is not part of Google's documentation, you can't take it as an official description of the URL language of Google Maps. However, the web page is also the work of a highly engaged community, actively working on uncovering every nook and cranny of Google Maps. With the list of parameters, you can learn some features that you might not have known from casual use of the Google Maps user interface. For instance:

---

10. http://mapki.com/wiki/Google_Map_Parameters, accessed as http://mapki.com/index.php?title=Google_Map_Parameters&oldid=4145

11. http://mapki.com/wiki/Google_Map_Parameters, accessed as http://maps.google.com/ maps?f=q&hl=en&q=1600+Pennsylvania+Ave,+Washington,+DC on April 14, 2007

- mrad lets you specify an additional destination address.

- output=kml gets a KML file to send to Google Earth.

- layer=t adds the traffic layer.

- mrt=kmlkmz shows "user-created content." For example, the following shows user-generated information about hotels around the White House:

```
http://maps.google.com/maps?f=q&hl=en&q=hotel&near=1600+Pennsylvania+Ave,
+Washington,+DC&sll=36.60585,-121.858956&sspn=0.006313,0.01133&ie=UTF8&z=16&om=1&
iwloc=addr&mrt=kmlkmz
```

Just as you can create mashups involving Flickr by using Flickr's URL language, you can create mashups with Google Maps by exploiting its URL structures. Let's consider a few examples.

Viewing KML Files in Google Maps

Many of the popular sources for KML (such as http://earth.google.com/gallery/) assume you will view KML in Google Earth. However, you can display a limited subset of KML in Google Maps. Consider, for instance, the KML file at the following location:

```
http://services.google.com/earth/kmz/global_heritage_fund_n.kmz
```

It can be viewed in Google Maps by passing in the URL of the KML file via the q parameter, as shown here:

```
http://maps.google.com/maps?q=http:%2F%2Fservices.google.com%2Fearth%2Fkmz%2Fglobal_
heritage_fund_n.kmz
```

Hence, in your own web site, you can give the option to your users of downloading KML to Google Earth or viewing the KML on Google Maps by linking to the following:

```
http://maps.google.com/maps?q={URL-of-KML}
```

Connecting Yahoo! Pipes and Google Maps

A specific case of displaying KML files is feeding KML from Yahoo! Pipes into Google Maps. (I describe Yahoo! Pipes in detail in Chapter 4. For the purposes of this discussion, you need to know only that Yahoo! Pipes can generate KML output.) Consider, for example, Apartment Near Something, configured specifically to list apartments that are close to cafes around UC Berkeley:

```
http://pipes.yahoo.com/pipes/pipe.info?location=94720&what=cafes&mindist=2&
=Run+Pipe&_id=1mrlkB232xGjJDdwXqIxGw&_run=1
```

You can get KML output from Yahoo! Pipes from the following:

```
http://pipes.yahoo.com/pipes/pipe.run?_id=1mrlkB232xGjJDdwXqIxGw&_render=kml&_run=1&
location=94720&mindist=2&what=cafes
```

which you can feed into Google Maps in the q={URL-of-KML} parameter:

```
http://maps.google.com/maps?f=q&hl=en&geocode=&q=http%3A%2F%2Fpipes.yahoo.com%2F
pipes%2Fpipe.run%3F_id%3D1mrlkB232xGjJDdwXqIxGw%26_render%3Dkml%26_run%3D1%26
location%3D94720%26mindist%3D2%26what%3Dcafes&ie=UTF8&ll=37.992916,-122.24556&
spn=0.189398,0.362549&z=12&om=1
```

Other Simple Applications of the Google Maps URL Language

Here are a few other examples of how to connect Google Maps to your applications by creating the appropriate URL:

- Let's not forget that by just using q={address}, you can now generate a URL to a map centered around that address. If such a map suffices, it's hard to imagine a simpler way to create a map corresponding to that address. No geocoding is needed.

- You can create a URL for custom driving directions for any source and destination address creating custom driving directions from your spreadsheet of addresses by making the URLs. For example, to generate driving directions from Apress to the Computer History Museum, you can use this:

  ```
  http://www.google.com/maps?saddr={source-address}&daddr=
  {destination-address}
  ```

  to generate this:

  ```
  http://www.google.com/maps?saddr=2855+Telegraph+Ave,+Berkeley,+CA+
  94705&daddr=1401+N+Shoreline+Blvd,+Mountain+View,+CA+94043
  ```

  Although driving directions have recently been added to the Google Maps API,[12] it is currently not possible to use the API to create directions to avoid highways, something you can do by using the dirflg=h parameter.[13] Hence, you can easily generate a scenic route for myself between the Apress offices and the Computer Museum, while avoiding the API altogether:

  ```
  http://www.google.com/maps?saddr=2855+Telegraph+Ave,+Berkeley,+CA
  +94705&daddr=1401+N+Shoreline+Blvd,+Mountain+View,+CA+94043&dirflg=h
  ```

  It pays to know the URL language of an application!

- You can use Google Maps as a nonprogrammer's geocoder. Center the map on the point for which you want to calculate its latitude and longitude, and read the values off the ll parameter. If the ll parameter is not present, you can double-click the center of the map, just enough to cause the map to recenter on the requested point.

---

12. http://www.google.com/apis/maps/documentation/#Driving_Directions
13. http://groups.google.com/group/Google-Maps-API/browse_thread/thread/279ee413e4e0309/
    0dabfb71863af712?lnk=gst&q=avoid+highway&rnum=2#0dabfb71863af712

Amazon

Amazon is the third major example in this chapter. Not only is Amazon a popular e-commerce site, but it is an e-commerce platform this is easily remixed with other content. Although you will study the Amazon APIs later in this book, you'll focus here on Amazon from the view of an end user. Moreover, the goal in this section is not to learn all the features of Amazon but rather to study its URL language.

■**Note** Although Amazon sells merchandise other than books, I use books in my examples. Moreover, I focus on Amazon, the site geared to the United States instead of Amazon's network of sites aimed to customers outside the United States.

The strategy you'll follow here is to discern the key entities of the Amazon site through a combination of using and experimenting with the site, sifting through documentation, and seeing what other users have done. You will see that figuring out the structure of Amazon's URLs is not as straightforward as working through the Flickr URL language. Since some of the conclusions here are not supported by official documentation from Amazon, I cannot make any long-term guarantee behind the URLs.

Amazon Items

It doesn't take much analysis of Amazon to see that the central entity of the site is an item for sale (akin to a photo in Flickr). By looking at the URL of a given item and looking throughout a page describing it, you will see that Amazon uses an Amazon Standard Identification Number (ASIN) as a unique identifier for its products.[14] For books that have an ISBN, the ASIN is the same as the ISBN-10 for the book. According to the Wikipedia article on ASIN, you can point to a product with an ASIN with the following URL:

```
http://www.amazon.com/gp/product/{ASIN}
```

Take for instance, Czesław Miłosz's *New and Collected Poems* (paperback edition), which has an ISBN-10 of 0060514485. You can find it on Amazon here:

```
http://www.amazon.com/gp/product/0060514485
```

It is important to know that the way to link to Amazon has changed in the past and will likely continue to change. For instance, you can also link to the book with this:

```
http://www.amazon.com/exec/obidos/ASIN/0060514485
```

or even with this shorter form:

```
http://amazon.com/o/ASIN/0060514485
```

---

14. http://en.wikipedia.org/wiki/Amazon_Standard_Identification_Number

Using this syntax would ideally be founded on some official documentation from Amazon. Where would you find definitive documentation on how to structure a link to a product of a given ASIN? My search through the Amazon developers' site led to the technical documentation,[15] whose latest version at the time of writing was the April 4, 2004, edition.[16] That trail leads ultimately to a page on the use of identifiers, which, alas, does not spell out how to formulate the URL for an item with a given ASIN.[17] The bottom line for now is that Wikipedia, combined with experimentation, is the best way to discern the URL structures of Amazon.

Let's apply this approach to other functions of Amazon. For instance, can you generate a URL for a full-text search? Go to Amazon, and enter your favorite search term. Take for example, `flower`. When I hit Submit, I got the following URL:

```
http://amazon.com/s/ref=nb_ss_gw/102-1755462-2944952?url=search-alias%3Daps&field-
keywords=flower&Go.x=0&Go.y=0
```

If I did the search again, say in a different browser, I got another URL:

```
http://amazon.com/s/ref=nb_ss_gw/102-8204915-1347316?url=search-alias%3Daps&field-
keywords=flower&Go.x=0&Go.y=0&Go=Go
```

Notice where things are similar and where they are different. Looking for what's common (the `http://amazon.com/s` prefix and the `?url=search-alias%3Daps&field-keywords=` `flower&Go.x=0&Go.y=0&Go=Go` argument), I eliminated the sections that were different to get the following:

```
http://amazon.com/s/?url=search-alias%3Daps&field-keywords=flower&Go.x=0&Go.y=0&
Go=Go
```

This URL seemed to work fine. You can even eliminate `&Go.x=0&Go.y=0&Go=Go` to boil the request down to this:

```
http://amazon.com/s/?url=search-alias%3Daps&field-keywords=flower
```

So, how do you limit the search to books? Going to Amazon, selecting the Book section, and using the `flower` keyword, you can get to the following URL:

```
http://amazon.com/s/ref=nb_ss_gw/102-6984159-2338509?url=search-
alias%3Dstripbooks&field-keywords=flower&Go.x=12&Go.y=6
```

Stripping away the parameters as before gave me this:

```
http://amazon.com/s/?url=search-alias%3Dstripbooks&field-keywords=flower
```

This trick works for the other departments. For example, to do a search on `flowers` in Home & Garden, use this:

```
http://amazon.com/s/?url=search-alias%3Dgarden&field-keywords=flower
```

---

15. `http://developer.amazonwebservices.com/connect/kbcategory.jspa?categoryID=19`

16. `http://developer.amazonwebservices.com/connect/entry.jspa?externalID=703&categoryID=19`

17. `http://docs.amazonwebservices.com/AWSECommerceService/2007-04-04/DG/ItemIdentifiers.html`

Based on these experiments, I would conclude that the URL for searching for a keyword in a department is as follows:

```
http://amazon.com/s/?url=search-alias%3D{amazon-dept}&field-keywords={keyword}
```

Let's run through the syntax of other organizational structures.

Lists

You can find the Wish List section at the following URL:

```
http://www.amazon.com/gp/registry/wishlist/
```

If you are logged in, you will see a list of your lists on the left. Look at the URL of one of the lists, which will look something like the one for my public wish list:

```
http://www.amazon.com/gp/registry/wishlist/1U5EXVPVS3WP5/ref=cm_wl_rlist_go/
102-5889202-4328156
```

Now look at another. I surmised that since the number on the right (102-5889202-4328156) remained the same and the other number (1U5EXVPVS3WP5) changed for each list, the unique 1U5EXVPVS3WP5 is the identifier for the list. You can point to a list using its list identifier by entering something similar to the following:

```
http://www.amazon.com/gp/registry/wishlist/1U5EXVPVS3WP5
```

Hence, you can conclude that the URL for a wish list is as follows:

```
http://www.amazon.com/gp/registry/wishlist/{wishlist-id}
```

Tags

Tags are a recent introduction to Amazon. You will see links like the following:

```
http://www.amazon.com/tag/czeslaw%20milosz/ref=tag_dp_ct/102-8204915-1347316
```

which can be reduced (following the strategy you took for other parts of Amazon) to this:

```
http://www.amazon.com/tag/czeslaw%20milosz/
```

The URL for books that correspond to a tag is as follows:

```
http://www.amazon.com/tag/{tag}/
```

Subject Headings

In looking through the Browse Subject section of Amazon (http://www.amazon.com/Subjects-Books/b/?ie=UTF8&node=1000), you can find a link such as the following:

```
http://www.amazon.com/b/ref=amb_link_1760642_21/104-0367717-
9318361?ie=UTF8&node=5&pf_rd_m=ATVPDKIKX0DER&pf_rd_s=center-
3&pf_rd_r=0J0MADEOYSN1VRBA6XZS&pf_rd_t=101&pf_rd_p=233185601&pf_rd_i=1000
```

This refers to the Computers & Internet Section, which you can reduce to the following:

```
http://www.amazon.com/b/?ie=UTF8&node=5
```

from which you can conclude that the URL for a section is as follows:

```
http://www.amazon.com/b/?ie=UTF8&node={node-number}
```

Caution The fact that the node is specified by number corresponding to its order by alphabetical listing rather than a unique key makes me concerned about the long-term stability of the link. Will 5 always refer to computers, or if there is another section added that goes before it alphabetically, will the link break?

There are plenty of other entities whose URL structures can be discerned, including the following:

- Listmania lists:

  ```
  http://www.amazon.com/lm/{list-mania-id}/
  ```

  For example:

  ```
  http://www.amazon.com/lm/1FHOE3G892IA/
  ```

- So You'd Like To guides:

  ```
  http://www.amazon.com/gp/richpub/syltguides/fullview/{slltg-id}
  ```

  For example:

  ```
  http://www.amazon.com/gp/richpub/syltguides/fullview/3T3I3YDBG889B
  ```

- Personal profiles:

  ```
  http://www.amazon.com/gp/pdp/profile/{user-id}/
  ```

  For example:

  ```
  http://www.amazon.com/gp/pdp/profile/A2D978B87TKMS2/
  ```

- Similar items for a book:

  ```
  http://amazon.com/sim/{ISBN-10}/1/ref=pd_sexpl_esi/
  ```

  For example:

  ```
  http://amazon.com/sim/0060514485/1/ref=pd_sexpl_esi/
  ```

In Chapter 1, you already studied how the Amazon URL language is used by the Library-Lookup bookmarklet to mash up Amazon and library catalogs. Linking to Amazon resources by a tag enables tag-based mashups, which I will describe in Chapter 3.

del.icio.us

The social-bookmarking site del.icio.us is a deeply influential site, credited by many for jump-starting the immense amount of activity around tagging.

The main resources of importance in del.icio.us (`http://del.ico.us`) are bookmarks, that is, URLs. You can associate tags with a given URL and look at an individual's collection of URLs and the tags they use. In this section, I again explain the URL structures by browsing through the site and noting the corresponding URLs.

You can look at the public bookmarks for a specific user (such as rdhyee) here:

```
http://del.icio.us/{user-id}
```

For example:

```
http://del.icio.us/rdhyee
```

You can see all the bookmarks of a user by tag here:

```
http://del.icio.us/{user-id}/{tag}
```

For example:

```
http://del.icio.us/rdhyee/NYTimes
```

You can see all the URLs that people have tagged with a given tag here:

```
http://del.icio.us/tag/{tag}
```

You can see just the popular URLs associated with the tag here:

```
http://del.icio.us/popular/{tag}
```

You can access today's popular items here:

```
http://del.icio.us/popular/
```

You can access just the newest popular ones here:

```
http://del.icio.us/popular/?new
```

Correlating a URL to a del.icio.us page is a bit trickier. Consider the following URL:

```
http://harpers.org/TheEcstasyOfInfluence.html
```

which you can reference from del.icio.us here:

```
http://del.icio.us/url/53113b15b14c90292a02c24b55c316e5
```

So, how do you get 53113b15b14c90292a02c24b55c316e5 from `http://harpers.org/TheEcstasyOfInfluence.html`? The answer is that the identifier is an md5 hash of the URL. In Python, the following line of code:

```
md5.new("http://harpers.org/TheEcstasyOfInfluence.html").hexdigest()
```

or the following PHP code:

```php
<?php
 $url = "http://harpers.org/TheEcstasyOfInfluence.html";
 print md5($url);
?>
```

yields 53113b15b14c90292a02c24b55c316e5.

Note that the following:

```
http://del.icio.us/url?url=http://harpers.org/TheEcstasyOfInfluence.html
```

also does work and redirects to the following:

```
http://del.icio.us/url/53113b15b14c90292a02c24b55c316e5
```

Screen-Scraping and Bots

The focus of this book is on creating mashups using public APIs and web services. If you want to mash up a web site, one of the first things to look for is a public API. A public API is specifically designed as an official channel for giving you programmatic access to data and services of the web site. In some cases, however, you may want to create mashups of services and data for which there is no public API. Even if there is a public API, it is extremely useful to look beyond just the API. An API is often incomplete. That is, there is functionality in the user interface that is not included in the API. Without a public API for a web site, you need to resort to other techniques to reuse the data and functionality of the application.

One such technique is screen-scraping, which involves extracting data from the user interface designed for display to human users. Let me define bots and spiders, which often use screen-scraping techniques. Bots (also known as an *Internet bots*, *web robots*, and *webbots*) are computer programs that "run automated tasks over the Internet," typically tasks that are "both simple and structurally repetitive."[18] Bots come in a variety of well-known types and engage in activities that range from positive and benign to illegal and destructive:

- "Chatterbots" that automatically reply to human users through instant messaging or IRC[19]

- Wikipedia bots that automate the monitoring, maintaining, and editing of the Wikipedia[20]

- Ticket-purchasing bots that buy tickets on behalf of ticket scalpers

- Bots that generate spam or launch distributed denial of service attacks

Web spiders (also known as *web crawlers* and *web harvesters*) are a special type of Internet bot. They typically focus on getting collections of web pages—up to billions of pages—rather than focused extraction of data on a given page. It's the spiders from search engines such as Google and Yahoo! that visit your web pages to collect your web pages with which to build their large indexes of the Web.

There are some important technical challenges to screen-scraping. The vast majority of data embedded in HTML is not marked up to be unambiguously and consistently parsed by bots. Hence, screen-scraping depends on making rather brittle assumptions about what the placement and presentation style of embedded data implies about the semantics of the data. The author of web pages often changes its visual style without intending to change any underlying semantics—but still ends up breaking, often inadvertently, screen-scraping code. In

---

18. http://en.wikipedia.org/wiki/Internet_bot, accessed on July 11, 2007, as http://en.wikipedia.org/w/index.php?title=Internet_bot&oldid=142845374

19. http://en.wikipedia.org/wiki/Chatterbot

20. http://en.wikipedia.org/wiki/Wikipedia:Bots

contrast, by packaging data in commonly understood formats such as XML geared to computer consumption, you are an implicit—if not explicit—commitment to the reliable transfer of data to others. Public API functions are controlled, defined programmatic interfaces between the creator of the site and you as the user. Hence, accessing data through the public API should theoretically be less fragile than screen-scraping/web-scraping a web site.

■**Caution** Since I'm not a lawyer, do not construe anything in this book, including the following discussion, as legal advice!

If you engage in screen-scraping, you need to be thoughtful about how you go about it and, in some cases, even whether you should do it in the first place. Start with reading the terms of service (ToS) of the web site. Some ToSs explicitly forbid the use of bots (such as automated crawling) of their sites. How should you respond to such terms of services? On the one hand, you could decide to take a conservative stance and not screen-scrape the site at all. Or you could go to the other extreme and screen-scrape the site at will, waging that you won't get sued and noting that if the web site owner is not happy, the owner could just use technical means to shut down your bot.

I think a middle ground is often in order, one that is well-stated by Bausch, Calishan, and Dornfest: "So use the API whenever you can, scrape only when you absolutely must, and mind your Ps and Qs when fiddling about with other people's data."[21] In other words, when you screen-scrape a web site, you should be efficient in how you use computational and network resources and respectful of the owner in how you reuse the data. Consider contacting the web site owners to ask for permission.

Even though bots have negative connotations, many do recognize the positive benefits of some bots, especially search engines. If everyone were to take an extremely conservative reading of the terms of services for web sites, wouldn't many of the things we take for granted on the Internet (such as search engines) simply disappear?

Since screen-scraping web sites without public APIs is largely beyond the scope of this book, I will refer you to the following books for more information:

- *Webbots, Spiders, and Screen Scrapers* by Michael Schrenk (No Starch Press, 2007)

- *Spidering Hacks* by Kevin Hemenway and Tara Calishain (O'Reilly and Associates, 2003)

■**Note** There's some recent research around end-user innovation that should encourage web site owners to make their sites extensible and even hackable. See Eric Von Hippel's books. Von Hippel argues that many products and innovations are originally created by users of products, not the manufacturers that then bake in those innovations after the fact (http://en.wikipedia.org/wiki/Eric_Von_Hippel).

---

21. *Google Hacks, Third Edition* by Paul Bausch, Tara Calishain, and Rael Dornfest (O'Reilly and Associates, 2006); http://proquest.safaribooksonline.com/0596527063/I_0596527063_CHP_8_SECT_8

Summary

In this chapter, I presented techniques for assessing and exploiting features of web sites that make them amenable to mashups. Specifically, you looked at web sites from the point of view of an end user. I presented a list of questions to use in analyzing web sites. Key questions include the following: What are the main resources and their URLs? How is the public being used in mashups? Does the site use tags, feeds, and weblogging features? What are the data formats for importing and exporting data? You applied these questions briefly when revisiting the mashups from the previous chapter.

The bulk of this chapter is devoted to studying URL languages of web sites and their importance in making mashups. Specifically, I presented an extensive analysis of Flickr, which has a rich URL language that covers a large part—but not all—of Flickr's functionality. I presented a simple pattern for creating that exploits the URL languages (the Mashup-by-URL-Templating-and-Embedding pattern) to create a mashup between Flickr and WordPress. I continued my examination of URL languages with a study of Google Maps, Amazon, and del.icio.us. I concluded the chapter with a discussion of screen-scraping and bots and how they can be used when public APIs are not available.

You'll turn in the next chapter to looking in depth at one group of issues raised in this chapter: tagging and folksonomies, their relationship to formal taxa, and how they can be used to knit together elements within and across sites.

CHAPTER 3

■ ■ ■

Understanding Tagging and Folksonomies

A major challenge of dealing with digital content—our own and others—is organizing it. We want to be able to find the piece of content we want, and we want to be able see its relationship to the whole and to other digital content. We might want to be able to reuse this content. Also, most important, we want other people to be able to understand the organization of our digital content so that they can find and reuse it.

Tags are one of the most popular mechanisms used in contemporary web sites for letting users organize digital content. A *tag* is a label, typically a word or short phrase, that a user can add to a piece of digital content, such as a photo, a URL, a video, or an e-mail (don't confuse these tags with the tags used to mark up pages, especially an HTML page's metatags). You can then search for digital content with those tags. As you saw in Chapter 2, when tags are embedded in URLs, you can link and embed content related by tags through those URLs.

The term *folksonomy* was coined to contrast tags with *taxonomies*, which are formal schemes typically created by communities with strict practices of classifying items. In other words, folksonomy uses an informal collection of tags provided by the community to build up a collaborative description of an item. There are few restrictions on the tags you can come up with to associate with your content. In fact, there are no preset categories or controlled vocabularies from which you must choose. Still, tags have proliferated; users have taken to them en masse, generating collections—or *clouds*—of tags that help order their own content as well as content throughout the Web. You can use these tags to relate content in your mashups, if you're mindful, however, that tags can often be idiosyncratic, ambiguous, and irregular.

For now at least, tags have not led to the anarchy predicted by some taxonomists, and there is more order to how people tag than you might think, created by rules such as personal and social conventions and the syntax of tags. On the other hand, the proliferation of tagging has certainly not obviated the need for formal classification schemes. There are rich opportunities to bring together user-generated, bottom-up folksonomic tags and controlled vocabularies and taxa.

This chapter will show you how to connect content by mashing things up, with tagging as the glue. Tags allow the aggregation of resources within a system (say, pictures in Flickr—your own and others) and across web sites (Technorati).

This chapter covers the following:

- It illustrates how tags are used in Flickr, del.icio.us, and Technorati.

- It shows how people are using tags to create interesting apps with tags.

- It discusses how people are hacking the tagging system to put more information into Flickr and other web sites, specifically *geotagging*, and now, more generally, machine tags.

- It covers some issues around the interoperability of tags across systems, specifically through a study of Technorati.

- It briefly shows how tagging relates to formal classification systems, using books as an example.

Tagging in Flickr

According to the Flickr FAQ,[1] "tags are like keywords or labels that you add to a photo to make it easier to find later." In other words, tagging is a central way of tying words to pictures. (Think about how search works—the user types in words and phrases.) Tagging is important for photos since computer vision/automatic scene recognition is in its infancy.

WILL WE HAVE VISUAL SEARCHING INSTEAD OF RELYING ON TAGS?

Note that companies such as Riya.com are hard at work to bring you visual search.[2] What might a non-word-based search look like? Draw something you want to look for, and the search engine will return pictures that look like what you drew? Or would you present a photo to the search engine, and it would return similar photos? The fact that we still have to type words in a search engine to search for pictures, video, or music shows how dependant we are on words for searching and for describing nontextual objects. That's why tags are so central in Flickr, where the dominant form of data is visual. That's not to say that there aren't interesting experiments in nontextual search such as the "search by sketch" system retreivr (`http://labs.systemone.at/retrievr/`).

Here are some practical skills related to tags in Flickr you will learn in the following sections:

- You'll see how tags are used in the Flickr community—by individuals and by subgroups—right across Flickr to bind photos together. (It's useful to study tags before creating your own.)

- You'll see how to tag a picture and thereby run into issues when you sit down to tag your pictures or those of others.

- You'll see how to deal with the syntax of tags in Flickr, how to use multiword tags, and how multiword tags get boiled down to canonical tags.

---

1. `http://flickr.com/help/tags/#37`

2. `http://riya.com` and `http://www.riya.com/riyaAPI` (for the Riya API)

Tags in Flickr

In Chapter 2, I presented an overview of how tags are used in Flickr, specifically how they manifest in the web site's URL language. Here, you'll look deeper at Flickr tags, specifically at the social context of tags in Flickr, the syntax and semantics of tags in Flickr, hacks of Flickr tags, and some remixes and mashups that build upon the Flickr tags.

Before I jump to those topics, let me present parts of the URL language concerning tags. For instance, you can see a list of popular tags in Flickr here:

```
http://www.flickr.com/photos/tags/
```

The URL for the most recent photos in Flickr associated with a tag is as follows:

```
http://www.flickr.com/photos/tags/{tag}/
```

For example:

```
http://www.flickr.com/photos/tags/flower/
```

Instead of sorting photos by the date uploaded, you can sort them by descending "interestingness" (a quantitative measure calculated by Flickr of how "interesting" a photo is):

```
http://www.flickr.com/photos/tags/{tag}/interesting/
```

Finally, for some tags, Flickr identifies distinct clusters of photos, which you can access here:

```
http://www.flickr.com/photos/tags/{tag}/clusters/
```

For example:

```
http://www.flickr.com/photos/tags/flower/clusters/
```

You can display the popular tags used by a specific user here:

```
http://www.flickr.com/photos/{user-id}/tags/
```

You can list all the user's tags here:

```
http://www.flickr.com/photos/{user-id}/alltags/
```

You can show all photos with a given tag for a specific user here:

```
http://www.flickr.com/photos/{user-id}/tags/{tag}/
```

How Tags Are Used in Practice

So, how do people actually use tags in Flickr? Look around to get a feel for how people have been tagging their photos. It is also helpful to draw upon the observations of seasoned Flickr users with respect to general trends for how tags are used—or should be used.[3]

---

3. http://www.flickr.com/groups/central/discuss/2026/ and http://www.flickr.com/groups/central/discuss/2730/

The issue of how tags are used is complicated. To get a feel for the issues involved, let's look at how people tag photos for July 4. You can probably imagine a number of different ways of tagging, including the following:

- july4 (for example, http://www.flickr.com/photos/tags/july4/)

- fourthofjuly (for example, http://www.flickr.com/photos/tags/fourthofjuly)

- july4th (for example, http://www.flickr.com/photos/tags/july4th)

- july04 (for example, http://www.flickr.com/photos/tags/july04)

- july4th2007 (for example, http://www.flickr.com/photos/tags/july4th2007)

As an end user, which tag should you use? It depends. Are you trying to use the most popular one? Flickr offers no guidance about which specific tag to use but attempts to make pictures related to July 4 all findable regardless of the exact tag used. The Flickr clustering algorithm, when applied to some of these specific tags (for example, http://www.flickr.com/photos/tags/july4th/clusters/), groups pictures with tags aimed at describing the same phenomenon.

It is significant that you can set a default permission that allows other people (which you can limit to your family, friends, contacts, or any registered Flickr user in general) to add tags and notes to your photos—but there is no provision for letting other people change the title or description of your photo. This suggests it might be a good idea to let other people tag your photos. Think of scenarios when it would be helpful to let others tag your photos. Consider why it might not be a good idea to let other people change the title or description of a photo.

Creating Your Own Tags

To add a tag to a photo for which you have permission, follow these steps:

1. Go to the Flickr page of the photo.

2. Click the Add a Tag link. A text box will open, and you can enter a single tag or a series of tags separated by spaces. You can also enter phrases by using double quote marks around the phrase.

3. You can also choose to add tags by selecting from tags you already use by clicking the Choose from Your Tags link instead of entering tags in the text box.

Syntax of Tags in Flickr

The Flickr tagging system is sufficiently well designed that you may never have occasion to think about the syntactical limitations of tags in Flickr. However, let's look at a simple case study. As noted earlier, you can add phrases as tags using double quotes, such as "San Francisco". The tag is displayed as "San Francisco", but internally, it is represented with spaces and with punctuation removed and letters turned to lowercase—that is, sanfrancisco. You can prove this by going to a picture and trying to enter "San Francisco" and sanfrancisco as tags. Flickr will take only one of the tags since it considers them to be the same tag.[4] Now, why should you care about the exact syntax of a tag? One reason is that tag syntax is going to be different among systems.

---

4. http://www.flickr.com/services/api/misc.tags.html draws the distinction between the "clean" version of a tag and the "raw" version of the tag.

To understand this, it helps to understand at least one system, such as Flickr, and then to figure out the syntax of tagging for these other web sites or applications. Also, it gives you insight into one issue that will challenge all tagging systems: figuring out which tags are the same and which are not.

Potential Weaknesses of Tags

Anyone who has spent much time using tags runs into the idiosyncrasies, inaccuracies, and irregularities often present in tagging. Drawing from an analysis in the Wikipedia, I list some possible causes for these problems:[5]

Polysemy: Since words often have multiple meanings, which meaning is supposed to be associated with a tag? (For example, does the tag apple refer to the fruit or to a computer?)

Synonymy: When multiple words can have the same or similar meaning, which tag should you use, and how do you find all the tags that mean the same? (For example, are "Independence Day" in the United States and "July 4th" the same?)

Word inflections: Since words are modified for specific grammatical contexts, which variation do you use for a tag? (For example, you might see mouse and mice.)

Syntactic constraints: How should you create tags out of phrases when spaces are not allowed? How should you deal with punctuation? How do you deal with non-ASCII words?

In this chapter, I cover the issue of word inflections (specifically the handling of single versus plural forms) and the syntax of tags, a topic that is not explicitly mentioned in this list but that presents practical difficulties in making mashups based on tags.

Singular and Plural Forms of Tags in Flickr

Web sites often leave it ambiguous whether users should use the singular or plural form for tags. When you use these tags, it's helpful to know whether tags created with the single and plural forms are treated as the same tag.

Here I describe a small experiment to figure out how Flickr deals with this issue, one you can adapt for other web sites. I tagged one of my photos with the tag mouse and did a full-text search and a tag search for mouse, mouses, and mice. Table 3-1 records whether the photo is returned in the search.

Table 3-1. *Stemming of Terms Related to* mouse *in Flickr*

Search Term	Full-Text or Tag Search?	Was the Picture Found?
mouse	Full text	Yes
mouse	Tag	Yes
mouses	Full text	Yes
mouses	Tag	No
mice	Full text	Yes
mice	Tag	No

5. http://en.wikipedia.org/wiki/Folksonomy as http://en.wikipedia.org/w/index.php?title= Folksonomy&oldid=145985651

Based on these limited observations, I can make the following tentative conclusions about how Flickr handles singular and plural English nouns in tags:

- Singular and plural forms of English nouns used are considered to be different tags.

- In full-text searches, Flickr uses some form of stemming to match singular and plural forms of English nouns. The Flickr stemming process is at least sophisticated enough to recognize that `mouse` and `mice` are related words.

Obviously, you would have to either find official documentation from Flickr or test with many more tags to validate these conclusions.[6] The point here is not to rigorously test these conclusions but to point out how simple experiments can sometimes reveal interesting aspects about a web site such as Flickr.

Hacking the Tagging System: Geotagging and Machine Tags

The Flickr map (`http://www.flickr.com/map/`), which displays Flickr photos on a map, is the official implementation of what started as a hack. Before the map, there was no official way to store the location information of a picture and display that location information on a map.

The ad hoc solution that became widely adopted was to insert geo-related information into the Flickr tags, specifically the `geotagged` tag along with `geo:lat` and `geo:lon`, to indicate the latitude and longitude of a photo.

This convention of geotagging worked well in many ways. Hundreds of thousands of Flickr photos were geotagged according to this convention. Tools such as the Google Maps in Flickr arose to use the geotagging data. On the downside, the Flickr user interface became cluttered with tags that were meant for programmatic consumption. There wasn't ideal support for such tags in the Flickr API (for instance, the only reason for the `geotagged` tag to be there was that the API did not allow you to look for tags that began with `geo:lat`).

It was to fix these problems that Flickr introduced machine tags, also known as *triple tags*. Machine tags are tags with a specific syntax aimed primarily for programmatic consumption and not directly for display to the typical end user. You can use machine tags to store extra data elements for a given photo. The most important example of such data has so far been the latitude and longitude associated with a photo; it's so important that Flickr ultimately introduced specialized functionality to handle this data to prevent people from shoehorning it into tags.

Machine tags are meant to support new types of applications along the lines of geotagging by adding functionality to the API that recognizes that machine tags have a different use pattern than standard tags. Also, the UI of Flickr has changed to hide the default machine tags from users.

The syntax of machine tags, which relates the triplets of `namespace`, `predicate`, and `value`, is as follows:

`namespace:predicate=value`

So, for example, `geo:lat=37.866276` is a machine tag, where `geo` is a namespace, `lat` is a predicate, and `37.866276` is a value.

---

6. The thread at `http://www.flickr.com/forums/bugs/31668/` includes a Flickr staff member confirming the use of stemming in titles and descriptions. `http://tech.groups.yahoo.com/group/yws-flickr/message/1913` mentions stemming in the context of tags. `http://www5.flickr.mud.yahoo.com/help/forum/37259/#reply211324` shows why these things happen.

Since machine tags are still in the early stages of uptake in Flickr, which is a pioneer in the field of letting people stick place in arbitrary data into their systems, I would be surprised to find other web applications that are further along. There are some nascent developments along these fronts in Google Base (which has attributes)[7] and Amazon S3 (with its item-level metadata).[8] In Chapter 16, I return to the topic of Amazon S3.

Interesting Apps Using Flickr Tags

A good way to understand how tags are used in Flickr is to study how others have built on top of the tagging system. Here are several to study:

- Flickr Related Tag Browser (`http://www.airtightinteractive.com/projects/related_ tag_browser/app/`) lets you browse relationships among related tags.

- findr (`http://www.forestandthetrees.com/findr/findr.html`) lets you display related tags and photos that have been tagged by a combination of related tags.

- fastr (`http://randomchaos.com/games/fastr/`) is a game in which you guess a tag based on the photo presented to you.

- ZoneTag (`http://zonetag.research.yahoo.com/`) is an example of Flickr tag hacking to insert location data of photos taken by cell phones.

- TagMaps (`http://tagmaps.research.yahoo.com/`) shows on a map popular tags correlated with geotagged Flickr photos for a region.

These examples show how Flickr calculates relationships among tags by mining information about how tags are being used. You can get a sense of how people use tags.

Tagging in del.icio.us

del.icio.us is a social-bookmarking application, the first of its kind and in many ways still the best. People use deli.cio.us to keep track of bookmarks, identified by URLs, and to follow other users' bookmarks. Tagging is an important part of del.icio.us, which pioneered tagging in general and has done much to popularize it.

In the discussion of Flickr, I show how tagging enables textual searching and browsing of nonverbal objects such as pictures. Why would tags be useful in del.icio.us for categorizing web pages, whose primary constituent still tends to be text? Tags capture essentials about a web page that cannot be easily uncovered by full-text searching. Useful tags might not even involve any of the words that are actually in the text of the web page. Tags often describe the relationship between the bookmark and the user (for example, the tag toread) rather than anything intrinsic to the web page. Nonetheless, you might get to the point in which computer summarization techniques could automatically generate tags for a given web page. For instance, Tagthe.net (`http://tagthe.net/`) provides such an API.

---

7. `http://base.google.com/support/bin/answer.py?answer=27882`

8. `http://docs.amazonwebservices.com/AmazonS3/2006-03-01/BasicsObjects.html` and `http:// docs.amazonwebservices.com/AmazonS3/2006-03-01/RESTObjectPUT.html`, where you can stick in user metadata (name/value pair).

Note a fundamental difference between tagging in Flickr and del.icio.us: in Flickr, each object being tagged (a photo) has only one set of tags, created by the object's owner and others granted permission to tag the photo. In del.icio.us, each object (a bookmark) being tagged could belong to many users, each having their own sets of tags. As Thomas Vander Wal explains, "broad" folksonomies such as that of del.icio.us (as opposed to the "narrow" folksonomies, such as Flickr's) enable one to compare how different people tag the same object.[9] For objects that are tagged by many people, del.icio.us is able to recommend tags to use, based solely on how others have already tagged the object. In Flickr, you can't get such recommendations since there is only one set of tags for any photo.

Chapter 2 documented the URL language of del.icio.us. In this chapter, I describe more about the mechanics of adding tags and the issues of multiple-word tags and multilingual tags.

Mechanics of Adding Tags in del.icio.us

Without the del.icio.us Firefox plug-in, you can use the web site's upload form:

1. Go to `http://del.icio.us/post/`, enter the URL (for example, `http://www.rubyonrails.org/`), and hit the Save button.

2. You will end up on a page that prompts you for the description, notes, and tags. Note that del.icio.us offers recommended tags and lists your tags, which are tags you have already used in del.icio.us—if any.

With the del.icio.us Firefox plug-in (`http://del.icio.us/help/firefox/extension`), it becomes easier to push a link into del.icio.us. You can also use a bookmarklet to put in pages (`http://del.icio.us/help/buttons`) or get Internet Explorer buttons (`http://del.icio.us/help/ie/extension`).

Dealing with Case and Multiword Phrases

In contrast to Flickr, del.icio.us tags are single-word labels. Tags in del.icio.us cannot contain any spaces, but they can contain punctuation. The example given in the documentation (`http://del.icio.us/help/tags`) is what to do with a multiword phrase such as *San Francisco*; the suggested tags are `sf`, `san-francisco`, `SanFrancisco`, `san.francisco`, or "whatever makes sense to you." Does it matter which of these tags you choose?

Let's gather some facts about how del.icio.us works with search phrases. There's some documentation at `http://del.icio.us/help/search`, but you can also do a little experiment. Let's look for *San Francisco* in del.icio.us. If you type **San Francisco** in the search box, selecting the option to search all of del.icio.us, you go here:

`http://del.icio.us/search/?fr=del_icio_us&p=san+francisco&type=all`

You can limit the domain of the search (to your own bookmarks, to all of del.icio.us, or to the Web). This search "goes through bookmark descriptions, notes, and tags." You can limit the search to tags via a `tag:` prefix (`tag:sanfrancisco`):

`http://del.icio.us/search/?fr=del_icio_us&p=tag%3Asanfrancisco&type=user`

---

9. `http://www.personalinfocloud.com/2005/02/explaining_and_.html`

What can you learn from this search?

- The case of tags is preserved in how a tag is displayed (that is, if you enter **SanFrancisco**, it will stay SanFrancisco). However, searches for tags are case insensitive; that is, if you enter **sanfrancisco** or **SanFrancisco**, you still get the same tags (http://del.icio.us/tag/SanFrancisco).

- On the other hand, punctuation is significant in search as well as in the display. Unlike Flickr, in which punctuation is stripped from the canonical representation of a tag, punctuation does not behave like whitespace.

In del.icio.us, because you can't have spaces in tags, there are many variations in dealing with multiword tags. Returning to the example of San Francisco and the variants sf, san-francisco, SanFrancisco, and san.francisco for a minute, contrast the syntax of tags in del.icio.us and Flickr:

- In del.icio.us, San Francisco is not a valid tag because it contains a space. sf, san-francisco, SanFrancisco, and san.francisco are all distinct tags.

- In Flickr, San Francisco is a permissible tag. However, you cannot tag the same photo with any of the following variants (san-francisco, SanFrancisco, and san.francisco) because the punctuation is stripped away to determine the clean version of a tag.

Getting More Information

The http://tech.groups.yahoo.com/group/ydn-del.icio.us/ site is a good place to get answers to developer-type technical questions. You'll often see Joshua Schachter, the founder of deli.cio.us, actively answering people's questions.

REPRESENTATION OF LATIN-8 AND UNICODE CHARACTERS

Let's see how tags work for Latin-8 characters first (for example, the French word *français*) and then for Chinese.

In Flickr

Let's look at http://flickr.com/photos/tags/fran%C3%A7ais/. There is no collapsing of *français* to *francais*. See the photo at http://flickr.com/photos/raymondyee/368644336/ to see that I can have both a français and francais tag; invoking the API[10] confirms that the two tags stay distinct.

It seems that Chinese works in a similar way. I don't know much Chinese, but I do know my name in Chinese (余俊雄). I managed to add it as a tag for one of my pictures.[11] You can pull up all pictures with that tag:

http://flickr.com/photos/raymondyee/tags/%E4%BD%99%E4%BF%8A%E9%9B%84/

---

10. http://api.flickr.com/services/rest/?method=flickr.tags.getListPhoto&api_key={api-key}&photo_id=368644336

Again, you can confirm that %E4%BD%99%E4%BF%8A%E9%9B%84 is a URL-encoded UTF-8 representation of my Chinese name. With Python, here's that code:

```
import urllib
print urllib.unquote('%E4%BD%99%E4%BF%8A%E9%9B%84').decode('utf-8')
u'\u4f59\u4fca\u96c4'
```

And you can see that the Unicode character point 4f59 is indeed 余.[12]

In del.icio.us

I added a URL for the France-Berkeley program:[13]

```
http://del.icio.us/tag/fran%C3%A7ais
```

does come up with many links with the tag français, as well as the corresponding full-text search for français.[14]

To test Chinese functionality in del.icio.us, I added my picture,[15] and as expected, I can pull up the picture via the tag of my Chinese name,[16] and a search works.[17] How do you get fran%C3%A7ais from français? With a bit of Python programming, you can convince yourself that it's a URL-encoding of the UTF-8 encoding of français:

```
>>> print chr(231)
ç
>>> print urllib.urlencode({'q':chr(231).decode('ISO-8859-1').➡
encode('utf-8')})
q=%C3%A7
```

YouTube copes well with Chinese characters too: I can find a video tagged with my Chinese name: http://www.youtube.com/results?search_query=%E4%BD%99%E4%BF%8A%E9%9B%84.

In rel-tag

The rel-tag specification gives the following example of how to encode tags:[18]

```
<a href="http://technorati.com/tag/Sant%C3%A9+et+bien-%C3%AAtre" rel="tag">
Santé et bien-être</a>
```

---

11. http://flickr.com/photos/raymondyee/79915850/ and http://flickr.com/photos/raymondyee/tags/%E4%BD%99%E4%BF%8A%E9%9B%84/

12. http://www.cojak.org/index.php?function=code_lookup&term=4F59 and http://www.unicode.org/cgi-bin/GetUnihanData.pl?codepoint=4F59

13. http://del.icio.us/url?url=http://ies.berkeley.edu/fbf/

14. http://del.icio.us/search/?fr=del_icio_us&p=fran%C3%A7ais&type=all

15. http://del.icio.us/url?url=http://flickr.com/photos/raymondyee/79915850/

16. http://del.icio.us/tag/%E4%BD%99%E4%BF%8A%E9%9B%84

17. http://del.icio.us/search/?fr=del_icio_us&p=%E4%BD%99%E4%BF%8A%E9%9B%84&type=all

18. http://microformats.org/wiki/rel-tag#Encoding_issues as http://microformats.org/wiki?title=rel-tag&diff=0&oldid=18625

You can verify that the tag is the URL encoding of the UTF-8 encoding of the tag string. In Python, the following code:

```
import urllib
s = "Santé et bien-être"
u = s.decode('iso-8859-1')
print urllib.urlencode({'q':u.encode('utf8')})
```

returns the following:

```
q=Sant%C3%A9+et+bien-%C3%AAtre
http://technorati.com/tag/Sant%C3%A9+et+bien-%C3%AAtre
```

which is a search on *Santé et bien-être*.

Gathering Content Through Tags in Technorati

Technorati is a search engine, focused primarily on searching weblogs but also "tagged social media" (specifically, photos in Flickr and videos in YouTube). Technorati is an excellent case study of how a web site crawls for tags on the Web and then uses those tags to organize digital content. (Think of Technorati as a big tag-based mashup.) Let's now look in detail at how Technorati presents tags to users and how it finds the tags in the first place.

Searching Technorati with Tags

The primary emphasis in the Technorati user interface is on searching by tag. In fact, the default search is a tag search. For instance, a search for the term *mashup* brings you to this page:

```
http://technorati.com/tag/mashup
```

Generally, items for a given tag are at the following URL:

```
http;//technorati.com/tag/{tag}
```

where {tag} is the URL-encoded version of the UTF-8 encoding of the tag. The items are broken as follows:

- Blog posts (`http://technorati.com/posts/tag/{tag}`)

- Videos (`http://technorati.com/videos/tag/{tag}`)

- Photos (`http://technorati.com/photos/tag/{tag}`)

- Weblogs (`http://technorati.com/blogs/tag/{tag}`)

Note that you can string tags together with OR to search for multiple tags.

A quick way to get a feel for Technorati is to look at the "most popular" search:

```
http://technorati.com/pop/
```

How Technorati Finds Tags on the Web

Technorati derives its tags from a variety of sources, as documented at `http://technorati.com/help/tags.html`:

- Categories embedded in Atom and RSS 2.0 feeds. (See Chapter 4 for more on feeds.)

- Tags in links using the rel-tag microformat, such as `<a href="http://technorati.com/tag/{tagname}" rel="tag">tagname</a>`. (See Chapter 18 for a complete description.)

- Tags from public photos in Flickr.

- Tags from public videos in YouTube.

Word Inflections and Syntactic Constraints in Technorati Tags

As with Flickr and deli.cio.us, singular and plural nouns in tags are not conflated. For example, the following:

`http://technorati.com/tag/mouse`

and the following:

`http://technorati.com/tag/mice`

return different results. Technorati is, however, able to recognize that `mouse` and `mice` are related tags, as are `peripherals` and `animals`. Unlike Flickr, but like del.icio.us, punctuation in Technorati tags is significant in tag-based searches. For example, the following:

`http://technorati.com/tag/san+francisco`

returns different results from the following:

`http://technorati.com/tag/san-francisco`

Tag searches are not case sensitive in Technorati, though other applications that use the `rel-tag` microformat may be case sensitive. Through `rel-tag`, you should be able to pass in the full range of non-ASCII words as tags. (See the "Representation of Latin-8 and Unicode Characters" sidebar on representing non-ASCII characters in tags to learn more.)

The next time you want to make a mashup of digital content based on tags, you can model what to do on how Technorati has dealt with making tags from different web sites work (*interoperate*) with one another. Moreover, you can leverage its work by linking directly to Technorati (through its URL language) or by using its API (`http://technorati.com/developers/api/`).

Using Tags to Mash Up Flickr and del.icio.us

In the following sections, I'll show how you can use tags in del.icio.us to collect Flickr pictures and make a simple visual collection. The idea is simple: you can use del.icio.us to gather pictures from Flickr by tagging Flickr URLs in del.icio.us and using a specific del.icio.us tag on all the pictures you want in the same set. Because del.icio.us shows thumbnails of photos from Flickr, you get a simple album maker using this combination of Flickr and del.icio.us and tagging.

Here's an example:

```
http://del.icio.us/rdhyee/set:Berkeley
```

In this case, I've tagged a selection of Flickr URLs with the tag `set:Berkeley`.

This mashup is certainly not a replacement for Picasa or iPhoto. You can't sort the pictures, for instance, though you could imagine adding another tag with a number and writing a Greasemonkey script that would sort the pictures for you (and allow you to edit the ordering). This mashup is a helpful supplement to Flickr, but you might ask, why not just use the Flickr favorites or collections to accomplish this goal? The problem that this little mashup solves is combining your own photos with those of others. Favorites must be other people's pictures; your collections can contain only your own photos.

Other Systems That Use Tagging

Many other applications use tags. If you look at the Wikipedia article on tags,[19] you will see some of the following mentioned:

- Other social-bookmarking sites.

- Other photo-sharing sites.

- Video sites such as YouTube.

- The Gmail and Thunderbird 2.0 email systems.

- You can generate tag clouds based on categories from your blog (for example, Ultimate Tag Warrior 3 WordPress plug-in[20]).

Relationship of Tags to Formal Classification Schemes

I don't think that folksonomies will supplant formal subject headings and taxonomies. There's plenty of room to experiment with the interplay between folksonomic and taxonomic approaches. Indeed, how can one combine some of the simplicity of tagging with the careful structures of formal classification schemes? In this section, I show a specific example to highlight some of the relevant challenges.

Let's return to an example I first used in Chapter 1, the book Czesław Miłosz's *New and Collected Poems 1931–2001*, specifically the hardcover edition with the ISBN-10 of 006019667X. You can search for the book at the Library of Congress here to learn how the Library of Congress has formally classified the book and its author:

```
http://catalog.loc.gov/cgi-bin/Pwebrecon.cgi?v3=1&DB=local&CMD=kisn+006019667X&
CNT=10+records+per+page
```

---

19. `http://en.wikipedia.org/wiki/Tags`
20. `http://www.neato.co.nz/ultimate-tag-warrior/`

The book is assigned to the Library of Congress Subject Heading (LCSH) `Miłosz, Czesław Translations into English`:

```
http://catalog.loc.gov/cgi-bin/Pwebrecon.cgi?SC=Subject&SA=Mi%C5%82osz%2C%20Czes
%C5%82aw%20Translations%20into%20English
```

Through this subject heading, which you can access through its corresponding URL, you can get all the books that are classified in the same group. In this specific case, you can reliably find a list of many, if not all, of the English translations of Miłosz's poetry published in the United States.

Why does this matter? By using the LCSH as a category, you get to leverage the careful and reliable work that the Library of Congress has done in classifying books. Just because you use tags doesn't mean you have to ignore formal classifications.

The LCSH is not the only formal classification scheme around for books. If you look the same book up at the Online Computer Library Center (OCLC) WorldCat.org site, like so:

```
http://worldcatlibraries.org/wcpa/isbn/006019667X
```

you will find the look listed under the subject of *Miłosz, Czesław*:

```
http://worldcatlibraries.org/search?q=su%3AMi%C5%82osz%2C+Czes%C5%82aw
```

The subject headers used by OCLC are based on its FAST project, which aims to simplify yet be upward compatible with LCSH:

```
http://www.oclc.org/research/projects/fast/
```

To see a sophisticated example of how tags can be effectively combined with formal classification, let's look at OCLC, where you can get a different subject category for the same book:

```
http://worldcatlibraries.org/search?q=su%3AMi%C5%82osz%2C+Czes%C5%82aw
```

You can feed an ISBN to LibraryThing, a social book-cataloging site, with this:

```
http://www.librarything.com/isbn/{isbn}
```

which will redirect to a URL with a `work-id` tag (different editions of a book, which can have different ISBNs, are collected under the same `work-id`):

```
http://www.librarything.com/work/{librarything-work-id}
```

Using our example, the following URL:

```
http://www.librarything.com/isbn/006019667X
```

redirects to the following:

```
http://www.librarything.com/work/161671
```

where you see tags that users of LibraryThing have applied to the book. At the same time, you can find LibraryThing lists here:

```
http://www.librarything.com/work-info/{librarything-work-id}
```

For example:

```
http://www.librarything.com/work-info/161671
```

The following is how the book has been formally classified (including such metadata as the Library of Congress Call Number and the Dewey Decimal classification) along with the LCSH:

```
http://www.librarything.com/subject.php?subject=Mi%B1osz%2C+Czes%B1aw%O9
Translations+into+English
```

■**Caution** There is an error in character encoding in LibraryThing that causes `Miłosz, Czesław` to be incorrectly displayed.[21]

Summary

In this chapter, you looked at how to use tags to create mashups. I first compared and contrasted how tags are used in Flickr and del.icio.us. Flickr's tagging system is an example of a narrow folksonomy, enabling textual searches to be done over visual media. As a broad taxonomy, del.icio.us involves many people tagging any given bookmark, creating multiple sets for tags for a bookmark. You considered some factors that reduce the reliability of tags and studied specifically the issue of singular versus plural nouns and the role played by syntactic constraints such as spaces, punctuation marks, multiple cases, and non-ASCII characters in Flickr and del.icio.us. You looked at Technorati as an example of a tag-based search engine as a case study of how to use tags to relate disparate digital content. I showed how you can create a simple mashup of Flickr and del.icio.us using del.icio.us tags to create sets of pictures that intermix your photos and other people's photos in Flickr. This chapter ended with an example of combining tags with formal classification schemes in the context of books.

---

21. http://www.librarything.com/talktopic.php?topic=12559#138896

CHAPTER 4

■ ■ ■

Working with Feeds, RSS, and Atom

A fundamental enabling technology for mashups is syndication feeds, especially those packaged in XML. *Feeds* are documents used to transfer frequently updated digital content to users. This chapter introduces feeds, focusing on the specific examples of RSS and Atom. RSS and Atom are arguably the most widely used XML formats in the world. Indeed, there's a good chance that any given web site provides some RSS or Atom feed—even if there is no XML-based API for the web site. Although RSS and Atom are the dominant feed format, other formats are also used to create feeds: JSON, PHP serialization, and CSV. I will also cover those formats in this chapter.

So, why do feeds matter? Feeds give you structured information from applications that is easy to parse and reuse. Not only are feeds readily available, but there are many applications that use those feeds—all requiring no or very little programming effort from you. Indeed, there is an entire ecology of web feeds (the data formats, applications, producers, and consumers) that provides great potential for the remix and mashup of information—some of which is starting to be realized today.

This chapter covers the following:

- What feeds are and how they are used

- The semantics and syntax of feeds, with a focus on RSS 2.0, RSS 1.0, and Atom 1.0

- The extension mechanism of RSS 2.0 and Atom 1.0

- How to get feeds from Flickr and other feed-producing applications and web sites

- Feed formats other than RSS and Atom in the context of Flickr feeds

- How feed autodiscovery can be used to find feeds

- News aggregators for reading feeds and tools for validating and scraping feeds

- How to remix and mashup feeds with Feedburner and Yahoo! Pipes

---

Note In this chapter, I assume you have an understanding of the basics of XML, including XML name-spaces and XML schemas. A decent tutorial on XML is available at `http://www.w3schools.com/xml/`. If you are new to the world of XML, working with RSS and Atom is an excellent way to get started with the XML family of technology.

What Are Feeds, and Why Are They Important?

Feeds are documents used to transfer frequently updated digital content to users. This content ranges from news items, weblog entries, installments of podcasts, and virtually any content that can be parceled out in discrete units. In keeping with this functionality, there is some commonly used terminology associated with feeds:

- You *syndicate*, or *publish*, content by producing a feed to distribute it.

- You *subscribe* to a feed by reading it and using it.

- You *aggregate* feeds by combining feeds from multiple sources.

Although feeds come in many data formats, I focus in the following sections on three formats that you are likely to see in current web sites: RSS 2.0, Atom 1.0, and RSS 1.0. (Later in the chapter, I will mention other feed formats.) The formats have fundamental conceptual and structural similarities but also are different in fundamental ways. In addition, they have a complicated, interdependent, and contested history—which I do not untangle here.

The examples of the three feed formats are adapted from the RSS 2.0 feed of new books from Apress (`http://www.apress.com/rss/whatsnew.xml`). They are meant to be (as much as possible) the same data packaged in different formats. They are minimalist, though not the absolute minimal, example to illustrate the core of each format. For instance, the description elements have embedded HTML. Also, I show two items to illustrate that channels (feeds) can contain more than one item (entries). I discuss extensions to RSS and Atom later in the chapter.

RSS 2.0

There are two main branches of formats in the RSS family. RSS 2.0 is the current inheritor of the line of XML formats that includes RSS versions 0.91, 0.92, 0.93, and 0.94. The "RSS 1.0" section covers the other branch. You can find the specification for RSS 2.0 here, from which you can get the details of required and optional elements and attributes:

`http://cyber.law.harvard.edu/rss/rss.html`

Here are some key aspects of RSS 2.0:

- The root element is `<rss>` (with the version="2.0" attribute).

- The `<rss>` element must contain a single `<channel>` element, which represents the source of the feed.

- A `<channel>` contains any number of `<item>` elements.

- A `<channel>` is described by three mandatory elements (`<title>`, `<link>`, and `<description>`) contained within `<channel>`.

- An `<item>` element is described by such optional elements, such as `<title>`, `<description>`, and `<link>`. An item must contain at least a `<title>` or `<description>` element.

- The tags in RSS 2.0 are not placed in any XML namespaces to retain backward compatibility with 0.91–0.94.

Here is an example of an RSS 2.0 feed with two `<item>` elements, each representing a new book. Each description contains entity-encoded HTML.[1]

```
<?xml version="1.0" ?>
<rss version="2.0">
  <channel>
    <title>Apress :: The Expert's Voice</title>
    <link>http://www.apress.com/</link>
    <description>
      Welcome to Apress.com. Books for Professionals, by Professionals(TM)...
      with what the professional needs to know(TM)</description>
    <item>
      <title>Excel 2007: Beyond the Manual</title>
      <link>http://www.apress.com/book/bookDisplay.html?bID=10232</link>
      <description>
        &lt;p&gt;&lt;i&gt;Excel 2007: Beyond the Manual&lt;/i&gt;
        will introduce those who are already familiar with Excel basics to more
        advanced features, like consolidation, what-if analysis, PivotTables,
        sorting and filtering, and some commonly used functions. You'll learn how to
        maximize your efficiency at producing professional-looking spreadsheets and
        charts and become competent at analyzing data using a variety of tools. The
        book includes practical examples to illustrate advanced features.&lt;/p&gt;
      </description>
    </item>
    <item>
      <title>Word 2007: Beyond the Manual</title>
      <link>http://www.apress.com/book/bookDisplay.html?bID=10249</link>
      <description>
```

---

1. http://examples.mashupguide.net/ch04/RSS2.0_Apress_simple_example.xml

```
&lt;p&gt;&lt;i&gt;Word 2007: Beyond the Manual&lt;/i&gt; focuses on new
features of Word 2007 as well as older features that were once less
accessible than they are now. This book also makes a point to include
examples of practical applications for all the new features. The book
assumes familiarity with Word 2003 or earlier versions, so you can focus on
becoming a confident 2007 user.&lt;/p&gt;
      </description>
    </item>
  </channel>
</rss>
```

RSS 1.0

As a data model, RSS 1.0 is similar to RSS 2.0, since both are designed to be represent feeds. In contrast to RSS 2.0, however, RSS 1.0 is expressed using the W3C RDF specification (http://www.w3.org/TR/REC-rdf-syntax/). Consequently, RSS 1.0 feeds are part of the Semantic Web, an ambitious effort of the W3C to build a "common framework that allows data to be shared and reused across application, enterprise, and community boundaries...based on the Resource Description Framework (RDF)."[2]

■**Note** Other than this description of RSS 1.0 and a brief analysis of RDFa in Chapter 18, the Semantic Web is beyond the scope of this book. Although I urge any serious student of mashups to track the Semantic Web for its long-term promise to transform the world of mashups, it has yet to make such an impact. Nonetheless, because RSS 1.0 is a concrete way to get started with RDF, I mention it here.

You can find the RDF 1.0 specification here:

```
http://web.resource.org/rss/1.0/spec
```

The RDF 1.0 format is associated with an RDF schema (http://www.w3.org/TR/rdf-schema/):

```
http://web.resource.org/rss/1.0/schema.rdf
```

Here I rewrite the RSS 2.0 feed to represent the same information as RSS 1.0 to give you a feel for the syntax of RSS 1.0:[3]

```
<?xml version="1.0" encoding="UTF-8"?>
<rdf:RDF
  xmlns:rdf="http://www.w3.org/1999/02/22-rdf-syntax-ns#"
  xmlns="http://purl.org/rss/1.0/">
  <channel rdf:about="http://www.apress.com/rss/whatsnew.xml">
```

---

2. http://www.w3.org/2001/sw/
3. http://examples.mashupguide.net/ch04/RSS1.0_Apress.xml

```
    <title>Apress :: The Expert's Voice</title>
    <link>http://www.apress.com/</link>
    <description>
      Welcome to Apress.com. Books for Professionals, by Professionals(TM)...
      with what the professional needs to know(TM)
    </description>
    <items>
      <rdf:Seq>
        <rdf:li rdf:resource="http://www.apress.com/book/bookDisplay.html?
bID=10232" />
        <rdf:li rdf:resource="http://www.apress.com/book/bookDisplay.html?
bID=10249" />
      </rdf:Seq>
    </items>
  </channel>
  <item rdf:about="http://www.apress.com/book/bookDisplay.html?bID=10232">
    <title>Excel 2007: Beyond the Manual</title>
    <link>http://www.apress.com/book/bookDisplay.html?bID=10232</link>
    <description>
      &lt;p&gt;&lt;i&gt;Excel 2007: Beyond the Manual&lt;/i&gt; will introduce those
      who are already familiar with Excel basics to more advanced features, like
      consolidation, what-if analysis, PivotTables, sorting and filtering, and some
      commonly used functions. You'll learn how to maximize your efficiency at
      producing professional-looking spreadsheets and charts and become competent at
      analyzing data using a variety of tools. The book includes practical examples
      to illustrate advanced features.&lt;/p&gt;
    </description>
  </item>
  <item rdf:about="http://www.apress.com/book/bookDisplay.html?bID=10249">
    <title>Word 2007: Beyond the Manual</title>
    <link>http://www.apress.com/book/bookDisplay.html?bID=10249</link>
    <description>
      &lt;p&gt;&lt;i&gt;Word 2007: Beyond the Manual&lt;/i&gt; focuses on new
      features of Word 2007 as well as older features that were once less accessible
      than they are now. This book also makes a point to include examples of
      practical applications for all the new features. The book assumes familiarity
      with Word 2003 or earlier versions, so you can focus on becoming a confident
      2007 user.&lt;/p&gt;
    </description>
  </item>
</rdf:RDF>
```

Consider the following aspects of RSS 1.0:

- Note the commonality in data structure between RSS 1.0 and RSS 2.0 in the use of such elements as <channel>, <item>, <title>, and <description>.

- It uses an XML namespace associated with RDF (http://www.w3.org/ 1999/02/22-rdf-syntax-ns#) and a default namespace related to RSS 1.0 (http://purl.org/rss/1.0/) to place all elements such as <channel>, <item>, and <title> into that namespace.

- It uses an enclosing <rdf:RDF> root element.

- Note the sequencing of <rdf:resources> contained by an <items> element.

- Note the placement of the <item> elements outside the <channel> element.

Since RSS 1.0 feeds are harder to find than RSS 2.0 and Atom 1.0 feeds, the following are some examples of RSS 1.0 feeds:

- http://rss.slashdot.org/Slashdot/slashdot

- http://www.nature.com/nature/current_issue/rss/index.html (drawn from a list at http://www.nature.com/webfeeds/index.html)

- http://www.w3.org/2000/08/w3c-synd/home.rss

- http://simile.mit.edu/blog/?feed=rdf

■**Note** There are efforts to update RSS. The RSS Advisory Board (http://www.rssboard.org/) has been designing updates to RSS 2.0, whereas RSS 1.1 (http://inamidst.com/rss1.1/) has been created by a small number of developers to enhance RSS 1.0. RSS 2.0 and RSS 1.0 remain the most important versions of the two major families of RSS specifications.

Atom 1.0

The name Atom applies to two related proposed standards: the Atom Syndication Format (whose current version is also known as Atom 1.0) and the Atom Publication Protocol (APP). Here, I discuss Atom 1.0 and return to APP later in this book in the context of various Google web services that use GData, an extension of APP.

Designed to overcome perceived shortcomings of the various RSS formats, Atom 1.0 is currently a proposed IETF standard:

http://tools.ietf.org/html/rfc4287

Atom 1.0, constructed to syndicate web content, has a similar semantics to RSS but a different naming scheme. In an Atom document, a `<feed>` element is composed of one or more `<entry>` elements, each described by a set of tags such as `<title>`, `<link>`, `<id>`, and `<summary>`.

Let me now rewrite the sample Apress "new books" feed into Atom 1.0:[4]

```
<?xml version="1.0" encoding="utf-8"?>
<feed xmlns="http://www.w3.org/2005/Atom">
  <title>Apress :: The Expert's Voice</title>
  <subtitle>
    Welcome to Apress.com. Books for Professionals, by Professionals(TM)...
    with what the professional needs to know(TM)
  </subtitle>
  <link rel="alternate" type="text/html" href="http://www.apress.com/"/>
  <link rel="self" href="http://examples.mashupguide.net/ch04/Atom1.0_Apress.xml"/>
  <updated>2007-07-25T12:57:02Z</updated>
  <author>
    <name>Apress, Inc.</name>
    <email>support@apress.com</email>
  </author>
  <id>http://apress.com/</id>
  <entry>
    <title>Excel 2007: Beyond the Manual</title>
    <link href="http://www.apress.com/book/bookDisplay.html?bID=10232"/>
    <id>http://www.apress.com/book/bookDisplay.html?bID=10232</id>
    <updated>2007-07-25T12:57:02Z</updated>
    <summary type="html">
      &lt;p&gt;&lt;i&gt;Excel 2007: Beyond the Manual&lt;/i&gt; will introduce those
      who are already familiar with Excel basics to more advanced features, like
      consolidation, what-if analysis, PivotTables, sorting and filtering, and some
      commonly used functions. You'll learn how to maximize your efficiency at
      producing professional-looking spreadsheets and charts and become competent at
      analyzing data using a variety of tools. The book includes practical examples
      to illustrate advanced features.&lt;/p&gt;
    </summary>
  </entry>
  <entry>
    <title>Word 2007: Beyond the Manual</title>
    <link href="http://www.apress.com/book/bookDisplay.html?bID=10249"/>
    <id>http://www.apress.com/book/bookDisplay.html?bID=10249</id>
    <updated>2007-07-25T12:57:10Z</updated>
    <summary type="html">
      &lt;p&gt;&lt;i&gt;Word 2007: Beyond the Manual&lt;/i&gt; focuses on new
      features of Word 2007 as well as older features that were once less accessible
      than they are now. This book also makes a point to include examples of
      practical applications for all the new features. The book assumes familiarity
```

---

4. http://examples.mashupguide.net/ch04/Atom1.0_Apress.xml

```
    with Word 2003 or earlier versions, so you can focus on becoming a confident
    2007 user.&lt;/p&gt;
  </summary>
  </entry>
</feed>
```

Note the following about this example:

- Note the use of a default Atom-related XML namespace (http://www.w3.org/2005/Atom).

- The <subtitle> element instead of <description> (in RSS) describes the feed.

- The <feed> and <entry> elements must both include an <updated> element.

- <link rel="alternate" type="text/html" href="http://www.apress.com/"/> indicates that the document is an "alternate" representation (that is, a feed) of the web page http://www.apress.com/.

- <link rel="self" href="http://examples.mashupguide.net/ch04/Atom1.0_Apress.xml"/> indicates the location of this feed document.

- The attribute type="html" in the <summary> elements indicates the use of entity-encoded HTML.

Writing a simple feed as RSS 2.0 and Atom 1.0 sheds some light on how the two formats compare. For a more detailed analysis, see the following:

```
http://en.wikipedia.org/wiki/Atom_%28standard%29#Atom_Compared_to_RSS_2.0
```

Finally, Atom 1.0 has an official RNG schema, defined in the appendix of RFC 4287:

```
http://atompub.org/rfc4287.html#schema
```

Extensions to RSS 2.0 and Atom 1.0

Extensions to RSS 2.0 and Atom 1.0 enable you to take advantage of the popular feed formats to be able to move information within the whole feed ecology while adding more information than is allowed in the simple base RSS or Atom vocabulary.

You can insert foreign XML elements (ones that are not defined in the respective specifications) into RSS 2.0 and Atom 1.0 by using XML namespaces. That is, with a few exceptions in Atom 1.0,[5] foreign tags are allowed as long as they are qualified in a namespace that is different from that of the base format. For RSS 2.0, that would mean the foreign tag would have to be placed in some namespace instead of having no namespace such as the core elements in RSS 2.0.

---

5. Foreign markup is permitted unless explicitly forbidden for specific contexts. See http://tools.ietf.org/html/rfc4287#section-6 for more details.

■Note I do not cover RSS 1.0 extensibility here other than to refer readers to RSS 1.0 Modules (`http://web.resource.org/rss/1.0/modules/`) and to note the standard modules: (`http://web.resource.org/rss/1.0/modules/dc/` (Dublin Core), `http://web.resource.org/rss/1.0/modules/syndication/` (Syndication), and `http://web.resource.org/rss/1.0/modules/content/` (Content).

Let's look at a simple example by adding a tag to the Atom 1.0 feed listed previously. Suppose you want to add a tag called <isbn> for each of the <entry> elements. You can do so by associating the <isbn> tag with a namespace (say, `http://mashupguide.net`):[6]

```
<?xml version="1.0" encoding="UTF-8"?>
<feed xmlns="http://www.w3.org/2005/Atom" xmlns:mg="http://mashupguide.net">
  [....]
  <entry>
    <title>Excel 2007: Beyond the Manual</title>
    <link href="http://www.apress.com/book/bookDisplay.html?bID=10232"/>
    <id>http://www.apress.com/book/bookDisplay.html?bID=10232</id>
    <updated>2007-07-25T12:57:02Z</updated>
    <mg:isbn>1590597982</mg:isbn>
  [....]
  </entry>
</feed>
```

This example is not meant to show the best way to encode an ISBN but to show how to extend Atom 1.0. Although inserting your own custom vocabulary results in a completely valid document, it doesn't necessarily help in terms of interoperability. How much software out there is set to interpret an <isbn> element in the `http://mashupguide.net` namespace—other than to ignore it? If you use a widely used extension, the better your chances that there is software that acts on those extensions. Some prominent RSS 2.0 extensions are as follows:

- Media RSS (`http://search.yahoo.com/mrss`), used in Flickr

- iTunes (`http://www.apple.com/itunes/store/podcaststechspecs.html`), used for podcasting

- OpenSearch (`http://www.opensearch.org/Specifications/OpenSearch/1.1`)

■Tip Other XML dialects use XML namespaces in a similar fashion to enable extensions, so it's useful to understand how extensions work in feeds to get a handle of how it works elsewhere.

---

6. `http://examples.mashupguide.net/ch04/Atom1.0_Apress_ISBN.xml`

There are few widely used Atom 1.0 extensions at this point. If you want to follow that topic, I suggest the series of articles by James Snell on Atom 1.0 and various proposed extensions.[7]

Now that you have studied three important formats for feeds (RSS 2.0, RSS 1.0, and Atom 1.0), you'll learn how feeds are implemented in Flickr and then in other web sites.

Feeds from Flickr

You can find feeds in Flickr in several ways. First, you can look throughout the Flickr UI for the orange feed icon and the text Subscribe To, as shown in Figure 4-1. You can then find out the feed's URL from the Feed link. Once you have that URL, you can subscribe to the feed and read the data it contains. For example, if you go to the following address:

```
http://flickr.com/groups/central/
```

you will find a the feed icon and link pointing here:

```
http://api.flickr.com/services/feeds/groups_discuss.gne?id=34427469792@N01&
lang=en-us&format=rss_200
```

■ Feed – Subscribe to

Figure 4-1. *Icon for subscribing to a feed in Flickr. (Reproduced with permission of Yahoo! Inc. ® 2007 by Yahoo! Inc. YAHOO! and the YAHOO! logo are trademarks of Yahoo! Inc.)*

A second way of finding feeds is to consult Flickr's documentation of its feeds:

```
http://www.flickr.com/services/feeds/
```

In a moment, I'll list the Flickr feeds that are available following the same convention of using URI templates as I did in Chapter 2. All the feeds share two common optional parameters: format and lang.

Flickr Feed Parameters

Let's look first at format, which can be one of the values listed in Table 4-1.

Table 4-1. *Values for the* format *Parameter in Flickr Feeds*

Format	Definition
rss_200 or rss2	RSS 2.0
atom_1 or atom	Atom 1.0
rss_091	RSS 0.91
rss_092 or rss	RSS 0.92

---

7. http://www-128.ibm.com/developerworks/xml/library/x-atom10.html, http://www-128.ibm.com/
developerworks/xml/library/x-extatom1/, and http://www-128.ibm.com/developerworks/xml/
library/x-extatom2.html

Format	Definition
rss_100 or rdf	RSS 1.0
rss_200_enc	RSS 2.0 with enclosures (but without enclosure sizes)
php	Code to represent feed as a PHP array
php_serial	Input to the PHP unserialize function
csv	Comma-separated value
json	JavaScript Object Notation (http://www.json.org/)
sql	Statements to store the feed data into a SQL database
yaml	YAML (http://en.wikipedia.org/wiki/YAML)
cdf	Channel Definition Format (http://en.wikipedia.org/wiki/Channel_Definition_Format)

If format is not specified, Atom 1.0 is assumed. Note that RSS 2.0, RSS 1.0, and Atom 1.0 (along with RSS 0.92 and RSS 0.91) are included among the formats. I'll present some samples of various formats later in this chapter, after I cover the rest of the URL language for Flickr feeds.

The second pervasive and optional parameter is lang, which represents the language you can use to query Flickr. Table 4-2 lists the values. The default language is en-us (English).

Table 4-2. *Values for the* lang *Parameter in Flickr Feeds*

Format	Definition
de-de	German
en-us	English
es-us	Spanish
fr-fr	French
it-it	Italian
ko-kr	Korean
pt-br	Portuguese (Brazilian)
zh-hk	Traditional Chinese (Hong Kong)

I'll now list the feeds available. Remember that all the feed URLs can include the optional format and lang parameters.

Examining the Flickr Feeds

Feeds for public photos in Flickr are available here:

```
http://api.flickr.com/services/feeds/photos_public.gne
```

with the following optional parameters:

- `id={user_nsid}`

- `ids={comma_delimited_user_nsids}`

- `tags={comma_delimited_tags}`

- `tagmode={mode}` where `mode` is `all` (the default value) or `any`

For example, the following:

```
http://api.flickr.com/services/feeds/photos_public.gne?tags=flower%2CBerkeley&
format=rss2&lang=fr-fr
```

returns a RSS 2.0 feed, annotated in French, of recent public photos tagged with both `flower` and `Berkeley` tags.

You can get a feed of recent photos of a user's friends here:

```
http://api.flickr.com/services/feeds/photos_friends.gne?user_id={user-nsid}
```

where `user-nsid` is the NSID of the user whose friends' photos you want to access. There are also optional parameters:

- `display_all` can be 1 to show multiple photos per friend, instead of the default value of one photo per friend.

- `friends` can be set to 1 to limit photos to only the family and friends for the requested user.

For example, the following:

```
http://api.flickr.com/services/feeds/photos_friends.gne?user_id=48600101146@N01&
friends=0&display_all=0&lang=en-us&format=atom_1
```

is an Atom 1.0 feed of up to one photo each from my Flickr friends, family, and contacts.

You can get feeds of a group discussion here:

```
http://api.flickr.com/services/feeds/groups_discuss.gne?id={group-nsid}
```

Feeds for the group photo pools are accessible here:

```
http://api.flickr.com/services/feeds/groups_pool.gne?{group-nsid}
```

Discussion feeds from the Help forum (`http://www.flickr.com/help/forum/en-us/`) are here:

```
http://api.flickr.com/services/feeds/forums.gne
```

You can track recent activity on a user's photos through feeds here:

```
http://api.flickr.com/services/feeds/activity.gne?user-id={user-nsid}
```

Feeds of recent comments made by a user are here:

```
http://api.flickr.com/services/feeds/photos_comments.gne?user-id={user-nsid}
```

You can track Flickr news bulletins here:

```
http://api.flickr.com/services/feeds/news.gne
```

Now that you know how to access the various feeds available in Flickr, you'll look at some examples of feeds to understand how various formats are implemented, including the role of extensions. Consider the following excerpt of a sample RSS 2.0 feed of recent public photos with the tag tree:

```
http://api.flickr.com/services/feeds/photos_public.gne?tags=tree&format=rss2
<?xml version="1.0" encoding="utf-8"?>
<rss version="2.0" xmlns:media="http://search.yahoo.com/mrss/"
     xmlns:dc="http://purl.org/dc/elements/1.1/">
  <channel>
    <title>tree - Everyone's Tagged Photos</title>
    <link>http://www.flickr.com/photos/tags/tree/</link>
    <description>A feed of tree - Everyone's Tagged Photos</description>
    <pubDate>Mon, 29 Jan 2007 06:40:42 -0800</pubDate>
    <lastBuildDate>Mon, 29 Jan 2007 06:40:42 -0800</lastBuildDate>
    <generator>http://www.flickr.com/</generator>
    <image>
      <url>http://www.flickr.com/images/buddyicon.jpg</url>
      <title>tree - Everyone's Tagged Photos</title>
      <link>http://www.flickr.com/photos/tags/tree/</link>
    </image>
    <item>
      <title>Odd Tree</title>
      <link>http://www.flickr.com/photos/davidleong/373343287/</link>
      <description>[....]</description>
      <pubDate>Mon, 29 Jan 2007 06:40:42 -0800</pubDate>
      <dc:date.Taken>2007-01-28T11:31:31-08:00</dc:date.Taken>
      <author>nobody@flickr.com (mountainhiker)</author>
      <guid isPermaLink="false">tag:flickr.com,2004:/photo/373343287</guid>
      <media:content
        url="http://farm1.static.flickr.com/127/373343287_df43da61f7_m.jpg"
        type="image/jpeg" height="160" width="240"/>
      <media:title>Odd Tree</media:title>
      <media:text type="html">[....]</media:text>
      <media:thumbnail
        url="http://farm1.static.flickr.com/127/373343287_df43da61f7_s.jpg"
        height="75" width="75"/>
      <media:credit role="photographer">mountainhiker</media:credit>
      <media:category scheme="urn:flickr:tags">snow tree vancouver northvancouver
                      grousemountain</media:category>
    </item>
    <item>
    [....]
    </item>
  </channel>
</rss>
```

Note the following about this XML fragment:

- Within an `<item>` element are some standard elements that you will find in RSS 2.0 feeds, namely, `<title>`, `<link>`, `<description>`, `<pubDate>`, and `<guid>`, as well as elements that are extensions of RSS 2.0, including `<dc.date.Taken>` and the tags in the media namespace such as `<media:thumbnail>`.

- Remember that RSS is basically a flat structure. That is, a `<channel>` consists of `<item>` elements—but an `<item>` doesn't consist of other `<item>` elements. This contrasts with other XML formats that you will learn about in later chapters of the book (such as the OpenDocument format).

Let's take a closer look at the extensions used in the RSS 2.0 Flickr feed:

- The `dc` prefix (for example, in `<dc:date.Taken>`), corresponding to the `http://purl.org/dc/elements/1.1/` namespace, denotes the Dublin Core (DC) metadata standard. DC is a vocabulary for a core set of metadata designed to be applicable to a wide range of digital content.

- Media RSS (`http://search.yahoo.com/mrss`), which supplements the `<enclosure>` element in RSS 2.0, is used by Flickr to store metadata of the photos, such as the following:

  - `<media:content>`, with the attributes `url`, `type`, `height`, and `width`

  - `<media:title>` to hold the photo's title

  - `<media:text>` with HTML to embed that picture into a web page

  - `<media:thumbnail>` to hold a URL to the thumbnail in the `url` attribute

  - `<media:credit>` to indicate the owner of the photo

  - `<media:category>` to holds tags

It's interesting to look at how all the Flickr metadata is expressed in the other feed formats. The following:

```
http://api.flickr.com/services/feeds/photos_public.gne?tags=tree&format=atom
```

shows that Atom 1.0 is natively able to encode much of the information for which Media RSS is being used in RSS 2.0. The Atom feed does, however, use a Dublin Core extension to mark up a date.

Exchange Formats Other Than RSS and Atom

Let's now return to the feed formats supported by Flickr other than RSS 2.0, RSS 1.0, and Atom 1.0. To get a start at understanding the various formats, load a Flickr feed, which will by default be in Atom 1.0, and replace the `format` parameter with the alternatives. For instance, if you are curious about CDF, change the following:

```
http://api.flickr.com/services/feeds/photos_public.gne?tags=tree
```

to the following:

```
http://api.flickr.com/services/feeds/photos_public.gne?tags=tree&format=cdf
```

In the following sections, I'll mention some but not all of formats supported in Flickr feeds.

RSS 0.91 and RSS 0.92

Although RSS 0.91 and RSS 0.92 have largely been superseded by RSS 2.0, you can still look at examples such as this:

```
http://api.flickr.com/services/feeds/photos_public.gne?tags=tree&format=rss_091
```

and this:

```
http://api.flickr.com/services/feeds/photos_public.gne?tags=tree&format=rss_092
```

to see how those older versions do not contain any of the Media RSS or Dublin Core extensions you find in the RSS 2.0 feeds.

JSON

The JSON format facilitates the consumption of Flickr feeds in JavaScript. I discuss JSON at greater length in Chapter 8. However, if you look at the following:

```
http://api.flickr.com/services/feeds/photos_public.gne?tags=tree&format=json
```

you can see that Flickr returns JavaScript code, specifically a call to a `jsonFlickrFeed()` function with one parameter. This parameter is a JavaScript object that holds the feed data. As a JavaScript programmer, you can use this JSON-formatted feed by supplying a `jsonFlickrFeed()` function to do something with the feed, such as displaying it on a web page.

Here's an example of some code that reads the Flickr JSON feed and renders the feed as HTML in the browser:[8]

```
<!DOCTYPE html PUBLIC "-//W3C//DTD XHTML 1.0 Strict//EN"
  "http://www.w3.org/TR/xhtml1/DTD/xhtml1-strict.dtd">
<html xmlns="http://www.w3.org/1999/xhtml">
  <head>
    <meta http-equiv="content-type" content="text/html; charset=utf-8"/>
    <title>Flickr JSON feed</title>
    <script type="text/javascript">
      //<![CDATA[

      function jsonFlickrFeed (feed) {
        var feed_div = document.getElementById("feed");
        var feed_html = '<p>' + '<a href="' + feed.link+ '">' +
          feed.title + '</a>'+ '</p>';
        for (x=0; x<feed.items.length; x++) {
          feed_html += '<a href="' + feed.items[x].link + '">' +
            '<img ' + 'src="' + feed.items[x].media["m"] + '"' + ' alt="' +
            feed.items[x].title + '"' + '/>' + '</a>'+ '<br/>';
        }
```

---

8. http://examples.mashupguide.net/ch04/Flickr.JSON.html

```
            feed_div.innerHTML = feed_html;
        }

        function load() {
            var head_element = document.getElementsByTagName("head")[0];
            var newScript = document.createElement('script');
            newScript.type = 'text/javascript';
            newScript.src = 'http://api.flickr.com/services/feeds/photos_public.gne?
tags=tree&format=json';
            head_element.appendChild(newScript);
        }

        //]]>
    </script>
  </head>
  <body onload="load()">
    <div id="feed" />
  </body>
</html>
```

In Chapter 8, I'll return to how to use JSON in mashups.

Other Feed Formats

The other available formats are less commonly used to represent feeds in web sites other than Flickr but come in handy depending on your specific needs. For example:

- You can use the php or php_serial format to generate a convenient representation of the feed for PHP programming. (These formats have roughly the relationship to PHP that the json format has to JavaScript.)

- You can use the sql format to quickly generate SQL code to get the Flickr feed into your SQL database.

- The csv format comes in handy for importing your feed into a spreadsheet.

- The rss_200_enc format is used to insert a reference to the original photo in an RSS 2.0 <enclosure> tag.

Feeds from Other Web Sites

Feeds are extremely helpful in creating mashups because feeds are packaged in formats designed to be accurately and automatically parsed by software. Not only do they not require programming to use—they are widely available, much more so than web APIs.

Nonetheless, feeds are still sometimes difficult to find. I first revisit the question of how to find feeds and the topic of autodiscovery. I then provide examples of feeds that are available from some specific web sites: a selection of blogs, Wikipedia, Google, and Yahoo! News. You will see how web sites other than Flickr use feeds. Moreover, I have focused in my examples on news-oriented web sites because I draw upon such sites in the feed mashups I create with Yahoo! Pipes later in the chapter.

Finding Feeds and Feed Autodiscovery

In the context of Flickr, I mention two ways of finding feeds that are applicable to other web sites:

- Looking in the user interface for features such as the common orange icon or the words *feed*, *RSS*, *subscribe*, and so on

- Finding documentation for a web site's feeds

Let's explore some other approaches to finding feeds. There are specialized feed directories and search engines such as the following, which also has an API (in case you find it useful):

```
http://www.syndic8.com/
```

Some of this feed search functionality has been incorporated into feed aggregators (which I describe more in a moment). For instance, you can browse and search for feeds from within Google Reader. This search functionality is also available from the Google AJAX Feed API.[9] Some have used general-purpose search engines to search for feeds, but it's hard to say how reliable such self-described hacks are.[10]

It seems sensible that if you know the URL of a web page, you should be able to easily figure out the URL for any feeds that are associated with it. Indeed, a mechanism called *RSS autodiscovery* (or more generally, *feed autodiscovery*) has become a de facto standard in associating web pages with feeds. To connect a web page to a feed, you add <link> elements to the <head> element, making appropriate use of the rel, href, and type (and optionally title) attributes of <link>:

- rel is set to the value alternate.

- href is the URL of the feed.

- type is set to the MIME type of the feed (either application/rss+xml or application/atom+xml).

- title is optionally set to be a title of the feed.

For example, in the following <head> element:

```
http://news.yahoo.com
```

you find the following <link>, which points to a corresponding RSS feed at http://rss.news.yahoo.com/rss/topstories:

```
<link rel="alternate" type="application/rss+xml" title="Yahoo! News - Top Stories"
href="http://rss.news.yahoo.com/rss/topstories" />
```

Many of the modern browsers support feed autodiscovery. If you use any of those browsers to go to a web page with a link to its feeds, you'll see an icon that leads to those feeds.

---

9. http://code.google.com/apis/ajaxfeeds/

10. http://www.xml.com/pub/a/2004/02/11/googlexml.html

Autodiscovery is similarly useful for creators of mashups. For example, if your program is fed the URL of a web page, you could look for the presence of associated feeds that might give you the data you need by using feed autodiscovery.

OFFICIAL STANDARDIZATION OF FEED AUTODISCOVERY?

Even though feed autodiscovery has been widely implemented, there is currently no de jure standard for this practice. Autodiscovery started as a collaboration carried out through weblogs (such as `http://diveintomark.org/archives/2002/06/02/important_change_to_the_link_tag`), progressed to being discussed as an IETF draft (whose last expired version was `http://www.ietf.org/internet-drafts/draft-snell-atompub-autodiscovery-00.txt`), and now is being considered in the context of standardization as part of HTML 5 (`http://www.whatwg.org/specs/web-apps/current-work/#alternate`).

In the meantime, some of the current practice around feed autodiscovery is documented in places such as the wiki at `http://www.feedautodiscovery.org/doku.php`.

Feeds from Weblogs

Weblogs are a major source of feeds because almost all modern weblog software produces feeds, which are often turned on by default. For example:

- Blogspot weblogs have Atom feeds[11] (for example, `http://googleblog.blogspot.com/atom.xml` and `http://googleblog.blogspot.com/feeds/posts/default`).

- WordPress blogs[12] (for example, `http://blog.mashupguide.net/feed/` and `http://blog.mashupguide.net/feed/atom/`).

- TypePad blogs support feeds.[13]

Wikipedia Feeds

Let's look at what Wikipedia has in the way of feeds to supplement Flickr as an example and to be of use in the following case studies. Wikipedia is a great source of information about the news and publishes RSS feeds. Here's some documentation for the feeds:

- `http://meta.wikimedia.org/wiki/RSS`

- `http://en.wikipedia.org/wiki/Wikipedia:Syndication`.

You can get a feed for the history of any regular page here:

`http://en.wikipedia.org/w/index.php?title={page-name}&action=history&feed={format}`

---

11. `http://help.blogger.com/bin/topic.py?topic=8927`

12. `http://codex.wordpress.org/WordPress_Feeds`

13. `http://support.typepad.com/cgi-bin/typepad.cfg/php/enduser/std_adp.php?p_faqid=86`

For example:

```
http://en.wikipedia.org/w/index.php?title=Hurricane_Katrina&action=history&
feed=atom
```

```
http://en.wikipedia.org/w/index.php?title=Mashup_%28web_application_hybrid%29&
action=history&feed=atom
```

Two of Wikipedia's special pages also have feeds. The first is of all recent changes to Wikipedia (which tends to have way too much data because Wikipedia is extremely active):

```
http://en.wikipedia.org/wiki/Special:Recentchanges?feed={format}
```

and the other lets you track the creation of new pages:

```
http://en.wikipedia.org/wiki/?Special:Newpagesfeed={format}
```

If you want to track news using Wikipedia, you might want to use Wikinews (`http://en.wikinews.org/wiki/Main_Page`), which has an RSS feed:

```
http://feeds.feedburner.com/WikinewsLatestNews
```

Finally, you can get at your Wikipedia watch list (when logged in) here:

```
http://en.wikipedia.org/w/api.php?action=feedwatchlist&feedformat={format}
```

where format is rss or atom.

Google and Yahoo! News

The feeds for Google News are documented here:

```
http://news.google.com/intl/en_us/news_feed_terms.html
```

You can access a variety of U.S.-oriented feeds here:

```
http://news.google.com/news?ned=us&topic={topic}&output={format}
```

where output is rss or atom and where topic is one of the values listed in Table 4-3.

Table 4-3. *Possible Values for* topic *in Google News Feeds*

Topic	Coverage
h	Top news
w	World
n	United States
b	Business
t	Science/technology
m	Health
s	Sports
e	Entertainment

For example, you can get the top news in RSS here:

```
http://news.google.com/news?ned=us&topic=h&output=rss
```

You can also get international news here:

```
http://news.google.com/news?ned={region}&topic=n&output={format}
```

where `region` is one of the values listed in Table 4-4.

Table 4-4. *Possible Values for* region *in Google News Feeds*

Region	Country
au	Australia
ca	Canada
in	India
ie	Ireland
nz	New Zealand
en_za	South Africa
uk	United Kingdom

In addition to feeds for general topics, you can generate a feed for a specific search term in Google News (an extremely useful feature you will use when constructing targeted feeds later in the chapter):

```
http://news.google.com/news?q={query}&output={output}
```

For example, to follow news on mashups, use this:

```
http://news.google.com/news?q=mashup&output=rss
```

Yahoo! News has some similarities to Google News. In addition to getting feeds by large categories, listed here:

```
http://news.yahoo.com/rss
```

you can also get feeds by keywords via `http://news.search.yahoo.com/news/rss?p={search-term}`. For example:

```
http://news.search.yahoo.com/news/rss?p=Hurricane+Katrina
```

News Aggregators: Showing Flickr Feeds Elsewhere

A primary use of feeds is to allow you as an end user to keep up with lots of information from many different sources—all in one place. News aggregators (also known as *feed readers*) gather items from the feeds you subscribe to and present them to you to read in a single interface.

Subscribing to feeds has become such a sufficiently mainstream activity for web users that modern web browsers now provide options for doing so when the user arrives at an RSS or Atom feed in the browser. For example, in Firefox 2.0+, you see options for how to subscribe to that feed, as shown in Figure 4-2.

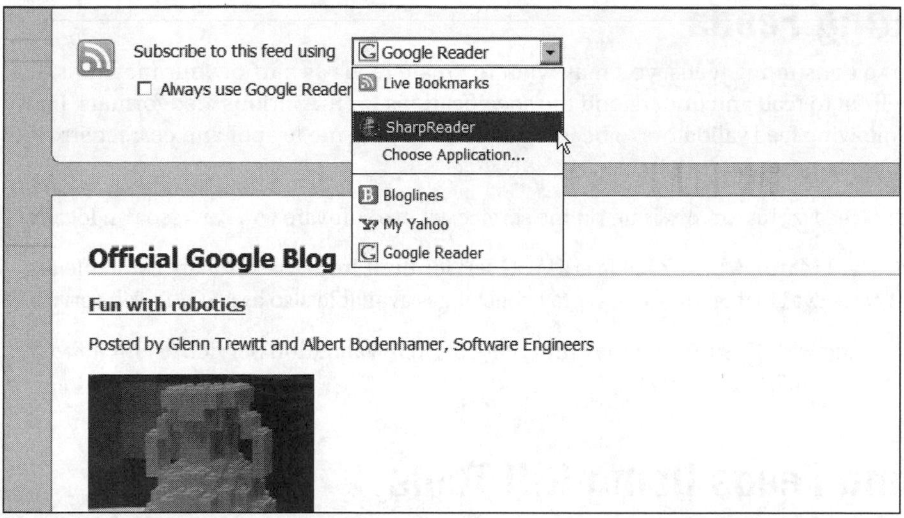

Figure 4-2. *Choosing a news aggregator with which to subscribe to a feed in Firefox*

There are different news/feed aggregators of note:

- Firefox Live Bookmarks. You can track feeds within the context of Firefox bookmarks.[14] There seem to be similar features in other browsers such as Safari[15] and Internet Explorer 7.[16]

- Bloglines (`http://www.bloglines.com/`).

- SharpReader, a desktop RSS aggregator/news reader for Windows (`http://www.sharpreader.net/`).

- NetNewsWire, a desktop news reader for the Mac. (`http://www.newsgator.com/NGOLProduct.aspx?ProdID=NetNewsWire`).

- Google Reader (`http://www.google.com/reader/view/`).

- My Yahoo! You can add an RSS feed to `http://my.yahoo.com`. You can, for instance, add an RSS feed with this URL: `http://e.my.yahoo.com/config/cstore?.opt=rss&.page=p1`. For more information, see the following:

  - `http://my.yahoo.com/s/faq/rss/`

  - `http://publisher.yahoo.com/rssguide`

---

14. `http://www.mozilla.com/en-US/firefox/livebookmarks.html`

15. `http://www.apple.com/macosx/features/safari/`

16. `http://www.microsoft.com/windows/rss/default.mspx`

Validating Feeds

In addition to consuming feeds, you may want to create feeds as part of your mashups. It's certainly helpful to read and understand the specifications for the various feed formats. I have found the following feed validators to be invaluable in helping me to spot and correct errors in feeds that I create or read from others:

- `http://feedvalidator.org` is an online service, whose software you can also run locally.[17]

- `http://validator.w3.org/feed/` is a W3C service built from the software available at `http://feedvalidator.org`. The syntax checking is available also as a SOAP web service.[18]

- For dealing with RSS 1.0, you may find the W3C RDF Validation Service useful (`http://www.w3.org/RDF/Validator/`).

Scraping Feeds Using GUI Tools

Feeds are available for many applications—but by no means for all applications. Because feeds are so useful, some services have arisen to generate feeds out of unstructured web sites. The goal of these services is to enable you to construct feeds more easily than you could screen-scrape the pages yourself—which, as I discuss in Chapter 2, is an option absent of APIs and feeds. Let's briefly consider one usage scenario to which we will apply two services. (I return to this topic of feed-scraping in Chapter 11.)

As I mention elsewhere in this book, perhaps the single most useful site on the Web for tracking web APIs is Programmableweb.com. Currently, it does not have an API and does not have a feed to represent all the APIs tracked by the site, but there is a feed for the latest changes in the list of APIs. The scenario I explore here is creating an RSS or Atom feed out of the list of APIs here:

`http://programmableweb.com/apis/directory`

Here I apply two services to this problem. The first is a specialized feed-creation web site:

`http://www.feedity.com/`

You can use Feedity to generate an RSS feed:

`http://feedity.com/?http://programmableweb.com/apis/directory%40%40%40CAT%40%40%406`

The feed is a perfectly fine feed except for the ads embedded in the feed. You need to use Pro (for-fee) level to get rid of the ads.

I used Openkapow.com's RoboMaker as a second approach to generate a feed. RoboMaker is a desktop visual tool to create bots hosted on Openkapow.com to generate feeds and APIs for web sites. In Chapter 11, I analyze RoboMaker and other tools that simplify mashup making. Here, I simply point out the end product of the Openkapow.com bot that converts the list of APIs into an RSS 2.0 feed:

`http://service.openkapow.com/rdhyee/programmablewebapis.rss`

---

17. `http://feedvalidator.org/docs/howto/install_and_run.html`
18. `http://validator.w3.org/feed/docs/soap`

There is a small image for Openkapow.com in the feed but no advertisements buried in the items themselves.

As you will see in the next section, being able to generate feeds for sites that don't have the feeds you want enables you to use the many tools that accept feeds as input.

Remixing Feeds with Feedburner

Feedburner (`http://feedburner.com`) lets users remix feeds and offers intermediary services based on feeds (such as tracking usage and advertising). It thus provides a useful illustration of the ways some users and companies are reusing and repackaging feeds.

The best way to understand Feedburner is to study the effect various options have on the feed you create with the service. Here's what happened when I created a Feedburner feed:

1. I signed up for an account and went to `http://www.feedburner.com/fb/a/myfeeds`. I entered the URL of my weblog `http://blog.mashupguide.net`, instead of the URL of a feed.

2. Feedburner prompted me to choose a feed from among the five feeds associated with my weblog via the feed autodiscovery mechanism (described earlier in this chapter). I chose the Mashup Guide Atom Feed (`http://blog.mashupguide.net/feed/atom/`).

3. I accepted the defaults for the title (`Mashup Guide`) and address (`http://feeds.feedburner.com/MashupGuide`).

Feedburner has various features for customizing your feed:

- You can customize the appearance of your feed in the browser. Feedburner attaches an XSLT style sheet to perform client-side transformation of the feed to HTML for a cleaner display of the feed in most browsers. For an example feed, you can explicitly see the HTML output using the W3C online XSLT service (`http://www.w3.org/2005/08/online_xslt/`) to generate this:

```
http://www.w3.org/2005/08/online_xslt/xslt?xslfile=
http%3A%2F%2Ffeeds.feedburner.com%2F%7Ed%2Fstyles%2
Fatom10full.xsl&xmlfile=http%3A%2F%2Ffeeds.feedburner.com%2FMashup
Guide+&content-type=&submit=transform
```

- You can get traffic statistics for the feeds you create.

- You can add tags from the iTunes or Media RSS extensions to your feeds to support podcasts.

- You can splice your feed with your links from various social-bookmarking sites (including del.icio.us) or your photos from various photo-sharing sites (such as Flickr).

- You can georeference your feed by having Feedburner attach the latitude and longitude of a given location to it.

- You can convert your feed to one of RSS 2.0, RSS 1.0, Atom 0.3, or Atom 1.0.

I list these features here not to advertise Feedburner (it seems to do well enough for itself given its acquisition by Google) but rather to present it as a model so you can study the many ways in which others are remixing and mashing up feeds. In fact, Feedburner provides an API (`http://www.feedburner.com/fb/a/developers`), which suggests the high level of automation in place (or at least anticipated) for feeds.

Remixing Feeds with Yahoo! Pipes

Yahoo! Pipes (`http://pipes.yahoo.com/pipes/`) is a "an interactive data aggregator and manipulator that lets you mash up your favorite online data sources." Yahoo! Pipes is focused on enabling end users to filter and combine feeds into new feeds. You construct pipes through dragging and dropping graphical widgets (called *modules*), entering parameters, and describing data flows through wiring these widgets together. Yahoo! Pipes is arguably more accessible to nonprogrammers because it does not involve typing code in a text editor. You'll see in practice whether the masses will be making mashups with Yahoo! Pipes.

Note I will say that as a programmer, Yahoo! Pipes does make it easier to remix feeds in many instances and got me to create feeds that I could have created programmatically but was not inspired to do so without the Yahoo! Pipes environment.

In this section, I describe how I built a series of pipes to solve a specific problem. In doing so, I hope to shed light on how to think about Yahoo! Pipes, specifically how to construct increasingly more complicated structures. For the basics of Yahoo! Pipes, please consult the official documentation:

`http://pipes.yahoo.com/pipes/docs`

especially the documentation of the modules available in Yahoo! Pipes:

`http://pipes.yahoo.com/pipes/docs?doc=modules`

The problem I address with Yahoo! Pipes is creating a single feed from diverse news sources, unified around a single topic or search term. In constructing my pipes, I had a concrete scenario in mind. I wanted a feed that enables one to follow the latest news about the aftermath of Hurricane Katrina. Though I generalized my Yahoo! Pipes where I could easily do so, I am not attempting here to develop a comprehensive solution.

The solution I devised was to synthesize a feed out of the following four sources:

- Yahoo! News

- Google News

- Wikinews

- The national section of *The New York Times*

This range of new sources enables me to illustrate how to overcome some of the challenges you'll likely face when using Yahoo! Pipes.

A Simple First Pipe with Yahoo! News

The first step I took was to build a pipe to handle the first source, Yahoo! News. I exploited the fact that you can generate an RSS Yahoo! News for a search term with this:

```
http://news.search.yahoo.com/news/rss?p={search-term}
```

I built two versions of a pipe to return a feed for a given search term. The first version—called "Yahoo! News by Search Term (First Version)"—is here:

```
http://pipes.yahoo.com/pipes/pipe.info?_id=Rg_rh3NA3BGdECIel7okhQ
```

You can run it and view the source if you are logged in. You can run a pipe to get an RSS 2.0 feed for a given search term here:

```
http://pipes.yahoo.com/pipes/pipe.run?_id={pipe-id}&_render=rss&search_term=
{search-term}
```

For example, to search for Hurricane Katrina, go here:

```
http://pipes.yahoo.com/pipes/pipe.run?_id=Rg_rh3NA3BGdECIel7okhQ&_render=rss&
search_term=Hurricane+Katrina
```

The pipe uses three widgets to enable a user to pass in a search term and return a feed of Yahoo! News (see Figure 4-3):

- A `Text Input` module that takes the search term from the user and is wired to feed this term to the `URL Builder` described next

- A `URL Builder` module that has a `Base` parameter of `http://news.search.yahoo.com/news/rss` and a query parameter of `p`

- A `Fetch Feed` that fetches the feed at the URL coming from the `URL Builder`

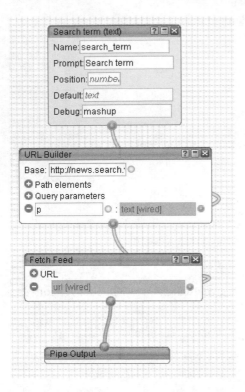

Figure 4-3. *Pipe for "Yahoo! News by Search Term (First Version)". (Reproduced with permission of Yahoo! Inc. ® 2007 by Yahoo! Inc. YAHOO! and the YAHOO! logo are trademarks of Yahoo! Inc.)*

Google News and Refactoring Pipes

The second news source that I need to pull in is Google News, which returns an Atom feed for a given search term here:

```
http://news.google.com/news?q={search-term}&output=atom
```

I use `output=atom` instead of `output=rss` to show that Yahoo! Pipes can handle Atom feeds.

One way to build a module to handle Google News is to clone the one for Yahoo! News and change the parameters in the `URL Builder` module. Instead, because I figured that there are plenty of feeds with URLs that consist of a single parameter and search term, I decided to build a utility pipe that would return feeds at URLs in the following form:

```
{base-URL}?{parameter_name}={parameter_value}{URL_suffix}
```

Constructing such a pipe is equivalent to writing a reusable function. By contrast, cloning a pipe is analogous to copying and pasting code. When you use pipes seriously, you begin to see patterns that can be captured and reused in a pipe.

The pipe I constructed for that purpose (called "Feed from a URL Constructed from One Variable Parameter") is located here:

```
http://pipes.yahoo.com/pipes/pipe.info?_id=VoLceXZA3BGkqcJZJxOyOQ
```

Note the intermixing of the `URL Builder` and `String Builder` modules to concatenate parameters and build a URL that can actually be fed to `Fetch Feed` module.

I used that pipe and the fact you can write the URLs to retrieve feeds from Yahoo! News and Google News in terms of these four parameters (see Table 4-5).

Table 4-5. *Parameters for Pipe Called "Feed from a URL Constructed from One Variable Parameter"*

base-URL	parameter_ name	parameter_ value	URL_ suffix
`http://news.google.com/news`	q	`{search-term}`	`&output=atom`
`http://news.search.yahoo.com/news/rss`	p	`{search-term}`	

The pipe that accesses Yahoo! News using the utility pipe (entitled "Yahoo! News by Search Term") is as follows:

`http://pipes.yahoo.com/pipes/pipe.info?_id=5NhmMndA3BGg5zQ5nOartA`

The "Google News by Search Term" pipe is here:

`http://pipes.yahoo.com/pipes/pipe.info?_id=OKWv6nNA3BGkPtA8qWIyXQ`

Wikinews and NY Times: Filtering Feeds

Now we come to the third and fourth sources: Wikinews, which has a single feed:

`http://feeds.feedburner.com/WikinewsLatestNews`

and the New York Times National News (I select the National News feed because of the focus on Hurricane Katrina):

`http://www.nytimes.com/services/xml/rss/nyt/National.xml`

In contrast to the Yahoo! News and Google News for which I can generate a feed for a given search term by constructing the appropriate URL, I use `search-term` to filter the feed. To that end, I use the `Filter` module in the Filter for Given Term in Feed Description and Title pipe here:

`http://pipes.yahoo.com/pipes/pipe.info?_id=KIYSv3pA3BGgloVbCB2yXQ`

to pass along only those items in the feed whose description or title contains the search term.

With that pipe as a foundation, I construct the "Wikinews Filtered by Search Term" pipe here:

`http://pipes.yahoo.com/pipes/pipe.info?_id=PA7iqHpA3BGbOAiVXOsBXw`

and the NY Times National News Filtered by a Search Term pipe here:

`http://pipes.yahoo.com/pipes/pipe.info?_id=yhBh7HxA3BGu_YRj1vC6Jw`

Pulling the Feeds Together

With a pipe each for my four news sources, each of which takes a search term as input, I then create a pipe here:

```
http://pipes.yahoo.com/pipes/pipe.info?_id=qlUkcn1A3BGeWlNQjknRlg
```

that does the following:

- Takes a search term as input and passes it to the individual news source pipes

- Concatenates the individual feeds with the Union module

- Gets rid of feed items that have the same link with the Unique module

You're done. You can search for Hurricane Katrina in the four news sources here:

```
http://pipes.yahoo.com/pipes/pipe.info?Search_term=Hurricane+Katrina&_cmd=Run+Pipe&
_id=qlUkcn1A3BGeWlNQjknRlg&_run=1
```

The corresponding feed is available here:

```
http://pipes.yahoo.com/pipes/pipe.run?Search_term=Hurricane+Katrina&
_id=qlUkcn1A3BGeWlNQjknRlg&_render=rss
```

Obviously, the pipes I created could be refined. Indeed, you can do so right now by going to the list of pipes I created for this chapter and cloning and modifying them for your own use:

```
http://pipes.yahoo.com/pipes/tag.info?namespace=user&tag=mashupguide
```

This section used feeds that are relatively easy to access. If you start to use tools such as Openkapow.com to screen-scrape new feeds, you have even more combinatorial possibilities for your mashups. Note that other tools that I discuss later in the book (such as the Google Mashup Editor) are able to consume feeds, such as those generated by Yahoo! Pipes and Feedburner.

Summary

Feeds provide the backbone of data exchange for mashups. Many web sites—including Flickr—generate feeds, particularly in the RSS and Atom formats. In this chapter, you learned about the ecosystem that has arisen around this plethora of feeds: news aggregators that gather feeds for reading, validators that help you produce good feeds, scrapers that let you generate feeds when a web site doesn't provide one, and remixing tools that let you generate elaborate mashups of feeds. In an extended example of mashups based on feeds, I showed how to use Yahoo! Pipes to generate a single topical news feed that is a mashup of several other appropriately filtered feeds.

## CHAPTER 5

Integrating with Blogs

Blogs (also known as *weblogs*) have become lightweight, general-purpose platforms for publication, self-expression, and collaboration. Bloggers push the limits of new-media production, especially in the area of integration, because they want ultimately to discuss anything they can see or think or hear—without any effort, of course. Because you can directly tie blogs in with other systems—often without any programming on your own part—you'll now study how to combine blogs with other applications and data sources. In this chapter, I cover end-user functionality that lets you publish content to a blog from a web site or a desktop application. In Chapter 7, you'll study how you can program the relevant web APIs to read and publish blog content. I close this chapter by applying lessons from blog integration to wikis, which I believe are ripe for a similar type of remixing.

In this chapter, you will do the following:

- You'll learn how to configure your WordPress or Blogger blog to receive pictures from Flickr through Flickr's Blog This button.

- You'll study the mechanisms behind blog integration by studying how it's done with Flickr.

- You'll learn how to use a desktop blogging client to take advantage of a richer writing environment for blogging.

- You'll see how the combination of syndication feeds and blogging can be recursive (that is, how content from blogs can be refashioned into new blog entries).

- You'll experience the forward-looking social browser integration of Flock, which combines a Web browser, Flickr photos, and blogging all in one user interface.

I'll first cover the mechanics of blogging from the point of view of the user, and then I'll cover what this means in terms of the back end (specifically the use of APIs once again, this time for blogs).

Integration Scenarios for Blogs

Essentially, blogs are online journals about a topic, a theme, or a person written by one person or a small group. Here are other general patterns:

- Blogs consist of entries that are typically displayed in reverse chronological order.

- These entries are often classified into categories.

- Most blogs provide their content via RSS or Atom syndication.

In Chapter 4, I discussed how RSS/Atom syndication makes the life of a reader simpler by allowing the reader to aggregate content. In this chapter, you'll examine how the lives of blog authors can be made simpler. Wouldn't it be great to be able to do the following?

1. First write or create some piece of digital content (it could be simple text, HTML, images, video, or a word-processed document) in the tool of your choice (Microsoft Word, OpenOffice.org, the rich-text editor of WordPress, vi, Thunderbird).

2. Then easily publish that content to a blog (or any other web site). That is, you could have the piece of content you wrote show up in a blog in a way that preserves the formatting— or at least translates that format appropriately to the new environment—without having to do much (or any) of the manual work of translating that formatting.

We have not pulled off such general seamless integration yet. However, we will examine some specific and useful cases of integration in this chapter. Figuring out how integration happens in these specific scenarios enables you to build not only your own tools for supporting similar circumstances but also solutions to the general integration problems.

FREE HOSTED BLOGS AS A WAY TO START BLOGGING

If you are not already using a blog, it's useful to set up an account with which to experiment. You can download blogging software, write your own, or pay for blog hosting, but the easiest way to get started is to use one of the following free hosted blogging services:

- WordPress (http://wordpress.com)

- Blogger (http://blogger.com)

- LiveJournal (http://livejournal.com)

There are others, but these three should get you started.[1]

Sending Flickr Pictures to Blogs

As you have seen in previous chapters, Flickr provides excellent functionality to display and add narration to your photos; you can create slide shows; create sets; tack titles, descriptions, and tags to photos; and create groups to collaborate with others with similar interests. Yet, it is natural to want to present your photos outside the world of Flickr. If you have a personal blog, would you not want to display your photos on your own blog and tell stories around them?

---

1. http://blogs.about.com/od/blogsoftwareandhosts/a/topfreeblogs.htm

As a Flickr user, you can automatically post a photo to your blog, provided you do the following:

1. First configure Flickr to work with your blog.

2. Hit the Blog This button for the desired photo.

The following sections are detailed instructions on the previous two steps. Before I cover how to use the automated process, I'll cover how you would manually present a photo from Flickr on your blog. You would do the following:

1. Generate the appropriate HTML for the photo in question. For this to work, you would need to know the URL for the actual image, as well as the URL for the photo page. You could grab the URL of the image from the web browser (through right-clicking the image and copying the image URL, for instance).

   If the photo in question is your own, Flickr provides some help in this department. For a given picture, hit the All Sizes button. For a given size of the photo, you can copy and paste the HTML given under the "Copy and Paste this HTML into Your Webpage" heading.

2. With the HTML now in hand, you would go to your blog to create a new post and then paste in that HTML.

Flickr helps automate this process by using blogging APIs. I'll now cover how.

Configuring Flickr for Integration with Blogs

Before you publish your photos from Flickr to a blog, you need to tell Flickr about the blogs you plan to use. Here are step-by-step instructions for configuring your blogs for access by Flickr:

1. Go to `http://flickr.com/blogs.gne`. You have to sign in to Flickr first.

2. Hit the Add Another Blog link (`http://flickr.com/blogs_add.gne`). You will see a list of weblogs that you have already configured. Note the types of blogs supported by Flickr:

   - Blogger
   - TypePad
   - Movable Type
   - LiveJournal
   - WordPress
   - Manila
   - Atom
   - Blogger API
   - MetaWeblog API
   - Vox

Depending on the type of blog you want to integrate with, the parameters you will need to fill in differ.

> ## WHY IS THERE A LIST OF BLOG TYPES IN THE FIRST PLACE?
>
> If all you are interested in is setting up Flickr to enable you to send a photo to your blog, you do not need to understand why there are so many blog types listed. If, however, you are interested in the mechanisms behind blogging integration, it's useful to ponder what you see here.
>
> For instance, why does Flickr ask about the type of blog you have? It's conceivable that Flickr would not have to ask that question at all if all blogs were the same in terms of the mechanics of integration. The fact that this question is asked indicates that there is some sort of dependency on the blog type that affects how Flickr connects to the blog. But if your blog type is not on the list, what are you supposed to do? What exactly are those dependencies, and can they be formulated in terms of parameters of the system? I'll return to these questions later in this chapter.

Let's take a look at two types of blog software to understand some of the necessary parameters involved in blogging integration: WordPress and Blogger.

WordPress

To add a WordPress blog to your Flickr configuration, do the following:

1. Go to `http://flickr.com/blogs_add.gne`. Make sure you have a WordPress blog that you own for this example. You can either install your own WordPress blog on your hosting service or use the free WordPress service (see the "Free Hosted Blogs As a Way to Start Blogging" sidebar).

2. Click WordPress Blog in response to the question "What kind of blog do you have?" Note that with this choice you end up at the URL `http://flickr.com/blogs_add_metaweblogapi.gne`—which suggests that WordPress is accessible through the MetaWeblog API.[2]

3. Enter the following parameters:

   - API endpoint (for WordPress blogs, the URL is `http://{url-of-your-blog}/xmlrpc.php`, for example, `http://blog.mashupguide.net/xmlrpc.php`)

   - Username

   - Password

4. After you hit Next—and assuming you entered the correct combination of API endpoint, username, and password—you have the choice of storing the password on Flickr and changing the URL or label. After you have entered your choices, click All Done.

5. You can now choose a template for your blog and customize it (if you know HTML and CSS).

6. You can test the blog configuration by issuing a test post. To do so, go to `http://flickr.com/blogs.gne`, and click the Test Post button that corresponds to the blog. If things go well, you'll get the message "A test post to [name of your blog] has been sent. Feel free to delete it once it's gone through," and you should see a test post on your blog.

---

2. `http://en.wikipedia.org/wiki/MetaWeblog`

Blogger Blogs

Blogger is another popular host of free blogs and is owned by Google. To add a new-style Blogger blog to Flickr, do the following:

1. Select Blogger Blog from the drop-down menu at `http://flickr.com/blogs_add.gne`. Make sure you have a Blogger blog, which you can sign up for at `http://www2.blogger.com/create-blog.g`.

2. At this point, you may be asked to head over to Google to authorize Flickr's access to your blog. If so, you will see a prompt like that in Figure 5-1. If not, skip to step 4.

Your account / Blogs / Add a blog

Authorize posting to your Blogger (beta) blog

If you're using the new beta.blogger.com, part of setting up your Blogger Beta blog to post from Flickr is you signing in at Google to establish permission.

So, here's the process:

1. Head to google.com and if you aren't already logged in you'll be asked to do so.
2. On the page you end up on, you need to "Grant Access" to flickr.com.
3. Return to Flickr, finish setting things up

Head over to Google now

Figure 5-1. *A prompt from Flickr explaining the authentication process required to enable you to send Flickr photos to new Blogger blogs. (Reproduced with permission of Yahoo! Inc. ® 2007 by Yahoo! Inc. YAHOO! and the YAHOO! logo are trademarks of Yahoo! Inc.)*

3. At Google, if you are not already logged in to Blogger, you will be prompted to log in. (Notice that it is Google/Blogger asking for the login, not Flickr here.) Once you are logged in, you'll be asked to grant access rights to Flickr, as shown in Figure 5-2. Note the comment "Flickr.com will not have access to your password or any personal information." There is a fuller explanation of how the authentication scheme works available on the Google web site.[3]

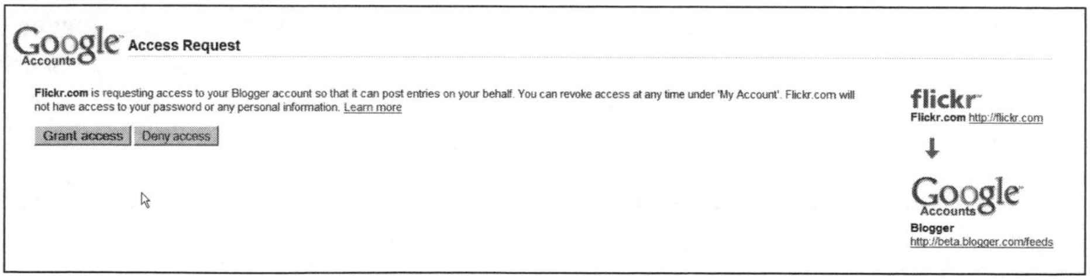

Google Accounts Access Request

Flickr.com is requesting access to your Blogger account so that it can post entries on your behalf. You can revoke access at any time under "My Account". Flickr.com will not have access to your password or any personal information. Learn more

Grant access   Deny access

flickr
Flickr.com http://flickr.com

↓

Google Accounts
Blogger
http://beta.blogger.com/feeds

Figure 5-2. *A prompt from Google requesting authorization to post to your Blogger blog from Flickr*

3. `https://www.google.com/support/accounts/bin/answer.py?answer=41192`

4. If you grant access to Google, your browser will be redirected to a page presenting you with a drop-down list of the blogs available at Blogger. Select the one you want.

5. Verify the settings (you can change the URL and label). Hit the All Done button.

6. Test your settings by making a test entry to your blog. Do you see a test entry on your blog? If so, your parameters are correct.

Notice that you never enter your username/password for your Blogger blogs to Flickr at any time during the process.

Blogging a Flickr Picture

Once you have a blog configured for blogging from Flickr, you are now ready to write a blog post based on a photo directly from Flickr. Here's how:

1. Go to a specific Flickr picture, and hit the Blog This button located above the picture.

2. Choose the blog from the list to which you want to send the picture.

3. Fill out the title and your post; I often find it helpful to copy and paste the description of the picture into the post. Hit Return.

If everything goes according to plan, you'll see the message from Flickr saying "Your blog entry has been posted!" and a URL to your blog so that you can check out your new post.

Note   Sometimes, you will get errors (such as timeouts). Often you can just try again. Sometimes Flickr reports an error when the post actually goes through and you can end up with multiple posts should you try again.

How Does the Flickr Blog Integration Work?

After you have configured a WordPress or Blogger blog and posted a picture, I encourage you to think about what must be happening underneath the hood to make the Flickr blogging interaction happen. Here are some specific issues to consider and questions to ask:

- Note the contrast in the parameters needed for a WordPress blog and a Blogger blog. For the WordPress blog, you need to enter an API endpoint along with the user and password, whereas for Blogger, you don't enter those credentials but are redirected to Google for authorization. Here are some issues to consider:

    - What do you think is happening differently to account for the contrast in functionality?

    - Why do you not need to type in an API endpoint for Blogger?

    - Where do you send username/passwords for each case?

    - What are the advantages and disadvantages of each approach?

- Note the wide variety of classes of blogs recognized by Flickr. You can try each type to study the parameters required to make each type of blog work.

- Note that once you blog a picture in the Flickr interface, a list dynamically pops up via Ajax.

- Study the types of templates available and how you can customize them via CSS and HTML.

After I describe web APIs in detail (for Flickr and for other web sites), I'll answer the questions I just posed in Chapter 7. There I explore in greater detail the use of blogging APIs. Still, without diving into technical details about the APIs, you can make several observations:

- Once you have configured a blog for access by Flickr, the process for publishing a photo is the same regardless of the actual blog you use.

- By contrast, Flickr is unable to smooth out the differences among weblogs to make the configuration process look identical. That means the protocols for connecting to Word-Press and to Blogger probably differ.

- Blogging protocol must address the important issue of authentication and authorization; the process in which you grant Flickr the power to post to your blog depends on the type of blog you use.

Desktop Blogging Tools

You have just seen how you can send HTML that encodes a photo and description from Flickr to a blog. It should not then be surprising to find out that you can send data to blogs from systems other than Flickr. Indeed, a whole genre of tools lets you compose and post blog entries in a more convenient environment (such as a desktop application) and then send those posts to your blog instead of having to use the native blog post interface. The following are examples of blogging clients:

- w.bloggar (http://www.wbloggar.com/) is a Windows desktop client.

- ecto (http://ecto.kung-foo.tv/) for Windows and Mac OS X.

- MarsEdit (http://www.red-sweater.com/marsedit/) is for Mac OS X.

- Windows Live Writer (http://windowslivewriter.spaces.live.com/) is a desktop client for Windows.

- BlogDesk (http://www.blogdesk.org/en/index.htm) is a Windows desktop client.

- ScribeFire (http://www.scribefire.com/) is a client right within Firefox.

- mo:Blog (http:www.moblogworld.net/) is a client for Palm OS devices.

Some brave souls such as Jon Udell are even doing cutting-edge experiments of blogging from Microsoft Word 2007.[4] Figure 5-3 shows how it looks to write a blog post in one of these clients.

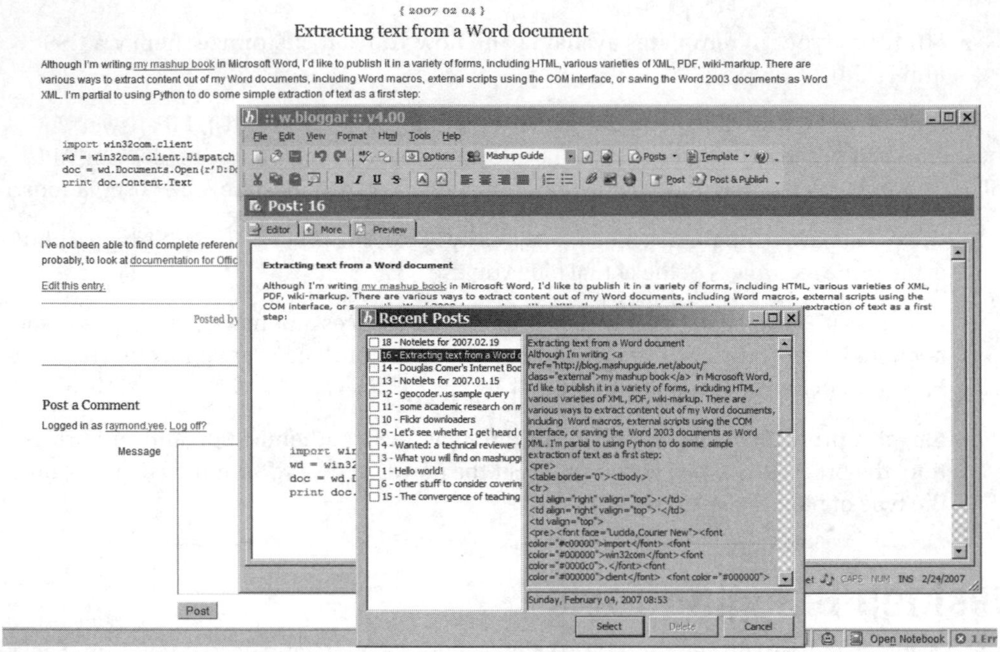

Figure 5-3. *Writing to a WordPress blog from the Windows w.bloggar client. Note that the post already exists on the blog and that w.bloggar is being used to post it for editing.*

It is instructive to ponder why there are so many tools in this area, what exactly is being integrated by the tools, and the exact list of functionality in these tools. Answers to these questions shed light on how users actually write blogs. For instance, Brent Simmons' description of MarsEdit, which he created, gives some insight into the genre:[5]

> *MarsEdit is weblog posting and editing software. It makes writing for the web like writing email: you open a window and write something, then send it to your weblog. It has many of the same features that email applications have: drafts, text editing commands, even AppleScript support. It also has features specific to weblogs: categories, text filters, trackbacks, pings, and so on. People that have more than one weblog find it especially useful because they have just one place to write and edit all their weblog posts, even if their weblogs are on different systems.*

---

4. http://blog.jonudell.net/2007/02/19/blogging-from-word-2007-crossing-the-chasm/#comments

5. http://www.newsgator.com/NGOLProduct.aspx?ProdID=MarsEdit

Combining Feeds and Blogging to Generate Feedback Flows

In blogging there is often tight coupling between reading other people's blogs and writing your own blog entries. If you happen to be reading other blogs through a feed reader, you might even be able to easily drop pieces of other people's blogs (that are coming in as RSS or Atom items) into your own blog editor.

For example, on Windows, using SharpReader[6] combined with w.bloggar[7] and the w.bloggar SharpReader plug-in,[8] you can directly write blog entries based on items coming into your SharpReader news feeds (in a process that has been called *reblogging*), as shown in Figure 5-4.

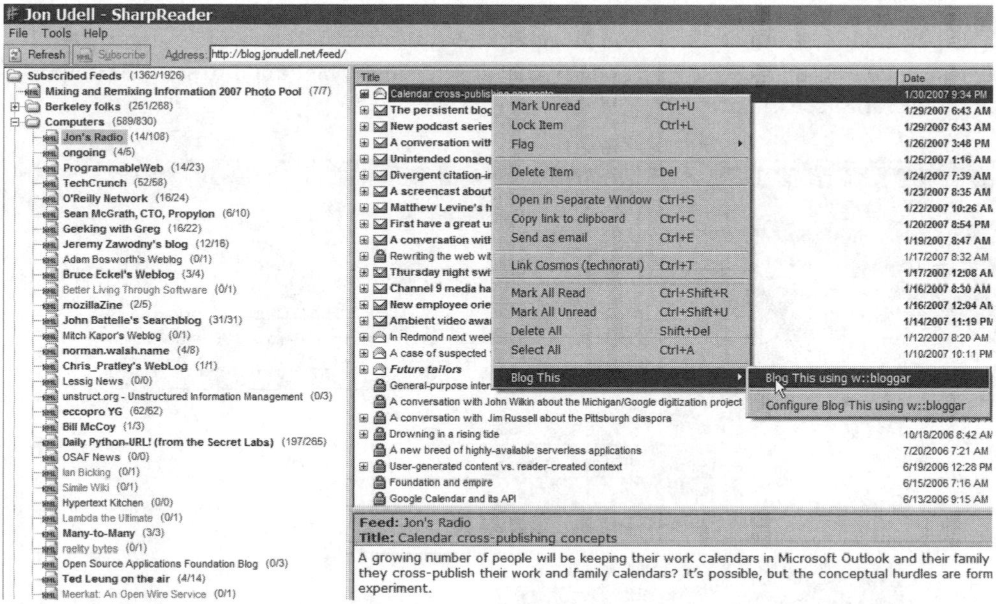

Figure 5-4. *On a Windows desktop, SharpReader is looking at one of Udell's posts, along with a right-click invocation of w.bloggar to send this entry to a blog.*

Since reblogging often produces nothing more than trivial republication of other people's words, it's easy to forget that this flow of content is actually undergird by a feedback loop of reading and writing. When you use Flickr's blog functionality, content goes from Flickr to a blog, but there's no easy flow of content from blogs back into Flickr. By contrast, the combination of weblogs that syndicate their contents through feeds and feed aggregators that are also blog clients means that what you read can flow easily into what you write. In the next section, I'll discuss Flock, a web browser that facilitates this flow between reading and writing by building in greater integration with blogging and various social media web sites.

---

6. http://www.sharpreader.net/

7. http://wbloggar.com/

8. http://www.sharpreader.net/plugins.html

Flock: Bringing Together Blogs and Flickr

Flock (http://flock.com) is advertised by its creators as the "social web browser." Built upon the Firefox code base, Flock incorporates the following in its own interface:

- Flickr, Photobucket, and YouTube integration

- Blogging integration (including Blogger, LiveJournal, TypePad, WordPress, and various self-hosted blogs), as shown in Figure 5-5

- Integration with your social bookmarks at del.icio.us and ma.gnolia.com

- Drag-and-drop functionality that allows you to drag Flickr photos into a writing toolbar that then connects to your blogs

Experimenting with the Flickr and blogging integration[9] in the Flock browser is a useful way to see the flow of data between systems that are starting to be built into service composition frameworks (see Chapter 11).

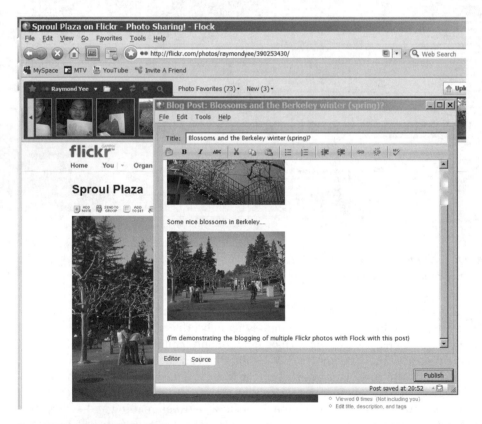

Figure 5-5. *Blogging Flickr photos from Flock by dragging and dropping multiple Flickr photos into an editing window and then posting that entry into a configured blog. (Reproduced with permission of Yahoo! Inc. ® 2007 by Yahoo! Inc. YAHOO! and the YAHOO! logo are trademarks of Yahoo! Inc.)*

---

9. http://www.flock.com/faq/show/29#q_8369

RSD: Discoverability of Blog APIs

If you configure Flock for blogging, you might wonder why some blogs can be configured by simply entering the URL of the blog only, while in Flickr, you sometimes need to enter the URL to the specific API endpoint. How is Flock able to find the URL endpoint from the URL of the blog? Finding the URL of the API endpoint is similar to the problem described in Chapter 4 of locating the URLs of feeds based on the URL of the web site. You won't be surprised then to discover that someone invented an autodiscovery mechanism for the existence of blogging APIs:

```
http://en.wikipedia.org/wiki/Really_Simple_Discovery
```

For detailed technical information on the mechanism, read the RSD specification:

```
http://cyber.law.harvard.edu/blogs/gems/tech/rsd.html
```

Here I point out how RSD has been implemented by at least two major blog publishing services: WordPress and Blogger. You can go to any of the blogs run by WordPress, such as the one for WordPress news:

```
http://wordpress.com/blog/
```

in which you will find the following link:

```
<link rel="EditURI" type="application/rsd+xml" title="RSD"
    href="http://wordpress.com/xmlrpc.php?rsd" />
```

From looking at `http://wordpress.com/xmlrpc.php?rsd`, which is as follows:

```
<?xml version="1.0" encoding="UTF-8"?><rsd version="1.0"
    xmlns="http://archipelago.phrasewise.com/rsd">
  <service>
    <engineName>WordPress</engineName>
    <engineLink>http://wordpress.org/</engineLink>
    <homePageLink>http://wordpress.com</homePageLink>
    <apis>
      <api name="WordPress" blogID="1" preferred="true"
          apiLink="http://wordpress.com/xmlrpc.php" />
      <api name="Movable Type" blogID="1" preferred="false"
          apiLink="http://wordpress.com/xmlrpc.php" />
      <api name="MetaWeblog" blogID="1" preferred="false"
          apiLink="http://wordpress.com/xmlrpc.php" />
      <api name="Blogger" blogID="1" preferred="false"
          apiLink="http://wordpress.com/xmlrpc.php" />
    </apis>
  </service>
</rsd>
```

you can see how the WordPress blog is advertising itself as having support for four blog APIs: WordPress, Movable Type, Metablog, and Blogger.

Similarly, for Blogger blogs such as `http://googleblog.blogspot.com/`, you'll get the following:

```
<link rel="EditURI" type="application/rsd+xml" title="RSD"
    href="http://www.blogger.com/rsd.g?blogID=10861780" />
```

And `http://www.blogger.com/rsd.g?blogID=10861780` shows support for one API, the Blogger API:

```
<api name="Blogger" preferred="true" apiLink="http://www.blogger.com/api"
    blogID="10861780"/>
```

Like feed autodiscovery, RSD functions as a reasonably well-implemented de facto standard without much formalization.

Linkbacks

I'll now explain a type of communication flow that you might notice from studying blogs (though not directly from how Flickr interacts with blogs). Among comments listed for a given blog post are often entries that come from other web sites. How is a blog able to track links that come from the outside? Weblogs use *linkbacks*, a family of methods for receiving notifications of inbound links to a web site.

As documented at `http://en.wikipedia.org/wiki/Linkback`, there are three major protocols for linkbacks: refback, trackback, and pingback. It's useful to know which of the protocols are supported by various blogging software so that you know which of the protocols to support if you set out to use linkbacks. Why might linkbacks be useful for mashups? You may want your mashup to either notify web sites that it links to or receive notifications of being linked to.

Note that Flickr doesn't support linkbacks, although it notifies you when someone else adds a comment to your picture or makes it a favorite.

Wiki Integration at an Early Stage

Wikis are web sites for bringing together user contributions, though they are designed to be more radically collaborative than blogs. According to the Wikipedia, a wiki is as follows:

> *A website that allows the visitors themselves to easily add, remove, and otherwise edit and change available content, typically without the need for registration.*[10]

The ideal scenario for wikis is allowing anyone to edit pages, combined with a lack of broken links. That is, when a user follows a link to a page that doesn't exist, the user is not given a 404 error but rather the opportunity to create that page.

I mention blogs and wikis together in this chapter because they are siblings. Indeed, there are hybrid blogs/wikis—or at least experimentation to bring them into hybrid structures.[11] And there are other similarities between blogs and wikis: both are used to publish web sites, both can have APIs that facilitate integration, and both tend to have plug-in infrastructures that make them more like platforms than simple software. This combination of APIs and plug-ins increases the mashup opportunities.

---

10. `http://en.wikipedia.org/wiki/Wiki`—accessed as `http://en.wikipedia.org/w/index.php?title=Wiki&oldid=109882004`

11. `http://www.docuverse.com/blog/donpark/2003/09/05/wiki-based-web` sites

You have seen some complicated ways in which the tools and data involved in blogs aren't being mashed up. Although the potential for wiki mashups is great, there are a lot fewer examples of such mashups. Much of the technical foundation is in place (for instance, many wikis have APIs and plug-in frameworks[12]), but the uptake of wikis is less than that for blogs.

The closest thing to a mass phenomenon we have in the world of wikis is Wikipedia. It's not surprising then to see some mashing up of Wikipedia, though not as much as you might expect. Let's look at one example of a remix of Wikipedia, FUTEF, which is a custom search engine that draws content from Wikipedia (`http://futef.com/`):

1. Go to `http://futef.com/`, and type **Bach** into the search engine.

2. Study the search results that come back, their order, and the categories listed.

3. Compare what you see in FUTEF with what you get from the same search in Wikipedia. In Wikipedia, you get an immediate redirection to the article on Johann Sebastian Bach. For other Bach-related terms, study the Bach disambiguation page.[13]

Curiously, FUTEF has built its own API that it has invited others to use.[14] Why, for instance, would anyone use FUTEF's API to access Wikipedia when Wikipedia provides its own? Well, once FUTEF fulfills its plans to offer content other than Wikipedia, I can see a good reason for trying the FUTEF API. At this point, I'd say FUTEF is useful primarily as a demonstration of how you can repackage Wikipedia.

Other places to look in terms of integration with Wikipedia is in authoring tools akin to blogging clients and in bots that have been written to support the editing of Wikipedia. You can find a list of such editors here:

`http://en.wikipedia.org/wiki/Wikipedia:Text_editor_support`

And you can find a discussion of Wikipedia bots here:

`http://meta.wikimedia.org/wiki/Bot`

Summary

Here are a few points to remember from this chapter:

- Flickr lets you blog a single picture. From this function, you can see a specific instance of data being sent to blogs.

- There are many types of blogs, and they require different type of configuration schemes.

- Flock tries to envision a future in which a whole bunch of tools are integrated: a web browser, Flickr, blogs, and social bookmarking.

---

12. `http://en.wikipedia.org/w/api.php` for MediaWiki and `http://api.pbwiki.com/` for PBWiki, which is a popular free wiki host provider

13. `http://en.wikipedia.org/wiki/Bach_%28disambiguation%29`

14. `http://www.programmableweb.com/api/FUTEFWikipedia`

- You can generate a feedback loop using RSS, news aggregators, and blogging, and most blogs automatically generate RSS.

- Blogs represent a type of remixing in a narrative, in contrast with the data-oriented remixing via tags and straight RSS so far discussed.

Now that you have studied how these tools work, you are in a good position in the coming chapters to start building your own tool. You will create some mashups step by step, remembering what you have seen as an end user of these tools.

■ ■ ■

## PART 2

Remixing a Single Web Application Using Its API

In Part I, we looked at how to recombine information without resorting to formal programming techniques. There is a lot that can be done by carefully examining various web applications from the perspective of an end user looking for integrative opportunities. We studied, for instance, how you can recombine information through manipulating URLs, introducing tags, and connecting feeds from one application to another.

In the rest of the book, we'll take on the programmer's perspective. In the first two chapters in this part, for example, we turn to learning about how to use web services, starting from the concrete example of Flickr (Chapter 6) and then contrasting and comparing Flickr to other examples (Chapter 7). In Chapter 8, we turn to Ajax-based and JavaScript-based widgets, building upon what we learn in Chapter 6 and Chapter 7.

CHAPTER 6

■ ■ ■

Learning Web Services APIs Through Flickr

Flickr is an excellent playground for learning XML web services. Among other reasons, Flickr offers clear documentation, an instructive API Explorer that lets you try the API through a browser, and lots of prior art to study in terms of remixes and mashups. Hundreds of third-party apps are using the Flickr API.

As I discussed in previous chapters (especially Chapter 2), application programming interfaces (APIs) are the preferred way of programming a website and accessing its data and services, although not all websites have APIs. We looked at a wide range of things you can do without doing much programming, which in many cases means not resorting to the API. But now we turn to using APIs. Don't forget what you learned while looking at end-user functionality, because you will need that knowledge in applying APIs.

By the end of this chapter, you will see that the Flickr API is an extensive API that can do many things using many options. The heart of the API is simple, though. I'll start this chapter by presenting and analyzing perhaps the simplest immediately useful thing you can do with the Flickr API. I'll walk you through that example in depth to show you conceptually how to use the search API and how to interpret the results you get. After walking you through how to make that specific request, I'll outline the various ways in which the example can be generalized.

After an overview of the policy and terms of service surrounding the API, I'll show you how to make sense of the Flickr documentation and how to use the excellent Flickr API Explorer to study the API. I'll revisit in depth the mechanics of making a basic call of a Flickr API method, using it as an opportunity to provide a tutorial on two fundamental techniques: processing HTTP requests and parsing XML. I then demonstrate how to knit those two techniques to create a simple HTML interface based on the photo search API.

With an understanding of how to exercise a single method in hand, you'll then look at all the API methods in Flickr. I'll demonstrate how to use the reflection methods in the Flickr API to tell you about the API itself. I'll next explain the ways in which you can choose alternative formats for the requests and responses in the API, laying the foundation for a discussion of REST and SOAP that I'll revisit in the next chapter.

By that point in the chapter, you will have done almost everything you can do with authorization, the trickiest part of the API. Flickr authorization can confusing if you do not understand the motivation behind the steps in the authorization dance. I'll explain the mechanics of the authorization scheme in terms of what Flickr must be accomplishing in authorization—and how all the technical pieces fit together to accomplish those design goals. It's an involved story but one that might elucidate for you other authentication schemes out there with similar design constraints. After the narrative, I've included some PHP code that implements the ideas.

For practical use of the Flickr API to make mashups, you probably do not want to work so close to the API itself but instead use API kits or third-party language-specific wrappers. Therefore, I'll survey briefly three of the PHP API kits for Flickr. I'll conclude this chapter by pointing out some of the limitations of the Flickr API with respect to what's possible with the Flickr user interface.

An Introduction to the Flickr API

It's useful to start with a simple yet illustrative example of the Flickr API before diving into the complexities that can easily obscure the simple idea at the heart of the API. The API is designed for you as a programmer to send *requests* to the API and get *responses* that are easy for you to decipher with your program. In earlier chapters, especially Chapter 2, you learned about you can use the URL language of Flickr to access resources from Flickr. However, for a computer program to use that information, it would have to screen-scrape the information. Screen-scraping is a fragile and cumbersome process. The Flickr API sets a framework for both making requests and getting responses that are well defined, stable, and convenient for computer programs.

Before you proceed any further, sign up for a Flickr API key so that you can follow along with this example (see "Obtaining a Flickr API Key").

OBTAINING A FLICKR API KEY

You need a key to use the Flickr API. A *key* is a string of numbers and letters that identifies you as the source of an API request. That is, when you make a call of the API, you typically need to pass in your key (or some other parameter derived from your key). You get a key through registering your application with Flickr:

```
http://www.flickr.com/services/api/keys/apply/
```

Get your own API key to try the exercises in this chapter and the following chapters. You can see the list of your current keys here:

```
http://www.flickr.com/services/api/keys/
```

In the next chapter, you will see that keys are a common mechanism used in other application APIs. Through keys, the API provider knows something about the identity of an API user (typically at least the API key holder's e-mail address if nothing else) and monitors the manner in which a user is accessing the API (such as the rate and volume of calls and the specific requests made). Through such tracking, the API provider might also choose to enforce the terms of use for the API—from contacting the user by e-mail to shutting down access by that key...to suing the user in extreme cases!

Once you have your key, let's make the simplest possible call to the Flickr API. Drop the following URL in your browser:

```
http://api.flickr.com/services/rest/?method=flickr.test.echo&api_key={api-key}
```

where api-key is your Flickr API key. For this request, there are two parameters: method, which indicates the part of the API to access, and api_key, which identifies the party making the API request. Flickr produces the following response corresponding to your request:

```
<?xml version="1.0" encoding="utf-8" ?>
<rsp stat="ok">
<method>flickr.test.echo</method>
<api_key>[API-KEY]</api_key>
</rsp>
```

Note that the entity body of the response is an XML document containing your key.

Let's now consider a slightly more complicated call to the Flickr API that returns something more interesting. Let's ask Flickr for photos with a given tag. You learned in Chapter 2 that the corresponding URL in the Flickr UI for pictures corresponding to a given tag (say, the tag puppy) is as follows:

```
http://www.flickr.com/photos/tags/{tag}/
```

For example:

```
http://www.flickr.com/photos/tags/puppy/
```

The corresponding way to get from the Flickr API to the most recently uploaded public photos for a tag is like so:

```
http://api.flickr.com/services/rest/?method=flickr.photos.search&api_key={api_key}
&tags={tag}&per_page={per_page}
```

When you substitute your API key, set tag to puppy, and set per_page to 3 to issue the following call:

```
http://api.flickr.com/services/rest/?method=flickr.photos.search&api_key={api_key}
&tags=puppy&per_page=3
```

you will get something similar to the following:

```
<?xml version="1.0" encoding="utf-8" ?>
<rsp stat="ok">
<photos page="1" pages="96293" perpage="3" total="288877">
  <photo id="1153699093" owner="7841384@N07" secret="d1fba451c9" server="1023"
         farm="2" title="willy after bath and haircut" ispublic="1" isfriend="0"
         isfamily="0" />
  <photo id="1154506492" owner="7841384@N07" secret="881ff7c4bc" server="1058"
         farm="2" title="rocky with broken leg" ispublic="1" isfriend="0"
         isfamily="0" />
  <photo id="1153588011" owner="90877382@N00" secret="8a7a559e68" server="1288"
         farm="2" title="DSC 6503" ispublic="1" isfriend="0" isfamily="0" />
</photos>
</rsp>
```

What happens in this Flickr API call? In the request, you ask for the three most recently uploaded public photos with the tag puppy via the flickr.photos.search method. You get back an XML document in the body of the response. I'll show you later in the chapter the mechanics of how to parse the XML document in languages such as PHP. For the moment, notice the information you are getting in the XML response:

- Within the `rsp root` element, you find a `photos` element containing three child `photo` elements.

- Attributes in the `photos` element tell you a number of facts about the photo: the `total` attribute is the number of public photos tagged with `puppy` (288,877), the `perpage` attribute is the number of photo elements actually returned in this response (3), the `page` attribute tells you which page corresponds to this response (1), and the `pages` attribute is the total number of pages (96,293), assuming a page size of `perpage`.

■**Note** Just as with the human user interface of Flickr, you get API results as a series of pages. (Imagine if the API were to send you data about every puppy picture in one shot!) The default value for `perpage` is `100`, and the maximum value is `500`. I choose `3` in this example so that you can easily study the entire response.

- Each of the `photo` elements has attributes that enable you to know a bit about what the photo is about (`title`), map them to the photo's various URLs (`id`, `owner`, `secret`, `server`, and `farm`), and tell you about the photo's visibility to classes of users (`ispublic`, `isfriend`, and `isfamily`).

Let's now consider two related issues about this pattern of request and response:

- What does this XML response mean?

- What can you do with the XML response?

What Does This XML Response Mean?

The user interface (UI) and the API give you much of the same information in different forms, meant for different purposes. The requests for the UI and the API are both HTTP `GET`s—but with their corresponding URLs and parameters. In the UI, the body of the response is HTML + JavaScript for display in a web browser. In the API, the response body is XML, meant for consumption by a computer program. (Remember, you learned about XML feeds in Chapter 4. The format of the XML is not the same as RSS or Atom, but you get the benefits of stuff coming back in XML instead of HTML—you don't have to screen-scrape the information. Also remember from the discussion in Chapter 2 that it is possible to screen-scrape HTML + JavaScript, but it's not ideal.)

Let's see how to convince ourselves of the correspondence of the information in the UI and the API. It's very powerful to see this correspondence—the same information is in the UI and from the API—because you'll get a vivid visual confirmation that you understand what's happening in the API. Let's return to comparing the following (when you are logged out of Flickr—to make sure you see only public photos):

```
http://www.flickr.com/photos/tags/puppy/
```

with the following:

```
http://api.flickr.com/services/rest/?method=flickr.photos.search&api_key={api_key}
&tags=puppy&per_page=3
```

What type of comparisons can you do?

- You can compare the total numbers of photos in the UI and the API (which you might expect to be same but are not quite the same because of privacy options—see the "Why Are Flickr UI Results Not the Same As Those in the API?" sidebar).

- You can map the information about the photo elements into the photo URLs in order to see what photos are actually being referred to by the API response.

With what you learned in Chapter 2 and with the attributes from the photo element, you can generate the URL for the photo. Take, for instance, the first photo element:

```
<photo id="1153699093" owner="7841384@N07" secret="d1fba451c9" server="1023"
    farm="2" title="willy after bath and haircut" ispublic="1" isfriend="0"
    isfamily="0" />
```

With this you can tabulate the parameters listed in Table 6-1.

Table 6-1. *Parameters Associated with Photo 1153699093*

Parameter	Value
photo-id	1153699093
farm-id	2
server-id	1023
photo-secret	d1fba451c9
file-suffix	jpg
user-id	7841384@N07

Remember, the URL templates for the context page of a photo is as follows:

```
http://www.flickr.com/photos/{user-id}/{photo-id}/
```

And the link to the medium-sized photo is as follows:

```
http://farm{farm-id}.static.flickr.com/{server-id}/{photo-id}_{photo-secret}.jpg
```

So, the following are the URLs:

```
http://www.flickr.com/photos/7841384@N07/1153699093/
http://farm2.static.flickr.com/1023/1153699093_d1fba451c9.jpg
```

You can follow the same procedure for all the photos—but one would probably be enough for you to use to compare with the photos in the UI. (You're likely to see the same photo from the API in the UI and hence confirm that the results are the same.)

■**Note** You might wonder how you derive the URL for the original image. Assuming that the original photo is publicly accessible at all, you add &extras=original_format to the query to get the originalsecret and originalformat attributes.

WHY ARE FLICKR UI RESULTS NOT THE SAME AS THOSE IN THE API?

The information available in the Flickr API and in the Flickr UI are closely aligned, so much so that it's easy to think they are the same. Not so. You as a Flickr user can set whether your photos are visible to site-wide searches in the Flickr UI and whether your photos are visible to other users via the API at the following location:

http://flickr.com/account/prefs/optout/?from=privacy

If any user with public photos tagged with puppy has enabled results from one type but not the other type of search to be visible, then what you get from the API and the UI will be different when you look for puppy-tagged photos. I still expect that the results will be similar since I would guess that most people have not hidden their public photos from the public search or the API.

What Can You Do with the XML Response?

Now that you know that you can generate an HTML representation of each photo, let's think about what you use flickr.photos.search for. Later in the chapter, I'll walk you through the details of how to generate a simple HTML interface written in PHP. Using that method alone and a bit of web programming, you can generate a simple Flickr search engine that lets you page through search results. You can do many other things as well. For example, you could generate an XML feed from this data. With feeds coming out the API, you'd be able to use all the techniques you learned in Chapter 4 (including mashing up feeds with Yahoo! Pipes). You might not have all the information you could ever want; there are other methods in the Flickr API that will give you more information about the photos, and I will show you how to use those methods later in the chapter.

Where to go from here? First, you won't be surprised to learn that many other parameters are available to you for flickr.photos.search given how many search options there are in the Flickr UI for search (see Chapter 2 for a review). You can learn more about those parameters by reading the documentation for the method here:

http://www.flickr.com/services/api/flickr.photos.search.html

Here you will see documented all the possible arguments you can pass to the method. In addition, you see an example response that, not surprisingly, should look similar to the XML response we studied earlier. In addition, you will see mention of two topics that I glossed over in my example:

Error handling: The carefully constructed simple request should work as described here. But errors do happen, and Flickr uses an error-handling process that includes the use of error codes and error messages. Any robust source code you write should take into account this error handling.

Authorization: The example we looked at involved only public photos. Things get a lot messier once you work with private photos. In the UI, that means having to establish a user account and being logged in. With the API, there is a conceptually parallel process with one twist. Three parties are involved in Flickr authentication; in addition to the user and Flickr, there is a third-party application that uses the API. To avoid users having to give their passwords to the third-party application to log in on their behalf, there's a complicated dance that could easily obscure the core ideas behind the API. We'll look at authentication later in this chapter.

As interesting as `flickr.photos.search` is (and it is probably the single most useful and functionally rich Flickr method), you'll want to see what other methods there are in the API. I'll show you how to learn about the diversity of functionality available in the Flickr API by using, among other things, the very cool Flickr API Explorer.

You'll find that a good understanding of Flickr's functionality will come in handy when you learn how to use the API. (This is a point I was stressing in Chapter 2.) There's the ad hoc method of learning the API that is to start with a specific problem you want to solve—and then look for a specific piece of functionality in the API that will solve it. You can consult the Flickr API documentation when you need it and use the Flickr API Explorer. You can also try to take a more systematic approach to outlining what's available in the Flickr API (a bit like the detailed discussion of Flickr's URL language I presented in Chapter 2). I will outline a method for doing this. This is cool, because such a method will involve the Flickr API telling us about itself! I will use that as an opportunity to talk about APIs in general.

A large part of this chapter will cover some of the programming details you will encounter working with the Flickr API and other APIs. The way I showed you to formulate the Flickr API through the use of the following:

```
http://api.flickr.com/services/rest/?method=flickr.photos.search&api_key={api_key}
&tags=puppy&per_page=3
```

is only one way of three ways to do so. There are also other formats for the response that Flickr can generate. I'll cover the different request and response formats in the "Request and Response Formats" section later in this chapter.

When working with these Flickr web services, you find that a detailed understanding of HTTP, XML, and request and response formats is helpful—but you're likely to want to work at a higher level of abstraction once you get down to doing some serious programming. That's when third-party wrappers to the API, what Flickr calls *API kits*, come into play. I will cover how to use a number of the PHP Flickr API kits later in this chapter.

There is a lot of complexity in using APIs, but just don't forget the essential pattern that you find in the Flickr API: *you make an HTTP request formatted with the correct parameters, and you get back in your response XML that you can then parse*. The rest is detail.

The bottom line is that you can learn a lot by using and studying the Flickr API. It's extremely well designed in so many ways. It's certainly not perfect—and there are other, sometimes better, ways of instantiating the certain functionality of an API. A close study of the Flickr API will help you understand the APIs of other systems—as you will see in Chapter 7.

API Documentation, Community, and Policy

You can find the official documentation for the Flickr API here:

`http://www.flickr.com/services/api/`

As you get familiar with the API, I recommend consulting or lurking in two communities:

- The Flickr API mailing list (`http://tech.groups.yahoo.com/group/yws-flickr/`)

- The Flickr API group on Flickr (`http://www.flickr.com/groups/api/`)

You can get a feel for what people are thinking about in terms of the API and get your questions answered too. When you become more proficient with the API, you can start answering other people's questions. (The first group is more technically oriented, and the second one is more focused on the workflow of Flickr.)

Terms of Use for the API

API providers, including Flickr, require assent to terms of service (ToS, also known as *terms of use*) for access to the API. The terms of use for the Flickr API are at the following location:

`http://www.flickr.com/services/api/tos/`

There is, of course, no substitute for reading the ToS carefully for yourself. Here I list a few highlights of the ToS, including what it tells you about Flickr and how you might find similar issues raised in the ToS of other web APIs. Here are some factors:

Commercial vs. noncommercial use: You need to apply for special permission to use the Flickr API for commercial purposes.

Payment for use: The Flickr API is free for noncommercial use, like many web APIs are.

Rate limits: The ToS states that you can't use an "unreasonable amount of bandwidth."

Compliance with the user-facing website ToS: Programmatic access to Flickr content must comply with all the terms that govern human users of Flickr. This includes, for instance, the requirement to link to Flickr when embedding Flickr-hosted photos.

Content ownership: You need to pay attention to the ownership of photos, including any Creative Commons licenses attached to the photos.

Caching: You are supposed to cache Flickr photos for only a "reasonable" period of time to provide your Flickr service.

Privacy policies: Your applications are supposed to respect (and by proxy enforce) Flickr's privacy policy and the photo owner's settings. You are supposed to have a clearly articulated privacy policy of your own for the photos you access through the Flickr API.

Using the Flickr API Explorer and Documentation

The column on the right at `http://www.flickr.com/services/api/` lists all the API methods available in the Flickr API. There are currently 106 methods in the API organized in the following 23 groups:

- Activity

- Auth

- Blogs

- Contacts

- Favorites

- Groups

- Groups.pools

- Interestingness

- People

- Photos

- Photos.comments

- Photos.geo

- Photos.licenses

- Photos.notes

- Photos.transform

- Photos.upload

- Photosets

- Photosets.comments

- Prefs

- Reflection

- Tags

- Test

- URLs

I've already used two methods in the early parts of the chapter: `flickr.test.echo` (part of the `test` group) and `flickr.photos.search` (part of the `photos` group). In this section, I'll show you how to exercise a specific API method in detail and return to looking at the full range of methods. Here I use `flickr.photos.search` for an example.

You can get the documentation for any method here:

```
http://www.flickr.com/services/api/{method-name}.html
```

For example:

```
http://www.flickr.com/services/api/flickr.photos.search.html
```

Notice the following subsections in the documentation of each method:

- A description of the method's functionality.

- Whether the method requires authentication and, if so, the minimum level of permission needed: one of none, read, write, or delete. read is permission to read private information; write is permission to add, edit, and delete metadata for photos in addition to the read permission; and delete is permission to delete photos in addition to the write and read permissions.

- Whether the method needs to be signed. All methods that require authentication require signing. Some methods, such as all the ones belonging to the auth group (for example, flickr.auth.getToken) don't need authentication but must be signed. I will describe the mechanics of signing later in the chapter.

- A list of arguments, the name of each argument, whether it is required or mandatory, and a short description of the argument.

- An example response.

- The error codes.

In the documentation, there is a link to the Flickr API Explorer:

```
http://www.flickr.com/services/api/explore/?method={method-name}
```

For example:

```
http://www.flickr.com/services/api/explore/?method=flickr.photos.search
```

The Flickr API Explorer is my favorite part of the Flickr API documentation. Figure 6-1 shows the API Explorer for flickr.photos.getInfo. For each method, the API Explorer not only documents the arguments but lets you fill in arguments and call the method (with your argument values) right within the browser. You have three choices for how to sign the call:

- You can leave the call unsigned.

- You can sign it without attaching any user information.

- You can sign it and grant the call write permission for yourself (as the logged-in user).

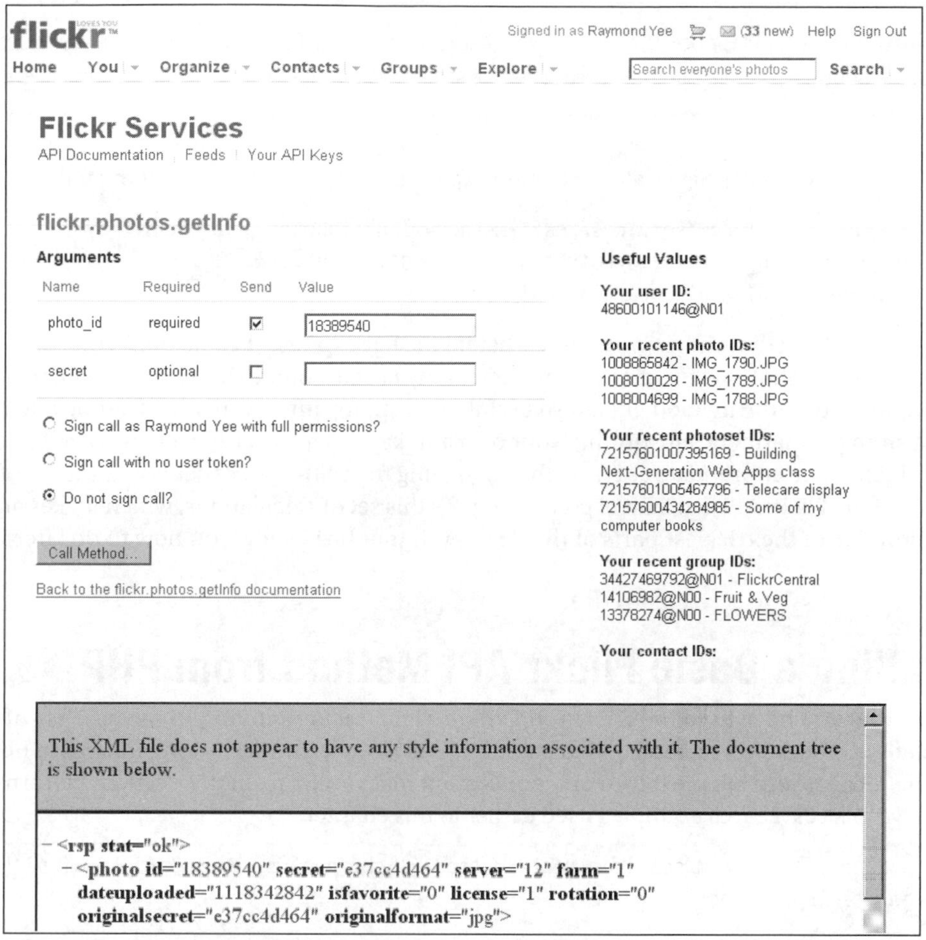

Figure 6-1. *The Flickr API Explorer for* flickr.photos.getInfo. *(Reproduced with permission of Yahoo! Inc. ® 2007 by Yahoo! Inc. YAHOO! and the YAHOO! logo are trademarks of Yahoo! Inc.)*

When you hit the Call Method button, the XML of the response is displayed in an iframe, and the URL for the call is displayed below the iframe. You can use the Flickr API Explorer to understand how a method works. In the case of the unsigned call, you can copy the URL and substitute your own API key to use it in your own programs.

For example, if you use the Flickr API Explorer to call flickr.photos.search with the tag set to puppy and then click the Do Not Sign Call button, you'll get a URL similar to this:

```
http://api.flickr.com/services/rest/?method=flickr.photos.search&api_key={api_key}
&tags=puppy
```

Copy and paste the URL you get from the Flickr API Explorer into a web browser to convince yourself that in this case of searching for public images, you can now call the Flickr API through a simple URL that returns results to you in XML.

Now when I click Sign Call As Raymond Yee with Full Permissions, I get the following URL:

```
http://api.flickr.com/services/rest/?method=flickr.photos.search&api_key={api_key}
&tags=puppy&auth_token=72157601583650732-e30f91f3313b3d14&
api_sig=3d7a2d1975e9699246a299d2deaf5b70
```

When I use that URL immediately—before the key expires—I get to perform searches for puppy-tagged photos with `write` permission for my user account. This URL is useful to test the functionality of the method. It's not so useful for dropping into a program. Getting it to work is not simply a matter of substituting your own `api_key` but also getting a new `auth_token` and calculating the appropriate `api_sig` (that is, signing the call)—tasks that take a couple of more calls to the Flickr API and a bit of computing. It's this set of calculations, which makes authorization one of the trickiest parts of the Flickr API, that I will show you how to do later in the chapter.

Calling a Basic Flickr API Method from PHP

Now that you have used the Flickr API Explorer and documentation to make sense of the details of a given API method and to package a call in the browser, you will now learn how to make a call from a simple third-party application that you write. In this section, I return to the `flickr.photos.search` example I used earlier in this chapter:

```
http://api.flickr.com/services/rest/?method=flickr.photos.search&api_key={api_key}
&tags={tag}&per_page={per_page}
```

Specifically, the following:

```
http://api.flickr.com/services/rest/?method=flickr.photos.search&api_key={api_key}
&tags=puppy&per_page=3
```

generates a response similar to this:

```
<?xml version="1.0" encoding="utf-8" ?>
<rsp stat="ok">
<photos page="1" pages="96293" perpage="3" total="288877">
  <photo id="1153699093" owner="7841384@N07" secret="d1fba451c9" server="1023"
         farm="2" title="willy after bath and haircut" ispublic="1" isfriend="0"
         isfamily="0" />
  <photo id="1154506492" owner="7841384@N07" secret="881ff7c4bc" server="1058"
         farm="2" title="rocky with broken leg" ispublic="1" isfriend="0"
         isfamily="0" />
  <photo id="1153588011" owner="90877382@N00" secret="8a7a559e68" server="1288"
         farm="2" title="DSC 6503" ispublic="1" isfriend="0" isfamily="0" />
</photos>
</rsp>
```

In the earlier narrative, I described to you how you can extract from the XML response such quantities as the total number of photos and how to derive from a photo element such as this:

```
<photo id="1153699093" owner="7841384@N07" secret="d1fba451c9" server="1023"
    farm="2" title="willy after bath and haircut" ispublic="1" isfriend="0"
    isfamily="0" />
```

Here are the URLs for the corresponding photo:

```
http://www.flickr.com/photos/7841384@N07/1153699093/
http://farm2.static.flickr.com/1023/1153699093_d1fba451c9.jpg
```

In the following sections, I'll show you how to instantiate that logic into code. Specifically, we will write a simple third-party Flickr app in PHP that makes a Flickr API call and converts the response to HTML. We'll use two important sets of techniques that I will elaborate on in some detail, HTTP clients and XML processing, after which I describe how to use these techniques to make the call to Flickr. Here I focus on PHP, but you can apply these ideas to your language of choice.

■**Tip** When debugging web services, I have found it helpful to use a network protocol analyzer such as Wireshark (`http://en.wikipedia.org/wiki/Wireshark`). Properly formulating a web service call often requires trial and error. Through its support of HTTP, Wireshark lets you see exactly what was sent and what was received, including HTTP headers, response codes, and entity bodies.

HTTP Clients

Let's consider first the issue of how to perform an HTTP GET request and retrieve the response in PHP. The function `file_get_contents` takes a URL and returns the corresponding content in a string, provided the `allow_url_fopen` option is set to `true` in the system-wide `php.ini`. For example:

```php
<?php
// retrieve Atom feed of recent flower-tagged photos in Flickr
$url = "http://api.flickr.com/services/feeds/photos_public.gne?tags=flower&lang=
en-us&format=atom";

$content = file_get_contents($url);
echo $content;
?>
```

If you are using an instance of PHP for which URL access for `file_get_contents` is disabled (which is not uncommon for shared hosting facilities with security concerns), then you might still be able to use the cURL extension for PHP (`libcurl`) to perform the same function. `libcurl` is documented here:

```
http://us3.php.net/curl
```

The following getResource function does what file_get_contents does. Note the four steps in using the curl library: initializing the call, configuring options, executing the call, and closing down the handle:

```php
<?php
function getResource($url){
// initialize a handle
        $chandle = curl_init();
// set URL
        curl_setopt($chandle, CURLOPT_URL, $url);
// return results a s string
        curl_setopt($chandle, CURLOPT_RETURNTRANSFER, 1);
// execute the call
        $result = curl_exec($chandle);
        curl_close($chandle);

        return $result;
}
?>
```

The many options you can configure in libcurl are documented here:

http://us3.php.net/manual/en/function.curl-setopt.php

In this book, I use libcurl for HTTP access in PHP. Should you not be able to use libcurl, you can use the libcurl Emulator, a pure-PHP implementation of libcurl:

http://code.blitzaffe.com/pages/phpclasses/files/libcurl_emulator_52-7

■**Note** I will often use curl to demonstrate HTTP requests in this book. More information is available at http://curl.haxx.se/.

A Refresher on HTTP

So, how would you configure the many options of a library such as libcurl? Doing so requires some understanding of HTTP. Although HTTP is a foundational protocol, it's really quite easy to get along, even as programmers, without knowing the subtleties of HTTP. My goal here is not to describe HTTP in great detail. When you need to understand the protocol in depth, I suggest reading the official specifications; here's the URL for HTTP 1.0 (RFC 1945):

http://tools.ietf.org/html/rfc1945

And here's the URL for HTTP 1.1:

http://tools.ietf.org/html/rfc2616

You can also consult the official W3C page:

http://www.w3.org/Protocols/

Reading and digesting the specification is not the best way to learn HTTP for most of us, however. Instead of formally learning HTTP all in one go in its formal glory, I've learned different aspects of HTTP at different times, and because that partial knowledge was sufficient for the situation at hand, I felt no need to explore the subtleties of the protocol. It was a new situation that prompted me to learn more. My first encounter with HTTP was simply surfing the Web and using URLs that had http for their prefix. For a little while, I didn't even know that http wasn't the only possible scheme in a URI—and that, technically, http:// is not a redundant part of a URI, even if on business cards it might be. (People understand www.apress.com means an address for a page in web browser—and the prefix http:// just looks geeky.)

Later when I learned about HTML forms, I learned that there are two possible values for the method attribute for FORM: get and post.[1] (It puzzled me why it wasn't get and put since put is often the complement to get.) For a long time, the only difference I perceived between get and post was that a form that uses the get method generates URLs that include the name/value pairs of the submitted form elements, whereas post doesn't. The practical upshot for me was that get produces addressable URLs, whereas post doesn't. I thought I had post figured out as a way of changing the state of resources (as opposed to using get for asking for information)—and then I learned about the formal way of distinguishing between safe and idempotent methods (see the "Safe Methods and Idempotent Methods" sidebar for a further explanation of these terms). Even with post, it turns out that there is a difference between two different forms of form encoding stated in the FORM enctype attribute (application/x-www-form-urlencoded vs. multipart/form-data), a distinction that is not technically part of HTTP but that will have a practical effect on how you programmatically make certain HTTP requests.[2]

SAFE METHODS AND IDEMPOTENT METHODS

The HTTP specification defines safe methods and idempotent methods here:

http://www.w3.org/Protocols/rfc2616/rfc2616-sec9.html

Safe methods "*should not* have the significance of taking an action other than retrieval" of a representation of a resource. You shouldn't be changing the resource through a safe method. In HTTP, GET and HEAD methods are supposed to be safe. Unsafe methods that have the potential of altering the state of the retrieved resource include POST, PUT, and DELETE.

Idempotent methods are those that have the same effect on the resource whether they are performed once or more than one time. It's akin to multiplying a number by zero—the result is the same whether you do it once or more than once. According to the HTTP standard, the GET, HEAD, PUT, and DELETE methods should be idempotent operations. Moreover, "the methods OPTIONS and TRACE *should not* have side effects and so are inherently idempotent."

---

1. http://www.w3.org/TR/html401/interact/forms.html#h-17.13.1

2. http://www.w3.org/TR/html401/interact/forms.html#h-17.13.4

Formal Structure of HTTP

When I moved from writing HTML to writing basic web applications, I then learned more about the formal structure of HTTP—and how what I had learned fit within a larger structure of what HTTP is capable of doing. For instance, I learned that, in addition to GET and POST, HTTP defines six other methods, among which was a PUT after all. (It's just that few, if any, web browsers support PUT.) Let me describe the parts of HTTP 1.1 request and response messages. (I draw some terminology in the following discussion from the excellent presentation of HTTP by Leonard Richardson and Sam Ruby in *Restful Web Services*.)

An HTTP request is composed of the following pieces:

- The *method* (also known as *verb* or *action*). In addition to GET and POST, there are six others defined in the HTTP specification: OPTIONS, HEAD, PUT, DELETE, TRACE, and CONNECT. GET and POST are widely used and supported in web browsers and programming libraries.

- The *path*—the part of the URL to the right of the hostname.

- A series of *request headers*. See http://www.w3.org/Protocols/rfc2616/rfc2616-sec14.html.

- A request *body*, which may be empty.

The parts of the HTTP response include the following:

- A *response code*. You can find a long list of codes at http://www.w3.org/Protocols/rfc2616/rfc2616-sec10.html. Examples include 200 OK, 400 Bad Request, and 500 Internal Server Error.

- *Response headers*. See http://www.w3.org/Protocols/rfc2616/rfc2616-sec6.html.

- A response *body*.

Let's consider the following example:

```
http://api.flickr.com/services/rest/?method=flickr.photos.search
&api_key={api-key}&tags=puppy&per_page=3
```

To track the HTTP traffic, I'm using curl (with the verbose option) to make the call. (You can also use Wireshark to read the parameters of the HTTP request and response):

```
curl --verbose "http://api.flickr.com/services/rest/?method=flickr.photos.search
&api_key={api-key}&tags=puppy&per_page=3"
```

This is an edited version of what I get:

```
* About to connect() to api.flickr.com port 80
*    Trying 68.142.214.24... * connected
* Connected to api.flickr.com (68.142.214.24) port 80
> GET /services/rest/?method=flickr.photos.search&api_key={api-key}&tags=puppy
&per_page=3 HTTP/1.1
User-Agent: curl/7.13.2 (i386-pc-linux-gnu) libcurl/7.13.2 OpenSSL/0.9.7e zlib/1.2.2
libidn/0.5.13
Host: api.flickr.com
Pragma: no-cache
Accept: */*
```

```
< HTTP/1.1 200 OK
< Date: Tue, 21 Aug 2007 20:42:54 GMT
< Server: Apache/2.0.52
< Set-Cookie: cookie_l10n=en-us%3Bus; expires=Friday, 20-Aug-10 20:42:54 GMT;
path=/; domain=flickr.com
< Set-Cookie: cookie_intl=deleted; expires=Monday, 21-Aug-06 20:42:53 GMT; path=/;
domain=flickr.com
< Content-Length: 570
< Connection: close
< Content-Type: text/xml; charset=utf-8
<?xml version="1.0" encoding="utf-8" ?>
<rsp stat="ok">
<photos page="1" pages="97168" perpage="3" total="291503">
        <photo id="1196703288" owner="69161261@N00" secret="d4e5a75664"
server="1412" farm="2" title="Pomeranian" ispublic="1" isfriend="0" isfamily="0" />
        <photo id="1196707012" owner="58944004@N00" secret="9d88253b87"
server="1200" farm="2" title="Fraggle" ispublic="1" isfriend="0" isfamily="0" />
        <photo id="1195805641" owner="21877391@N00" secret="311d276ec7"
server="1177" farm="2" title="Blue" ispublic="1" isfriend="0" isfamily="0" />
</photos>
</rsp>
```

Let's break down the specifics of this request/response exchange, as shown in Table 6-2 and Table 6-3, respectively.

Table 6-2. *The HTTP Request Parameters in a Flickr Call*

Parameter	Value
method	GET
path	/services/rest/?method=flickr.photos.search&api_key={api-key}&tags= puppy&per_page=3
headers	Four headers of the following types: User-Agent, Host (which identifies api.flickr.com), Pragma, and Accept
response	Empty (typical of GET requests)

Table 6-3. *The HTTP Response Parameters in a Flickr Call*

Parameter	Value
Response code	200 OK
Response headers	Seven headers of the following types: Date, Server, Set-Cookie (twice), Content-Length, Connection, Content-Type
Response body	The XML document representing the photos that match the query

Keep this example in mind to see how the HTTP request and response are broken down as you continue through this chapter. Notice the structure of having a document (in the body) and a set of headers in both the HTTP request and response structure.

Even though you now understand the basic structure of HTTP, the point is to not have to understand the intricacies of the protocol. You can shield yourself from the details while still taking advantage of the rich functionality of HTTP with the right choice of tools and libraries. Richardson and Ruby provide a helpful shopping list of desirable features in an HTTP client library:

- Support for HTTPS and SSL certificate validation.

- Support for what they consider to be the five main HTTP methods: GET, HEAD, POST, PUT, and DELETE. Some give you only GET. Others let you use GET and POST.

- Lets you customize the request body of POST and PUT requests.

- Lets you customize the HTTP request headers.

- Gives you access to the response code and HTTP response headers—not just the body of the response.

- Lets you communicate through an HTTP proxy.

They list the following features as nice options:

- Lets you request and handle data *compression*. The relevant HTTP request/response headers are Accept-Encoding and Encoding.

- Lets you deal with *caching*. The relevant HTTP headers are ETag and If-Modified-Since and ETag and Last-Modified.

- Lets you deal with the most common forms of HTTP *authentication*: Basic, Digest, and WSSE.

- Lets you deal with HTTP *redirects*.

- Helps you deal with HTTP *cookies*.

They also make specific recommendations for what to use in various languages, including the following:

- The httplib2 library (http://code.google.com/p/httplib2/) for Python

- HttpClient in the Apache Jakarta project (http://jakarta.apache.org/commons/httpclient/)

- rest-open-uri, a modification of Ruby's open-uri to support more than the GET method (http://rubyforge.org/projects/rest-open-uri/)

XML Processing

Once you have made the HTTP request to the Flickr API, you are left with the second big task of processing the XML document contained in the response body. The topic of how to process XML is a large subject, especially when you consider techniques in multiple languages. What I show you here is one way of parsing XML in PHP 5 through an example involving a reasonably complicated XML document (with namespaces and attributes).

The simpleXML library is built into PHP 5, which is documented here:

http://us3.php.net/simplexml

I found the following article particularly helpful to me in understanding how to handle namespaces and mixed content in simpleXML:

http://devzone.zend.com/node/view/id/688

In the following example, I parse an Atom feed (an example from Chapter 4) and print various parts of the document. I access XML elements as though they are PHP object properties (using ->element-name) and the attributes as though they are members of an array (using ["attribute-name"]), for example, $xml->title and $entry->link["href"]. First I list the code and then the output from the code:

```php
<?php
// An example to show how to parse an Atom feed (with multiple namespaces)
// with SimpleXML
# create the XML document in the $feed string
$feed=<<<EOT
<?xml version="1.0" encoding="utf-8"?>
<feed xmlns="http://www.w3.org/2005/Atom"
      xmlns:dc="http://purl.org/dc/elements/1.1/">
  <title>Apress :: The Expert's Voice</title>
  <subtitle>Welcome to Apress.com. Books for Professionals,
    by Professionals(TM)...with what the
    professional needs to know(TM)</subtitle>
  <link rel="alternate" type="text/html" href="http://www.apress.com/"/>
  <link rel="self"
        href="http://examples.mashupguide.net/ch06/Apress.Atom.with.DC.xml"/>
  <updated>2007-07-25T12:57:02Z</updated>
  <author>
    <name>Apress, Inc.</name>
    <email>support@apress.com</email>
  </author>
  <id>http://apress.com/</id>
  <entry>
    <title>Excel 2007: Beyond the Manual</title>
    <link href="http://www.apress.com/book/bookDisplay.html?bID=10232"/>
    <id>http://www.apress.com/book/bookDisplay.html?bID=10232</id>
    <updated>2007-07-25T12:57:02Z</updated>
    <dc:date>2007-03</dc:date>
    <summary type="html"
      >&lt;p&gt;&lt;i&gt;Excel 2007: Beyond the Manual&lt;/i&gt; will introduce
those who are already familiar with Excel basics to more advanced features, like
consolidation, what-if analysis, PivotTables, sorting and filtering, and some
commonly used functions. You'll learn how to maximize your efficiency at producing
professional-looking spreadsheets and charts and become competent at analyzing data
using a variety of tools. The book includes practical examples to illustrate
advanced features.&lt;/p&gt;</summary>
```

```
    </entry>
    <entry>
      <title>Word 2007: Beyond the Manual</title>
      <link href="http://www.apress.com/book/bookDisplay.html?bID=10249"/>
      <id>http://www.apress.com/book/bookDisplay.html?bID=10249</id>
      <updated>2007-07-25T12:57:10Z</updated>
      <dc:date>2007-03-01</dc:date>
      <summary type="html"
        >&lt;p&gt;&lt;i&gt;Word 2007: Beyond the Manual&lt;/i&gt; focuses on new
features of Word 2007 as well as older features that were once less accessible than
they are now. This book also makes a point to include examples of practical
applications for all the new features. The book assumes familiarity with Word 2003
or earlier versions, so you can focus on becoming a confident 2007
user.&lt;/p&gt;</summary>
    </entry>
</feed>
EOT;

# instantiate a simpleXML object based on the $feed XML
$xml = simplexml_load_string($feed);

# access the title and subtitle elements
print "title: {$xml->title}\n";
print "subtitle: {$xml->subtitle}\n";

# loop through the two link elements, printing all the attributes for each link.

print "processing links\n";
foreach ($xml->link as $link) {
  print "attribute:\t";
  foreach ($link->attributes() as $a => $b) {
    print "{$a}=>{$b}\t";
  }
  print "\n";
}
print "author: {$xml->author->name}\n";

# let's check out the namespace situation

$ns_array = $xml->getDocNamespaces(true);

# display the namespaces that are in the document
print "namespaces in the document\n";
foreach ($ns_array as $ns_prefix=>$ns_uri) {
  print "namespace: ${ns_prefix}->${ns_uri}\n";
}
print "\n";
```

```
# loop over all the entry elements
foreach ($xml->entry as $entry) {
  print "entry has the following elements in the global namespace: \t";

  // won't be able to access tags that aren't in the global namespace.
  foreach ($entry->children() as $child) {
    print $child->getName(). " ";
  }
  print "\n";
  print "entry title: {$entry->title}\t link: {$entry->link["href"]}\n";

  // show how to use xpath to get date
  // note dc is registered already to $xml.
  $date = $entry->xpath("./dc:date");
  print "date (via XPath): {$date[0]}\n";

  // use children() to get at date
  $date1 = $entry->children("http://purl.org/dc/elements/1.1/");
  print "date (from children()): {$date[0]}\n";

}


# add <category term="books" /> to feed -- adding the element will work
# but the tag is in the wrong place to make a valid Atom feed.
# It is supposed to go before the entry elements
$category = $xml->addChild("category");
$category->addAttribute('term','books');

# output the XML to show that category has been added.
$newxmlstring = $xml->asXML();
print "new xml (with category tag): \n$newxmlstring\n";
?>
```

The output from the code is as follows:

```
title: Apress :: The Expert's Voice
subtitle: Welcome to Apress.com. Books for Professionals,
by Professionals(TM)...with what the professional needs to know(TM)
processing links
attribute: rel=>alternate type=>text/html href=>http://www.apress.com/
attribute: rel=>self
href=>http://examples.mashupguide.net/ch06/Apress.Atom.with.DC.xml
author: Apress, Inc.
namespaces in the document
namespace: ->http://www.w3.org/2005/Atom
namespace: dc->http://purl.org/dc/elements/1.1/
```

entry has the following elements in the global namespace: title link id
updated summary
entry title: Excel 2007: Beyond the Manual link:
http://www.apress.com/book/bookDisplay.html?bID=10232
date (via XPath): 2007-03
date (from children()): 2007-03
entry has the following elements in the global namespace: title link id
updated summary
entry title: Word 2007: Beyond the Manual link:
http://www.apress.com/book/bookDisplay.html?bID=10249
date (via XPath): 2007-03-01
date (from children()): 2007-03-01
new xml (with category tag):

```
<?xml version="1.0" encoding="utf-8"?>
<feed xmlns="http://www.w3.org/2005/Atom"
        xmlns:dc="http://purl.org/dc/elements/1.1/">
  <title>Apress :: The Expert's Voice</title>
  <subtitle>Welcome to Apress.com. Books for Professionals,
by Professionals(TM)...with what the professional needs to know(TM)</subtitle>
  <link rel="alternate" type="text/html" href="http://www.apress.com/"/>
  <link rel="self"
        href="http://examples.mashupguide.net/ch06/Apress.Atom.with.DC.xml"/>
  <updated>2007-07-25T12:57:02Z</updated>
  <author>
    <name>Apress, Inc.</name>
    <email>support@apress.com</email>
  </author>
  <id>http://apress.com/</id>
  <entry>
    <title>Excel 2007: Beyond the Manual</title>
    <link href="http://www.apress.com/book/bookDisplay.html?bID=10232"/>
    <id>http://www.apress.com/book/bookDisplay.html?bID=10232</id>
    <updated>2007-07-25T12:57:02Z</updated>
    <dc:date>2007-03</dc:date>
    <summary type="html">&lt;p&gt;&lt;i&gt;Excel 2007: Beyond the
Manual&lt;/i&gt; will introduce those who are already familiar with Excel basics to
more advanced features, like consolidation, what-if analysis, PivotTables, sorting
and filtering, and some commonly used functions. You'll learn how to maximize your
efficiency at producing professional-looking spreadsheets and charts and become
competent at analyzing data using a variety of tools. The book includes practical
examples to illustrate advanced features.&lt;/p&gt;</summary>
  </entry>
  <entry>
    <title>Word 2007: Beyond the Manual</title>
    <link href="http://www.apress.com/book/bookDisplay.html?bID=10249"/>
    <id>http://www.apress.com/book/bookDisplay.html?bID=10249</id>
    <updated>2007-07-25T12:57:10Z</updated>
```

```
<dc:date>2007-03-01</dc:date>
<summary type="html">&lt;p&gt;&lt;i&gt;Word 2007: Beyond the
Manual&lt;/i&gt; focuses on new features of Word 2007 as well as older features that
were once less accessible than they are now. This book also makes a point to include
examples of practical applications for all the new features. The book assumes
familiarity with Word 2003 or earlier versions, so you can focus on becoming a
confident 2007 user.&lt;/p&gt;</summary>
  </entry>
<category term="books"/></feed>
```

There are certainly alternatives to simpleXML for processing XML in PHP 5, but it provides a comfortable interface for a PHP programmer to XML documents.

■**Note** When trying to figure out the structures of PHP objects, consider using one of the following functions: print_r, var_dump, or var_export.

Pulling It All Together: Generating Simple HTML Representations of the Photos

Now we have the two pieces of technology to send an HTTP request to Flickr and parse the XML in the response:

- The getResource function I displayed earlier that uses the libcurl library of PHP 5

- The simpleXML library to parse the XML response

I'll now show you a PHP script that uses these two pieces of functionality to prompt a user for a tag and that returns the list of five HTML-formatted photos for that tag.

Here's a breakdown of the logical steps that take place in the following script:

1. It displays the total number of pictures ($xml->photos['total']).

2. It iterates through the array of photos through an elaboration of the following loop:

```
foreach ($xml->photos->photo as $photo) {
  $id = $photo['id'];
}
```

3. It forms the URL of the thumbnail and the URL of the photo page through the logic contained in the following line:

```
$thumb_url =
  "http://farm{$farmid}.static.flickr.com/{$serverid}/{$id}_{$secret}_t.jpg";
```

The following is one possible version of such a script.[3] (Note the Content-Type HTTP response header of text/html to keep Internet Explorer happy with XHTML, but the output is XHTML 1.0 Strict.)

---

3. http://examples.mashupguide.net/ch06/flickrsearch.php

```php
<?php
header("Content-Type:text/html");
echo '<?xml version="1.0" encoding="utf-8"?>';
?>
<!DOCTYPE html PUBLIC "-//W3C//DTD XHTML 1.0 Strict//EN"
"http://www.w3.org/TR/xhtml1/DTD/xhtml1-strict.dtd">
<html xmlns="http://www.w3.org/1999/xhtml" xml:lang="en" lang="en">
  <head>
    <meta http-equiv="Content-Type" content="text/html;charset=utf-8" />
    <title>flickrsearch.php</title>
  </head>
  <body>
<?php
if (isset($_GET['tag'])) {
   do_search($_GET['tag']);
} else {
?>
    <form action="<?php echo $_SERVER['PHP_SELF']?>" method="get">
    <p>Search for photos with the following tag:
    <input type="text" size="20" name="tag"/> <input type="submit" value="Go!"/></p>
    </form>
<?php
}
?>
<?php

# uses libcurl to return the response body of a GET request on $url
function getResource($url){
  $chandle = curl_init();
  curl_setopt($chandle, CURLOPT_URL, $url);
  curl_setopt($chandle, CURLOPT_RETURNTRANSFER, 1);
  $result = curl_exec($chandle);
  curl_close($chandle);

  return $result;
}

function do_search($tag) {
  $tag = urlencode($tag);

#insert your own Flickr API KEY here

  $api_key = "[API-Key]";
  $per_page="5";
  $url = "http://api.flickr.com/services/rest/?method=flickr.photos.search
&api_key={$api_key}&tags={$tag}&per_page={$per_page}";
```

```
$feed = getResource($url);
$xml = simplexml_load_string($feed);
print "<p>Total number of photos for {$tag}: {$xml->photos['total']}</p>";


# http://www.flickr.com/services/api/misc.urls.html
# http://farm{farm-id}.static.flickr.com/{server-id}/{id}_{secret}.jpg
foreach ($xml->photos->photo as $photo) {
  $title = $photo['title'];
  $farmid = $photo['farm'];
  $serverid = $photo['server'];
  $id = $photo['id'];
  $secret = $photo['secret'];
  $owner = $photo['owner'];
  $thumb_url = "http://farm{$farmid}.static.flickr.com/{$serverid}/
{$id}_{$secret}_t.jpg";
  $page_url = "http://www.flickr.com/photos/{$owner}/{$id}";
  $image_html= "<a href='{$page_url}'><img alt='{$title}' src='{$thumb_url}'/></a>";
  print "<p>$image_html</p>";
}


} # do_search
?>
  </body>
</html>
```

Where Does This Leave Us?

This code allows you to search and display some pictures from Flickr. More important, it is an example of a class of Flickr methods: those that require neither signing nor authorization to be called. You will see in the next section how to determine which of the Flickr API methods fall in that category. In the following sections, you'll look at generalizing the techniques you have used in studying flickr.photos.search to the other capabilities of the Flickr API.

The Flickr API in General

What are some approaches to learning the Flickr API? My first suggestion is to look around the documentation and glance through the list of API methods here:

http://www.flickr.com/services/api/

While you are doing so, you should think back to all the things you know about Flickr as an end user (aspects I discussed in Chapter 2) and see whether they are reflected in the API. For example, can you come up with an API call to calculate the NSID of your own account? What is a URL to return that information? Hint: flickr.people.findByUsername.

Perhaps the best way to learn about the API is to have a specific problem in mind and then let that problem drive your learning of the API. Don't try to learn commit the entire API to memory—that's what the documentation is for.

As I argued earlier, calls that require neither signing nor authorization (such as flickr.photos.search) are the easiest place to start. How would you figure out which calls those are? You can make pretty good guesses from the names of methods. For instance, you won't be surprised that the method flickr.photos.geo.setLocation would need authorization: you would be using it to change the geolocation of a photo, an act that would require Flickr to determine whether you have the permission to do so. On the other hand, the method flickr.groups.pools.getPhotos allows you to retrieve photos for a given group. A reasonably proficient Flickr user knows that there are public groups whose photos would be visible to everybody, including those who are not logged in to Flickr at all. Hence, it's not surprising that this method would not require signing or authorization.

Using flickr.reflection Methods

You can get fairly far by eyeballing the list of Flickr methods for ones that do not require any permission to execute. (Recall the levels of permissions within the Flickr API: none, read, write, and delete.) It turns out that the Flickr API has a feature that you won't find in too many other web APIs: *the Flickr API has methods that return information about the API itself.* flickr.reflection.getMethods returns a list of all the Flickr methods available. flickr.reflection.getMethodInfo takes a given method name and returns the following:

- A description of the method

- Whether the method needs to be signed

- Whether the method needs to be authorized

- The minimal permission level needed by the method (0 = none, 1 = read, 2= write, 3=delete)

- The list of arguments for the method, including a description of the argument and whether it is optional

- The list of possible errors arising from calling the method

For example, let's look at what the Flickr API tells us about flickr.photos.geo.setLocation. You can use this format:

```
http://api.flickr.com/services/rest/?method= flickr.reflection.getMethodInfo
&api_key={api-key}&method_name={method-name}
```

Specifically, you can use this:

```
http://api.flickr.com/services/rest/?method=flickr.reflection.getMethodInfo
&api_key={api-key}&method_name=flickr.photos.geo.setLocation
```

to generate this:

```
<?xml version="1.0" encoding="utf-8" ?>
<rsp stat="ok">
<method name="flickr.photos.geo.setLocation" needslogin="1" needssigning="1"
        requiredperms="2">
  <description>Sets the geo data (latitude and longitude and, optionally,
the accuracy level) for a photo.
```

Before users may assign location data to a photo they must define who, by default, may view that information. Users can edit this preference at <a href="http://www.flickr.com/account/geo/privacy/">http://www.flickr.com /account/geo/privacy/</a>. If a user has not set this preference, the API method will return an error.</description>
</method>
<arguments>
  <argument name="api_key" optional="0">Your API application key. <a href="/services/api/misc.api_keys.html">See here</a> for more details.</argument>
  <argument name="photo_id" optional="0">The id of the photo to set location data for.</argument>
  <argument name="lat" optional="0">The latitude whose valid range is -90 to 90. Anything more than 6 decimal places will be truncated.</argument>
  <argument name="lon" optional="0">The longitude whose valid range is -180 to 180. Anything more than 6 decimal places will be truncated.</argument>
  <argument name="accuracy" optional="1">Recorded accuracy level of the location information. World level is 1, Country is ~3, Region ~6, City ~11, Street ~16. Current range is 1-16. Defaults to 16 if not specified.</argument>
</arguments>
<errors>
  <error code="1" message="Photo not found">The photo id was either invalid or was for a photo not viewable by the calling user.</error>
  <error code="2" message="Required arguments missing.">Some or all of the required arguments were not supplied.</error>
  <error code="3" message="Not a valid latitude.">The latitude argument failed validation.</error>
  <error code="4" message="Not a valid longitude.">The longitude argument failed validation.</error>
  <error code="5" message="Not a valid accuracy.">The accuracy argument failed validation.</error>
  <error code="6" message="Server error.">There was an unexpected problem setting location information to the photo.</error>
  <error code="7" message="User has not configured default viewing settings for location data.">Before users may assign location data to a photo they must define who, by default, may view that information. Users can edit this preference at <a href="http://www.flickr.com/account/geo/privacy/"> http://www.flickr.com/account/geo/privacy/</a></error>
  <error code="96" message="Invalid signature">The passed signature was invalid.</error>
  <error code="97" message="Missing signature">The call required signing but no signature was sent.</error>
  <error code="98" message="Login failed / Invalid auth token">The login details or auth token passed were invalid.</error>
  <error code="99" message="User not logged in / Insufficient permissions">The method requires user authentication but the user was not logged in, or the authenticated method call did not have the required permissions.</error>
  <error code="100" message="Invalid API Key">The API key passed was not

```
valid or has expired.</error>
  <error code="105" message="Service currently unavailable">The requested
service is temporarily unavailable.</error>
  <error code="111" message="Format &quot;xxx&quot; not found">The requested
response format was not found.</error>
  <error code="112" message="Method &quot;xxx&quot; not found">The requested
method was not found.</error>
  <error code="114" message="Invalid SOAP envelope">The SOAP envelope send in
the request could not be parsed.</error>
  <error code="115" message="Invalid XML-RPC Method Call">The XML-RPC request
document could not be parsed.</error>
</errors>
</rsp>
```

Note specifically that the following:

```
<method name="flickr.photos.geo.setLocation" needslogin="1" needssigning="1"
        requiredperms="2">
```

confirms what we had surmised—that it needs authorization and signing because it requires a minimum permission level of write. Compare that to what we would get for flickr.photos. search, which is the method that we have used throughout this chapter as an easy place to start in the API:

```
<method name="flickr.photos.search" needslogin="0" needssigning="0"
        requiredperms="0">
```

These reflection methods give rise to many interesting possibilities, especially to those of us interested in the issue of automating and simplifying the way we access web APIs. Methods in the API are both similar and different from the other methods. It would be helpful to be able to query the API with the following specific questions:

- What are all the methods that do not require any permissions to be used?

- Which methods need to be signed?

- What is an entire list of all arguments used in the Flickr API? Which method uses which argument? Which methods have in common the same arguments?

■**Caution** These reflection methods in the Flickr API are useful only if they are kept up-to-date and provide accurate information. In working with the reflection APIs, I have run into some problems (for example, http://tech.groups.yahoo.com/group/yws-flickr/message/3263) that make me wonder the degree to which the reflection methods are a first-class member of the APIs.

Querying the Flickr Reflection Methods with PHP

As a first step toward building a database of the Flickr API methods that would support such queries, I wrote the following PHP script to generate a summary table of the API methods. First there is a flickr_methods.php class that has functions to read the list of methods using flickr.methods. getMethods and, for each method, convert the data from flickr.reflection.getMethodInfo into a form that can be serialized and unserialized from a local file.

```php
<?php
# flickr_methods.php
# can use this class to return a $methods (an array of methods) and $methods_info --
# directly from the Flickr API or via a cached copy

class flickr_methods {

  protected $api_key;

  public function __construct($api_key) {
    $this->api_key = $api_key;
  }

  public function test() {
    return $this->api_key;
  }

# generic method for retrieving content for a given url.
  protected function getResource($url){
    $chandle = curl_init();
    curl_setopt($chandle, CURLOPT_URL, $url);
    curl_setopt($chandle, CURLOPT_RETURNTRANSFER, 1);
    $result = curl_exec($chandle);
    curl_close($chandle);

    return $result;
  }

# return simplexml object for $url if successful with specified number of retries
  protected function flickrCall($url,$retries) {
    $success = false;
    for ($retry = 0; $retry < $retries; $retry++) {
      $rsp = $this->getResource($url);
      $xml = simplexml_load_string($rsp);
      if ($xml["stat"] == 'ok') {
        $success = true;
        break;
      }
    } // for
```

```php
    if ($success) {
      return $xml;
    } else {
      throw new Exception("Could not successfully call Flickr");
    }
  }

# go through all the methods and list

  public function getMethods() {

    // would be useful to return this as an array (later on, I can have another
    // method to group them under common prefixes.)

    $url = "http://api.flickr.com/services/rest/?method=flickr.reflection.getMethods
&api_key={$this->api_key}";
    $xml = $this->flickrCall($url, 3);
    foreach ($xml->methods->method as $method) {
      //print "${method}\n";
      $method_list[] = (string) $method;
    }
    return $method_list;
  }

# get info about a given method($api_key, $method_name)

  public function getMethodInfo($method_name) {

    $url =
    "http://api.flickr.com/services/rest/?method=flickr.reflection.getMethodInfo
&api_key={$this->api_key}&method_name={$method_name}";
    $xml = $this->flickrCall($url, 3);
    return $xml;
  }

# get directly from Flickr the method data
# returns an array with data
  public function download_flickr_methods () {

    $methods = $this->getMethods();

    // now loop to grab info for each method

# this counter lets me limit the number of calls I make -- useful for testing
    $limit = 1000;
    $count = 0;
```

```php
    foreach ($methods as $method) {

      $count += 1;
      if ($count > $limit) {
        break;
      }

      $xml = $this->getMethodInfo($method);
      $method_array["needslogin"] = (integer) $xml->method["needslogin"];
      $method_array["needssigning"] = (integer) $xml->method["needssigning"];
      $method_array["requiredperms"] = (integer) $xml->method["requiredperms"];
      $method_array["description"] = (string) $xml->method->description;
      $method_array["response"] = (string) $xml->method->response;
    // loop through the arguments
      $args = array();
      foreach ($xml->arguments->argument as $argument) {
        $arg["name"] = (string) $argument["name"];
        $arg["optional"] = (integer) $argument["optional"];
        $arg["text"] = (string) $argument;
        $args[] = $arg;
      }
      $method_array["arguments"] = $args;

    // loop through errors
      $errors = array();
      foreach ($xml->errors->error as $error) {
        $err["code"] = (string) $error["code"];
        $err["message"] = (integer) $error["message"];
        $err["text"] = (string) $error;
        $errors[] = $err;
      }
      $method_array["errors"] = $errors;

      $methods_info[$method] = $method_array;
    }

    $to_store['methods'] = $methods;
    $to_store['methods_info'] = $methods_info;
    return $to_store;

  } // download_Flickr_API

# store the data
  public function store_api_data($fname, $to_store) {

    $to_store_str = serialize($to_store);
    $fh = fopen($fname,'wb') OR die ("can't open $fname!");
```

```php
    $numbytes = fwrite($fh, $to_store_str);
    fclose($fh);
  }

# convenience method for updating the cache
  public function update_api_data($fname) {

    $to_store = $this->download_flickr_methods();
    $this->store_api_data($fname,$to_store);
  }

# restore the data

  public function restore_api_data($fname) {

    $fh = fopen($fname,'rb') OR die ("can't open $fname!");
    $contents = fread($fh, filesize($fname));
    fclose($fh);
    return unserialize($contents);


  }

} //flickr_methods
```

This form of serialization in the flickr_method class provides some basic caching so that you don't have to make more than 100 calls (one for each method) each time you want to display a summary table—which is what the following code does:

```php
<?php

  require_once("flickr_methods.php");
  $API_KEY = "[API_KEY]";

  $fname = 'flickr.methods.info.txt';

  $fm = new flickr_methods($API_KEY);

  if (!file_exists($fname)) {
    $fm->update_api_data($fname);
  }
  $m = $fm->restore_api_data($fname);

    $methods = $m["methods"];
    $methods_info = $m["methods_info"];

    header("Content-Type:text/html");
    echo '<?xml version="1.0" encoding="utf-8"?>';
?>
```

```php
<!DOCTYPE html PUBLIC "-//W3C//DTD XHTML 1.0 Strict//EN"
"http://www.w3.org/TR/xhtml1/DTD/xhtml1-strict.dtd">
<html xmlns="http://www.w3.org/1999/xhtml" xml:lang="en" lang="en">
  <head>
    <title>Flickr methods</title>
    <meta http-equiv="Content-Type" content="text/html;charset=utf-8" />
  </head>
  <body>
    <table>
      <tr>
        <th>method name</th>
        <th>description</th>
        <th>needs login</th>
        <th>needs signing</th>
        <th>permissions</th>
        <th>args (mandatory)</th>
        <th>args (optional)</th>
      </tr>
<?php
  foreach ($methods_info as $name=>$method) {
    $description = $method["description"];
# calc mandatory and optional arguments
    $m_args = "";
    $o_args = "";
    foreach ($method["arguments"] as $arg){
      //print "arg: {$arg['name']}\n";
      //print_r ($arg);
      // don't list api_key since it is mandatory for all calls
      if ($arg['name'] != 'api_key') {
        if ($arg["optional"] == '1') {
          $o_args .= " {$arg['name']}";
        } else {
          $m_args .= " {$arg['name']}";
        }
      } //if
    }
    print <<<EOT
      <tr>
        <td>
          <a href="http://www.flickr.com/services/api/{$name}.html">{$name}</a>
        </td>
        <td>{$description}</td>
        <td>{$method["needslogin"]}</td>
        <td>{$method["needssigning"]}</td>
        <td>{$method["requiredperms"]}</td>
        <td>{$m_args}</td>
        <td>{$o_args}</td>
```

```
        </tr>
EOT;
  }
?>
    </table>
  </body>
</html>
```

What Else Can Be Done with Reflection?

There's certainly a lot more you can do with this code. Let me suggest a few ideas:

- Store the data in a database (relational or XML) that can support a query language for making the queries that I listed earlier. (A poor person's approach is to copy the output of the script into a spreadsheet and work from there.)

- Create your own version of the Flickr API Explorer, perhaps as a desktop application, to help you learn about pieces of the API as you have specific questions.

- Use the reflection methods as the basis of a new third-party API wrapper that is able to update itself as the API changes.

Note In all the examples I have shown of the Flickr API, I have used HTTP GET because none of the examples so far has required any write or delete permissions. If your calls do require write or delete permissions, you must issue your Flickr call with HTTP POST.

Request and Response Formats

So far in this chapter, I have limited myself to one particular way of formulating a request to call a Flickr API method and the corresponding default format for the response. The Flickr API actually supports three different ways of packaging a request and five different formats for the response. In this section, I describe the choices you have with respect to request and response formats. Understanding these choices will help you make sense of APIs other than Flickr's since you will face similar choices in working with them.

Regardless of the request or response format used, the Flickr API rests on HTTP. Hence, we need to remember that making a Flickr API call involves two steps, which is a reflection of the request and response pattern of the underlying HTTP protocol of the API:

- You formulate an HTTP *request* corresponding to API method and parameters you want to use. With Flickr, you have a choice of three formats for the request format: REST (what we have used so far), XML-RPC, and SOAP.

- You process the HTTP *response* that includes a payload that is by default XML but that also can contain JavaScript (JSON) or PHP (input for the PHP unserialize method).

Note Although web services are not necessarily tied to HTTP (for instance, SOAP can be bound to SMTP), HTTP is the only transport protocol supported for the Flickr API. However, the vast majority of web services used, especially for mashups, are made over HTTP. Hence, I don't cover the use of transport protocols other than HTTP in this book.

Flickr supports three different request formats to call the methods of the API (REST, SOAP, and XML-RPC):

- The REST request format, the simplest one to work with, is similar conceptually and practically to submitting a request through an HTML form. (That is, you submit a request through either HTTP GET or POST and use named parameters.) In the simplest cases, that could be equivalent to setting parameters for a URL to which you get back some XML that you can parse. Think about the examples I have presented so far to confirm that this is what has been happening. For Flickr, I recommend starting with its REST request format.

Note In Chapter 7, I revisit and refine the term REST. What Flickr calls the REST approach is a commonly used pattern of structuring web services but is more accurately described as a REST-RPC hybrid.

- SOAP has an envelope around the request and enables higher levels of abstraction, but it is more complicated and typically takes more specialized libraries and tools to deal with than REST. We will return to this subject in the next chapter, both in the context of Flickr's SOAP request format and in other APIs' SOAP interfaces. SOAP is an important web services technique, especially among folks who use web services for enterprise work.[4]

Note In version 1.1 of SOAP, SOAP is an acronym for Simple Object Access Protocol. Version 1.2 of the SOAP specification indicates that SOAP is no longer an acronym.

- XML-RPC was, in many ways, the proto-SOAP. It's most convenient to use XML-RPC from a library, of which there are many in a variety of languages.

There are current five different formats for Flickr responses: the three corresponding default response formats (REST, XML-RPC, SOAP) and two specialized response formats (json and php_serial). In other words, a REST-formatted request generates by default a REST-formatted response. You can change the format for the response by using the format parameter.

The default behavior of tying the request and request format is typical for web APIs. With the exception of the REST-to-JSON pairing, which we will return to in our discussion of Ajax programming in Chapter 8, the ability to decouple the request format from the response format

---

4. http://en.wikipedia.org/wiki/SOAP

is unusual. For instance, with the Flickr API, you issue a SOAP-formatted request that asks for a REST-formatted response. I'm not aware of any standard SOAP libraries that can handle such a pairing.

You can see for yourself these five formats in action through a simple REST-formatted request:

```
http://api.flickr.com/services/rest/?method=flickr.test.echo
&api_key={api-ky}&format={format}
```

where `format` = `rest`, `xmlrpc`, `soap`, `json`, `php_serial`, or blank (for the default response format).

Flickr Authorization

Authentication is a bit tricky to follow, and ultimately you may want to leave the details to one of the Flickr API kits (covered later in the chapter). However, you may still be interested in working through the details at least once so that you know what's going on below the hood before you use someone else's library. Besides, there will be other authentication schemes out there besides Flickr's that you will want to use. Getting a solid handle on Flickr's authentication scheme is good preparation for more quickly understanding those other authentication schemes.

You can find the specification for Flickr authentication here:

```
http://www.flickr.com/services/api/auth.spec.html
```

There are three types of authentication cases to handle with Flickr:

- Web applications

- Desktop applications

- Mobile applications

Each scheme is different because of the differing natures of each type of application. For example, the author of a web application can configure it to have a URL through which Flickr would be able to communicate. It's hard to guarantee that a desktop application would have a URL through which such communication could happen. In this book, I cover only the specific case of authentication for web applications. Once you understand this case, you will be able to understand the others without much problem.

Three parties are involved in the authentication dance:

- Flickr

- A third-party application that is using the Flickr API and that I refer to as the *app*

- A person who is both a user of the app and a Flickr user

Authorization is required when an app is calling a Flickr method that requires a permission level of `read`, `write`, or `delete`—anything but none. Through authorization, the app is granted a specific *permission* level by the *user* to access the Flickr API on the user's behalf. Flickr creates a *token* that ties a specific app with a specific user and a specific permission level to embody this authorization act. The authentication dance is all about how that token gets created, used in conjunction with specific API calls, and can be managed and possibly revoked by the user. The details are a bit complicated because this process must also fulfill certain design criteria, which you can surmise from how the authorization scheme is designed:

- The three parties need to be reliably and securely identified and associated in the process of authorization.

- The user must be able to undo an authorization act given to a specific app.

- The protocol must be done using HTTP and not HTTPS. That is, all the parameters being passed are visible to potential third-party interlopers. In other words, knowledge of the token itself should not allow another app to have the token's permissions.

- The app should not need to know anything *a priori* about a person's Flickr identity to secure permission.

Why Passing Passwords Around Doesn't Work Too Well

The current Flickr authorization scheme is not the first one it used. In the early days of Flickr, users granted the power to an app to act on their behalf by giving the apps their Flickr username and password. Doing so meant that in order to revoke an app's permission, users would have to change their Flickr password. Of course, doing that would also instantly revoke permissions of other third-party apps with knowledge of the user's password. The new authorization scheme is meant to correct obvious problems with the old scheme. Why should you as a user have to use your Flickr password for anything other than your dealings with Flickr? Why should revoking permissions to one app mean revoking permissions to other apps?

Authorization for Web Apps

Let's now look at the authorization scheme used with Flickr. We first need to set up some permissions.

Setting Up the Example of Lois and ContactLister

Let's now get down to the details of the process of authentication for web-based applications, keeping the authorization design criteria in mind. Let's have a specific example in mind. The app, which I will call ContactLister, displays the list of contacts for a given Flickr user. It specifically uses the `flickr.contacts.getList` method, which requires authorization with `read` permission. (A Flickr user's contacts list is private.) Let's also make up a hypothetical user called Lois.

Basic Lesson: Flickr Needs to Mediate the Authorization Dance

For ContactLister to get permission from Lois, why couldn't ContactLister just directly display a screen asking Lois to give it permission to read her contact list—and then relay that fact to Flickr? For starters, how does ContactLister prove to Flickr that Lois did in fact give ContactLister permission to access her photos? In the old days of Flickr, ContactLister would have Lois's Flickr username and password. At that time, ContactLister might as well have been Lois since it's the Flickr username/password that Flickr used to authenticate a user.

The solution that Flickr came up with is based on that Flickr needs to establish unambiguously that Lois is with full knowledge of (that is, not being tricked into) giving ContactLister (and not some other third-party app) `read` (and not some other) permission. To do that, Flickr needs to mediate communication between Lois and ContactLister.

Step 1: ContactLister Directs Flickr to Ask Lois for Permission

So instead of ContactLister directly prompting Lois for permission, ContactLister directs Flickr to prompt Lois for read permission by formulating the following Flickr URL that it directs Lois to:

```
http://flickr.com/services/auth?api_key={api_key}&perms={perms}&api_sig={api_sig}
```

Let's look at the various arguments. You are familiar with the api_key; perms would be set to read in this circumstance.

Signing a Call: How Does ContactLister Create and Send One?

The part that is new in this chapter is the api_sig. It is the act of calculating the api_sig and attaching it to method calls in the Flickr API that we refer to as *signing* the call. The purpose of signing a call is to reliably establish the identity of the signer, the one formulating the URL. Why isn't the api_key enough to establish the identity of the caller? In some circumstances, it would be if no one but the author of ContactLister and Flickr knew this api_key. On another level, Flickr API keys are sent unencrypted every time a call is made to the Flickr API, akin to passwords being sent in plain text. Hence, the api_key alone is an insufficient foundation for signing this call. You shouldn't be able to easily fake a signature.

When you sign up for a Flickr API key, in addition to getting a key, you get a corresponding string: secret. As the name implies, you are supposed to keep secret secret so that in theory only you and Flickr know it. Go to http://www.flickr.com/services/api/keys/ to see your own keys and secrets.

ContactLister has to use this secret to calculate the api_sig and thereby sign the call. The api_sig is calculated according to the following algorithm for any Flickr API call:

- Make a signature string that starts with the secret followed by a concatenation of all the name/value pairs of the arguments to be passed to Flickr, sorted alphabetically by name— excluding the api_sig but including method. The values need to UTF-8 encoded but not URL-encoded.

- The api_sig is then the hexadecimal digest of the md5 hash of the signature string.

The following is a Python function that takes a secret and a dictionary of name/value pairs and returns the corresponding api_sig:

```python
def calcSig(secret,params):
    import md5
    l = params.keys()
    l.sort()
    hash = ''
    for key in l:
        hash += str(key) + params[key].encode('utf-8')
    hash = secret + hash
    api_sig = md5.new(hash).hexdigest()
    return api_sig
```

Let's first run through a concrete example and then discuss how this process constitutes signing the call. Consider the following sample key and secret:

- Key: 020338ddabd2f41ae7ce9413a8d51429

- Shared secret: f0fc085289c7677a

The signature string is then as follows:

{secret}api_key{api_key}perms{perms}

which is as follows:

f0fc085289c7677aapi_key{api_key}permsread

The md5 hexadecimal digest of the string is then as follows:

f9258a76e4ad3cb5fa40bd8b0098d119

Therefore, the signed call is as follows:

http://flickr.com/services/auth?api_key={api_key}&perms=read
&api_sig=f9258a76e4ad3cb5fa40bd8b0098d119

What Flickr Makes of the Signed Call

So when ContactLister directs Lois to go to this URL, Flickr first determines the integrity of this call by performing the same signature calculation as ContactLister did in the first place: find the secret that corresponds to the api_key, sort all the parameters by key (except for the api_sig parameter), form the signature string, and then compare it to the value of the api_sig parameter. If two match up, then Flickr can conclude the call did indeed come from ContactLister because presumably the author of ContactLister is the only one other than Flickr who knows the key/secret combination.

You might ask, why can't someone take the api_sig from the call and reverse the md5 calculation to derive the secret? Although it's straightforward to calculate the md5 hash of a string, it's much more difficult computationally to go in the other direction. For the purposes here, you should think of this reverse direction for md5 as practically—but not theoretically—impossible. Moreover, using md5 makes it difficult to change the parameters of the call. If you change, say, perms=read to perms=delete, you get a different api_sig, which is very hard to calculate without knowing secret.

▌Note md5, it turns out, does have limitations as a cryptographic hash function. Researchers have demonstrated how to take an md5 hash and create another string that will give you the same md5 hash. Can this weakness be used to issue fake Flickr calls? I don't know; see http://en.wikipedia.org/wiki/MD5 for more information.

Step 2: Flickr Asks Lois for Permission on Behalf of ContactLister

At any rate, assuming a properly signed call to http://flickr.com/services/auth, Flickr now knows reliably that it is indeed ContactLister asking for read permission. Remember, though, that the end goal, a token, ties three things together: an app, a permission level, and a user.

The call reliably ties the app and permission together for Flickr. However, the call has no explicit mention of a user at all. There's no parameter for user_id, for instance.

That ContactLister doesn't have to pass to Flickr anything about Lois's Flickr account is a virtue—not a problem. Why should a third-party app have to know anything *a priori* about a person's relationship to Flickr? So, how does Flickr figure out the user to tie to the request by ContactLister for the read permission? The fact is that it's Lois—and not someone else—who uses the authorization URL:

```
http://flickr.com/services/auth?api_key={api_key}&perms=read
&api_sig=f9258a76e4ad3cb5fa40bd8b0098d119
```

When Lois loads the authorization URL in her browser, Flickr then determines the user in question. If Lois is logged in, then Flickr knows the user in question is Lois. If no one is logged in to Flickr, then Lois will be sent through the login process. In either case, it's Flickr that is figuring out Lois's identity as a Flickr user and taking care of her authenticating to Flickr. In that way, Flickr can establish to its own satisfaction the identity of the user involved in the authorization dance—rather than trusting ContactLister to do so.

Now that Flickr knows for sure the identity of the app, the permission level requested, and the user involved, it still needs to actually ask Lois whether it's OK to let ContactLister have the requested read permission. If Lois had not already granted ContactLister such permission, then Flickr presents to Lois a screen that clearly informs her of ContactLister's request. The fact that such a display comes from Flickr instead of ContactLister directly should give Lois some confidence that Flickr can track what ContactLister will do with any permissions she grants to it and thereby hold the authors of ContactLister accountable.

Step 3: Flickr Lets ContactLister Know to Pick Up a Token

Assuming that Lois grants ContactLister read permission, Flickr must now inform ContactLister of this fact. (Remember, the permission granting is happening on the Flickr site.) Flickr communicates this authorization act by sending the HTTP GET request to the callback-URL for ContactLister with what Flickr calls a *frob*. Flickr knows the callback-URL to use because part of registering a web application to handle authorization is specifying a callback URL at the following location:

```
http://www.flickr.com/services/api/keys/{api-key}/
```

where the api-key is that for the app. In other words, ContactLister must handle a call from Flickr of the following form:

```
callback-URL?frob={frob}
```

A frob is akin to a session ID. It lets ContactLister know that some form of authorization has been granted to ContactLister. To actually get the token that ContactLister needs to use the requested read permission, ContactLister needs to use flickr.auth.getToken to exchange the frob for the token. Frobs aren't meant to be the permanent representation of an authorization act. Frobs expire after 60 minutes or after flickr.auth.getToken is used to redeem the frob for a token. This exchange ensures that ContactLister receives a token and that Flickr knows that ContactLister has received the token. Note that flickr.auth.getToken is also a signed call with two mandatory arguments: api_key and frob—in addition to api_sig, of course. The returned token is expressed in the following form (quoting from http://www.flickr.com/services/api/flickr.auth.getToken.html):

```
<auth>
  <token>976598454353455</token>
  <perms>write</perms>
  <user nsid="12037949754@N01" username="Bees" fullname="Cal H" />
</auth>
```

Note that it's the token that tells ContactLister the details of what is being authorized: the Flickr user and the permission granted. Now, ContactLister knows the Flickr identity of Lois—without ever needing Lois to tell ContactLister directly.

Step 4: ContactLister Can Now Make an Authorized and Signed Call

ContactLister can now actually make the call to `flickr.contacts.getList`. How so? In addition to signing a call to `flickr.contacts.getList`, ContactLister adds the appropriate authorization information by adding the following argument to the call and signing it appropriately:

```
auth-token={token}
```

We should note moreover that Lois, like all users, can revoke any permission she had previously granted here:

```
http://flickr.com/services/auth/list.gne
```

It's nice for Lois to know that she doesn't have to convince ContactLister to stop accessing her account. She just tells Flickr.

Implementation of Authorization in PHP

That's the narrative of how to do Flickr authorization for web applications. Now let's look at it implemented in PHP. There are two pieces of code. The first generates the authorization URL. (To use it, use your own API key and secret.)

```php
<?php
  $api_key = "";
  $secret = "f0fc085289c7677a";
  $perms = "read";

  function login_link($api_key,$secret,$perms) {
    # calculate API SIG
    # sig string = secret + [arguments listed alphabetically name/value --
    # including api_key and perms]

    $sig_string = "{$secret}api_key{$api_key}perms{$perms}";
    $api_sig = md5($sig_string);

    $url = "http://flickr.com/services/auth?api_key={$api_key}&perms={$perms}
&api_sig={$api_sig}";
    return $url;
  }
```

```php
  $url = login_link($api_key,$secret,$perms);
?>
<html>
  <body><a href="<?php print($url);?>">Login to Flickr</a></body>
</html>
```

To confirm that you have things set up correctly, if you run the app, you should get a prompt from the Flickr site asking for access (see Figure 6-2).[5]

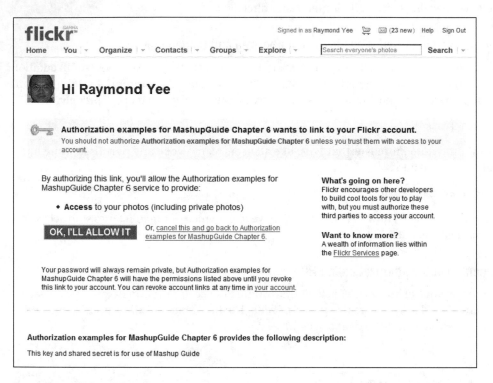

Figure 6-2. *Flickr authorization screen. (Reproduced with permission of Yahoo! Inc. ® 2007 by Yahoo! Inc. YAHOO! and the YAHOO! logo are trademarks of Yahoo! Inc.)*

The second piece of code is the authentication-handling script whose URL is the callback URL registered to the API key. It reads the frob, gets the token, and then lists the contacts of the user (a type of access that demonstrates that authorization is working, since without authorization, an app will not be able to access a user's contact list). To try this yourself, you will need to create this file and then enter its URL in the Callback URL field of your app's key configuration screen at Flickr:[6]

---

5. http://examples.mashupguide.net/ch06/auth.php

6. http://examples.mashupguide.net/ch06/auth_cb.php

```php
<?php
##insert your own Flickr API KEY here
$api_key = "[API_KEY]";
$secret = "[SECRET]";

$perms = "read";

$frob = $_GET['frob'];

function getResource($url){
  $chandle = curl_init();
  curl_setopt($chandle, CURLOPT_URL, $url);
  curl_setopt($chandle, CURLOPT_RETURNTRANSFER, 1);
  $result = curl_exec($chandle);
  curl_close($chandle);

  return $result;
}

function getContactList($api_key, $secret, $auth_token)  {
  # calculate API SIG
  # sig string = secret + [arguments listed alphabetically name/value --
  # including api_key and perms]; don't forget the method call

  $method = "flickr.contacts.getList";
  $sig_string =
    "{$secret}api_key{$api_key}auth_token{$auth_token}method{$method}";
  $api_sig = md5($sig_string);

  $token_url =
    "http://api.flickr.com/services/rest/?method=flickr.contacts.getList
&api_key={$api_key}&auth_token={$auth_token}&api_sig={$api_sig}";
  $feed = getResource($token_url);
  $rsp = simplexml_load_string($feed);

  return $rsp;
}

function getToken($api_key,$secret,$frob) {
  # calculate API SIG
  # sig string = secret + [arguments listed alphabetically name/value --
  # including api_key and perms]; don't forget the method call

  $method = "flickr.auth.getToken";
  $sig_string = "{$secret}api_key{$api_key}frob{$frob}method{$method}";
  $api_sig = md5($sig_string);
```

```php
  $token_url =
    "http://api.flickr.com/services/rest/?method=flickr.auth.getToken
&api_key={$api_key}&frob={$frob}&api_sig={$api_sig}";
  $feed = getResource($token_url);
  $rsp = simplexml_load_string($feed);

  return $rsp;
}

$token_rsp = getToken($api_key,$secret,$frob);
$nsid = $token_rsp->auth->user["nsid"];
$username = $token_rsp->auth->user["username"];
$auth_token = $token_rsp->auth->token;
$perms = $token_rsp->auth->perms;

# display some user info
echo "You are: ", $token_rsp->auth->user["fullname"],"<br>";
echo "Your nsid: ", $nsid, "<br>";
echo "Your username: ", $username,"<br>";
echo "auth token: ", $auth_token, "<br>";
echo "perms: ", $perms, "<br>";

# make a call to getContactList

$contact_rsp = (getContactList($api_key,$secret,$auth_token));
$n_contacts = $contact_rsp->contacts["total"];
$s = "<table>";
foreach ($contact_rsp->contacts->contact as $contact) {
  $nsid = $contact['nsid'];
  $username = $contact['username'];
  $realname = $contact['realname'];
  $s = $s . "<tr><td>{$realname}</td><td>{$username}</td><td>{$nsid}</td></tr>";
}

$s = $s . "</table>";
echo "Your contact list (which requires read permission) <br>";
echo "Number of contacts: {$n_contacts}<br>";
echo $s;
?>
```

Note Uploading photos to Flickr is a major part of the Flickr API that is not covered in this book. I suggest reading the documentation (`http://www.flickr.com/services/api/upload.api.html`) and using one of the API kits.

Using Flickr API Kits

Once you get the hang of the APIs using REST, you'll likely get tired of using it directly in your programming. The details of authorizing users, uploading photos, and managing a cache of Flickr results (to speed up access) are not things you want to deal with all the time.

API kits in various programming languages have been written to make it more comfortable for you to use the API in your language. These tools often express the Flickr API in terms that are more natural for a given language, by abstracting data, maintaining sessions, and taking care of some of the trickier bits of the API.

You can find a list of API kits for Flickr here:

```
http://www.flickr.com/services/api/
```

In this section I'll describe briefly some options of API kits for PHP. Currently, three Flickr API kits are publicized on the Flickr services page. This section shows how to set them up to do a simple example of a working program for each of the API kits. You then need to figure out which is the best to use for your given situation.

SETTING UP INCLUDE_PATH AND FLICKR KEYS

Whenever you use third-party libraries, you need to ensure that your PHP path (the `include_path` variable) is set properly so that your PHP code can find your libraries. If you have access to `php.ini`, by all means use it. You can also use the `ini_set()` function in PHP to set your `include_path` variable within your code. In the following code, I assume that `include_path` is properly set.

Also, it's convenient to store your Flickr key and secret in an external file that you can then include. For the following examples, I have a file named `fickr_key.php` containing the following:

```php
<?php
define('API_KEY', '[YOUR_KEY]');
define('API_SECRET', '[YOUR_SECRET]');
?>
```

PEAR::Flickr_API

This kit,[7] written by Cal Henderson, is the earliest and simplest of the API kits. To try it on your hosting platform, make sure you have PEAR installed, and install the library using the following command:

```
pear install -of http://code.iamcal.com/php/flickr/Flickr_API-Latest.tgz
```

Here's a little code snippet to show you its structure:

```php
<?php
  include("flickr_key.php");
  require_once 'Flickr/API.php';
  # create a new api object
```

---

7. http://code.iamcal.com/php/flickr/readme.htm

```php
$api =& new Flickr_API(array(
    'api_key'    => API_KEY,
    'api_secret' => API_SECRET
));

# call a method

$response = $api->callMethod('flickr.photos.search', array(
    'tags'     => 'flower',
    'per_page' => '10'
));

# check the response

if ($response){
  # response is an XML_Tree root object
  echo "total number of photos: ", $response->children[0]->attributes["total"];
}else{
  # fetch the error
  $code = $api->getErrorCode();
  $message = $api->getErrorMessage();
}
?>
```

Why might you want to use PEAR::Flickr_API? It's a simple wrapper with some defining characteristics:

- There's not much of an abstraction of the method calls. You pass in the method name. The advantage is that the API will not be out-of-date with the addition of new Flickr methods. The disadvantage is that one can imagine abstractions that are more idiomatic PHP.

- You pass in the API key when creating a new Flickr_API object.

- The response is an XML_Tree root object.[8]

My conclusion is that it makes sense to use one of the newer, richer PHP API kits: phpFlickr or Phlickr; also, more people are actively working on them.

phpFlickr

You can find Dan Coulter's toolkit at http://phpflickr.com/. It is written in PHP 4, which is currently an advantage, since PHP 5 is not always readily available. Moreover, there seems to be a continued active community around phpFlickr. To install and test the library, following these steps:

---

8. http://pear.php.net/package/XML_Tree—this package has been superseded by XML_Serializer (http://pear.php.net/package/XML_Serializer)

1. Follow the detailed instructions at http://phpflickr.com/docs/?page=install. Download the latest ZIP file from http://sourceforge.net/projects/phpflickr. At the time of writing, the latest is the following:[9]

   http://downloads.sourceforge.net/phpflickr/phpFlickr-2.1.0.tar.gz

   or the following:

   http://downloads.sourceforge.net/phpflickr/phpFlickr-2.1.0.zip

2. In theory, PEAR should let me install it, but I was not been able to get it to install phpFlickr.[10] Uncompress the file into a directory so that you can include it. I put it in a non-PEAR phplib directory and renamed the file to phpFlickr.

3. Copy and paste the following code as a demonstration of working code:

   ```php
   <?php

   include("flickr_key.php");
   require_once("phpFlickr/phpFlickr.php");

   $api = new phpFlickr(API_KEY, API_SECRET);

   #
   # Get user's ID
   #
   $username = 'Raymond Yee';
   if (isset($_GET['username']))
       $username = $_GET['username'];
   $user_id = $api->people_findByUsername($username);
   $user_id = $user_id['id'];

   print $user_id;

   ?>
   ```

Let's see how phpFlickr works:

- The constructor has three arguments: the mandatory API key and two optional parameters, secret and die_on_error (a Boolean for whether to die on an error condition). Remember that you can use the getErrorCode() and getErrorMsg() functions of $api.[11]

---

9. http://sourceforge.net/project/showfiles.php?group_id=139987&package_id=153541&release_id=488387

10. pear install -of http://downloads.sourceforge.net/phpflickr/phpFlickr-2.1.0.tar.gz gets me "Could not extract the package.xml file from /home/rdhyee/pear/temp/download/phpFlickr-2.1.0.tar.gz."

11. http://phpflickr.com/docs/?page=install

- This is from the official documentation:

  - Apparently, all of the API methods have been implemented in the phpFlickr class.

  - To call a method, remove the flickr. part of the name, and replace any periods with underscores. You call the functions with parameters in the order listed in the Flickr documentation—with the exception of flickr.photos.search, for which you pass in an associative array.

  - To enable caching, use the phpFlickr::enableCache() function.

Because the naming convention of phpFlickr, which is closely related to that of the Flickr API, you can translate what you know from working with the API pretty directly into using phpFlickr.

Phlickr

Phlickr requires PHP 5 and is not just a facile wrapper around the Flickr API; it provides new classes that significantly abstract the API. There are significant advantages to this approach; if the abstraction is done well, you should be able to program Flickr in a more convenient and natural method in the context of PHP 5 (for example, you can work with objects and not XML, which you can then turn into objects). The downside is that you might need to juggle between the Flickr API's way of organizing Flickr functionality and the viewpoint of the Phlickr author. Moreover, if Flickr adds new methods, there is a greater chance of Phlickr breaking as a result— or at least not being able to keep up with such changes.

The home page for the project is as follows:

http://drewish.com/projects/phlickr/

You can get the latest version of Phlickr from here:

http://sourceforge.net/project/showfiles.php?group_id=129880

The following code is a simple demonstration of Phlickr in action—it uses the flickr.test.echo method:

```php
<?php
ini_set(
  'include_path',
  ini_get( 'include_path' ) . PATH_SEPARATOR . "/home/rdhyee/pear/lib/php"
);

require_once 'Phlickr/Api.php';

#insert your own Flickr API KEY here
define('FLICKR_API_KEY', '[API-KEY]''');
define('FLICKR_API_SECRET', '[SECRET]''');

$api = new Phlickr_Api(FLICKR_API_KEY, FLICKR_API_SECRET);
$response = $api->ExecuteMethod(
  'flickr.test.echo',
  array('message' => 'It worked!'));
```

```
print "<h1>{$response->xml->message}</h1>";
?>
```

http://drewish.com/projects/phlickr/docs/ documents the objects of the library. To learn more about Phlickr, buy and read *Building Flickr Applications with PHP* by Rob Kunkle and Andrew Morton (Apress, 2006). Andrew Morton is the author of Phlickr.

■Note Phlickr must be in a folder called exactly Phlickr for operating systems (such as Linux) whose filenames are case-sensitive.

Limitations of the Flickr API

The Flickr API is extensive. The methods of the Flickr API are a fairly stable, well-supported way for your program to access data about most resources from Flickr. As one would expect, the functionality of the Flickr API overlaps strongly with that of the Flickr UI—but the two are not identical. There are currently things you can do in the UI that you can't do in the API. For example:

- Although you can access a Flickr group's photo pool, you can't read or write to the group discussions with the API (though you can get at the latest comments in a group discussion through Flickr feeds).

- You can't add, delete, and configure a weblog for your Flickr account including layout and settings with the API.

- You can't add or delete contacts via the API.

- You can't delete your Flickr account with the API or do most of the account management elements such as changing your e-mail or using a different Yahoo! ID for this Flickr account.

- There is no support for Flickr collections in the API.

- I don't think there is currently support for tag clusters in the API (http://tech.groups. yahoo.com/group/yws-flickr/message/1596).

Some of limitations of the API are probably intentional design decisions that are unlikely to change (such as not being able to programmatically delete your entire account). Other discrepancies reflect that new features in Flickr tend to show up first in the UI and then in the API. I would guess, for instance, that there will eventually be support for Flickr collections in the API.

I will point out another class of differences between the API and UI. There is, however, some information from Flickr that is available from both the UI and the API—but that is easier to derive from screen-scraping the UI and through using the API. Take this, for example:

http://www.flickr.com/photos/{user-id}/archives/

This lists for every year and month the number of photos that the user has taken or uploaded. Accessing this information from the UI involves one HTTP GET and screen-scraping the HTML. In contrast, generating the same dataset using the Flickr API requires calculating Unix timestamps for the beginnings and ends of months (for the time zone of the user, which is not available via the API) so that you can feed those time boundaries to `flickr.photos.getCounts`.

What's the point here? Although the API provides the flexibility to calculate the number of photos taken or uploaded between any two arbitrary times, the UI for the archives provides a count of the photos for a very useful default case (that by month), which turns out to require a bit of work to get from the API. In other words, the UI of an application gives insight into what the mainstream use cases for the API are.

I've found such examples about limitations of APIs with respect to the UI a bit surprising at first. I would have expected a given functionality to be purposely excluded from the API (because of a policy decision) or easier to programmatically access via the UI—but not harder than screen-scraping using the API. Otherwise, there's a disincentive to use the API in that case.

Summary

If you have read this long chapter and studied the examples in depth, you should now be able to see both the conceptual heart of the Flickr API—a bunch of HTTP requests that look like HTML form submissions and responses that by default return nice-to-parse XML—and the complexities that arise when dealing with various cases (different request and response formats, authorization, and the need to abstract the API when using them in practice). I'm a big believer in learning as much as you can from the API before taking on authorization. You can use simple calls to solidify your understanding of HTTP and XML processing. Then you can move on to the more complicated cases when you are ready.

If you want to make sense of the Flickr API as a whole, focus on tackling specific problems that get you into exploring parts of the API. The reflection methods, though, do give you the potential to computationally support your understanding of the API as well as make more robust libraries for interacting with Flickr.

Understanding the underlying details of Flickr authorization is something you don't have to deal with if you don't want to—turn to your favorite API kit for help. However, understanding it brings not only intellectual satisfaction but also enables you to better understand other authorization schemes you may encounter (such as the one for Amazon S3).

In the next chapter, we'll turn to web APIs other than Flickr. I will use the lens of the Flickr API to show you how to explore the bigger world of APIs in general.

CHAPTER 7

■ ■ ■

Exploring Other Web APIs

In Chapter 6, you examined the Flickr API in great detail, so I'll turn now to other web APIs. Studying the Flickr API in depth is obviously useful if you plan to use it in your mashups, but I argue here that it's useful in your study of other APIs because you can draw from your understanding of the Flickr API as a point of comparison. (I'll cover the subject of HTTP web APIs bound to a JavaScript context in the next chapter. You'll take what you learn in Chapter 6 and this chapter and study the specific context of working within the modern web browser using JavaScript.)

How do you generalize from what you know about the Flickr API to other web APIs? I will use three major axes/categories for organizing my presentation of web APIs. (I'm presenting some heuristics for thinking about the subject rather than a watertight formula. This scheme won't magically enable you to instantly understand all the various APIs out there.) The categories I use are as follows:

- The *protocols* used by the API. Some questions that I'll discuss include the following: Is the API available with a REST interface? Does it use SOAP or XML-RPC?

- The *popularity* or *influence* of the API. It's helpful to understand some of the more popular APIs because of their influence on the field in general and also because popularity is an indicator of some utility. We'll look at how you might figure out what's popular.

- The *subject matter* of the APIs. Since APIs are often tied to specific subject matter, you'll naturally need to understand the basics of the subject to make sense of the APIs. What are some of those subject areas?

It doesn't take being too long in the field of web services to hear about REST vs. SOAP as a great divide—and hence the impetus for classifying web services by the *protocols* used. You already saw the terms REST and SOAP (as well as XML-RPC) in Chapter 6 to describe the request and response formats available to developers of the Flickr API. I focused on the Flickr REST formats because they are not only the easiest ones to work with but also they are the ones that are most helpful for learning other APIs.

In this chapter, I'll cover what XML-RPC and SOAP are about. Understanding just Flickr's REST request/response structure can get you far—but there are web APIs that have only XML-RPC or SOAP interfaces. So, I'll start by discussing XML-RPC and SOAP and show you the basics of how to use those two protocols. Also, I'll lay out tips for dealing with the practical complexities that sometimes arise in consuming SOAP services.

Note The term REST (an acronym for Representational State Transfer) was coined by Roy Fielding to describe a set of architectural principles for networks. In Fielding's usage, REST is not specifically tied to HTTP or the Web. At the same time, a popular usage has arisen for REST to refer to exchanging messages over HTTP without using such protocols as SOAP and XML-RPC, which introduce an additional envelope around these messages. These two different usages of the term REST have caused confusion since it is possible to use HTTP to exchange messages without additional envelopes in a way that nonetheless does not conform to REST principles. If a creator of a service associates the service with the term REST (such as the Flickr REST interface), I will also refer to it as REST in this chapter.

Once you have a good understanding of the protocols and architectural issues behind HTTP web services, you're in a good position to consume any web API you come across—at least on a technical level. You still have to understand what a service is about and which services you might want to use. I will cover how to use Programmableweb.com as a great resource to learn about APIs in general. Programmableweb.com helps you understand which are the popular APIs as well as how APIs can be categorized by subject matter. I conclude the chapter with a study of two APIs: the API for YouTube as a simple REST interface and the Blogger API as a specific case of an entire class of APIs that share a uniform interface based on a strict usage of the HTTP methods.

XML-RPC

Although Flickr provides the option of using the XML-RPC and SOAP request and response formats in addition to REST, I wrote all my examples using the Flickr REST request format in Chapter 6. I'll show you how to use the XML-RPC protocol in this section and cover SOAP in the following section.

Tip Before taking on this section, it might be helpful to review Chapter 6's "A Refresher on HTTP" section and remind yourself of the structure of an HTTP request and response and the variety of HTTP request methods.

XML-RPC is defined at `http://www.xmlrpc.com/` as "remote procedure calling using HTTP as the transport and XML as the encoding." XML-RPC specifies how to form remote procedure calls in terms of requests and responses, each of which has parameters composed of some basic data types. There are XML-RPC libraries written in many languages, including PHP and Python.

A central point of having an XML-RPC interface for a web API is akin to that of an API kit—getting an interface that is a closer fit to the native structures and found in the programming language you are using. Let's consider a specific example to make this point.

Recall from Chapter 6 how to use the Flickr REST interface to search for public photos. You do an HTTP GET request on the following URL:

```
http://api.flickr.com/services/rest/?method=flickr.test.echo&api_key={api-key}
```

and parse the resulting XML (using, say, the `libcurl` and `simpleXML` libraries in PHP). Let's see how you do the same query using XML-RPC in Python and PHP for comparison. In Python, you can use `xmlrpclib`, which is part of the standard Python distribution and is documented at

```
http://docs.python.org/lib/module-xmlrpclib.html
```

Here's a program to illustrate how to make a call to Flickr: one to `flickr.search.photos`. Note how parameters are passed in and how you can use the `ElementTree` library to parse the output. To use the `xmlrpclib` to make this call, you need to know that the XML-RPC server endpoint URL is as follows:

```
http://api.flickr.com/services/xmlrpc/
```

and you need to name your parameters and stick them into a dictionary. When I ran the following:

```
API_KEY = "[API-KEY]"

from xmlrpclib import ServerProxy, Error, Fault
server = ServerProxy("http://api.flickr.com/services/xmlrpc/")

try:
    from xml.etree import ElementTree as et
except:
    from elementtree import ElementTree as et

# call flickr.search.photos

args = {'api_key': API_KEY, 'tags':'flower', 'per_page':3}
try:
    rsp = server.flickr.photos.search(args)
except Fault, f:
    print "Error code %s: %s" % (f.faultCode, f.faultString)

# show a bit of XML parsing using elementtree
# useful examples:  http://www.amk.ca/talks/2006-02-07/
# context page for photo: http://www.flickr.com/photos/{user-id}/{photo-id}

# fixes parsing errors when accented characters are present
rsp = rsp.encode('utf-8')
print rsp
tree = et.XML(rsp)
print "total number of photos: %s" %(tree.get('total'))
for p in tree.getiterator('photo'):
    print "%s: http://www.flickr.com/photos/%s/%s" % (p.get("title"),➥
p.get("owner"), p.get("id"))
```

I got this:

```
<photos page="1" pages="485798" perpage="3" total="1457392">
  <photo id="1236197537" owner="7823684@N06" secret="f58310acf3"
          server="1178" farm="2" title="Rainbow over flower" ispublic="1"
          isfriend="0" isfamily="0" />
  <photo id="1236134903" owner="27238986@N00" secret="fa461fb8e3" server="1036"
          farm="2" title="Watercolor" ispublic="1" isfriend="0"
          isfamily="0" />
  <photo id="1237043346" owner="33121739@N00" secret="7a116ff4af" server="1066"
          farm="2" title="Flowers" ispublic="1" isfriend="0" isfamily="0" />
</photos>
```

```
total number of photos: 1457392
Rainbow over flower: http://www.flickr.com/photos/7823684@N06/1236197537
Watercolor: http://www.flickr.com/photos/27238986@N00/1236134903
Flowers: http://www.flickr.com/photos/33121739@N00/1237043346
```

Note how the xmlrpclib library takes care of packaging the response and sending you back the XML payload (which doesn't have the <rsp> root node that is in the Flickr REST response). However, you still have to parse the XML payload. Whether using XML-RPC or REST is more convenient, you can judge for yourself.

Let's take a look at how some PHP code looks. There are two major PHP libraries for XML-RPC:

- http://phpxmlrpc.sourceforge.net/

- http://pear.php.net/package/XML_RPC/

Here I show how to use the PEAR::XML_RPC package. You can install it using PEAR:

```
pear install XML_RPC
```

The following program shows how to use PEAR::XML-RPC to do a number of things:

- You can retrieve the current time by making a call that requires no parameters (currentTime.getCurrentTime) from http://time.xmlrpc.com.

- In search_example(), you can make a specific call to flickr.photos.search.

- The class flickr_client shows how to generalize search_example() to handle more of the Flickr methods.

Here's the program:

```
<?php

// flickr_xmlrpc.php
// This code demonstrates how to use XML-RPC using the PEAR::XML-RPC library.
// gettime() is the simple example that involves
// calling a timeserver without passing in any parameters.
// search_example() shows a specific case of how to pass in some parameters
// for flickr.photos.search
```

```
// the flickr_client class generalizes search_example() to handle Flickr methods
// in general.

require_once('XML/RPC.php');
$API_KEY ='[API-KEY]';

function process_xmlrpc_resp($resp) {
  if (!$resp->faultCode()) {
      $val = $resp->value()->scalarval();
      return $val;
  } else {
    $errormsg = 'Fault Code: ' . $resp->faultCode() . "\n" . 'Fault Reason: ' .
      $resp->faultString() . "\n";
    throw new Exception ($errormsg);
  }
}

class flickr_client {

  protected $api_key;
  protected $server;

  public function __construct($api_key, $debug) {
    $this->api_key = $api_key;
    $this->server =
      new XML_RPC_Client('/services/xmlrpc','http://api.flickr.com',80);
    $this->server->setDebug($debug);
  }

  public function call($method,$params) {

    # add the api_key to $params
    $params['api_key'] = $this->api_key;

    # build the struct parameter needed
    foreach ($params as $key=>$val) {
      $xrv_array[$key] = new XML_RPC_Value($val,"string");
    }
    $xmlrpc_val = new XML_RPC_Value ($xrv_array,'struct');

    $msg = new XML_RPC_Message($method, array($xmlrpc_val));
    $resp = $this->server->send($msg);

    return process_xmlrpc_resp($resp);

  } //call

} //class flickr_client
```

```
function search_example () {
  GLOBAL $API_KEY;
  $server = new XML_RPC_Client('/services/xmlrpc','http://api.flickr.com',80);
  $server->setDebug(0);

  $myStruct = new XML_RPC_Value(array(
      "api_key" => new XML_RPC_Value($API_KEY, "string"),
      "tags" => new XML_RPC_Value('flower',"string"),
      "per_page" => new XML_RPC_Value('2',"string"),
      ), "struct");

  $msg = new XML_RPC_Message('flickr.photos.search', array($myStruct));
  $resp = $server->send($msg);

  return process_xmlrpc_resp($resp);
}

function gettime() {

  # http://www.xmlrpc.com/currentTime
  $server = new XML_RPC_Client('/RPC2','http://time.xmlrpc.com',80);
  $server->setDebug(0);

  $msg = new XML_RPC_Message('currentTime.getCurrentTime');
  $resp = $server->send($msg);

  return process_xmlrpc_resp($resp);

}

print "current time: ".gettime();
print "output from search_example \n" . search_example(). "\n";

$flickr = new flickr_client($API_KEY,0);

print "output from generalized Flickr client using XML-RPC\n";
print $flickr->call('flickr.photos.search',array('tags'=>'dog','per_page'=>'2'));
?>
```

What's Happening on the Wire?

XML-RPC is meant to abstract away how a remote procedure call is translated into an exchange of XML documents over HTTP so that you as a user of XML-RPC don't have to understand the underlying process. That's the theory with XML-RPC and especially with SOAP, an expansive elaboration on XML-RPC out of which it originally evolved. In practice, with the right tools and under certain circumstances, consuming services with XML-RPC or SOAP is a very simple, trouble-free experience.

At other times, however, you'll find yourself having to know more about the underlying protocol than you really need to know. For that reason, in the following sections I'll show you techniques for making sense of what XML is actually being exchanged and how it's being exchanged over HTTP. This discussion is meant as an explication of XML-RPC in its own right but also as preparation for studying the yet more complicated SOAP later in the chapter. But first, let's look at two tools that I use to analyze XML-RPC and SOAP: Wireshark and `curl`.

Using Wireshark and curl to Analyze and Formulate HTTP Messages

Wireshark (`http://www.wireshark.org/`) is an open source network protocol analyzer that runs on Windows, OS X, and Linux. With it, you can analyze network traffic flowing through your computer, including any HTTP traffic—making it incredibly useful for seeing what's happening when you are using web APIs (or, if you are curious, merely surfing the Web). Refer to the Wireshark site for instructions about how to install and run Wireshark for your platform.

■**Tip** With Wireshark, I found it helpful to *turn off* the Capture Packets in Promiscuous Mode option. Also, for studying web service traffic, I filter for only HTTP traffic—otherwise, there is too much data to view.

---

curl (`http://curl.haxx.se/`) is another highly useful command-line tool for working with HTTP—among many other things:

> *curl is a command line tool for transferring files with URL syntax, supporting FTP, FTPS, HTTP, HTTPS, SCP, SFTP, TFTP, TELNET, DICT, FILE and LDAP. curl supports SSL certificates, HTTP POST, HTTP PUT, FTP uploading, HTTP form based upload, proxies, cookies, user+password authentication (Basic, Digest, NTLM, Negotiate, kerberos . . .), file transfer resume, proxy tunneling, and a busload of other useful tricks.*

Go to `http://curl.haxx.se/download.html` to find a package for your platform. Be sure to look for packages that support SSL—you'll need it when you come to some examples later this chapter. Remember in particular the following documentation:

- `http://curl.haxx.se/docs/manpage.html` is the man page for `curl`.

- `http://curl.haxx.se/docs/httpscripting.html` is the most helpful page in many ways because it gives concrete examples.

To learn these tools, I suggest using `curl` to issue an HTTP request and using Wireshark to analyze the resulting traffic. For instance, you can start with the following:

```
curl http://www.yahoo.com
```

to see how to retrieve the contents of a web page. To see the details about the HTTP request and response, turn on the `verbose` option and make explicit what was implicit (that fetching the content of `http://www.yahoo.com` uses the HTTP GET method):

```
curl -v -X GET http://www.yahoo.com
```

You can get more practice studying Wireshark and the Flickr API by performing some function in the Flickr UI or in the Flickr API Explorer and seeing what HTTP traffic is exchanged. Try operations that don't require any Flickr permissions, and then try ones that require escalating levels of permissions. You can see certainly see the Flickr API being invoked and when HTTP GET vs. HTTP POST is used by Flickr—and specifically what is being sent back and forth.

I'll teach you more about `curl` in the context of the following examples.

Parsing XML-RPC Traffic

When you look at the documentation for the XML-RPC request format for Flickr (http://www.flickr.com/services/api/request.xmlrpc.html) and for the response format (http://www.flickr.com/services/api/response.xmlrpc.html), you'll find confirmation that the transport mechanism is indeed HTTP (just as it for the REST request and response). However, the request parameters and response are wrapped in many layers of XML tags. I'll show you how to use Wireshark and `curl` to confirm for yourself what's happening when you use XML-RPC.

Here I use Wireshark to monitor what happens when I run the Python example that uses the `flickr.photos.search` method and then use `curl` to manually duplicate the same request to show how you can formulate XML-RPC requests without calling an XML-RPC library per se. Again, I'm not advocating this as a practical way of using XML-RPC but as a way of understanding what's happening when you do use XML-RPC.

When I ran the Python program and monitored the HTTP traffic, I saw the following request (an HTTP POST to `/services/xmlrpc/`):

```
POST /services/xmlrpc/ HTTP/1.0
```

It had the following HTTP request headers:

```
Host: api.flickr.com
User-Agent: xmlrpclib.py/1.0.1 (by www.pythonware.com)
Content-Type: text/xml
Content-Length: 415
```

and the following request body (reformatted here for clarity):

```
<?xml version='1.0'?>
<methodCall>
  <methodName>flickr.photos.search</methodName>
  <params>
    <param>
      <value><struct>
        <member>
          <name>per_page</name>
          <value><int>3</int></value>
        </member>
        <member>
          <name>api_key</name>
          <value><string>[API-KEY]</string></value>
        </member>
        <member>
```

```
      <name>tags</name>
      <value><string>flower</string></value>
    </member>
  </struct></value>
 </param>
</params>
</methodCall>
```

The HTTP response (edited here for clarity) was as follows:

```
HTTP/1.1 200 OK
Date: Sun, 26 Aug 2007 04:33:29 GMT
Server: Apache/2.0.52
[...some cookies....]
Content-Length: 1044
Connection: close
Content-Type: text/xml; charset=utf-8

<?xml version="1.0" encoding="utf-8" ?>
<methodResponse>
  <params>
    <param>
      <value>
        <string>
          &lt;photos page=&quot;1&quot; pages=&quot;485823&quot;
          perpage=&quot;3&quot; total=&quot;1457468&quot;&gt;
          &lt;photo id=&quot;1237314286&quot; owner=&quot;41336703@N00&quot;
          secret=&quot;372291c5f7&quot; server=&quot;1088&quot; farm=&quot;2&quot;
          title=&quot;250807 047&quot; ispublic=&quot;1&quot; isfriend=&quot;0&quot;
          isfamily=&quot;0&quot; /&gt;
          &lt;photo id=&quot;1236382563&quot; owner=&quot;70983346@N00&quot;
          secret=&quot;459e79fde3&quot; server=&quot;1376&quot; farm=&quot;2&quot;
          title=&quot;Darling daisy necklace&quot; ispublic=&quot;1&quot;
          isfriend=&quot;0&quot; isfamily=&quot;0&quot; /&gt;
          &lt;photo id=&quot;1237257850&quot; owner=&quot;39312862@N00&quot;
          secret=&quot;fa9d15f9c3&quot; server=&quot;1272&quot; farm=&quot;2&quot;
          title=&quot;Peperomia species&quot; ispublic=&quot;1&quot;
          isfriend=&quot;0&quot; isfamily=&quot;0&quot; /&gt;
          &lt;/photos&gt;
        </string>
      </value>
    </param>
  </params>
</methodResponse>
```

To make sense of the interchange, it's useful to study the XML-RPC specification (http://www.xmlrpc.com/spec) to learn that the Flickr XML-RPC request is passing in one struct that holds all the parameters. The request uses HTTP POST. What comes back in the response is an entity-encoded XML <photos> element (the results that we wanted from the API), wrapped in a series of XML elements used in the XML-RPC protocol to encapsulate the response. This process of serializing the request and deserializing the response is what an XML-RPC library does for you.

We can take this study of XML-RPC one more step. You can use curl (or another HTTP client) to confirm that you can synthesize an XML-RPC request independently of any XML-RPC library to handle the work for you. This is not a convenient way to do things, and it defeats the purpose of using a protocol such as XML-RPC—but this technique is helpful for proving to yourself that you really understand what is really happening with a protocol.

To wit, to call flickr.photos.search using XML-RPC, you need to send an HTTP POST request to http://api.flickr.com/services/xmlrpc/ whose body is the same as what I pulled out using Wireshark. The call, formulated as an invocation of curl, is as follows:

```
curl -v -X  POST --data-binary "<?xml version='1.0' encoding='UTF-8'?>➡
  <methodCall><methodName>flickr.photos.search</methodName><params><param><value>➡
  <struct><member><name>per_page</name><value><int>3</int></value></member><member>➡
  <name>api_key</name><value><string>[API-KEY]</string></value></member><member>➡
  <name>tags</name><value><string>flower</string></value></member></struct></value>➡
  </param></params></methodCall>"  http://api.flickr.com/services/xmlrpc/
```

■Note To write curl invocations that work from the command line of Windows, OS X, and Linux, I rewrote the XML to use single quotes to allow me to use double quotes to wrap the XML.

You can issue this request through curl to convince yourself that you are now speaking and understanding XML-RPC responses!

An XML-RPC library is supposed to hide the details you just looked at from you. One of the major practical problems that I have run into when using XML-RPC (and SOAP) is understanding for a given language and library how exactly to formulate a request. Notice some important lines from the examples. An essentialist rendition of the Python example is as follows:

```
server = ServerProxy("http://api.flickr.com/services/xmlrpc/")
args = {'api_key': API_KEY, 'tags':'flower', 'per_page':3}
rsp = server.flickr.photos.search(args)
rsp = rsp.encode('utf-8')
tree = et.XML(rsp)
print "total number of photos: %s" %(tree.get('total'))
```

Besides the mechanics of calling the right libraries, you had to know how to pass in the URL endpoint of the XML-RPC server—which is usually not too hard—but also how to package up the parameters. Here, I had to use a Python dictionary, whose keys are the names of the Flickr parameters. I then call flickr.photos.search as a method of server and get back XML.

The PHP example can be boiled down to this:

```
$server = new XML_RPC_Client('/services/xmlrpc','http://api.flickr.com',80);
$myStruct = new XML_RPC_Value(array(
    "api_key" => new XML_RPC_Value($API_KEY, "string"),
    "tags" => new XML_RPC_Value('flower',"string"),
```

```
        "per_page" => new XML_RPC_Value('2',"string"),
        ), "struct");
$msg = new XML_RPC_Message('flickr.photos.search', array($myStruct));
$resp = $server->send($msg);
$val = $resp->value()->scalarval();
```

Again, I knew what I had to tell PHP and the `PEAR::XML_RPC` library, and once someone provides you with skeletal code like I did here, it's not hard to use. However, it has been my experience with XML-RPC and especially SOAP that it takes a lot of work to come up with the incantation that works. Complexity is moved from having to process HTTP and XML directly (as you would have using the Flickr REST interface) to understanding how to express methods and their parameters in the way a given higher-level toolkit wants from you.

SOAP

SOAP is a complicated topic of which I readily admit to having only a limited understanding. SOAP and the layers of technologies built on top of SOAP—WSDL, UDDI, and the various WS-* specifications (`http://en.wikipedia.org/wiki/WS-%2A`)—are clearly getting lots of attention, especially in enterprise computing, which deals with needs addressed by this technology stack. I cover SOAP and WSDL (and leave out the other specifications) in this book because some of the APIs you may want to use in creating mashups are expressed in terms of SOAP and WSDL. My goal is to provide practical guidance as to how to consume such services, primarily from the perspective of a PHP and Python programmer.

As with XML-RPC, SOAP and WSDL are supposed to make your life as a programmer easier by abstracting away the underlying HTTP and XML exchanges so that web services look a lot like making a local procedure call. I'll start with simple examples, using tools that make using SOAP and WSDL pretty easy to use, in order to highlight the benefits of SOAP and WSDL, and then I'll move to more complicated examples that show some of the challenges. Specifically, I'll show you first how to use a relatively straightforward SOAP service (geocoder.us), proceeding to a more complicated service (Amazon.com's ECS AWS), and then discussing what turns out to be unexpectedly complicated (the Flickr SOAP interface).

The Dream: Plug-and-Go Functionality Through WSDL and SOAP

As you learned in Chapter 6, the process of using the Flickr REST interface generally involves the following steps:

1. Finding the right Flickr method to use

2. Figuring out what parameters to pass in and how to package up the values

3. Parsing the XML payload

Although these steps are not conceptually difficult, they do tend to require a fair amount of manual inspection of the Flickr documentation by any developer working directly with the Flickr API. A Flickr API kit in the language of your choice might make it easier because it makes Flickr look like an object in that language. Accordingly, you might then be able to use the facilities of the language itself to tell you what Flickr methods are available and what parameters they take and be able to get access to the results without having to directly parse XML yourself.

You might be happy as a user of the third-party kit, but the author of any third-party kit for Flickr must still deal with the original problem of manually translating the logic and semantics of the Flickr documentation and API into code to abstract it away for the user of the API kit. It's a potentially tedious and error-prone process. In Chapter 6, I showed you how you could use the flickr.reflection methods to automatically list the available API methods and their parameters. Assuming that Flickr keeps the information coming out of those methods up-to-date, there is plenty of potential to exploit with the reflection methods.

However, flickr.reflection.getMethodInfo does not currently give us information about the formal data typing of the parameters or the XML payload. For instance, http://www.flickr.com/services/api/flickr.photos.search.html tells us the following about the per_page argument: "Number of photos to return per page. If this argument is omitted, it defaults to 100. The maximum allowed value is 500." Although this information enables a human interpreter to properly formulate the per_page argument, it would be difficult to write a program that takes advantage of this fact about per_page. In fact, it would be useful even if flickr.reflections.getMethodInfo could tell us that the argument is an integer without letting us know about its range.

That's where Web Services Definition Language (WSDL) comes in as a potential solution, along with its typical companion, SOAP. There are currently two noteworthy versions of WSDL. Although WSDL 2.0 (documented at http://www.w3.org/TR/2007/REC-wsdl20-20070626/) is a W3C recommendation, it seems to me that WSDL 1.1, which never became a *de jure* standard, will remain the dominant version of WSDL for some time (both in WSDL documents you come across and the tools with which you will have easy access). WSDL 1.1 is documented at http://www.w3.org/TR/wsdl.

A WSDL document specifies the methods (or in WSDL-speak *operations*) that are available to you, their associated *messages*, and how they turned in concrete calls you can make, typically through SOAP. (There is support in WSDL 2.0 for invoking calls using HTTP without using SOAP.) Let me first show you concretely how to use WSDL, and I'll then discuss some details of its structure that you might want to know even if you choose never to look in depth at how it works.

geocoder.us

Consider the geocoder.us service (http://geocoder.us/) that offers both free noncommercial and for-pay commercial geocoding for U.S. addresses. You can turn to the API documentation (http://geocoder.us/help/) to learn how to use its free REST-RDF, XML-RPC, and SOAP interface. There are three methods supported by geocoder.us:

geocode: Takes a U.S. address or intersection and returns a list of results

geocode_address: Works just like geocode except that it accepts only an address

geocode_intersection: Works just like geocode except that it accepts only an intersection

Let's first use the interface that is most familiar to you, which is its REST-RDF interface, and consider the geocode method specifically. To find the latitude and longitude of an address, you make an HTTP GET request of the following form:

```
http://geocoder.us/service/rest/geocode?address={address}
```

For example, applying the method to the address of Apress:

```
http://geocoder.us/service/rest/geocode?address=2855+Telegraph+Ave%2C+Berkeley%2C+CA
```

gets you this:

```
<?xml version="1.0"?>
<rdf:RDF
  xmlns:dc="http://purl.org/dc/elements/1.1/"
  xmlns:geo="http://www.w3.org/2003/01/geo/wgs84_pos#"
  xmlns:rdf="http://www.w3.org/1999/02/22-rdf-syntax-ns#"
>
<geo:Point rdf:nodeID="aid78384162">
    <dc:description>2855 Telegraph Ave, Berkeley CA 94705</dc:description>
    <geo:long>-122.260070</geo:long>
    <geo:lat>37.858276</geo:lat>
</geo:Point>
</rdf:RDF>
```

Now let's make the same call using the SOAP interface. Instead of making the SOAP call directly to the geocode method, let's use the WSDL document for the service:

```
http://geocoder.us/dist/eg/clients/GeoCoderPHP.wsdl
```

■**Note** Because the first WSDL document (`http://geocoder.us/dist/eg/clients/GeoCoder.wsdl`) referenced by geocoder.us apparently gives PHP 5 heartburn, I instead use the second WSDL document (`GeoCoderPHP.wsdl`) in this chapter.

I will use the WSDL document in a variety of ways to teach you the ideal usage pattern for WSDL, which involves the following steps:

- A SOAP/WSDL tool/library takes a given WSDL document and makes transparent the operations that are available to you.

- For a given operation, the SOAP/WSDL tool makes it easy for you to understand the possible input parameters and formulate the appropriate request message.

- The SOAP/WSDL tool then returns the response to you in some easy-to-parse format and handles any *faults* that come up in the course of the operation.

Using the oXygen XML Editor

My favorite way of testing a WSDL file and issuing SOAP calls is to use a visual IDE such as oXygen (`http://www.oxygenxml.com/`). Among the plethora of XML-related technologies supported by oXygen is the WSDL SOAP Analyser. I describe how you can use it to invoke the geocoder.us geocode operation to illustrate a core workflow.

■**Note** oXygen is a commercial product. You can evaluate it for 30 days free of charge. XML Spy (`http://www.altova.com/`), another commercial product, provides a similar WSDL tool. I know of one open source project that lets you visually explore a WSDL document and invoke operations: the Web Services Explorer for the Eclipse project that is part of the Web Tools project (`http://www.eclipse.org/webtools/`).

When you start the WSDL SOAP Analyser, you are prompted for the URL of a WSDL file. You enter the URL for the geocoder.us WSDL (listed earlier), and oXygen reads the WSDL file and displays a panel with four subpanels. (Figure 7-1 shows the setup of this panel.) The first subpanel contains three drop-down menus for three types of entities defined in the WSDL file:

- Services

- Ports

- Operations

The geocoder.us WSDL file follows a pattern typical for many WSDL files: it has one *service* (`GeoCode_Service`) tied to one *port* (`GeoCode_Port`), which is tied, through a specific *binding*, to one or more *operations*. It's this list of operations that is the heart of the matter if you want to use any of the SOAP services. The panel shows three operations (`geocode`, `geocode_address`, and `geocode_intersection`) corresponding to the three methods available from geocoder.us.

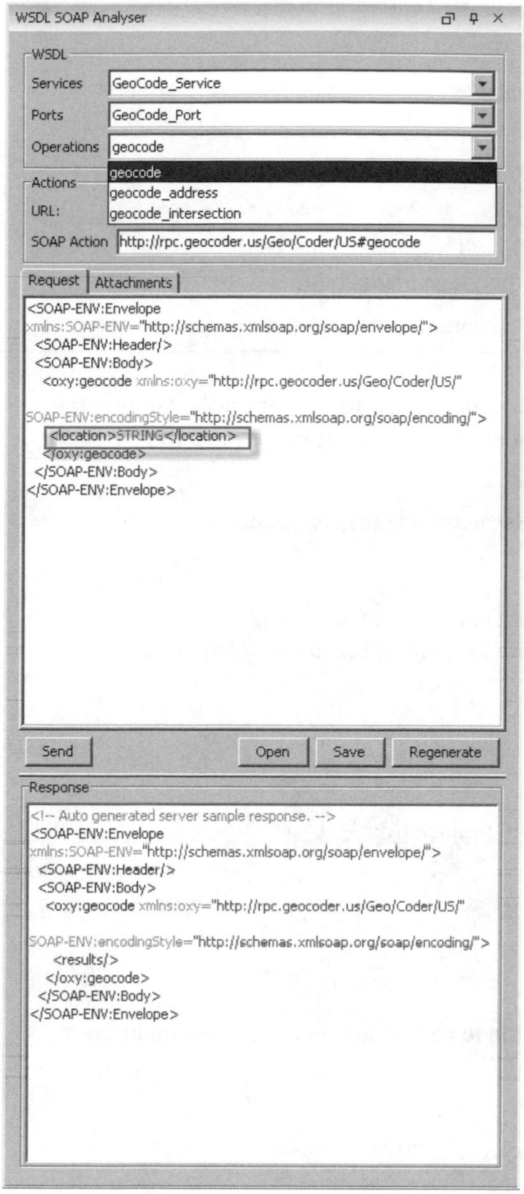

Figure 7-1. *The WSDL SOAP Analyser panel loaded with the geocoder.us WSDL*

The values shown in the three other subpanels depend on the *operation* you select. The four subpanels list the parameters described in Table 7-1.

Table 7-1. *Panels and Parameters from the WSDL Soap Analyser in oXygen*

Panel	Parameter	Explanation
WSDL	Services	Drop-down menu of services (for example, GeoCode_Service)
	Ports	Drop-down menu of ports (for example, GeoCode_Port)
	Operations	Drop-down menu of operations (for example, geocode)
Actions	URL	For example, http://rpc.geocoder.us/service/soap/
	SOAP action	For example, http://rpc.geocoder.us/Geo/Coder/US#geocode
Request		The body of the request (you fill in the parameters)
Response		The body of the response (this is the result of the operation)

As someone interested in just using the geocode operation (rather understanding the underlying mechanics), you would jump immediately to the sample request that oXygen generates:

```
<SOAP-ENV:Envelope xmlns:SOAP-ENV="http://schemas.xmlsoap.org/soap/envelope/">
  <SOAP-ENV:Header/>
  <SOAP-ENV:Body>
    <oxy:geocode xmlns:oxy="http://rpc.geocoder.us/Geo/Coder/US/"
      SOAP-ENV:encodingStyle="http://schemas.xmlsoap.org/soap/encoding/">
      <location>STRING</location>
    </oxy:geocode>
  </SOAP-ENV:Body>
</SOAP-ENV:Envelope>
```

To look up the address of Apress, you would replace this:

```
<location>STRING</location>
```

with the following:

```
<location>2855 Telegraph Ave, Berkeley CA 94705</location>
```

and hit the Send button on the Request subpanel to get the following to show up in the Response subpanel:

```
<?xml version="1.0" encoding="UTF-8"?>
<SOAP-ENV:Envelope xmlns:xsi="http://www.w3.org/2001/XMLSchema-instance"
  xmlns:SOAP-ENC="http://schemas.xmlsoap.org/soap/encoding/"
  xmlns:SOAP-ENV="http://schemas.xmlsoap.org/soap/envelope/"
  xmlns:xsd="http://www.w3.org/2001/XMLSchema"
  SOAP-ENV:encodingStyle="http://schemas.xmlsoap.org/soap/encoding/">
  <SOAP-ENV:Body>
    <namesp6:geocodeResponse xmlns:namesp6="http://rpc.geocoder.us/Geo/Coder/US/">
      <geo:s-gensym23 xsi:type="SOAP-ENC:Array"
                      xmlns:geo="http://rpc.geocoder.us/Geo/Coder/US/"
        SOAP-ENC:arrayType="geo:GeocoderAddressResult[1]">
        <item xsi:type="geo:GeocoderAddressResult">
          <number xsi:type="xsd:int">2855</number>
```

```
                <lat xsi:type="xsd:float">37.858276</lat>
                <street xsi:type="xsd:string">Telegraph</street>
                <state xsi:type="xsd:string">CA</state>
                <zip xsi:type="xsd:int">94705</zip>
                <city xsi:type="xsd:string">Berkeley</city>
                <suffix xsi:type="xsd:string"/>
                <long xsi:type="xsd:float">-122.260070</long>
                <type xsi:type="xsd:string">Ave</type>
                <prefix xsi:type="xsd:string"/>
            </item>
        </geo:s-gensym23>
    </namesp6:geocodeResponse>
  </SOAP-ENV:Body>
</SOAP-ENV:Envelope>
```

There you have it. Let's review what oXygen and a WSDL document could accomplish for you:

- You can get a list of *operations* available for the services and ports defined in the WSDL (not atypically one service and port combination).

- You are given a template for the body of the request with an indication of the data type of what you need to fill in.

- oXygen packages up the request, issues the HTTP request, handles the response, and presents you with the results.

To confirm that you understand the nuances of the geocode SOAP call, you can rewrite the SOAP request as a curl invocation—once you notice the role played by the two parameters that oXygen does pick up from the WSDL document:

- The SOAP action of http://rpc.geocoder.us/Geo/Coder/US#geocode. In SOAP 1.1, the version of SOAP used for geocoder.us, the SOAP action is transmitted as a SOAPAction HTTP request header.

- The URL (or *location*) to target the SOAP call: http://rpc.geocoder.us/service/soap/.

SOAP 1.1 AND SOAP 1.2

Ideally, one wouldn't need to dive too much into the SOAP protocol—after all, the whole point of SOAP is to make access to web services look like programming objects on your own desktop or server. But libraries and services do seem to have crucial dependences on the actual version of SOAP being used (for example).

SOAP has become a W3C Recommendation. The latest version of SOAP is 1.2:

http://www.w3.org/TR/soap12-part1/

Earlier versions of SOAP are still very much in use—maybe even more so than version 1.2. Version 1.1 is specified here:

http://www.w3.org/TR/2000/NOTE-SOAP-20000508/

Here are a few salient differences between the two specifications (the differences are described in detail at `http://www.w3.org/TR/2007/REC-soap12-part0-20070427/#L4697`):

- Different namespaces for the SOAP envelope (`http://www.w3.org/2003/05/soap-envelope` for version 1.2 and `http://schemas.xmlsoap.org/soap/envelope/` for version 1.1)—a practical heuristic to help spot which version of SOAP you are dealing with.

- Different use of the `SOAPAction` parameter for the SOAP HTTP binding. In SOAP 1.2, a `SOAPAction` HTTP request header is no longer used.

- The use of an HTTP response header of `Content-Type` "application/soap+xml" to identify SOAP 1.2.

I point out these differences because libraries and toolsets support different versions of SOAP.

You can now replicate this call with `curl`:

```
curl -v -X POST -H "SOAPAction: http://rpc.geocoder.us/Geo/Coder/US#geocode"➡
--data-binary "<SOAP-ENV:Envelope xmlns:SOAP-ENV='http://schemas.xmlsoap.org/soap/➡
envelope/'><SOAP-ENV:Header/><SOAP-ENV:Body><oxy:geocode xmlns:oxy=➡
'http://rpc.geocoder.us/Geo/Coder/US/' SOAP-ENV:encodingStyle='http://schemas.➡
xmlsoap.org/soap/encoding/'><location>2855 Telegraph Ave, Berkeley, CA</location>➡
</oxy:geocode></SOAP-ENV:Body></SOAP-ENV:Envelope>"➡
http://rpc.geocoder.us/service/soap/
```

Note that you need to know the `SOAPaction` header and URL of the SOAP call *only* if you are trying to understand all the details of the HTTP request and response. oXygen was just being helpful in pointing out those parameters. They, however, were not needed to fill out an address or interpret the latitude or longitude contained in the response.

■Note If you're wondering why I'm not using Flickr for my concrete example, Flickr does not offer a WSDL document even though it does present a SOAP interface. I'll return to discussing Flickr in the later section called "The Flickr API via SOAP."

Even without access to oXygen or the Eclipse Web Services Explorer, you can use Tomi Vanek's WSDL XSLT-based viewer (`http://tomi.vanek.sk/index.php?page=wsdl-viewer`) to make sense of a WSDL document. For example, take a look at the results for the geocoder.us WSDL document:

```
http://www.w3.org/2000/06/webdata/xslt?xslfile=http://tomi.vanek.sk/xml/➡
wsdl-viewer.xsl&amp;xmlfile=http://geocoder.us/dist/eg/clients/GeoCoderPHP.wsdl&amp;➡
transform=Submit
```

Using Python's SOAPpy

Let's take a look how to use the geocoder.us WSDL using the `SOAPpy` library in Python.

■**Note** You can download SOAPpy from `http://pywebsvcs.sourceforge.net/`. Mark Pilgrim's *Dive Into Python* provides a tutorial for SOAPpy at `http://www.diveintopython.org/soap_web_services/index.html`.

The following piece of Python code shows the process of creating a WSDL proxy, asking for the methods (or operations) that are defined in the WSDL document, and then calling the geocode method and parsing the results:

```python
from SOAPpy import WSDL

wsdl_url = r'http://geocoder.us/dist/eg/clients/GeoCoderPHP.wsdl'
server = WSDL.Proxy(wsdl_url)

# let's see what operations are supported
server.show_methods()

# geocode the Apress address
address = "2855 Telegraph Ave, Berkeley, CA"
result = server.geocode(location=address)
print "latitude and longitude: %s, %s" % (result[0]['lat'], result[0]['long'])
```

This produces the following output (edited for clarity):

```
Method Name: geocode_intersection
   In #0: intersection  ((u'http://www.w3.org/2001/XMLSchema', u'string'))
   Out #0: results  ((u'http://rpc.geocoder.us/Geo/Coder/US/',
u'ArrayOfGeocoderIntersectionResult'))

Method Name: geocode_address
   In #0: address  ((u'http://www.w3.org/2001/XMLSchema', u'string'))
   Out #0: results  ((u'http://rpc.geocoder.us/Geo/Coder/US/',
u'ArrayOfGeocoderAddressResult'))

Method Name: geocode
   In #0: location  ((u'http://www.w3.org/2001/XMLSchema', u'string'))
   Out #0: results  ((u'http://rpc.geocoder.us/Geo/Coder/US/',
u'ArrayOfGeocoderResult'))

latitude and longitude: 37.858276, -122.26007
```

Notice the reference to XML schema types in describing the location parameter for geocode. The type definitions come, as one expects, from the WSDL document.

The concision of this code shows WSDL and SOAP in good light.

USING SOAP FROM PHP

There are several choices of libraries for consuming SOAP in PHP:

- NuSOAP (http://sourceforge.net/projects/nusoap/)

- PEAR::SOAP package (http://pear.php.net/package/SOAP)

- The built-in SOAP library in PHP 5 (http://us2.php.net/soap), which is available if PHP is installed with the enable-soap flag

In this book, I use the PEAR::SOAP library.

Using PHP PEAR::SOAP

Let's do the straight-ahead PHP PEAR::SOAP invocation of geocode.us. You'll the same pattern of loading the WSDL document using a SOAP/WSDL library, packaging up a named parameter (location) in the request, and then parsing the results.

```php
<?php
# example using PEAR::SOAP + Geocoder SOAP search
require 'SOAP/Client.php';

# let's look up Apress
$address = '2855 Telegraph Avenue, Berkeley, CA 94705'; // your Google search terms

$wsdl_url = "http://geocoder.us/dist/eg/clients/GeoCoderPHP.wsdl";

# true to indicate that it is a WSDL url.
$soap = new SOAP_Client($wsdl_url,true);

$params = array(
    'location'=>$address
  );

$results = $soap->call('geocode', $params);

# include some fault handling code
if(PEAR::isError($results)) {
    $fault = $results->getFault();
    print "Error number " . $fault->faultcode . " occurred\n";
    print "      " . $fault->faultstring . "\n";
} else {
    print "The latitude and longitude for address is: {$results[0]->lat},
{$results[0]->long}";
}
?>
```

■**Note** I have not been able to figure out how to use `PEAR::SOAP` to tell me the operations that are available for a given WSDL file.

Amazon ECS

Now that you have studied the `geocoder.us` service, which has three SOAP methods, each with a single input parameter, let's turn to a more complicated example, the Amazon E-Commerce Service (ECS):

```
http://www.amazon.com/E-Commerce-Service-AWS-home-page/b?ie=UTF8&node=12738641
```

See the "Setting Up an Amazon ECS Account" sidebar to learn about how to set up an Amazon ECS account.

SETTING UP AN AMAZON ECS ACCOUNT

To use the service, you need to obtain keys by registering an account (like with Flickr):

```
http://www.amazon.com/gp/aws/registration/registration-form.html
```

If you already have an account, you can find your keys again:

```
http://aws-portal.amazon.com/gp/aws/developer/account/index.html/?ie=UTF8&
action=access-key
```

You get an access key ID and a secret access key to identify yourself and your agents to AWS. You can also use an X.509 certificate, which the Amazon interface can generate for you.

Although I focus here on the SOAP interface, ECS also has a REST interface. The WSDL for AWS-ECS is found at

```
http://webservices.amazon.com/AWSECommerceService/AWSECommerceService.wsdl?
```

Using one of the SOAP/WSDL toolkits I presented in the previous section (for example, oXygen, the Eclipse Web Services Explorer, or Vanek's WSDL viewer), you can easily determine the 20 operations that are currently defined by the WSDL document. Here I show you how to use the `ItemSearch` operation.

If you use oXygen to formulate a template for a SOAP request, you'll get the following:

```
<?xml version="1.0" encoding="UTF-8"?>
<SOAP-ENV:Envelope xmlns:SOAP-ENV="http://schemas.xmlsoap.org/soap/envelope/">
  <SOAP-ENV:Header/>
  <SOAP-ENV:Body>
    <ItemSearch
      xmlns="http://webservices.amazon.com/AWSECommerceService/2007-07-16">
      <AWSAccessKeyId>STRING</AWSAccessKeyId>
```

```
        [5 tags]
      <Shared>
          [40 tags]
      </Shared>
      <Request>
          [40 tags]
      </Request>
    </ItemSearch>
  </SOAP-ENV:Body>
</SOAP-ENV:Envelope>
```

Let's say you wanted to look for books with the keyword flower. To create the proper request, you'll need to figure out which of the many tags you must keep and how to fill out the values that you need to fill out. Through reading the documentation for ItemSearch (http://docs.amazonwebservices.com/AWSECommerceService/2007-07-16/DG/ItemSearch.html) and trial and error, you can boil down the request template to the following:

```
<SOAP-ENV:Envelope xmlns:SOAP-ENV="http://schemas.xmlsoap.org/soap/envelope/">
  <SOAP-ENV:Header/>
  <SOAP-ENV:Body>
    <ItemSearch
      xmlns="http://webservices.amazon.com/AWSECommerceService/2007-07-16">
      <AWSAccessKeyId>STRING</AWSAccessKeyId>
      <Request>
        <Keywords>STRING</Keywords>
        <SearchIndex>STRING</SearchIndex>
      </Request>
    </ItemSearch>
  </SOAP-ENV:Body>
</SOAP-ENV:Envelope>
```

You can pull together a full request by filling out your Amazon key and entering flower and Books for the <Keywords> and <SearchIndex> into a curl invocation:

```
curl -H "SOAPAction: http://soap.amazon.com" -d "<?xml version='1.0'➥
encoding='UTF-8'?><SOAP-ENV:Envelope xmlns:SOAP-ENV='http://schemas.xmlsoap.org/➥
soap/envelope/'><SOAP-ENV:Header/><SOAP-ENV:Body><ItemSearch➥
xmlns='http://webservices.amazon.com/AWSECommerceService/2007-07-16'>➥
<AWSAccessKeyId>[AMAZON-KEY]</AWSAccessKeyId><Request><Keywords>flower</Keywords>➥
<SearchIndex>Books</SearchIndex></Request></ItemSearch></SOAP-ENV:Body>➥
</SOAP-ENV:Envelope>" http://soap.amazon.com/onca/soap?Service=AWSECommerceService
```

to which you get something like this:

```
<?xml version="1.0" encoding="UTF-8"?>
<SOAP-ENV:Envelope xmlns:SOAP-ENV="http://schemas.xmlsoap.org/soap/envelope/"
  xmlns:SOAP-ENC="http://schemas.xmlsoap.org/soap/encoding/"
  xmlns:xsi="http://www.w3.org/2001/XMLSchema-instance"
  xmlns:xsd="http://www.w3.org/2001/XMLSchema">
```

```
  <SOAP-ENV:Body>
    <ItemSearchResponse
      xmlns="http://webservices.amazon.com/AWSECommerceService/2007-07-16">
      <OperationRequest>
[....]
      </OperationRequest>
      <Items>
        <Request>
          <IsValid>True</IsValid>
          <ItemSearchRequest>
            <Keywords>flower</Keywords>
            <SearchIndex>Books</SearchIndex>
          </ItemSearchRequest>
        </Request>
        <TotalResults>34489</TotalResults>
        <TotalPages>3449</TotalPages>
        <Item>
          <ASIN>0812968069</ASIN>
        <DetailPageURL>
          http://www.amazon.com/gp/redirect.html%3FASIN=0812968069%26➥
tag=ws%26lcode=sp1%26cID=2025%26ccmID=165953%26location=/o/ASIN/0812968069%253F➥
SubscriptionId=0Z8Z8FYGP01Q0OKF5802</DetailPageURL>
          <ItemAttributes>
            <Author>Lisa See</Author>
            <Manufacturer>Random House Trade Paperbacks</Manufacturer>
            <ProductGroup>Book</ProductGroup>
            <Title>Snow Flower and the Secret Fan: A Novel</Title>
          </ItemAttributes>
        </Item>
[...]
      </Items>
    </ItemSearchResponse>
  </SOAP-ENV:Body>
</SOAP-ENV:Envelope>
```

Notice what makes this example more complicated than geocoder.us:

- There are many more operations.

- There are many more parameters, and it's not obvious what is mandatory without reading the documentation and experimenting.

- The XML in the request and response involve complex types. Notice that <Keywords> and <SearchIndex> are wrapped within <Request>. This representation means you have to understand how to get your favorite SOAP library to package up the request and handle the response.

Using the Python SOAPpy library, you perform the same SOAP call with the following:

```
# amazon search using WSDL
KEY = "[AMAZON-KEY]"

from SOAPpy import WSDL

class amazon_ecs(object):
    def __init__(self, key):
        AMAZON_WSDL =
"http://webservices.amazon.com/AWSECommerceService/AWSECommerceService.wsdl?"
        self.key = key
        self.server = WSDL.Proxy(AMAZON_WSDL)
    def ItemSearch(self,Keywords,SearchIndex):
        return self.server.ItemSearch(AWSAccessKeyId=self.key,Request=➡
{'Keywords':Keywords,'SearchIndex':SearchIndex})


if __name__ == "__main__":
    aws = amazon_ecs(KEY)
    results= aws.ItemSearch('flower','Books')
    print results.Items.TotalPages,  results.Items.TotalResults
    for item in results.Items.Item:
        print item.ASIN, item.DetailPageURL, item.ItemAttributes.Author
```

Notice in particular how to represent the nested parameters in this:

```
self.server.ItemSearch(AWSAccessKeyId=self.key,Request=➡
{'Keywords':Keywords,'SearchIndex':SearchIndex})
```

Also notice how to read off the nested elements in the XML response:

```
print results.Items.TotalPages,  results.Items.TotalResults
for item in results.Items.Item:
    print item.ASIN, item.DetailPageURL, item.ItemAttributes.Author
```

When you look at this Python code and my description of how to use oXygen to interface with Amazon ECS via WSDL and SOAP, you might think to yourself that doing so doesn't look that hard. The combination of WSDL and SOAP does indeed bring some undeniable conveniences such as the automated discovery of what methods are available to you as a programmer. However, my experience of SOAP and WSDL is that they are still a long way from plug-and-go technology—at least in the world of scripting languages such as PHP and Python. It took me a great amount of trial and error, reverse engineering, reading source code, and hunting around to even get to the point of distilling for you the various examples of how to use SOAP and WSDL you see here. I would have wanted to reduce using SOAP and WSDL to full-proof recipes that hid from you what was happening underneath.

For instance—returning to the example—I was not able to able to craft a satisfactory working example of using PEAR::SOAP to call ItemSearch. Some of the issues I struggled with included how to pass in parameters with complex types to a SOAP call, how to parse the results, and how to debug the entire process. I'd be willing to bet that there is in fact a way to make this call work with PEAR::SOAP or in some other PHP toolkit. However, if I had wanted to call this SOAP service only for a mashup, I would likely have given up even earlier on figuring out how to make it work.

Note It might be true that if you use Java or .NET, programming environments for which there is deep support for SOAP and WSDL, you might have an easier time using this technology. Don't let me discourage you from trying those tools. I hope to find out for myself whether libraries such as Axis from the Apache Project (http://ws.apache.org/axis/java/index.html) or the WSDL functionality in .NET do indeed make my life as a SOAP developer easier.

The Flickr API via SOAP

The Flickr SOAP request and response formats are documented here:

```
http://www.flickr.com/services/api/request.soap.html
http://www.flickr.com/services/api/response.soap.html
```

The first thing to notice about the Flickr SOAP interface is that *Flickr provides no WSDL document to tell us how to use it*. Hence, if you want to use Flickr SOAP, you need to figure out how call it directly yourself. But why bother? Flickr has a wonderfully supported REST interface that you already know how to use. If you go down the road of using the SOAP interface, you'll have to deal with many challenges, some of which I have already discussed.

Learning About Specific Web APIs

In the previous section, I showed you how to call web APIs that use XML-RPC and SOAP. That still leaves many APIs that fall under the name of REST—ones that look a lot like the Flickr REST interface. These APIs take some things we are familiar with from web browsers, such as going to a specific URL to get back some results and submitting HTML forms to make a query, but they have one important difference: instead of sending mostly HTML (which is directed at human consumption), you send primarily XML, a *lingua franca* of computer data exchange. For that reason, you should remind yourself of what you've learned from the previous chapters as you embark on a study of other REST APIs.

In the following sections, I'll make sense of the world of web APIs, covering how to find out what APIs are available and then how to use a particular API. I'll start my discussion by introducing perhaps the single most useful website about web APIs: Programmableweb.com. There's a lot of information that is both readily apparent and waiting to be discovered in this treasure trove of data.

Note Other directories of web services that are worth exploring are http://www.xmethods.net/, which lists publicly available SOAP services, and http://strikeiron.com/, a provider of commercial web services that you can try for free.

Programmableweb.com

Programmableweb.com, started and maintained by Jon Musser, is an excellent resource for learning about what APIs are available, the basic parameters for the APIs, and the mashups that use any given API. Some noteworthy sections are as follows:

- `http://www.programmableweb.com/apis` is the "API dashboard" that lists the latest APIs to be registered and the most popular APIs being used in mashups.

- `http://www.programmableweb.com/apilist/bycat` lists APIs by categories. Understanding the various categories that have emerged is helpful for understanding for which fields of endeavor people are making APIs.

- `http://www.programmableweb.com/apilist/bymashups` lists APIs by how many times they are used in the mashups registered at Programmableweb.com.

I highly recommend a close and periodic study of Programmableweb.com for anybody wanting to learn about web APIs and mashups. Let me show some of the things you can learn from the website, based both on what is directly presented on the site and on data that John Musser has sent me. Although web APIs and corresponding mashups are rapidly changing, the data (and derived results), accurate for August 11, 2007, demonstrates some trends that I think will hold for a while yet.

The first thing to know is that of the 494 web APIs in the database, we get the distribution of number of APIs by protocol supported shown in Table 7-2. Note that some APIs are multiply represented.

Table 7-2. *Number of APIs vs. Protocol in Programmableweb.com*

Protocol	Number of APIs with Support
REST	255
SOAP	131
XML-RPC	19
JavaScript	30
Other	16

Some other observations drawn from the database are as follows:

- Ninety-three APIs have WSDL files associated with them.

- Of the 131 APIs that support SOAP, 42 also support REST—leaving 89 that support SOAP but not REST. Eighty-eight APIs support only SOAP.

- XML-RPC is the only choice for nine APIs.

- JavaScript is listed as the exclusive protocol for 25 APIs.

The following are my conclusions based on this data:

- REST is the dominant mode of presenting web APIs, but a significant number of APIs exist where your only choice is SOAP.

- There are a relatively small number of APIs listing XML-RPC as the only choice of protocol.

It's therefore useful to know how to use SOAP and XML-RPC, even if they are not your first choice.

Note A large number of APIs list JavaScript as a protocol. I'll cover such APIs in the next chapter.

Table 7-3 lists the top 20 APIs on Programmableweb.com by mashup count and also lists the type of protocols supported by the API.

Table 7-3. *Top 21 APIs by Mashup Count*

API Name	Number of Mashups	Protocols Support
Google Maps	1110	JavaScript
Flickr	243	REST, SOAP, XML-RPC
Amazon E-Commerce Service	174	REST, SOAP
YouTube	149	REST, XML-RPC
Microsoft Virtual Earth	97	JavaScript
Yahoo! Maps	95	REST, JavaScript, Flash
411Sync	89	RSS input over HTTP, SOAP
eBay	89	SOAP, REST
del.icio.us	83	REST
Google Search	79	SOAP
Yahoo! Search	78	REST
Yahoo! Geocoding	66	REST
Technorati	40	REST
Yahoo! Image Search	31	REST
Yahoo! Local Search	30	REST
Last.fm	28	REST
Google home page	27	JavaScript
Google Ajax Search	24	JavaScript
Upcoming.org	21	REST
Windows Live Search	21	SOAP
Feedburner	21	REST

What can you do with this information? To learn about popular APIs, one approach would be to go down the list systematically to figure out how each works. Indeed, through the rest of the book, I'll cover many of the APIs in the table. The Flickr API is the second most used API in mashups and is a main subject throughout this book. I'll cover the JavaScript-based maps (first and foremost Google Maps but also Yahoo! Maps and Virtual Earth) first in Chapter 8 and then in depth in Chapter 13. I'll cover the Yahoo! Geocoding API extensively also in Chapter 13. I'll cover various search APIs (Google Search, Yahoo! Search, Yahoo! Image Search, and Windows

Live Search) in Chapter 19. Finally, I'll cover the del.icio.us API in Chapter 14 on social book-marking. Indeed, the fact that I cover many APIs clustered by subject matter indicates that it is a natural way to think about APIs.

YouTube

YouTube is probably the most famous video-sharing site on the Web—and it also uses tagging as one way of organizing content. The YouTube API is documented at http://www.youtube.com/dev.

The YouTube API supports both a REST interface and an XML-RPC interface. The examples I give in this section use the REST interface. You can find a list of methods at http://www.youtube.com/dev_docs.

To use the API, you need to set up your own development profile; see http://www.youtube.com/my_profile_dev.

An interesting feature of the registration process is that you enter your own secret (instead of having one set by YouTube). When you submit your profile information, you then get a "developer ID." The following are some sample calls. To get the user profile for a user (for example, rdhyee), you do an HTTP GET on the following:

```
http://www.youtube.com/api2_rest?method=youtube.users.get_profile&➥
dev_id={youtube-key}&user=rdhyee
```

YouTube will send you a response something like this:

```
<?xml version="1.0" encoding="utf-8"?>
<ut_response status="ok">
  <user_profile>
    <first_name>Raymond</first_name>
    <last_name/>
    <about_me/>
    <age>40</age>
    <video_upload_count>2</video_upload_count>
    <video_watch_count>102</video_watch_count>
    [....]
  </user_profile>
</ut_response>
```

To get the list of rdhyee's favorite videos, use this:

```
http://www.youtube.com/api2_rest?method=youtube.users.list_favorite_videos&➥
dev_id={youtube-key}&user=rdhyee
```

To get details of a video with an ID of XHnE4umovw4, use this:

```
http://www.youtube.com/api2_rest?method=youtube.videos.get_details&➥
dev_id={youtube-key} &video_id=XHnE4umovw4
```

To get videos for the tag HolidayWeekend, use this:

```
http://www.youtube.com/api2_rest?method=youtube.videos.list_by_tag&➥
dev_id={youtube-key}&tag=HolidayWeekend&page=1&per_page=100
```

There's more to the API, but you can get a feel for how it works through these examples.

■**Caution** Expect the YouTube API to evolve into something more like the rest of Google's APIs: `http://code.google.com/apis/youtube/overview.html`.

GData and the Blogger API

The Atom Publishing Protocol (APP), a companion to the Atom Syndication Format (Atom 1.0) described in Chapter 2, represents the next generation of the blogging APIs. APP is currently a draft IETF proposal:

`http://tools.ietf.org/wg/atompub/draft-ietf-atompub-protocol/`

which is linked from here:

`http://tools.ietf.org/wg/atompub/`

One of APP's biggest supporters thus far has been Google, which has implemented GData, which is based on Atom 1.0 and RSS 2.0 feeds, combined with APP. GData, which incorporates Google-specific extensions, is the foundation of the APIs for many of its services, including Google Base, Blogger, Google Calendar, Google Code Search, and Google Notebook:

`http://code.google.com/apis/gdata/index.html`

The API for Blogger is documented here:

`http://code.google.com/apis/blogger/developers_guide_protocol.html`

In the following sections, you'll learn the basics of the API for Blogger as a way of understanding GData and APP in general.

Obtaining an Authorization Token

The first thing you need to have is a Google account to use Blogger. If you don't have one, go to the following location to create one:

`https://www.google.com/accounts/NewAccount`

Next, with a Google account, you obtain an authorization token. One way to do so is to follow the procedure for ClientLogin (one of two Google authorization mechanisms) detailed here:

`http://code.google.com/apis/blogger/developers_guide_protocol.html#client_login`

Specifically, you make an HTTP POST request to the following location:

`https://www.google.com/accounts/ClientLogin`

The body must contain the following parameters (using the `application/x-www-form-urlencoded` content type):

`Email`: Your Google email (for example, `raymond.yee@gmail.com`)

Password: Your Google password

source: A string of the form *companyName-applicationName-versionID* to identify your program (for example, `mashupguide.net-Chap7-v1`)

service: The name of the Google service, which in this case is `blogger`

Using the example parameters listed here, you can package up the authorization request as the following `curl` invocation:

```
curl -v -X POST -d "Passwd={passwd}&source=mashupguide.net-Chap7-v1&➥
Email=raymond.yee%40gmail.com&service=blogger"➥
https://www.google.com/accounts/ClientLogin
```

If this call succeeds, you will get in the body of the response an `Auth` token (of the form `Auth=[AUTH-TOKEN]`). Retain the `AUTH-TOKEN` for your next calls.

Figuring Out Your Blogger User ID

If you don't have a blog on Blogger.com, create one here:

```
http://www.blogger.com/create-blog.g
```

Now figure out your Blogger user ID by going to and noting the URL associated with the View link (beside the Edit Profile link):

```
http://www.blogger.com/home
```

Your View link will be of the following form:

```
http://www.blogger.com/profile/{userID}
```

For example, my blog profile is as follows:

```
http://www.blogger.com/profile/13847941708302188690
```

So, my user ID is `13847941708302188690`.

Getting a List of a User's Blogs and a Blog's Posts

Note that Blogger lists user blogs in a user's profile:

```
http://www.blogger.com/profile/{userID}
```

From an API point of view, you can retrieve an Atom feed of a user's blog here:

```
http://www.blogger.com/feeds/{userID}/blogs
```

That the list of blogs is an Atom feed and not some custom-purpose XML (such as that coming out of the Flickr API) is useful. You can look at the feed of your blogs to pull out the blog ID for one of your blogs. For instance, one of my blogs is entitled "Hypotyposis Redux" and is listed in the feed with the following tag:

```
<id>tag:blogger.com,1999:user-354598769533.blog-5586336</id>
```

From this you can determine its blog ID of 5586336. With this `blogID`, you can now send HTTP `GET` requests to retrieve an Atom feed of posts here:

```
http://www.blogger.com/feeds/{blogID}/posts/default
```

For example:

```
http://www.blogger.com/feeds/5586336/posts/default
```

Creating a New Blog Entry

Let's now look at how to create a new post. A central design idea behind the Atom Publishing Protocol and hence its derivatives—GData generally and the Blogger API specifically—is the notion of a *uniform interface* based on the standard HTTP methods. At this point, it's useful to refer to the "Methods Definition" of the HTTP 1.1 specification (`http://www.w3.org/Protocols/rfc2616/rfc2616-sec9.html`), specifically the definition for `POST`:

> *The POST method is used to request that the origin server accept the entity enclosed in the request as a new subordinate of the resource identified by the Request-URI in the Request-Line.*

You may be surprised to read this definition of the `POST` method, considering, for instance, how POST is used for every single SOAP 1.1 call bound to HTTP—whether the call is for retrieving a simple piece of information, creating a new resource, or deleting it.

Let's see how to create an HTTP `POST` request to create a new blog entry and confirm how the process follows the earlier definition:

1. Create a blog entry formatted as an `<entry>` Atom element, something like this:

```
<entry xmlns='http://www.w3.org/2005/Atom'>
  <title type='text'>Using Blogger to demo APP</title>
  <content type='xhtml'>
    <div xmlns='http://www.w3.org/1999/xhtml'>
      <p>This message is being created from invoking the blogger
APP-based API.</p>
      <p>This process is documented at <a href="http://code.google.com/
apis/blogger/developers_guide_protocol.html#CreatingPosts">Blogger Data
API -- Creating Posts</a></p>
    </div>
  </content>
  <author>
    <name>Raymond Yee</name>
    <email>raymond.yee@gmail.com</email>
  </author>
</entry>
```

2. Save the file, say with the filename `blogger.message.1.xml`.

3. Issue the following `curl` invocation to `POST` the contents of your file to `http://www.blogger.com/feeds/{blogID}/posts/default`—which is the feed of all your entries for the blog—to create a new entry for the blog (a "new subordinate of the resource identified by the Request-URI").

```
curl -X POST -v --data-binary "@blogger.message.1.xml" -H "Content-Type:➥
application/atom+xml " -H "Authorization: GoogleLogin  auth=[AUTH-TOKEN]"➥
http://www.blogger.com/feeds/{blogID}/posts/default
```

4. If things go fine, you'll get an HTTP 201 Created code and an `<entry>` holding the new post. This `<entry>` tells you things such as the post ID of your new entry. The response will look like the following:

```
HTTP/1.1 201 Created
Content-Type: application/atom+xml; charset=UTF-8
Cache-Control: max-age=0, must-revalidate, private
Location: http://www.blogger.com/feeds/5586336/posts/default/409227349217351
7704
Content-Location: http://www.blogger.com/feeds/5586336/posts/default/4092273
492173517704
Transfer-Encoding: chunked
Date: Sat, 25 Aug 2007 14:38:49 GMT
Server: GFE/1.3
<?xml version='1.0' encoding='UTF-8'?><?xml-stylesheet href="http://www.b
logger.com/styles/atom.css" type="text/css"?><entryxmlns='http://www.w3.o
rg/2005/Atom'><id>tag:blogger.com,1999:blog-5586336.post-4092273492173517
704</id><published>2007-08-25T07:38:00.001-07:00</published><updated>2007
-08-25T07:38:49.607-07:00</updated><title type='text'>Using Blogger to de
mo APP</title><content type='html'>&lt;br /&gt;    &lt;div xmlns='http://
www.w3.org/1999/xhtml'&gt;&lt;br /&gt;
    &lt;p&gt;This message is being created from invoking the blogger APP-
based API.&lt;/p&gt;&lt;br /&gt;        &lt;p&gt;This process is documented
at &lt;a href='http://code.google.com/apis/blogger/developers_guide_proto
col.html#CreatingPosts'&gt;Blogger Data API -- Creating Posts&lt;/a&gt;&l
t;/p&gt;&lt;br /&gt;    &lt;/div&gt;&lt;br /&gt; </content><link rel='al
ternate' type='text/html' href='http://hypotyposis.blogspot.com/2007_08_0
1_archive.html#4092273492173517704' title='Using Blogger to demo APP'/><l
ink rel='replies' type='applicati* Connection #0to host www.blogger.com l
eft intact* Closing connection #0
```

5. In this example, the POST request created a new blog entry with a post ID of 40922734921735177.

Updating the Blog Entry

You can update your blog entry using an HTTP PUT request, in accordance to the HTTP 1.1 specification that states the following:

> *The PUT method requests that the enclosed entity be stored under the supplied Request-URI. If the Request-URI refers to an already existing resource, the enclosed entity SHOULD be considered as a modified version of the one residing on the origin server.*

Let's package this request for curl after first creating an updated message in the blogger.message.2.xml file:

```
curl -X PUT -v --data-binary "@blogger.message.2.xml" -H "Content-Type:➥
application/atom+xml " -H "Authorization: GoogleLogin  auth=[AUTH-TOKEN]"➥
http://www.blogger.com/feeds/{blogID}/posts/default/{postID}
```

If you are unfamiliar with using the HTTP PUT method, you're hardly alone. As mentioned in Chapter 6, there is little support for it. (Remember, for instance, that the HTML forms define the GET and POST methods.) Recognizing that PUT might not be supported by the client doing the entry update (or that firewalls might block PUT requests), you can tunnel the PUT request through a POST request like so:

```
curl -X POST -v --data-binary "@blogger.message.2.xml" -H "X-HTTP-Method-Override:➥
PUT"  -H "Content-Type: application/atom+xml " -H "Authorization: GoogleLogin➥
auth=[AUTH-TOKEN]"   http://www.blogger.com/feeds/{blogID}/posts/default/{postID}
```

Deleting a Blog Entry

You can use the HTTP DELETE method to delete an entry but send that request to the URL of the entry itself. As a curl invocation, the request looks like this:

```
curl -X DELETE -v -H "Content-Type: application/atom+xml " -H "Authorization:➥
GoogleLogin  auth=[AUTH-TOKEN]"➥
http://www.blogger.com/feeds/{blogID}/posts/default/{postID}
```

As with updating a blog entry, you can tunnel a DELETE request through an HTTP POST request using an "X-HTTP-Method-Override: DELETE" request header.

Using the Blogger API As a Uniform Interface Based on HTTP Methods

Now that you have seen how to use the Blogger API to retrieve feeds of blogs and blog entries, create new blog entries, update an entry, and delete an entry, you should notice how all these actions are performed while hewing closely to HTTP methods as they are actually defined in the HTTP specification. This pattern of using the HTTP methods as the fundamental methods of the API, in fact, repeats itself in all the APIs that are based on the Atom Publishing Protocol and therefore GData. Thus, the uniform interface of GData is the full collection of standard HTTP methods.

Summary

In this chapter, I discussed how to consume web APIs that use the XML-RPC and SOAP/WSDL protocols. Although these protocols, especially SOAP and WSDL, are geared toward simplifying the process for making calls to web services, they sometimes are fragile in practice. Consequently, if you use them, you should learn how to debug them with the techniques I showed you in this chapter.

With techniques to work with REST, XML-RPC, and SOAP web APIs in hand, you can then start moving beyond Flickr to look at a wide range of APIs. I showed you how to use Programmableweb.com to learn about those APIs and to draw some broad conclusions about APIs, the protocols they use, which ones are popular, and which subject matter they cover. I concluded this chapter with a study of the YouTube API (as an example of a simple REST API other than Flickr) and the Blogger API (as an instance of a uniform interface intimately tied to the HTTP methods). In the next chapter, you'll study JavaScript-based APIs and look at how to consume web APIs in the browser.

CHAPTER 8

■ ■ ■

Learning Ajax/JavaScript Widgets and Their APIs

In the previous two chapters, you studied web APIs, first that of Flickr and then of other applications. I showed you how to call APIs using REST, SOAP, and XML-RPC interfaces from PHP and Python. In this chapter, I'll begin an analysis of one extremely important context where web APIs are used: JavaScript inside the modern web browser—the stuff called Ajax.

The term Ajax was coined as shorthand for *Asynchronous JavaScript and XML*. In Chapter 10, I'll show you some of the underlying flow of data of Ajax when you learn how to fully exercise the Flickr API from JavaScript to create a mashup. In this chapter, I'll teach you how to use Ajax *widgets*, JavaScript-based programs created by others to express some functionality, as a way to a study of Ajax. Along the way, you'll learn how to use some debugging tools such as Firebug and the JavaScript Shell that will help you make sense of these widgets and, as I'll show you later, the whole range of Ajax programming.

In the context of contemporary Web 2.0 development, Ajax is a big deal, particularly for how it allows you to mash up data and services in new and easier ways. Ajax exploits the fact that modern web browsers are programmable and that they are inherently network applications. In addition to sending static HTML to web browsers, programmers can send JavaScript programs to run in the web browser. What can be done with this type of JavaScript-based client-side programming?

- You can achieve more dynamic interaction without having to reload the entire web page. This capability can be used, for instance, for drop-down menus and other widgets that we are used to having on the desktop.

- In particular, JavaScript can be used to get data via formal and informal web APIs from a server without having to reload the entire web page.

- Widgets can be created and deployed by other people. These widgets can be used to combine data and services and shown to other people. (Google Maps is the single most mashed-up API/service on the public Internet.)

JavaScript and DHTML are not new phenomena but have become extremely popular under the banner of Ajax. Jesse James Garrett says it well:[1]

But seeing Ajax as a purely technological phenomenon misses the point. If anything, Ajax is even more of a sea change for designers than it is for developers. Sure, there are a lot of ways in which developers need to change their thinking as they make the transition from building traditional web applications to building Ajax applications. But for those of us who design user experiences, the change brought about by Ajax is even more profound.

This chapter concentrates on helping you use Ajax to mash up data and services by doing the following:

- Pointing out the Ajax-based parts of Flickr and contrasting the old style of web development that involved the reloading of an entire page to new-style development in which more logic is pushed to the client, opening up more opportunities for integration

- Pointing out ways to see the difference between Ajax and non-Ajax apps by turning off JavaScript in the browser

- Introducing the Yahoo! UI Library as a specific example of various JavaScript widget libraries

- Introducing Google Maps, the single most used API as an example of a JavaScript widget

- Using one of the JavaScript widget libraries to demonstrate how to use a widget (for example, the TreeView widget)

- Showing how to write a basic Greasemonkey script as a way of mashing up services and data in the browser

What You Need to Know

Ajax, along with all its attendant use of JavaScript and the modern web browser, is a rich subject, as can be seen in the myriad of books that have been published recently on the subject. I'll put Ajax in the larger context of the programmable web browser. To become a master programmer of the web browser, you should understand the following:

- Both how an ideal W3C DOM standards-compliant browser works and how various browsers actually work in various areas: how JavaScript is implemented, object model behavior, CSS, and events

- JavaScript-based APIs and widgets such as Google Maps—what they are and how to use them

- Nonbrowser environments for JavaScript, such as Google Gadgets, Yahoo! Widgets, and Adobe Acrobat

---

1. *Ajax Hacks* by Bruce Perry (O'Reilly & Associates, 2006)

- Extension mechanisms in browsers (such as Firefox add-ons)

- JavaScript and browser debugging tools such as Firebug

- JavaScript libraries: how they relate and what can be intermixed—and which ones are tied to which web programming frameworks

- What people have done already on all these fronts using JavaScript and remixing the browser

- How to write JavaScript and JavaScript widgets that can be reused by other people, including cross-platform JavaScript

- What you can do in terms of mashups

Fortunately, you do not need to know all these things to merely get started.

What Difference Does Ajax Make?

To convince yourself that JavaScript is at work in web applications such as Flickr, Google Maps, and Gmail, you can turn off JavaScript in your browser and see what changes in the behavior of the application.

To turn off JavaScript in your browser, do the following, depending on which browser you're using:

- In Firefox, uncheck Tools ➤ Options ➤ Content ➤ Enable JavaScript.

- In Internet Explorer, check Tools ➤ Internet Options ➤ Security ➤ Custom Level ➤ Scripting ➤ Active Scripting ➤ Disable.

- In Opera, uncheck Tools ➤ Quick Preferences ➤ Enable JavaScript.

- In Safari, uncheck Safari ➤ Preferences ➤ Security ➤ Enable JavaScript.

Once you have JavaScript turned off, notice the following changes in Flickr and Google Maps:

- In Flickr pages for a specific photo (in other words, `http://flickr.com/photos/{user-d}/{photo-id}/`), you will see the message "To take full advantage of Flickr, you should use a JavaScript-enabled browser and install the latest version of the Macromedia Flash Player." All the buttons on top of the picture no longer function. Instead of clicking the title, description, and tags to start editing them, you have to click a link (Edit Title, Description, and Tags) before doing so.

- Notice that some apps will gracefully support non-JavaScript-enabled browsers— particularly Google Maps. With JavaScript turned off, you no longer see the pan and zoom new-style maps but an old-style map that provides links to move north, south, east, or west or to change the zoom level.

When using JavaScript, there are interesting and important issues regarding usability/ accessibility. Many computers, including mobile devices, do not use JavaScript. How should apps gracefully deal with browsers that don't use JavaScript? Some apps are so dependent on JavaScript that a non-JavaScript version would look drastically different.

Now that you have seen the effects of turning off JavaScript in the browser, be sure to turn it back on if you want to learn how to use JavaScript-based widgets and APIs.

Learning Firebug, DOM Inspector, and JavaScript Shell

In learning Ajax and widgets/applications based on Ajax, I recommend using Firefox, the DOM Inspector, and the JavaScript Shell (bookmarklet) to manipulate live web pages and widgets. This combination allows for live interaction with the little apps; you can load a running map, analyze the details of how it is working while running, and issue commands that take immediate effect.

■**Note**   Even if you work primarily in a web browser other than Firefox, you can still gain a tremendous amount of insight about JavaScript programming using the Firefox-based tools.

Moreover, the right tools can help you make sense of complicated stuff such as the Browser Object Model and the Document Object Model (DOM) by letting you interact with the browser, test code, and so on. I will use these tools in the rest of the chapter to support this experimental/reverse-engineering approach.

Using the DOM Inspector

The DOM Inspector allows you to look at the HTML DOM as a tree and make changes in that DOM. The DOM Inspector comes with Firefox but is not installed by default in Windows. To install it in Windows, you need to choose explicitly to install the DOM Inspector in the installation process. Consult the following documentation to learn how to use the DOM Inspector:

`http://kb.mozillazine.org/DOM_Inspector`

Remember, you can invoke the DOM Inspector by selecting Tools ➤ DOM Inspector from the Firefox menu.

Using the Firebug Extension for Firefox

I highly recommend installing the Firefox add-on called Firebug. In many ways, Firebug is an enhancement of the DOM Inspector. In addition to being able to view and edit the contents of the DOM, you also get some very nice JavaScript debugging functionality.

To install this extension in Firefox, navigate to `http://getfirebug.com`, give permission to Firefox to install the extensions from that domain, and then install the extension. (As with installing all Firefox add-ons, you need to restart the browser to complete the installation.)

Figure 8-1 shows Firebug when I was using its Inspect HTML functionality to examine the title of a Flickr photo.

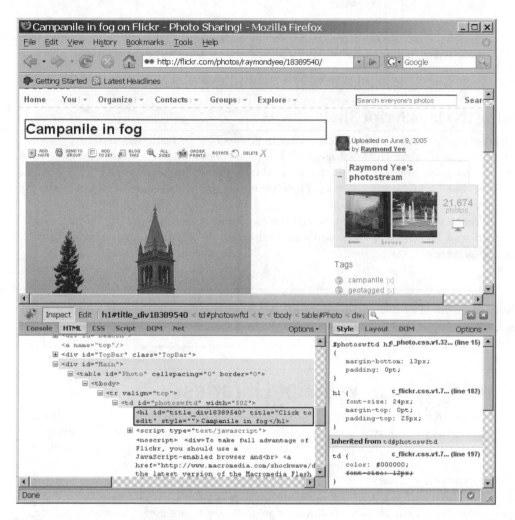

Figure 8-1. *Firebug applied to a Flickr photo page. (Reproduced with permission of Yahoo! Inc. ® 2007 by Yahoo! Inc. YAHOO! and the YAHOO! logo are trademarks of Yahoo! Inc.)*

Important features of Firebug include the following:

- The ability to view live source (that is, what the HTML of the DOM is at the moment, not what the original source was).

- Instant HTML editing (you can edit the HTML in Firebug and see the changes reflected on the page).

- You can see the request and response headers, which is invaluable during debugging.

Firebug can therefore be useful for the following tasks:

- Learning CSS by changing <style> elements and seeing the effects (for example, the cascading process is shown, and overridden properties are struck out).

- Tracking uses of the XMLHttpRequest object (the object, which we will see in the next chapters, is the one often responsible for the exchange of XML or JSON by the browser). You can use Firebug to see whether and what data is actually being loaded.

- Using inspect mode to mouse over a piece of a web page and see the corresponding HTML.

Using the JavaScript Shell

The JavaScript Shell is a bookmarklet to use in Firefox that you can find at https://www.squarefree.com/bookmarklets/webdevel.html. A *bookmarklet* is a short piece of JavaScript that you can treat like a browser bookmark but that does some function when you click it. With the JavaScript Shell, you can run snippets of JavaScript code that will execute in the context of the page in which you invoked the shell.

To install the JavaScript Shell, just drag it to your Links toolbar in Firefox. To invoke the JavaScript Shell, put the page you want in the foreground, and click the JavaScript Shell bookmarklet.

■**Note** In addition to the tools already mentioned, there is Firebug Lite to use with Internet Explorer, Opera, and Safari.[2] You might consider using the Venkman JavaScript Debugger.[3]

Working with JavaScript Libraries

Instead of programming directly for a specific browser, it is often useful to work at a higher level of abstraction by working with a JavaScript library. There are many cross-browser differences and fine technical details that are best left to the JavaScript specialist. JavaScript libraries typically allow you to program the browser as a generic entity rather than having to account for the differences among browsers.

Ideally there would be one obvious choice for an excellent JavaScript library, and everyone would use it. The current situation is that there are many JavaScript libraries, and it is not at all obvious how they compare. For instance, Simon Willison, a well-respected web developer, wrote that the big four are the following:[4]

- Dojo

- Mochikit

- Prototype/script.aculo.us

- Yahoo! UI Library (YUI)

Others have pointed out Rico (which is built on top of Protoype) and OpenLaszlo.[5] In this chapter and those that follow, I will concentrate on using YUI.

---

2. http://www.getfirebug.com/lite.html

3. http://www.mozilla.org/projects/venkman/

4. http://simonwillison.net/2006/Jun/26/libraries/

5. http://www.openlaszlo.org/

YUI Widgets

You can find the Yahoo UI Library at `http://developer.yahoo.com/yui/` where you can read "Yahoo! UI Library—Getting Started."[6] The best way is to learn about the library is to look around and try the various examples. Also use the JavaScript Shell and Firebug extension to learn how things work.

Try the pieces on the Yahoo! site (for example, the TreeView controller at `http://developer.yahoo.com/yui/examples/treeview/index.html`), and enter some commands on the JavaScript Shell. To help you out, we will walk through the use of two YUI widgets: the calendar and the TreeView widget.

Using the YUI Calendar

The YUI Calendar component (`http://developer.yahoo.com/yui/calendar/`) presents a browser-based calendar interface from which users can select one or more dates. To learn how to use it, you can try the calendar examples:

- `http://developer.yahoo.com/yui/examples/calendar/index.html` (refer to the API documentation)

- `http://developer.yahoo.com/yui/docs/YAHOO.widget.Calendar.html` (to get a list of methods for the widget)

You can use the Firebug extension or JavaScript Shell to get a feel for how to program the component:

1. Go to `http://developer.yahoo.com/yui/examples/calendar/quickstart.html`.

2. Click a date.

3. In the console of Firebug or the JavaScript Shell, type the following to get back the date you selected (see Figure 8-2):

```
YAHOO.example.calendar.cal1.getSelectedDates()
```

4. Try other methods to see how the calendar works:

```
YAHOO.example.calendar.cal1.hide() // Hides the control
YAHOO.example.calendar.cal1.show() // Shows the control
// Sets month to February (change not visible until redrawn)
YAHOO.example.calendar.cal1.setMonth(1)
// Redraws the control using the YUI TreeView
YAHOO.example.calendar.cal1.render()
```

---

6. `http://developer.yahoo.com/yui/#start`

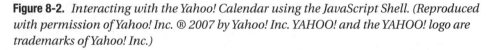

Figure 8-2. *Interacting with the Yahoo! Calendar using the JavaScript Shell. (Reproduced with permission of Yahoo! Inc. ® 2007 by Yahoo! Inc. YAHOO! and the YAHOO! logo are trademarks of Yahoo! Inc.)*

The TreeView component is a UI control that lets users interact with a tree structure (by, for instance, expanding or collapsing branches of the tree):

```
http://developer.yahoo.com/yui/treeview/
```

In addition to reading the API documentation for the TreeView component,[7] you can use Firebug and the JavaScript Shell to experiment with the component. To do so, follow these steps:

1. Go to `http://developer.yahoo.com/yui/examples/treeview/default_tree.html`.

2. In the console of Firebug or the JavaScript Shell, type the following to expand and collapse the tree, respectively:

   ```
   tree.expandAll()
   tree.collapseAll()
   ```

See how you can interactively learn how to use the YUI JavaScript widgets through using Firebug and the JavaScript Shell.

Installing YUI on Your Host

To use YUI in your own applications, you should set up YUI on your own web host. I will use a concrete example, `http://examples.mashupguide.net`, which is mapped to the Unix directory `~/examples.mashupguide.net`. Substitute your own values. My goal is to set up YUI so that it is accessible at `http://examples.mashupguide.net/lib/yui/`.

---

7. `http://developer.yahoo.com/yui/docs/YAHOO.widget.TreeView.html`

1. Download the library to your machine or your web hosting environment. Go to `http://developer.yahoo.com/yui/download/`.

2. Unzip and copy the files to the right location. In my case, I unzipped and copied the unzipped directory (which is named `yui`) to `/home/rdhyee/examples.mashupguide.net/lib/yui`, which maps to the `yui` directory at `http://examples.mashupguide.net/lib/yui/`. The important part of the library for runtime purposes is the `yui/build` directory.

With the files in your own directory, you can, for instance, look at the calendar example on my own server:

`http://examples.mashupguide.net/lib/yui/examples/calendar/quickstart.html`

Learning Google Maps

Just as there are different UI elements packaged up in one of the major JavaScript libraries, vendors have already started to create reusable JavaScript components. The most famous of these Ajax widgets is Google Maps. In this section, we'll look at how to embed a Google map using the Google Maps API. The online documentation on how to get started with the maps at the Google web site is good.[8] The approach given there, one that I can certainly recommend, is to give you source code for increasingly more complex examples, which you can copy and paste to your own site.

Here we will set up a simple map and then use the JavaScript Shell to work with a live map so that you can invoke a command and see an immediate response. The intended effect is that you see the widgets as dynamic programs that respond to commands, whether that command comes in a program or from you entering that command.

Use the Google Maps API to make a simple map:

1. Make sure you have a public web directory to host your map and know the URL of that directory. Any Google map that uses the free, public API needs to be publicly visible.

2. Go to the sign-up page for a key to access Google Maps.[9] You will need a key for any given domain in which you host Google Maps. (It is through these keys that Google regulates the use of the Google Maps API.)

3. Read the terms of service,[10] and if you agree to them, enter the URL directory on the host where you want to place your test file. For example, in my case, the URL is `http://examples.mashupguide.net/ch08`. Write down the resultant key.

4. Copy and paste the HTML code into your own page in your web-hosting directory. You should get something like the following (except that the code will have your API key):[11]

---

8. `http://www.google.com/apis/maps/documentation/#Introduction`

9. `http://www.google.com/apis/maps/signup.html`

10. `http://www.google.com/apis/maps/terms.html`

11. `http://maps.google.com/maps/api_signup?url=http%3A%2F%2Fexamples.mashupguide.net%2Fch08`

```
<!DOCTYPE html PUBLIC "-//W3C//DTD XHTML 1.0 Strict//EN"
  "http://www.w3.org/TR/xhtml1/DTD/xhtml1-strict.dtd">
<html xmlns="http://www.w3.org/1999/xhtml">
  <head>
    <meta http-equiv="content-type" content="text/html; charset=utf-8"/>
    <title>Google Maps JavaScript API Example</title>
    <script
      src="http://maps.google.com/maps?file=api&amp;v=2&amp;key=[API_key]"
      type="text/JavaScript"></script>
    <script type="text/JavaScript">

    //<![CDATA[

    function load() {
      if (GBrowserIsCompatible()) {
        var map = new GMap2(document.getElementById("map"));
        map.setCenter(new GLatLng(37.4419, -122.1419), 13);
      }
    }

    //]]>
    </script>
  </head>
  <body onload="load()" onunload="GUnload()">
    <div id="map" style="width: 500px; height: 300px"></div>
  </body>
</html>
```

5. Now make one modification to the example by removing the var keyword in front of map to make it a global variable that is thus accessible to the JavaScript Shell. That is, change the following:

```
var map = new GMap2(document.getElementById("map"));
to map = new GMap2(document.getElementById("map"));
```

to expose the map object to the JavaScript Shell utility.[12]

6. Invoke the JavaScript Shell for your map by hitting the JavaScript Shell bookmarklet in the context of your map. Type the following code fragments, and see what happens. (Note that another approach is to modify your code directly with these code fragments and reload your page.) One can correlate the actions to the documentation for version 2 of the Google Maps API.[13]

---

12. http://examples.mashupguide.net/ch08/google.map.html
13. http://www.google.com/apis/maps/documentation/reference.html#GMap2

To return the current zoom level of the map (which goes from 0 to 17, with 17 for the most detailed), use this:

```
map.getZoom()
```

13

To obtain the latitude and longitude of the center of the map, enter the following:

```
map.getCenter()
```

(37.4419, -122.1419)

To center the map around the Campanile for UC Berkeley, use this:

```
map.setCenter(new GLatLng(37.872035,-122.257844), 13);
```

You can pan to that location instead:

```
map.panTo(new GLatLng(37.872035,-122.257844));
```

To add a small map control (to control the zoom level), use the following:

```
map.addControl(new GSmallMapControl())
map.addControl(new GMapTypeControl())
```

To add GMap keyboard navigation so that you can pan and zoom with the keyboard, use this:

```
window.kh = new GKeyboardHandler(map)
```

[object Object]

To fully zoom out the map, use this:

```
map.setZoom(0)
```

To zoom in all the way, use the following:

```
map.setZoom(17)
```

To set the variable maptypes to an array holding three objects, use this:

```
maptypes = map.getMapTypes()
```

[object Object],[object Object],[object Object]

To get the name of the first entry in maptypes (1 corresponds to satellite, while 2 corresponds to the hybrid map type):

```
map.getMapTypes()[0].getName()
```

Map

To get the current map type, you can get the object and the name of that type object:

```
map.getCurrentMapType()
```

[object Object]

```
map.getCurrentMapType().getName()
```

Map

To set the map type to satellite, use the following:

```
map.setMapType(maptypes[1]);
```

You can zoom one level in and out if you are not already at the max or min zoom level:

```
map.zoomIn()
map.zoomOut()
```

To make an overlay, try the following:

```
point = new GLatLng (37.87309185260284, -122.25508689880371)
```

```
(37.87309185260284, -122.25508689880371)
```

```
marker = new GMarker(point)
```

[object Object]

```
map.addOverlay(marker);
```

To make something happen when you click the marker, type the following:

```
GEvent.addListener(marker, 'click', function() {
  marker.openInfoWindowHtml('hello'); })
```

[object Object]

There are many more features to explore, such as polylines, overlays, and draggable points. To learn more, I certainly recommend the "Google Maps API: Introduction" documentation.[14] I will also return to the topic of Google Maps in Chapters 10 and 13.

---

14. http://www.google.com/apis/maps/documentation/#Introduction

Accessing Flickr via JavaScript

In Chapter 10, we will be building a mashup that integrates Flickr data and Google Maps within the browser context. That is, we will need to call the Flickr API from JavaScript within the browser (in true Ajax style). Flickr provides JSON output to its API.[15]

In Chapter 4, I already presented some code that reads a Flickr feed in JSON format and renders it in HTML. In this section, I'll show you one basic way to use this JSON data from the Flickr API via JavaScript. Let's jump into how it works:

1. Go to the `flickr.photos.search` page in the Flickr Explorer (`http://www.flickr.com/ services/api/explore/?method=flickr.photos.search`), set the `tag` parameter to `flower`, and set the `per_page` parameter to 3 (to make for a more manageable number of photos for now). Do not sign the call. Hit the Call Method button, and grab the REST URL (below the results box). Substitute the `api_key` parameter with your own Flickr API key. You will get something like this:

   ```
   http://api.flickr.com/services/rest/?method=flickr.photos.search&➥
   api_key=<API_key>&tags=flower&per_page=3
   ```

   from which you get the Flickr XML output with which you are familiar from previous chapters.

2. Let's now study the JSON output by tacking on the parameter `format=json` to the URL.[16] Now you get the following (in a prettified rendition):

   ```
   jsonFlickrApi( {
      "photos" : {
         "page" : 1, "pages" : 283266, "perpage" : 3, "total" : "849797",
         "photo" : [ {"id" : "397677823", "owner" : "28374750@N00",
         "secret" : "cab3f3db01", "server" : "124", "farm" : 1, "
         title" : "DSC_0026", "ispublic" : 1, "isfriend" : 0, "isfamily" : 0}
         , {
            "id" : "397677820", "owner" : "28374750@N00",
            "secret" : "f70cf0bb19", "server" : "174", "farm" : 1,
            "title" : "red flowers", "ispublic" : 1, "isfriend" :
   0, "isfamily" : 0}
         , {
            "id" : "397677553", "owner" : "37015070@N00",
            "secret" : "7329c71748", "server" : "158", "farm" : 1,
            "title" : "Rose In Vase", "ispublic" : 1, "isfriend" : 0,
            "isfamily" : 0}
         ]}
      , "stat" : "ok"}
   )
   ```

---

15. `http://www.flickr.com/services/api/response.json.html`

16. `http://api.flickr.com/services/rest/?method=flickr.photos.search&api_key={api-key}&tags= flower&per_page=3&format=json`

Note what is being returned: a piece of JavaScript containing the function named jsonFlickrApi() with a single parameter, which is a JavaScript object that represents the photos.

3. Let's now write a bit of HTML and JavaScript to test how to write JavaScript to access the various pieces of the Flickr response:

```
<!DOCTYPE html PUBLIC "-//W3C//DTD XHTML 1.0 Transitional//EN"
"http://www.w3.org/TR/xhtml1/DTD/xhtml1-transitional.dtd">
<html xmlns="http://www.w3.org/1999/xhtml" xml:lang="en" lang="en">
  <head>
    <title>Flickr JSON</title>
  </head>
<script>
function jsonFlickrApi(rsp) {
  window.rsp = rsp;
}
</script>
<script src="http://api.flickr.com/services/rest/?method=flickr.photos.search➥
&api_key=<API_key>&tags=flower&per_page=3&format=json"></script>
</html>
```

You can load this page in your browser and invoke the JavaScript Shell to learn a few key lines to access parts of the response:

```
props(rsp.photos)
Fields: page, pages, perpage, photo, total
rsp.photos.perpage
3
rsp.photos.photo[0].id
397694840
```

4. Let's now have jsonFlickrApi() produce a display of the photos:

```
<!DOCTYPE html PUBLIC "-//W3C//DTD XHTML 1.0 Transitional//EN"
"http://www.w3.org/TR/xhtml1/DTD/xhtml1-transitional.dtd">
<html xmlns="http://www.w3.org/1999/xhtml" xml:lang="en" lang="en">
  <head>
    <title>Flickr JSON</title>
  </head>
<body>
  <script>
  function jsonFlickrApi(rsp) {
    window.rsp = rsp;
    var s = "";
    // http://farm{id}.static.flickr.com/{server-id}/{id}_{secret}_[mstb].jpg
    // http://www.flickr.com/photos/{user-id}/{photo-id}
    s = "total number is: " + rsp.photos.photo.length + "<br/>";
```

```
      for (var i=0; i < rsp.photos.photo.length; i++) {
        photo = rsp.photos.photo[i];
        t_url = "http://farm" + photo.farm + ".static.flickr.com/" +
          photo.server + "/" + photo.id + "_" + photo.secret + "_" + "t.jpg";
        p_url = "http://www.flickr.com/photos/" + photo.owner + "/" + photo.id;
        s +=  '<a href="' + p_url + '">' + '<img alt="'+ photo.title +
          '"src="' + t_url + '"/>' + '</a>';
      }
      document.writeln(s);
    }
    </script>
    <script src="http://api.flickr.com/services/rest/?method=flickr.photos.➥
    search&api_key=<API_key>&tags=flower&per_page=50&format=json"></script>
    </body>

  </html>
```

5. The previous example is simple but limited by the fact that loading JSON data immediately calls the function jsonFlickrApi(). You can customize the name of the callback function with the jsoncallback parameter (for example, jsoncallback=MyHandler). You can also use the nojsoncallback=1 parameter[17] to return raw JSON:

```
{
    "photos" : {
        "page" : 1, "pages" : 283353, "perpage" : 3, "total" : "850057",
        "photo" : [ {"id" : "397750427", "owner" : "98559475@N00",
        "secret" : "f59b1ae9e1", "server" : "180", "farm" : 1,
        "title" : "sakura", "ispublic" : 1, "isfriend" : 0, "isfamily" : 0}
        , {
            "id" : "397750433", "owner" : "81222973@N00",
            "secret" : "0023e79dff", "server" : "133", "farm" : 1,
            "title" : "just before spring", "ispublic" : 1,
            "isfriend" : 0, "isfamily" : 0}
        ]}
, "stat" : "ok"}
```

Given this information, you might be wondering why should you use the jsonFlickrApi() callback in the first place instead of using a pattern based on the examples I showed you in Chapter 6 of how to use PHP to interact with the Flickr API. That is, why not use JavaScript to do the following:

1. Do an HTTP GET on this:

   ```
   http://api.flickr.com/services/rest/?method=flickr.photos.search➥
   &api_key={api-key}&tags=flower&per_page=3&format=json&nojsoncallback=1
   ```

2. Instantiate the response as a JavaScript object that you can then parse at your leisure.

---

17. http://api.flickr.com/services/rest/?method=flickr.photos.search&api_key={api-key}&tags=flower&per_page=3&format=json&nojsoncallback=1

I will, in fact, walk you through such an approach in Chapter 10. I defer the discussion until then because we will need to deal with security issues particular to web browsers in order to make our examples work.

Using Greasemonkey to Access *New York Times* Permalinks

Greasemonkey is an add-on for Firefox that allows you to change the behavior of web pages in your browser. That includes creating mashups. You already saw an example of a Greasemonkey script in Chapter 1—the Google Maps in Flickr Greasemonkey script. And here are some good references you can use to get the best out of Greasemonkey:

- `http://diveintogreasemonkey.org/`

- *Greasemonkey Hacks* by Mark Pilgrim (O'Reilly Media, 2005)

- `http://en.wikipedia.org/wiki/Greasemonkey`

- `http://www.greasespot.net/` (the official blog of the Greasemonkey project)

Links that show up on the *New York Times* online site typically expire after a week. That is, instead of going to the article, you are given an excerpt and a chance to purchase a copy of the article. However, in 2003, Dave Winer struck a deal with the *New York Times* to provide a mechanism to get weblog-safe permalinks to articles.[18] Aaron Swartz wrote a *New York Times* link generator that compiles those permalinks and makes them available for lookup via a web form or a JavaScript bookmarklet.[19] That is, you give it a URL to a *New York Times* article, and it will return to you a more permanent link.

Let's look at an example. Consider the following URL:

```
http://www.nytimes.com/2007/04/04/education/04colleges.html
```

This corresponds to the following:

```
http://www.nytimes.com/2007/04/04/education/04colleges.html?ex=1333339200&➥
en=3b7aac16a1ce4512&ei=5090&partner=rssuserland&emc=rss
```

You can see this for yourself by going to the link generator:

```
http://nytimes.blogspace.com/genlink?q=http://www.nytimes.com/2007/04/04/education/➥
04colleges.html
```

When there is no permalink for an article, you will see a different type of output from the *New York Times* link generator. For example, consider the following:

```
http://www.nytimes.com/aponline/us/AP-Imus-Protests.html
```

---

18. `http://www.scripting.com/davenet/2003/06/06/newYorkTimesArchiveAndWebl.html`

19. `http://nytimes.blogspace.com/genlink`

This doesn't have a permalink, as you can see from this:

```
http://nytimes.blogspace.com/genlink?q=http://www.nytimes.com/aponline/us/➥
AP-Imus-Protests.html
```

Where's a good place to stick a UI element for the permanent link on the *New York Times* page? There are lots of choices, but a good one is a toolbar with such elements as e-mail/print/single-page/save/share.

The basic logic of the Greasemonkey script we want to write consists of the following:

1. If you are on a *New York Times* article, send the link to the *New York Times* link generator.

2. If there is a permalink (which you will know is true if the `href` attribute of the first `<a>` tag starts with `http:` and not `genlink`), insert a new `<li>` element at the end of the `<ul id="toolsList">`.

Now let's walk through the steps to get this functionality working in your own Firefox browser installation:

1. Install the Greasemonkey extension if you don't already have it installed.[20]

2. Create a new script in Greasemonkey in one of two ways:

    a. You can go to `http://examples.mashupguide.net/ch08/newyorktimespermalinker.user.js` and click Install.

    b. Select Tools ➤ Greasemonkey ➤ New User Script, fill in Name/Namespace/Description/Includes, and then enter the following code. (Note the use of `GM_xmlhttpRequest` to find out what a more permanent link is. You will see in Chapter 10 the logic behind `xmlhttpRequest`.[21])

```
// ==UserScript==
// @name         New York Times Permlinker
// @namespace    http://mashupguide.net
// @description  Adds a link to a "permalink" or  "weblog-safe" URL
// for the NY Times article, if such a link exists
// @include      http://*.nytimes.com/*
// ==/UserScript==

function rd(){

    // the following code is based on the bookmarklet written by Aaron Swartz
    // at http://nytimes.blogspace.com/genlink

    var x,t,i,j;
    // change %3A -> : and %2F -> '/'
    t=location.href.replace(/[%]3A/ig,':').replace(/[%]2f/ig,'/');
```

---

20. `https://addons.mozilla.org/en-US/firefox/addon/748`

21. `http://wiki.greasespot.net/GM_xmlhttpRequest` and `http://diveintogreasemonkey.org/api/gm_xmlhttprequest.html`

```
// get last occurrence of "http://"
i=t.lastIndexOf('http://');

// lop off stuff after '&'
if(i>0){
  t=t.substring(i);
  j=t.indexOf('&');
  if(j>0)t=t.substring(0,j);
}

var url = 'http://nytimes.blogspace.com/genlink?q='+t;

// send the NY Times link to the nytimes.blogspace.com service.
// If there is a permalink, then the href attribute of the first tag
//  will start with 'http:' and not 'genlink'.
// if there is a permalink, then insert a new li element at the end of the
// <ul id="toolsList">.

GM_xmlhttpRequest({
method:"GET",
url:url,
headers:{
  "User-Agent":"monkeyagent",
  "Accept":"text/html",
},
onload:function(details) {
  var s = details.responseText;
  var p = /a href="(.*)"/;
  var plink = s.match(p)[1];
  if ( plink.match(/^http:/) &&
      (tl = document.getElementById('toolsList')) )  {
    plink = plink + "&pagewanted=all";
    plinkItem = document.createElement('li');
    plinkItem.innerHTML = '<a href="' + plink + '">PermaLink</a>';
    tl.appendChild(plinkItem);
  }
}
});

}

rd();
```

3. What you will see now with this Greasemonkey script if you go to http://www.nytimes.com/2007/04/04/education/04colleges.html is the new entry Permalink underneath the Share button. The link may take a few seconds to appear while the permalink is retrieved.

Note that this Greasemonkey script is sensitive to changes in the way *New York Times* articles are laid out: older articles have a different page structure and therefore need some other logic to put the permalink in the right place.

Learning More About JavaScript and Ajax

It's good to have some handy references on JavaScript programming while working on Ajax-related projects:

- *JavaScript, the Definitive Guide, Fifth Edition* by David Flanagan (O'Reilly Media, 2006)

- *Pro JavaScript Techniques* by John Resig (Apress, 2006)

- *Learning JavaScript* by Shelley Powers (O'Reilly Media, 2007)

I'm particularly fond of Peter-Paul Koch's web site, which has tons of useful resources:

- The general resource page.[22] See also his introduction to JavaScript.[23]

- He has all the example scripts from his book (http://www.quirksmode.org/book/) that you can study at http://www.quirksmode.org/book/examplescripts.html.

Summary

In this chapter, you learned about how Ajax has changed the style of programming in contemporary web applications. You did so by turning off JavaScript in your browser and seeing what happens to Flickr and Google Maps. You studied the functionality of a JavaScript library (Yahoo! UI Library) and Google Maps via the Firebug Firefox extension and the JavaScript Shell. You also learned the basics of invoking the Flickr API in Ajax. Finally, you learned how to create a basic Greasemonkey script that inserts a permanent link into a *New York Times* online article. Although there is much more to learn concerning JavaScript and Ajax, this chapter provides the necessary background to the following chapters.

---

22. http://www.quirksmode.org/resources.html
23 http://www.quirksmode.org/js/intro.html

PART 3

■ ■ ■

Making Mashups

Part 3 is the heart of the book. The previous chapters explained how to work with individual APIs and widgets, which are the raw materials of mashups. In this part, Chapter 9 talks about mashups in general and their relationship to APIs; the primary technique shown is to use ProgrammableWeb to learn about mashups. Chapter 10 covers the nitty-gritty of creating a mashup—using a specific example of mashing up Flickr and Google Maps. In Chapter 11, we'll study the tools that help you create mashups, while in Chapter 12, we'll look at the subject of mashup making from the point of view of API creators.

## CHAPTER 9

Moving from APIs and Remixable Elements to Mashups

Now that you understand the pieces that go into mashups (remixable elements such as a rich URL language, tags, and feeds—all the subjects of Part 1) and APIs (the subject matter of Part 2), this chapter teaches you how to get a feel for how mashups are created from their pieces. To learn how to create mashups, you should study a lot of examples of mashups. In the next chapter, we will work out all the technical details of how to create a specific mashup. In this chapter, we'll step back to look at a broad range of problems that can be addressed with mashups. I won't work through all the details of how to create the mashup, but by thinking about a variety of problems—how others have created mashups to solve the problems themselves or related ones—you can learn about how to create mashups, what's possible, and what goes into them.

The primary technique we'll use to learn about mashups and APIs in this chapter is to mine ProgrammableWeb for information. ProgrammableWeb is the most useful web site for keeping up with the world of mashups, specifically, the relationships between all the APIs and mashups out there. It's by no means the only resource; you can't learn all you need from using it alone. However, learning how to use it effectively is a great way to make sense of the world of mashups as a whole.

To effectively understand mashup making, you should have a specific problem in mind that you want to solve. There's so much you can do with mashups that you will be overwhelmed if you set out to assimilate 2,000+ mashups in ProgrammableWeb without a set purpose. In this chapter, I will use some specific problems and show how ProgrammableWeb can help you understand how to use mashups to solve these problems.

Specifically, I'll cover the following situations in this chapter:

Books: Integrating my varied interactions with books through mashups

Real estate search: Tracking houses coming onto the market and comparing them to estimates of worth

Travel search: Knowing when is a good time to buy airplane tickets

News: Using maps to understand current events around the world

Getting Oriented to ProgrammableWeb

You have already learned about ProgrammableWeb (`http://www.programmableweb.com/`) in this book. In Chapter 7, I discussed what you can learn about APIs, which are the major raw ingredients mashups, from ProgrammableWeb.

Here, I'll show you how to use ProgrammableWeb to learn about mashups. ProgrammableWeb is probably the most comprehensive database of web APIs and mashups and how they are related to one another. ProgrammableWeb and this book are complementary resources to learn about mashups. This book is focused on the nitty-gritty programming details of how to use APIs in creating mashups, and ProgrammableWeb covers the field in breadth and keeps pace with the fast-changing field. Note, however, that ProgrammableWeb doesn't claim to be comprehensive:[1]

You list a lot of mashups on this site. Are these all the mashups there are?

No. This is a subset, or sample, of all mashups. The universe of web mashups is too large and dynamic to be cataloged in one place. And even that assumes that there's an agreed-upon single definition of what a mashup is. Which there isn't. That being said, this is probably the most diverse and structured collection available.

One of the great features of ProgrammableWeb is that it covers APIs and mashups across a wide range of fields. Whereas API providers often link to applications that build upon their own APIs, ProgrammableWeb not only makes that information organized in a nice fashion, but it also lets you see how these APIs work with other APIs, which is really not usually of interest to any given API provider.

User-Generated Data in ProgrammableWeb

ProgrammableWeb depends deeply on user-generated profiles, as well as content entered by the people who run ProgrammableWeb. To participate in commenting or creating mashup or API entries, you can create an account on ProgrammableWeb here:

`http://www.programmableweb.com/register`

Registered users can create an entry for APIs or mashups and enter data about it here:

`http://www.programmableweb.com/add`

When you list a mashup at ProgrammableWeb, you can indicate what APIs are being used by the mashup.

Can Any Directory of Mashups Keep Up?

As mashups become more commonplace, we're going to be in a parallel situation to when Yahoo! went from being able to list every web site in a directory to needing search engines to crawl the Web to figure out what's on the Web. There will be way too many web sites that will use APIs in the future. Nonetheless, the practice you get here with the examples listed on

---

1. `http://www.programmableweb.com/faq#PWHowMany`

ProgrammableWeb will help you recognize others in the wild. Until there is such a search engine for APIs and mashups that can automatically crawl for APIs, we will need a manual approach such as ProgrammableWeb.

Learning About the Overall Mashup Scene

You can follow ProgrammableWeb's own overview here:

```
http://www.programmableweb.com/tour
```

I will also highlight for you how to use it specifically to learn about mashups. Figure 9-1 shows the portal page for mashups on ProgrammableWeb.

```
http://www.programmableweb.com/mashups
```

Figure 9-1. *ProgrammableWeb Mashup Dashboard*

That page is a useful snapshot of the world of mashups that are in the ProgrammableWeb database. Here are some statistics listed on the page (as of January 13, 2008):

- The total number of mashups listed (2,661)

- The average rate of new mashups being added to the database (the six-month average was 3.14 per day)

I have found that this rapid growth of mashups makes it a challenge to keep up with everything that happens, even though some trends have remained quite stable (such as the popularity of map-based mashups).

Directory of Mashups

You can get a list of all the mashups in the database (by page) here:

```
http://www.programmableweb.com/mashups/directory
```

You can sort the list of mashups by the name of a mashup (which is the default view), the date when the mashup's profile was last updated, and the popularity of the mashup (the number of page views on ProgrammableWeb for that mashup). You can view the list as text, as "descriptive" (a mix of text and a thumbnail), or as a pure thumbnail view:

```
http://www.programmableweb.com/mashups/directory/{page}?sort={sort}&view={view}
```

where sort is one of name, date, or popular and where view is one of text, desc, or images.
For example:

```
http://www.programmableweb.com/mashups/directory/5?sort=popular&view=desc
```

Note that the popularity of APIs is measured by the number of mashups using that API:

```
http://www.programmableweb.com/popular
```

I like the idea of looking at the newest (if you are up on a field and want to see the latest) and the most popular (if you are new to a field and want to get a quick glance of what the scene is like). Comparing the newest and most popular mashups often helps to see what trends are afoot.

Indeed, you might be able to get the best of both by viewing a list of the top "popular new mashups" at http://www.programmableweb.com/mashups.

Using Feeds to Track Mashups

ProgrammableWeb uses techniques detailed in earlier chapters to help users not only track mashups but to create data about mashups. For instance, you can use the following RSS 2.0 feed to track new mashups on ProgrammableWeb:

```
http://feeds.feedburner.com/programmableweb/mashup
```

There are other feeds available such as the RSS 2.0 feed for blog entries:

```
http://feeds.feedburner.com/ProgrammableWeb
```

Here is the RSS 2.0 feed for the latest APIs:

```
http://feeds.feedburner.com/programmableweb/apis
```

You will find in the ProgrammableWeb blog (`http://blog.programmableweb.com/`) references to the APIs and mashup profile pages themselves. The ProgrammableWeb blog is an excellent place to read about the latest APIs and mashups of note, and it's also a thoughtful commentary about what these APIs and mashups mean.

Using Tags to Describe Mashups

Tags serve in ProgrammableWeb as thumbnail descriptions of what a given mashup or API is about. They are normalized to some degree to enable comparisons among mashups, in other words, to find similarities and patterns. I'll use these tags in this chapter to relate various mashups.

Tags associated with a given mashup are user-generated. That is, the user who creates a profile for a given mashup is allowed to use up to six tags that can be associated with the mashup. Note the caveat on the link addition page, specifically, the admonition to "[u]se spaces between tags, no punctuation and limit to six tags please":

```
http://www.programmableweb.com/add
```

Also, the site will edit the entry to limit spam and ensure consistency—say, among tags. You can see popular tags for mashups here:

```
http://www.programmableweb.com/mashups
```

Specifically, on this page you can see a pie chart of the top mashup tags for the last 14 days and for all time; this allows you to see how the current trends may or may not be deviating from long-term averages. Table 9-1 reproduces that information.

Table 9-1. *The Percentage of Mashups in ProgrammableWeb Grouped by Tags (January 13, 2008)*

Category	All	Last 14 Days
Mapping	40%	27%
Photo	10%	n/a
Shopping	9%	12%
Video	6%	12%
RSS	n/a	6%

This quick comparison attests to the long-term and short-term popularity of mapping. It looks like video mashups are on the rise—but you have to track it more to be sure. At any rate, if you keep an eye on the popular tags associated with mashups over time, you can get a feel for both short-term and long-term trends.

You can find the tag cloud of tags associated with the mashups here:

`http://www.programmableweb.com/search`

There you will find a short list of the top ten tags. Another worthwhile page is here:

`http://www.programmableweb.com/mashups/directory`

On the left side, you will find a list of the top 20 tags for mashups, along with the number of mashups for that tag. Here's a list of the ten most popular tags for mashups as of January 13, 2008:

- `mapping`
- `photo`
- `shopping`
- `search`
- `travel`
- `video`
- `news`
- `sports`
- `realestate`
- `messaging`

Note that the URL template to access the list of mashups by tag is as follows:

`http://www.programmableweb.com/tag/{tag}`

For example:

`http://www.programmableweb.com/tag/mapping`

You can page and sort and change views, too:

`http://www.programmableweb.com/tag/{tag}/{page}?sort={sort}&view={view}`

where `sort` is one of `name`, `date`, or `popular` and where `view` is one of `text`, `desc`, or `images`.

For example:

`http://www.programmableweb.com/tag/mapping/2?sort=date&view=desc`

Note that the tags associated with mashups are not necessarily the same as those for API tags, though you can expect some overlap. For example:

`http://www.programmableweb.com/apitag/mapping`

That brings up APIs that have been tagged with `mapping` and brings up mashups tagged with `mapping`:

`http://www.programmableweb.com/tag/mapping`

Note APIs are also classified in categories:

```
http://www.programmableweb.com/apis/directory/1?sort=category
```

API and Mashup Verticals

ProgrammableWeb calls out certain fields or segments with high activity as vertical markets for special attention:

```
http://www.programmableweb.com/markets
```

As of this writing, the special vertical markets (which are correlated to popular tags but not exactly) are as follows with upcoming markets for search, enterprise, and widgets:

- `http://www.programmableweb.com/shopping`

- `http://www.programmableweb.com/government`

- `http://www.programmableweb.com/mapping`

- `http://www.programmableweb.com/telephony`

- `http://www.programmableweb.com/social`

- `http://www.programmableweb.com/video`

If you take a look at one of these segments, you will see a dashboard (much like the main Mashup Dashboard) focused on that segment. One helpful extra is a description of the "big picture" for a segment, such as the one for telephony:

```
http://www.programmableweb.com/featured/telephony-mobile-apis-and-mashups
```

Why are verticals significant? That is, what does distinguishing verticals offer beyond just looking at the top mashup tags? You shouldn't be surprised that there would be significant overlap between the top mashup tags and the verticals. Certain verticals (such as government and telephony) are identified whose importance is not immediately apparent from tag popularity.

Looking at a Specific Mashup Profile

So far we've looked at the directory of mashups or collections of mashups grouped by tags or vertical markets. Let's consider how ProgrammableWeb displays a mashup profile.

You can find a profile for a given mashup here:

```
http://www.programmableweb.com/mashup/{mashup-handle}
```

For example, the profile for the Flash Earth mashup is here:

```
http://www.programmableweb.com/mashup/flash-earth
```

What do you find on the mashup profile page? For each mashup, you get the following:

- A description

- A screenshot

- The APIs involved in the mashup

- Any tags for the mashup

- The URL of the mashup

- When it was added and who added it

- Related mashups

- Associated comments and a rating (as a registered user, you can contribute comments and rate the mashup)

In this case, you learn that Flash Earth is a "[z]oomable mashup of Google Maps, Virtual Earth, and other satellite imagery through a Flash application" found here:

```
http://www.flashearth.com/
```

Tagged with the tag mashup, it involves the following APIs: Google Maps, Microsoft Virtual Earth, NASA, OpenLayers, and Yahoo! Maps. Moreover, you learn that Flash Earth is one of the most popular mashups on ProgrammableWeb.

In Chapter 13, you will take a closer look at online maps. Without figuring out how the various online map APIs actually work, you can—through playing with Flash Earth—learn that it is possible to extract tiles that make up various mapping APIs (for example, Google Maps, Yahoo! Maps, and Microsoft Virtual Earth) and recombine them in a Flash interface. (Figuring out exactly how it's done is not necessarily so easy to do, though.) Flash Earth is a powerful demonstration of what is technically possible with online maps in a mashup.

Going from a Specific API to Mashups

In the previous section, you saw how a mashup profile lists the APIs that are used in the mashup. You can take a given API and find out all the mashups that use that API. For example, you start with a list of the most used APIs:

```
http://www.programmableweb.com/apis/directory/1?sort=mashups
```

Then you find the profile for the Google Maps API, the most popular of all APIs in ProgrammableWeb:

```
http://www.programmableweb.com/api/google-maps
```

From that link, you can click the Mashups link to arrive at the list of the 1,200+ mashups registered that use the Google Maps API:

```
http://www.programmableweb.com/api/google-maps/mashups
```

Sample Problems to Solve Using Mashups

Through a number of scenarios in which I describe some problems that are particularly suited to be solved through mashups, I'll show how you can use ProgrammableWeb to figure out what mashups might already exist to solve these problems. Often, there won't be a perfect—or even a good—solution, but the existing ones show you what is possible, what is easy to do, and what might be difficult to do. Moreover, by using ProgrammableWeb, you can immediately see what APIs are being used, as well as what mashups have gotten a following in the community of ProgrammableWeb readers.

Tracking Interesting Books

One scenario is to develop a system to handle book-related information in all the ways you might deal with books. Such a system would track books that

- you own,

- you have out from the various libraries and when they are due,

- you've lent to others or borrowed from others,

- you would like to read one day,

- you would buy if they dropped below a certain price,

- you'd buy from a used bookstore,

- you have just been published,

- you have just shown up your local libraries, or

- you cite in your writing.

Moreover, you probably want to keep some of this information private, some available only to friends, and some pieces of information completely public.

For my own books, I currently use a mishmash of web sites, desktop applications, and web applications to track books—all of which I would like to mash together:

- Amazon.com to look up and buy new books

- Amazon.com wishlists to store books that I would like to buy, borrow, or just ponder

- http://worldcatlibraries.org/ to locate the book in my local library

- The online card catalogs of my local libraries (that of Berkeley Public Library and UC Berkeley)

- LibraryThing, a web site where I often enter books I'm reading and follow what others are reading

- Zotero (http://zotero.org), a Firefox extension that I use to track references

- Bn.com and other online bookstores

- http://www.half.ebay.com/ to buy used books

What would I like to a complete book mashup to do? Lots of things—but some scenarios are as follows:

- If I place a book in my Amazon.com wishlist, I want to be informed whenever that book becomes available at any of the bookstores for which I have borrowing privileges.

- I want to synchronize books that I have listed in Zotero and LibraryThing.

- I want the due dates of all my library books to show up on my Google Calendar.

- I want to be able to format any subset of books from anywhere into a citation for the bibliography I'm compiling.

In some ways, the problem I'd like to solve is an elaboration of the problem I first discussed in Chapter 1. There I talked about the LibraryLookup bookmarklet that shows you how to find a library book in your local library catalog based on an ISBN. Here, I'd like my book information to flow easily among all the places I am referring to books.

I don't actually expect any existing mashup to bring them altogether—partly because mashups generally aren't that all-encompassing yet and partly because the mix of elements I want mashed up is rather idiosyncratic. But let's look at what mashups are out there, what they bring together, and whether we can mash up the mashups themselves.

Let's use ProgrammableWeb to help us to find possible solutions. One approach is to do a full-text search for *book* among the mashup profiles, sorting the results by popularity:

```
http://www.programmableweb.com/mashups/directory/1?q=book&sort=popular
```

Another approach is to use the tags. You can look through the tag cloud here to get a sense of popular book-related tags:

```
http://www.programmableweb.com/search
```

You'll see a link listed to the tag `books`. I recommend sorting by popularity first:

```
http://www.programmableweb.com/tag/books/1?sort=popular
```

and then by date to see the latest developments among mashups tagged with `books`:

```
http://www.programmableweb.com/tag/books/1?sort=date
```

I recommend looking through the results and reading the descriptions of each mashup. Try some. You'll get a feel for the range of possibilities among book-related mashups.

Here, I'll highlight ones that stand out in my viewing. One question to ask while looking through the mashup profiles is, what are the important APIs involved in these mashups? It would be nice to have ProgrammableWeb return the list of APIs involved in a given set of mashups sorted by the number of times it is used. In this case, such a feature would make it easy to see what the most commonly used APIs for mashups tagged with `books` are. However, even with a casual glance through this:

```
http://www.programmableweb.com/tag/books/1?sort=popular
```

you'll see several mentions of the Amazon.com E-Commerce Service API among the various APIs:

```
http://www.programmableweb.com/api/amazon-ecommerce
```

I'm sure you won't be surprised to see the Amazon.com web services show up in this context, given Amazon.com's prominence in two areas: online book retailing and web APIs. It's still helpful, though, to see how people have used the Amazon.com APIs in book-related mashups. You can use the advanced search on ProgrammableWeb (see the "Using the Advanced Search for Mashups and APIs" sidebar) to narrow down the list of mashups tagged with books to ones that use the Amazon.com E-Commerce Service API:

```
http://www.programmableweb.com/tag/books/1?apis=Amazon+eCommerce&sort=popular
```

This ability to focus a search on a specific API (or a combination of APIs) in conjunction with a specific mashup tag can often demonstrate the capabilities of an API for a specific context more vividly than reading the documentation for the API!

USING THE ADVANCED SEARCH FOR MASHUPS AND APIS

You can use an advanced search form to search for mashup and API profiles. For mashups, go here:

```
http://www.programmableweb.com/mashups/directory
```

Then hit the Advanced Search link, which will then open an Advanced Search option. With the Advanced Search option, you can specify the following:

- Up to three APIs used by the mashup (as you type the name of an API, the name will be autocompleted)

- Up to three tags associated with the mashup

- One of an optional date range when the mashup profile was created

For searching APIs, go here first:

```
http://www.programmableweb.com/apis/directory
```

Then click the Advanced Search link, which opens an Advanced Search form that lets you specify the following:

- Up to three tags associated with the API

- A category

- A company

- A protocol (for example, REST or JavaScript)

- An optional date range when the API profile was created

Let's now look at a few of the books-tagged mashups and how they can help in my quest to bring together all aspects of my book-related activities.

BlueOrganizer

BlueOrganizer is a Firefox extension that attempts to recognize when a web page is referring to items of certain categories such as wine, music, stocks, and—most important in this context—books:

http://www.programmableweb.com/mashup/blueorganizer

This ProgrammableWeb profile links to the URL for BlueOrganizer:

http://www.adaptiveblue.com/

specifically:

http://www.adaptiveblue.com/smartlinks_books.html

From reading the documentation for the plug-in, or actually installing it and trying it, you'll see that it recognizes books and gives you a button to take a variety of actions, including the following:

- Adding the book to the Amazon.com wishlist

- Adding the book to LibraryThing or Shelfari (a LibraryThing competitor)

From studying BlueOrganizer, you can learn about web sites that might provide useful sources of book information such as AbeBooks, which advertises an API in its affiliate program (but you need to contact them: http://www.abebooks.com/docs/AffiliateProgram/).

GuruLib, BookBump, and Other LibraryThing Analogs

Although I am a fan of LibraryThing, I follow the development of other web sites that allow readers to track books that they read and share that information with friends or the world. The *New York Times* covered this genre here:

http://www.nytimes.com/2007/03/04/business/yourmoney/04novel.html

Although I knew about Shelfari (http://www.shelfari.com) and Goodreads (http://www.goodreads.com) before consulting ProgrammableWeb, I learned about GuruLib and Book-Bump from ProgrammableWeb:

- http://www.programmableweb.com/mashup/gurulib

- http://www.programmableweb.com/mashup/bookbump

One thing that keeps me from investing too heavily in these sites is the struggle of how to move my book data in and out of any of these sites. For any given site, I look for APIs that help in that regard as well as any feeds that might allow users to easily import and export data.

Some Conclusions About Book Mashups

Here are some things that we learned by thinking through how to create a full-featured book mashup with the help of ProgrammableWeb:

- When it comes to book-related information, Amazon.com is a good API to start with in regard to book searching. The API gives you access to the Amazon.com wishlist (as you will see in Chapter 17).

- Don't expect all APIs of interest to be listed on ProgrammableWeb. As of writing, there is no mention of Zotero, WorldCat, and LibraryThing—even though they are all programmable to one degree or another.

- Lots of web sites I use don't have APIs at all, such as Bn.com and my local library catalogs. We are left with the question of how to deal with those sites. Should we screen-scrape the sites?

- There are other angles that won't be covered by looking only at ProgrammableWeb. For example, for the latest books at my library, I have to look at `http://www.berkeley-public.org/ftlist` for recent arrivals. There is no API.

Knowing When to Buy Airplane Tickets

Let's move from tracking books to tracking plane tickets. Suppose I want to buy a round-trip ticket between San Francisco and New York City. I know roughly when I want to travel but have some flexibility in terms of exactly when I can leave and return (within a day or two) and which airlines I can take. I'm planning far ahead of time to try to get the best price. However, I really don't want to have to leave before 8 a.m. or arrive in New York City after 9 p.m.

For a long time, it would be difficult for me as a typical consumer to be able to monitor over periods of weeks or months airfares for trips that meet such criteria so that I could wait for a good time to buy. However, some of the newer travel sites are giving users the ability to perform increasingly sophisticated searches, filter results by such criteria as the time of day of departure, and receive e-mail alerts for canned searches. Now, given that there are even travel web sites with APIs, I'm wondering whether I could use these APIs to get closer to finding the plane tickets at the prices I want.

We can use ProgrammableWeb to look through a collection of travel-tagged mashups:

`http://www.programmableweb.com/tag/travel`

John Musser wrote a recent analysis of the travel APIs:

`http://blog.programmableweb.com/2007/10/29/5-travel-apis-from-comparison-to-booking/`

You can search for travel-tagged APIs here:

`http://www.programmableweb.com/apis/directory/1?q=travel`

but if you limit the display to APIs tied to any mashup profiles (and sorting by popularity), like so:

`http://www.programmableweb.com/apis/directory/1?q=travel&sort=mashups`

you quickly find only two APIs at the time of writing:

- `http://www.programmableweb.com/api/yahoo-travel`

- `http://www.programmableweb.com/api/kayak`

Since the Yahoo! Travel API is focused on travel plans made by users on the Yahoo! Travel web site, and not on the purchase of airplane tickets, we'll focus then on the Kayak Search API:

```
http://www.kayak.com/labs/api/search/
```

Kayak (`http://www.kayak.com/`) is a web site like Expedia and Travelocity that allows users to search for flights. Given that APIs for travel sites are a new concept, I wasn't surprised that there were few mashups listed as using the Kayak Search API (`http://www.programmableweb.com/api/kayak/mashups`). Kayak's deals from cell phones profiled here made me think of alternate interfaces to Kayak's travel information:

```
http://www.programmableweb.com/mashup/kayak.com-deals-from-cell-phone
```

One mashup that I have yet to see is one of Kayak with Google Calendar. When I schedule flights, it's useful to see what else I have going on in my personal schedule. A Kayak/Google Calendar mashup could present possible flights as a Google calendar that I could juxtapose with my personal calendar. The mashup might even read my personal schedule to filter out prospective flights to begin with. (See Chapter 15 for how to use the Google Calendar API.)

Apart from connecting Kayak to alternative interfaces such as cell phones and calendars, a mashup of Kayak could allow you to conduct a more thorough search through the complicated combinations of parameters possible when flying. I found that manually varying parameters such as departure dates and return dates and keeping the best deals in my head got rather tiring after five to ten tries. I suspect that a mashup of the Kayak Search API and a smart search algorithm could possibly find better flights than I could find manually.

Finding That Dream House

Real estate–oriented APIs and mashups promise to make home buying a bit easier and maybe more fun. Specifically, let's look at how we might use a variety of web feeds and APIs to track houses that come on the market in a given area.

You can start on ProgrammableWeb by searching for mashups tagged with `realestate` and sorting the results by popularity:

```
http://www.programmableweb.com/tag/realestate/1?view=desc
```

More to the point, by searching for APIs tagged with `realestate` and listing them by popularity by going here:

```
http://www.programmableweb.com/apitag/realestate/1?sort=mashups
```

you find two relevant APIs for American real estate:

- Zillow (`http://www.programmableweb.com/api/zillow`)

- Trulia (`http://www.programmableweb.com/api/trulia`)

Zillow (`http://www.zillow.com/`) focuses on providing estimates of home valuations and details of properties, while also listing homes for sale and that have been recently sold. Trulia (`http://www.trulia.com/`) aggregates listings of homes for sale. Note that although the Trulia API (`http://developer.trulia.com/`) doesn't currently return any individual listings, you can use Trulia feeds to access some of the listings. For example, the following is an RSS 2.0 feed of some of the current properties available in Berkeley, California:

```
http://www.trulia.com/rss2/CA/Berkeley/
```

Currently, I do not know of what seems to be an obvious combination—a mashup of the Zillow and Trulia APIs, one that, for instance, would compare the sale price of houses listed for sale on Trulia with what Zillow estimates to be the value of the house. ProgrammableWeb doesn't list any such mashup:

```
http://www.programmableweb.com/mashups/directory/1?apis=trulia%2Czillow
```

Something I learned by looking through the `realestate` mashups is that Google Base is an interesting source of real estate data. Take a look at mashups tagged by `realestate` using the Google Base API:

```
http://www.programmableweb.com/tag/realestate?apis=Google+Base
```

Mapping Breaking News

In Chapter 4, you learned how to use Yahoo! Pipes to pull together various news feeds into a single feed. In this section, I'll cover how to plot those current events on a map.

I often read about places in the world for which I have only the vaguest idea where they are located. Online maps certainly make it easy to look places up now. But much like how Housingmaps.com helps with visualizing real estate on a map, perhaps displaying news on a map of the world could have the similar benefits.

Let's see what ProgrammableWeb has to say about mashups of news and maps. The `news` tag is a popular tag for mashups on ProgrammableWeb.

```
http://www.programmableweb.com/tag/news/1?view=desc
```

When you look through this section, you'll see several mashups of interest:

- `http://www.programmableweb.com/mashup/bbc-news-map` points to a now-defunct mashup that mapped BBC News items about the United Kingdom on a map.

- `http://www.programmableweb.com/mashup/ap-national-news-google-maps` points to `http://www.81nassau.com/apnews/`, which displays items from a choice of Associated Press feeds (including national news, sports, and business) on a Google map.

- `http://www.programmableweb.com/mashup/mapified-rss` points to `http://o.gosselin.free.fr/Projects/MapifiedRss/`, which maps to Google Maps entries from one of the preconfigured RSS feeds (for example, Reuters, Associated Press top headlines, or Google News) or from the URL of a feed entered the user.

Seeing these mashups reminded me how easy it is now to display feeds that contain geographic locations on a map. Let's use Yahoo! Pipes, which you have already learned how to use in Chapter 4. The key to georeferencing a feed so that it can be displayed on a map is the Location Extractor Operator in Yahoo! Pipes:

```
http://pipes.yahoo.com/pipes/docs?doc=operators#LocationExtractor
```

Another thing you need to know is that Yahoo! Pipes is able to output KML that can then be displayed on Google Earth and Google Maps. (Chapter 13 contains more details about KML.) I constructed a Yahoo! pipe that takes as input a URL to a feed to be georeferenced:

```
http://pipes.yahoo.com/raymondyee/locationextractor
```

The default value for this URL is that for the *New York Times* International News feed:

```
http://www.nytimes.com/services/xml/rss/nyt/International.xml
```

The KML output for this default feed is as follows:

```
http://pipes.yahoo.com/pipes/pipe.run?InputURL=http%3A%2F%2Fwww.nytimes.com%2Fservices➡
%2Fxml%2Frss%2Fnyt%2FInternational.xml&_id=cInT4D7B3BGMoxPNiXrLOA&_render=kml
```

or as follows:

```
http://tinyurl.com/yvx8qy
```

You can display this KML feed on a Google map, like so:

```
http://maps.google.com/maps?f=q&hl=en&geocode=&time=&date=&ttype=&q=http:%2F%2F➡
pipes.yahoo.com%2Fpipes%2Fpipe.run%3FInputURL%3Dhttp%253A%252F%252Fwww.nytimes.com%252F➡
services%252Fxml%252Frss%252Fnyt%252FInternational.xml%26_id%3DcInT4D7B3BGMoxPNiXrLOA%➡
26_render%3Dkml&ie=UTF8&ll=28.921631,53.4375&spn=150.976999,360&z=2&om=1
```

or like so:

```
http://tinyurl.com/yp8k2b
```

Since in this section we're looking at mapping, it's helpful to look at the mapping vertical market coverage on ProgrammableWeb:

```
http://www.programmableweb.com/mapping
```

Summary

In this chapter, you learned about mashups and their relationships to APIs by studying a series of specific problems for which mashups can provide useful solutions. You looked at how you can track books, real estate, airfare, and current events by combining various APIs. You used ProgrammableWeb to help analyze these problems.

CHAPTER 10

■■■

Creating Mashups of Several Services

In previous chapters, you learned about the raw ingredients of mashups. This chapter teaches you how to write mashups by walking you through a detailed example of mashing up Flickr photos with Google Maps. This chapter draws upon what you have learned in previous chapters. In Chapter 1, you learned about how geotagging photos started in Flickr and how people such as Rev. Dan Catt and C.K. Yuan built tools—essentially mashups, such as Geobloggers and GMiF—to display those geotagged photos. In Chapter 2, you learned about how such features were baked into Flickr. In Chapter 6, you learned about how to program the Flickr API, while in Chapter 8, you learned the basics of Ajax and how to program Google Maps. We will draw upon all those pieces of knowledge in this chapter.

Given that you can already display Flickr photos on a Yahoo! map, why would you still build any Flickr-map mashup? Well, you might for a number of reasons. You might have a preference for Google Maps over the default maps. Making such a mashup is an instructive process. What better way to learn about mashups than to mash up the two most mashed up services: GMap and Flickr?

What you learn in this chapter will be useful for other mashups. The type of mashup shown here is an extremely common one: getting data from somewhere and putting that data on a map. (Here, we're not screen-scraping that data but rather getting that directly out of an API. There are mashups that require screen-scraping, but that's largely outside the scope of this book.)

You will also learn about the interaction of server-side and client-side programming, another major issue in many mashups. In addition, you will learn about the central process of dealing with impedance matching between APIs. That is, you will find how to make APIs that have different conceptual and implementation details fit together so that data can flow between them. You will learn where to find the common matching points (for example, latitudes and longitudes are common in both the Flickr API and Google Maps) and create interfaces (channel adapters) that bridge the APIs. Finally, there is also the process of taking the work you did and then recasting the same logic into a different environment.

The bulk of this chapter is devoted to writing a simple mashup of Flickr photos with Google Maps using the Google Maps API, but we finish by creating a Flickr/Google Maps mashup using the Google Mapplets API. Since the Mapplets API is similar but not identical to the Google Map API, you will be able to use some of the programming you will do for Google Maps. You'll see how mapplets eliminate the need for server-side programming on your part; the solution we will come up with will be a pure HTML/JavaScript combination.

The goals of this chapter are as follows:

- To enable you to build a significant end-to-end mashup that gives you knowledge about building other mashups

- To cover and reinforce the materials beforehand, which was background material building up to this mashup building

The Design

For both the Google Maps and the Google Mapplets–based mashup, you will want to let your users search for geotagged photos in Flickr and to display them on a Google map. When the user changes the bounding box (that is, the rectangular region of a map often defined by the coordinates of the map's southwest and northeast corners) of the map (by panning and zooming or by changing the zoom level of the map), a new search for geotagged photos is done, and the resulting pictures are displayed on the map.

We will build the mashups in manageable chunks:

- You'll review what you have already learned about geotagging in Flickr and then see how to use the Flickr API to associate locations with photos and how to find geotagged photos.

- You'll study how to access XML web services from the browser using the XMLHttpRequest browser object, both natively and wrapped in the Yahoo! UI library.

- You'll study how the security constraints on the browser necessitate a server-side proxy for accessing web services.

- You'll build a server-side proxy to get Flickr geotagged photos.

- You'll work toward building a mashup of the client-side Google Maps API with the Flickr API by first building a simple client-side framework.

- You'll elaborate the client-side framework to translate a search for Flickr geotagged photos into an HTML display of the results.

- You'll transform this framework into a mashup of the Google Maps API and Flickr through a series of steps: setting up a basic map; having the map respond to changes in the viewport of the map; bringing together the Flickr and Google Maps into the same page, first as independent pieces; wiring the bounding box of the Google map to be the source of lat/long coordinates; and finally, making the pictures show up in the map.

- You'll refactor this work into a Flickr/Google mapplet to create a pure client-side solution.

- You'll draw conclusions about what you learned in making these mashups and see how they can be applied to creating other mashups.

■**Note** Chapter 13 provides greater detail on maps and further elaborates on the core examples of this chapter—by mashing up Flickr and Google Earth via KML.

Background: Geotagging in Flickr

As you learned in Chapter 1, geotagging in Flickr started with people using tags (specifically, geotagged and geo:lon, geo:lat) to associate a latitude and longitude with a given photo. This way of geotagging was very popular. Lots of people started creating geotagged photos. Moreover, programs arose to both display geotagged photos (such as GMiF and Geobloggers) and create geotagged photos.

This approach (what I refer here as *old-style geotagging*), as cool as it was, was a hack. Flickr moved to institutionalize geotagging, into what I refer to as *new-style geotagging*. First, Flickr created the framework of *machine tags* to clean up the clutter. Clearly, there was a desire for developers (spurred on by serving users) to add extra metadata to Flickr photos. The result was that data meant for machine consumption was pushed into tags, which were geared more for people manually sticking in descriptions. Flickr decided to take tags of the following form and make them into machine tags:

```
namespace:predicate=value
```

For example, the geo:lat= and geo:lon= tags have become machine tags. This means they are not displayed by default in the UI. Rather, a user needs to click the "Show machine tags" link to see these machine tags. (The thinking is that machine tags weren't really for human consumption—so why display them?)

Let's consider a geotagged photo that we already looked at in Chapter 1 ("Campanile in the Fog"):

```
http://flickr.com/photos/raymondyee/18389540/
```

You can see the relevant geotags under Tags by clicking "Show machine tags" to reveal this:

```
geo:lon=-122.257704
geo:lat=37.8721
```

You can use the Flickr API to get at these regular and machine tags. Remember that Flickr geotagging was based originally on the geotagged tag and tags of the form geo:lon=[LONGITUDE] and geo:lat=[LATITUDE] that became machine tags. For example, to use the Flickr API to look up the tags for the photo whose ID is 18389540, you issue the following HTTP GET request:

```
http://api.flickr.com/services/rest/?method=flickr.tags.getListPhoto➥
&api_key={api_key}&photo_id=18389540
```

whose response is as follows:

```
<?xml version="1.0" encoding="utf-8" ?>
<rsp stat="ok">
  <photo id="18389540">
    <tags>
      <tag id="29475-18389540-11787" author="48600101146@N01"
          authorname="Raymond Yee" raw="campanile" machine_tag="0">campanile</tag>
      <tag id="29475-18389540-1700" author="48600101146@N01"
          authorname="Raymond Yee" raw="geotagged" machine_tag="0">geotagged</tag>
      <tag id="29475-18389540-10860922" author="48600101146@N01"
          authorname="Raymond Yee" raw="geo:lon=-122.257704"
          machine_tag="1">geo:lon=122257704</tag>
```

```
          <tag id="29475-18389540-10860930" author="48600101146@N01"
              authorname="Raymond Yee" raw="geo:lat=37.8721"
              machine_tag="1">geo:lat=378721</tag>
          <tag id="29475-18389540-88988" author="48600101146@N01"
              authorname="Raymond Yee" raw="UC Berkeley"
              machine_tag="0">ucberkeley</tag>
          <tag id="29475-18389540-9233381" author="48600101146@N01"
              authorname="Raymond Yee" raw="mashupguide"
              machine_tag="0">mashupguide</tag>
        </tags>
      </photo>
    </rsp>
```

■**Note** You might wonder why you get machine tags for latitude and longitude since using geo:lat and geo:lon has been superceded. I'm showing this technique for historic interest and also because it's still used by older pieces of software (such as the Google Maps in Flickr Greasemonkey script that uses old-style geotagging).

With new-style geotagging, support for geotagging was built into the core of Flickr (geo-information became a first-class citizen of the Flickr data world). Each photo can optionally be associated with a location (that is, a latitude and longitude) and permissions about who can see this location.

There are some major advantages of the new-style geotagging:

- You can search for photos in a given bounding box. There was no way to do so with regular tags unless you crawled a whole bunch of geotagged photos and built your own database of those photos and their locations and built geosearching on top of that database. Flickr does that for you.

- You can control the visibility of the location independently of that photo (that is, the photo can be visible but not the location). In the old-style geotagging, if the photo is visible, then its tags are also visible, thus rendering any geo:lat/geo:lon visible.

- The new style is the official way to do geotagging, whereas the old style never had official support. Along with it being the official way comes a lot of supporting features: the Flickr map, a link to a map for any georeferenced photo, and so on.

By setting a location, you give a photo a latitude, longitude, and accuracy (1–16): world level equals 1, country equals approximately 3, and street equals approximately 16. The default accuracy is 16. Permissions are the values for four parameters: is_public, is_contact, is_friend, and is_family (0 or 1). (See Chapter 2 for a discussion of the permission system in Flickr.) There are five methods under flickr.photos.geo: getting, setting, deleting the location of a given photo (flickr.photos.geo.getLocation, flickr.photos.geo.setLocation, and flickr.photos.geo.removeLocation), and getting and setting the permission (flickr.photos.geo.getPerms and flickr.photos.geo.getPerms).

You'll notice that for the following, in addition to using the old-style geotagging in the example photo, I am also using the new-style geotagging:

```
http://flickr.com/photos/raymondyee/18389540/
```

Since this photo is public, anyone can use `flickr.photos.geo.getLocation` to access the photo's latitude and longitude. (All the other geo.* methods require authorization.) Let's use the API to get the location. Issue an HTTP GET request on this:

```
http://api.flickr.com/services/rest/?method=flickr.photos.geo.getLocation
&api_key={api_key}&photo_id=18389540
```

You will get the following:

```
<?xml version="1.0" encoding="utf-8" ?>
<rsp stat="ok">
  <photo id="18389540">
    <location latitude="37.8721" longitude="-122.257704" accuracy="16">
      <locality>Oakland</locality>
      <county>Alameda</county>
      <region>California</region>
      <country>United States</country>
    </location>
  </photo>
</rsp>
```

For the other methods, it's easier to demonstrate using a Flickr API kit that helps you with the Flickr authentication process (which is covered in detail in Chapter 6). I'll now display some code to show how to use Python to manipulate a photo's location and geopermission. Here, `flickr.client` is an authenticated instance of the Flickr client using Beej's Python Flickr API (http://flickrapi.sourceforge.net/).

Let's retrieve the location of the photo:

```
>>> rsp = flickr.client.photos_geo_getLocation(photo_id=18389540)
```

Now let's remove the location of the photo:

```
>>> rsp = flickr.client.photos_geo_removeLocation(photo_id=18389540)
```

Let's write the location back to the photo:

```
>>> rsp = flickr.client.photos_geo_setLocation(photo_id=18389540,lat=37.8721,
lon=-122.257704,accuracy=16)
```

In addition to reading and writing the location and geopermissions of an individual photo, you can use the Flickr API to search for photos that have an associated location. You do so by using the `flickr.photos.search` method (the one to which you were introduced in Chapter 6), documented here:

```
http://www.flickr.com/services/api/flickr.photos.search.html
```

To do a search for geotagged photos, you add the search parameters of the following form:

```
bbox=lon0,lat0,lon1,lat1
```

Here `lon0,lat0` and `lon1,lat1` are the longitude and latitude of the southwest and northeast corners of the bounding box, respectively. Note that you can also use the `accuracy` parameter to specify the minimum accuracy level you demand of the specified locations.

Let's consider the example of searching for photos around Berkeley in a bounding box with the following parameters:

```
SW:   37.81778516606761, -122.34374999999999
NE:   37.92619056937629, -122.17208862304686
```

The following will get the first page of all the publicly available geotagged photos in Flickr, including photos of all accuracies (with this call, you can get at the total number of such photos):

```
http://api.flickr.com/services/rest/?api_key={api_key}&method=flickr.photos.search➡
&bbox=-180%2C-90%2C180%2C90&min_upload_date=820483200&accuracy=1
```

You can get the first page of photos with a bounding box around the UC Berkeley campus:

```
http://api.flickr.com/services/rest/?api_key={api_key}&method=flickr.photos.search➡
&bbox=-122.34374999999999%2C+37.81778516606761%2C+-122.17208862304686➡
%2C+37.92619056937629&min_upload_date=820483200&accuracy=1
```

The Flickr API doesn't like unqualified searches for geotagged photos. That is, you can't just, say, search for photos in a certain bounding box—you need to use at least one other search parameter to reduce the strain on the Flickr database caused by unqualified searches. Here I'm using the `min_upload_date` parameter to convince Flickr to give some results.

Background: XMLHttpRequest and Containing Libraries

In the previous chapters, especially Chapters 6 and 7, I concentrated on showing you how to make web service requests using server-side languages such as PHP and Python. In this section, I will show you how to make HTTP requests from JavaScript in the browser. The key piece of technology is the `XMLHttpRequest` (XHR) object (or XHR-like objects in Internet Explorer). I will outline the basics of XHR, covering briefly how to use XHR in the raw and then in the form of a library (specifically the YUI Connection Manager) that abstracts the details of XHR for you.

Using XMLHttpRequest Directly

The XHR object is an API for JavaScript for transferring XML and other textual data between the (client-side) browser and a server. There are differences in naming the object between Internet Explorer and the other browsers. Moreover, there are subtle issues that are easiest to handle by using a good wrapper around XHR, such as the Yahoo! Connection Manager.

Even though we will be using the Yahoo! Connection Manager to access XHR, it's still useful to look at how to use XHR before relying on a library. Drawing from Peter-Paul Koch's description of XHR at `http://www.quirksmode.org/js/xmlhttp.html` and noting that the following proxies an RSS feed of weather in the 94720 ZIP code (see the discussion after the code for an explanation of the script) . . .

```
http://examples.mashupguide.net/ch10/weather.php?p=94720
```

then I present the following, which shows a typical usage of XHR to read the RSS feed:

```
http://examples.mashupguide.net/ch10/xhr.html
```

This extracts and displays an HTML excerpt from the feed:

```html
<!DOCTYPE html PUBLIC "-//W3C//DTD HTML 4.01 Transitional//EN"
"http://www.w3.org/TR/html4/loose.dtd">
<html>
  <head>
    <title>xhr.html</title>
    <meta http-equiv="content-type" content="text/html; charset=utf-8" >
    <script type="text/javascript">
    //<![CDATA[

  // based on http://www.quirksmode.org/js/xmlhttp.html

  var XMLHttpFactories = [
    function () {
        xhr = new XMLHttpRequest(); xhr.overrideMimeType('text/xml'); return xhr;
    },
    function () {return new ActiveXObject("Msxml2.XMLHTTP")},
    function () {return new ActiveXObject("Msxml3.XMLHTTP")},
    function () {return new ActiveXObject("Microsoft.XMLHTTP")}
  ];

  function getXmlHttpRequest() {
    var xmlhttp = false;
    for (var i=0;i<XMLHttpFactories.length;i++) {
      try {
        xmlhttp = XMLHttpFactories[i]();
      }
      catch (e) {
        continue;
      }
      break;
    }
    return xmlhttp;
  }

    function writeResults() {

      if (xmlhttp.readyState == 4 && xmlhttp.status == 200) {
        resultsDiv = document.getElementById('results');
        //alert(xmlhttp.responseText);
        var response = xmlhttp.responseXML;
        resultsDiv.innerHTML =
            response.getElementsByTagName('description')[1].firstChild.nodeValue;
```

```
      }

   }

   function load() {

      // http://examples.mashupguide.net/ch10/weather.php?p=94720
      xmlhttp = getXmlHttpRequest();
      if (xmlhttp) {
         zip = "94720";
         url = "weather.php?p=" + zip;
         xmlhttp.open('GET', url, true);
         xmlhttp.onreadystatechange = writeResults;
         xmlhttp.send(null);
      }

   }

   //]]>
   </script>
</head>
<body onload="load()" >
<!-- retrieve -->
<div id="results"></div>
</body>
</html>
```

Note the following:

- The code attempts to instantiate XHR by trying various ways to do so until it succeeds—
  or finally fails if none of the methods works.

- Through the use of the following:

  ```
  xmlhttp.onreadystatechange = writeResults;
  ```

  the writeResults() method is the callback for the HTTP GET request. That is, XHR feeds
  writeResults with its state (xmlhttp.readyState). A typical usage pattern is for the
  callback routine to wait until the call is complete (xmlhttp.readyState == 4) and for
  the return of an HTTP response code of 200 (to indicate a successful call).

- xmlhttp.responseXML returns the body of the HTTP response in the form of an XML DOM.

Using the YUI Connection Manager

The main goal of this section is to again use JavaScript to call the Flickr API to get photos from
a given bounding box. In the previous section, you learned how to use XHR directly; here, I show
you how to use a library that wraps XHR: the Yahoo! UI (YUI) Library's Connection Manager,
which is documented here:

```
http://developer.yahoo.com/yui/connection/
```

The official examples page for the Connection Manager is here:

```
http://developer.yahoo.com/yui/examples/connection/index.html
```

Let's look at the weather example provided by the YUI:

```
http://developer.yahoo.com/yui/examples/connection/weather.html
```

Our ultimate goal is to use the Connection Manager to hook up the Flickr API. Instead of jumping directly to that goal, I'll first explain the weather example. The server-side part is relatively easy to understand, thus letting you concentrate on the XHR part of the example. The example is built in with the YUI download, and therefore you can immediately see an example of a client-side JavaScript invocation of the Yahoo! weather web service.

Enter a ZIP code, and hit Get Weather RSS. The web page uses XHR (wrapped by the Connection Manager) to retrieve an RSS 2.0 feed for the ZIP code, parses the weather information, and displays it on the page. Note that this happens without a page reload—remember that is what XHR (and Ajax) can do for you.

One thing to notice about weather.html is that its JavaScript code invokes assets/weather.php running from the same server. That is, if you have a version of the YUI example loaded on examples.mashupguide.net:

```
http://examples.mashupguide.net/lib/yui/examples/connection/weather.html
```

you'll see that it calls the following:

```
http://examples.mashupguide.net/lib/yui/examples/connection/assets/weather.php
```

What does weather.php do?

A quick study shows that weather.php takes the ZIP code (that is, 94720), does an HTTP GET request on the Yahoo! Weather API (http://developer.yahoo.com/weather/), and echoes the feed back.

For example, suppose you make the following request:

```
http://examples.mashupguide.net/lib/yui/examples/connection/assets/weather.php?➥
p=94720
```

The script echoes back the following:

```
http://xml.weather.yahoo.com/forecastrss?p=94720
```

This will be something of the following form:

```
<?xml version="1.0" encoding="UTF-8" standalone="yes" ?>
<rss version="2.0" xmlns:yweather="http://xml.weather.yahoo.com/ns/rss/1.0"
xmlns:geo="http://www.w3.org/2003/01/geo/wgs84_pos#">
  <channel>
    <title>Yahoo! Weather - Berkeley, CA</title>
    <link>http://us.rd.yahoo.com/dailynews/rss/weather/Berkeley__CA/➥
*http://weather.yahoo.com/forecast/94720_f.html</link>
    <description>Yahoo! Weather for Berkeley, CA</description>
    <language>en-us</language>
    <lastBuildDate>Mon, 05 Nov 2007 12:53 pm PST</lastBuildDate>
    <ttl>60</ttl>
```

```
    <yweather:location city="Berkeley" region="CA" country="US"/>
    <yweather:units temperature="F" distance="mi" pressure="in" speed="mph"/>
    <yweather:wind chill="62" direction="300" speed="10"/>
    <yweather:atmosphere humidity="65" visibility="1287" pressure="30.03"
                        rising="2"/>
    <yweather:astronomy sunrise="6:39 am" sunset="5:06 pm"/>
    <image>
      <title>Yahoo! Weather</title>
      <width>142</width>
      <height>18</height>
      <link>http://weather.yahoo.com/</link>
      <url>http://l.yimg.com/us.yimg.com/i/us/nws/th/main_142b.gif</url>
    </image>
    <item>
      <title>Conditions for Berkeley, CA at 12:53 pm PST</title>
      <geo:lat>37.87</geo:lat>
      <geo:long>-122.3</geo:long>
      <link>http://us.rd.yahoo.com/dailynews/rss/weather/Berkeley__CA/➥
*http://weather.yahoo.com/forecast/94720_f.html</link>
      <pubDate>Mon, 05 Nov 2007 12:53 pm PST</pubDate>
      <yweather:condition text="Fair" code="34" temp="62"
                        date="Mon, 05 Nov 2007 12:53 pm PST"/>
      <description><![CDATA[
<img src="http://l.yimg.com/us.yimg.com/i/us/we/52/34.gif" /><br />
 <b>Current Conditions:</b><br />
 Fair, 62 F<BR /><BR />
 <b>Forecast:</b><BR />
  Mon - Sunny. High: 69 Low: 46<br />
  Tue - Partly Cloudy. High: 70 Low: 47<br />
 <br />
<a href="http://us.rd.yahoo.com/dailynews/rss/weather/Berkeley__CA/➥
*http://weather.yahoo.com/forecast/94720_f.html">
Full Forecast at Yahoo! Weather</a><BR/>
 (provided by The Weather Channel)<br/>
 ]]></description>
      <yweather:forecast day="Mon" date="05 Nov 2007" low="46" high="69"
                        text="Sunny" code="32"/>
      <yweather:forecast day="Tue" date="06 Nov 2007" low="47" high="70"
                        text="Partly Cloudy" code="30"/>
      <guid isPermaLink="false">94720_2007_11_05_12_53_PST</guid>
    </item>
  </channel>
</rss>
```

Building a Server-Side Proxy

In the previous section, you learned how to use XHR to talk to a local weather.php file that in turn calls the Yahoo! Weather API. You might wonder why XHR doesn't go directly to the Yahoo! Weather API. It turns out that because of cross-domain security issues in the browser, you can't use the XHR object to make a request to a server that is different from the originating server of the JavaScript code. That would apply to the Flickr API as it does to the Yahoo! Weather API. To get around this issue, you will need a little help from a server-side proxy in the form of a PHP script whose job it is to take a tag and bounding box as input, call the Flickr API to get photos, and return that in XML or JSON to the calling script.

I'll show you how to write a server-side proxy to the Flickr API to get geotagged photos, but first I'll prove to you that you can't use XHR to go directly to the Yahoo! Weather API.

What Happens with XHR and Direct API Calls?

Let's see why weather.html can't just call Yahoo! directly. You can find out what happens by running the following code, which instead of calling the local weather.php goes directly to http://xml.weather.yahoo.com/forecastrss?94720:[1]

```
<!DOCTYPE html PUBLIC "-//W3C//DTD XHTML 1.0 Transitional//EN"
"http://www.w3.org/TR/xhtml1/DTD/xhtml1-transitional.dtd">
<html xmlns="http://www.w3.org/1999/xhtml" xml:lang="en" lang="en">
  <head>
    <title>Direct connect</title>
    <script type="text/javascript" src="/lib/yui/build/yahoo/yahoo.js"></script>
    <script type="text/javascript" src="/lib/yui/build/event/event.js"></script>
    <script type="text/javascript"
            src="/lib/yui/build/connection/connection.js"></script>
  </head>
  <body>
  <div id="status"></div>
  <script>
    div = document.getElementById('status');

    var handleSuccess = function(o){

      function parseHeaders(headerStr){

        var headers = headerStr.split("\n");
        for(var i=0; i < headers.length; i++){
          var delimitPos = headers[i].indexOf(':');
          if(delimitPos != -1){
            headers[i] = "<p>" +
            headers[i].substring(0,delimitPos) + ":"+
            headers[i].substring(delimitPos+1) + "</p>";
```

---

1. http://examples.mashupguide.net/ch10/direct.connect.html

```
        }
        return headers;
        }
    }

    if(o.responseText !== undefined){
        div.innerHTML = "Transaction id: " + o.tId;
        div.innerHTML += "HTTP status: " + o.status;
        div.innerHTML += "Status code message: " + o.statusText;
        div.innerHTML += "HTTP headers: " + parseHeaders(o.getAllResponseHeaders);
        div.innerHTML += "Server response: " + o.responseText;
        div.innerHTML += "Argument object: property foo = " + o.argument.foo +
                "and property bar = " + o.argument.bar;
    }

    }

    var handleFailure = function(o){
        if(o.responseText !== undefined){
            div.innerHTML = "<li>Transaction id: " + o.tId + "</li>";
            div.innerHTML += "<li>HTTP status: " + o.status + "</li>";
            div.innerHTML += "<li>Status code message: " + o.statusText + "</li>";
        }
    }

    var callback =
    {
        success:handleSuccess, failure: handleFailure,
        argument: { foo:"foo", bar:"bar" }
    };

    var sUrl = "http://xml.weather.yahoo.com/forecastrss?p=94720";
    var request = YAHOO.util.Connect.asyncRequest('GET', sUrl, callback);
  </script>
  <div id="status"></div>
</body>
</html>
```

If you try to run this, you will get a JavaScript error. In Firefox, if you look in the Firefox error console, you'll see the following:

```
Error: uncaught exception: Permission denied to call method XMLHttpRequest.open
```

The main lesson here is that XHR lets you access URLs only from the same domain—for security reasons. Let's prove that by making a new HTML file in the same directory as a local copy of weather.php. This security issue, and the workaround by the server-side proxy, is explained here:

http://developer.yahoo.com/javascript/howto-proxy.html

In case you are still skeptical, you can change the JavaScript in your HTML to access weather.php from this:

var sUrl = "http://xml.weather.yahooapis.com/forecastrss?p=94720";

to this:

var sUrl = "./weather.php?p=94720";

When you load weather.proxy.html,[2] you no longer get the error. Instead, you get information about the weather—that means communication is happening between your JavaScript and the Yahoo! weather system. Using Firebug, you can actually see the RSS embedded in the <div>—but that's not very nice. Let's now move toward getting Flickr information.

Building a Server-Side Script for Geolocated Photos

Based on what you just learned, you now know that you need to get results about Flickr geo-tagged photos from the Flickr API into the browser using XHR. Hence, you'll need a server-side proxy for bridging any client-side script with Flickr. That's the aim of this section.

As an exercise, I recommend you write this code yourself before studying the solution presented. Think about how weather.php works and how you can use flickr.photos.search to look for geotagged photos. You can imagine a PHP script that gives access to the full range of input parameters for flickr.photos.search in searches of public photos and returns the search results in a variety of useful formats. You can find a list of the input parameters for flickr.photos.search here:

http://www.flickr.com/services/api/flickr.photos.search.html

A script that I wrote to serve as a server-side proxy for flickr.photos.search is flickrgeo.php. You can run the script here:

http://examples.mashupguide.net/ch10/flickrgeo.php

The code is listed here:

http://examples.mashupguide.net/ch10/flickrgeo.php.txt

Moreover, you will find a complete listing of the code in Chapter 13, including a description of how it handles KML and KML network links (which is beyond what is covered here). In this section, I'll describe the overall structure of flickrgeo.php and discuss some example usage.

---

2. http://examples.mashupguide.net/ch10/weather.proxy.html

With several exceptions, all the parameters for flickr.photos.search are also parameters for flickrgeo.php:

- user_id

- tags

- tag_mode

- text

- min_upload_date

- max_upload_date

- min_taken_date

- max_taken_date

- license

- sort

- privacy_filter

- accuracy

- safe_search

- content_type

- machine_tags

- machine_tag_mode

- group_id

- place_id

- extras

- per_page

- page

There are three differences between the parameters for flickr.photos.search and for flickrgeo.php. First, the api_key is hardwired for flickrgeo.php. Second, instead of using the single bbox parameter from flickr.photos.search to specify the bounding box for geotagged photos, flickrgeo.php takes four parameters: lat0, lon0, lat1, and lon1 where lat0, lon0 and lat1, lon1 are, respectively, the southwest and northeast corners of the bounding box. Hence, the value of the bbox parameter for flickr.photos.search is {lon0},{lat0},{lon1},{lat1}.

Second, instead of using the format parameter for Flickr API methods, which takes one of rest (the default value), xml-rpc, soap, json, or php, flickrgeo.php uses an o_format parameter to control the output of the script. These are the values recognized by the script:

- `rest` returns the default (rest) output from the Flickr API.

- `json` returns the JSON output from the Flickr API.

- `html` returns an HTML form and list of photos.

- `kml` returns the search results as KML (see Chapter 13 for more details).

- `nl` returns the results as a KML network link (see Chapter 13 for more details).

If the `o_format` is not set or is equal to `html`, then you want to return the HTML form and a display of the photos. If the `o_format` is `rest`, return the default output from the Flickr API (rest). If it's `json`, you want to return the JSON output with no callback.

For example, a sample invocation of this script shows the first page of geotagged photos tagged with `cat` from all over the world:

```
http://examples.mashupguide.net/ch10/flickrgeo.php?tags=cat&lat0=-90&lon0=-180&lat1=➡
90&lon1=180&page=1&per_page=10&o_format=html
```

If you change the `o_format` to `json`, you get JSON output:

```
http://examples.mashupguide.net/ch10/flickrgeo.php?tags=cat&lat0=-90&lon0=-180&lat1=➡
90&lon1=180&page=1&per_page=10&o_format=json
```

This script generates a simple user interface so that you can test the input parameters. That is, you can use the `html` interface to see what photos are coming back and then switch the output to `json`, `rest`, `kml`, or `nl` to be used in your server-side proxy. Much of the code is devoted to generating KML and KML network links, functionality used in Chapter 13. There's also some other convenience functionality: automatic form generation, error checking, and some useful default values for the `bbox` parameter. Again, consult Chapter 13 for more details.

Building a Simple Client-Side Frame

You now have `flickrgeo.php`, a server-side proxy for talking to Flickr. Before you turn your attention to directly connecting Google Maps with Flickr, I'll remind you about two basic interactions between the DOM and JavaScript:

- Reading and writing DOM elements, `<div>` elements, and form elements

- Handling simple events to connect form input and displaying calculations

Reading and Writing Elements

In this section, I will remind you how to do some basic things in browser-based JavaScript. Specifically, I'll review how to manipulate certain DOM elements. This section will seem trivial to experienced JavaScript developers, but the example provides a starting point for the rest of the chapter.

To that end of learning some basic JavaScript techniques, create the following HTML file:[3]

```
<!DOCTYPE html PUBLIC "-//W3C//DTD XHTML 1.0 Transitional//EN"
"http://www.w3.org/TR/xhtml1/DTD/xhtml1-transitional.dtd">
<html xmlns="http://www.w3.org/1999/xhtml" xml:lang="en" lang="en">
  <head>
    <title>Dom Play</title>
  </head>
  <body>
    <div id="container"></div>
  </body>
</html>
```

Fire up the JavaScript Shell and the Firebug extension to follow what happens when you type the following commands:

```
document
```

```
[object HTMLDocument]
```

```
div = document.getElementById('container')
```

```
[object HTMLDivElement]
```

```
div.innerHTML = 'hello';
```

```
hello
```

Notice that the word *hello* shows up on the web page now. You've just used JavaScript to write to the DOM, specifically *hello* to the innerHTML of the <div> element with the ID of container.

The next step is to write an example with an input box and a submit button. When you hit submit, the calc_square() JavaScript function calculates the square of the number and updates the result box (the answer span). Start with the following, though we'll leave the calc_square() function empty for now:[4]

```
<!DOCTYPE html PUBLIC "-//W3C//DTD XHTML 1.0 Transitional//EN"
"http://www.w3.org/TR/xhtml1/DTD/xhtml1-transitional.dtd">
<html xmlns="http://www.w3.org/1999/xhtml" xml:lang="en" lang="en">
```

---

3. http://examples.mashupguide.net/ch10/dom.html
4. http://examples.mashupguide.net/ch10/square1.html

```
<head>
  <title>Squaring the input(square1.html)</title>
  <meta http-equiv="Content-Type" content="text/html;charset=utf-8" />
</head>
<body>
  <script type="text/javascript">
  //<![CDATA[
    function calc_square() {
    }
  //]]>
  </script>
  <form action="#" onsubmit="calc_square(); return false;">
    <label>Input a number:</label>
    <input type="text" size="5" name="num" value="0" />
    <input type="submit" value="Square it!" />
  </form>
  <p>The square of the input is: <span id="answer">0</span></p>
</body>
</html>
```

In the JavaScript Shell, try the following pieces of code:

```
document
```

```
[object HTMLDocument]
```

```
document.forms[0].innerHTML
```

```
<label>Input a number:</label><input size="5" name="num" value="0" type="text">
<input value="Square it!" type="submit">
```

```
document.forms[0].elements[0].value
```

```
0
```

Change the value in the text box, and try it again to see the new value reflected (note num is the ID of the <input> element):

```
document.forms[0].num.value
```

```
8
```

The following gets you the <answer> element:

```
span.document.getElementById('answer')
```

```
[object HTMLSpanElement]
```

Finally, this will fill in 16 to the <answer> element:

```
span.document.getElementById('answer').innerHTML = 16
```

```
16
```

Handling Simple Events to Connect Form Input and Display Calculations

Next, you'll want to figure out how to programmatically submit the form (you'll use this logic later). Instead of having to hit the submit button, you will create a method that responds to the button submission event. Remember, in the previous example, it is the job of the calc_square() method (which was left empty) to read the input, calculate the square of the input, and write the answer to the answer box. Let's fill in calc_square with something like this:[5]

```
<script type="text/javascript">
//<![CDATA[
 function calc_square() {
     var n = document.forms[0].num.value;
     document.getElementById('answer').innerHTML = n*n;
 }
//]]>
</script>
<form action="#" onsubmit="calc_square(); return false;">
  <label>Input a number:</label>
  <input type="text" size="5" name="num" value="0" />
  <input type="submit" value="Square it!" />
</form>
<p>The square of the input is: <span id="answer">0</span></p>
<script type="text/javascript">
//<![CDATA[
  document.forms[0].num.onchange = calc_square;  //register an event
//]]>
</script>
```

---

5. http://examples.mashupguide.net/ch10/square2.html

Hooking the Client-Side Framework to Flickr

Now that you've constructed some simple JavaScript code to read form elements and do a calculation in response to a button submission event, you're ready to wire up a form to use XHR to access the flickrgeo.php server-side proxy. That is, you'll let the user fill in new values and do the form submission by JavaScript. Once the user hits Go!, the script returns a URL to use flickrgeo.php to search for geotagged photos. We'll build up the example in three steps:

1. Translate the form parameters into a query to flickrgeo.php.

2. Use XHR to do the request to flickrgeo.php and display the resulting JSON response.

3. Translate that JSON into HTML for display.

Let's start with the following:

```
<!DOCTYPE html PUBLIC "-//W3C//DTD XHTML 1.0 Transitional//EN"
"http://www.w3.org/TR/xhtml1/DTD/xhtml1-transitional.dtd">
<html xmlns="http://www.w3.org/1999/xhtml" xml:lang="en" lang="en">
  <head>
    <title>flickrgeo.1.html</title>
    <meta http-equiv="Content-Type" content="text/html;charset=utf-8" />
  </head>
  <body>
    <script type="text/javascript">
    //<![CDATA[
    function get_pictures() {
    /*
    We're aiming for the following:
    flickrgeo.php?tags=flower&lat0=-90&lon0=-180&lat1=90&lon1=180&page=1➥
&per_page=10&o_format=json
    */
    }
    //]]>
    </script>
    <form action="#" onsubmit="get_pictures(); return false;">
      <label>Search for photos with the following tag:</label>
      <input type="text" size="20" name="tag" value="flower" />
      <label> located at: lat0,lon0,lat1,lon1:</label>
      <input type="text" size="10" name="lat0" value="-90.0" />
      <input type="text" size="10" name="lon0" value="-180.0" />
      <input type="text" size="10" name="lat1" value="90.0" />
      <input type="text" size="10" name="lon1" value="180.0" />
      <label>at page</label>
      <input type="text" size="4" name="page" value="1" />
      <label>with</label>
      <input type="text" size="3" name="per_page" value="1" />
      <label> per page.</label>
      <button type="submit">Go!</button>
    </form>
```

```
    <div id="pics"></div>
  </body>
</html>
```

Writing a URL for Querying flickrgeo.php

Your goal is to figure out how to fill in get_pictues() to translate the input parameters from the form into a URL of the correct form. Here's one possible approach:[6]

```
<script type="text/javascript">
//<![CDATA[
function get_pictures() {
// flickrgeo.php?tags=flower&lat0=-90&lon0=-180&lat1=90&lon1=180&page=1&per_page
// =10&o_format=json
  var s = "";
  f = document.forms[0].getElementsByTagName('input'); // get all input fields
  for (i = 0; i < f.length; i++)
    if (i < f.length - 1) {
      s = s + f[i].name + "=" + escape(f[i].value) + "&amp;";
    } else {
      s = s + f[i].name + "=" + escape(f[i].value);
    }
  var url = "flickrgeo.php?" + s + "&o_format=json";
  document.getElementById('pics').innerHTML = "<a href=" + url + ">URL</a>";
}
//]]>
</script>
```

The get_pictures function iterates through all the <input> tags in the form, extracting the name and value of each tag, out of which to create a URL (with parameters) to flickrgeo.php. This URL is an HTTP GET request for JSON-formatted results for the given parameters.

Using XHR via the YUI Connection Manager to Read the JSON

The next step is to actually grab the JSON that is available at the URL. Using what you learned earlier (in the section "What Happens with XHR and Direct API Calls"), let's use the YUI Connection Manager to call flickrgeo.php and display the raw JSON:[7]

```
<!DOCTYPE html PUBLIC "-//W3C//DTD XHTML 1.0 Transitional//EN"
"http://www.w3.org/TR/xhtml1/DTD/xhtml1-transitional.dtd">
<html xmlns="http://www.w3.org/1999/xhtml" xml:lang="en" lang="en">
  <head>
    <title>flickrgeo.2.html</title>
    <meta http-equiv="Content-Type" content="text/html;charset=utf-8" />
    <script type="text/javascript" src="/lib/yui/build/yahoo/yahoo.js"></script>
```

---

6. http://examples.mashupguide.net/ch10/flickrgeo.1.html

7. http://examples.mashupguide.net/ch10/flickrgeo.2.html

```
    <script type="text/javascript" src="/lib/yui/build/event/event.js"></script>
    <script type="text/javascript" src="/lib/yui/build/connection/connection.js">
    </script>
</head>
<body>
    <script type="text/javascript">
    //<![CDATA[

    var handleSuccess = function(o){

      div = document.getElementById('pics');
      div.innerHTML = "";  // blank out the div

      if(o.responseText !== undefined){

        div.innerHTML += "Server response: " + o.responseText + "<br/>";
      }

    }


    var handleFailure = function(o){
      if(o.responseText !== undefined){
          alert("failure");
      }
    }

    var callback =
    {
      success:handleSuccess, failure: handleFailure, argument: {}
    };

function get_pictures() {
// flickrgeo.php?tags=flower&lat0=-90&lon0=-180&lat1=90&lon1=180&page=1&per_page
// =10&o_format=json
  var s = "";
  f = document.forms[0].getElementsByTagName('input'); // get all input fields
  for (i = 0; i < f.length; i++)
    if (i < f.length - 1) {
      s = s + f[i].name + "=" + escape(f[i].value) + "&";
    } else {
      s = s + f[i].name + "=" + escape(f[i].value);
    }
  var url = "flickrgeo.php?" + s + "&o_format=json";
  var request = YAHOO.util.Connect.asyncRequest('GET', url, callback);

}
//]]>
```

```
    </script>
    <form action="#" onsubmit="get_pictures(); return false;">
<label>Search for photos with the following tag:</label>
<input type="text" size="20" name="tags" value="flower" />
<label> located at: lat0,lon0,lat1,lon1:</label>
<input type="text" size="10" name="lat0" value="-90.0" />
<input type="text" size="10" name="lon0" value="-180.0" />
<input type="text" size="10" name="lat1" value="90.0" />
<input type="text" size="10" name="lon1" value="180.0" />
<label>at page</label><input type="text" size="4" name="page" value="1" />
<label>with</label>
<input type="text" size="3" name="per_page" value="1" /><label> per page.</label>
<button type="submit">Go!</button>
    </form>
    <div id="pics"></div>
  </body>
</html>
```

Note what was added:

- <script> elements to include the relevant parts of the Yahoo! UI Library to enable the use of the Connection Manager.

- The definition of callback functions (handleSuccess and handleFailure), which are referenced by the callback object, to handle successful and failed calls, respectively, to flickrgeo.php. If the call is successful, the JSON output from flickrgeo.php is written into the <div id="pics"></div>.

- A call to the Yahoo! Connection Manager in the line var request = YAHOO.util.Connect. asyncRequest('GET', url, callback);. Remember that an HTTP GET request is made to url and the HTTP response is fed to the functions contained in the callback object.

Converting the JSON to HTML

The next step is to convert the JSON input to HTML so that you can use it to display the photos. Note how you can use eval() to convert the JSON coming back from Flickr to a JavaScript object because you trust the source of this JSON. An alternative to eval() is JSON stringify().[8]

Here's some code:[9]

```
  <body>
    <script type="text/javascript">
    //<![CDATA[

    function rspToHTML(rsp) {
      var s = "";
```

___

8. http://www.json.org/js.html

9. http://examples.mashupguide.net/ch10/flickrgeo.3.html

```
  // http://farm{farm-id}.static.flickr.com/{server-id}/{id}_{secret}_[mstb].jpg
  // http://www.flickr.com/photos/{user-id}/{photo-id}
  s = "total number is: " + rsp.photos.photo.length + "<br/>";

  for (var i=0; i < rsp.photos.photo.length; i++) {
    photo = rsp.photos.photo[i];
    t_url = "http://farm" + photo.farm + ".static.flickr.com/" + photo.server +
      "/" + photo.id + "_" + photo.secret + "_" + "t.jpg";
    p_url = "http://www.flickr.com/photos/" + photo.owner + "/" + photo.id;
    s +=  '<a href="' + p_url + '">' + '<img alt="'+ photo.title + '"src="' +
      t_url + '"/>' + '</a>';
  }
  return s;
}

var handleSuccess = function(o){
  div = document.getElementById('pics');
  div.innerHTML = "";  // blank out the div

  if(o.responseText !== undefined){
    div.innerHTML += "Server response: " + o.responseText + "<br/>";

    //let's deposit the response in a global variable
    //so that we can look at it via the shell.
    window.response = o.responseText;
    window.rsp = eval('(' + o.responseText + ')');
    div.innerHTML = rspToHTML(window.rsp);
  }
}

var handleFailure = function(o){
  ...
}

var callback =
{
  ...
};

function get_pictures() {

  ...
}
//]]>
</script>
<form action="#" onsubmit="get_pictures(); return false;">
  ...
```

```
  </form>
  <div id="pics"></div>
</body>
```

You now have a client-side form that uses XHR to query the Flickr API, get back results in JSON, convert the JSON to HTML, and insert that HTML into the page—without a page reload (see Figure 10-1). The next steps are to integrate these results with Google Maps—the work of the next section.

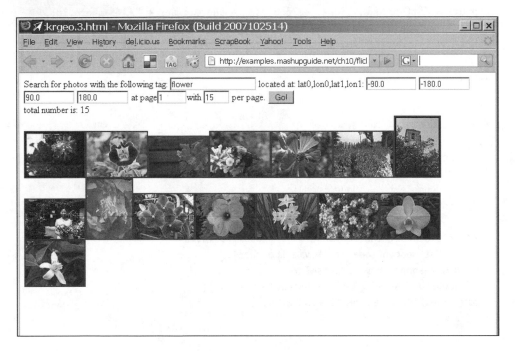

Figure 10-1. *Results of* flickrgeo.3.html. *Geotagged photos are displayed as HTML in response to the XHR request.*

Mashing Up Google Maps API with Flickr

You now have all the pieces needed to finish up the Flickr and Google Maps mashup. Here's a step-by-step walk-through of the big steps:

1. Set up a basic Google map.

2. Have the map respond to changes in the viewport of the map.

3. Bring together Flickr and GMap into the same HTML page by combining the code into one file—the two pieces are just together but don't interact.

4. Wire up the bounding box of the Google map to be the source of the lat/long coordinates.

5. Write the coordinates into the lat0/lon0 and lat1/lon1 boxes.

6. Make the pictures show up in the map.

Setting Up a Basic Google Map

To start with, let's just get a simple Google map set up by using the Google Maps API (which you learned about in Chapter 8):

1. Make sure you have the Google Maps key needed for your domain. The domain I have is `http://examples.mashupguide.net/ch10`. You can calculate the corresponding API key:

   ```
   http://www.google.com/maps/api_signup?url=http%3A%2F%2Fexamples.mashup➥
   guide.net%2Fch10
   ```

2. Copy the following code, substituting your key, to get a map centered on UC Berkeley with the size, map-type control, and keyboard handlers (you can use the arrow keys to control the map):[10]

```
<!DOCTYPE html PUBLIC "-//W3C//DTD XHTML 1.0 Strict//EN"
  "http://www.w3.org/TR/xhtml1/DTD/xhtml1-strict.dtd">
<html xmlns="http://www.w3.org/1999/xhtml">
  <head>
    <meta http-equiv="content-type" content="text/html; charset=utf-8"/>
    <title>Google Maps JavaScript API Example</title>
    <script src="http://maps.google.com/maps?file=api&amp;v=2&amp;key=➥
[API_KEY]"
       type="text/javascript"></script>
    <script type="text/javascript">

    //<![CDATA[

    function load() {
      if (GBrowserIsCompatible()) {
        var map = new GMap2(document.getElementById("map"));
        window.map = map;
        map.setCenter(new GLatLng(37.872035,-122.257844), 13);
        map.addControl(new GSmallMapControl());
        map.addControl(new GMapTypeControl());
      }
    }

    //]]>
    </script>
  </head>
  <body onload="load()" onunload="GUnload()">
    <div id="map" style="width: 800px; height: 600px"></div>
  </body>
</html>
```

---

10. `http://examples.mashupguide.net/ch10/gmap.1.html`

Making the Map Respond to Changes in the Viewport of the Map

The next thing to pull off is to have the map respond to changes in the viewport of the map (that is, when the user has panned or zoomed the map). The mechanism to use is Google Maps events:

```
http://www.google.com/apis/maps/documentation/#Events_overview
```

You can get a list of supported events here:

```
http://www.google.com/apis/maps/documentation/reference.html#GMap2
```

The relevant event we need here is the moveend event, the one that is fired once the viewport of the map has stopped changing (as opposed to the move event, which is fired during the changing of the viewport). To see this event in action, load the Google map you just created and use the JavaScript Shell to add a listener for the moveend event:

```
onMapMoveEnd = function () {alert("You moved or zoomed the map");}
```

```
function () { alert("You moved or zoomed the map"); }
```

```
GEvent.addListener(map,'moveend', onMapMoveEnd);
```

```
[object Object]
```

With that event listener added, every time you finish panning or zooming the map, an alert box pops up with the message "You moved or zoomed the map."

Let's now write some code that displays the bounding box in a <div> element, updating this information every time the map is moved. We are doing this as a stepping-stone to feeding the bounding box information to flickrgeo.php. Here's the code:[11]

```
<!DOCTYPE html PUBLIC "-//W3C//DTD XHTML 1.0 Strict//EN"
  "http://www.w3.org/TR/xhtml1/DTD/xhtml1-strict.dtd">
<html xmlns="http://www.w3.org/1999/xhtml">
  <head>
    <meta http-equiv="content-type" content="text/html; charset=utf-8"/>
    <title>gmap.2.html</title>
    <script src="http://maps.google.com/maps?file=api&amp;v=2&amp;key=[API_KEY]"
      type="text/javascript"></script>
    <script type="text/javascript">

    //<![CDATA[
```

---

11. http://examples.mashupguide.net/ch10/gmap.2.html

```
        function updateStatus() {
          var div = document.getElementById('mapinfo');
          div.innerHTML = map.getBounds();
          return (1);
        }

        function onMapMove() {

          updateStatus();
        }

        function onMapZoom(oldZoom, newZoom) {

          updateStatus();
        }

        function load() {
          if (GBrowserIsCompatible()) {
            var map = new GMap2(document.getElementById("map"));
            window.map = map;
            map.setCenter(new GLatLng(37.872035,-122.257844), 13);
            map.addControl(new GSmallMapControl());
            map.addControl(new GMapTypeControl());
            window.kh = new GKeyboardHandler(map);

            GEvent.addListener(map,'moveend',onMapMove);
            GEvent.addListener(map,'zoomend',onMapZoom);
            updateStatus();
          }
        }

      //]]>
      </script>
    </head>

  <body onload="load()" onunload="GUnload()">
    <div id="map" style="width: 800px; height: 600px"></div>
    <div id="mapinfo"></div>
  </body>
</html>
```

Bringing Together the Flickr and GMap Code

At this point, you are now ready to bring together the Flickr elements (the input form hooked up to flickrgeo.php) and the Google map. The first thing to do is to display the two parts on the same page without having them interact. Getting things displaying side by side ensures that you have the proper dependencies worked out. Once you get there, then you can wire the two pieces together. The first thing to do is to copy and paste code from your Flickr code and GMap code into one file. Here is one possible way to do it:

```
http://examples.mashupguide.net/ch10/gmapflickr1.html
```

Wiring Up the Bounding Box of the Google Map

Let's get some interaction going between the Flickr parts and the Google map, now that they are contained in the same HTML page. Let's wire up the bounding box of the Google map to be the source of the lat/long coordinates. Now, when you move or zoom the Google map, the new coordinates are written into the form elements (the lat0/lon0 and lat1/lon1 boxes) for the Flickr search.[12]

```
<!DOCTYPE html PUBLIC "-//W3C//DTD XHTML 1.0 Transitional//EN"
"http://www.w3.org/TR/xhtml1/DTD/xhtml1-transitional.dtd">
<html xmlns="http://www.w3.org/1999/xhtml" xml:lang="en" lang="en">
  <head>
    <meta http-equiv="content-type" content="text/html; charset=utf-8" />
    <title>gmapflickr.2.html</title>
    <script src="http://maps.google.com/maps?file=api&amp;v=2&amp;key=[API_KEY]"
      type="text/javascript"></script>
    <script type="text/javascript">

    //<![CDATA[

    function updateStatus() {
      var div = document.getElementById('mapinfo');
      div.innerHTML = map.getBounds();

      document.forms[0].lat0.value = map.getBounds().getSouthWest().lat();
      document.forms[0].lon0.value = map.getBounds().getSouthWest().lng();
      document.forms[0].lat1.value = map.getBounds().getNorthEast().lat();
      document.forms[0].lon1.value = map.getBounds().getNorthEast().lng();

      get_pictures();
    }

    function onMapMove() {
      updateStatus();
    }

    function onMapZoom(oldZoom, newZoom) {
      updateStatus();
    }

    function load() {
```

---

12. http://examples.mashupguide.net/ch10/gmapflickr2.html

```
    ...
}

//]]>
</script>
<script type="text/javascript" src="/lib/yui/build/yahoo/yahoo.js"></script>
<script type="text/javascript" src="/lib/yui/build/event/event.js"></script>
<script type="text/javascript"
        src="/lib/yui/build/connection/connection.js"></script>
<script type="text/javascript">
//<![CDATA[
function rspToHTML(rsp) {
  var s = "";
  // http://farm{farm-id}.static.flickr.com/{server-id}/{id}_{secret}_[mstb].jpg
  // http://www.flickr.com/photos/{user-id}/{photo-id}
  s = "total number available is: " + rsp.photos.total + "<br/>";

  for (var i=0; i < rsp.photos.photo.length; i++) {
    photo = rsp.photos.photo[i];
    t_url = "http://farm" + photo.farm + ".static.flickr.com/" + photo.server +
      "/" + photo.id + "_" + photo.secret + "_" + "t.jpg";
    p_url = "http://www.flickr.com/photos/" + photo.owner + "/" + photo.id;
    s += '<a href="' + p_url + '">' + '<img alt="'+ photo.title + '"src="' +
      t_url + '"/>' + '</a>';
  }
  return s;
}

var handleSuccess = function(o){


    ...
  }
}

var handleFailure = function(o){

  ...
}

var callback =
{
  ...
};

function get_pictures() {
```

```
        ...
      }
      //]]>
      </script>
  </head>

  <body onload="load()" onunload="GUnload()">
    <form action="#" onsubmit="get_pictures(); return false;">
      <label>Search for photos with the following tag:</label>
      <input type="text" size="20" name="tags" value="flower" />
      <label> located at: lat0,lon0,lat1,lon1:</label>
      <input type="text" size="10" name="lat0" value="-90.0" />
      <input type="text" size="10" name="lon0" value="-180.0" />
      <input type="text" size="10" name="lat1" value="90.0" />
      <input type="text" size="10" name="lon1" value="180.0" />
      <label>at page</label><input type="text" size="4" name="page" value="1" />
      <label>with</label>
      <input type="text" size="3" name="per_page" value="1" />
      <label> per page.</label>
      <button type="submit">Go!</button>
    </form>
  <div id="pics"></div>
  <div id="map" style="width: 800px; height: 600px"></div>
  <div id="mapinfo"></div>
  </body>
</html>
```

Note that as soon as the page is loaded, the load function is called, which in turn calls updateStatus. The result is a search for photos using the starting parameters in the form. That is, geotagged photos tagged with flower are retrieved and displayed. You can change the starting photos by changing the default value for the <input> element to tags.

Making the Pictures Show Up in the Map

In this section, you'll complete the wiring between the Flickr results and the map. I'll show you how to display the images in the list on the map. This is done by creating markers for each of the photos and adding those markers as overlays to the map. That involves generating HTML to put into the markers.

I'll remind you how to add overlays to a Google map using the API:

```
point = new GLatLng (37.87309185260284, -122.25508689880371);
marker = new GMarker(point);
map.addOverlay(marker);
```

Here's the code with the new stuff in bold (see Figure 10-2):[13]

```
<!DOCTYPE html PUBLIC "-//W3C//DTD XHTML 1.0 Transitional//EN"
"http://www.w3.org/TR/xhtml1/DTD/xhtml1-transitional.dtd">
<html xmlns="http://www.w3.org/1999/xhtml" xml:lang="en" lang="en">
  <head>
    <meta http-equiv="content-type" content="text/html; charset=utf-8" />
    <title>gmapflickr.html</title>
    <script src="http://maps.google.com/maps?file=api&amp;v=2&amp;key=[API_KEY]"
      type="text/javascript"></script>
    <script type="text/javascript">

    //<![CDATA[
    // set up a blank object to hold markers that are added to the map
    markersInMap = {}

    function updateStatus() {
      var div = document.getElementById('mapinfo');
      div.innerHTML = map.getBounds();

      document.forms[0].lat0.value = map.getBounds().getSouthWest().lat();
      document.forms[0].lon0.value = map.getBounds().getSouthWest().lng();
      document.forms[0].lat1.value = map.getBounds().getNorthEast().lat();
      document.forms[0].lon1.value = map.getBounds().getNorthEast().lng();

      get_pictures();
    }

    // Creates a marker at the given point with the given msg.
    function createMarker(point, msg) {
      var marker = new GMarker(point);
      GEvent.addListener(marker, "click", function() {
        marker.openInfoWindowHtml(msg);
      });
      return marker;
    }

    function photos_to_markers(rsp) {

      // loop through the photos
      for (var i=0; i < rsp.photos.photo.length; i++) {
        var photo = rsp.photos.photo[i];
        // check whether marker already exists
```

---

13. http://examples.mashupguide.net/ch10/gmapflickr.html

```
      if (!(photo.id in markersInMap)) {
        var point = new GLatLng (photo.latitude, photo.longitude);
        var msg = photo.title + "<br>" + genPhotoLink(photo);
        map.addOverlay(createMarker(point, msg));
        markersInMap[photo.id] = "";  // don't know what to store so far.
      }
    }
  }
}

function onMapMove() {
  updateStatus();
}

function onMapZoom(oldZoom, newZoom) {
  updateStatus();
}

function load() {

  ...

}

//]]>
</script>
<script type="text/javascript" src="/lib/yui/build/yahoo/yahoo.js"></script>
<script type="text/javascript" src="/lib/yui/build/event/event.js"></script>
<script type="text/javascript"
        src="/lib/yui/build/connection/connection.js"></script>
<script type="text/javascript">
//<![CDATA[

function genPhotoLink(photo) {
    var t_url = "http://farm" + photo.farm + ".static.flickr.com/" +
      photo.server + "/" + photo.id + "_" + photo.secret + "_" + "t.jpg";
    var p_url = "http://www.flickr.com/photos/" + photo.owner + "/" + photo.id;

    return '<a href="' + p_url + '">' + '<img alt="'+ photo.title + '"src="' +
      t_url + '"/>' + '</a>';
}

function rspToHTML(rsp) {

  ...

}
```

```
  var handleSuccess = function(o){
    div = document.getElementById('pics');
    div.innerHTML = "";  // blank out the div

    if(o.responseText !== undefined){
      //let's deposit the response in a global variable
      //so that we can look at it via the shell.
      window.response = o.responseText;
      window.rsp = eval('(' + o.responseText + ')');
      div.innerHTML = rspToHTML(window.rsp);
      photos_to_markers(window.rsp);
    }
  }

  var handleFailure = function(o){

    ...
  }

  var callback =
  {
    ...
  };

  function get_pictures() {

    ...
  }
  //]]>
  </script>
</head>

<body onload="load()" onunload="GUnload()">
  <form action="#" onsubmit="get_pictures(); return false;">
    <label>Search for photos with the following tag:</label>
    <input type="text" size="20" name="tags" value="flower" />
    <label> located at: lat0,lon0,lat1,lon1:</label>
    <input type="text" size="10" name="lat0" value="-90.0" />
    <input type="text" size="10" name="lon0" value="-180.0" />
    <input type="text" size="10" name="lat1" value="90.0" />
    <input type="text" size="10" name="lon1" value="180.0" />
    <label>at page</label><input type="text" size="4" name="page" value="1" />
    <label>with</label>
    <input type="text" size="3" name="per_page" value="1" />
    <label> per page.</label>
```

```
        <button type="submit">Go!</button>
      </form>
    <div id="pics"></div>
    <div id="map" style="width: 800px; height: 600px"></div>
    <div id="mapinfo"></div>
    </body>
</html>
```

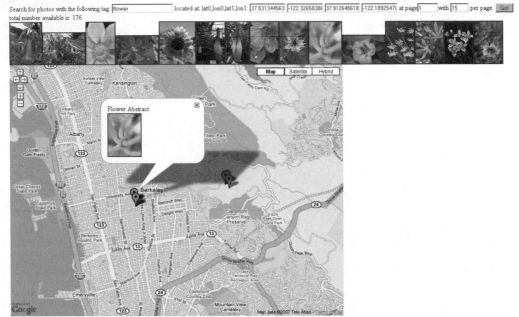

Figure 10-2. *The Flickr Google Maps mashup*

This is just a beginning of a mashup between Flickr geotagged photos and Google Maps. Some ideas for elaborating this mashup include the following:

- Refining the look and feel of the mashup (including removing `<div id="mapinfo">`, which currently displays the bounding box of the map)

- Dealing with the fact that clicking a marker and its consequent window opening moves the map

- Clustering photos that are at the same location (as is done in the Flickr map interface)

Google Mapplet That Shows Flickr Photos

In addition to the Google Maps API, which allows a developer to embed Google Maps on a third-party site, Google recently introduced Google Mapplets as a way of adding extensions to Google Maps directly as little applications that run in a side panel. (Any mapplet you install and turn on interacts with the same map. For example, if you are using a mapplet for displaying flower shops and another one that displays restaurants, the resulting Google map shows both flower shops and restaurants.) You can find developer information here:

```
http://www.google.com/apis/maps/documentation/mapplets/
```

In this section, I'll show you how to create a basic mapplet to display Flickr geotagged photos. Mapplets are a combination of JavaScript and HTML, embedded in an XML file. The methods you use are similar but not identical to those found in the Google Maps API, and there's no need to write any server-side components. The Mapplets API provides wrappers for XHR that talk to the Google servers (which in turn act like server-side proxies that we wrote in PHP).

You can find the source for a mapplet that allows users to search for Flickr pictures of a certain tag here:

```
http://examples.mashupguide.net/ch10/flickr.mapplet.xml
```

Add the mapplet to your collection of maps. (See "Adding a Google Mapplet to Your Google My Maps.")

ADDING A GOOGLE MAPPLET TO YOUR GOOGLE MY MAPS

1. Go to `http://maps.google.com/`, and log in to Google Maps if you are not already logged in.

2. Click the My Maps tab.

3. Click Browse the Directory button or link.

4. Click the Add by URL link to the right of the Search Google Maps Content button.

5. Enter the URL of the mapplet source (for example, `http://examples.mashupguide.net/ch10/flickr.mapplet.xml`), and hit the Add button.

6. Click Back to Google Maps.

7. Now you should now see on the My Maps tab under Created by Others a map called "Flickr Geotagged Photos." You can use the check box to turn it off and on.

Figure 10-3 shows the mapplet in action.

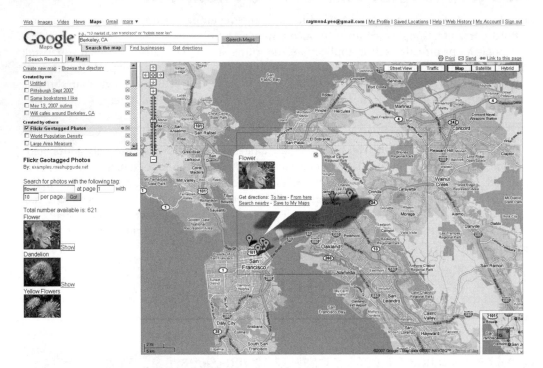

Figure 10-3. *The Flickr Google Maps mapplet mashup*

The source is as follows:

```
<?xml version="1.0" encoding="UTF-8"?>
<Module>
<ModulePrefs title="Flickr Geotagged Photos"
            description="Show Flickr photos"
            author="Raymond Yee"
            author_email="raymondyee@mashupguide.net"
            height="150">
  <Require feature="sharedmap"/>
</ModulePrefs>
<Content type="html"><![CDATA[

<script>

  var map = new GMap2();
  var border = null;

function genPhotoLink(photo) {
    var t_url = "http://farm" + photo.farm + ".static.flickr.com/" + photo.server +
      "/" + photo.id + "_" + photo.secret + "_" + "t.jpg";
    var p_url = "http://www.flickr.com/photos/" + photo.owner + "/" + photo.id;
```

```
      return '<a href="' + p_url + '">' + '<img alt="'+ photo.title + '"src="' +
        t_url + '"/>' + '</a>';
}

// Creates a marker at the given point with the given msg.
function createMarker(point, msg) {
  var marker = new GMarker(point);
  GEvent.addListener(marker, "click", function() {
    marker.openInfoWindowHtml(msg);
  });
  return marker;
}

function createMarkerAndDiv (point,msg) {
    var marker, e, anchors, alink

    marker = createMarker(point, msg);
    e = document.createElement("div");

    e.innerHTML = msg +  "<a href='#'>Show</a><br>"
    anchors = e.getElementsByTagName('a')
    alink = anchors[anchors.length-1];
    alink.onclick = function(){marker.openInfoWindowHtml(msg);}

    return [marker,e];
}

function cb(s) {
    var rsp = eval('(' + s + ')');
    var marker, e

    // clear the photos
    map.clearOverlays();

    // add border
    map.addOverlay(border);

    var pdiv = document.getElementById("pictures");
    pdiv.innerHTML = "Total number available is: " + rsp.photos.total + "<br/>";;

    // put the pictures on the map
    for (var i=0; i < rsp.photos.photo.length; i++) {
        var photo = rsp.photos.photo[i];

        var point = new GLatLng (photo.latitude, photo.longitude);
        var msg = photo.title + "<br>" + genPhotoLink(photo);
```

```
        md =  createMarkerAndDiv(point,msg);
        marker = md[0];
        e=md[1];

        map.addOverlay(marker);
        pdiv.appendChild(e);
    }
}

function get_pictures() {
    var API_KEY = "[API_KEY]";
    fForm = document.getElementById('FlickrForm');

    map.getBoundsAsync(function(bounds) {
      var lat0 = bounds.getSouthWest().lat();
      var lon0 = bounds.getSouthWest().lng();
      var lat1 = bounds.getNorthEast().lat();
      var lon1 = bounds.getNorthEast().lng();

      // add polyline to mark the search boundaries
      border  = new GPolygon([
        new GLatLng(lat0, lon0),
        new GLatLng(lat1, lon0),
        new GLatLng(lat1, lon1),
        new GLatLng(lat0,lon1),
        new GLatLng(lat0,lon0)
      ], "#ff0000", 2);

      var url = "http://api.flickr.com/services/rest/?method=flickr.photos.search" +
        "&api_key=" + API_KEY +
        "&bbox=" + lon0 + "%2C" + lat0 + "%2C" + lon1 + "%2C" + lat1  +
        "&per_page=" + fForm.per_page.value +
        "&page=" + fForm.page.value +
        "&format=json&nojsoncallback=1&extras=geo";

      var tagValue = fForm.tag.value;
      // search by tag only if the box is not blank.
      if (tagValue.length) {
        url = url + "&tags=" + fForm.tag.value;
      } else {
        url = url + "&min_upload_date=820483200";
      }

      _IG_FetchContent(url, cb);

    } //anonymous function
    ); //map.getBoundsAsync
```

```
} //get_pictures

</script>

<form action="#" onsubmit="get_pictures(); return false;" id="FlickrForm">
  <p>Search for photos with the following tag:
  <input type="text" size="20" name="tag" value="flower">
  at page <input type="text" size="4" name="page" value="1"> with
  <input type="text" size="3" name="per_page" value="10"> per page.
  <button type="submit">Go!</button></p>
</form>
<div id="pictures"></div>

]]></Content>
</Module>
```

A few words about the logic of this code:

- This code is compact partly because the _IG_FetchContent() method makes accessing the Flickr API fairly straightforward because you can code the URL directly to the Flickr API instead of having to create your own server-side proxy (such as flickrgeo.php).

- Mapplets do not provide much room to display content in the sidebar. Hence, the mapplet can be better optimized to make use of the small space.

Summary

In this chapter, you learned how to create a mashup of two different APIs, the Flickr API and the Google Maps API, to display geotagged Flickr photos on a Google map. After reviewing geotagging in Flickr, you learned how to access XML web services using the XMLHttpRequest browser object (XHR) and deal with security constraints in the browser by creating server-side proxies to access web services. You then looked at how to use flickrgeo.php, a server-side proxy to search photos in Flickr. You then set up a simple client-side framework that we transformed one step at a time into a mashup between Flickr and Google Maps. Finally, you refactored that work into a Flickr/Google mapplet to create a pure client-side solution.

Although this chapter focused on Flickr and Google Maps, what you learned in this chapter can be generalized for other mashups. For instance, you'll continue to see repeated interactions between server-side and client-side components. Building mashups in controlled steps, adding functionality one piece at a time, is a good way to work. Frameworks such as Google Mapplets let you write widgets in HTML and JavaScript by providing server-side proxies to access web services from other parties (such as the _IG_FetchContent() method in Google Mapplets).

When creating mashups, you are often faced with issues of "impedance matching"—that is, how to translate information from one source into a form that is usable by the consumer of that information. In this chapter, we focused on extracting geocoding information from Flickr and then translating it for use by Google Maps. Data flow went the other way too: how to get the viewport of the Google map to define the bounding box for a query for geotagged photos in Flickr. You will see the need to deal with impedance matching throughout the rest of the book.

■ ■ ■

## CHAPTER 11

Using Tools to Create Mashups

In the previous chapters, we focused on creating mashups through combining a number of technologies: XML, PHP, JavaScript, Python, and so on. As you've seen, creating mashups takes some amount of skill and knowledge. Can specialized tools make it easier to create mashups? In this chapter, I'll introduce several mashup-making tools and show the basics of how to use a few of them. My goal in this chapter is to pick ones that are popular, useful, and illustrative of some important issues or trends.

The focus of this chapter will be on using the Google Mashup Editor (GME) (in conjunction with Yahoo! Pipes) to build a Flickr/Google Maps mashup; it's like the one you saw in Chapter 10, but this one will show you how mashup-making tools make it easier (or different) from straight-up PHP and JavaScript programming, which you saw in Chapter 10. Specifically, this chapter includes the following:

- A tutorial on the GME

- A way of comparing mashup-making tools with the straight-up programming you did in previous chapters

I'll briefly describe some other tools (Microsoft Popfly, Dapper, and others). By essentially re-creating the Flickr/Google Maps mashup using the GME and Yahoo! Pipes, you'll see what mashup tools get you and what they don't get you.

The Problem Mashup Tools Solve

With a mashup-oriented mind-set in which you prize being able to integrate data and services (because integration brings value), you care about how to introduce new things that can be well integrated with the stuff you already use, without a high cost (in learning or effort to make those bridges).

Currently, creating mashups takes a lot of work to knit APIs together. You've already seen that work in the previous chapters and will see it again in the chapters that follow. APIs are similar to one another, but they are all somewhat different. One day, perhaps, you'll be able to mash up different APIs the same way that you can surf from one web site to another and make sense of them all. It may never be that easy, but it should be easier than how it is today.

Case in point: although WSDL is not perfect, something like WADL (roughly WSDL for RESTful APIs) would be really helpful in alleviating the syntactic complications of connecting stuff, if not exactly making autosemantic connections possible.

Another major problem is that getting data to work together from different APIs requires translating among them. RDF promises to be a close-to-universal data representation. I have always thought there is some merit to the semantic web stack, at the bottom of which is RDF. Hence, I'm keeping an eye on RDF and other semantic web tools. I can certainly believe that if more and more data were expressed in RDF, things would connect better. RDF is, however, not a panacea. (That's why I think a study of the SIMILE project (`http://simile.mit.edu`) is a practical way to start looking at semantic web technology.)

Specifically, when you use a new API, you want to minimize the type of new learning; you want the API to be similar to what you've already seen before. I think of the DRY ("don't repeat yourself") principle: it's nice to not have to tackle the same thing repeatedly—solve it once, run it anywhere. For example, if you write code to access the Flickr API in one language and in one framework, wouldn't it be nice to be able to not have to redo that code when you have another need? That's the ideal anyway.

Tools and services can help you reach these goals. The key aspect of good tools is that they simplify the routine stuff and let you concentrate on the essence of the problem. There are always trade-offs, however—and we'll look at them as we look at the various tools.

What You Are Making in This Chapter

As mentioned, the focus of this chapter will be using the GME in conjunction with Yahoo! Pipes to build a Flickr/Google Maps mashup. Let's first look at the final product that I will show you how to build step by step. Doing so will teach you about the GME and Yahoo! Pipes (when you load the mashup, you will be asked to log in using your Google e-mail address because this app requires authentication):

```
http://mashup-raymond-yee-flickrfeed4.googlemashups.com/
```

This mashup displays geotagged photos on a Google map. There are two tabs: Search and Saved Results. Let's consider the Search tab (see Figure 11-1). Upon loading, the map is set to Berkeley, California—and recent geotagged photos around that area are loaded in a list form and also displayed on a Google map. Remember that when you use the Flickr API to search for geotagged photos, you need to specify a geographic region (a *bounding box*) in which you are searching for photos. This mashup map shows a rectangle to denote this search bounding box.

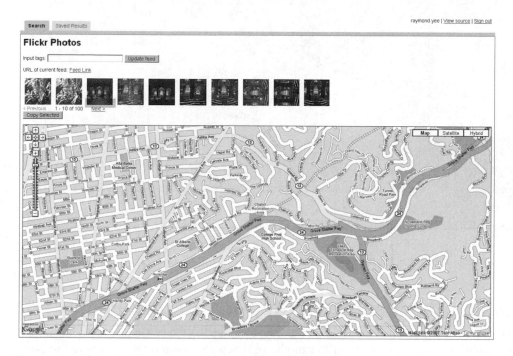

Figure 11-1. *The Search tab of the Flickr/Google Maps mashup*

When you enter a tag, a search is done on geotagged photos with the specified tag within the current bounding box of the map. Up to 100 results are loaded at a time; you can page through the photos.

Notice that there is a Copy Selected button. You can select a photo and hit that button, which saves the selected photo to your saved entries feed, which you can then see on the Saved Results tab (see Figure 11-2). On this second tab, you find a list of the Flickr photos that you have saved in addition to a map showing the locations of the saved photos. You'll also see a Delete Selected button that lets you remove a selected photo from your feed of saved entries.

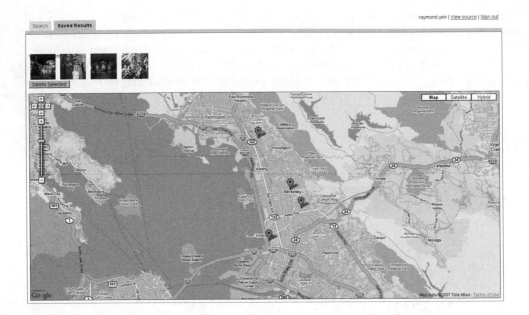

Figure 11-2. *The Saved Results tab of the Flickr/Google Maps mashup*

Now let's build this mashup step by step.

Making the Mashup: A Step-by-Step Example

In this section, you will be redoing and extending Chapter 10's Flickr/Google Maps mashup. First you'll see how to reproduce the example, and then you'll extend it because of the data persistence that is possible with the GME. One of the distinctive elements of the GME is its ability to persist data with feeds, which is an elegant approach. It allows for the extensibility of data elements in an easy-to-fashion way (for example, you'll see that there's no need to predefine a data schema).

Even though this chapter is about mashup tools in general, I will use the GME and Yahoo! Pipes first and then survey a few others. Yahoo! Pipes has been out for a while and has proven itself to be very useful. Though the GME is a new product, it is a promising one, backed also by a big company. There are similarities but also important differences with Yahoo! Pipes; the two are actually complementary, as I will show in the extended example of this chapter. That example will cover the following:

- Familiarizing yourself with the GME

- Reading and displaying a feed

- Introducing a custom template

- Using Yahoo! Pipes to access the Flickr API

- Displaying Flickr photos using `<gm:map>`

- Adding JavaScript to update the feed parameters and give the coordinates of the map

- Learning how to persist feeds and use tabs

- Making the final product

Familiarizing Yourself with the Google Mashup Editor

The GME (`http://editor.googlemashups.com/editor`) is a browser-based environment that makes it easier to create mashups that are hosted on Google.

You can find documentation on how to use the GME here:

```
http://code.google.com/gme/
```

The GME is targeted at programmers familiar with HTML, CSS, and JavaScript, and it is a programming environment. You can intermix browser-side techniques in HTML, CSS, and JavaScript with GME tags. This combination is compiled into web pages (with HTML, CSS, and JavaScript) that run on modern browsers—the GME tags are converted into JavaScript.

■**Note** As this book goes to press, the Google Mashup Editor is still under closed beta.

You don't have to use the browser-based editor to use the GME. See the sidebar "Using Subversion (SVN) to Access Your Project" to learn about accessing your code via SVN.

You should keep the tag reference located at the following URL handy while programming with the GME:

```
http://editor.googlemashups.com/docs/reference.html
```

Contrast the GME to Yahoo! Pipes. The GME is a text-based programming environment, while Yahoo! Pipes is a visual programming environment.

The first step is to save a new project and give it a display title (for example, "Flickr on Google Maps") and a single-word/lowercase string for a project name (`flickrgmap`). Look at the starter code for `index.gml` for a new project:

```
<gm:page title="My App" authenticate="false">

</gm:page>
```

The next step is to customize it to have it say something like this:

```
<gm:page title="Flickr Photos on Google Maps" authenticate="false">

<!--
Displaying Flickr Photos on a Google Map
@author: Raymond Yee
-->

<h1>Flickr Photos</h1>

</gm:page>
```

After you have copied and pasted the previous code, I suggest just getting familiar with the environment. That is, hit Save, and enter a display name and project name. Then hit Test to see your basic application compile; you'll be brought to the Sandbox tab to see the application run.

Reading and Displaying a Feed (Simple Template)

The GME makes it easy to read and write Atom and RSS feeds. Let's get a Flickr Atom or RSS feed flowing into the GME. Go to the Feed Browser tab in the GME; in the list of GData feeds, you can choose from the Test feed (which you can use to test your code), the Remote Feed feed, and the Google Base feed.

■**Note** Currently, the GME is unable to read in XML data other than RSS and Atom 2.0 feeds. You can use Yahoo! Pipes to convert XML to RSS 2.0, which can in turn be processed by GME.

Let's give it a feed of geotagged photos from Flickr Central:

```
http://api.flickr.com/services/feeds/geo/?g=34427469792@N01➥
&lang=en-us&format=rss_200
```

Use the Feed Browser tab's Remote Feed to read it in and see how the RSS 2.0 feed is converted to Atom 1.0. The native format for the GME is Atom 1.0, but the GME can accept RSS 2.0 and Atom 1.0. Feeding the RSS 2.0 feed to the GME Feed Browser tab shows how feeds are converted to Atom 1.0, and you refer to the data elements in the Atom format. For example, the GME makes extensive use of *GPath*, a small subset of XPath expressions, to refer to specific elements or attributes in a feed.[1] For instance, the GPath expression `atom:title` will return the title of an RSS item, which has been converted to an Atom element.

Let's create a simple GME application that reads and displays the feed, using a `<gm:list>` tag to specify the URL of the feed. You tell GME how to display this feed by using a *template*. In the next section, I'll show you how to create a custom template. In this section, you'll use one of the built-in templates (specifically `simple`) to display the feed, as shown here:

```
<gm:page title="Flickr Photos on Google Maps" authenticate="false">

<!--
Displaying Flickr Photos on a Google Map
@author: Raymond Yee
-->

<h1>Flickr Photos</h1>

<gm:list id="flickrList" template="simple"
        data="http://api.flickr.com/services/feeds/geo/?g=34427469792@N01
```

---

1. http://code.google.com/gme/docs/data.html#xpath

```
&lang=en-us&format=rss_200"
         pagesize="10"/>
```

```
</gm:page>
```

Note the types of built-in templates: `simple` (which lists only the title of each entry), `task` (which displays a check box to mark a task as done, the due date, and the priority), and `blog` (which is a template particularly suited to feeds coming from blogs).

Introducing a Custom Template

Now let's use `<gm:template>` to customize how the feed is displayed—specifically to get the image in the list:

```
<gm:page title="Flickr Photos on Google Maps" authenticate="false">

<!--
Displaying Flickr Photos on a Google Map
@author: Raymond Yee
-->

<h1>Flickr Photos</h1>

  <gm:list id="flickrList" template="flickrTemplate"
           data="http://api.flickr.com/services/feeds/geo/?g=34427469792@N01&lang=➥
en-us&format=rss_200" pagesize="10"/>

  <gm:template id="flickrTemplate">
    <table class="blue-theme" style="width:50%">
      <tr repeat="true">
        <td style="padding-bottom:10px">
          <b><gm:text ref="atom:title"/></b>
          <br/>
          <gm:html ref="atom:summary"/>
          <br/>
          <span style="color:#3366cc">
            location: (<gm:text ref="geo:Point/geo:lat"/>,
                       <gm:text ref="geo:Point/geo:long"/>)
          </span>
        </td>
      </tr>
    </table>
  </gm:template>

</gm:page>
```

You can see the code here:

```
http://mashup-raymond-yee-flickrfeed1.googlecode.com/svn/trunk/index.gml
```

And you can run the app here:

```
http://mashup-raymond-yee-flickrfeed1.googlemashups.com/
```

Note the following about this template:

- There are built-in CSS classes; this example uses `blue-theme`.

- This example uses `<tr repeat="true">` to repeat a `<tr>` for each Atom entry. This is useful because there is no need to write a loop explicitly.

- The template for each entry displays the text of the title (`<gm:text ref="atom:title">`) and the HTML in the summary (`<gm:html ref="atom:summary"/>`).

- See how you can get at the geotag of each entry through the GPath entries `geo:Point/geo:lat` and `geo:Point/geo:long`. You can use the Feed Browser tab to help you figure out the XPath by hovering over the element you want to access.

USING SUBVERSION (SVN) TO ACCESS YOUR PROJECT

Instead of using the browser-based editor to edit your code, you can use Subversion (`http://en.wikipedia.org/wiki/Subversion_(software)`) to download and check in your edits. You will find basic documentation of how to use SVN in the context of the GME here:

```
http://code.google.com/support/bin/answer.py?answer=76145&topic=11689
```

Each mashup project you create with the GME generates a separate project hosted by Google Code. To find a list of these projects on Google Code, visit the following URL:

```
http://code.google.com/hosting/
```

Click Settings to get your Google Code password, which you need for Subversion. Click the My Profile tab to go to your list of projects. In my case, the My Profile tab leads to the following:

```
http://code.google.com/u/raymond.yee/
```

Consider a specific project. One project I created through GME is available here:

```
http://code.google.com/p/mashup-raymond-yee-flickrfeed2/
```

You can browse the code here:

```
http://mashup-raymond-yee-flickrfeed2.googlecode.com/svn/
```

The code `index.gml` for the project is available here:

```
http://mashup-raymond-yee-flickrfeed2.googlecode.com/svn/trunk/index.gml
```

Note that, by default, the code you produce using GME is licensed under an Apache 2.0 license. You can change it on the Administer tab:

```
http://code.google.com/p/mashup-raymond-yee-flickrfeed2/admin
```

You can find instructions for using SVN to check out the code here:

```
http://code.google.com/p/mashup-raymond-yee-flickrfeed2/source
```

Once your code is checked out, you use your favorite desktop editor instead of being confined to editing source through a web browser. Moreover, it's also easier to edit many files simultaneously rather than depending on the browser-based editor in which you can currently edit only one file at a time.

Using Yahoo! Pipes to Access Flickr

The GME needs RSS 2.0 or Atom—and cannot read XML feeds in general. Yahoo! Pipes, on the other hand, can be used to read XML in general and emit RSS 2.0. The Flickr API doesn't currently output RSS 2.0 and Atom 1.0, but rather its own custom XML (although as we learned in Chapter 4, there is an extensive selection of feeds from Flickr).

Here I'll show you a Yahoo! Pipe that is created to be an interface to `flickr.photos.search`. That is, you can input the same parameters as you can to `flickr.photos.search`, but instead of getting Flickr XML, you get RSS 2.0. Here's the pipe I generated:

```
http://pipes.yahoo.com/raymondyee/flickr_photos_search
```

You can also find it here:

```
http://pipes.yahoo.com/pipes/pipe.info?_id=YG9eZGWO3BGukZGJTqoASA
```

The parameters for this pipe are similar to the `flickrgeo.php` server-side proxy that you wrote for Chapter 10 (and will see again in Chapter 13). The parameters are almost the same as the parameters you'll find for `flickr.photos.search` with the following exceptions:

- This pipe handles only unauthenticated searches.

- Instead of `bbox` to denote the bounding box, the pipe uses `lat0,lon0,lat1,lat1`.

- There is no use of a `format` or `o_format` parameter (as for `flickrgeo.php`) since the pipe controls the output.

- The pipe has some default parameters to search for geotagged photos around downtown Berkeley, California.

As to how to create this pipe, refer to the tutorial on pipes in Chapter 4. I'll mention a few possibly tricky parts here. (You can check out the source of the pipe on the Yahoo! Pipes site.) First, you need to create a text input or number input for each of the parameters (this process is a bit tedious given there are 24 input parameters).

To convert the Flickr XML to RSS 2.0, you can use several *loops*:

- A loop to create an `item.image_prefix` for each item. The `item.image_prefix` is used as the first part of a URL to point to Flickr images of various sizes.

- A second loop to create `item.image_small_URL` by concatenating `item.image_prefix` with `_s`.

- A third loop to calculate and assign item.link—a link to the Flickr page of the photo.

- A fourth loop to calculate and assign item.description, which holds HTML for the small square version of the Flickr photo.

Note that the last two loops are the ones that directly affect the translation of the Flickr XML to RSS 2.0. Finally, the pipe uses the Location Extractor module[2] to extract the longitude and latitude from the Flickr results into <geo:lat> and <geo:long> for each photo.

Using the default parameters with RSS 2.0 output, here's the code:

```
http://pipes.yahoo.com/pipes/pipe.run?_id=YG9eZGWO3BGukZGJTqoASA&_render=rss➡
&api_key={api_key}&extras=geo&lat0=37.817785166068&lat1=37.926190569376&lon0=➡
-122.34375&lon1=-122.17208862305&min_upload_date=820483200&per_page=10
```

If you wanted KML output, you'd use the following:

```
http://pipes.yahoo.com/pipes/pipe.run?_id=YG9eZGWO3BGukZGJTqoASA&_render=kml
```

RETAINING NONCORE RSS 2.0 ELEMENTS IN YAHOO! PIPES

I was hoping that the RSS 2.0 feed emitted by the pipe would retain nonstandard elements calculated by the pipe (for example, <image_prefix>) that would make calculating the URL for various image sizes more straightforward. It turns out that the RSS 2.0 feed doesn't have this information—although the JSON feed does indeed contain the extra parameters.

```
http://pipes.yahoo.com/pipes/pipe.run?_id=YG9eZGWO3BGukZGJTqoASA&_render=➡
json&api_key={api_key}&extras=geo&lat0=37.817785166068&lat1=37.926190569376&➡
lon0=-122.34375&lon1=-122.17208862305&min_upload_date=820483200&per_page=10
```

One way to solve this problem is to write a web service in PHP to transform the JSON to RSS 2.0 with extension elements—but that defeats the purpose of trying to make this stuff easier.[3]

Displaying Flickr Photos Using <gm:map>

Remember that the overall goal in this iteration is to display the Flickr photos on a Google map. Now that you have access to the Flickr API (via the pipe you just created), you can change the source of Flickr photos to the pipe that accesses flickr.photos.search as the source of images:

```
http://pipes.yahoo.com/pipes/pipe.run?_id=YG9eZGWO3BGukZGJTqoASA&_render=rss➡
&api_key={api_key}&extras=geo&lat0=37.817785166068&lat1=37.926190569376&lon0=➡
-122.34375&lon1=-122.17208862305&min_upload_date=820483200&per_page=100
```

---

2. http://pipes.yahoo.com/pipes/docs?doc=operators#LocationExtractor

3. http://discuss.pipes.yahoo.com/Message_Boards_for_Pipes/threadview?m=tm&bn=pip-DeveloperHelp&tid=2513&mid=2517&tof=-1&rt=2&frt=2&off=1

Here the parameters to the pipe are hard-coded; later I'll show you how to construct a form to let a user change the parameters.

I'll first show you the resultant code for this iteration and then explain the pieces:

```
<gm:page title="Flickr Photos on Google Maps" authenticate="false">


<!--
Displaying Flickr Thumbnails on a Google Map (hardwired parameters)
@author: Raymond Yee
-->


  <h1>Flickr Photos</h1>

  <gm:list id="flickrList" template="flickrTemplate"
           data="http://pipes.yahoo.com/pipes/pipe.run?_id=YG9eZGWO3BGukZGJTqoAS➥
A&_render=rss&api_key=e81ef8102a5160154ef4662adcc9046b&extras=geo&lat0=37.817785➥
166068&lat1=37.926190569376&lon0=-122.34375&lon1=-122.17208862305&min_upload_➥
date=820483200&per_page=100" pagesize="10">
      <gm:handleEvent event="select" src="flickrMap"/>
  </gm:list>


  <gm:map id="flickrMap" style="border:solid black 1px" control="large"
          maptypes="true" data="${flickrList}" latref="geo:lat" lngref="geo:long"
            infotemplate="FlickrMapDetailsTemplate" height="600">
      <gm:handleEvent event="select" src="flickrList"/>
   </gm:map>


  <!-- flickrTemplate -->

  <gm:template id="flickrTemplate" class="blue-theme">
    <div style="float:left; width:85px" repeat="true">
      <gm:html ref="atom:summary"/>
    </div>
    <br style="clear:both"/>
    <gm:pager/>
  </gm:template>


  <!-- FlickrMapDetailsTemplate -->

  <gm:template id="FlickrMapDetailsTemplate">
    <div >
      <b><gm:link ref="atom:link[@rel='alternate']/@href" labelref="atom:title" />
      </b>
      <br/>
      <gm:html ref="atom:summary"/>
      <br/>
      Lat: <gm:text ref="geo:lat"/><br/>
      Long: <gm:text ref="geo:long"/>
```

```
      </div>
   </gm:template>

</gm:page>
```

I published this app at the following location:

http://mashup-raymond-yee-flickrfeed2.googlemashups.com/

You'll see how I changed the data attribute in <gm:list> to point to the new source of data. In addition, I revised <gm:template> to use <div> instead of a <table> and to display only the thumbnail. Moreover, I added a <gm:pager/> to enable the user to page through the images ten at a time.

Next, you use a <gm:map> element to instantiate a map:

```
<gm:map id="flickrMap" style="border:solid black 1px" control="large"
      maptypes="true" data="${flickrList}" latref="geo:lat" lngref="geo:long"
      infotemplate="FlickrMapDetailsTemplate" height="600">
   <gm:handleEvent event="select" src="flickrList"/>
</gm:map>
```

Note how the parameters for <gm:map> are constructed:

- The data attribute (set to ${flickrList}, which is the ID of your <gm:list>) makes the tie to the input data source defined in the <gm:list> element.

- The latref and lngref attributes are the XPath (or in the parlance of the GME, the GPath) expressions relative to a feed entry to get at the latitude and longitude. (You can use the Feed Browser tab to determine this quantity.)

- The <gm:handleEvent> tells the map to respond to a select event from the flickrList. That is, when a user clicks a photo in the <gm:list>, the corresponding marker on the map pops open.

- In a fashion similar to the template for the Flickr thumbnails, you can create a template to control how the bubbles on the map are displayed.

Note in general how this declarative approach replaces having to write a lot of HTML and JavaScript. Indeed, the mashup we created in Chapter 10 doesn't have this interaction between the display of thumbnails and the markers on the map.

Adding JavaScript to the Mashup

The goals of the next pass of development are as follows:

- Pass a subset of the parameters (instead of having hard-coded parameters) to Yahoo! Pipes.

- Let the user set the bounding box of the search, and draw a bounding box on the map to indicate this bounding box.

Before jumping into doing this, you might want to consult the sidebar "Introducing Custom JavaScript into the GME."

INTRODUCING CUSTOM JAVASCRIPT INTO THE GME

Before I try to introduce a new element (in this case some JavaScript event handling) into the main code I'm working on, I often like to write a little side program to test this idea. The following is a simple program that involves an input form and a submission event, reminiscent of a simple example from Chapter 10 (`http://examples.mashupguide.net/ch10/square2.html`):

```
<gm:page title="Squaring Input and Flickr feed" authenticate="false">
<!--
  Introducing custom JavaScript into a GME mashup
-->

    <form action="#" onsubmit="calc_square(); return false;">
      <label>Input a number:</label>
      <input type="text" size="5" name="num" value="4" />
      <input type="submit" value="Square it!" />
    </form>

    <p>The square of the input is: <span id="answer">16</span></p>

  <gm:list id="flickrList" template="flickrTemplate"
          data="http://pipes.yahoo.com/pipes/pipe.run?_id=YG9eZGWO3BGukZGJTqoA➥
SA&_render=rss&api_key={api_key}&extras=geo➥
&lat0=37.817785166068&lat1=37.926190569376&lon0=-122.34375&lon1=-122.17208862305➥
&min_upload_date=820483200&per_page=100"
          pagesize="10" />

  <!-- flickrTemplate -->

  <gm:template id="flickrTemplate" class="blue-theme">
    <div>
      <span repeat="true" style="padding: 5px">
        <gm:html ref="atom:summary"/>
      </span>
      <gm:pager/>
    </div>
  </gm:template>

  <script type="text/javascript">
    //<![CDATA[
      function calc_square() {
          var n = document.forms[0].num.value;
          document.getElementById('answer').innerHTML = n*n;
      }

      document.forms[0].num.onchange = calc_square;  //register an event
```

```
    //]]>
  </script>
</gm:page>
```

When you run this code, you'll see that a lot of the JavaScript techniques for event handling can be directly interspersed with the GME tags.

You can find the code I created to accomplish these goals here:

http://mashup-raymond-yee-flickrfeed3.googlecode.com/svn/trunk/index.gml

You can run the code here:

http://mashup-raymond-yee-flickrfeed3.googlemashups.com/

Here's the code:

```
<gm:page title="Flickr Photos on Google Maps" authenticate="false"
         onload="init_data();">

<!--
Displaying Flickr Thumbnails on a Google Map
@author: Raymond Yee
-->

  <h1>Flickr Photos</h1>

  <form action="#" onsubmit="update_feed(); return false;">
    <label>Input tags:</label><input type="text" size="30" name="tags" value="" />
    <input type="submit" value="Update feed" />
  </form>

  <p>URL of current feed: <span id="current_tags">.</span></p>

  <gm:list id="flickrList" template="flickrTemplate" pagesize="10">
    <gm:handleEvent event="select" src="flickrMap"/>
  </gm:list>

  <gm:map id="flickrMap" style="border:solid black 1px" control="large"
          maptypes="true" data="${flickrList}" latref="geo:lat" lngref="geo:long"
            infotemplate="FlickrMapDetailsTemplate" height="600">
      <gm:handleEvent event="select" src="flickrList"/>
  </gm:map>

  <!-- flickrTemplate -->

  <gm:template id="flickrTemplate" class="blue-theme">
    <div style="float:left; width:85px" repeat="true">
```

```
    <gm:html ref="atom:summary"/>
  </div>
  <br style="clear:both"/>
  <gm:pager/>
</gm:template>

<!-- FlickrMapDetailsTemplate -->

<gm:template id="FlickrMapDetailsTemplate">
  <div >
    <b><gm:link ref="atom:link[@rel='alternate']/@href" labelref="atom:title" />
    </b>
    <br/>
    <gm:html ref="atom:summary"/>
    <br/>
    Lat: <gm:text ref="geo:lat"/><br/>
    Long: <gm:text ref="geo:long"/>
  </div>
</gm:template>

<script type="text/javascript">
  //<![CDATA[
    function update_feed() {
        var tags = document.forms[0].tags.value;

    // let's get the bounds of the map
        var flickrMap = google.mashups.getObjectById('flickrMap');

        var bounds = flickrMap.getBounds();
        var lat0 = bounds.getSouthWest().lat();
        var lon0 = bounds.getSouthWest().lng();
        var lat1 = bounds.getNorthEast().lat();
        var lon1 = bounds.getNorthEast().lng();

        update_feed0 (tags,lat0,lon0,lat1,lon1);

    } // update_feed

  function update_feed0(tags,lat0,lon0,lat1,lon1) {

      var flickrList = google.mashups.getObjectById('flickrList');
      var flickrMap = google.mashups.getObjectById('flickrMap');
      var url = 'http://pipes.yahoo.com/pipes/pipe.run?_id=YG9eZGWO3BGukZGJ➥
TqoASA&_render=rss&api_key=e81ef8102a5160154ef4662adcc9046b&extras=geo&min_➥
upload_date=820483200&per_page=100' + '&tags=' + escape (tags) + "&lat0="➥
        + lat0 + "&lon0=" + lon0 + "&lat1=" + lat1 + "&lon1=" + lon1;
```

```
        // clear the old overlays (I'm doing this to get rid of the boundary

        flickrMap.getMap().clearOverlays();

        document.getElementById('current_tags').innerHTML =
          "<a href='" + url + "'>Feed Link</a>";

        flickrList.setData(url);
        flickrList.setPage(0);   // reset the pager

        // now draw a bounding box

        border = new GPolygon([
        new GLatLng(lat0, lon0),
        new GLatLng(lat1, lon0),
        new GLatLng(lat1, lon1),
        new GLatLng(lat0,lon1),
        new GLatLng(lat0,lon0)
        ], "#ff0000", 2);

        flickrMap.getMap().addOverlay(border);

    } // update_feed0

      function init_data() {

          var lat0=37.817785166068;
          var lat1=37.926190569376
          var lon0=-122.34375;
          var lon1=-122.17208862305;

          update_feed0("",lat0,lon0,lat1,lon1);

      } // init_data

    //]]>
    </script>

  </gm:page>
```

The code in bold was what changed from the previous code. Recall that the overall goal of this iteration is to go from a hard-coded Flickr search with a set of hard-coded parameters to a search that uses the map to determine the bounding box and also that allows the user to specify the Flickr tag on which to search. To implement this functionality, you can add an HTML form to accept input tags. You also create the function update_feed() to respond to a form submission in the following ways:

- Calculates the appropriate URL to the Yahoo! Pipes to search for geotagged Flickr photos that match the tags and are found in the given bounding box. The init_data() method, which sets the initial location for the map, calls update_feed(), which in turn calculates the URL to Yahoo! Pipes and uses the setData(url) method of the <gm:list> to load the data.

- Draws a bounding box on the map to mark the current search area.

How to Persist Feeds and Use Tabs

The next major task to try is the data persistence aspects of the GME. In this section, you'll learn how to create a simple database, specifically, a feed to save Flickr images that a user finds interesting. These feeds persist between sessions. (That is, when users log out and return to the mashup, they can find their saved results as they left them.) You will learn also how to copy data from one feed to another. Finally, you will learn how to use the tab support in the GME.

Specifically, I'll show you how to build a mashup that has two tabs. The first tab (Search) shows Flickr images from a hard-coded feed. Each photo is displayed with a button to let a user copy the image to a feed of saved photos. The second tab (Saved Results) displays this feed of saved photos.

The code I wrote to implement this design, which can be found here:

```
http://mashup-raymond-yee-tabs0.googlecode.com/svn/trunk/index.gml
```

is shown here:

```
<gm:page title="Tabs0" authenticate="true">
  <!--
  Load the feeds in one tab and allow to copy selected entries to a data source
  in another tab
  -->

  <gm:tabs target="myContainer"/>

  <gm:container id="myContainer"
                style="padding:3px;border:1px solid #369;width:600px;">

    <gm:section id="sectionFlickrSearch" title="Search">
      <gm:list id="myList" template="flickrTemplate"
               data="http://pipes.yahoo.com/pipes/pipe.run?_id=YG9eZGWO3BGukZGJTqoA➥
SA&_render=rss&extras=geo&lat0=37.817785166068&lat1=37.926190569376&lon0=-122.34375&➥
lon1=-122.17208862305&min_upload_date=820483200&per_page=10" pagesize="10"/>
    </gm:section>

    <gm:section id="sectionSavedEntries" title="Saved Results">
      <gm:list id="savedEntries" data="${user}/crud"
               template="savedEntryTemplate" />
    </gm:section>

  </gm:container>
```

```
<gm:template id="flickrTemplate">
  <table class="blue-theme" style="width:50%">
    <tr repeat="true">
      <td style="padding-bottom:10px">
        <b><gm:text ref="atom:title"/></b>
        <br/>
        <gm:html ref="atom:summary"/>
        <br/>
        <span style="color:#3366cc">
            location: (<gm:text ref="geo:lat"/>, <gm:text ref="geo:long"/>)
        </span>
        <br/>
        <input type="button" value="Copy" onclick="copy_this(this)" />
      </td>
    </tr>
  </table>
</gm:template>

 <gm:template id="savedEntryTemplate">
   <div>Your saved entries</div>
   <table class="blue-theme" style="width:50%">
     <tr repeat="true">
       <td style="padding-bottom:10px">
         <b><gm:text ref="atom:title"/></b>
         <br/>
         <gm:html ref="atom:summary"/>
         <br/>
         <span style="color:#3366cc">
             location: (<gm:text ref="geo:lat"/>, <gm:text ref="geo:long"/>)
         </span>
         <gm:editButtons deleteonly="true" />
       </td>
     </tr>
   </table>
 </gm:template>

<script type="text/javascript">
//<![CDATA[

function copy_this(DOMElement) {
  var entry = google.mashups.getEntryForElement(DOMElement);
  var myList = google.mashups.getObjectById('myList');
  var savedEntries = google.mashups.getObjectById('savedEntries');
  savedEntries.getData().addEntry(entry);
}
```

```
//]]>
</script>

</gm:page>
```

You can run this mashup here:

`http://mashup-raymond-yee-tabs0a.googlemashups.com/`

Let's look at how this code works:

- Three tags are used to create the two tabs. A `<gm:tabs>` tag is used to instantiate a set of tabs, with a target attribute pointing to a `<gm:container>` element that in turn holds a `<gm:section>` for each tab.[4]

- The `copy_this()` function is invoked when the Copy button corresponding to a thumbnail is clicked. This function identifies the feed entry matching the selected DOM element and copies the element to the feed whose ID is `savedEntries`.

- The `authenticate` attribute of the `<gm:page>` element is set to `true`, so users must sign in to a Google account to use the application.

Once a user creates a collection, you can access the resulting feeds. See the instructions here:

`http://code.google.com/support/bin/answer.py?answer=76140&topic=11689`

The generic URL of a user feed is as follows:

`{PUBLISHED_MASHUP_NAME}.googlemashups.com/feeds/public/user/{USER_EMAIL}/➥`
`<STRIPE_NAME>`

`STRIPE_NAME` is essentially an identifier for a feed. In the case of our mashup, the feed of my saved entries is available here:

`http://mashup-raymond-yee-tabs0a.googlemashups.com/feeds/public/user/raymond.yee➥`
`%40gmail.com/crud`

The following relative URL—relative to the logged-in user, that is—also works:

`http://mashup-raymond-yee-tabs0a.googlemashups.com/feeds/user/crud`

This feed works only from a browser with the right credentials (that is, cookies from a logged-in user in a browser).

■Note When writing GME feeds, keep in mind that the maximum number of entries in a custom feed is 1000.

---

4. `http://code.google.com/gme/docs/samples.html#tabs`

Changing the Selection and Deletion Process for the Photos

The previous code attaches a copy button to each image. In this section, you'll rewrite the code to switch to showing small thumbnails horizontally and to have a Copy Selected button on the Search tab. Similarly, let's add a Delete Selected button to the Saved Results tab.

The code for the new version, available from here:

```
http://mashup-raymond-yee-tabs1.googlecode.com/svn/trunk/index.gml
```

is as follows:

```
<gm:page title="Tabs1" authenticate="true">
  <!--
  Load the feeds in one tab and allow to copy selected entries to a data source
  in another tab
  -->

  <gm:tabs target="myContainer"/>

  <gm:container id="myContainer" style="padding:3px;border:1px solid #369;">

    <gm:section id="sectionFlickrSearch" title="Search">
      <gm:list id="flickrList" template="flickrTemplate"
               data="http://pipes.yahoo.com/pipes/pipe.run?_id=YG9eZGWO3BGukZGJTqoAS➥
A&_render=rss&api_key=e81ef8102a5160154ef4662adcc9046b&extras=geo&lat0=37.8177851660➥
68&lat1=37.926190569376&lon0=-122.34375&lon1=-122.17208862305&min_upload_date=820483➥
200&per_page=100"
               pagesize="10" />
      <input type="button" value="Copy Selected" onclick="copy_selected()" />
    </gm:section>

    <gm:section id="sectionSavedEntries" title="Saved Results">
      <gm:list id="savedEntries" data="${user}/crud"
               template="savedEntryTemplate" />
      <input type="button" value="Delete Selected" onclick="delete_selected()" />
    </gm:section>

  </gm:container>

  <!-- flickrTemplate -->

  <gm:template id="flickrTemplate" class="blue-theme">
    <div style="float:left; width:85px" repeat="true">
      <gm:html ref="atom:summary"/>
    </div>
    <br style="clear:both"/>
    <gm:pager/>
  </gm:template>
```

```
<!-- savedEntryTemplate -->

<gm:template id="savedEntryTemplate">
    <div>Your saved entries</div>
    <div style="float:left; width:85px" repeat="true">
     <gm:html ref="atom:summary"/>
    </div>
    <br style="clear:both"/>
    <gm:pager/>
</gm:template>

<script type="text/javascript">
//<![CDATA[

// figure what is the currently selected entry and copy that over
function copy_selected() {

  var flickrList = google.mashups.getObjectById('flickrList');
  var entry = flickrList.getSelectedEntry();
  if (entry) {
    var savedEntries = google.mashups.getObjectById('savedEntries');
    savedEntries.getData().addEntry(entry);
  }

} // copy_selected

function delete_selected() {

  var savedEntries = google.mashups.getObjectById('savedEntries');
  var entry = savedEntries.getSelectedEntry();
  if (entry) {
    savedEntries.getData().removeEntry(entry);
  }

} // delete_selected

//]]>
</script>

</gm:page>
```

You can run the new code here:

```
http://mashup-raymond-yee-tabs1.googlemashups.com/
```

The key changes to the code are as follows:

- Switching from a vertical to a horizontal template and adding a single Save Selected button and Delete Selected button to the tabs—instead of having a separate button for each photo entry

- Adding the appropriate event handlers (copy_selected() and delete_selected())

The Final Product: Showing the Saved Entries on a Map

You are now ready to create the final product with the GME. You can do so by embedding the search and display of geotagged Flickr photos on a Google map from here:

http://mashup-raymond-yee-tabs1.googlemashups.com/

with the overall framework of two tabs to hold search results and saved entries:

http://mashup-raymond-yee-flickrfeed3.googlemashups.com/

The final product is at http://mashup-raymond-yee-flickrfeed4.googlemashups.com/.

The code is at http://mashup-raymond-yee-flickrfeed4.googlecode.com/svn/trunk/index.gml; it's as follows:

```
<gm:page title="Flickr Photos on Google Maps" authenticate="true"
         onload="init_data();">

<!--
Displaying Flickr Thumbnails on a Google Map (flickrfeed4)
@author: Raymond Yee
-->

  <gm:tabs target="myContainer"/>

  <gm:container id="myContainer" style="padding:3px;border:1px solid #369;">

      <!-- searchFlickrSearch section
      -->

    <gm:section id="sectionFlickrSearch" title="Search">

      <h1>Flickr Photos</h1>

      <form action="#" onsubmit="update_feed(); return false;">
        <label>Input tags:</label>
        <input type="text" size="30" name="tags" value="" />
        <input type="submit" value="Update feed" />
      </form>

      <p>URL of current feed: <span id="current_tags">.</span></p>
```

```
      <gm:list id="flickrList" template="flickrTemplate" pagesize="10">
        <gm:handleEvent event="select" src="flickrMap"/>
      </gm:list>
      <input type="button" value="Copy Selected" onclick="copy_selected()" />

      <gm:map id="flickrMap" style="border:solid black 1px" control="large"
              maptypes="true" data="${flickrList}" latref="geo:lat"
              lngref="geo:long"
              infotemplate="FlickrMapDetailsTemplate" height="600">
          <gm:handleEvent event="select" src="flickrList"/>
        </gm:map>

    </gm:section>

    <!-- sectionSavedEntries -->

    <gm:section id="sectionSavedEntries" title="Saved Results">

      <gm:list id="savedEntries" data="${user}/crud" template="savedEntryTemplate"
/>

      <input type="button" value="Delete Selected" onclick="delete_selected()" />

      <gm:map id="flickrMap2" style="border:solid black 1px" control="large"
              maptypes="true" data="${savedEntries}" latref="geo:lat"
              lngref="geo:long"
              infotemplate="FlickrMapDetailsTemplate" he1ght="600">
          <gm:handleEvent event="select" src="savedEntries"/>
        </gm:map>

    </gm:section>

  </gm:container>

<!-- flickrTemplate -->

  <gm:template id="flickrTemplate" class="blue-theme">
    <div style="float:left; width:85px" repeat="true">
      <gm:html ref="atom:summary"/>
    </div>
    <br style="clear:both"/>
    <gm:pager/>
  </gm:template>

<!-- FlickrMapDetailsTemplate -->
```

```
<gm:template id="FlickrMapDetailsTemplate">
  <div >
    <b><gm:link ref="atom:link[@rel='alternate']/@href" labelref="atom:title" />
    </b>
    <br/>
    <gm:html ref="atom:summary"/>
    <br/>
    Lat: <gm:text ref="geo:lat"/><br/>
    Long: <gm:text ref="geo:long"/>
  </div>
</gm:template>

<!-- savedEntryTemplate -->

<gm:template id="savedEntryTemplate">
  <div>Your saved entries</div>
  <div style="float:left; width:85px" repeat="true">
  <gm:html ref="atom:summary"/>
  </div>
  <br style="clear:both"/>
  <gm:pager/>
</gm:template>

<script type="text/javascript">
  //<![CDATA[
  function update_feed() {
      var tags = document.forms[0].tags.value;

    // let's get the bounds of the map
      var flickrMap = google.mashups.getObjectById('flickrMap');

      var bounds = flickrMap.getBounds();
      var lat0 = bounds.getSouthWest().lat();
      var lon0 = bounds.getSouthWest().lng();
      var lat1 = bounds.getNorthEast().lat();
      var lon1 = bounds.getNorthEast().lng();

      update_feed0 (tags,lat0,lon0,lat1,lon1);

    } // update_feed

  function update_feed0(tags,lat0,lon0,lat1,lon1) {

    var flickrList = google.mashups.getObjectById('flickrList');
    var flickrMap = google.mashups.getObjectById('flickrMap');
```

```
    var url =
        'http://pipes.yahoo.com/pipes/pipe.run?_id=YG9eZGWO3BGukZGJTqoASA&_render=➥
rss&api_key=e81ef8102a5160154ef4662adcc9046b&extras=geo&min_upload_date=820483200&➥
per_page=100'
        + '&tags=' + escape (tags) + "&lat0=" + lat0 + "&lon0=" + lon0
        + "&lat1=" + lat1 + "&lon1=" + lon1;

    // clear the old overlays (I'm doing this to get rid of the boundary)

    flickrMap.getMap().clearOverlays();

    document.getElementById('current_tags').innerHTML =
        "<a href='" + url + "'>Feed Link</a>";

    //a lert('flickrList' + flickrList);
    // alert('url' + url);

    flickrList.setData(url);
    flickrList.setPage(0);  // reset the pager

    // now draw a bounding box

    border = new GPolygon([
    new GLatLng(lat0, lon0),
    new GLatLng(lat1, lon0),
    new GLatLng(lat1, lon1),
    new GLatLng(lat0,lon1),
    new GLatLng(lat0,lon0)
    ], "#ff0000", 2);

    flickrMap.getMap().addOverlay(border);

} // update_feed0

    function init_data() {

        var lat0=37.817785166068;
        var lat1=37.926190569376;
        var lon0=-122.34375;
        var lon1=-122.17208862305;

        update_feed0("",lat0,lon0,lat1,lon1);

    } // init_data

// figure what is the currently selected entry and copy that over
    function copy_selected() {
```

```
      var flickrList = google.mashups.getObjectById('flickrList');
      var entry = flickrList.getSelectedEntry();
      if (entry) {
        var savedEntries = google.mashups.getObjectById('savedEntries');
        savedEntries.getData().addEntry(entry);
      }

    } // copy_selected

    function delete_selected() {

      var savedEntries = google.mashups.getObjectById('savedEntries');
      var entry = savedEntries.getSelectedEntry();
      if (entry) {
        savedEntries.getData().removeEntry(entry);
      }

    } // delete_selected

    //]]>
  </script>

</gm:page>
```

Note When writing your first apps, you might wonder why the data doesn't persist between sessions. Publish your mashup first.

At this point, you have a mashup that covers much of the GME's capabilities, and you can continue developing this mashup. Some possible further steps include the following:

- You could incorporate the GME's annotation support, which would allow users to add tags and ratings to feed entries (http://code.google.com/gme/docs/data.html#annotations).

- You could create a better input form to let a user enter any of the input parameters that can be fed to the Yahoo! pipe. It would be nice to have collapsible input boxes for a streamlined interface. Connecting the GME to some nice Ajax widget libraries would be helpful.

- You could minimize redundancy by packaging reusable code into modules. Currently, GME files cannot include other GME files. Once the GME lets programmers create reusable modules, you can then rewrite the mashups in this chapter to pull out common features in different tabs.

Analysis of Trade-Offs in Using GME and Yahoo! Pipes

Now that you have created mashups of Flickr and Google Maps using both specialized mashup tools (a combination of the GME and Yahoo! Pipes) and general-purpose web programming techniques (PHP and JavaScript), let's compare these two approaches. First, consider that the GME and Yahoo! Pipes provide the following to you as a developer:

- Hosting is provided; you don't need to use your own server.

- Instead of PHP and JavaScript, you program only in JavaScript. This can be considered an advantage in that you don't have to know PHP to use the GME and Yahoo! Pipes. Google and Yahoo! are doing the server-side proxying for you.

- You don't need to register for separate API keys for Google Maps to use the maps.

- You get access to a Subversion interface, to issue tracking, and to the other features of Google Code, which is used to host the GME code.

- Both the GME and Yahoo! Pipes make it easier to see what others are building; hence, they promote the sharing of tips, ideas, and code.

There are, of course, trade-offs you make by using the GME, Yahoo! Pipes, and possibly other third-party tools:

- Each tool generally presents a new framework to learn. Some are easier to learn than others, often by building on what you are likely to know from other contexts. However, there is always something new to learn.

- Sometimes the abstractions used by a given tool are not quite what you want. For instance, the central data exchange format is Atom feeds, which can be either an apt simplification or a burdensome limitation.

- Having your application hosted on the GME or Yahoo! Pipes means revealing your data and code to Google or Yahoo!

- The identity and branding of your mashup will be associated with Google or Yahoo!

- You become dependent on the infrastructure of Google and Yahoo! Lock-in could become a problem.

There are a couple of things that it would be nice to get from Yahoo! Pipes and the GME:

- Being able to host your code on your own server. If Google were one day to let you compile GME code into HTML and JavaScript that could then be modified and run independently of the GME, that would increase GME's attractiveness to many developers and users.

- GME does not have the ability to read in information other than RSS and Atom feeds. Right now, Yahoo! Pipes fills that niche well—by using pipes to read in XML and then converting it to feeds, you can then process that data in GME. However, the GME being able to process XML beyond RSS and Atom would be a useful feature.

I think a measure of success for tools such as the GME and Yahoo! Pipes is the degree to which they let you easily build applications for a specific purpose; and these are applications that you don't even mind throwing away after a single use because they were so easy to write. By this measure, the GME and Yahoo! Pipes moves you toward tools to create such apps. I think that the GME and Yahoo! Pipes makes it easier for programmers to create certain types of mashups, though it's not so clear whether they open up mashup development for a nonprogramming audience.

Other Mashup Tools

Many other tools are designed to help in creating mashups. There are so many mashup tools to look at—more than I can do justice to here. Table 11-1 lists a number of them along with a brief description and a URL for how you can learn more. Some use browser-based interfaces, while others are desktop tools. Some focus on specific aspects of creating mashups, while others aim to be a unifying framework.

Table 11-1. *Other Mashup Tools*

Name	Description	URL
Apatar	Open source software designed for business users and programmers to integrate data sources and formats	`http://www.apatar.com/product.html`
BEA AquaLogic Pages	Browser-based tools for authoring web pages and web applications	`http://www.bea.com/framework.jsp?CNT=index.jsp&FP=/content/products/aqualogic/pages/`
Bungee Connect	Browser-based environment for building web applications	`http://www.bungeelabs.com/`
Chickenfoot	Firefox extension (similar to Greasemonkey) that allows users to write scripts to "manipulate web pages and automate web browsing"	`http://groups.csail.mit.edu/uid/chickenfoot/index.php`
Coghead	Browser-based GUI for creating and hosting business applications	`http://www.coghead.com/`
CoScripter	Firefox extension "that automates the process of recording and playing back processes"	`http://services.alphaworks.ibm.com/coscripter/browse/about`
Dapper	Browser-based GUI for producing screen-scrapers that output Atom, RSS, Google Maps, and other formats	`http://www.dapper.net`
Data Mashups Online Service	Browser-based GUI to create custom business applications, especially for mashing up data and web services	`http://datamashups.com/`
Denodo data mashup	A platform focused on creating new business services by integrating existing data	`http://www.denodo.com/`
Extensio	A platform for data extraction, integration, and delivery	`http://www.extensio.com/`

Name	Description	URL
Intel Mash Maker	A experimental research project for enabling the easy creation of mashups ("mashups for the masses")	`http://mashmaker.intel.com/`
JackBe Presto Enterprise Edition	Software to let users "create, consume, and customize enterprise mashups"	`http://jackbe.com/resources/download.php`
Marmite	A research prototype of a mashup creation tool for nonprogrammers	`http://www.cs.cmu.edu/~jasonh/projects/marmite/`
Microsoft Popfly	A browser mashup tool whose drag-and-drop widgets have some similarity to Yahoo! Pipes but that puts more of an emphasis on presentation gadgets	`http://popfly.ms`
Openkapow	Desktop software for creating bots hosted by openkapow	`http://openkapow.com/`
Potluck	The mashup-making tool for SIMILE, a research project focused on the application of the semantic Web for manipulating digital assets	`http://simile.mit.edu/potluck`
Proto	Desktop mashups, especially for business intelligence applications	`http://www.protosw.com/`
QEDWiki	A browser-based interface for creating mashups	`http://services.alphaworks.ibm.com/qedwiki/`
RSSBus	Tools to "generate, manage, orchestrate, and pipeline RSS feeds"	`http://rssbus.com/`
Serena Mashup Composer	Software for creating business mashups	`http://www.serena.com/mashups/testdrive.html`
StrikeIron SOA Express for Excel	An add-on to enable easy access to web services from within Microsoft Excel	`http://strikeiron.com/tools/tools_soaexpress.aspx`
WSO2 Mashup Server	An open source platform for creating and deploying "web services mashups"	`http://wso2.org/projects/mashup`

Summary

Several tools are available that make it easier to create mashups. In this chapter, you explored the topic primarily by using a combination of two such tools, the Google Mashup Editor and Yahoo! Pipes, to create a mashup of geotagged Flickr photos and Google Maps. By creating this mashup in a number of manageable steps, you learned how to use the GME and incorporate Yahoo! Pipes. Moreover, by comparing the process used in this chapter to that used in the previous chapter, you get to see some of the advantages and trade-offs involved in using mashup tools instead of general-purpose web programming techniques.

CHAPTER 12

■ ■ ■

Making Your Web Site Mashable

This chapter is a guide to content producers who want to make their web sites friendly to mashups. That is, this chapter answers the question, how would you as a content producer make your digital content most effectively remixable and mashable to users and developers?

Most of this book is addressed to creators of mashups who are therefore *consumers* of data and services. Why then should I shift in this chapter to addressing *producers* of data and services? Well, you have already seen aspects of APIs and web content that make it either easier or harder to remix, and you've seen what makes APIs easy and enjoyable to use. Showing content and data producers what would make life easier for consumers of their content provides useful guidance to service providers who might not be fully aware of what it's like for consumers.

The main audience for the book—as *consumers* (as opposed to producers) of services— should still find this chapter a helpful distillation of best practices for creating mashups. In some ways, this chapter is a review of Chapters 1–11 and a preview of Chapters 13–19. Chapters 1–11 prepared you for how to create mashups in general. I presented a lot of the technologies and showed how to build a reasonably sophisticated mashup with PHP and JavaScript as well as using mashup tools. Some of the discussion in this chapter will be amplified by in-depth discussions in Chapters 13–19. For example, I'll refer to topics such as geoRSS, iCalendar, and microformats that I discuss in greater detail in those later chapters. Since I don't assume that you will have read any of those chapters, I will give you enough context in this chapter to understand the points I'm making.

Specifically, in this chapter, I will outline what content producers can do in two major categories:

- Ways in which they can make their web sites and content mashable without even producing a formal API

- Ways in which they can shape their API (features that are friendly to mashups)

Before content producers can decide how to act on any of this advice, they need to consider how remixability fits in with what they're trying to accomplish. We look at some of these issues first.

■**Tip** For detailed notes on how to create, run, and maintain an API from the perspective of a seasoned API creator, please consult Chapter 11 of *Building Scalable Web Sites* (O'Reilly Media, 2006), written by Cal Henderson of Flickr.

Why Make Your Web Site Mashable?

To decide on how remixable you want to make your content, you need to understand what you want to accomplish. There is a wide range of interest with respect to making APIs. Some content producers (such as Amazon, Google, and Yahoo!) set out to develop a platform and therefore invest huge amounts of effort in creating an API. Others are interested in making things convenient for users of their content and create an API if it's not too difficult. Other content producers want to work actively against any remixing of their content. The course of action you take as a content producer will certainly depend heavily on your level of interest in the mashability of your content to others as well as the resources you have at your disposal to create an API.

Here are some arguments for why you might want to make your content remixable (in other words, why it's good not only for content users but also for you as a content producer):

- With a good API, developers and users can extend what you provide. Look at how the vast majority of the API kits for Flickr are developed by third parties rather than Flickr.

- Third-party developers can develop applications you haven't even thought of or are too busy to create. (I'd say geotagging is a huge example of this for Flickr—it opened up a whole new vein of activity for Flickr.)

- APIs appeal to users who are concerned about lock-in and want to use their content in places other than your web site.

- Many users are starting to expect to have APIs; as a result, having an API is a selling point to prospective users.

- With an API, you might be able to extend your presence and point others to you (for example, Flickr photos are distributed all over the Web, but they all link back to Flickr). Indeed, Flickr is *the* platform for photo sharing on the Web. But Flickr's attribution requirement (in other words, the photos served from Flickr need to link back to Flickr) keeps Flickr from being commoditized as a file-hosting service.

- If the API is of sufficient economic value to your users, it is possible to charge for using your API.

- In some cases, you might be able to create something like Amazon.com, which as a platform for e-commerce takes a cut of purchases built on top of its platform.

- Making your data more open is contributing to the common goals of the entire Web.

Using Techniques That Do Not Depend on APIs

Without creating a formal API for your web site, you can nonetheless make things friendly for mashups while creating a highly usable site for your users.

Use a Consistent and Rich URL Language

Chapter 2 analyzed the URL language of Flickr and showed how its highly addressable, granular, transparent, and persistent URL language opens up a lot of opportunities to mash up content from Flickr merely by exploiting Flickr's URL structures. The human-readable, transparent URLs of Flickr lets developers link deeply into the fabric of the web site, even in the absence of formal documentation. The fact that Flickr works hard to keep the URLs permanent allows mashup creators to depend on the URLs to keep working. Granular URLs give mashups very fine-grained access and control over resources at Flickr. You will learn in Chapter 14 how these same qualities make it possible to use a social bookmarking system such as del.icio.us to bookmark content from Flickr. Hence, developing your own web site with a rich URL language avails your content to similar mashup techniques.

Moreover, the discipline of creating a consistent and human-readable URL structure benefits you as a content producer. It forces you to abstract the interface of your application (for example, the URL structures) from your back-end implementation, thus making your web site more maintainable and flexible.

Use W3C Standards to Develop Your Web Site

The use of good standards helps bring clarity to your web design, especially standards that insist on separating concerns (such as content from design). For instance, disentangling formatting from the markup and sticking it into CSS has a side benefit for mashup folks of producing content that is clearly laid out. Even generating well-formed XHTML (instead of tag-soup HTML) would be a huge boon since it allows for more error-free scraping of data. All this makes things more parsable even in the absence of explicit XML feeds.

Pay Attention to Web Accessibility

An accessible site lets more people access your content. You might be required by law to make your web site accessible to people with disabilities (see http://section508.gov/). Even if you aren't legally obliged to produce accessible content, adhering to modern web design such as producing valid (X)HTML naturally contributes to producing better accessibility. The end product of increased accessibility (for example, clean separation of content from style) is more mashable than nonaccessible sites.

Consider Allowing Users to Tag Your Content

Tagging provides a lightweight way for users to interact with and label and annotate content. As I demonstrated in Chapter 3, those tags can be the basis of simple mashups. There are some tricky issues to consider when you create a system for tagging—for example, how to incorporate multiple words and what to do about singular vs. plural tags. There is no universally accepted way to do this, so you need to weigh the possibilities (I covered some in Chapter 3). Having a strategy for multilingual tags is helpful (in other words, how to handle Unicode).

Consider also whether you have built enough structure to allow the hacking of tags. Could a user have jump-started geotagging as was done in Flickr with your site? Do you have something equivalent to machine tags?

Make Feeds Available

In Chapter 4, you learned about syndication feeds, their syntax, and how they can be used to represent your content in different formats to be exported to other applications. Feeds are becoming ubiquitous on the Web—they're the closest thing to the lingua franca of data exchange. Users by and large are beginning to expect feeds to be available from web sites. Users like syndication; they spend more time away from your site than on yours. Feeds let people access data from your site in their preferred local context (such as a feed reader). Moreover, there is a whole ecosystem built around feeds. By producing feeds, your data becomes part of that ecosystem.

Creating feeds out of your web site should be very high on a priority list. In fact, depending on what systems you are using to publish, you might already be generating them (for example, weblogs or many content management systems). By virtue of pushing your photos to Flickr, YouTube, and many other social sharing systems, you have the option of autogenerating feeds.

Feeds sound intimidating, but don't worry. You can start small and grow them. You might have a single feed for the most recent content. See how that works for you. Then you can consider generating feeds throughout your system. (Remember that Flickr has an extensive selection of feeds.)

If you need to programmatically generate feeds, they represent a good place to start in the business of generating XML. You might ask which feed type to generate. Ideally, you should generate many types like Flickr does, which takes little effort. That is possible if you have an abstract model of the data that you then format for different format types by writing a template for each format. If you don't want to go through that effort, then Atom 1.0 is a good place to start. Atom 1.0 is now recognized by lots of feed aggregators. It's also a good stepping-stone toward building an API. (You would have the Atom Publishing Protocol, covered in Chapter 7, and GData as good prior art to start.) Moreover, Atom feeds can flow into Yahoo! Pipes and the Google Mashup Editor (GME). RSS 2.0 wouldn't be far behind in my priority list. Also, if you want to get a start on experimenting with RDF and the semantic Web, a good place to start is to produce RSS 1.0.

Let's return briefly to the issue of the feed ecosystem. As you have seen, Yahoo! Pipes and the GME use feeds natively. The Flickr API puts out many formats (as you saw in Chapter 6) but not RSS 2.0 or Atom, although there are many Flickr feeds. You saw in Chapter 11 that even with the extensive number of Flickr feeds to access the Flickr API, I still had to convert Flickr XML to RSS 2.0, which I did with Yahoo! Pipes. That conversion made the data available to the GME.

As a final note, try using feed autodiscovery to enable easier access to feeds by users (which was discussed in Chapter 4).

Finally, be friendly to extensions to feeds. Remember that RSS 2.0, Atom 1.0, and RSS 1.0 are all extensible. Make use of this extensibility. If your system consumes feeds that have extensions, don't strip them out.

Make It Easy to Post Your Content to Blogs and Other Web Sites

In Chapter 5, you learned about how blogs can be integrated with web sites such as Flickr. Flickr's Blog button allows users to post a photo to a weblog. Moreover, the Flickr All Sizes button makes it easy for users to embed a photo into a blog or other web site by providing HTML fragments that they readily copy and paste elsewhere. In a similar fashion, YouTube provides HTML to embed a video, and Google provides HTML to embed its maps and calendars. You as a content producer can emulate the practice of making it easy to post your content to other sites while linking back to your own web site, where the content originates. In addition to facilitating the flow of content from your web site, you track comments originating from other web sites through a variety of *linkback* mechanisms. (See Chapter 5 for more information.)

Encourage the Sharing of Content with Explicit Licenses

Licensing digital content clears away important barriers to creating mashups with that content. In your web site, you should allow users to explicitly set the licensing of content and data to use, such as the Creative Commons licenses do, for instance. Set defaults that encourage sharing, but always give your users the choice to change those defaults. Build functionality to enable users to search and browse content according to a license.

As you learned in Chapter 2, Flickr is a good model here. Flickr has done a huge amount to promote open content specifically licensed through a Creative Commons license. That users can explicitly tie a Creative Commons license to a piece of content has been a tremendous enabler for remixing. If you don't give a mechanism for your users to assert a certain license, there might be too much ambiguity around the reuse of content. Even if you don't have granular control over the licensing of content on the site, it's very helpful to have a global statement about intellectual property issues. That is, some content producers license an entire site in a certain way. For example, the Wikipedia is licensed under GFDL:

```
http://en.wikipedia.org/wiki/Wikipedia:Copyrights
```

Freebase is licensed under CC-By:

```
http://www.freebase.com/signin/licensing
```

In Chapter 2, we discussed the barriers to screen-scraping. If you don't have an API but don't mind your users accessing your data, consider creating some bot-friendly terms of service (ToS).

Develop Extensive Import and Export Options for User Content

The more ways you have to get data in and out of an application, the better. Ideally, you would support protocols and data formats that would help your users. As a bonus, let your users embed their data hosted on your site somewhere else on the Web (for example, through a JavaScript *badge*). Super-flexible badges can be used themselves to access data for mashups and can hint at the existence of a feature-rich API.

Study How Users Remix Your Content and Make It Easier to Do So

Be prepared to be surprised by how people might use and reuse your content. See how people are using your content, and make it easier to do so. The primary example I have in mind here is when people started to hack the Google Maps API. Google, instead of stopping those people, actually formalized the API.

At the least, if you don't want to develop an API, when you see people use your web site in unusual ways, you should think about what's really go on and whether to make it easier to carry out this reuse.

Creating a Mashup-Friendly API

Some web APIs are easier than others to use for creating mashups. In the following sections, I'll give advice to content producers aiming to make their APIs friendlier for consumption.

Learn From and Emulate Other APIs

You can learn a lot from studying what other API providers are doing. That's why this book is useful; you will learn about what API makers are doing—at least from the outside.

What are some great examples to study? Flickr is a good one obviously. Recently, I've come to appreciate the Google documentation as being really good too. It has a lot of copy-and-paste code, plenty of getting-started sections, and the API references. Often there are API kits in a number of languages; of course, a lot of time and energy went into creating this documentation.

Moreover, if you are a little player, consider making your API look a lot like those of the big players. For example, 23hq.com, a photo-sharing site, decided to mimic Flickr's API instead of developing its own:

```
http://www.23hq.com/doc/api/
```

That enabled Dan Coulter to support that API in addition to Flickr's API in `phpFlickr`:

```
http://phpflickr.com/phpFlickr/README.txt
```

If 23hq.com had built its own API, it would not be able to leverage the work of the much-larger Flickr development community.

Whether the creator of an API is flattered or irritated by the sincere imitation of the API by other players surely depends on context. Consumers of the API, however, will be all too happy to not have to learn yet another API to access essentially the same functionality from different web sites.

Keep in Mind Your Audiences for the API

You need to consider two distinct audiences when deploying a public API. The first is the direct audience for the API; this is the developer community, which includes those who will directly program against your API. The second is the indirect audience for the API but perhaps a direct audience for your web site: the possible audience for those third-party applications. Remember that although you have a direct audience in the developers, you are ultimately trying to reach the second, potentially much larger, audience.

Make Your API Easy to Learn

Good documentation of the features, the API, data formats, and any other aspect of the web site makes it much easier to understand and recombine its data and functionality. You should clearly document the input and output data expected. Do you provide pointers to schemas or ways to validate data? Documentation reduces the amount of guesswork involved. Moreover, it brings certainty to whether a function you uncover through reverse engineering is an official feature or an undocumented hack that has no guarantee of working for any length of time.

Why, for instance, do I recommend people using the Flickr API as a starting point (and maybe for the long term)?

- It's well-documented and has structures that make it easy to learn, such as the Flickr API Explorer at `http://www.flickr.com/services/api/explore/?method=flickr.photos`. (I don't know of any documentation for APIs that is as clear as this. You can try a query and see it happen.)

- It has lots of code samples.

- It has toolkits that implement the API in your favorite language. Flickr is ahead of the game here with more than ten language-specific implementations of the Flickr API.

The Flickr API Explorer is excellent and should be more widely emulated. It lets you invoke a method in the browser and see the response. The documentation lists not only the methods but also the input parameters and error codes. The great thing is that you can read the documentation and try something. Moreover, the Flickr API Explorer shows you a URL coming out of the REST API that you can copy and paste elsewhere.

Test the Usability of Your API

Use the techniques from Chapters 7 and 8 to remix your own site to see how mashable your site is and how well your API works. Review Chapter 11, and read in the feeds from your site into Yahoo! Pipes or the Google Mashup Editor.

You might be using your own APIs in an Ajax interface—but it's helpful to think like a mashup creator who is coming to your site for the first time and who will use more generic tools to analyze your site. It's interesting to see how your site looks from that point of view.

You can go further by extrapolating techniques from usability testing (http://www.useit.com/alertbox/20000319.html) to testing your API, instead of the UI of your web site. For instance, you could recruit a group of developers and give them a problem to be solved using your API. See what these developers actually do. Make changes to your API in response to feedback.

Build a Granular, Loosely Coupled Architecture So That Creating an API Serves You As Much As It Does Others

A public API for your web site does not have to be something you build only for others. Rather, it can be the natural outcome of creating a scalable and adaptable web site. One architectural pattern that has proven effective in creating such web sites—that of service-oriented architectures—is to decompose functionality into independent, fine-grained components (called *services*) that can then be stitched together to create applications. By defining clear interfaces among the services, one can change the internal workings of individual services while minimizing the effect on other services and applications that consume those services. It is this loose coupling of the components that makes the whole web site scalable.

With a set of granular services in place, you as a content producer have the building blocks of a public API. You can always start with a private API—which many Ajax interfaces demand. That way, you can decide to roll out a public API. (For instance, you use Firebug to study how the Flickr API is often being called by Ajax parts of the Flickr interface.)

If you decide to go for an API, make APIs an integral part of your site. The fact that the system depends on the APIs ensures that the APIs aren't just throwaway parts of the system. This provides assurance that the API is an integral part of the system.

For more insight into how service orientation benefits Amazon.com, which is a major consumer of its own services, read an interview with Werner Vogels, CTO of Amazon.com:

http://www.acmqueue.com/modules.php?name=Content&pa=showpage&pid=388

Embrace REST But Also Support SOAP and XML-RPC If You Can

From Chapters 6 and 7, you know that REST is much easier for your users to get started with. (Amazon S3 in Chapter 16 provides another concrete case study of REST.) The use of REST and not just SOAP or XML-RPC lowers the barrier to entry. With REST, you can see results in the web browser without having to invoke a SOAP client (which is bound to be less available than a web browser). There's a strong argument to be made that by building a good RESTful human web API, you are already building a good API:

http://blog.whatfettle.com/2007/01/11/good-web-apis-are-just-web-sites/

However, if your primary developer audience is oriented toward enterprise development and is equipped with the right tooling, you might have to prefer SOAP/WSDL over REST. Remember that SOAP without WSDL isn't that useful. And if you do SOAP, be strictly observant of the version you are using.

Again, if you build an abstraction layer underneath, you might be able to handle multiple transport protocols. Your favorite programming frameworks might autogenerate REST or SOAP interfaces for your web application.

Consider Using the Atom Publishing Protocol As a Specific Instantiation of REST

If you build Atom 1.0 feeds, you're already on the road to building an API. Recall that there's plenty of prior art to be studied in the Google GData APIs if you want to go down this road. (Chapter 7 has a study of GData; Chapter 15 on the Google Calendar API is another study of GData.)

Encourage the Development of API Kits: Third Party or In-House

It's nice to have both the raw XML web services and the language-specific API kits. In theory, according to the argument of REST or the SOAP/WSDL camp folks, having the right web services should obviate the need for language-specific API kits. My own experience is the opposite. Sure, the Google GData APIs (see Chapters 7, 8, and 10) are RESTful, but having PHP and Python libraries is very useful. Even with WSDL, a language-specific API kit is handy.

Ideally you would have API packets for every possible language. Of course this is not practical—and not even the largest companies such as Google provide that many API kits. The priority is to have a good well-documented API. After that, I would say if you can put out an API kit in the language that you use in-house, that's already a great service. Google puts out API kits for its in-house languages. Microsoft puts out API kits in the languages it supports. Beyond that you need to talk to your potential developers and see what's important to them. (It's nice to have API kits that cover a range of languages.) Remember you don't have to develop all the API kits yourself—Flickr doesn't develop that many but provides a place to publicize them and promotes those API kits in the community of developers.

If you can provide both, it's nice to have a server-side language API kit and JavaScript API kit for client-side access.

Support Extensive Error Reporting in Your APIs

Note that for better or worse, it's very easy for developers to ignore error handling. You have to encourage them to handle errors. It starts with having good documentation of errors.

I'm of mixed minds about whether to embed the error in the XML body or as an HTTP response code. HTTP error codes are a standard way of dealing with errors, but it's not necessarily the easiest thing for new developers to understand. At any rate, in SOAP you can do fault handling in the fault code of the SOAP body. In XML-RPC, it's dealt with in the error body. I might suggest that even if you put error codes in the response body that you use the HTTP error codes as a starting point to build your own error response functionality.

Note The specification for the latest version of SOAP (1.2) now provides guidance on how to use the various 2xx, 3xx, 4xx HTTP status codes.[1]

Accept Multiple Formats for Output and Input

It's nice to have multiple ways of getting content in and out of an application. For example, Flickr has many ways to upload photos: the web interface, the desktop Uploadr, the API, and e-mail. Even so, some people have requested FTP and some type of mass downloading. Flickr doesn't offer FTP capabilities, but some people have worked to simulate it:

```
http://blog.wired.com/monkeybites/2007/06/upload_to_flick.html
```

For calendaring, you'll see the use of iCalendar and CSV in Chapter 15. In Chapter 13, you'll see how the proliferation of KML and geoRSS has been a boon.

Support UI Functionality in the API

As a consumer of APIs, I advocate support for all the elements available to users in the UI—and then some. It's frustrating for mashup creators to not be able to do something in the API that is clearly allowed by the user interface. There are sometimes good reasons to not enable certain actions in the API—but apart from such reasons, having a complete API is really helpful. As you saw in Chapter 6, there is a strong overlap between the capabilities of the Flickr API and the UI. There are some discrepancies between the API and UI—they got close but not an exact alignment.

Include a Search API for Your Own Site

You might consider adding an API to specifically enable searching of your web site. See Chapter 19 for how OpenSearch can then be used to integrate your web site's search functionality in other frameworks.

---

1. http://www.w3.org/TR/2007/REC-soap12-part2-20070427/#http-reqbindwaitstate

Version Your API

APIs, like all programming artifacts, are likely to change. Instead of having only one version of your API that can change, support multiple versioning of your API. That doesn't mean you will have to support every version indefinitely. Publishing a timeline for when you plan to retire a specific version of your API and documenting changes between versions allows the consumers of your API to make an orderly transition and adapt to changes in your API. Flickr doesn't explicitly version its API; for an example of an API with support of multiple versions, see the following:

```
http://developer.amazonwebservices.com/connect/kbcategory.jspa?categoryID=118
```

Foster a Community of Developers

A vibrant and active community makes a lot of mashup work practical. When making mashups, there are things that are theoretically possible to do—if you had the time, energy, and resources—but are practically impossible for you as an individual to pull off. A community of developers means that there are other people to work with, lots of examples of what other people have done, and often code libraries that you can build upon.

Don't Try to Be Too Controlling in Your API

You should have a clear ToS for the API—see Chapter 6 for a discussion of the ToS for the Flickr API. Don't try to be too controlling of your API. For instance, you might be tempted to forbid a user of your API from combining data from your site with that of other sites, such as those of your competitors. That's very much against the spirit of mashups and is likely to antagonize your developers. I would argue that asking a user of your API to reference your web site is a good balance between the interests of the API consumer and API producer.

There are a lot of issues when it comes to establishing a policy for your API—but one is worthy of special consideration is that of commercial use. It's not uncommon to make a basic distinction between the commercial and noncommercial use of an API, especially if you are not charging for the noncommercial use of an API. It's useful to reflect on how Flickr and others handle the distinction in the context of your own business model. Remember, though, that it's sometimes tricky to distinguish between commercial and noncommercial use; you will need to set up a process to make such a distinction.

Consider Producing a Service-Level Agreement (SLA)

A service-level agreement formally spells out the level of service a user can expect from a service and the remedies for failures to meet the expected level of service. It's debatable whether most SLAs are of much practical use. What I really want is perfectly reliable service. Can any remedy offered by most service providers adequately compensate for disappointing that desire?

Nonetheless, as a user, I find that a thoughtfully constructed SLA reassuring because it gives me a sense of the level of reliability to expect from a service provider. A specific measurable target of performance is likely better than none at all. As an example, Amazon.com recently introduced an SLA for its S3 service:

```
http://www.amazon.com/b?ie=UTF8&node=379654011
```

Help API Users Consume Your Resources Wisely

Encourage the users of your API to consume compute cycles and bandwidth parsimoniously—most developers will want to cooperate. Document your expectations on the limits you set for the total volume or rate of API calls. Error messages from your API to indicate the throttling of API calls are very useful to consumers of an API.

When developing an API, it's not unusual for you to issue keys to developers. However, tracking usage by the key alone is sometimes insufficient to manage the level of usage—keys are often leaked. You might track API usage based on a combination of key and originating IP address.

Both server- and client-side caching help with the performance of an API. You will want to help the users of your API to cache results properly. It's extremely useful to have APIs that tell you when something has been updated and to return changes in the state of the data since a given time.

Consider Open Sourcing Your Application

If you want to open up your site to deeper remixability, you might even publish the source for your web site. Users will then have the option of studying the source directly should reverse engineering—or reading the relevant documentation—not give you the answers they need.

Easy-to-Understand Data Standards

The use of open data standards by content producers and consumers is a good thing, but it's hard for someone outside a field of endeavor to understand what those standards are and exactly how important they are. (For instance, it doesn't take a lot of time working with online calendars to grasp that iCalendar is an important standard, but it did take me some study to grasp how central it really is.) Hence, it is helpful if for every subject you could find a simple, clear articulation of the standards for a given field. In the absence of a clear consensus about what the relevant standards are, a trustworthy and clear-headed outline of the main contenders and the perceived strengths and weaknesses would be really helpful to an outsider or newbie.

The Cover Pages (`http://xml.coverpages.org/`) hosted by OASIS is the closest thing to such a resource that I've seen:

> *OASIS provides the Cover Pages as a public resource to document and encourage the use of open standards that enhance the intelligibility, quality, and longevity of digital information.*

Complementing a wide use of open standards is a concerted effort to generate API kits that comprehensively and accurately interpret these standards. For example, as you'll see in Chapter 15 in the discussion iCalendar, it's hard to tell how good any given API kit is at interpreting and creating that data format.

Moreover, the presence of good validators and schemas for any data formats would be extremely helpful to mashup developers. For example, the early days of working with KML were hard because there was so much trial and error with writing something and then feeding it to Google Earth to see whether it would work. With good validators in place, data producers can debug their data without less experimentation. Some examples of useful validators are as follows:

- http://feedvalidator.org/, which helps with KML as well as RSS and Atom feeds (remember Chapter 4)

- W3C validators (http://validator.w3.org/ and http://jigsaw.w3.org/css-validator/) to check on the validity of (X)HTML and CSS, respectively

Summary

This chapter presented a series of techniques for making a web site more mashable. After explaining why content producers would want to make their data and services remixable, I then presented some techniques that do not depend on creating a formal API. The heart of creating a mashable web site is producing an API that is friendly to developers. I presented techniques for creating such an API, drawing from what you learned from the process of creating mashups in various contexts.

PART 4

■■■

Exploring Other Mashup Topics

Now that you've had some experience of the anatomy of a mashup and come to grips with some specifics, this part will apply what you've learned to a range of different APIs and technologies. We'll examine a different category in each chapter, starting with online maps in Chapter 13 and moving onto social bookmarking, online calendars, online storage, office documents, microformats, and searches.

Remixing Online Maps and 3D Digital Globes

It would be difficult to overstate the importance of maps in the course of human civilization. Maps help us place ourselves in a spatial context with regard to everything else on the planet. With the advent of the Web, we have been able to access online maps, which have proven to be both useful and fascinating. There are many practical daily uses for these maps, including getting driving directions, locating a restaurant in the neighborhood, thinking of places to go for travel. Online maps let us explore parts of the world in new ways too. Moreover, maps provide an intuitive conceptual and visual metaphor/space for connecting other things; as part of our cultural development, we have all developed a strong intuition for maps.

It is no wonder then that online maps have been used extensively in many mashups. One reason for this extensive activity is that contemporary online maps are designed for easy customization. In this chapter, you will learn how to customize maps. It is an exciting time for web-based mapping, and we really are only at the beginning of developing this immersive space. Add the Global Positioning System (GPS), more immersive systems/platforms such as Google Earth and Second Life, ubiquitous computing, and GPS devices, and we're going to get amazing stuff.

Note We're good at reading maps, and we know how things on maps are related to each other. We're used to adding dots and drawing lines. Hence, it's not much of a stretch for us to add other things—dots, lines, pictures, and even more abstract data to maps. Things that are located in space have a natural spot on maps. That's what I mean by saying that maps are a powerful metaphor.

The goal of this chapter is to introduce how to use some leading systems for remix purposes (Google Maps, Yahoo! Maps, Microsoft Maps, MapQuest, and Google Earth), looking for commonalities and differences. A potential framing question, technically, is how to write a wrapper so that one can substitute one system for another—and I will tell you about a couple of such efforts. However, most people want to use just one of these maps and do some easy customization; hence, I will show how you can do that. Each system has strengths, and it's useful to be able to interchange information among them without much effort. Obviously, I will not attempt to exhaust this very rich subject, but I'll provide you with a strong starting point to build on.

In this chapter, I will cover the following:

- I'll describe how to use the APIs of the major map providers, such as Google Maps, Yahoo! Maps, and Microsoft's Live Search Maps.

- I'll describe how you can make web-based maps without programming.

- I'll describe declarative approaches to working with maps, such as creating KML and GeoRSS and CSV.

- I'll teach you the fundamentals of KML and how to do some basic programming of Google Earth.

- I'll show you how to create a mashup of Flickr, Google Earth, and Google Maps using KML.

To learn more about the subject of online maps, please read the following:

- *Beginning Google Maps Applications with PHP and Ajax: From Novice to Professional* by Michael Purvis, Jeffrey Sambells, and Cameron Turner (Apress, 2006)

- *Beginning Google Maps Applications with Rails and Ajax: From Novice to Professional* by Andre Lewis, Michael Purvis, Jeffrey Sambells, and Cameron Turner (Apress, 2007)

The Number of Online Maps

The capability of individual users to make web-based digital maps has been rapidly increasing over the past several years. Online maps have evolved quickly from maps with only predefined purposes (for example, driving directions) to increasingly customizable platforms. That is, we are close to having map-making for the masses—Geographic Information System (GIS) for dummies (so to speak).

Perhaps the most dramatic revelation of the capabilities of what would later be known as Ajax was the emergence of Google Maps in February 2005.[1] It was a watershed event for all web apps and showed that it was possible to have highly interactive apps on a large scale. (Yes, people had been using JavaScript for menus but not for shipping a substantial amount of real-time data.) In the area of maps, this event marked the beginning of what I will refer to as *new-style* online maps as opposed to old-style online maps (which are an endangered species it would seem; even MapQuest has switched over to Ajax-type maps). By old-style online maps, I mean non-JavaScript-powered maps—ones in which moving around or zooming means reloading the page.

The most obvious aspect of the new-style maps is the substantial increase in interactivity (with the fluid drag-and-drop capabilities, instead of clicking and waiting for a page reload). However, hackers quickly realized that the Ajax technology also allowed Google Maps to be extended to new purposes.[2] Apps that showed up included Housingmaps.com. These apps, however, involved the extensive reverse engineering of Google Maps; the techniques that emerged could break anytime, and the whole enterprise was of questionable legality and longevity.

---

1. http://en.wikipedia.org/wiki/Google_maps and http://www.adaptivepath.com/publications/essays/archives/000385.php

2. http://www.oreillynet.com/etel/blog/2005/05/hackers_tap_into_the_functiona.html

What Google did was then smart and novel: it released an API to formalize and regulate the usage of its maps, transforming Google Maps mashups into legitimate business. Google really did transform the whole endeavor of GIS through Google Maps by making online maps accessible to and customizable by the masses. Competitors soon followed. Yahoo!, Microsoft, and eventually MapQuest all went new-style, with the release of not only Ajax implementations but APIs to boot.

Examples of Map-Based Mashups

Before we figure out how to make map-based mashups, it's handy to look at a number of examples to understand what is possible. As discussed in Chapter 1, there are many map-based mashups, including Housingmaps.com, Chicagocrime.org, and the 1,000+ map-based mashups listed on Programmableweb.com (`http://www.programmableweb.com/tag/mapping`). Here are some specific examples:

- `http://tutorlinker.com/` connects tutors to students via a mapping interface.

- `http://flashearth.com` is a mashup of various major online map services displayed through a Flash interface.

Programmableweb.com lists Google Maps as by far the most popular API used in mashups. Mapping as a category is very popular. Yahoo! Maps and Microsoft's Live Search Maps are also in the top ten.

Making Maps Without Programming

In this chapter, I'll show you how to create online maps without any programming before we jump into programming online maps. Then I'll show you how to use Mapbuilder.net as an example of a third-party authoring tool for Google Maps before discussing the functionality available directly in Google Maps and Virtual Earth for making custom maps. Along the way, I'll explain how you can transform a collection from Yahoo! Local into CSV format that you can send to Mapbuilder.net.

Mapbuilder.net

The scenario I'll focus on in this chapter is building a map with dots pointing to a list of places for which you have addresses in the United States. We will look at more sophisticated scenarios later.

Let's see how much of a Google map you can build without any programming. For the first two years after Google Maps was released, there was no built-in user functionality to create custom maps. You could use the Google Maps API to create custom maps, but that's beyond the skill or energy level of most users. Andriy Bidochko built Mapbuilder.net, a free service to let users create Google and Yahoo! Maps with custom markers through an interface that does not require knowledge of JavaScript. In this section, I'll show you how to use Mapbuilder.net as an easy way to create your own map.

In April 2007, Google introduced the My Maps feature into its online maps. Moreover, Microsoft's Live Search Maps has similar collection-making functionality in its maps. That the big players have incorporated functionality that allows its end users to create maps beyond locating a single location or displaying driving directions between two points is validation of the map builder concept. I also describe how to use those functions.

What are some sites built using Mapbuilder.net? Drawing from the list of featured maps,[3] I see ones like Edinburgh Pub Guide.[4] Note some have been heavily used in commercial contexts: the most popular of all time for Mapbuilder.net-built maps[5] is the "Find a Distributor" map for Pacific Wireless.[6]

Mapbuilder.net How-To

The following are the step-by-step instructions for how to create a map using Mapbuilder.net:

1. Sign up for an account.[7]

2. Click the New Map link.[8] (Note that the map name must contain only letters, numbers, underscores, and dashes.)

3. You can create a dot in one of two ways:

   a. Start typing addresses to add (under Location Search & Quick Navigation).

   b. Click the map to indicate a spot's location.

4. When you add a new dot, it will be flashing. Click any marker on the map to update its information or delete it (using the Update or Delete button). Remember to hit the Add button to save the location.

5. Use the Save Center, Zoom, MapType button located on the map to save the center of your map, zoom level, and map type (regular map, satellite, hybrid) as well. (You will have to adjust the scale and center of the map by using the zoom control and dragging the mouse to fit your taste; the default is not that helpful.)

6. Click the Preview link (located at the upper right) to take a look at the map.

7. To embed the map on your own site as a Google map, click the Source Code link, and copy the displayed code to your own site. (You will need to enter the appropriate API key in the code. See the "Google Maps API" section later in this chapter for how to get a key.) Note that you can use the options listed under Map Controls and Map Implementation to set other options for the map, including getting access to code to create a Yahoo! Map version of your map.

With a bit of futzing and by doing a series of searches on Yahoo! Local for addresses, I created "Some of my favorite bookstores around Berkeley,"[9] as hosted on Mapbuilder.net. I also embedded the map elsewhere using both Yahoo! Maps and Google Maps:

---

3. http://www.mapbuilder.net/About.php

4. http://www.imkblue.pwp.blueyonder.co.uk/index.html

5. http://www.mapbuilder.net/Popular.php?OP=ALL

6. http://www.pacwireless.com/distributor-locations.shtml

7. http://www.mapbuilder.net/SignUp.php

8. http://www.mapbuilder.net/Map.Add.php

9. http://www.mapbuilder.net/users/rdhyee/9329

- "Some bookstores I like" (Google version),[10] kept up-to-date via JavaScript injection[11]

- "Some bookstores I like" (Yahoo! version)[12]

Overall, I recommend Mapbuilder.net as a way to quickly build custom Google maps or Yahoo! maps or as a way to get started learning the APIs.[13]

Google My Maps

In addition to Mapbuilder.net, consider using Google's built-in My Maps functionality to create a custom Google map, which is documented here:

`http://local.google.com/support/bin/answer.py?hl=en&answer=68480`

I created a Google map with the same three bookstores as the previous example. I could either show the map hosted under the Google domain here:

`http://maps.google.com/maps/ms?f=q&hl=en&geocode=&ie=UTF8&msa=0`➡
`&msid=116029721704976049577.0000011345e68993fc0e7&z=14&om=1`

or embed it elsewhere by copying and pasting HTML for an embeddable iframe to generate the following, for example:[14]

`http://examples.mashupguide.net/ch13/embedded.GMap.html`

There are some major advantages of using My Maps. It's well integrated into Google Maps with its Search the Map functionality for looking up addresses and the Find Businesses option for locating businesses by name. If a marker comes up in your search results, you can click the Save to My Maps link to save the location on one of your custom maps. In addition, My Maps also lets you edit the markers and draw lines and polygons on your maps. Altogether, Google My Maps goes a long way to letting end users create custom maps (based on Google Maps, of course) without knowing JavaScript.

From a mashup point of view, you should know that you can generate a KML version of one of any of the maps produced by My Maps. The `msid` parameter of the Google Maps URL holds an identifier for a My Map–produced map (for example, `116029721704976049577.0000011345e68993fc0e7` for the map I produced). A URL of this format:

`http://maps.google.com/maps/ms?f=q&msa=0&output=kml&msid={my-map-id}`

such as the following:

`http://maps.google.com/maps/ms?f=q&msa=0&output=kml`➡
`&msid=116029721704976049577.0000011345e68993fc0e7`

---

10. `http://examples.mashupguide.net/ch13/SomeBookstoresGMap.html`

11. For an explanation of how to use JavaScript injection, see `http://www.mapbuilder.net/Map.Implemenation.php`.

12. `http://examples.mashupguide.net/ch13/SomeBookstoresYMap.html`

13. I ran into one snag: I wasn't able to delete a certain point using Firefox 1.5.0.7 on Windows XP no matter what I did. I finally deleted the point by logging in to Mapbuilder.net using Opera.

14. `http://local.google.com/support/bin/answer.py?answer=72644`

returns a KML version of the map. As I describe in greater detail later in this chapter, KML (an XML vocabulary for displaying geospatial information) lets you easily parse details of the map.

A Mashup Opportunity: Mapping Yahoo! Local Collections

Yahoo! Local makes it easy to make collections of places, but it does not allow easy mapping of those places. For instance, I assembled a collection of bookstores around Berkeley,[15] but the Yahoo! interface does not allow me to easily map those bookstores. In this section, we will create this by transforming one data format to another (specifically, transforming the addresses of stores selling used books offered in the XML that comes from the Yahoo! Local API into CSV, which is understood by Mapbuilder.net). There are two steps to this, which I will cover in more detail in the following sections:

1. Get information out via the Yahoo! Local API.

2. Transform the collection appropriately (XML to CSV) to feed into Mapbuilder.net.

Getting XML Out of Yahoo! Local via getCollection

We will use the getCollection method of the Yahoo! Local web service, which "enables you to get detailed information about a collection created with Yahoo! Local collections, through a REST-like API."[16] So, how do we use it?

The base URL is as follows:

```
http://collections.local.yahooapis.com/LocalSearchService/V1/getCollection
```

There are four parameters, as shown in Table 13-1.

Table 13-1. getCollection *Parameters*

Parameter	Description of Parameter	Value of the Parameter
appid	Application ID	raymondyee.net
collection_id	ID of the collection to be retrieved	1000014156
output	Output type	Unspecified, thus returning the default of XML
callback	Callback function	Unspecified

In other words, we can formulate the following query:

```
http://collections.local.yahooapis.com/LocalSearchService/V1/getCollection?➥
appid={app-id}&collection_id=1000014156
```

■**Tip** You can get your Yahoo! addid at https://developer.yahoo.com/wsregapp/index.php.

---

15. http://local.yahoo.com/collections?cid=1000014156
16. http://developer.yahoo.com/local/V1/getCollection.html

This request returns the code shown in Listing 13-1.

Listing 13-1. *XML for a Collection from Yahoo! Local*

```xml
<?xml version="1.0" encoding="UTF-8" ?>
<Result id="1000014156" xmlns="urn:yahoo:travel"
        xmlns:xsi="http://www.w3.org/2001/XMLSchema-instance"
        xsi:schemaLocation="unknown">
  <Title>bookstores around Berkeley</Title>
  <Description>some of my favorite bookstores around Berkeley.</Description>
  <CreatedTime>2006-10-24 13:29:40</CreatedTime>
  <Username>Raymond Yee</Username>
  <CommentCount>0</CommentCount>
  <Item>
    <Address>
      <Address1>2476 Telegraph Ave</Address1>
      <Address2 />
      <City>Berkeley</City>
      <State>CA</State>
      <PostalCode>94704</PostalCode>
    </Address>
    <id>21518795</id>
    <Title>Moe&apos;s Books</Title>
    <CreatedTime>2006-10-24 13:29:41</CreatedTime>
    <Description>
      * The Bay Area&apos;s Largest Selection of Used Scholarly Books
    </Description>
    <Url>
http://local.yahoo.com/details?id=21518795&amp;stx=&amp;csz=Berkeley+CA&amp;
ed=xoDOxa160SyYoswS6OvDhQk64pj4Q8RHG5PQhcSqprzxVT6mDHMezwfQ2U244pugG4LDSdibA78iSw--
    </Url>
    <type>Retail Shopping</type>
    <Category>Used &amp; Rare Bookstores</Category>
    <Photo />
    <Tag />
    <Phone>(510) 849-2087</Phone>
  </Item>
  <Item>
    <Address>
      <Address1>1730 4th St</Address1>
      <Address2 />
      <City>Berkeley</City>
      <State>CA</State>
      <PostalCode>94710</PostalCode>
    </Address>
    <id>21512172</id>
    <Title>Cody&apos;s Books</Title>
    <CreatedTime>2006-10-24 14:07:28</CreatedTime>
```

```
      <Description />
      <Url>
http://local.yahoo.com/details?id=21512172&amp;stx=&amp;csz=Berkeley+CA&amp;
ed=3uqWba16OSzFEqntYzu46yunejqBEmJnCBEi_I7QbD68sZTEVRYl4WkOGEf6alVIaEB3</Url>
      <type>Retail Shopping</type>
      <Category>Bookstores</Category>
      <Photo />
      <Tag />
      <Phone>(510) 559-9500</Phone>
    </Item>
    <Item>
      <Address>
        <Address1>6060 El Cerrito Plz</Address1>
        <Address2 />
        <City>El Cerrito</City>
        <State>CA</State>
        <PostalCode>94530</PostalCode>
      </Address>
      <id>21414999</id>
      <Title>Barnes &amp; Noble Booksellers</Title>
      <CreatedTime>2006-10-24 14:07:56</CreatedTime>
      <Description />
      <Url>
http://local.yahoo.com/details?id=21414999&amp;stx=&amp;csz=El+Cerrito+CA&amp;
ed=Fo51gq16OSy24fPx_u7IvyZen3kxQq5wR9ZOi_Aos2J.pPlJ75D_th3K2MHtNCWF_V5k_nOq62ssy3I-
      </Url>
      <type>Retail Shopping</type>
      <Category>Bookstores</Category>
      <Photo />
      <Tag />
      <Phone>(510) 524-0087</Phone>
    </Item>
</Result>
```

Transforming the Yahoo! Local XML into CSV for Mapbuilder.net

Our goal is to convert the XML data from Listing 13-1 into CSV. There are various techniques you could consider to do this. One way is to write a PHP script that takes a collection ID and outputs CSV, as shown in Listing 13-2.[17]

Listing 13-2. *PHP Script to Convert Yahoo! Local XML to CSV*

```
<?php

function getResource($url){
  $chandle = curl_init();
```

---

17. http://examples.mashupguide.net/ch13/yahooCollectionToCSV.php

```php
    curl_setopt($chandle, CURLOPT_URL, $url);
    curl_setopt($chandle, CURLOPT_RETURNTRANSFER, 1);
    $result = curl_exec($chandle);
    curl_close($chandle);
    return $result;
}

// get a collection_id
//default to my own
    $cid  = isset($_REQUEST['cid']) ? $_REQUEST['cid'] : "1000014156";

    $url = ➥
      "http://collections.local.yahooapis.com/LocalSearchService/V1/getCollection?➥
appid=[app-id]&collection_id=". urlencode($cid);
    $feed = getResource($url);
    $xml = simplexml_load_string($feed);

    //header("Content-Type:text/csv");
    $out = fopen('php://output', 'w');

    $header = array("Caption","Street Address","City","State","Zip");
    fputcsv($out, $header);

     foreach ($xml->Item as $item) {
      $caption = $item->Title;
      $street_address = $item->Address->Address1;
      $city = $item->Address->City;
      $state = $item->Address->State;
      $zip = $item->Address->PostalCode;
      fputcsv($out, array($caption,$street_address,$city,$state,$zip));
    }

      fclose($out);
?>
```

With this code in hand, we can generate a CSV file that we can feed to Mapbuilder.net:

```
http://examples.mashupguide.net/ch13/yahooCollectionToCSV.php?cid=1000014156
```

To try this, we can go to our collections here:

```
http://local.yahoo.com/userreviews?target=pOTJ1rUjf64lpQPwpZGZmXVTOyaM➥
&rvwtype=COLLECTION
```

and pull out collection ID numbers to feed to the script to generate the CSV:

```
Caption,"Street Address",City,State,Zip
"Moe's Books","2476 Telegraph Ave",Berkeley,CA,94704
```

```
"Cody's Books","1730 4th St",Berkeley,CA,94710
"Barnes & Noble Booksellers","6060 El Cerrito Plz","El Cerrito",CA,94530
```

We can then take the CSV and feed it to Mapbuilder.net to create our map.

Note You might say that writing such a script gets you only CSV and you still have to manually create a map with Mapbuilder.net—and you're right. Later, we'll transform this collection into formats that are easier to work with in terms of generating maps.

Collection Building in Microsoft's Live Search Maps

For Microsoft's Live Search Maps (http://local.live.com), powered by Microsoft's Virtual Earth, the story is a bit more complicated. Live Search Maps has excellent collection-building facilities. I was surprised how easy it was to look up bookstores and save them to collections and then to see those bookstores on the map all within the Microsoft map environment. If you make a collection public, anyone can access it here:

```
http://maps.live.com/?v=2&cid={collection-id}&encType=1
```

For example:

```
http://maps.live.com/?v=2&cid=74B8FFD299EDD840!106&encType=1
```

Moreover, you are able to get a GeoRSS representation of a Live Search Maps collection here:

```
http://maps.live.com/GeoCommunity.aspx?action=retrieverss&mkt=en-us➡
&cid={collection-id}
```

As you will see later in the chapter, GeoRSS is an XML vocabulary for embedding geographic information into RSS and Atom feeds. For a preview of what GeoRSS is, you can look at the following URL, which is shown in Listing 13-3.[18]

```
http://maps.live.com/GeoCommunity.aspx?action=retrieverss➡
&mkt=en-us&cid=74B8FFD299EDD840!10
```

Listing 13-3. *GeoRSS of a Map from Microsoft's Live Search Maps*

```
<rss version="2.0" xmlns:georss="http://www.georss.org/georss"
  xmlns:gml="http://www.opengis.net/gml"
  xmlns:Cml2GeoRssHelper="urn:Cml2GeoRssHelper">
  <channel>
    <title>Bookstores around Berkeley</title>
    <description>An example for mashupguide.net</description>
    <link>http://local.live.com/?v=2&amp;cid=74B8FFD299EDD840!106</link>
    <pubDate>Wed, 29 Aug 2007 23:32:51 GMT</pubDate>
```

---

18. The file is cached at http://examples.mashupguide.net/ch13/ve.bookstores.georss.xml.

```
    <item>
      <title>Moe's Books</title>
      <link>http://local.live.com/?v=2&amp;cid=74B8FFD299EDD840!106</link>
      <guid>74B8FFD299EDD840!128</guid>
      <pubDate>Wed, 29 Aug 2007 23:32:18 GMT</pubDate>
      <description>
      &lt;div style="padding:4px;"&gt; 2476 Telegraph Ave, Berkeley, CA
      &lt;/div&gt; &lt;br/&gt;
  </description>
      <georss:point>37.865523 -122.258492</georss:point>
    </item>
    <item>
      <title>Barnes &amp; Noble Booksellers</title>
      <link>http://local.live.com/?v=2&amp;cid=74B8FFD299EDD840!106</link>
      <guid>74B8FFD299EDD840!112</guid>
      <pubDate>Sat, 06 Jan 2007 16:47:10 GMT</pubDate>
      <description>
      &lt;div style="padding:4px;"&gt; 6060 El Cerrito Plz, El Cerrito, CA
      &lt;/div&gt; &lt;br/&gt;
  </description>
      <georss:point>37.899299 -122.300926</georss:point>
    </item>
    <item>
      <title>Cody's Books</title>
      <link>http://local.live.com/?v=2&amp;cid=74B8FFD299EDD840!106</link>
      <guid>74B8FFD299EDD840!107</guid>
      <pubDate>Wed, 25 Oct 2006 01:27:14 GMT</pubDate>
      <description>
      &lt;div style="padding:4px;"&gt; 1730 4th St, Berkeley, CA 94710
      &lt;/div&gt; &lt;br/&gt;
  </description>
      <georss:point>37.870975 -122.301021</georss:point>
    </item>
  </channel>
</rss>
```

Notice that each of the three bookstores is now associated with a georss:point element containing the latitude and longitude of the place (georss corresponds to the http://www.georss.org/georss namespace). For example, the element for Moe's Books is as follows:

```
<georss:point>37.865523 -122.258492</georss:point>
```

Notice a crucial difference between the GeoRSS originating from Live Search Maps and the XML of Yahoo! Local: the former contains the latitude and longitude of the bookstores, whereas the latter contains the addresses. We'll return to studying the implications of these differences later in the chapter.

Summary of Making Maps Without Programming

What can you conclude from these exercises? Mapbuilder.net is not so easy to use if you want to create a lot of markers but you don't already have those addresses laid out as CSV-formatted data. It would be nice to use a service like Yahoo! Local to pull up addresses and then pass the data into Mapbuilder.net. Live.local.com is surprisingly easy to use for building maps, but it's not easy to extract address information to create maps on competing map services. Google My Maps allows you to search for businesses and make maps of those results if you are content to make a Google map based on Google business data. Remember, however, that you can get a representation of the maps you make with Google My Maps as KML, which you can reuse elsewhere.

Data Exchange Formats

Before you study the details of specific APIs, you should understand the formats used to get data in and out of maps. Sometimes you can make a map by formatting what you want to place on a map in the right format. You already saw this approach in the previous section where I showed you how to transform the Yahoo! Local collection XML into CSV to feed to Mapbuilder.net. In the following sections, I'll examine some common data formats for online maps:

- CSV

- Microformats and other metatags

- GeoRSS

- KML

CSV

CSV stands for *comma-separated values*. It is a simple and widely supported format across many operating systems and applications. For tabular data, it is conceptually simpler and more compact than XML. In the case of Mapbuilder.net, you can upload the data for a set of markers using CSV format. For each marker, you can specify the caption, street address, city, state, and ZIP code. Mapbuilder.net can then geocode the addresses (that is, calculate the latitude and longitude of the address) to place them on a map. The built-in geocoding functionality of Mapbuilder.net is a major convenience for users.

For example, you can use a simple use of CSV by Geocoder.us (a service to convert U.S. addresses to latitude and longitude). The following:

```
http://rpc.geocoder.us/service/csv?address=2855+Telegraph+Ave.,+Berkeley,+CA
```

returns this:

```
37.858276,-122.260070,2855 Telegraph Ave,Berkeley,CA,94705
```

Microformats and Metatags for HTML

Some web sites have taken to embedding geographic information in HTML. As I will discuss in Chapter 18, microformats are little parcels of structured data that are seamlessly embedded in web pages—making them easily parsed by computer programs so that the data can be reused in other contexts. There are two relevant microformats in this context: geo and adr.

Consider the case of geotagged photos in Flickr, specifically the example I have already used in this book:

```
http://www.flickr.com/photos/raymondyee/18389540/
```

in which you will see the use of both the geo and adr microformats as instantiated in the following pieces of HTML, respectively:

```
<span class='geo' style='display:none'><span class='latitude'>37.8721</span>
<span class='longitude'>-122.257704</span></span>
```

```
<li id="li_location" class="Stats adr">
[....]
<span class='locality'>Oakland</span>, <span class='region'>California</span>
[....]
</li>
```

■**Caution** Although the latitude and longitude are correct, the placement of the address in Oakland, California, is inaccurate unless Berkeley is being subsumed as part of Oakland. This inaccuracy doesn't take away from the syntactic correctness of the adr example.

You might notice also the use of two metatags that embed the latitude and longitude corresponding to the photo. The ICBM <meta> tag, which in this case is as follows, is documented at http://geourl.org/add.html:

```
<meta name="ICBM" content="37.8721, -122.257704">
```

You can learn more about the geo.position metatag, such as the following:

```
<meta name="geo.position" content="37.8721; -122.257704">
```

at http://geotags.com/geo/. Both the <meta> tags (located in the <head> section) are used to associate a latitude and longitude with a web page as a whole.

GeoRSS

GeoRSS (http://georss.org/) is a way of embedding location information within RSS 2.0, RSS 1.0, Atom 1.0, and potentially other XML formats. GeoRSS seems to be a standard—or at least an emerging one. In GeoRSS, you can represent points, lines, boxes, and polygons. Let's look in more detail at how to work with points.

GeoRSS is conceptually simple, but you might get confused by the fact that there are at least four ways to encode GeoRSS points in XML. The first two are the recommended encodings going forward, while the second set of two are considered legacy formats that are nonetheless widely used and therefore recommended for support. I list them here with examples:

- The *GeoRSS GML* encoding (http://georss.org/gml) wraps the gml:pos element in a gml:Point element within georss:where—where the gml prefix corresponds to http://www.opengis.net/gml and the georss prefix corresponds to http://www.georss.org/georss:

```
<georss:where>
  <gml:Point>
    <gml:pos>37.8721 -122.257704</gml:pos>
  </gml:Point>
</georss:where>
```

- The *GeoRSS Simple* encoding (http://georss.org/simple) uses a single georss:point element to contain the latitude and longitude, where georss corresponds to the same namespace as for the GeoRSS GML encoding (that is, http://www.georss.org/georss):

```
<georss:point>37.8721 -122.257704</georss:point>
```

- The *W3C Basic Geo* encoding (http://georss.org/w3c) uses geo:Point to wrap the geo:lat and geo:long elements—where the geo namespace prefix refers to http://www.w3.org/2003/01/geo/wgs84_pos#._gml:

```
<geo:Point>
<geo:lat>37.8721 </geo:lat>
<geo:long>-122.257704</geo:long>
</geo:Point>
```

- A common variant of the previous, which I call here the *Compact W3C Basic Geo* encoding, drops the enclosing geo:Point:

```
<geo:lat>37.8721</geo:lat>
<geo:long>-122.257704</geo:long>
```

If you refer to Listing 13-3, you will note that the Live Search Maps collection uses the *GeoRSS Simple* encoding. Let's also look at Flickr GeoFeed, which you can currently get for a given user here:

```
http://api.flickr.com/services/feeds/geo/?id={user-nsid} &lang=en-us&format=rss_200
```

For example, the GeoFeed for Rev. Dan Catt (the driving force behind Flickr geotagging) is as follows:

```
http://api.flickr.com/services/feeds/geo/?id=35468159852@N01&lang=en-us➥
&format=rss_200
```

You can also get a GeoFeed for a given Flickr group here:

```
http://api.flickr.com/services/feeds/geo/?g={group-nsid} &lang=en-us&format=rss_200
```

For example, the GeoFeed for the FlickrCentral group is as follows:

```
http://api.flickr.com/services/feeds/geo/?g=34427469792@N01&lang=en-us➥
&format=rss_200
```

Studying the GeoFeeds, you'll notice the use of two GeoRSS encodings, the GeoRSS Simple and W3C Basic Geo encodings, within the GeoFeeds:

```
<?xml version="1.0" encoding="utf-8"?>
<rss version="2.0" xmlns:media="http://search.yahoo.com/mrss/"
  xmlns:dc="http://purl.org/dc/elements/1.1/"
  xmlns:geo="http://www.w3.org/2003/01/geo/wgs84_pos#"
  xmlns:georss="http://www.georss.org/georss">
  <channel>
    [....]
    <item>
      <title>maybe not</title>
      <link>http://www.flickr.com/photos/solidether/1270523097/</link>
      [....]
      <georss:point>51.269057 12.345714</georss:point>
      <geo:Point>
        <geo:lat>51.269057</geo:lat>
        <geo:long>12.345714</geo:long>
      </geo:Point>
      [....]
    </item>
    [....]
  </channel>
</rss>
```

Yahoo!'s Use of GeoRSS and Yahoo! YMaps Extensions

When you read Yahoo!'s documentation at the following locations about its support for GeoRSS, you might get confused by the conflation of its own set of extensions to RSS 2.0 that use YMaps (corresponding to `http://api.maps.yahoo.com/Maps/V1/AnnotatedMaps.xsd` or `http://api.maps.yahoo.com/Maps/V2/AnnotatedMaps.xsd`—depending on which API you are using):

- `http://developer.yahoo.com/maps/simple/V1/reference.html` (for the Yahoo! Maps Simple API)

- `http://developer.yahoo.com/maps/georss/index.html` (for its Ajax API)

There are a whole bunch of tags, but I'll focus here on the ones for marking up addresses: `<ymaps:Address>`, `<ymaps:CityState>`, `<ymaps:Zip>`, and `<ymaps:Country>` to denote an address associated with an `<item>`.

The Yahoo! Simple API[19] lets you pass in the URL of an RSS 2.0 feed that has Compact W3C Basic Geo encoding and Yahoo!-specific extensions. See, for instance, the example given in the Yahoo! documentation:

```
http://api.maps.yahoo.com/Maps/V1/annotatedMaps?appid=YahooDemo➥
&xmlsrc=http://developer.yahoo.com/maps/sample.xml
```

This ability to use a mix of Geo and YMaps extensions reflects the ability of Yahoo! Maps to do the geocoding for you: you can still place a point on a map without knowing the latitude

---

19. `http://developer.yahoo.com/maps/simple/V1/reference.html`

and longitude as long as you have an address that you can mark up with the appropriate ymaps tag. (We will look later at how to call on services to do explicit geocoding.) However, you must not conflate the YMaps extension with GeoRSS—they are not the same. For instance, I don't know of any applications outside of Yahoo! Maps that supports the YMaps extensions.

Let's look at a working example of how to use the YMaps extension. Recall that you can use the Yahoo! Local API to get the XML for a collection here:

```
http://collections.local.yahooapis.com/LocalSearchService/V1/getCollection?➥
appid={app-id}&collection_id={collection-id}
```

For example, the following is the URL for the collection of bookstores that I have assembled:

```
http://collections.local.yahooapis.com/LocalSearchService/V1/getCollection?➥
appid={appp-id}&collection_id=1000014156
```

I have cached the results of the API call here:

```
http://examples.mashupguide.net/ch13/bookstores.yahoo.local.xml
```

You can convert this XML to RSS 2.0 with the YMaps extension either by hand or by using some XSLT code that I wrote for that purpose. What you get, which is cached here:

```
http://examples.mashupguide.net/ch13/yahoo.local.to.georss.xsl
```

is the following:

```xml
<?xml version="1.0" encoding="UTF-8"?>
<rss xmlns:xsi="http://www.w3.org/2001/XMLSchema-instance"
    xmlns:yahoo="urn:yahoo:travel"
    xmlns:ymaps="http://api.maps.yahoo.com/Maps/V1/AnnotatedMaps.xsd"
    xmlns:geo="http://www.w3.org/2003/01/geo/wgs84_pos#"
    version="2.0">
  <channel>
    <title>bookstores around Berkeley</title>
    <link>http://local.yahoo.com/collections?cid=1000014156</link>
    <description>some of my favorite bookstores around Berkeley.</description>
    <item>
        <title>Moe's Books</title>
        <link>http://local.yahoo.com/details?id=21518795&amp;stx=➥
&amp;csz=Berkeley+CA&amp;ed=xoDOxa160SyYoswS6OvDhQk64pj4Q8RHG5PQhcSqprzxVT6mDHMezwfQ➥
2U244pugG4LDSdibA78iSw--</link>
        <description>
          * The Bay Area's Largest Selection of Used Scholarly Books
        </description>
        <ymaps:Address>2476 Telegraph Ave</ymaps:Address>
        <ymaps:CityState>Berkeley, CA</ymaps:CityState>
        <ymaps:Zip>94704</ymaps:Zip>
        <ymaps:Country>US</ymaps:Country>
    </item>
    <item>
        <title>Cody's Books</title>
```

```
            <link>http://local.yahoo.com/details?id=21512172&amp;stx=➡
&amp;csz=Berkeley+CA&amp;ed=3uqWba16OSzFEqntYzu46yunejqBEmJnCBEi_I7QbD68sZTEVRYl4WkO➡
GEf6alVIaEB3</link>
            <description/>
            <ymaps:Address>1730 4th St</ymaps:Address>
            <ymaps:CityState>Berkeley, CA</ymaps:CityState>
            <ymaps:Zip>94710</ymaps:Zip>
            <ymaps:Country>US</ymaps:Country>
        </item>
        <item>
            <title>Barnes &amp; Noble Booksellers</title>
            <link>http://local.yahoo.com/details?id=21414999&amp;stx=➡
&amp;csz=El+Cerrito+CA&amp;ed=Fo51gq16OSy24fPx_u7IvyZen3kxQq5wR9ZOi_Aos2J.pPlJ75D_th➡
3K2MHtNCWF_V5k_nOq62ssy3I-</link>
            <description/>
            <ymaps:Address>6060 El Cerrito Plz</ymaps:Address>
            <ymaps:CityState>El Cerrito, CA</ymaps:CityState>
            <ymaps:Zip>94530</ymaps:Zip>
            <ymaps:Country>US</ymaps:Country>
        </item>
    </channel>
</rss>
```

Tip You can use the W3C XSLT services to perform online XSLT transformations at `http://www.w3.org/2001/05/xslt` and `http://www.w3.org/2005/08/online_xslt/` (for XSLT 2.0).

Go to the following URL to see the rendition of the location data in version 1 of Yahoo! Maps:

`http://api.maps.yahoo.com/Maps/V1/annotatedMaps?appid={app-id}➡`
`&xmlsrc=http://examples.mashupguide.net/ch13/bookstores.georss.xml`

You can also pass the geocoded RSS 2.0 to the Ajax Yahoo! Maps.[20] One way to see this functionality at work is to follow these steps:

1. Adapt code from one of the Yahoo! examples[21] by centering it on the UC Berkeley campus and using your own Yahoo! API key.[22]

2. Bring up that example. Invoke the JavaScript Shell on it,[23] and type the following to load the RSS file (with the YMaps extensions) into the map:

```
map.addOverlay(➡
    new YGeoRSS('http://examples.mashupguide.net/ch13/bookstores.georsss.xml'));
```

---

20. `http://developer.yahoo.com/maps/georss/index.html`

21. `http://developer.yahoo.com/maps/ajax/V3/ajaxexample1.html`

22. `http://examples.mashupguide.net/ch13/yahoo.map.berkeley.html`

23. `http://www.squarefree.com/shell/`, a technique introduced in Chapter 8.

Caution If you plan to feed GeoRSS to the Yahoo! Maps APIs, use the Compact W3C Basic Geo encoding since that's the encoding implied by the documentation for Yahoo! Maps. Moreover, you may find the error messages from the Yahoo! Maps Simple API to be rather terse. I have found using Feedvalidator.org to be useful in debugging my GeoRSS.

GeoRSS in Virtual Earth

Virtual Earth also has the capacity to handle GeoRSS files using any of the four encodings, according to this:

http://dev.live.com/virtualearth/sdk/Ref/HTML/WorkingWithLayers.htm

Now we should be able to feed that file to Virtual Earth. Making a slight modification to some sample code[24] to read a cached version of my own Flickr GeoFeed,[25] I come up with the following demo code:

```
<!DOCTYPE html PUBLIC "-//W3C//DTD XHTML 1.0 Transitional//EN"
"http://www.w3.org/TR/xhtml1/DTD/xhtml1-transitional.dtd">
<html>
  <head>
    <title></title>
    <meta http-equiv="Content-Type" content="text/html; charset=utf-8">
    <script src="http://dev.virtualearth.net/mapcontrol/mapcontrol.ashx?v=5">
    </script>
    <script>
      var map = null;
      var layerid=1;

      function GetMap()
      {
        map = new VEMap('myMap');
        map.LoadMap();
      }

      function AddMyLayer(type)
      {
        var l = new VEShapeLayer();
        var txtSource = document.getElementById('txtSource');
        var veLayerSpec =
          new VEShapeSourceSpecification(type, txtSource.value, l);
        map.ImportShapeLayerData(veLayerSpec, onFeedLoad);
      }
```

---

24. http://msdn2.microsoft.com/en-us/library/bb429606.aspx

25. http://examples.mashupguide.net/ch13/flickr.geofeed.xml

```
        function onFeedLoad(feed)
        {
            feed0 = feed;
            alert('RSS or Collection loaded. There are '+feed.GetShapeCount()+
                  ' items in this list.');
        }
    </script>
  </head>
  <body onload="GetMap();">
    <div id='myMap' style="position:relative; width:400px; height:400px;"></div>
    <input id="txtSource" type="text" value="flickr.geofeed.xml" name="txtSource">
    <input id="loadFeed" type="button" value="Load RSS"
           onclick="AddMyLayer(VEDataType.GeoRSS);">
  </body>
</html>
```

This is available here:

```
http://examples.mashupguide.net/ch13/virtualearth.flickrgeofeed.v5.html
```

KML

Keyhole Markup Language (KML) "is an XML grammar and file format for modeling and storing geographic features such as points, lines, images, and polygons for display in Google Earth, Google Maps, and Google Maps for mobile."[26] Google's backing of KML makes it an important format for the exchange of geographic information.

KML has moved beyond its use in Google Earth alone. For instance, you can display KML files and export search results and one of your My Maps from Google Maps in KML. Other applications are beginning to support KML. For instance, you can get KML coming out of Yahoo! Pipes;[27] also, there is support for KML in Feed Validator.[28] KML is being shepherded through a standards process.[29] Google is advising people to use KML so that its geosearch can index KML—in KML 2.2, there is an <attribution> element. Google apparently will also index GeoRSS.

I'll cover the syntax KML in greater detail in the "Google Earth and KML" section. It's helpful, nonetheless, to see a simple example of a KML document so that you have something concrete to bounce off of:

```
<?xml version="1.0" encoding="UTF-8"?>
<kml xmlns="http://earth.google.com/kml/2.1">
  <Placemark id="berkeley">
    <description>Berkeley, CA</description>
    <name>Berkeley</name>
    <Point>
```

---

26. http://earth.google.com/kml/
27. http://blog.pipes.yahoo.com/2007/05/02/pipes-adds-interactive-yahoo-maps-kml-support-and-more/
28. http://googleearthuser.blogspot.com/2007/05/feed-validator.html
29. http://geotips.blogspot.com/2007/04/kml-ogc.html

```
      <coordinates>-122.257704,37.8721,0</coordinates>
    </Point>
  </Placemark>
</kml>
```

Interoperability Among Formats: GeoRSS vs. KML

In commenting on the Where 2.0 conference, Benjamin Christen wrote this: "There are two important XML schemas covered today at Where 2.0—GeoRSS and KML.[30] Can we get these two formats—and others of importance—to work together?"[31] Mikal Maron provides an intriguing portrait of the relationship among various formats:[32]

> *There are of course other geodata formats in use, which deserve a look as alternatives to GeoRSS. KML is used in Google Earth, and loads of data layers have been published by an active community. However, KML is very tied to its application, with features specifically aimed for 3D spinny globes, and the spec is controlled by a single organization. GPX, for data interchange between GPS units, is again very tied to specifics of GPS units. GML is a feature-rich vocabulary for encoding geographic information, but its complexity has been daunting for unversed developers and its proper use misunderstood. GML is similar to RDF, defining a number of primitive objects that can be assembled into profiles for particular purposes. In fact, a GML profile for GeoRSS is a result of the new standard.*

Not surprisingly, Maron was involved in such interoperability efforts as MGeoRSS, an extension that "integrates basic GeoRSS support directly into Google Maps."[33] Someone from Google might have been listening to him—in March 2007, Google added native support for GeoRSS to its maps.

We're at a point now that since both GeoRSS and KML are getting a good amount of traction, some good interconversion utilities between them would be timely.

Creating Maps by API Programming

In the following sections, I will discuss the APIs of various popular online services, specifically, Google, Yahoo!, and Microsoft. In the previous section, I discussed data formats with an eye to making maps without any (or much) programming. In the following sections, we will do a bit of programming.

I'll now summarize what these maps can do in general. The four covered here all allow you to do the following:

- Embed an Ajax-based map, to which you can add custom locations with pop-up windows

- Geocode addresses (translate an address to latitude and longitude), at least for U.S. and Canadian addresses

---

30. http://www.oreillynet.com/conferences/blog/2006/06/georss_and_kml.html

31. http://www.ogleearth.com/2006/05/georss_is_here.html is a good summary of some of the issues.

32. http://xtech06.usefulinc.com/schedule/paper/56

33. http://brainoff.com/gmaps/mgeorss.html

- Show the maps at various zoom levels and of various types (road, aerial, or hybrid)

- Add lines to the maps to represent features such as driving directions

With a bit of copying and pasting, you can get working examples of each of the maps. You can then modify them incrementally. Using the DOM Inspector and the JavaScript Shell, you can even make changes to live working examples within the browser. I will also use those mechanisms to highlight important capabilities and functions of the maps.

Google Maps API

Let's look at the Google Maps API. We will start with how to embed a Google map using the Google Maps API. The online documentation on how to get started with the maps at the Google web site is good.[34]

We'll set up a simple map and then use the JavaScript Shell to work with a live map so that you can invoke a command and see an immediate response. The intended effect is that you see the widgets as dynamic programs that respond to commands, whether that command comes in a program or from you entering the commands one by one.

■**Note** This tutorial on the Google Maps API is essentially the same as that in Chapter 8 and is repeated here for your convenience.

Getting Started with Google Maps and the JavaScript Shell

We will use the Google Maps API to make a simple map:

1. Make sure you have a public web directory to host your map and know the URL of that directory. Any Google map that uses the free, public API needs to be publicly visible.

2. Go to the sign-up page for a key to access Google Maps.[35] You will need a key for any given domain in which you host Google Maps. (It is through these keys that Google regulates the use of the Google Maps API.)

3. Read the terms of service,[36] and if you agree to them, enter the URL directory on the host that you want to place your test file. For example, in my case, the URL is `http://examples.mashupguide.net/ch13/`. Note that key.

4. Copy and paste the HTML code into your own page on your web-hosting directory. You should get something like my own example:[37]

```
<!DOCTYPE html PUBLIC "-//W3C//DTD XHTML 1.0 Strict//EN"
  "http://www.w3.org/TR/xhtml1/DTD/xhtml1-strict.dtd">
<html xmlns="http://www.w3.org/1999/xhtml">
```

---

34. http://www.google.com/apis/maps/documentation/#Introduction

35. http://www.google.com/apis/maps/signup.html

36. http://www.google.com/apis/maps/terms.html

37. http://www.google.com/maps/api_signup?url=http%3A%2F%2Fexamples.mashupguide.net%2Fch13%2F

```
<head>
  <meta http-equiv="content-type" content="text/html; charset=utf-8"/>
  <title>Google Maps JavaScript API Example</title>
  <script src="http://maps.google.com/maps?file=api&amp;v=2&amp;key=<API_KEY>"
    type="text/javascript"></script>
  <script type="text/javascript">

  //<![CDATA[

  function load() {
    if (GBrowserIsCompatible()) {
      var map = new GMap2(document.getElementById("map"));
      map.setCenter(new GLatLng(37.4419, -122.1419), 13);
    }
  }

  //]]>
  </script>
</head>
<body onload="load()" onunload="GUnload()">
  <div id="map" style="width: 500px; height: 300px"></div>
</body>
</html>
```

5. Now make one modification to the example by removing the var keyword in front of map to make it a global variable that is thus accessible to the JavaScript Shell. That is, change this:

```
var map = new GMap2(document.getElementById("map"));
```

to the following:

```
map = new GMap2(document.getElementById("map"));
```

to expose the map object to the JavaScript Shell utility.[38]

6. Invoke the JavaScript Shell for your map by hitting the JavaScript Shell bookmarklet in the context of your map. Type the code fragments in the following steps, and see what happens. (Note that another approach is to modify your code directly with these code fragments and reload your page.) These actions use version 2 of the Google Maps API.[39]

7. To return the current zoom level of the map (which goes from 0 to 17, with 17 being the most detailed), type the following command (the response from the JavaScript Shell is shown right after the code):

```
map.getZoom()
```

13

8. To obtain the latitude and longitude of the center of the map, do this:

```
map.getCenter()
```

```
(37.4419, -122.1419)
```

9. To center the map around the Campanile for UC Berkeley, use this:

```
map.setCenter(new GLatLng(37.872035,-122.257844), 13);
```

10. You can pan to that location instead:

```
map.panTo(new GLatLng(37.872035,-122.257844));
```

11. To add a small map control (to control the zoom level), run these two commands:

```
map.addControl(new GSmallMapControl());
map.addControl(new GMapTypeControl());
```

12. To turn GMap keyboard navigation on, use this:

```
window.kh = new GKeyboardHandler(map);
```

```
[object Object]
```

13. To fully zoom out the map, use this:

```
map.setZoom(0)
```

14. To zoom in all the way (maximum zoom level may go from 15 to 17), do this:

```
map.setZoom(17)
```

15. To set the variable `maptypes` to an array holding three objects, use this:

```
maptypes = map.getMapTypes()
```

```
[object Object],[object Object],[object Object]
```

16. To get the name of the first entry in `maptypes`, use this:

```
map.getMapTypes()[0].getName()[40]
```

```
Map
```

17. To get the current map type, you can get the object and the name of that type object:

```
map.getCurrentMapType()
```

```
[object Object]
```

---

40. 1 corresponds to satellite, while 2 corresponds to the hybrid map type.

```
map.getCurrentMapType().getName()
```

Map

---

18. To set maptype to satellite, do this:

```
map.setMapType(maptypes[1]);
```

19. You can zoom one level in and out if you are not already at the max or min zoom level:

```
map.zoomIn();
map.zoomOut();
```

20. To make an overlay, try this:

```
point = new GLatLng (37.87309185260284, -122.25508689880371);
```

(37.87309185260284, -122.25508689880371)

```
marker = new GMarker(point);
```

[object Object]

```
map.addOverlay(marker);
```

21. To make something happen when you click the marker, do this:

```
GEvent.addListener(marker, 'click', function() {
marker.openInfoWindowHtml('hello'); });
```

[object Object]

---

22. To add a new layer of pins from a GeoRSS feed, use this:

```
map.addOverlay(new GGeoXml('http://api.flickr.com/services/feeds/geo/➥
?id=48600101146@N01&lang=en-us&format=rss_200'));
```

There are many more things to explore, such as polylines and overlays and draggable points. To learn more, I certainly recommend the "Google Maps API: Introduction" document.[41] Note that "this documentation is designed for people familiar with JavaScript programming and object-oriented programming concepts. You should also be familiar with Google Maps from a user's point of view."

---

41. http://www.google.com/apis/maps/documentation/#Introduction

Yahoo! Maps API

The Yahoo! Maps can be programmed with its API. You can find the core documentation, "Yahoo! Maps Web Services: Introducing the Yahoo! Maps APIs," on the Yahoo! web site.[42] As I described in the previous sections, the Simple API[43] is useful to get started with because the declarative approach does not involve any JavaScript programming but creates only the right XML file.

■**Note** If you want to learn about the Flash APIs for Yahoo! Maps, which are outside the scope of this book, please refer to the official documentation at `http://developer.yahoo.net/maps/flash/index.html`.

Getting Started with Yahoo! Maps and the JavaScript Shell

In this exercise, I will present a step-by-step introduction to the Ajax APIs for Yahoo! Maps:[44]

1. Apply for a Yahoo! application key.[45] You are told not to use the `appid` for the example code in the Yahoo! documentation (which is `YahooDemo`).

2. Copy and paste the following code for your web site:[46]

```
<html>
  <head>
    <script type="text/javascript"
src="http://api.maps.yahoo.com/ajaxymap?v=3.0&appid=<API_Key>"></script>
    <style type="text/css">
      #mapContainer {
      height: 500px;
      width: 80%;
      }
    </style>
  </head>
<body>
  <div id="mapContainer"></div>
  <script type="text/javascript">
    // Create a lat/lon object
    var myPoint = new YGeoPoint(37.4041960114344,-122.008194923401);
    // Create a map object
    var map = new YMap(document.getElementById('mapContainer'));
    // Display the map centered on a latitude and longitude
    map.drawZoomAndCenter(myPoint, 3);
```

---

42. http://developer.yahoo.net/maps/

43. http://developer.yahoo.net/maps/simple/index.html

44. http://developer.yahoo.net/maps/ajax/index.html

45. https://developer.yahoo.com/wsregapp/index.php

46. I have my code at http://examples.mashupguide.net/ch13/yahoo.map.simple.1.html.

```
        // Add map type control
        map.addTypeControl();

        // Set map type to either of: YAHOO_MAP_SAT YAHOO_MAP_HYB YAHOO_MAP_REG
        map.setMapType(YAHOO_MAP_SAT);

        //Get valid map types,
        //returns array [YAHOO_MAP_REG, YAHOO_MAP_SAT, YAHOO_MAP_HYB]
        var myMapTypes = map.getMapTypes();
      </script>
  </body>
  </html>
```

3. Invoke the JavaScript Shell for your map by hitting the JavaScript Shell bookmarklet in the context of your map. Type the code fragments in the following steps, and see what happens. (If you don't use your own map, try the JavaScript Shell on the example on the Yahoo! web site.)[47]

4. To get the zoom level, use this:

```
map.getZoomLevel()
```

3

---

5. To get the center location, specifically, the latitude and longitude, use this:

```
map.getCenterLatLon()
```

```
[object Object]
```

```
    props(map.getCenterLatLon())
```

```
Fields: Lat, Lon
Methods of prototype: distance, equal, getRad, greater, middle, pointDiff,
setgeobox, valid
```

```
    map.getCenterLatLon().Lat
```

```
37.4041960114344
```

```
    map.getCenterLatLon().Lon
```

```
-122.008194923401
```

---

47. http://developer.yahoo.com/maps/ajax/V3/ajaxexample1.html

6. To set the zoom level (15 for largest scale, 1 for most zoomed in), use this:

```
map.setZoomLevel(15)
map.setZoomLevel(1)
```

7. To move the map to a new center (in this case, the UC Berkeley campus), do this:

```
p = new YGeoPoint(37.87309185260284, -122.25508689880371)
```

[object Object]

```
map.panToLatLon(p)
```

8. To add some navigation and zoom controls, use this:

```
map.addPanControl();
map.addZoomLong();
```

9. To add a marker, labeled *H*, use the following:

```
marker = new YMarker(p);
```

[object Object]

```
marker.addLabel("H");
map.addOverlay(marker);
```

10. To make a click event invoke a pop-up, use this:

```
function onSmartWinEvent() {var words = "Yeah Yahoo maps!"; ➥
marker.openSmartWindow(words); }
YEvent.Capture(marker, EventsList.MouseClick, onSmartWinEvent);
```

11. To add a marker to a specific address, in this case, 2195 Hearst Ave, you can use either of the following three alternatives:

```
map.addMarker("2855 Telegraph Ave, Berkeley, CA");
```

or

```
map.addOverlay(new YMarker("2855 Telegraph Ave, Berkeley, CA "));
```

or

```
marker = new YMarker("2855 Telegraph Ave, Berkeley, CA ");
marker.addLabel("Apress");
map.addOverlay(marker);
marker.reLabel("<b>hello</b>");
```

12. To add a GeoRSS feed (that uses either the Yahoo! YMaps extensions or the Compact W3C Basic Geo encoding) to the map, use this:

```
map.addOverlay(new YGeoRSS('http://examples.mashupguide.net/ch13/➥
bookstores.georsss.xml'));
```

These examples do not exhaust the Yahoo! Ajax API, which has features such as polylines and more complete overlay functionality.

Microsoft's Live Search Maps/Virtual Earth

Microsoft's Live Search Maps, the company's latest offering in online maps, has gone by quite a few other names (Windows Live Map and Windows Live Local). The name of the service is also not to be confused with Virtual Earth, the name Microsoft has given to the technology that "powers" Live Search Maps. None of this technology is to be confused with MSN Maps, also run by Microsoft.[48]

The Virtual Earth Map control is an Ajax widget, well documented at the following locations:

- The official central place for the Microsoft Virtual Earth docs.[49]

- The Virtual Earth Interactive SDK[50] is a great place to learn about Virtual Earth because it combines a live demo with relevant source code and links to the reference documentation. (Think of it as a counterpart to the Flickr API Explorer.)

Getting Started with Virtual Earth and the JavaScript Shell

1. Copy and paste the following code (this is the simplest piece of code given at the Virtual Earth Interactive SDK):[51]

```
<html>
  <head>
    <title>ve.map.1.html</title>
    <meta http-equiv="Content-Type" content="text/html; charset=utf-8">
    <script src="http://dev.virtualearth.net/mapcontrol/v5/mapcontrol.js">
    </script>
    <script>
    var map = null;

    function GetMap()
    {
       map = new VEMap('myMap');
       map.LoadMap();
    }
```

---

48. http://mappoint.msn.com/

49. http://dev.live.com/virtualearth

50. http://dev.live.com/virtualearth/sdk/

51. http://examples.mashupguide.net/ch13/ve.map.1.html

```
        </script>
      </head>
      <body onload="GetMap();">
        <div id="myMap"
             style="position:relative; width:400px; height:400px;"></div>
      </body>
    </html>
```

2. Invoke the JavaScript Shell for your map by hitting the JavaScript Shell bookmarklet in the context of your map. Type the code fragments in the following steps, and see what happens.

3. To get the zoom level, use this:

```
map.GetZoomLevel()
```

4

---

4. To zoom in and out, use this:

```
map.ZoomIn();
map.ZoomOut();
```

5. To get the style of the map, use this:

```
map.GetMapStyle()
```

---

r

---

6. To set the map style (a = aerial, r = road, h = hybrid, and o = bird's-eye), use this:

```
map.SetMapStyle('a');
```

3D Aspects of Virtual Earth

One cool distinguishing feature of the Virtual Earth is its 3D mode, accessible via JavaScript. This 3D mode is akin to wrapping Google Earth functionality into Google Maps. The 3D mode is available if you are running Firefox or Internet Explorer version 6 or 7 on Windows and have the appropriate 3D add-ons installed. The requirements are documented here:

http://msdn2.microsoft.com/en-us/library/bb429547.aspx

Continuing the exercise, you can put the map into 3D mode with the following command in the JavaScript Shell:

```
map.SetMapMode(VEMapMode.Mode3D);
```

Remember to use the Virtual Earth Interactive SDK (http://dev.live.com/virtualearth/sdk/) to learn about the other capabilities in Virtual Earth, including working with shapes and driving directions.

Geocoding

A common task in using online maps is to geocode addresses—that is, converting street addresses to the corresponding latitude and longitude. In the following sections, I will walk through the basics of geocoding in Yahoo!, Google, Geocoder.us, and Virtual Earth maps, which is enough to get you started. For the following examples, I use the address of Apress, which is 2855 Telegraph Ave., Berkeley, CA.

■**Caution** There are subtleties that I won't go in detail about: the precision and accuracy of the APIs, dealing with ambiguities in the addresses, and which geocoder is best for a given geographic location.

Yahoo! Maps

Yahoo! provides a REST geocoding method here:

```
http://developer.yahoo.com/maps/rest/V1/geocode.html
```

whose base URL is `http://api.local.yahoo.com/MapsService/V1/geocode` and whose parameters include the `appid` to identify your application and two ways of identifying the address:

- A combination of `street`, `city`, `state`, and `zip`:

  ```
  http://api.local.yahoo.com/MapsService/V1/geocode?appid={app-id}➥
  &street=2855+Telegraph+Ave.&city=Berkeley&state=CA
  ```

- `location`, which is free text that consists of one string that holds a combination of `street`, `city`, `state`, and `zip`. The `location` string has priority for determining the placement of this:

  ```
  http://api.local.yahoo.com/MapsService/V1/geocode?appid={app-id}➥
  &location=2855+Telegraph+Ave.%2C+Berkeley%2C+CA
  ```

When you use these two methods to geocode the location of the Apress office, you get the same result. Using `street`, `city`, and `state` returns this:

```
<?xml version="1.0"?>
<ResultSet xmlns:xsi="http://www.w3.org/2001/XMLSchema-instance"
           xmlns="urn:yahoo:maps"
           xsi:schemaLocation="urn:yahoo:maps
http://api.local.yahoo.com/MapsService/V1/GeocodeResponse.xsd">
  <Result precision="address">
    <Latitude>37.858377</Latitude>
    <Longitude>-122.259171</Longitude>
    <Address>2855 TELEGRAPH AVE</Address>
    <City>BERKELEY</City>
    <State>CA</State>
    <Zip>94705-1128</Zip>
    <Country>US</Country>
  </Result>
</ResultSet>
```

Note the following characteristics of the output:

- You get the same results with the two methods in this case.

- You can compare the output address and the input address to make sure the geocoder is interpreting the address the way you think it should be.

- The default output format is XML when no output parameter is specified.

- You get the latitude and longitude in the `<Latitude>` and `<Longitude>` elements, respectively.

A good way to see how the API behaves is to try various parameters. See what happens in the following cases:

- Specify only `city=Berkeley` to get several results corresponding to the cities that go by the name of Berkeley.[52]

- Use the `output=php` option to get serialized PHP.[53]

- Enter a nonexistent street address for a given city.[54]

Geocoder.us

Geocoder.us provides a free gecoding service for U.S. addresses. Refer to Chapter 7 for a detailed discussion of the REST and SOAP interfaces to the Geocoder.us API, which is documented here:

`http://geocoder.us/help/`

Let's calculate the latitude and longitude for the Apress office with different aspects of the Geocoder.us service:

- The Geocoder.us user interface, invoked with this:

  `http://geocoder.us/demo.cgi?address=2855+Telegraph+Ave.%2C+Berkeley%2C+CA`

  shows that the latitude and longitude of the address is the following:

  `(37.858276, -122.260070)`

- The CSV interface, invoked with this:

  `http://rpc.geocoder.us/service/csv?address=2855+Telegraph+Ave.%2C+Berkeley%2C+CA`

  returns the following:

  `37.858276,-122.260070,2855 Telegraph Ave,Berkeley,CA,94705`

---

52. `http://api.local.yahoo.com/MapsService/V1/geocode?appid={app-id}&city=Berkeley`

53. `http://api.local.yahoo.com/MapsService/V1/geocode?appid={app-id}&location=350+5th+Ave,`
    `+New+York,+NY&output=php`

54. `http://api.local.yahoo.com/MapsService/V1/geocode?appid={app-id}&location=350000+main+Street,`
    `+Berkeley,+CA`

- The REST interface, through this:

```
http://geocoder.us/service/rest/?address=2855+Telegraph+Ave.%2C+Berkeley%2C+CA
```

returns the following:

```
<?xml version="1.0"?>
<rdf:RDF xmlns:dc="http://purl.org/dc/elements/1.1/"
  xmlns:geo="http://www.w3.org/2003/01/geo/wgs84_pos#"
  xmlns:rdf="http://www.w3.org/1999/02/22-rdf-syntax-ns#">
  <geo:Point rdf:nodeID="aid33483656">
    <dc:description>2855 Telegraph Ave, Berkeley CA 94705</dc:description>
    <geo:long>-122.260070</geo:long>
    <geo:lat>37.858276</geo:lat>
  </geo:Point>
</rdf:RDF>
```

Notice the use of the W3 Basic Geo encoding for the latitude and longitude in the response.

Google Geocoder

The Google Geocoder provides two interfaces: a REST interface and a JavaScript-accessible interface:

```
http://www.google.com/apis/maps/documentation/#Geocoding_Examples
```

I'll cover each in turn.

REST Interface

We'll first look at the REST method, whose base URL is `http://maps.google.com/maps/geo` and whose parameters are as follows:

- q is the address to geocode.

- key is your API key.[55]

- output is the format of the output—one of xml, kml, csv, or json.

Let's look at some example output. The xml and kml output for 2855 Telegraph Ave., Berkeley, CA, produces the same body (listed next) but different Content-Type headers ("text/xml" and "application/vnd.google-earth.kml+xml"), respectively:[56]

---

55. You can get your key at http://www.google.com/apis/maps/signup.html. ABQIAAAAdjiS7YH6Pzk2Nrli02b5xxR10RG5t-vK3TwPKbpNUO2c5sYb4RTmySs_TEFzYvlZrCaYJKlmTzJ5lA is the key for http://examples.mashupguide.net/ch13/.

56. http://maps.google.com/maps/geo?q=2855+Telegraph+Ave.%2C+Berkeley%2C+CA.&output=xml&key= ABQIAAAAdjiS7YH6Pzk2Nrli02b5xxR10RG5t-vK3TwPKbpNUO2c5sYb4RTmySs_TEFzYvlZrCaYJKlmTzJ5lA

```xml
<?xml version="1.0" encoding="UTF-8"?>
<kml xmlns="http://earth.google.com/kml/2.0">
  <Response>
    <name>2855 Telegraph Ave., Berkeley, CA.</name>
    <Status>
      <code>200</code>
      <request>geocode</request>
    </Status>
    <Placemark id="p1">
      <address>2855 Telegraph Ave, Berkeley, CA 94705, USA</address>
      <AddressDetails Accuracy="8" xmlns="urn:oasis:names:tc:ciq:xsdschema:xAL:2.0">
        <Country>
          <CountryNameCode>US</CountryNameCode>
          <AdministrativeArea>
            <AdministrativeAreaName>CA</AdministrativeAreaName>
            <SubAdministrativeArea>
              <SubAdministrativeAreaName>Alameda</SubAdministrativeAreaName>
              <Locality>
                <LocalityName>Berkeley</LocalityName>
                <Thoroughfare>
                  <ThoroughfareName>2855 Telegraph Ave</ThoroughfareName>
                </Thoroughfare>
                <PostalCode>
                  <PostalCodeNumber>94705</PostalCodeNumber>
                </PostalCode>
              </Locality>
            </SubAdministrativeArea>
          </AdministrativeArea>
        </Country>
      </AddressDetails>
      <Point>
        <coordinates>-122.259310,37.858517,0</coordinates>
      </Point>
    </Placemark>
  </Response>
</kml>
```

■**Caution** Even though the XML output does include a `</Placemark>` element, which is valid KML, the `</Response>` element in the output precludes the output from being valid KML.

Here is the json output for convenient use in JavaScript:[57]

```
{"name":"2855 Telegraph Ave., Berkeley, CA.","Status":{"code":200,"request":
"geocode"},"Placemark":[{"id":"p1","address":"2855 Telegraph Ave, Berkeley,
CA 94705, USA","AddressDetails":{"Country":{"CountryNameCode":"US",
"AdministrativeArea":{"AdministrativeAreaName":"CA","SubAdministrativeArea":
{"SubAdministrativeAreaName":"Alameda","Locality":{"LocalityName":"Berkeley",
"Thoroughfare":{"ThoroughfareName":"2855 Telegraph Ave"},"PostalCode":
{"PostalCodeNumber":"94705"}}}}},"Accuracy": 8},"Point":{"coordinates":
[-122.259310,37.858517,0]}}]}
```

JavaScript Interface

As for the JavaScript methods available in the Google mapping system, consult the documentation provided by Google,[58] which points to using the GClientGeocoder object. You can use the JavaScript Shell to see this object in action:

1. Open the simple Google map from the previous section.[59]

2. In the JavaScript Shell, set up the address and an instance of GClientGeocoder:

   ```
   address = "2855 Telegraph Ave., Berkeley, CA"
   ```

   ```
   2855 Telegraph Ave., Berkeley, CA
   ```

   ```
   geocoder = new GClientGeocoder();
   ```

   ```
   [object Object]
   ```

3. Compose a call to GClientGeocoder.getLatLng, which takes an address and a callback function, which in turn takes the point geocoded from the address:

   ```
   geocoder.getLatLng(address, function(point) {
       if (!point) {
         alert(address + " not found");}
       else {
         map.setCenter(point, 13);
         var marker = new GMarker(point);
         map.addOverlay(marker);
         marker.openInfoWindowHtml(address);
       }
     }
   );
   ```

---

57. http://maps.google.com/maps/geo?q=2855+Telegraph+Ave.%2C+Berkeley%2C+CA.&output=json&key=
ABQIAAAAdjiS7YH6Pzk2NrliO2b5xxR10RG5t-vK3TwPKbpNUO2c5sYb4RTmySs_TEFzYvlZrCaYJKlmTzJ5lA

58. http://www.google.com/apis/maps/documentation/#Geocoding_JavaScript

59. http://examples.mashupguide.net/ch13/google.map.1.html

If you get rid of the whitespace in the function, you can easily invoke it in the JavaScript Shell:

```
geocoder.getLatLng( address, function(point) {
  if (!point) { alert(address + " not found");}
  else {
    map.setCenter(point, 13);
    var marker = new GMarker(point);
    map.addOverlay(marker);
    marker.openInfoWindowHtml(address);
  }
} );
```

4. You will then see that Google Maps adds an overlay marking 2855 Telegraph Ave., Berkeley, CA (as shown in Figure 13-1).

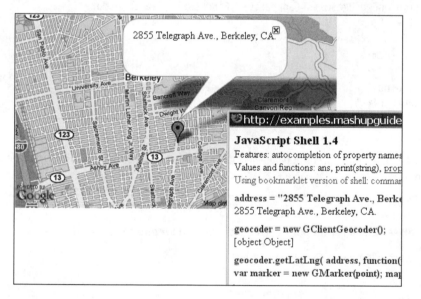

Figure 13-1. *Invoking the JavaScript Google Geocoder with the JavaScript Shell*

Virtual Earth

Virtual Earth provides geocoding functionality in the VEMap.Find method of version 5 of the Virtual Earth SDK,[60] which takes two parameters: a location string and a callback function. Let's illustrate this at work with the JavaScript Shell:

1. Open the basic Virtual Earth example.[61]

2. Let's create a callback function that pops up an alert with the latitude/longitude of the found locations:

---

60. http://msdn2.microsoft.com/en-US/library/bb429645.aspx

61. http://examples.mashupguide.net/ch13/ve.map.1.html

```
function onFoundResults (ShapeLayer,FindResult,Place,HasMore) {
  html = "";
  for (x=0; x<Place.length; x++) {
    html = html + Place[x].LatLong + "";
  }
  alert (html);
}
```

3. In the JavaScript Shell, type the following:

```
address = "2855 Telegraph Ave., Berkeley, CA"
```

```
2855 Telegraph Ave., Berkeley, CA
```

```
function onFoundResults (ShapeLayer,FindResult,Place,HasMore) {
  html = "";
  for (x=0; x<Place.length; x++) {html = html + Place[x].LatLong + "";}
  alert (html);
}
map.Find(null,address,null,null,null,null,null,null,null,null,
onFoundResults);
```

Note The last line with the many `null` parameters might look surprising, but it is an officially recommended invocation from `http://msdn2.microsoft.com/en-us/library/bb545008.aspx`.

4. You will see an alert that pops up the latitude and longitude of the address.

I packaged this logic in a simple example:[62]

```
<html>
  <head>
    <title>VE Map showing VEMap.Find (ve.map.find.html)</title>
    <meta http-equiv="Content-Type" content="text/html; charset=utf-8">
    <script src="http://dev.virtualearth.net/mapcontrol/v5/mapcontrol.js"></script>
    <script>
    var map = null;

    function onFoundResults (ShapeLayer,FindResult,Place,HasMore) {
      html = "";
      //alert("Place: " + Place);
```

---

62. `http://examples.mashupguide.net/ch13/ve.map.find.html`

```
      for (x=0; x<Place.length; x++) {
        html = html + Place[x].LatLong + "";
      }
      alert (html);
    }

    function GetMap()
    {
      map = new VEMap('myMap');
      map.LoadMap();

      address = "2855 Telegraph Ave., Berkeley, CA";
      map.Find(null,address,null,null,null,null,null,null,null,
               null, onFoundResults);
    }
    </script>
  </head>
  <body onload="GetMap();">
    <div id='myMap' style="position:relative; width:400px; height:400px;"></div>
  </body>
</html>
```

Geocoding Non-U.S. Addresses

As I have implied in my previous examples, the Google, Yahoo!, Microsoft, and Geocoder.us geocoders are built to handle American addresses. What if you want to geocode street-level addresses in other countries? It would be great to have a single geocoding API that would return a reliable latitude and longitude for an address from anywhere in the world. That service doesn't currently exist. Here, however, are some starting points to geocoding addresses from around the world:

- The Google geocoder can geocode addresses in countries listed here:

  http://code.google.com/support/bin/answer.py?answer=62668&topic=12266

  The list currently includes Austria, Australia, Belgium, Brazil, Canada, The Czech Republic, Denmark, Finland, France, Germany, Hong Kong, Hungary, India, Ireland, Italy, Japan, Luxembourg, The Netherlands, New Zealand, Poland, Portugal, Singapore, Spain, Sweden, Switzerland, Taiwan, the United Kingdom, and the United States. Note the caveat that the accuracy of the results can vary per country.

- The best list I could find for Yahoo!'s coverage is here:

  http://ylocalblog.com/blog/2007/05/16/yahoo-maps-global-rollout-gets-a-new-look-➥ %e2%80%93-and-a-new-platform/

This blog entry lists the following countries in Western Europe as having "complete coverage": Austria, Belgium, Denmark, Finland, Germany, Great Britain, Luxembourg, Netherlands, Ireland, Norway, Portugal, Spain, Sweden, Switzerland, France, and Italy.

- Consult the following for lists of other geocoders:

  ```
  http://groups.google.com/group/Google-Maps-API/web/resources-non-google-➥
  geocoders
  http://mapki.com/wiki/FAQs#Geocoding
  ```

Google Earth and KML

Google Earth (`http://earth.google.com/`) is a virtual globe, which means it is a desktop environment that simulates the three-dimensional aspects of the earth. It runs on Windows, Mac OS X, and Linux. Google Earth is a cool application, rightfully described as *immersive*. There are other virtual globes,[63] but I wouldn't be surprised if Google Earth remains the dominant virtual globe platform for geodata sharing.[64]

Google Earth is also a great mashup platform. What makes it so?

- The three-dimensional space of a planet is an organizing framework that is easy to understand—everyone knows his or her place in the world, so to speak.

- KML—the XML data format for getting data in and out of Google Earth is easy to read and write.

- There are other APIs to Google Earth, including a COM interface in Windows and an AppleScript interface in Mac OS X.

Displaying and Handling KML As End Users

I introduced KML earlier in the chapter but reserved a full discussion of it in the context of Google Earth. The main reason for this organizational choice is that although KML is steadily growing beyond its origins as the markup language for Keyhole, the precursor to Google Earth, the natural home for KML remains Google Earth. Google Earth is the fullest user interface for displaying and interacting with KML. You can also use it to create KML. At the same time, since Google Earth is not the only tool for working with KML, I'll describe some useful tips for using those other tools.

A good and fun way to start with KML is to download and install Google Earth and to use it to look at a variety of KML files. Here are some sources of KML:

- The Google Earth Gallery (`http://earth.google.com/gallery/index.html`)

- The Google Earth Community (`http://bbs.keyhole.com/ubb/ubbthreads.php/Cat/0`)

---

63. `http://en.wikipedia.org/wiki/Virtual_globe`

64. `http://www.technologyreview.com/read_article.aspx?ch=specialsections&sc=personal&id=17537` makes the argument that Google Earth will be exactly that dominant platform.

It turns out that Google Maps and Flickr are also great sources of KML. After walking you through a specific example to demonstrate the mechanics of interacting with KML, I will describe how to get KML out of Flickr and Google Maps—and how to use Google Maps to display KML.

Let me walk you through the mechanics with one example:

```
http://maps.google.com/maps/ms?f=q&hl=en&geocode=&ie=UTF8&msa=0➥
&msid=116029721704976049577.0000011345e68993fc0e7&z=14&om=1
http://maps.google.com/maps/ms?f=q&msa=0&output=kml&msid=116029721704976049577.➥
0000011345e68993fc0e7
```

Downloading KML into Google Earth

1. Make sure you have Google Earth installed. You can download it from here:

   ```
   http://earth.google.com/
   ```

2. After you have installed Google Earth, learn how to navigate the interface. At the least, you should get comfortable with typing addresses or business names, causing the Google interface to go to those places. Also learn how to use the Save to My Places functionality to create collections of individual items and how to change the properties of individual items, including the latitude, longitude, icon, and view of the item. Finally, you should be to be able to get KML corresponding to the collection.[65] With the KML in hand and an understanding of what a collection looks like in Google Earth, you are in a good position not only to read KML but also to write KML.

3. The classic way that most Google Earth users interact with KML is through clicking a link that causes a KML file to be downloaded and fed into Google Earth. (I'll cover the technical mechanism for how that happens later in the chapter.) Here, I'll walk through one such example of a KML file that you can download.

   Go to the map of bookstores I created with Google My Maps:

   ```
   http://maps.google.com/maps/ms?f=q&msa=0&msid=116029721704976049577.➥
   0000011345e68993fc0e7&z=14&om=1
   ```

4. Click the KML link, which is as follows:

   ```
   http://maps.google.com/maps/ms?f=q&om=1&ie=UTF8&msa=0&output=nl➥
   &msid=116029721704976049577.0000011345e68993fc0e7
   ```

5. If your browser and Google Earth are set up in the typical configuration (in which Google Earth is registered to handle files with a `Content-Type` header of "application/vnd.google-earth.kml+xml"), you will be prompted to let Google Earth open the downloaded KML. If you accept, the collection of points representing the bookstores is loaded into Temporary Places. Double-clicking the link of the collection spins the markers into view in Google Earth. See Figure 13-2 to see the Google Maps collection displayed in Google Earth.

---

65. To start with, you should know the default locations of your stored KML files: `C:\Documents and Settings\[USERNAME]\Application Data\Google\GoogleEarth\myplaces.kml` (Win32) and `~/Library/ Google Earth/myplaces.kml` (OS X).

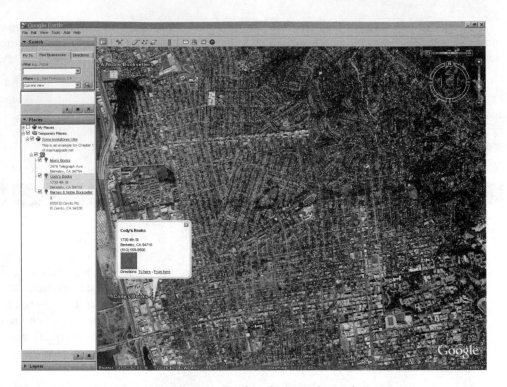

Figure 13-2. *A Google Maps collection displayed in Google Earth*

Now that you have downloaded a KML file into Google Earth, let's look at other tools that are useful for your study of KML.

Google Maps As a KML Renderer

You can use Google Maps to display the contents of a KML file. The easiest way to do so is to go to the Google Maps page (http://maps.google.com) and enter the URL of the KML file as though it were an address or other search term. Such a query results in the following URL:

```
http://maps.google.com?q={kml-url}
```

For example, feeding the KML for the bookstore map back into Google Maps, we get the following:

```
http://maps.google.com/maps?q=http:%2F%2Fmaps.google.com%2Fmaps%2Fms%3Ff%3Dq%26om%3D➥
1%26ie%3DUTF8%26msa%3D0%26output%3Dnl%26msid%3D116029721704976049577.0000011345e6899➥
3fc0e7
```

I have found using Google Maps to be an incredibly useful KML renderer. First, you can test KML files without having access to Google Earth. Second, you can let others look at the content of KML files without requiring them to have Google Earth installed. You should be aware, however, of two caveats in using Google Earth to render KML:

- Google Maps does not implement KML in total—so don't expect to replace Google Earth with Google Maps for working with KML.

- Google Maps caches KML files that you render with it. That is, if you are using Google Maps to test the KML that you are changing, be aware that Google Maps might not be reading the latest version of your KML file.

KML from Flickr

You can now use Flickr to learn more about KML. Currently, although there's no official documentation, you can refer to Rev. Dan Catt's weblog entry to learn some of the details about getting KML out of Flickr:

`http://geobloggers.com/archives/2007/05/31/flickr-kml-and-a-stroll-down-memory-lane/`

The following KML feeds contain at most 20 entries. You have two choices about the format to use:

- `format=kml_nl` for the KML network link that refreshes periodically to show the latest photos. (I will discuss the KML `<NetworkLink>` element in a moment.)

- `format=kml` for the static KML that contains the data about the locations.

So, anywhere I write `format=kml_nl`, you can substitute `format=kml`.

When you are looking at these feeds, it's helpful to remember that in addition to using Google Earth as a KML viewer, you can use Google Maps, which I find very convenient. Just drop the URL for the KML file into the search box for Google Maps, and you can have the KML file displayed in Google Maps. For instance, you can take the KML for the 20 most recent geo-tagged photos in Flickr, like so:

`http://api.flickr.com/services/feeds/geo/?format=kml_nl`

and drop it into Google Maps, which you can access here:

`http://maps.google.com/maps?q=http:%2F%2Fapi.flickr.com%2Fservices%2Ffeeds%2Fgeo%2F%`➡
`3Fformat%3Dkml_nl`

Currently, you can get a KML feed for an individual user with this:

`http://api.flickr.com/services/feeds/geo/?id={user-nsid}&format=kml_nl`

For example, here's the feed for Rev. Dan Catt:

`http://api.flickr.com/services/feeds/geo/?id=35468159852@N01&format=kml_nl`

You can get the KML feed for a group here:

`http://api.flickr.com/services/feeds/geo/?g={group-nsid}&format=kml_nl`

For example, here's the KML feed for the Flickr Geotagging group:

`http://api.flickr.com/services/feeds/geo/?g=94823070@N00&format=kml_nl`

You can get KML feeds for a tag, such as `flower`:

`http://api.flickr.com/services/feeds/geo/&tags=flower&format=kml_nl`

You can get KML feeds for locations. Here are some examples:

```
http://api.flickr.com/services/feeds/geo/us/?format=kml_nl
http://api.flickr.com/services/feeds/geo/us/ca/berkeley/?format=kml_nl
http://api.flickr.com/services/feeds/geo/uk/london/?format=kml_nl
http://api.flickr.com/services/feeds/geo/ca/on/toronto/?format=kml_nl
http://api.flickr.com/services/feeds/geo/FR/%C3%8Ele-de-France/Paris?format=kml_nl
http://api.flickr.com/services/feeds/geo/cn/beijing/?format=kml_nl
http://api.flickr.com/services/feeds/geo/cn/%E5%8C%97%E4%BA%AC/?format=kml_nl
```

Note that the last two links are both for Beijing (北京).

You can do a combined search on a user, location, and tags. For example, to get Raymond Yee's photos in Berkeley, California, tagged with `flower`, use this:

```
http://api.flickr.com/services/feeds/geo/us/ca/berkeley/?id=48600101146@N01➥
&tags=flower&format=kml_nl
```

■**Caution**   Look for official documentation on KML in Flickr to see how it evolves beyond its early beginnings.

KML

Although KML at its heart is a simple dialect of XML, Google is steadily adding features to do more and more through KML. The home for KML documentation is here:

```
http://code.google.com/apis/kml/documentation/
```

Don't overlook the file of KML samples that the documentation refers to, because the examples are very useful:

```
http://code.google.com/apis/kml/documentation/KML_Samples.kml
```

You can have these rendered in Google Maps:

```
http://maps.google.com/maps?q=http%3A%2F%2Fkmlscribe.googlepages.com%2F➥
SamplesInMaps.kml
```

The goal in this section is to get you started with how to read and write KML. Let's start with a simple example of KML that contains a single `<Placemark>` element, whose associated `<Point>` element is located at the Campanile of the UC Berkeley campus:[66]

```
<?xml version="1.0" encoding="UTF-8"?>
<kml xmlns="http://earth.google.com/kml/2.1">
  <Placemark id="berkeley">
    <description>Berkeley, CA</description>
    <name>Berkeley</name>
    <Point>
      <coordinates>-122.257704,37.8721,0</coordinates>
```

---

66. http://examples.mashupguide.net/ch13/berkeley.simple.kml

```
    </Point>
  </Placemark>
</kml>
```

The `<Point>` element defines the position of the placemark's name and icon. You can read the file into Google Earth to display it or use Google Maps to render it:

```
http://maps.google.com/maps?q=http:%2F%2Fexamples.mashupguide.net%2Fch13%2F➥
berkeley.simple.kml
```

You can validate the KML using the techniques described here:

```
http://googlemapsapi.blogspot.com/2007/06/validate-your-kml-online-or-offline.html
```

For instance, you can feed to the file to Feedvalidator.org, which validates KML (in addition to RSS and Atom feeds):

```
http://feedvalidator.org/check.cgi?url=http%3A%2F%2Fexamples.mashupguide.net%2F➥
ch13%2Fberkeley.simple.kml
```

Using your favorite XML validator, you can also validate the KML against the XML Schema for KML 2.1 located here:

```
http://code.google.com/apis/kml/schema/kml21.xsd
```

Adding a View to a Placemark: LookAt and Camera

The previous KML document defined a specific point for positioning the placemark's name and icon but did not specify a viewpoint for the placemark. Given that you can zoom around the virtual globe from many angles, you won't be surprised that KML allows you to define a viewpoint associated with a placemark. There are two ways to do so: the `<LookAt>` element and the `<Camera>` element (defined in KML 2.2 and later). You will find excellent introductory documentation for these two elements here:

```
http://code.google.com/apis/kml/documentation/cameras.html
```

Here I use a series of examples to illustrate the central difference between `<LookAt>` and `<Camera>`: `<LookAt>` specifies the viewpoint in terms of the location being viewed, whereas `<Camera>` specifies the viewpoint in terms of the viewer's location and orientation. I have gathered the examples in a single KML file:

```
http://examples.mashupguide.net/ch13/berkeley.campanile.evans.kml
```

which you can view through Google Earth or Google Maps here:

```
http://maps.google.com/maps?f=q&hl=en&geocode=&q=http:%2F%2Fexamples.mashupguide.net➥
%2Fch13%2Fberkeley.campanile.evans.kml&ie=UTF8&ll=37.872507,-122.257565➥
&spn=0.006581,0.01133&z=17&om=1
```

or here:

```
http://tinyurl.com/38oawy
```

I recommend loading the KML into Google Earth and in Google Maps so that you can follow along. See Figure 13-3 for how this KML file looks in Google Maps. Notice that there are three `<Placemark>` elements for two buildings: the Campanile, which sits almost due south of Evans Hall, and Evans Hall, both on the UC Berkeley campus.

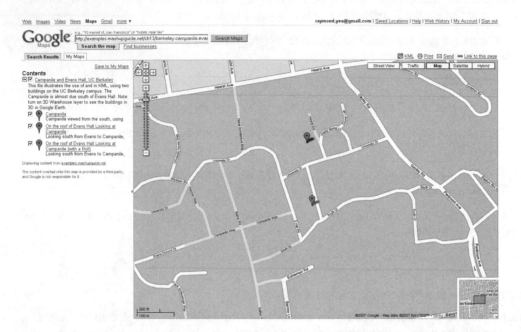

Figure 13-3. *KML for the Campanile and Evans Hall in Google Maps*

The first placemark is placed at the Campanile and uses a `<LookAt>` element to specify a viewpoint for the Campanile (see Figure 13-4 for a rendering of this placemark in Google Earth):

```
<Placemark id="Campanile">
  <name>Campanile</name>
  <description><![CDATA[Campanile viewed from the South, using  <LookAt> (range=200,
tilt=45, heading=0)]]></description>
  <LookAt>
    <longitude>-122.257704</longitude>
    <latitude>37.8721</latitude>
    <altitude>0</altitude>
    <altitudeMode>relativeToGround</altitudeMode>
    <range>200</range>
    <tilt>45</tilt>
    <heading>0</heading>
  </LookAt>
  <Point>
    <coordinates>-122.257704,37.8721,0</coordinates>
  </Point>
</Placemark>
```

Figure 13-4. *View of the Campanile in Google Earth defined by the* <LookAt> *element*

In addition to the <Point> element, which specifies a marker to click for the placemark, the KML defines a point of focus whose latitude and longitude are 37.8721 and -122.257704 and whose altitude is 0 meters (relative to the ground). The distance between this point of focus and the viewer is specified in meters by the range element. (In this example, the virtual camera of the viewpoint is 200 meters away from the point.) Two further parameters control the orientation the viewpoint:

- tilt specifies the angle of the virtual camera relative to an axis running perpendicular to the ground. In other words, 0 degrees means you are looking straight down at the ground; 90 degrees means you're looking at the horizon. In the case of our example, tilt is 45 degrees, which you can pick out from Figure 13-4. (tilt is limited to the range of 0 to 90 degrees.) Note that the default value is 0 degrees, which is, in fact, the only value that is supported in Google Maps.

- heading (which ranges from 0 to 360 degrees) specifies the geographic direction you are looking at. Zero degrees, the default value, means the virtual camera is pointed north. In this example, heading is indeed 0—we are looking at the Campanile from the south. We can see Evans Hall to the north. In Google Maps, the rendered heading is fixed to 0 degrees—north is always up.

Now let's consider a second placemark, which appears as Figure 13-5 when rendered in Google Earth:

```
<Placemark id="Evans">
  <name>On the roof of  Evans Hall  Looking at Campanile</name>
  <description><![CDATA[Looking south from Evans to Campanile, using <Camera>
(heading=180,  tilt=90, roll=0)]]></description>
  <Camera>
    <longitude>-122.2578687854004</longitude>
    <latitude>37.87363451913904</latitude>
    <altitude>50</altitude>
    <altitudeMode>relativeToGround</altitudeMode>
    <heading>180</heading>
    <tilt>90</tilt>
    <roll>0</roll>
  </Camera>
  <Point>
    <coordinates>-122.2578687854004,37.87363451913904,0</coordinates>
  </Point>
</Placemark>
```

Figure 13-5. *View of the Campanile in Google Earth defined by the* <Camera> *element*

You set up the <Camera> element by specifying the location and orientation of the viewer instead of the point of focus. The latitude/longitude for the camera corresponds to Evans Hall, a point north of the Campanile. The altitude (50 m) is roughly roof height for Evans Hall. Let's look at the three angles that are part of a <Camera> element definition:

- heading is set to 180 degrees, meaning the virtual camera is pointing south. Thus, the Campanile is in view.

- tilt is set to 90 degrees, meaning it is looking parallel to the ground. (In contrast to the tilt for <LookAt>, which is constrained to a value between 0 and 90 degrees, the tilt for <Camera> can go from 0 to 180 degrees.) It can even be negative, which results in an upside-down view. This difference in the range for tilt allows a <Camera> element to be aimed at the sky, whereas a <LookAt> element could at most be aimed at the horizon but not above it.

- roll is set to 0 degrees, which is the default value. You can look at the third placemark defined here:

  http://examples.mashupguide.net/ch13/berkeley.campanile.evans.kml

  in which roll is 45 degrees to get a sense of the effect that roll has on a view (refer to Figure 13-6 to see the third placemark).

Figure 13-6. *View of the Campanile in Google Earth defined by the* <Camera> *element with a 45-degree roll*

The final KML file uses a folder to group the three <Placemark> elements, and it associates a <LookAt> element for the folder to give the folder a view.

Programming Google Earth via COM and AppleScript

In addition to controlling Google Earth through the user interface or through feeding it KML, you can also program Google Earth. In Windows, you can do so through the COM interface and on Mac OS X via AppleScript.[67] Little information is publicly available for these APIs. In the following sections, I'll show you some small samples to get you started and to show you some of the capabilities of the API.

COM Interface

You can find documentation of the COM interface to Google Earth here:

http://earth.google.com/comapi/index.html

The following is a small sample Python snippet (running on Windows with the Win32 extension) to load the previous KML example, highlight each of the placemarks, and render their respective views in turn. Note that the code uses the OpenKmlFile method to read a local file so that it can then get features using the GetFeatureByHref method.

```
# demonstrate the Google Earth COM interface
#
import win32com.client
ge = win32com.client.Dispatch("GoogleEarth.ApplicationGE")

fn = r'D:/Document/PersonalInfoRemixBook/examples/ch13/berkeley.campanile.evans.kml'
ge.OpenKmlFile(fn,True)

features = ['Campanile', 'Evans', 'Evans_Roll']

for feature in features:s
    p = ge.GetFeatureByHref(fn + "#" + feature)
    p.Highlight()
    ge.SetFeatureView(p,0.1)
    raw_input('hit to continue')
```

The following is a Python code example to demonstrate the use of SetCameraParams to set the current view of Google Earth. Notice how the parameters correspond to those of the <LookAt> element. At some point, perhaps, the Google Earth COM interface will support the parameters corresponding to the <Camera> element in KML.

```
# demonstrate the Google Earth COM interface
#
import win32com.client
ge = win32com.client.Dispatch("GoogleEarth.ApplicationGE")
```

---

67. http://www.ogleearth.com/2006/09/google_earth_fo_6.html

```
# send to UC Berkeley Campanile
lat = 37.8721
long = -122.257704

#altitude in meters
altitude = 0

# http://earth.google.com/comapi/earth_8idl.html#5513db866b1fce4e039f09957f57f8b7
# AltitudeModeGE { RelativeToGroundAltitudeGE = 1, AbsoluteAltitudeGE = 2 }
altitudeMode = 1

#range in meters; tilt in degrees, heading in degres
range = 200
tilt = 45
heading = 0 # aka azimuth

#set how fast to send Google Earth to the view
speed = 0.1

ge.SetCameraParams(lat,long,altitude,altitudeMode,range,tilt,heading,speed)
```

AppleScript Interface to Google Earth

In Mac OS X, you would use AppleScript to control Google Earth or something like appscript, an Apple event bridge that allows you to write Python scripts in place of AppleScript:

```
http://appscript.sourceforge.net/
```

Here's a little code segment in AppleScript to get you started—It will send you to the Empire State Building:

```
tell application "Google Earth"
  activate
  set viewInfo to (GetViewInfo)
  set dest to {latitude:57.68, longitude:-95.4, distance:1.0E+5,
tilt:90.0, azimuth:180}
  SetViewInfo dest speed 0.1
end tell
```

This moves the view to 57.68 N and 95.4 degrees W.

Using appscript, the following Python script also steers Google Earth in Mac OS X:

```
#!/Library/Frameworks/Python.framework/Versions/Current/bin/pythonw
from appscript import *
ge = app("Google Earth")
#h = ge.GetViewInfo()
h = {k.latitude: 36.510468818615237, k.distance: 5815328.0829986408,➡
k.azimuth: ➡
10.049582258046936, k.longitude: -78.864908202209094, k.tilt:➡
```

```
3.0293063358608456e-14}
ge.SetViewInfo(h,speed=0.5)
```

Mapstraction and OpenLayers

In this chapter, I've covered how to use some of the major mapping APIs: Google Maps, Yahoo!, MapQuest, and Microsoft. It would be convenient to be able to not worry about the differences among the maps and easily switch among the various maps. That's the promise of a mapping abstraction library such as Mapstraction (`http://mapstraction.com`). We'll have to wait and see how and whether it is widely used to gauge the library's effectiveness.

Along a different vein is OpenLayers (`http://www.openlayers.org/`), which is defined as follows:

> *A pure JavaScript library for displaying map data in most modern web browsers, with no server-side dependencies. OpenLayers implements a (still-developing) JavaScript API for building rich web-based geographic applications, similar to the Google Maps and MSN Virtual Earth APIs, with one important difference—OpenLayers is free software, developed for and by the open source software community.*

You can try OpenLayers in FlashEarth (`http://www.flashearth.com/`). Go to the site, and select OpenLayers. You might have to zoom out sufficiently to see any tiles (for example, go to `http://www.flashearth.com/?lat=38.417308&lon=-122.271821&z=9.9&r=0&src=ol`). You can also check out other examples in the OpenLayers gallery at `http://www.openlayers.org/gallery/`.

An Integrative Example: Showing Flickr Pictures in Google Earth

In this section of this chapter, I'll walk you through an example that mashes up Flickr, Google Earth, and Google Maps. Specifically, I'll show you how to query Flickr for public geotagged photos and convert the response to KML that can then be channeled to either Google Earth or Google Maps.

You can see the program that combines this functionality here:

`http://examples.mashupguide.net/ch13/flickrgeo.php`

And you can see the PHP code here:

`http://examples.mashupguide.net/ch13/flickrgeo.php.txt`

The `flickrgeo.php` script described in this chapter is the same code as that in Chapter 10.

What you will see is a basic HTML form aimed at a user who already understands the parameters for the `flickr.photos.search` method (`http://examples.mashupguide.net/ch13/flickrgeo.php`). There are two differences between the parameters used for Flickrgeo and the Flickr API:

- The `bbox` parameter used by the Flickr API is broken out into four individual parameters for Flickrgeo: `lat0`, `lon0` for the southwest corner and `lat1`, `lon1` for the northeast corner of the bounding box. This approach will be familiar to you from Chapter 10, which focuses in detail on how to query Flickr for geotagged photos.

- Flickrgeo has an `o_format` parameter to set the requested output. Recognized values are `html` (for the simple user interface), `rest` (to return the Flickr API in REST format), `json` (to return the results as JSON), `nl` (to return a KML NetworkLink), and `kml` (to return the photo data as KML). The appropriate value for `format` is passed to `flickr.photos.search`.

When the Flickrgeo form loads, `o_format` is set by default to `html` so that you can use the form to enter some values and see some search results rendered as HTML. For example, the following:

```
http://examples.mashupguide.net/ch13/flickrgeo.php?user_id=48600101146%40N01&tags=➥
&text=&lat0=37.817785166068&lon0=-122.34375&lat1=37.926190569376&lon1=-122.17208862305➥
&page=1&per_page=10&min_upload_date=820483200&extras=geo&o_format=html
```

or

```
http://tinyurl.com/2nbjbb
```

displays my public geotagged photos in the Berkeley area. You can change `o_format` to `json` and `rest` to get JavaScript and XML versions of this data, respectively; Flickrgeo just passes back the data that comes from Flickr.

If you set `o_format` to `kml`, you get the results as a KML feed. For example, here's a KML feed of my public geotagged photos in the Berkeley area:

```
http://examples.mashupguide.net/ch13/flickrgeo.php?user_id=48600101146%40N01&tags=➥
&text=&lat0=37.817785166068&lon0=-122.34375&lat1=37.926190569376&lon1=-122.17208862305&➥
page=1&per_page=10&min_upload_date=820483200&extras=geo&o_format=kml
```

or

```
http://tinyurl.com/36hu2j
```

which you can see on Google Maps (see Figure 13-7):[68]

```
http://maps.google.com/maps?f=q&hl=en&geocode=&q=http:%2F%2Fexamples.mashupguide.net➥
%2Fch13%2Fflickrgeo.php%3Fuser_id%3D48600101146%2540N01%26tags%3D%26text%3D%26lat0%➥
3D37.817785166068%26lon0%3D-122.34375%26lat1%3D37.926190569376%26lon1%3D-122.17208862305➥
%26page%3D1%26per_page%3D10%26min_upload_date%3D820483200%26extras%3Dgeo%26o_format%➥
3Dkml&ie=UTF8&z=14&om=1
```

or

---

68. `http://tinyurl.com/2fmhh5`

Figure 13-7. *Flickr photos displayed in Google Maps via a KML feed*

If you set o_format to nl, you get a KML NetworkLink that enables you to use Google Earth to interact with Flickrgeo. That is, if you change your viewpoint on Google Earth, Google Earth will send to Flickrgeo the parameters of your new viewpoint to get pictures for that new viewpoint.

Hence, Flickrgeo does four major tasks to pull off the mashup:

1. Querying Flickr for geotagged photos

2. Converting Flickr results from a single flickr.photos.search into the corresponding KML

3. Generating a KML NetworkLink to feed your actions in Google Earth to Flickrgeo

4. Knitting together the various possibilities for o_format into one script

For the first topic, I refer you to Chapter 10 for a detailed discussion and remind you that the essential point is that you use the bbox parameter to specify a bounding box, add geo to the extras parameter to get the latitude and longitude, and set a minimum upload time to something like 820483200 (for January 1, 1996 Pacific Time) to coax some photos from the API when you are not searching on tags or text.

For the final topic, you can see the logic of what is done by studying the source code. Next I'll discuss the topics of KML NetworkLink and generating KML from flickr.photos.search results.

KML NetworkLink

So far I have shown you how to write a KML document and render it with Google Earth and Google Maps. In many situations, including the mashup I create here, it's extremely helpful to get information flowing from Google Earth back to the program that generated the KML in the first place. Foremost among that data would be the current viewpoint of the user. If you as the generator of the KML know the region that the user is focused on, you can generate data that would be visible in that viewpoint.

That's the purpose of the `<NetworkLink>` element in KML. Here I'll show you how to use it by example. Load the following into Google Earth:

```
http://examples.mashupguide.net/ch13/hello.world.networklink.kml
```

You will see a pin appear in the middle of your current viewpoint announcing the current time. If you click the pin, you'll see a list of parameters corresponding to the current viewpoint. If you change the viewpoint and wait a couple of seconds, the pin is refreshed to be located in the center of the new viewpoint. How does this happen?

Let's look first at this:

```
http://examples.mashupguide.net/ch13/hello.world.networklink.kml
```

which is the following:

```
<?xml version="1.0" encoding="UTF-8"?>
 <kml xmlns="http://earth.google.com/kml/2.2">
   <NetworkLink>
     <flyToView>0</flyToView>
     <name>Hello World</name>
     <open>1</open>
     <visibility>1</visibility>
     <Link>
       <href>http://examples.mashupguide.net/ch13/hello.world.networklink.php</href>
       <viewRefreshMode>onStop</viewRefreshMode>
       <viewRefreshTime>2</viewRefreshTime>➡
<viewFormat>bboxWest=[bboxWest]&amp;bboxSouth=[bboxSouth]&amp;bboxEast=[bboxEast]➡
&amp;bboxNorth=[bboxNorth]&amp;lookatLon=[lookatLon]&amp;lookatLat=[lookatLat]➡
&amp;lookatRange=[lookatRange]&amp;lookatTilt=[lookatTilt]&amp;lookatHeading=➡
[lookatHeading]&amp;lookatTerrainLon=[lookatTerrainLon]&amp;lookatTerrainLat=➡
[lookatTerrainLat]&amp;lookatTerrainAlt=[lookatTerrainAlt]&amp;cameraLon=[cameraLon]➡
&amp;cameraLat=[cameraLat]&amp;cameraAlt=[cameraAlt]&amp;horizFov=[horizFov]➡
&amp;vertFov=[vertFov]&amp;horizPixels=[horizPixels]&amp;vertPixels=[vertPixels]➡
&amp;terrainEnabled=[terrainEnabled]</viewFormat>
     </Link>
   </NetworkLink>
 </kml>
```

A KML NetworkLink defines how often refreshing occurs or the conditions under which it happens. I'll discuss what a refresh actually does in the next paragraph. There are two modes of refreshing that can be specified in a NetworkLink. The first, based on time, uses the `<refreshMode>` and `<refreshInterval>` elements. With those tags, you can, for instance, set a refresh to happen every ten seconds. For the KML I present here, I use refreshing based on changes in the viewpoint, which are parameterized by two tags: <viewRefreshMode> and <viewRefreshTime>. If you consult the KML documentation, you'll see that one choice for <viewRefreshMode> is onStop—which means a refresh event happens once the viewpoint stops changing for the amount of time specified by the <viewRefreshTime> element—in this case two seconds.

So, what happens during a refresh event? Google Earth does an HTTP GET request on the URL specified by the href element with parameters specified in the <viewFormat> element, which contains something akin to a URI template. That is, Google Earth substitutes the values that correspond to the viewpoint at the time of the refresh event for the value templates such as [bboxWest], [bboxSouth], [bboxEast], and so on. Consult the documentation for a comprehensive list of parameters supported in KML. The template I specify here has the complete current list of parameters. Note that there is no requirement that the parameter names match the naming scheme given by Google. In fact, you should match the parameter names to the ones recognized by the script specified by the href element.

Let's now turn to the script here:

```
http://examples.mashupguide.net/ch13/hello.world.networklink.php
```

to see how the HTTP GET request is processed. Here's the PHP code:

```php
<?php
// get the time
$timesnap = date("H:i:s");

// for clarity, place each coordinate into a clearly marked bottom-left
// or top-right variable

$bboxWest  = isset($_GET['bboxWest'])  ? $_GET['bboxWest']  : "-180.0";
$bboxSouth = isset($_GET['bboxSouth']) ? $_GET['bboxSouth'] : "-90.0";
$bboxEast  = isset($_GET['bboxEast'])  ? $_GET['bboxEast']  : "180.0";
$bboxNorth = isset($_GET['bboxNorth']) ? $_GET['bboxNorth'] : "90.0";

// calculate the approx center of the view -- note that this is inaccurate
// if the user is not looking straight down
$userlon = (($bboxEast - $bboxWest)/2) + $bboxWest;
$userlat = (($bboxNorth - $bboxSouth)/2) + $bboxSouth;

$response = '<?xml version="1.0" encoding="UTF-8"?>';
$response .= '<kml xmlns="http://earth.google.com/kml/2.2">';
$response .= '<Placemark>';
$response .= "<name>Hello at: $timesnap</name>";

# calculate all the parameters

$arg_text = "";
foreach ($_GET as $key => $val) {
  $arg_text .= "<b>{$key}</b>:{$val}<br>";
}
```

```php
$description_text = $arg_text;
$description = "<![CDATA[{$description_text}]]>";
$response .= "<description>{$description}</description>";

$response .= '<Point>';
$response .= "<coordinates>$userlon,$userlat,0</coordinates>";
$response .= '</Point>';
$response .= '</Placemark>';
$response .= '</kml>';
# set $myKMLCode together as a string
 $downloadfile="myKml.kml"; # give a name to appear at the client
 header("Content-disposition: attachment; filename=$downloadfile");
 header("Content-Type: application/vnd.google-earth.kml+xml; charset=utf8");
 header("Content-Transfer-Encoding: binary");
 header("Content-Length: ".strlen($response));
 header("Pragma: no-cache");
 header("Expires: 0");
echo $response;
?>
```

hello.world.networklink.php reads all the parameters that are passed to it and displays them to the user. This is accomplished by generating the KML for a <Placemark> element with a <description> element with all the parameters.

Let's return to how I use the KML NetworkLink in flickrgeo.php. In that script, I needed to generate <NetworkLink> elements that looked like this:

```xml
<?xml version="1.0" encoding="UTF-8"?>
<kml xmlns="http://earth.google.com/kml/2.2">
  <NetworkLink>
    <flyToView>0</flyToView>
    <name>Pictures from Flickr</name>
    <description>
      <![CDATA[<a href='http://examples.mashupguide.net/ch13/flickrgeo.php?
text=stop+sign&page=1&per_page=10&min_upload_date=820483200&extras=geo%2Clicense
%2Cowner_name%2Cicon_server%2Ctags&o_format=html'>Search Something Different</a>]]>
    </description>
    <open>1</open>
    <visibility>1</visibility>
    <Link>
      <href>http://examples.mashupguide.net/ch13/flickrgeo.php?
text=stop+sign&amp;page=1&amp;per_page=10&amp;min_upload_date=820483200
&amp;extras=geo&amp;o_format=kml</href>
      <viewRefreshMode>onStop</viewRefreshMode>
      <viewRefreshTime>3</viewRefreshTime>
<viewFormat>lat0=[bboxSouth]&amp;lon0=[bboxWest]&amp;lat1=[bboxNorth]
&amp;lon1=[bboxEast]</viewFormat>
    </Link>
  </NetworkLink>
</kml>
```

This is a `<NetworkLink>` element for generating refreshable KML on photos that match a full-text search for `stop sign`. Notice how the viewpoint is passed from Google Earth to http://examples.mashupguide.net/ch13/flickrgeo.php by the `viewFormat` element:

```
lat0=[bboxSouth]&amp;lon0=[bboxWest]&amp;lat1=[bboxNorth]&amp;lon1=[bboxEast]
```

Generating the KML for the Photos

The following excerpt of KML shows the structure of the KML that `flickrgeo.php` generates to display the photos in Google Earth or Google Maps (I have put some KML elements in bold that I have yet to introduce.):

```
<?xml version="1.0" encoding="UTF-8"?>
<kml xmlns="http://earth.google.com/kml/2.2">
  <Document>
    <Style id="118550863">
      <IconStyle>
       <Icon>
       <href>http://farm1.static.flickr.com/56/118550863_1b8f5a26aa_s.jpg</href>
       </Icon>
      </IconStyle>
    </Style>
    [....]
    <Folder>
      <name>Flickr Photos</name>
      <description>Total Number of Photos available: 72 &lt;➥
a href='http://examples.mashupguide.net/ch13/flickrgeo.php?➥
user_id=48600101146%40N01&amp;lat0=37.75976100792328&amp;lon0=-122.➥
4470955684774&amp;lat1=37.95649244418595&amp;lon1=-122.1471302328438➥
&amp;page=1&amp;per_page=10&amp;min_upload_date=820483200&amp;extras=geo%2Clicense➥
%2Cowner_name%2Cicon_server%2Ctags&amp;o_format=kml'&gt;KML&lt;/a&gt; &lt;➥
a href='http://maps.google.com?q=http%3A%2F%2Fexamples.mashupguide.net%2F➥
ch13%2Fflickrgeo.php%3Fuser_id%3D48600101146%2540N01%26lat0%3D37.75976100792328%26➥
lon0%3D-122.4470955684774%26lat1%3D37.95649244418595%26lon1%3D-122.➥
1471302328438%26page%3D1%26per_page%3D10%26min_upload_date%3D820483200%26extras%3D➥
geo%252Clicense%252Cowner_name%252Cicon_server%252Ctags%26o_format%3Dkml'&gt;GMap➥
&lt;/a&gt;</description>
      <Placemark>
        <name>shrink wrap car</name>
        <description>
          <![CDATA[<a href='http://www.flickr.com/photos/48600101146@N01/118550863'>
<img src='http://farm1.static.flickr.com/56/118550863_1b8f5a26aa.jpg'></a>]]>
        </description>
        <LookAt>
          <longitude>-122.300915</longitude>
          <latitude>37.898562</latitude>
          <altitude>0</altitude>
          <altitudeMode>relativeToGround</altitudeMode>
```

```
        <range>2000</range>
        <tilt>0</tilt>
        <heading>0</heading>
      </LookAt>
      <styleUrl>#118550863</styleUrl>
      <Point>
        <coordinates>-122.300915,37.898562,0</coordinates>
      </Point>
    </Placemark>
    [....]
  </Folder>
  </Document>
</kml>
```

Note the following features of the KML:

- There is a `<Placemark>` element for each photo, whose name element holds the title for the photo. In the `<description>` element is HTML for the medium-sized version of the photo. The latitude and longitude, drawn from the geo information provided by Flickr, goes into two places: the coordinates element for the `<Point>` element and a `<LookAt>` view.

- Each `<Placemark>` element is tied to a `<Style>` element to generate custom icons for each photo. The icon is the square version of the Flickr photo. The association is made through the `<styleUrl>` element.

- There is a `<Folder>` element that groups all the `<Placemark>` elements. The `<description>` element for the `<Folder>` element contains links to the KML itself and to a Google Map showing this KML. These links provide you with a way of getting hold of what you are seeing in Google Earth.

The flickrgeo.php Code

Here's an edited listing of the `flickrgeo.php` code:

```php
<?php
# flickrgeo.php
# copyright Raymond Yee, 2007
# http://examples.mashupguide.net/ch13/flickrgeo.php

# xmlentities substitutes characters in $string that can be expressed
# as the predefined XML entities.

function xmlentities ($string)
{ return str_replace (
        array ( '&', '"', "'", '<', '>' ),
        array ( '&amp;' , '&quot;', '&apos;' , '&lt;' , '&gt;' ),
        $string );
}
```

```
# converts an associative array representing form parameters
# and values into the request part of a URL.

function form_url_params($arg_list, $rid_empty_value=TRUE) {
    $list = array();

    foreach ($arg_list as $arg => $val) {
     if (!($rid_empty_value) || (strlen($val) > 0)) {
        $list[] = $arg . "=" . urlencode($val);
     }
    }
    return join("&",$list);
  }

# a simple wrapper around flickr.photos.search for public photos.
# It deals a request for either the Flickr REST or JSON formats

class flickrwrapper {
  protected $api_key;

  public function __construct($api_key) {
    $this->api_key = $api_key;
  }

  # generic method for retrieving content for a given URL.
  protected function getResource($url){
    $chandle = curl_init();
    curl_setopt($chandle, CURLOPT_URL, $url);
    curl_setopt($chandle, CURLOPT_RETURNTRANSFER, 1);
    $result = curl_exec($chandle);
    curl_close($chandle);

    return $result;
  }

  # returns an HTTP response body and headers
  public function search($arg_list) {
    # attach API key
    $arg_list['api_key'] = $this->api_key;

    # attach parameters specific to the format request, which is either JSON or REST.
    $format = $arg_list["format"];
    if ($format == "rest") {
      $url = "http://api.flickr.com/services/rest/?method=flickr.photos.search&" .
form_url_params($arg_list);
      $rsp = $this->getResource($url);
```

```php
      $response["body"] = $rsp;
      $response["headers"] = array("Content-Type"=>"application/xml");
      return $response;
    } elseif ($format == "json") {
      $arg_list["nojsoncallback"] = 1;
      $url = "http://api.flickr.com/services/rest/?method=flickr.photos.search&" .
form_url_params($arg_list);
      $rsp = $this->getResource($url);
      $response["headers"] = array("Content-Type"=>"text/javascript");
      $response["body"] = $rsp;
      return $response;
    }
  } // search
} //flickrwrapper

class flickr_html {

# generates a simple form based on the parameters
# and values of the input associative array $arg_array
# uses $path as the target of the form's action attribute

  public function generate_form($arg_array, $path) {
    $form_html = "";
    foreach ($arg_array as $arg => $default) {
      $form_html .= <<<EOT
{$arg}:<input type="text" size="20" name="{$arg}" value="{$default}"><br>
EOT;
    }

    $form_html = <<<EOT
<form action="{$path}" method="get">
{$form_html}<br>
<input type="submit" value="Go!">
</form>
EOT;

    return $form_html;
  } //generate_form

  # generates a simple HTML representation of the results of flickr.photos.search
  public function html_from_pics($rsp) {

    $xml = simplexml_load_string($rsp);
    #print_r($xml);
    #var_dump($xml);
    $s = "";
    $s .= "Total number of photos: " . $xml->photos['total'] . "<br>";
```

```
  # http://www.flickr.com/services/api/misc.urls.html
  # http://farm{farm-id}.static.flickr.com/{server-id}/{id}_{secret}.jpg
  foreach ($xml->photos->photo as $photo) {
    $farmid = $photo['farm'];
    $serverid = $photo['server'];
    $id = $photo['id'];
    $secret = $photo['secret'];
    $owner = $photo['owner'];
    $thumb_url =
      "http://farm{$farmid}.static.flickr.com/{$serverid}/{$id}_{$secret}_t.jpg";
    $page_url = "http://www.flickr.com/photos/{$owner}/{$id}";
    $image_html= "<a href='{$page_url}'><img src='{$thumb_url}'></a>";
    $s .= $image_html;
  }
  return $s;
}
} // flickr_html


# a class to handle conversion of Flickr results to KML

class flickr_kml {

# helper function to create a new text node with $string that is wrapped by an
# element named by $childName -- and then attach the whole thing to $parentNode.
# allow for a namespace to be specified for $childName

  protected function attachNewTextNode($parentNode,
                                      $childName,$childNS="",$string="") {
    $childNode = $parentNode->appendChild(new DOMElement($childName,$childNS));
    $childNode->appendChild(new DOMText($string));
    return $childNode;
  }

  # create the subelements for Style
  /*
  e.g.,
    <Style id="118550863">
      <IconStyle>
        <Icon>
          <href>http://farm1.static.flickr.com/56/118550863_1b8f5a26aa_s.jpg</href>
        </Icon>
      </IconStyle>
    </Style>
  */

  protected function populate_style($style,$photo) {
    $id = $photo['id'];
    $farmid = $photo['farm'];
```

```php
  $serverid = $photo['server'];
  $secret = $photo['secret'];
  $square_url =
    "http://farm{$farmid}.static.flickr.com/{$serverid}/{$id}_{$secret}_s.jpg";


  $id_attr = $style->setAttributeNode(new DOMAttr('id', $id));
  $iconstyle = $style->appendChild(new DOMElement("IconStyle"));
  $icon = $iconstyle->appendChild (new DOMElement("Icon"));
  $href = $this->attachNewTextNode($icon,"href","",$square_url);

  return $style;
}


# converts the response from the Flickr photo search ($rsp),
# the arguments from the original search ($arg_array),
# the $path of the script to KML

public function kml_from_pics($arg_array, $path, $rsp) {

  $xml = simplexml_load_string($rsp);
  $dom = new DOMDocument('1.0', 'UTF-8');
  $kml = $dom->appendChild(new DOMElement('kml'));
  $attr = $kml->setAttributeNode(new DOMAttr('xmlns',
                                        'http://earth.google.com/kml/2.2'));
  $document = $kml->appendChild(new DOMElement('Document'));

  # See http://www.flickr.com/services/api/misc.urls.html
  # Remember http://farm{farm-id}.static.flickr.com/{server-id}/{1d}_{secret}.jpg
  # syntax for URLs


  # parameters for LookAt -- hard-coded in this instance
  $range = 2000;
  $altitude = 0;
  $heading =0;
  $tilt = 0;

  # make the <Style> elements first
  foreach ($xml->photos->photo as $photo) {
    $style = $document->appendChild(new DOMElement('Style'));
    $this->populate_style($style,$photo);
  }

  # now make the <Placemark> elements -- but tuck them under one Folder
  # in the Folder, add URLs for the KML document and how to send
  # the KML document to Google Maps
```

```php
    $folder = $document->appendChild(new DOMElement('Folder'));
    $folder_name_node = $this->attachNewTextNode($folder,"name","","Flickr Photos");
    $kml_url =  $path . "?" . form_url_params($arg_array,TRUE);
    $description_string = "Total Number of Photos available: {$xml->
photos['total']}" . " <a href='{$kml_url}'>KML</a>";
    $description_string .= " <a href='" . "http://maps.google.com?q=" .
urlencode($kml_url) .  "'>GMap</a>";
    $folder_description_node = $this->
attachNewTextNode($folder,"description","",$description_string);

    # loop through the photos to convert to a Placemark KML element
    foreach ($xml->photos->photo as $photo) {
      $farmid = $photo['farm'];
      $serverid = $photo['server'];
      $id = $photo['id'];
      $secret = $photo['secret'];
      $owner = $photo['owner'];
      $thumb_url =
        "http://farm{$farmid}.static.flickr.com/{$serverid}/{$id}_{$secret}_t.jpg";
      $med_url =
        "http://farm{$farmid}.static.flickr.com/{$serverid}/{$id}_{$secret}.jpg";
      $page_url = "http://www.flickr.com/photos/{$owner}/{$id}";
      $image_html= "<a href='{$page_url}'><img src='{$med_url}'></a>";
      $title = $photo['title'];
      $latitude = $photo['latitude'];
      $longitude = $photo['longitude'];

      $placemark = $folder->appendChild(new DOMElement('Placemark'));

      # place the photo title into the <name> KML element
      $name = $this->attachNewTextNode($placemark,"name","",$title);

      # drop the title and thumbnail into description and wrap in CDATA
      # to work around encoding issues
      $description_string = "{$image_html}";
      $description = $placemark->appendChild(new DOMElement('description'));
      $description->appendChild($dom->createCDATASection($description_string));

      $lookat = $placemark->appendChild(new DOMElement('LookAt'));
      $longitude_node = $this->attachNewTextNode($lookat,"longitude","",$longitude);
      $latitude_node = $this->attachNewTextNode($lookat,"latitude","",$latitude);
      $altitudeNode = $this->attachNewTextNode($lookat,"altitude","",$altitude);
      $altitudeMode =
        $this->attachNewTextNode($lookat,"altitudeMode","","relativeToGround");
      $rangeNode = $this->attachNewTextNode($lookat,"range","",$range);
      $tiltNode = $this->attachNewTextNode($lookat,"tilt","",$tilt);
      $headingNode = $this->attachNewTextNode($lookat,"heading","",$heading);
```

```
        $styleurl = $this->attachNewTextNode($placemark, "styleUrl","","#".$id);

        $point = $placemark->appendChild(new DOMElement('Point'));
        $coordinates_string = "{$longitude},{$latitude},{$altitude}";
        $coordinates =
          $this->attachNewTextNode($point,"coordinates","",$coordinates_string);
    }
    return $dom->saveXML();
}


# generate a network link based on the user search parameters ($arg_list)
# and the $path to this script
public function generate_network_link ($arg_list, $path) {

    # look through the $arg_list but get rid of lat/long and blanks
    unset ($arg_list['lat0']);
    unset ($arg_list['lat1']);
    unset ($arg_list['lon0']);
    unset ($arg_list['lon1']);

    $arg_list['o_format'] = 'kml';   //set to KML
    $url = $path . "?" . form_url_params($arg_list,TRUE);
    $url = xmlentities($url);

    # generate a description string to guide user
    # to reparameterizing the network link
    $arg_list['o_format'] = 'html';
    $url2 = $path . "?" . form_url_params($arg_list,TRUE);
    $description = "<a href='{$url2}'>Search Something Different</a>";

    $nl = <<<EOT
<?xml version="1.0" encoding="UTF-8"?>
<kml xmlns="http://earth.google.com/kml/2.2">
  <NetworkLink>
    <flyToView>0</flyToView>
    <name>Pictures from Flickr</name>
    <description><![CDATA[{$description}]]></description>
    <open>1</open>
    <visibility>1</visibility>
    <Link>
      <href>{$url}</href>
      <viewRefreshMode>onStop</viewRefreshMode>
      <viewRefreshTime>3</viewRefreshTime>
      <viewFormat>lat0=[bboxSouth]&amp;lon0=[bboxWest]&amp;lat1=[bboxNorth]
&amp;lon1=[bboxEast]</viewFormat>
    </Link>
  </NetworkLink>
```

```
</kml>
EOT;
   return $nl;
  }
} // flickr_kml

# this class translates what comes in on the URL and from form values
# to parameters to submit to Flickr

class flickr_view {

  # this function filters $_GET passed in as $get by parameters
  # that are in $defaults
  # only parameters named in $defaults are allowed -- and if that value isn't set in
  # $get, then this function passes back the default value

  public function form_input_to_user_inputs($get,$defaults) {
    $params = array();
    foreach ($defaults as $arg => $default_value) {
      $params[$arg] = isset($get[$arg]) ? $get[$arg] : $default_value;
    }
    return $params;
  }

  # translate the user inputs to the appropriate ones for Flickr.
  # for example -- fold the latitudes and longitude coordinates into bbox
  # get rid of o_format  for Flickr

  public function user_inputs_to_flickr_params($user_inputs) {
    $search_params = $user_inputs;

    $o_format = $user_inputs["o_format"];
    unset ($search_params["o_format"]);

    if (($o_format == "json") || ($o_format == "rest")) {
      $search_params["format"] = $o_format;
    } else {
      $search_params["format"] = "rest";
    }

    #recast the lat and long parameters in bbox

    $bbox = "{$search_params['lon0']},{$search_params['lat0']},
            {$search_params['lon1']},{$search_params['lat1']}";
    $search_params['bbox'] = $bbox;
    unset($search_params['lon0']);
    unset($search_params['lon1']);
```

```php
        unset($search_params['lat0']);
        unset($search_params['lat1']);

        return $search_params;
    } // user_inputs_to_flickr_params
} //flickr_view

// API key here
$api_key = "[API-KEY]";

# a set of defaults -- center the search around Berkeley by default
# and any geotagged photo in that bounding box.
# BTW, this script needs at least geo in extras.
# min_upload_date corresponds to Jan 1, 1996 (Pacific time)
$default_args = array(
    "user_id" => '',
    "tags" => '',
    "tag_mode" => '',
    "text" => '',
    "min_upload_date" => '820483200',
    "max_upload_date" => '',
    "min_taken_date" => '',
    "max_taken_date" => '',
    "license" => '',
    "sort" => '',
    "privacy_filter" => '',
    "lat0" => 37.81778516606761,
    "lon0" => -122.34374999999999,
    "lat1" => 37.92619056937629,
    "lon1" => -122.17208862304686,
    "accuracy" => '',
    "safe_search" => '',
    "content_type" => '',
    "machine_tags" => '',
    "machine_tag_mode" => '',
    "group_id" => '',
    "place_id" => '',
    "extras" => "geo",
    "per_page" => 10,
    "page" => 1,
    "o_format" => 'html'
);

# calculate the path to this script as a URL.
$path = "http://" . $_SERVER['SERVER_NAME'] . $_SERVER['PHP_SELF'];

# instantiate the Flickr wrapper and the view object
$fw = new flickrwrapper($api_key);
```

```php
$fv = new flickr_view();

# get the parameters that have been submitted to it.
$user_inputs = $fv->form_input_to_user_inputs($_GET,$default_args);
$search_params = $fv->user_inputs_to_flickr_params($user_inputs);

# see what the requested format is
$o_format = $user_inputs["o_format"];

# if the user is looking for a network link,
# calculate the Networklink KML and return it
# with the appropriate Content-Type for KML

if ($o_format == 'nl') {
  $fk = new flickr_kml();
  header("Content-Type:application/vnd.google-earth.kml+xml");
  $downloadfile="flickr.kml"; # give a name to appear at the client
  header("Content-disposition: attachment; filename=$downloadfile");
  print $fk->generate_network_link($user_inputs,$path);
  exit();
}

# If the user is looking instead for JSON, REST, HTML, or KML, we query Flickr

$response = $fw->search($search_params);

# If the request is for JSON or REST,
# just pass back the results of the Flickr search
if (($o_format == "json") || ($o_format == "rest")) {
  foreach ($response["headers"] as $header => $val) {
    header("{$header}:{$val}");
  }
  print $response["body"];

  # if the request is for HTML or KML, do the appropriate transformations.

} elseif ($o_format == "html") {

  # now translate to HTML
  $fh = new flickr_html();
  header("Content-Type:text/html");
  print $fh->generate_form($user_inputs, $_SERVER['PHP_SELF']);
  print $fh->html_from_pics($response["body"]);

} elseif ($o_format == "kml") {

  $fk = new flickr_kml();
  header("Content-Type:application/vnd.google-earth.kml+xml");
```

```
$downloadfile="flickr.kml"; # give a name to appear at the client
header("Content-disposition: attachment; filename=$downloadfile");
print $fk->kml_from_pics($user_inputs, $path, $response["body"]);

}
?>
```

Summary

The online mapping arena is changing very quickly, and I obviously am not able to cover the details of all these changes. Nonetheless, here's what I believe will be the long-term trends in this area:

- You'll see a migration of many features found in typical full-fledged GIS system—for example, shading of layers—into programmable web applications.

- Not surprisingly, you'll see the platform players (such as Google Maps) incorporate functionality that started off as extensions to the platform into the platform itself. For example, sites such as Mapbuilder.net provided a user interface for building a Google (or Yahoo!) map before Google made it easier to build a Google map via its My Maps functionality. Google's My Maps doesn't exactly duplicate Mapbuilder.net, but it's bound to win a major audience by virtue of its tight integration with Google Maps.

- You will see increased merging in 2D and 3D representations of the globe. As you've already seen in this chapter, Microsoft's Live Search Maps has both 3D and 2D views. You can use KML as a way of moving data between Google Earth and Google Maps. KML is finding support from competitors to Google such Yahoo!'s Flickr and Yahoo! Pipes.

- We're going to see more native support of GPS devices as they become ubiquitous.

Here are some references where you can find more information:

- *Beginning Google Maps Applications with PHP and Ajax: From Novice to Professional* (Apress, 2006)

- *Beginning Google Maps Applications with PHP and Ajax: From Novice to Professional* (Apress, 2006)

- *Google Maps Hacks: Tips & Tools for Geographic Searching and Remixing* (O'Reilly, 2006)

- *Hacking Google Maps and Google Earth* (Wiley, 2006)

- *Web Mapping Illustrated: Using Open Source GIS Toolkits* (O'Reilly, 2005)

- *Mapping Hacks: Tips & Tools for Electronic Cartography* (O'Reilly, 2005)

- Google Mapki[69] (a great wiki and source of information on Google Maps)

---

69. http://mapki.com/wiki/Main_Page

CHAPTER 14

■ ■ ■

Exploring Social Bookmarking and Bibliographic Systems

Ⓞne of the fundamental challenges of using the Web is keeping found things found, whether it be at the basic level of simple URLs or other digital content such as images and data sets. Social bookmarking has arisen to be a popular solution to this problem. According to "7 things you should know about social bookmarking,"[1] social bookmarking "is the practice of saving bookmarks to a public Web site and 'tagging' them with keywords." A specific type of reference is a *bookmark* or *favorite*, which is a URL stored by the user. You can try to manage these URLs in the browser by storing them as favorites or bookmarks. Social bookmarking involves storing one's references online and making bookmarking a collaborative process.

There are several reasons for using social bookmarking:

- To keep track of interesting items (URLs) you find on the Web in the hopes you will be able to find them again. This process is nicely described as "keeping found things found" by the words of a research project.[2]

- To have basic metadata or citation information about bookmarks, including metadata about the item so that you can cite the item and tell others about these items.

- To find materials that are similar to what you already have. The ability to find more and related materials is a major reason for the existence of social bookmarking. You can certainly save bookmarks in your own browser. Of course, you can just copy down the URL, paste it in a Word document, and drop the document in an e-mail message, but doing so either keeps this information to yourself or keeps it to just a select group of friends. Social bookmarks put the focus on sharing bookmarks with others so that others can find and learn from you. Tagging is widely used to forge connections among disparate sources. (Think about applying this to all we talked about in Chapter 3.)

Social bookmarking is an area in flux. At `http://www.irox.de/file_download/3` you can find a helpful chart (from 2006) comparing features of 19 systems. Wikipedia also has a list of

---

1. `http://www.educause.edu/ir/library/pdf/ELI7001.pdf`
2. `http://kftf.ischool.washington.edu/`

social bookmarking sites,[3] but it's difficult to keep track of the many sites that come and go. A list that is reasonably up-to-date (last updated April 16, 2007) lists 200+ sites.[4]

Social bookmarking is of further interest in the context of this book because of the extensibility/remixability being built into these systems. Social bookmarks also lend insight into other systems. For instance, del.icio.us, the granddaddy of social bookmarking sites, is generally credited with kicking off the latest wave of social, or *folksonomic*, tagging, which has taken many Web 2.0 sites by storm.

This chapter does the following:

- Provides an overview of the social bookmarking landscape

- Walks through a select set of social bookmarking systems: del.icio.us, Yahoo!'s MyWeb 2.0, and Connotea

- Walks through the APIs, focusing in detail on del.icio.us (which is influential and the model for other social bookmarking sites) and then comparing it to those of Yahoo! and Connotea

- Discusses how you can use the del.icio.us API to enhance Flickr through a mashup of the two web sites

The Social Bookmarking Scene

As mentioned, there are a lot of social bookmarking sites. A reasonable approach is to focus on del.icio.us, the one to which all other social bookmarking systems are compared. Moreover, del.icio.us has an API, and there is much to learn from it.

Here are some other social bookmarking sites I will mention and examine briefly:

- Yahoo! MyWeb 2.0 and Bookmarks because Yahoo! is pursuing these properties despite already owning del.icio.us. Functionally, Yahoo! MyWeb allows you to store pages and to use the Yahoo! identity network, a major social network.

- Connotea is a more scholarly social bookmarking site. Connotea is backed up by Nature Publishing, and therefore it's likely to have some longevity.

Using Programmableweb.com to Examine the Popularity of APIs

A good way to figure out what to focus on is to see what is listed on Programmableweb.com— and to focus on the systems that actually have APIs. Go to the following location, and look for services that are in the Bookmarks category:

```
http://www.programmableweb.com/apilist/bycat
```

As of August 11, 2007, they are as follows:

- del.icio.us

- Simpy

---

3. http://en.wikipedia.org/wiki/List_of_social_software#Social_bookmarking

4. http://3spots.blogspot.com/2006/01/all-social-that-can-bookmark.html

- Blogmarks

- Scribble

- Shadows

- Jots

- Rrove

- OnlyWire

- linkaGoGo

- Ma.gnolia

Table 14-1 sorts them by mashup count.[5]

Table 14-1. *A Summary of Bookmarking APIs**

API	Description	Category	Mashups
del.icio.us	Social bookmarking	Bookmarks	83
Ma.gnolia	Social bookmarking service	Bookmarks	4
Shadows	Social bookmarking and community	Bookmarks	2
Simpy	Social bookmarking	Bookmarks	1
Rrove	Social bookmarking for places; create and share maps	Bookmarks	1
Jots	Social bookmarking	Bookmarks	1

* Table generated on August 11, 2007

The fact that del.icio.us has an order of magnitude more mashup activity than the rest of bookmark services combined is why we're focusing on del.icio.us.

del.icio.us

del.icio.us is the granddaddy of social bookmarking sites; in fact, it's the site that kicked off the whole folksonomic craze. Its web site is at `http://del.icio.us/`.

The main objects of importance in del.icio.us are bookmarks, that is, URLs. You can associate tags with a given URL. You can look at an individual's collection of URLs and the tags they use. Let's look again at the URL structures by browsing through the site and noting the corresponding URLs.

You can look at the public bookmarks for a specific user (for example, for `rdhyee`) by using this:

`http://del.icio.us/rdhyee`

---

5. `http://www.programmableweb.com/apilist/bymashups`

You can see all the bookmarks tagged `NYTimes` by `rdhyee` by using this:

`http://del.icio.us/rdhyee/NYTimes`

You can see all the URLs that people have tagged with `NYTimes` by using this:

`http://del.icio.us/tag/NYTimes`

And you can see just the popular ones by using this:

`http://del.icio.us/popular/NYTimes`

Here are today's popular items:

`http://del.icio.us/popular/`

Or here are just the fresh popular ones:

`http://del.icio.us/popular/?new`

Now, correlating a URL to a del.icio.us page is a bit trickier. Consider the following URL:

`http://harpers.org/TheEcstasyOfInfluence.html`

You can reference this from del.icio.us here:

`http://del.icio.us/url/53113b15b14c90292a02c24b55c316e5`

How do you get `53113b15b14c90292a02c24b55c316e5` from `http://harpers.org/`
`TheEcstasyOfInfluence.html`? Answer—it's an md5 hash. In Python the following yields
`53113b15b14c90292a02c24b55c316e5`:

`md5.new("http://harpers.org/TheEcstasyOfInfluence.html").hexdigest()`.

Note that the following does work:

`http://del.icio.us/url?url=http://harpers.org/TheEcstasyOfInfluence.html`

It redirects to this location:

`http://del.icio.us/url/53113b15b14c90292a02c24b55c316e5`

Using the del.icio.us API

From the documentation for the API (`http://del.icio.us/help/api/`) you can learn the
following:

- All del.icio.us API calls must be sent over HTTPS.

- All calls require HTTP-Auth—that means there are no API keys *per se*, but all API calls
  are tied to a specific user account.

- You need to watch for the 503 HTTP error (which would mean that your calls are being
  throttled and that you need to slow down the rate of your calls).

■**Note** This implies you can work on your own del.icio.us references but not on others unless they give you their credentials. All API calls to del.icio.us are made in the context of a specific user. There are no unauthenticated calls as there are on Flickr.

There are four major sections of the API:[6]

Update: Check to see when a user last posted an item.

Tags: Get a list of tags, and rename them.

Posts: Get a list of posts, add, and delete.

Bundles: Get bundles, create, and delete.

In the following sections, I'll give you a flavor of the capabilities of the del.icio.us API, but I won't comprehensively document it.

Update

You can find the documentation for the update method here:

```
http://del.icio.us/help/api/update
```

The update method tells you the last time a user updated his posts.

Let's look at three ways to work through various methods listed in the API. The first is to use a web browser, while the second and third use curl. Let's use the update method as an example:

- With a web browser, go to the following location, and when prompted, enter your del.icio.us username and password:

  ```
  https://api.del.icio.us/v1/posts/update
  ```

- With curl, you would run the following where USER and PASSWORD are your username and password:

  ```
  curl -u USER:PASSWORD https://api.del.icio.us/v1/posts/update
  ```

- Finally, you can embed the username and password into the URL:

  ```
  curl "https://{user}:{password}@api.del.icio.us/v1/posts/update"
  ```

In any of these cases, if your username and password are correct, you should get a response like the following:

```
<?xml version='1.0' standalone='yes'?>
<update time="2007-04-29T22:49:55Z" />
```

---

6. http://del.icio.us/help/api/

■**Note** For the following examples, we will use the second method only.

Tags

To get the complete list of tags used by a user and the number of times a given tag is used, use this:

```
curl -u USER:PASSWORD  https://api.del.icio.us/v1/tags/get
```

To rename the tag FEDORA to fedora, use this:

```
curl -u USER:PASSWORD "https://api.del.icio.us/v1/tags/rename?old=FEDORA&new=Fedora"
```

Posts

The posts method has several submethods: get, recent, all, dates, and delete.[7]

The get Submethod

You can use the get submethod with the optional parameters tag, dt (for the date in CCYY-MM-DDThh:mm:ssZ format), and url to return posts matching the arguments:

```
https://api.del.icio.us/v1/posts/get?
```

For example, to get posts with the tag mashup, use this:

```
curl -u USER:PASSWORD https://api.del.icio.us/v1/posts/get?tag=mashup
```

You can use this submethod to figure out the number of times an article has been posted. Consider the following scenario. Say you've posted the following URL to del.icio.us:

```
http://www.ala.org/ala/acrl/acrlissues/future/changingroles.htm
```

and want to track the number of times it has been posted to del.icio.us. You do so through this:

```
curl -u USER:PASSWORD  https://api.del.icio.us/v1/posts/get?➡
url=http://www.ala.org/ala/acrl/acrlissues/future/changingroles.htm
```

which returns the following:

```
<?xml version="1.0" standalone="yes"?>
<posts dt="2007-04-26" tag="" user="rdhyee">
  <post href="http://www.ala.org/ala/acrl/acrlissues/future/changingroles.htm"
        description="ALA | Changing Roles of Academic and Research Libraries"
        hash="fa5be4b4401acf147ff6c8634b55cdda" others="49"
        tag="library2.0 libraries academic future" time="2007-04-26T19:45:56Z"/>
</posts>
```

---

7. http://del.icio.us/help/api/posts

The `others` attribute in the `post` tag gives 49, which means that 49 users have added the URL to their collection of bookmarks.

If I don't have the URL in the library, it returns this:

```
<?xml version='1.0' standalone='yes'?>
<posts dt="" tag="" user="rdhyee">
</posts>
```

You need to add a URL to your library to inquire about a given URL in the API. Another way to calculate the number of users who have a given URL in their collection of bookmarks is to note the number of `rdf:item` elements in the RSS feed for the URL. As I describe in a moment, you can access the RSS feed for a given URL here:

```
http://del.icio.us/rss/url?url={url}
```

For example:

```
http://del.icio.us/rss/url?url=http://www.ala.org/ala/acrl/acrlissues/future/➥
changingroles.htm
```

The major advantages of this method are that you don't need to authenticate yourself to access the RSS feed and that you don't need to have the URL in your own set of bookmarks.

The recent Submethod

The `recent` submethod returns a list of the user's recent posts (up to 100), filtered by the optional arguments `tag` and `count`:

```
https://api.del.icio.us/v1/posts/recent?
```

For example, the following returns the last five posts:

```
curl -u USER:PASSWORD https://api.del.icio.us/v1/posts/recent?count=5
```

The all Submethod

The `all` submethod returns all your posts. You are advised to use this call sparingly (since it can generate a lot of data) and use the `update` function to see whether you need to do this call at all. You can filter by tag, such as in the following call (to get all posts with the tag `architecture`):

```
curl -u USER:PASSWORD    https://api.del.icio.us/v1/posts/all?tag=architecture
```

The add Submethod

You can use `add` to add posts to del.icio.us. It has two required parameters:

- `&url` (required) is the URL of the item.

- `&description` (required) is the description of the item.

The rest of its parameters are optional:

- &extended (optional) is notes for the item.

- &tags (optional) is tags for the item (space delimited).

- &dt (optional) is a date stamp of the item (with the format CCYY-MM-DDThh:mm:ssZ). It requires a literal T and Z as in ISO8601 at http://www.cl.cam.ac.uk/~mgk25/iso-time.html. This is an example: 1984-09-01T14:21:31Z.

- &replace=no (optional) doesn't replace post if the given URL has already been posted.

- &shared=no (optional) makes the item private.

Let's set the description to be ALA | Changing Roles of Academic and Research Libraries and the tags to library 2.0 academic ACRL technology:

```
curl -u USER:PASSWORD "https://api.del.icio.us/v1/posts/add?➥
url=http://www.ala.org/ala/acrl/acrlissues/future/changingroles.htm➥
&description=ALA+%7C+Changing+Roles+of+Academic+and+Research+Libraries➥
&tags=library+2.0+academic+ACRL+technology"
```

This command returns this:

```
<?xml version='1.0' standalone='yes'?>
<result code="done" />
```

The dates Submethod

The dates submethod returns a list of dates, along with the number of posts for each date. You can optionally filter the search with a tag.

For instance, the following:

```
curl -u USER:PASSWORD https://api.del.icio.us/v1/posts/dates?tag=mashup
```

returns something like this:

```
<?xml version='1.0' standalone='yes'?>
<dates tag="mashup" user="rdhyee">
  <date count="1" date="2007-09-20" />
  <date count="1" date="2007-05-28" />
[...]
</dates>
```

The delete Submethod

To delete a post with a given URL, issue the following GET:

```
curl -u USER:PASSWORD "https://api.del.icio.us/v1/posts/delete?➥
url={url}"
```

If the action is successful, then the result will be as follows:

```
<?xml version='1.0' standalone='yes'?>
<result code="done" />
```

Bundles

When using del.icio.us, you may quickly accumulate many tags. *Bundles* allow you to group tags into organizational sets, which you can manipulate through the del.icio.us API. I'll now illustrate how to use the API to control bundles through some examples.

The following request retrieves all the bundles for a user:

```
curl -u USER:PASSWORD https://api.del.icio.us/v1/tags/bundles/all
```

To create a bundle called `Google` to group the tags `GoogleMaps` and `GoogleEarth`, you can issue the following command:

```
curl -u USER:PASSWORD "https://api.del.icio.us/v1/tags/bundles/set?➥
bundle=Google&tags=GoogleMaps+GoogleEarth"
```

You can delete the Google bundle with this:

```
curl -u USER:PASSWORD "https://api.del.icio.us/v1/tags/bundles/delete?➥
bundle=Google"
```

RSS and JSON

In addition to the API, you can get RSS 1.0 feeds from del.icio.us:

```
http://del.icio.us/help/rss
```

Don't overlook them in your del.icio.us mashup work. Currently, the API returns information about the bookmarks of the authenticating user only. The RSS feeds, on the other hand, give you public information about bookmarks and how they are used by all users. Accessing RSS feeds does not require any authentication. However, you should observe the admonition to not access any given RSS feed more than once every 30 minutes.

The `del.icio.us` "hotlist" is at:

```
http://del.icio.us/rss/
```

The most recent postings (that have at least two posters) is here:

```
http://del.icio.us/rss/recent
```

Popular posts are here:

```
http://del.icio.us/rss/popular
```

You can get recent postings by a user here:

```
http://del.icio.us/rss/{user}
```

The RSS feed for a given tag is here:

```
http://del.icio.us/rss/tag/{tag}
```

For example, to get the RSS feed for the tag `mashup`, use this:

```
http://del.icio.us/rss/tag/mashup
```

You can get a feed for posts that are tagged with both mashup and computer using this:

http://del.icio.us/rss/tag/mashup+computer

You can a feed for a specific tag and user using this:

http://del.icio.us/rss/{user}/{tag}

For example:

http://del.icio.us/rss/rdhyee/mashup+computer

Finally, you can track the history of postings for a given URL here:

http://del.icio.us/rss/url?url={url}

For example:

http://del.icio.us/rss/url?url=http://www.ala.org/ala/acrl/acrlissues/future/➥
changingroles.htm

You can track this feed also here:

http://del.icio.us/rss/url/fa5be4b4401acf147ff6c8634b55cdda

noting that fa5be4b4401acf147ff6c8634b55cdda is the md5 hash of http://www.ala.org/
ala/acrl/acrlissues/future/changingroles.htm.

Several RSS feeds are not in the official documentation. Posting for a user's subscription is available here:

http://del.icio.us/rss/subscriptions/{user}

A feed of a user's network (which has private information) is accessible here:

http://del.icio.us/rss/network/{user}?private={private-key}

where the private-key is discoverable through the del.icio.us user interface for the authenticated user. Similarly, a feed for the "links for me" feature is here:

http://del.icio.us/rss/for/{user}?private={private-key}

In addition to these RSS feeds, you can get some feeds in JSON format, which is convenient for JavaScript programming:

http://del.icio.us/help/json/

There are JSON analogs to the RSS feeds to get a user's list of posts and list of tags and details about the posting history for a given URL. Moreover, there are JSON feeds that present information about a user's social network that's not available in the RSS feeds:

- A listing of the names of people in a user's *network* at http://del.icio.us/feeds/json/
  network/{user}. That is, the list of people being tracked by the user.

- A user's *fans* at http://del.icio.us/feeds/json/fans/{user}. That is, the list of people tracking the user.

With these JSON feeds, you can visualize the graph of social networks in del.icio.us such as done by the tools here:

```
http://www.twoantennas.com/projects/delicious-network-explorer/
```

Third-Party Tools for del.icio.us

You can find a useful reference for what others have done with the del.icio.us API here:

```
http://del.icio.us/help/thirdpartytools
```

Of the various tools, I find useful these three useful:

- The official Firefox add-on for del.icio.us (`http://del.icio.us/help/firefox/extension`), which enables you to access your bookmarks and tags from a browser sidebar.

- MySQLicious (`http://nanovivid.com/projects/mysqlicious/`), a PHP library for copying your del.icio.us bookmarks to a MySQL database. You download the code and follow the instructions. What you end up with is a MySQL database containing all the data for your bookmarks. The documentation says PHP 4—but it works for PHP 5 in my experience.

- freshDel.icio.us (`http://freshdelicious.googlepages.com/`), a utility to check your links and prune your bookmarks.

Third-Party API Kits

Here are some of the third-party API kits listed at `http://del.icio.us/help/thirdpartytools`:

- PHPDelicious (`http://www.ejeliot.com/pages/5`).

- Pydelicious (`http://code.google.com/p/pydelicious/`).

- Cocoalicious (a Cocoa del.icio.us client for Mac OS X that might be a good desktop tool).

- When it comes time to mirror del.icio.us to a local database, you can look at MySQLicious for "del.icio.us to MySQL mirroring."

To give you a sense of how PHPDelicious works, the following is the code to crawl through your bookmarks and tag each bookmark with the hostname of the URL (for example, `host:www.nytimes.com`). Once you have such tags, you can look at all of your bookmarks from a specific domain.

```php
<?php
# a file storing DELICIOUS_USER and DELICIOUS_PASSWORD
include("delicious.cred.php");
require_once('php-delicious/php-delicious.inc.php');

$del_obj = new PhpDelicious(DELICIOUS_USER, DELICIOUS_PASSWORD);

# get all your bookmarks (and check for errors in the request)
#$aPosts = $del_obj->GetAllPosts();
```

```php
if (!$aPosts = $del_obj->GetAllPosts()){

  echo $del_obj->LastError(), $del_obj->LastErrorString();
  exit();

}

# go through them and extract the hostname.
# set a limit for the number of links the program does -- for debugging

$maxcount = 5;
$count = 0;

$hosts = array();

foreach ($aPosts as $post) {

  $count += 1;
  if ($count > $maxcount) {
    break;
  }

  $url = $post['url'];
  $tags = $post['tags'];

  $url_parts = parse_url($url);
  $host = $url_parts['host'];

  # make a new tag
  $host_tag = "host:" . $host;
  echo $url, " ", $host_tag, "\n";

  # add the post with the new tag
  # parameters of a post

  $sUrl = $post['url'];
  $aTags = $post['tags'];

  # add host_tag to it
  $aTags[] = $host_tag;

  # track hosts that we are seeing
  if (isset($hosts[$host_tag])) {
    $hosts[$host_tag] += 1;
  } else {
    $hosts[$host_tag] = 1;
  }
```

```php
    $sDescription = $post['desc'];
    $sNotes = $post['notes'];
    $sDate = $post['updated'];
    $bReplace = true;
    echo $sUrl, $sDescription, " ", $sNotes, " ", $sDate, " ", $bReplace;
    print_r (array_unique($aTags));
    print "\n";
    if ($del_obj->AddPost($sUrl, $sDescription, $sNotes, array_unique($aTags), $sDate,
$bReplace)) {
        print "added $sUrl successfully\n";
    } else {
        print "problem in adding $sUrl\n";
    }
}
?>
```

To give you a flavor for Pydelicious, the following is a code snippet to delete all bookmarks with a certain tag (in this example, FlickrFavorite):

```python
USER = '[USER]'
PASSWORD = '[PASSWORD]'

import pydelicious
pyd = pydelicious.apiNew(USER,PASSWORD)

posts = pyd.posts_all(tag='FlickrFavorite')
for post in posts['posts']:
    print post['href'], "\n"
    pyd.posts_delete(post['href'])
```

Yahoo! Bookmarks and MyWeb

Yahoo!'s social bookmarking system is worth looking at because Yahoo! is a big company (with tons of users) that is adamant about getting heavily into the folksonomic space (by buying del.icio.us and Flickr, for instance). Yahoo!'s MyWeb 2.0 certainly has attractive features, including the ability to save web pages. In addition to del.icio.us, Yahoo! also has two other bookmarking services:

- http://bookmarks.yahoo.com/

- http://myweb2.search.Yahoo.com/

The relationship between the various Yahoo!-owned services is a bit confusing. The following is according to an explanation by one Yahoo! employee involved with the various bookmarking systems:[8]

- Yahoo! Bookmarks is for personal bookmarking, while del.icio.us is for social bookmarking.

- Yahoo! is extending the social bookmarking platform built for MyWeb to store the data for Yahoo! Bookmarks and soon del.icio.us. This will allow for seamless migration from one service to another while preserving existing bookmarks.

- MyWeb and Yahoo! Bookmarks share the same back-end database. In other words, they are two interfaces to the same underlying data.

Let's look at using the API documentation (`http://developer.yahoo.com/search/myweb/`). The following are the three calls currently available in the API (`yahooid=rdhyee&appid=mashupguide.net`):

- To the list of a user's (`rdhyee`) tags, use this:[9]

  ```
  http://api.search.yahoo.com/MyWebService/V1/tagSearch?➥
  appid=mashupguide.net&yahooid=rdhyee&results=50
  ```

- To do a search for URLs with a certain tag (`mashup`), use this:

  ```
  http://search.yahooapis.com/MyWebService/V1/urlSearch?➥
  appid=mashupguide.net&tag=mashup
  ```

- You can search for tags related to the given tag (for example, `mashup`) using this:[10]

  ```
  http://search.yahooapis.com/MyWebService/V1/relatedTags?➥
  appid=mashupguide.net&tag=mashup&results=50
  ```

Unfortunately, there's currently no method in the API to add bookmarks to one's collection.

Connotea

Connotea is an academically oriented social bookmarking system that is run by Nature Publishing and that specializes in scientific literature:

```
http://www.connotea.org/
```

You can find the documentation for the Connotea API here:

```
http://www.connotea.org/wiki/WebAPI
```

I should distinguish between a *bookmark* and a *post* in Connotea terminology. A bookmark is a URL along with corresponding metadata, such as the title and md5 hash of the URL. A post represents an event: the adding of a bookmark to a specific user's library. Accordingly,

---

8. `http://www.techcrunch.com/2006/10/24/Yahoo!-bookmarks-enters-21st-century/#comment-297657`

9. `http://developer.yahoo.com/search/myweb/V1/tagSearch.html`

10. `http://developer.yahoo.com/search/myweb/V1/relatedTags.html`

a post contains metadata about the name of the user, the tags the user has assigned to the bookmark, and the date of the event. A bookmark may belong to many users, but a post is tied to one and only one user. You can access the bookmarks in a given user's library here:

```
http://www.connotea.org/user/{user}
```

For example, you can find the bookmarks of Timo Hannay, the publishing director of Nature.com, here:

```
http://www.connotea.org/user/timo
```

There are some major conceptual similarities between the Connotea API and the del.icio.us API. For instance, both require authentication. However, in the Connotea API, you can access other users' posts.

To see whether the Connotea API recognizes your username/password combination, issue the following request:

```
curl -v -u USER:PASSWORD http://www.connotea.org/data/noop
```

Let's look next at how to get data from Connotea. You do so by forming the URL that concatenates four parts:

- The base URL of `http://www.connotea.org/data`

- An indicator of the type of data you want (bookmarks, tags, or posts), that is, `/bookmarks` or `/tags` or an empty string, which means *posts*

- Filters, any part of which is optional, specified in order by `user`, `tag`, `date`, and `uri` (that is, `/user/{username}/tag/{tagname}/date/{YYYY-MM-DD}/uri/{uri-or-hash}`)

- Optional text search parameter, number of results to return, and number to start at (that is, `?q={free-text-string}&num={number-of-results}&start={starting-index}`)

Let's look at some specific examples.
To get tags for `timo`, use this:

```
curl -u USER:PASSWORD http://www.connotea.org/data/tags/user/timo
```

In contrast to the del.icio.us API, you can get the tags of other users.
To get all the bookmarks for user `timo`, issue the following call:

```
curl -u USER:PASSWORD http://www.connotea.org/data/bookmarks/user/timo
```

To get the posts for user `timo`, issue the following call:

```
curl -u USER:PASSWORD http://www.connotea.org/data/user/timo
```

You can compare how a given URL is described as a bookmark and as a post in the two calls to see the differences between what posts and bookmarks are. A *bookmark* contains information about a given URI, its title, and which users have included (or "posted") it into their own libraries:

```
<dcterms:URI rdf:about="http://jdupuis.blogspot.com/2007/07/interview-with-timo-➥
hannay-head-of-web.html">
    <link>http://jdupuis.blogspot.com/2007/07/interview-with-timo-hannay-head-of-➥
web.html</link>
    <dc:title>Confessions of a Science Librarian: Interview with Timo Hannay, Head ➥
of Web Publishing, Nature Publishing Group</dc:title>
    <tag>npg</tag>
    <postedBy>timo</postedBy>
    <postedBy>bk66</postedBy>
    <postedBy>andi70</postedBy>
    <postedBy>marchitelli</postedBy>
    <postedBy>darrenjones</postedBy>
    <postedBy>hjaqu001</postedBy>
    <postedBy>duncan</postedBy>
    <postedBy>bgood</postedBy>
    <postedBy>bonnieswoger</postedBy>
    <postCount>8</postCount>
    <hash>07ccdc14de0e2efee719e55c22a223b5</hash>
    <bookmarkID>1047762</bookmarkID>
    <created>2007-07-04T07:29:21Z</created>
    <updated>2007-08-14T22:00:50Z</updated>
    <firstUser>timo</firstUser>
        <citation>
          <rdf:Description>
            <citationID>465002</citationID>
            <prism:title>Interview with Timo Hannay, Head of Web Publishing, Nature ➥
Publishing Group</prism:title>
            <foaf:maker>
              <foaf:Person>
                <foaf:name>John Dupuis</foaf:name>
              </foaf:Person>
            </foaf:maker>
            <dc:date>2007-07-03T00:00:00Z</dc:date>
            <journalID>433043</journalID>
            <prism:publicationName>Confessions of a Science Librarian
            </prism:publicationName>
          </rdf:Description>
        </citation>
    <rdfs:seeAlso rdf:resource="http://www.connotea.org/data/uri/07ccdc14de0e2efee71➥
9e55c22a223b5" /> <!-- GET this URI to retrieve further information -->
  </dcterms:URI>
```

In addition to having some overlapping metadata, the corresponding post tells you when the given URL was put into the user's library:

```
<Post rdf:about="http://www.connotea.org/user/timo/uri/07ccdc14de0e2efee719e55c22➥
a223b5">
  <title>Interview with Timo Hannay, Head of Web Publishing, Nature Publishing ➥
Group</title>
  <dc:subject>npg</dc:subject>
  <userBookmarkID>504437</userBookmarkID>
  <dc:creator>timo</dc:creator>
  <private>0</private>
  <created>2007-07-04T07:30:01Z</created>
  <updated>2007-08-09T11:33:43Z</updated>
  <uri>
    <dcterms:URI
      rdf:about="http://jdupuis.blogspot.com/2007/07/interview-with-timo-hannay-➥
head-of-web.html">
      <dc:title>Confessions of a Science Librarian: Interview with Timo Hannay, Head ➥
of Web Publishing, Nature Publishing Group</dc:title>
      <link>http://jdupuis.blogspot.com/2007/07/interview-with-timo-hannay-head-of-➥
web.html</link>
      <hash>07ccdc14de0e2efee719e55c22a223b5</hash>
      <citation>
        <rdf:Description>
          <citationID>465002</citationID>
          <prism:title>Interview with Timo Hannay, Head of Web Publishing, Nature ➥
Publishing Group</prism:title>
          <foaf:maker>
            <foaf:Person>
              <foaf:name>John Dupuis</foaf:name>
            </foaf:Person>
          </foaf:maker>
          <dc:date>2007-07-03T00:00:00Z</dc:date>
          <journalID>433043</journalID>
          <prism:publicationName>Confessions of a Science Librarian
          </prism:publicationName>
        </rdf:Description>
      </citation>
    </dcterms:URI>
  </uri>
</Post>
```

To get bookmarks that timo has tagged with chemistry, use this:

```
curl -u USER:PASSWORD http://www.connotea.org/data/bookmarks/user/timo/tag/chemistry
```

To add a URL to your collection, do an HTTP post to this location:

```
http://www.connotea.org/data/add
```

with the mandatory parameters `uri` and `tags` and optional parameters such as `usertitle`, `description`, `myworks`, `private`, and `comment`. For instance:

```
curl -v -u USER:PASSWORD --data-binary "uri=http://www.ala.org/ala/acrl/acrlissues/➥
future/changingroles.htm&tags=library2.0+academic+ACRL+technology&description=ALA+%7➥
C+Changing+Roles+of+Academic+and+Research+Libraries&usertitle=Changing+Roles+of+Acad➥
emic+and+Research+Libraries" http://www.connotea.org/data/add
```

To edit an existing post (for example, to change the description), use this:

```
curl -v -u USER:PASSWORD --data-binary "uri=http://www.ala.org/ala/acrl/acrlissues/➥
future/changingroles.htm&tags=library2.0+academic+ACRL+technology&usertitle=Essay%3A➥
+Changing+Roles+of+Academic+and+Research+Libraries" ➥
http://www.connotea.org/data/edit
```

To delete the post by its URL, use this:

```
curl -v -u USER:PASSWORD --data-binary "uri=http://www.ala.org/ala/acrl/acrlissues/➥
future/changingroles.htm"  http://www.connotea.org/data/remove
```

A Flickr and del.icio.us Mashup

In this section, I'll return to an idea I first wrote about in Chapter 3—demonstrating how you can create a mashup using the del.icio.us API to enhance the functionality of Flickr. There are many ways to organize the photos that you own in Flickr: you can tag them, put them in sets and collections, and send them to specific groups. With photos that belong to others, you have a lot fewer options. Generally, you're limited to making a photo a favorite. (If a photo has been placed into a group pool, you as a member of that group are able to tag the photo.) Moreover, you can't make any groupings of photos within Flickr that contain both your own photos and those of others. You can't "favorite" your own photos, and you can't place other users' photos in your sets. (You can say that group pools are an exception, but the owner of the photo has to send the photo to the pool.)

You can use del.icio.us to increase your ability to annotate Flickr photos and to intermix your own photos with those of others. A nice supporting feature of del.icio.us is that Flickr photos that are bookmarked in del.icio.us are shown with a thumbnail of the image—making deli.cio.us a simple photo display mechanism.

To use del.icio.us to track and annotate Flickr photos, you have to bookmark the photo. For bookmarking individual photos, you can simply use the same del.icio.us bookmarklets you would use to bookmark any other URL. However, if you have a large number of Flickr photos to manage with del.icio.us, it's more convenient to programmatically bookmark the photos.

Here I demonstrate how to send your Flickr favorites into del.icio.us so that you set your own tags and descriptions for the photos. The following code uses phpFlickr (see Chapter 6) and PHPDelicious:

```php
<?php

# This PHP script pushes a Flickr user's favorites into a del.icio.us account

# a function for appending two input strings separated by a comma.
function aconcat ($v, $w)
{
    return $v . "," . $w;
}

# read in passwords for Flickr, the MySQL cache for phpFlickr, and del.icio.us
include("flickr_key.php");
include("mysql_cred.php");
include("delicious.cred.php");

# use phpFlickr with caching
require_once("phpFlickr/phpFlickr.php");

$api = new phpFlickr(API_KEY, API_SECRET);
$db_string =
  "mysql://" . DB_USER . ":" . DB_PASSWORD. "@" . DB_SERVER . "/". DB_NAME;
$api->enableCache(
    "db", $db_string, 10
);

# instantiate a del.icio.us object via the phpDelicious library
require_once('php-delicious/php-delicious.inc.php');
$del_obj = new PhpDelicious(DELICIOUS_USER, DELICIOUS_PASSWORD);

$username = 'Raymond Yee';

if ($user_id = $api->people_findByUsername($username)) {
  $user_id = $user_id['id'];
} else {
  print 'error on looking up $username';
  exit();
}

#print $user_id;

# get a list of the user's favorites (public ones first)
# http://www.flickr.com/services/api/flickr.favorites.getPublicList.html

# allow a maximum number of photos to be copied over -- useful for testing.
$maxcount = 2;
$count = 0;
```

```php
# set the page size and the page number to start with
$per_page = 500;
$page = 1;

# loop over the pages of photos and the photos within each page

do {

if (!$photos = $api->favorites_getPublicList($user_id,"owner_name,last_update,tags",
$per_page, $page)) {

  echo "Problem in favorites_getPublicList call: ", $api->getErrorCode(), " ",
$api->getErrorMsg();
  exit();
}

$max_page = $photos['pages'];

foreach ($photos['photo'] as $photo) {

  $count += 1;
  if ($count > $maxcount) {
    break;
  }

  echo $photo['id'], "\n";

  # Map Flickr metadata to del.icio.us fields

  # use the URL of the context page as the del.icio.us URL
  $sUrl = "http://www.flickr.com/photos/$photo[owner]/$photo[id]/";

  # copy the photo title as the del.icio.us description
  $sDescription = $photo['title']. " (on Flickr)";

  # set del.icio.us note to empty
  $sNotes = '';

  # use the default date of now.
  $sDate = '';

  # replace previous del.icio.us posts with this URL
  $bReplace = true;

  # copy over the tags and add FlickrFavorite
  $aTags = split(' ', $photo['tags']);
  $aTags[] = 'FlickrFavorite';
```

```
    echo $sUrl, $sDescription, " ", $sNotes, " ", array_reduce($aTags, "aconcat") ,
" ", $sDate, " ", $bReplace;
    print "\n";

    if ($del_obj->AddPost($sUrl, $sDescription, $sNotes, $aTags, $sDate, $bReplace)) {
      print "added $sUrl successfully\n";
    } else {
      print "problem in adding $sUrl\n";
    }

} // foreach

  $page += 1;

} while (($page <= $max_page) && ($count <= $maxcount)) // do

?>
```

When you run this script, you will see something akin to Figure 14-1.

Figure 14-1. *Mashup of Flickr favorites and deli.cio.us. (Reproduced with permission of Yahoo! Inc. ® 2007 by Yahoo! Inc. YAHOO! and the YAHOO! logo are trademarks of Yahoo! Inc.)*

Once you have your Flickr favorites in del.icio.us, you can use all the del.ico.us functionality to manipulate them; for example, you can edit the tags (which have been copied over from Flickr), title, and description of a photo—something you couldn't do directly to the Flickr photos you don't own. In addition, you can use tags to group pictures—whether they are your own or someone else's.

These are some ways in which you can expand the functionality of the script presented here:

- You can use the del.icio.us API to help you gather your groups of Flickr photos by their del.icio.us tags and present them as slide shows.

- You can change the script to push all of a user's favorites instead of just the public favorites.

- In addition to favorites, you can add any individual photo or group of your own photos or any arbitrary Flickr aggregation of photos to del.icio.us.

- You can keep favorites synchronized between Flickr and del.icio.us.

Summary

In this chapter, you learned about social bookmarking as a whole, especially about sites that have APIs. You then concentrated on how to use the APIs of del.icio.us, Yahoo! MyWeb, and Connotea. The chapter concluded with a mashup of Flickr and del.icio.us that demonstrates how social bookmarking can be used to enhance Flickr.

CHAPTER 15

■ ■ ■

Accessing Online Calendars and Event Aggregators

Online calendars will move from being merely trendy to virtually indispensable as our lives move increasingly to the network. Calendaring (scheduling appointments and coordinating calendars) is something most of us can relate to since we all have appointments that we make and keep.

As we use electronic calendars, there is a good chance that we will have more than one calendar to synchronize—people use different calendars or work with people with other calendars, no matter how much Microsoft, Apple, Google, or Yahoo! might want everyone to use its calendar alone. A lot of this calendaring activity has moved to not only digital form but specifically to a networked digital form. In addition to the old calendars, new generations of online calendars are coming into existence—that's the focus of this chapter.

Online calendars exist in the context of other digital calendars: desktop calendars such as Microsoft Outlook and Apple iCal and calendars on handheld devices such as the Palm calendar. Much work has been done on synchronizing these calendars. Of course, calendar synchronization has been operant for a while, but these approaches (specialized conduits/SyncML[1]) have been more opaque than the APIs now available.[2] Today's online calendars with APIs generally make synchronization easier.

In addition to the proliferation of online calendars, event aggregation sites such as Upcoming.yahoo.com and Eventful.com are starting to create a marketplace of event data. They are focused on public events, whereas online calendars have as their focal point individuals and private events. These worlds intersect, of course, because individual users often track the public events they attend on their individual calendars.

When it comes to public events, the point of focus is different, depending on whether you are an attendee (and consumer of information about the event) or are a publisher or purveyor of event information. As an individual viewer, you want to browse, aggregate, and select events, typically from multiple sources. You might be conducting these tasks in a social context. What are your friends interested in? What do they invite you to, and vice versa? Your friends might know what you care about and direct you to events you'll find interesting. As a publisher of events, you probably want to disseminate information about

---

1. SyncML is now known as Open Mobile Alliance Data Synchronization and Device Management.
2. http://www.coldsync.org/description.html

the event as widely as possible. There are technical mechanisms for supporting the interchange of data between publishers of event data and consumers of event data, which is one of the subjects of this chapter.

This chapter shows the first steps to take in learning this subject:

- It covers what data you can get in and out of calendars without programming using iCalendar and various XML feeds as examples.

- It covers how to program individual calendars using Google Calendar and 30boxes.com, how to move data from a source of event data into calendars, and how to write event information to event aggregators such as Upcoming.yahoo.com and Eventful.com.

Google Calendar

Google Calendar is fast increasing in popularity among online calendars.[3] Not only does it have some clever features, but it is highly remixable with its extensive API and use of feeds and excellent data import and export functionality.

Let's talk about how to use Google Calendar as a user first and then look at how to program it.

Setting Up Google Calendar As an End User

Log in to your Google account here:

http://calendar.google.com

Google Calendar has some noteworthy features:

- In addition to creating a main calendar, you can create secondary calendars and subscribe to calendars belonging to others. Because you can turn the visibility of any given calendar on and off, you get a composite view of the events of all your visible calendars. (Think of each calendar as a layer.) On the sidebar, you get a list of your own calendars and the other calendars to which you are subscribing.

- You can search for public events and look for public calendars.[4] You can also make your events publicly searchable right within your own calendar—tightly coupling the process of publishing and consuming events.

- You can set the visibility of your calendars to one of three options: make it publicly available to everyone; show only the Free/Busy information availability, that is, show only whether a block of time is occupied; or set it to the Do Not Share with Everyone level, in which case the calendar is visible only to those people with whom you explicitly share your calendar.[5]

- To delete a calendar, you have to click the Manage Calendars link.

---

3. http://www.techcrunch.com/2007/01/04/online-calendar-wiars/

4. http://www.google.com/calendar/render?mode=gallery&cat=POPULAR

5. http://www.google.com/support/calendar/bin/answer.py?answer=34577&hl=en

- There is Gmail/Google Calendar integration: "Gmail users can send event invitations directly from their Gmail accounts without accessing Google Calendar."[6]

- There is currently no direct offline access to Google Calendar.[7]

Some Usage Patterns for Google Calendar

To show some use case scenarios for Google Calendar, here I list some of the calendars that I have set up and the reasons why:

- A strictly personal calendar for events. I have set this calendar to Do Not Share with Everyone.

- A family and friends calendar for my closest friends. I also use the Do Not Share with Everyone setting here but then add the e-mail addresses of individual friends and family members.

- A calendar called Raymond Yee's Public Events to list events that I plan to be at and don't mind the world knowing about. I use the Share All Information on This Calendar with Everyone setting.

- A calendar called Mashup Guide Demo Calendar, a public calendar I'll use in this chapter to demonstrate how to program Google Calendar.

When I create a new Google calendar, I consider the following factors:

- Who I want to share the calendar with (that is, is the calendar for myself, a specific group of people, or for the whole world?)

- The broad topic of that calendar

Sharing Calendars

There are calendar addresses that are visible to others if the calendar is public. There are three formats:[8]

- HTML

- iCalendar (also known colloquially as iCal)[9]

- XML (specifically, Atom feed)

To illustrate the different feed formats, I'll use a publicly available calendar that I created: the Mashup Guide Demo Calendar, whose sharing status I have set to Share All Information on This Calendar with Everyone.

---

6. http://www.google.com/support/calendar/bin/answer.py?answer=53231&topic=8556

7. http://www.google.com/support/calendar/bin/answer.py?answer=61527&topic=8556

8. http://www.google.com/support/calendar/bin/answer.py?answer=34578&hl=en and
   http://www.google.com/support/calendar/bin/answer.py?answer=37104&ctx=sibling

9. http://en.wikipedia.org/wiki/ICalendar

Every Google calendar has an *identifier*. The user ID for a user's main calendar is the user's e-mail address. For other calendars, the user ID is a more complicated e-mail address. For instance, the user ID for the Mashup Guide Demo Calendar is as follows:

```
9imfjk71chkcs66t1i436je0s0%40group.calendar.google.com
```

You can get the HTML feed for a calendar here:

```
http://www.google.com/calendar/embed?src={userID}
```

For example:

```
http://www.google.com/calendar/embed?src=9imfjk71chkcs66t1i436je0s0%40group.calendar.➥
google.com
```

Associated with the iCalendar and XML feeds are two parameters (visibility and projection) that I'll explain in greater detail in a moment. For instance, you can access an iCalendar feed here:

```
http://www.google.com/calendar/ical/{userID}/{visibility}/{projection}.ics
```

For example:

```
http://www.google.com/calendar/ical/9imfjk71chkcs66t1i436je0s0%40group.calendar.➥
google.com/public/full.ics
```

and for example:

```
http://www.google.com/calendar/ical/9imfjk71chkcs66t1i436je0s0%40group.calendar.➥
google.com/public/basic.ics
```

The Atom feeds are found here:

```
http://www.google.com/calendar/feeds/{userID}/{visibility}/{projection}
```

For example:

```
http://www.google.com/calendar/feeds/9imfjk71chkcs66t1i436je0s0%40group.calendar.➥
google.com/public/basic
```

If your calendar is not public, there are still private addresses that other applications can use to access the calendar. Note that you can reset these URLs too in case you want to reset access.[10]

Exploring the Feed Formats from Google Calendar

The Google Calendar API is built upon GData, the RESTful protocol based on the Atom Publishing Protocol (APP) combined with the Google-specific extensions introduced in Chapter 7.[11] There are API kits for various languages, including PHP and Python (as well as Java, .NET, and JavaScript).[12]

---

10. http://www.google.com/support/calendar/bin/answer.py?answer=34576&hl=en

11. http://code.google.com/apis/calendar/overview.html

12. http://code.google.com/apis/calendar/developers_guide_protocol.html

Before I cover how to programmatically interact with the Google Calendar, I'll first cover what you can do by changing documents. It's useful to take a look at specific instances of iCalendar and the XML feeds.

iCalendar/iCal

iCalendar is a dominant standard for the exchange of calendar data. Based on the older vCalendar standard, iCalendar is sometimes referred to as iCal, which might be confused with the name of the Apple calendaring program of the same name. The iCalendar standard is supported in a wide range of products.

The official documentation for iCalendar is RFC 2445:

```
http://tools.ietf.org/html/rfc2445
```

Some other allied standards are built around RFC 2445, but they are beyond the scope of this book:

- iCalendar Transport-Independent Interoperability Protocol (iTIP) Scheduling Events, BusyTime, To-dos and Journal Entries (RFC 2446) lays out how calendar servers can exchange calendaring events.[13]

- iCalendar Message-Based Interoperability Protocol (iMIP) (RFC 2447) covers the exchange of calendaring data by e-mail.[14]

See the Wikipedia article on iCalendar for a list of the wide range of products that support iCalendar.[15] Calendaring standards are complex. I recommend a good overview of how standards relate.[16]

The structure of an iCalendar file is *not* based on XML like many of the data exchange formats covered in this book. There have been attempts to cast the iCalendar data model into XML (such as xCal[17]), but none has reached the level of wide adoption that iCalendar has.

iCalendar has many features, but there are a few basic things to know about it:

- iCalendar has a top-level object: VCALENDAR.

- There are subobjects, including VEVENT, VTODO, VJOURNAL, and VFREEBUSY.

I'll focus mostly on the VEVENT object here—though VFREEBUSY is generated in Google Calendar when one uses the "Share only my free/busy information (hide details)" mode.

This is a simple example of iCalendar data (with one VEVENT), quoted from RFC 2445:[18]

```
BEGIN:VCALENDAR
VERSION:2.0
PRODID:-//hacksw/handcal//NONSGML v1.0//EN
```

---

13. http://tools.ietf.org/html/rfc2446

14. http://tools.ietf.org/html/rfc2447

15. http://en.wikipedia.org/wiki/ICalendar

16. http://www.calconnect.org/calendaringstandards.shtml

17. http://en.wikipedia.org/wiki/XCal

18. http://tools.ietf.org/html/rfc2445#section-4.4

```
BEGIN:VEVENT
DTSTART:19970714T170000Z
DTEND:19970715T035959Z
SUMMARY:Bastille Day Party
END:VEVENT
END:VCALENDAR
```

To see a more complicated instance of an iCalendar document, you can use Google Calendar via this:

```
curl "http://www.google.com/calendar/ical/9imfjk71chkcs66t1i436je0s0%40group.➥
calendar.google.com/public/basic.ics"
```

This gets the iCalendar rendition of my public Mashup Guide Demo Calendar, a version of which is as follows:

```
BEGIN:VCALENDAR
PRODID:-//Google Inc//Google Calendar 70.9054//EN
VERSION:2.0
CALSCALE:GREGORIAN
METHOD:PUBLISH
X-WR-CALNAME:Mashup Guide Demo Calendar
X-WR-TIMEZONE:America/Los_Angeles
X-WR-CALDESC:a Google Calendar to support mashupguide.net
BEGIN:VTIMEZONE
TZID:America/Los_Angeles
X-LIC-LOCATION:America/Los_Angeles
BEGIN:DAYLIGHT
TZOFFSETFROM:-0800
TZOFFSETTO:-0700
TZNAME:PDT
DTSTART:19700308T020000
RRULE:FREQ=YEARLY;BYMONTH=3;BYDAY=2SU
END:DAYLIGHT
BEGIN:STANDARD
TZOFFSETFROM:-0700
TZOFFSETTO:-0800
TZNAME:PST
DTSTART:19701101T020000
RRULE:FREQ=YEARLY;BYMONTH=11;BYDAY=1SU
END:STANDARD
END:VTIMEZONE
BEGIN:VEVENT
DTSTART;TZID=America/Los_Angeles:20070507T130000
DTEND;TZID=America/Los_Angeles:20070507T140000
DTSTAMP:20070510T155641Z
ORGANIZER;CN=Mashup Guide Demo Calendar:MAILTO:9imfjk71chkcs66t1i436je0s0@➥
group.calendar.google.com
UID:vk021kggr20ba2jhc3vjg6p8ek@google.com
```

```
CLASS:PUBLIC
CREATED:20070510T021623Z
DESCRIPTION:
LAST-MODIFIED:20070510T021623Z
LOCATION:110 South Hall\, UC Berkeley
SEQUENCE:0
STATUS:CONFIRMED
SUMMARY:Mixing and Remixing Information Class Open House
TRANSP:OPAQUE
END:VEVENT
BEGIN:VEVENT
DTSTART;TZID=America/Los_Angeles:20070411T123000
DTEND;TZID=America/Los_Angeles:20070411T140000
DTSTAMP:20070510T155641Z
ORGANIZER;CN=Mashup Guide Demo Calendar:MAILTO:9imfjk71chkcs66t1i436je0s0@➥
group.calendar.google.com
UID:d9btebsfd121lhqc4arhj9727s@google.com
CLASS:PUBLIC
CREATED:20070411T144226Z
DESCRIPTION:
LAST-MODIFIED:20070411T144226Z
LOCATION:
SEQUENCE:0
STATUS:CONFIRMED
SUMMARY:Day 22
TRANSP:OPAQUE
END:VEVENT
END:VCALENDAR
```

This chapter does not cover the ins and outs of the iCalendar format. I recommend the following ways to learn more about iCalendar:

- Read the "Guide to Internet Calendaring" (http://www.ietf.org/rfc/rfc3283.txt).

- There are many standards (http://www.calconnect.org/calendaringstandards.shtml), but keep especially RFC 2445 in mind.

- Know that since iCalendar is rich in features, these features are not evenly implemented among calendars, servers, or libraries that claim to work with iCalendar.

- The community is wrestling with a lot of subtleties. That's why you have organizations such as CalConnect making recommendations about handling recurring events and time zones (http://calconnect.org/recommendations.shtml).

- Interoperability among iCalendar implementations remains a challenge,[19] so don't be surprised if you run into problems using one system to interpret an iCalendar file produced by another system.

---

19. http://www.calconnect.org/ioptesting.shtml and http://www.calconnect.org/interop/uc%20berkeley%20interop%20testing.pdf

- Have some good programming libraries on hand to parse and create iCalendar (although it's hard to know for sure the quality of any given iCalendar library).

- Note that work is underway to update the standards: `http://www.ietf.org/html.charters/calsify-charter.html`.

In working with iCalendar, I've found the iCalendar Validator (`http://severinghaus.org/projects/icv/`), based on the iCal4j library (`http://ical4j.sourceforge.net/`), to be useful. You can use it to validate the iCalendar feed for the Mashup Guide Demo Calendar:

```
http://severinghaus.org/projects/icv/?url=http%3A%2F%2Fwww.google.com%2Fcalendar%2Fi➥
cal%2F9imfjk71chkcs66t1i436je0s0%2540group.calendar.google.com%2Fpublic%2Fbasic.ics
```

Google Calendar Atom Data

Now compare Google Calendar data formatted as an Atom XML feed, which you can get using this:

```
curl http://www.google.com/calendar/feeds/9imfjk71chkcs66t1i436je0s0%40group.➥
calendar.google.com/public/basic
```

This will return a feed that looks something like this:

```
<?xml version="1.0" encoding="UTF-8"?>
<feed xmlns="http://www.w3.org/2005/Atom" xmlns:openSearch="http://a9.com/-/spec/➥
opensearchrss/1.0/"
      xmlns:gd="http://schemas.google.com/g/2005"
      xmlns:gCal="http://schemas.google.com/gCal/2005">

<id>http://www.google.com/calendar/feeds/9imfjk71chkcs66t1i436je0s0%40group.calendar.➥
google.com/public/basic</id>
  <updated>2007-05-10T02:16:23.000Z</updated>
  <category scheme="http://schemas.google.com/g/2005#kind"
            term="http://schemas.google.com/g/2005#event"/>
  <title type="text">Mashup Guide Demo Calendar</title>
  <subtitle type="text">a Google Calendar to support mashupguide.net</subtitle>
  <link rel="http://schemas.google.com/g/2005#feed" type="application/atom+xml"
        href="http://www.google.com/calendar/feeds/9imfjk71chkcs66t1i436je0s0%40
group.calendar.google.com/public/basic"/>
  <link rel="self" type="application/atom+xml"
        href="http://www.google.com/calendar/feeds/9imfjk71chkcs66t1i436je0s0%40
group.calendar.google.com/public/basic?max-results=25"/>
  <author>
    <name>Raymond Yee</name>
    <email>raymond.yee@gmail.com</email>
  </author>
  <generator version="1.0" uri="http://www.google.com/calendar">Google Calendar
</generator>
  <openSearch:totalResults>2</openSearch:totalResults>
  <openSearch:startIndex>1</openSearch:startIndex>
```

```
<openSearch:itemsPerPage>25</openSearch:itemsPerPage>
<gd:where valueString=""/>
<gCal:timezone value="America/Los_Angeles"/>
<entry>
    <id>http://www.google.com/calendar/feeds/9imfjk71chkcs66t1i436je0s0%40group.➥
calendar.google.com/public/basic/vk021kggr20ba2jhc3vjg6p8ek</id>
    <published>2007-05-10T02:16:23.000Z</published>
    <updated>2007-05-10T02:16:23.000Z</updated>
    <category scheme="http://schemas.google.com/g/2005#kind"
             term="http://schemas.google.com/g/2005#event"/>
    <title type="text">Mixing and Remixing Information Class Open House</title>
    <summary type="html">When: Mon May 7, 2007 1pm to 2pm  PDT&lt;br&gt;
&lt;br&gt;Where: 110 South Hall, UC Berkeley &lt;br&gt;Event Status:
confirmed</summary>
    <content type="text">When: Mon May 7, 2007 1pm to 2pm  PDT&lt;br&gt;
&lt;br&gt;Where: 110 South Hall, UC Berkeley &lt;br&gt;Event Status:
confirmed</content>
    <link rel="alternate" type="text/html" ➥
          href="http://www.google.com/calendar/event?eid=dmswMjFrZ2dyMjBiYTJqaGMzd➥
mpnNnA4ZWsgOWltZmprNzFjaGtjczY2dDFpNDM2amUwczBAZw" title="alternate"/>
    <link rel="self" type="application/atom+xml" ➥
          href="http://www.google.com/calendar/feeds/9imfjk71chkcs66t1i436je0s0%40➥
group.calendar.google.com/public/basic/vk021kggr20ba2jhc3vjg6p8ek"/>
    <author>
      <name>Mashup Guide Demo Calendar</name>
    </author>
    <gCal:sendEventNotifications value="false"/>
  </entry>
  <entry>

<id>http://www.google.com/calendar/feeds/9imfjk71chkcs66t1i436je0s0%40group.calendar.➥
google.com/public/basic/d9btebsfd121lhqc4arhj9727s</id>
    <published>2007-04-11T14:42:26.000Z</published>
    <updated>2007-04-11T14:42:26.000Z</updated>
    <category scheme="http://schemas.google.com/g/2005#kind"
             term="http://schemas.google.com/g/2005#event"/>
    <title type="text">Day 22</title>
    <summary type="html">When: Wed Apr 11, 2007 12:30pm to 2pm 
PDT&lt;br&gt;   &lt;br&gt;Event Status:    confirmed</summary>
    <content type="text">When: Wed Apr 11, 2007 12:30pm to 2pm 
PDT&lt;br&gt;   &lt;br&gt;Event Status:    confirmed</content>
    <link rel="alternate" type="text/html" ➥
          href="http://www.google.com/calendar/event?eid=ZDlidGVic2ZkMTIxbGhxYzRhcmh➥
qOTcyN3MgOWltZmprNzFjaGtjczY2dDFpNDM2amUwczBAZw" title="alternate"/>
    <link rel="self" type="application/atom+xml" ➥
          href="http://www.google.com/calendar/feeds/9imfjk71chkcs66t1i436je0s0%40➥
group.calendar.google.com/public/basic/d9btebsfd121lhqc4arhj9727s"/>
```

```
      <author>
        <name>Mashup Guide Demo Calendar</name>
      </author>
      <gCal:sendEventNotifications value="false"/>
    </entry>
</feed>
```

Note the following about this data:

- The feed is expressed in Atom format (which you learned about in Chapter 4).

- It uses common GData extension elements,[20] OpenSearch, and Google Calendar extensions.[21]

Using the GData-Based Calendar API Directly

In this section, I will lead you through the basics of programming the Google Calendar API. Since I won't cover all the details of the API, I refer you to "Google Calendar Data API Developer's Guide: Protocol" documentation as an excellent place to start. You'll learn how to set up some calendars and access the right URLs for various feeds.[22]

As with most APIs, you can take two basic approaches: you can work directly with the protocol, which in this case is based on the GData protocol that underlies many Google APIs, including that for Blogger (see Chapter 7), or you can use a language-specific API kit. Here I'll show you both approaches. Although the latter approach is often more practical, I'll use this explication of the Calendar API as a chance to review GData (and the concepts of REST in general). To work with the specific language-specific libraries, consult the documentation here:

```
http://code.google.com/apis/gdata/clientlibs.html
```

Later, I'll give a quick rundown on how to use the PHP and Python API kits. You can get started with the documentation for the Calendar API here:

```
http://code.google.com/apis/calendar/developers_guide_protocol.html
```

The reference for the API is here:

```
http://code.google.com/apis/calendar/reference.html
```

The Google Calendar API is based on GData, which in turn is based on APP with Google-specific extensions. APP is a strictly REST protocol; remember, that means resources are represented as Atom feeds, and you use standard HTTP methods (GET, POST, PUT, and DELETE) to read, update, create, and delete elements. Here I'll show you some of the key feeds and how to use them. Before diving into doing so, I'll first show you how to obtain an authentication token, which you need in order to make full use of these feeds (that is, beyond issuing GET requests for public feeds).

---

20. http://code.google.com/apis/gdata/elements.html

21. http://code.google.com/apis/calendar/reference.html#Elements

22. http://code.google.com/apis/calendar/developers_guide_protocol.html

Obtaining an Authentication Token

One of the two authentication methods available to you is documented here:

```
http://code.google.com/apis/gdata/auth.html
```

I'll show you how to use the `ClientLogin` technique here. To make authorized access to the API, you will need an authentication token, which you can obtain by making an HTTP POST request (using the `application/x-www-form-urlencoded` content type) to here:

```
https://www.google.com/accounts/ClientLogin
```

with a body that contains the following parameters:

`Email`: Your Google e-mail (for example, raymond.yee@gmail.com)

`Password`: Your Google password

`source`: A string of the form *companyName-applicationName-versionID* to identify your program (for example, mashupguide.net-Chap15-v1)

`service`: The name of the Google service, which in this case is `cl`

Using the example parameters listed here, you can package the authentication request with the following `curl` invocation:

```
curl -v -X POST -d "Passwd={passwd}&source=mashupguide.net-Chap15-v1&Email=➥
raymond.yee%40gmail.com&service=cl" https://www.google.com/accounts/ClientLogin
```

If this call succeeds, you will get in the body of the response an `Auth` token (of the form `Auth=[AUTH-TOKEN]`). Retain the `Auth` token for your next calls. You will embed the authentication token in your calls by including the following HTTP request header:

```
Authorization: GoogleLogin auth=[AUTH-TOKEN]
```

Tip In `curl`, you do so with the `-H` option: `-H "Authorization: GoogleLogin auth=[AUTH-TOKEN]"`.

On occasion, you will need to handle HTTP 302 redirects from the API. That is, instead of fulfilling a request, the Google Calendar API sends you a response with a *redirect URL* appended with the new query parameter `gsessionid`. You then reissue your request to this new URL.

Tip For HTTP GET, use the `-L` option in `curl` to automatically handle a redirect.

Feeds Available from Google Calendar

There are three feed types: *calendar* (for managing calendars), *event* (for events contained by calendars), and *comment* (for representing comments attached to events). Each of the feeds is qualified by two parameters: `visibility` and `projection`. After I describe `visibility` and projection, I'll list the various feeds and show how you can access them via `curl`. For more details about the feeds, consult this page:

```
http://code.google.com/apis/calendar/reference.html#Feeds
```

visibility and projection

There are two parameters for "specifying" the representation of feeds: `visibility` and `projection`. The `visibility` parameter can be one of `public`, `private`, or `private-[magicCookie]`. Feeds that are public do not require authorization and are always read-only; public feeds are inaccessible if the user has turned off sharing for the calendar. Feeds that are private do require authentication to use and are potentially writable in addition to being readable (that is, read/write). Finally, feeds that have a visibility of `private-[magicCookie]` are read-only and enable private information to be read without authorization. (The `magicCookie` encapsulates authentication information.)

The `projection` values are listed here:

```
http://code.google.com/apis/calendar/reference.html#Projection
```

They include the following:

- `full` (potentially read/write).

- `free-busy` (always read-only). This feed shows minimal information about events but does include data about the duration of events (in other words, the `<gd:when>` element).

- `basic` (always read-only). The basic projection produces Atom feeds without any extension elements; the `<atom:summary>` and `<atom:content>` elements contain HTML descriptions with embedded data about the events.

Calendar Feeds

There are three types of calendar feeds—*meta-feed*, *allcalendars*, and *owncalendars*—which I'll cover in turn.

meta-feed

The private and read-only meta-feed contains an `<entry>` element for each calendar to which the user has access. This list includes both calendars that are owned by the user and ones to which the user is subscribed. You can access the feed at the following URL:

```
http://www.google.com/calendar/feeds/default
```

by using this:

```
curl -L -X GET -H "Authorization: GoogleLogin  auth=[AUTH-TOKEN]"  ➥
http://www.google.com/calendar/feeds/default
```

Let's look at an instance of an `<entry>`. Here is my own default calendar:

```
<entry>
    <id>http://www.google.com/calendar/feeds/default/raymond.yee%40gmail.com</id>
    <published>2007-10-20T18:46:01.839Z</published>
```

```
    <updated>2007-10-19T23:18:04.000Z</updated>
    <title type="text">Raymond Yee</title>
    <link rel="alternate" type="application/atom+xml" ➥
        href="http://www.google.com/calendar/feeds/raymond.yee%40gmail.com/➥
private/full"/>
    <link rel="http://schemas.google.com/acl/2007#accessControlList" ➥
        type="application/atom+xml"➥
        href="http://www.google.com/calendar/feeds/raymond.yee%40gmail.com/acl/➥
full"/>
    <link rel="self" type="application/atom+xml"
      href="http://www.google.com/calendar/feeds/default/raymond.yee%40gmail.com"/>
    <author>
      <name>Raymond Yee</name>
      <email>raymond.yee@gmail.com</email>
    </author>
    <gCal:timezone value="America/Los_Angeles"/>
    <gCal:hidden value="false"/>
    <gCal:color value="#2952A3"/>
    <gCal:selected value="true"/>
    <gCal:accesslevel value="owner"/>
  </entry>
```

Note the three link elements in the entry for the meta-feed:

- rel="alternate" whose href is as follows:

```
http://www.google.com/calendar/feeds/raymond.yee%40gmail.com/private/full
```

If you were to do an authenticated GET on this feed, you'd see that this is an event feed containing all the events for the default calendar.

Note how the URL of this feed maps to the following form:

```
http://www.google.com/calendar/feeds/{userID}/{privacy}/{projection}
```

Here the user ID is raymond.yee%40gmail.com, visibility is private, and projection is full.

- rel="http://schemas.google.com/acl/2007#accessControlList". The following feed gives you the access control list for the given calendar.

```
http://www.google.com/calendar/feeds/raymond.yee%40gmail.com/acl/full
```

For this calendar, there is a single entry (I'm the only person who has permissions associated with my default calendar):

```
<entry> <id>http://www.google.com/calendar/feeds/raymond.yee%40gmail.com/acl/➥
full/user%3Araymond.yee%40gmail.com</id>
    <updated>2007-10-20T23:14:47.000Z</updated>
    <category scheme="http://schemas.google.com/g/2005#kind"
      term="http://schemas.google.com/acl/2007#accessRule"/>
    <title type="text">owner</title>
```

```
    <content type="text"/>
    <link rel="self" type="application/atom+xml" ➡
          href="http://www.google.com/calendar/feeds/raymond.yee%40gmail.com/acl/➡
full/user%3Araymond.yee%40gmail.com"/>
    <link rel="edit" type="application/atom+xml" ➡
          href="http://www.google.com/calendar/feeds/raymond.yee%40gmail.com/acl/➡
full/user%3Araymond.yee%40gmail.com"/>
    <author>
      <name>Raymond Yee</name>
      <email>raymond.yee@gmail.com</email>
    </author>
    <gAcl:scope type="user" value="raymond.yee@gmail.com"/>
    <gAcl:role value="http://schemas.google.com/gCal/2005#owner"/>
  </entry>
```

- rel="self"

  http://www.google.com/calendar/feeds/default/raymond.yee%40gmail.com

  This feed returns one entry for the default calendar—instead of all the calendars to which the user (raymond.yee@gmail.com) has access.

allcalendars

The allcalendars feed is a private, potentially read/write feed for controlling subscriptions and settings (such as the display color) for calendars. Inserting or deleting entries to the allcalendars feed is tantamount to subscribing or unsubscribing to existing calendars. You can update personalization settings for your calendars: the color, whether it is hidden, and whether it is selected. You can't create or delete calendars by manipulating the allcalendars feed; for those actions, you need to use the owncalendars feed.

The URL for the allcalendars feed is here:

```
http://www.google.com/calendar/feeds/default/allcalendars/full
```

which you can access with this:

```
curl -L -X GET -H "Authorization: GoogleLogin  auth=[AUTH-TOKEN]"  ➡
http://www.google.com/calendar/feeds/default/allcalendars/full
```

■**Note** You might wonder about the difference between meta-feed and allcalendars since both of them list all the calendars to which a user has access. The allcalendars feed with a `projection` value of `full` is read/write, while the meta-feed is read-only. If you try to access the allcalendars feed with a `projection` value of `basic` (to get something akin to the meta-feed), you'll get an "unknown visibility found" error.

I'll now walk you through how to manipulate the allcalendars feed to add and delete a subscription to the Phases of the Moon calendar, one of Google's public calendars, which is available here:

```
http://www.google.com/calendar/embed?src=ht3jlfaac5lfd6263ulfh4tql8%40group.calendar.➥
google.com
```

Note the user ID of the calendar:

```
ht3jlfaac5lfd6263ulfh4tql8%40group.calendar.google.com
```

To subscribe to the calendar, create a file (called phases_moon_entry.xml) with the minimal entry element needed to be the body of the post as follows:

```
<?xml version='1.0' encoding='UTF-8'?>
<atom:entry xmlns:atom="http://www.w3.org/2005/Atom">
  <atom:id>ht3jlfaac5lfd6263ulfh4tql8%40group.calendar.google.com</atom:id>
</atom:entry>
```

Next, issue an HTTP POST request:

```
curl -v  -X POST --data-binary "@phases_of_moon_entry.xml"  -H "Content-Type: ➥
application/atom+xml "  -H "Authorization: GoogleLogin  auth=[AUTH-TOKEN]" ➥
http://www.google.com/calendar/feeds/default/allcalendars/full
```

As mentioned earlier, there's a good chance you'll get a 302 HTTP response code to this call:

```
http://www.google.com/calendar/feeds/default/allcalendars/full?gsessionid=➥
{gessionid}
```

For example:

```
http://www.google.com/calendar/feeds/default/allcalendars/full?gsessionid=➥
GUWxgPh61GQ
```

If you do get a 302 HTTP response code, reissue the call to the new URL with this:

```
curl -v  -X POST --data-binary "@phases_of_moon_entry.xml" -H "Content-Type: ➥
application/atom+xml "  -H "Authorization: GoogleLogin  auth=[AUTH-TOKEN]" ➥
http://www.google.com/calendar/feeds/default/allcalendars/full?gsessionid=➥
{gessionid}
```

If the request to subscribe to the Phases of the Moon calendar is successful, you'll get a 201 HTTP response code to indicate a created calendar, along with a response body akin to this:

```
  <entry> <id>http://www.google.com/calendar/feeds/default/allcalendars/full/➥
ht3jlfaac5lfd6263ulfh4tql8%40group.calendar.google.com</id>
    <published>2007-10-20T23:55:52.611Z</published>
    <updated>2007-10-14T07:19:30.000Z</updated>
    <title type="text">Phases of the Moon</title>
    <summary type="text"/>
    <link rel="alternate" type="application/atom+xml" ➥
        href="http://www.google.com/calendar/feeds/ht3jlfaac5lfd6263ulfh4tql8%40➥
group.calendar.google.com/private/full"/>
    <link rel="self" type="application/atom+xml"➥
        href="http://www.google.com/calendar/feeds/default/allcalendars/full/➥
ht3jlfaac5lfd6263ulfh4tql8%40group.calendar.google.com"/>
```

```
    <link rel="edit" type="application/atom+xml" ➥
        href="http://www.google.com/calendar/feeds/default/allcalendars/full/➥
ht3jlfaac5lfd6263ulfh4tql8%40group.calendar.google.com"/>
    <author>
      <name>Phases of the Moon</name>
    </author>
    <gCal:timezone value="Etc/GMT"/>
    <gCal:hidden value="false"/>
    <gCal:color value="#7A367A"/>
    <gCal:selected value="false"/>
    <gCal:accesslevel value="read"/>
    <gd:where valueString=""/>
  </entry>
```

You can then unsubscribe to the Phases of the Moon calendar with the following HTTP
DELETE request:

```
curl -v -X DELETE -H "Authorization: GoogleLogin  auth=[AUTH-TOKEN]" ➥
http://www.google.com/calendar/feeds/default/allcalendars/full/ht3jlfaac5lfd6263ulfh➥
4tql8%40group.calendar.google.com?gsessionid={gsessionid}
```

owncalendars

The owncalendars feeds hold data about the calendars that a user owns. This feed is conceptually similar to the allcalendars feed, with one important difference. Instead of subscribing
and unsubscribing to calendars, actions on the owncalendars feed are equivalent to creating
and destroying calendars. The syntax for manipulating the owncalendars feed is similar to that
for the allcallendars feed. For instance, to retrieve the feed, do a GET to this:

```
http://www.google.com/calendar/feeds/default/owncalendars/full
```

For example:

```
curl -v -L -X GET -H "Authorization: GoogleLogin  auth=[AUTH-TOKEN]" ➥
http://www.google.com/calendar/feeds/default/owncalendars/full
```

To create a new book-writing calendar, create a file entitled book_writing_calendar_entry.xml:

```
<?xml version="1.0" encoding="UTF-8"?>
<entry xmlns='http://www.w3.org/2005/Atom'
  xmlns:gd='http://schemas.google.com/g/2005'
  xmlns:gCal='http://schemas.google.com/gCal/2005'>
  <title type='text'>Book Writing Schedule</title>
  <summary type='text'>A calendar to track when I write my book.</summary>
  <gCal:timezone value='America/Los_Angeles'></gCal:timezone>
  <gCal:hidden value='false'></gCal:hidden>
  <gCal:color value='#2952A3'></gCal:color>
  <gd:where rel='' label='' valueString='Berkeley, CA'></gd:where>
</entry>
```

and do the following POST (after handling the HTTP 302 redirect):

```
curl -v  -X POST --data-binary "@book_writing_calendar_entry.xml"  -H "Content-Type: ➥
application/atom+xml "  -H "Authorization: GoogleLogin  auth=[AUTH-TOKEN]" ➥
http://www.google.com/calendar/feeds/default/owncalendars/full?gsessionid=➥
{gsession-id}
```

Furthermore, you can then update an existing calendar by issuing the appropriate PUT:

```
http://www.google.com/calendar/feeds/default/owncalendars/full/{userID}
```

And you can delete an existing calendar by using DELETE:

```
http://www.google.com/calendar/feeds/default/owncalendars/full/{userID}
```

Event Feeds

Now that you have studied the three types of calendar feeds, you'll look at how to use the
event feeds. (I won't cover comment feeds in this book.) Specifically, let's look at the simple
case of retrieving all the events from a given feed for which you have write privileges. To work
with a given calendar, you need to know its user ID. In the instance of my own calendars (the
Mashup Guide Demo calendar), the user ID is as follows:

```
9imfjk71chkcs66t1i436je0s0%40group.calendar.google.com
```

The syntax of the URL to the feed of the events is as follows:

```
http://www.google.com/calendar/feeds/{userID}/{privacy}/{projection}
```

Specifically, you can use a privacy value of public and a projection value of full since
the calendar is a public one to arrive here:

```
http://www.google.com/calendar/feeds/{userID}/public/full
```

For example:

```
http://www.google.com/calendar/feeds/9imfjk71chkcs66t1i436je0s0%40group.calendar.➥
google.com/public/full
```

which you can confirm is a URL to a feed of all the events on the calendar. To add an event, you
need to send an HTTP POST request (with the proper authentication) here:

```
http://www.google.com/calendar/feeds/{userID}/private/full
```

For example:

```
http://www.google.com/calendar/feeds/9imfjk71chkcs66t1i436je0s0%40group.calendar.➥
google.com/private/full
```

That is, you create a file by the name of project_showcase_event.xml with the following
content:

```
<?xml version='1.0' encoding='UTF-8'?>
<entry xmlns='http://www.w3.org/2005/Atom'
  xmlns:gd='http://schemas.google.com/g/2005'>
```

```
<category scheme='http://schemas.google.com/g/2005#kind'
    term='http://schemas.google.com/g/2005#event'></category>
<title type='text'>Project Showcase</title>
<content type='text'>A chance for the class to show off their projects</content>
<gd:where valueString='110 South Hall'></gd:where>
<gd:when startTime="2008-05-12T13:00:00.000-07:00"
        endTime="2008-05-12T14:00:00.000-07:00"/>
</entry>
```

and issue the following request:

```
curl -v  -X POST  --data-binary "@project_showcase_event.xml"  -H "Content-Type: ➥
application/atom+xml "  -H "Authorization: GoogleLogin  auth=[AUTH-TOKEN]" ➥
http://www.google.com/calendar/feeds/{userID}/private/full?gsessionid={gsessionid}
```

where the gsessionid is the one given in the 302 redirect to create an event on the Mashup Guide Demo calendar.

With an analogous procedure to how you subscribe or unsubscribe to calendars in the all-calendars feed or create calendars through the owncalendars feed, you can create and delete events through the events feed.

Using the PHP API Kit for Google Calendar

Working directly with the GData interface to Google Calendar gives you a lot of flexibility at the cost of tedium. Now we'll turn to studying how to use two of the API wrappers for Google Calendar. In the next section, I'll show you how to use the Python API kit. Here, we'll study the PHP wrapper.

The PHP API kit is documented here:

```
http://code.google.com/apis/calendar/developers_guide_php.html
```

The PHP library for accessing Google Calendar is part of the Zend Google Data Client Library, which, in turn, is available as part of the Zend Framework or as a separate download. Note that the library is developed by Zend and works with PHP 5.1.4 or newer. You can download the Zend Framework from this location:

```
http://framework.zend.com/
```

You can read about how to use the Zend Framework to access Google Calendar here:

```
http://framework.zend.com/manual/en/zend.gdata.calendar.html
```

You install the Zend framework by copying the files to a directory of your choice. I set up the Zend Framework in this location:

```
http://examples.mashupguide.net/lib/ZendFramework/
```

I'll now illustrate the basics of using this library through two code snippets. Both use the ClientLogin form of authorization. The first example retrieves a list of a user's calendars:

```php
<?php

require_once 'Zend/Loader.php';
Zend_Loader::loadClass('Zend_Gdata');
Zend_Loader::loadClass('Zend_Gdata_ClientLogin');
Zend_Loader::loadClass('Zend_Gdata_Calendar');

function getGDataClient($user, $pass)
{
  $service = Zend_Gdata_Calendar::AUTH_SERVICE_NAME;

  $client = Zend_Gdata_ClientLogin::getHttpClient($user, $pass, $service);
  return $client;
}

function printCalendarList($client)
{
  $gdataCal = new Zend_Gdata_Calendar($client);
  $calFeed = $gdataCal->getCalendarListFeed();
  echo $calFeed->title->text . "\n";
  echo "\n";
  foreach ($calFeed as $calendar) {
    echo $calendar->title->text, "\n";
  }
}

$USER = "[USER]";
$PASSWORD = "[PASSWORD]";

$client = getGDataClient($USER, $PASSWORD);
printCalendarList($client);

?>
```

The second code sample retrieves a list of events for a given calendar and prints basic elements for a given event: its ID, title, content, and details about the "where" and "when" of the event:

```php
<?php

require_once 'Zend/Loader.php';
Zend_Loader::loadClass('Zend_Gdata');
Zend_Loader::loadClass('Zend_Gdata_ClientLogin');
Zend_Loader::loadClass('Zend_Gdata_Calendar');
```

```php
function getGDataClient($user, $pass)
{
  $service = Zend_Gdata_Calendar::AUTH_SERVICE_NAME;

  $client = Zend_Gdata_ClientLogin::getHttpClient($user, $pass, $service);
  return $client;
}

function printEventsForCalendar($client, $userID)
{
  $gdataCal = new Zend_Gdata_Calendar($client);

  $query = $gdataCal->newEventQuery();
  $query->setUser($userID);
  $query->setVisibility('private');
  $query->setProjection('full');

  $eventFeed = $gdataCal->getCalendarEventFeed($query);

  echo $eventFeed->title->text . "\n";
  echo "\n";
  foreach ($eventFeed as $event) {
    echo $event->title->text, "\t", $event->id->text, "\n" ;
    echo $event->content->text, "\n";
    foreach ($event->where as $where) {
      echo $where, "\n";
    }
    foreach ($event->when as $when) {
      echo "Starts: " . $when->startTime . "\n";
      echo "Ends: " . $when->endTime . "\n";
    }

    # check for recurring events
    if ($recurrence = $event->getRecurrence()) {
      echo "recurrence: ", $recurrence, "\n";
    }

    print "\n";
  }
}

$USER = "[USER]";
$PASSWORD = "[PASSWORD]";

# userID for the Mashup Guide Demo calendar
$userID = "9imfjk71chkcs66t1i436je0sO%40group.calendar.google.com";
```

```
$client = getGDataClient($USER, $PASSWORD);
printEventsForCalendar($client, $userID);

?>
```

Later in the chapter, you will see how to use the PHP Google Calendar library to create events.

Using the Python API Kit for Google Calendar

You can find the documentation on the Python API kit here:

```
http://code.google.com/apis/calendar/developers_guide_python.html
```

To install the library, you can download it from here:

```
http://code.google.com/p/gdata-python-client/downloads/list
```

Or you can access the access the Subversion repository for the project here:

```
http://gdata-python-client.googlecode.com/svn/trunk/
```

■**Note** The following code depends on the ElementTree library, which ships with Python 2.5 and newer. You can find instructions for downloading ElementTree at http://effbot.org/zone/element-index.htm.

Here's some Python code to demonstrate how to list all of your calendars and to list the events on a specific calendar:

```python
"""
Chapter 15:  simple facade for Python Google Calendar library
"""

__author__ = 'raymond.yee@gmail.com (Raymond Yee)'

EMAIL = '[USER]'
PASSWORD = '[PASSWORD]'

try:
  from xml.etree import ElementTree
except ImportError:
  from elementtree import ElementTree

import gdata.calendar.service
import gdata.calendar
import atom
```

```python
class MyGCal:
    def __init__(self):
        self.client = gdata.calendar.service.CalendarService()
        self.client.email = EMAIL
        self.client.password = PASSWORD
        self.client.source = 'GCalendarUtil-raymondyee.net-v1.0'
        self.client.ProgrammaticLogin()
    def listAllCalendars(self):
        feed = self.client.GetAllCalendarsFeed()
        print 'Printing allcalendars: %s' % feed.title.text
        for calendar in feed.entry:
            print calendar.title.text
    def listOwnCalendars(self):
        feed = self.client.GetOwnCalendarsFeed()
        print 'Printing owncalendars: %s' % feed.title.text
        for calendar in feed.entry:
            print calendar.title.text
    def listEventsOnCalendar(self,userID='default'):
        """
        list all events on the calendar with userID
        """
        query = gdata.calendar.service.CalendarEventQuery(userID, 'private', 'full')
        feed =  self.client.CalendarQuery(query)
        for event in feed.entry:
            print event.title.text, event.id.text, event.content.text
            for where in event.where:
                print where.value_string
            for when in event.when:
                print when.start_time, when.end_time
            if event.recurrence:
                print "recurrence:", event.recurrence.text

if __name__ == '__main__':
    gc = MyGCal()
    gc.listAllCalendars()
    # userID for Mashup Guide Demo calendar
    userID = '9imfjk71chkcs66t1i436je0s0%40group.calendar.google.com'
    gc.listEventsOnCalendar(userID)
```

30boxes.com

30boxes.com is another online calendar service, one that has won some rave reviews.[23] It has very noteworthy features, in addition to an API, making it worthwhile to describe it here.

---

23. http://30boxes.com/press

For information about the 30boxes.com API, go here:

- `http://30boxes.com/developers`

- `http://30boxes.com/api/`

An End User Tutorial

Before programming 30boxes.com, it's useful of course to view it as an end user:

1. Sign up for an account if you don't already have one:

   `http://30boxes.com/signup`

2. Once you have an account, log into it:

   `http://30boxes.com/login`

3. You can learn how to do various tasks at 30boxes.com by consulting the help section (`http://30boxes.com/help`).

One noteworthy feature from an end user's point of view is that, in terms of sharing, it seems that all calendars are completely private by default. You can add buddies and set options as to how much a given buddy can see:

- Buddies can see your entire calendar unless you mark an event as private.

- Buddies can see events that are marked with a certain tag.

- Buddies can see only the stuff on the buddy page.

30boxes.com API

The main documentation is at this location:

`http://30boxes.com/api/`

You have to get a key here:

`http://30boxes.com/api/api.php?method=getKeyForUser`

In this section, we'll exercise the API. Please substitute your own [APIKEY] and [AUTHTOKEN]. You can do HTTP GET requests on the following URLs:

- `test.ping`:[24]

  `http://30boxes.com/api/api.php?method=test.Ping&apiKey={APIKEY}`

- `user.FindByEmail`:

  `http://30boxes.com/api/api.php?method=user.FindByEmail&apiKey={APIKEY}&email=yee@`➡
  `berkeley.edu`

---

24. `http://30boxes.com/api/#t`

- user.Authorize: Many methods require authorization, which then yields an authorization token. In this example, I use a small picture of me as the application icon.[25] When calling user.FindByEmail, I also drop the optional returnURL argument:

```
http://30boxes.com/api/api.php?method=user.Authorize&apiKey={APIKEY}➟
&applicationName={application-name}&applicationLogoUrl={url}
```

For example:

```
http://30boxes.com/api/api.php?method=user.Authorize&apiKey={APIKEY}➟
&applicationName=Raymond+Yee&applicationLogoUrl=http%3A%2F%2Ffarm1.static.➟
flickr.com%2F4➟%2F5530475_48f80eece8_s.jpg
```

You will get an authentication token, which I show here as {AUTHTOKEN}.

- user.GetAllInfo:

```
http://30boxes.com/api/api.php?method=user.GetAllInfo&apiKey={APIKEY}➟
&authorizedUserToken={AUTHTOKEN}
```

to which you will get something like this:

```xml
<?xml version="1.0" encoding="utf-8"?>
<rsp stat="ok">
  <user>
    <id>40756</id>
    <facebookId>1229336</facebookId>
    <firstName>Raymond</firstName>
    <lastName>Yee</lastName>
    <avatar>http://farm1.static.flickr.com/4/5530475_48f80eece8_s.jpg</avatar>
    <status>sweeping stuff under the carpet while he writes.</status>
    <bio/>
    <dateFormat>MM-DD-YYYY</dateFormat>
    <timeZone>US/Pacific</timeZone>
    <createDate>2006-03-17</createDate>
    <startDay>0</startDay>
    <use24HourClock>0</use24HourClock>
    <feed>
      <name>Raymond - MySpace Blog</name>
      <url>http://blog.myspace.com/blog/rss.cfm?friendID=82943257</url>
    </feed>
    <email>
      <address>yee@berkeley.edu</address>
      <primary>1</primary>
    </email>
```

---

25. http://farm1.static.flickr.com/4/5530475_48f80eece8_s.jpg

```
    <email>
      <address>raymond.yee@gmail.com</address>
      <primary>0</primary>
    </email>
    <otherContact>
      <type>Yahoo</type>
      <value>rdhyee</value>
    </otherContact>
    <otherContact>
      <type>Personal Site</type>
      <value>http://hypotyposis.net/blog</value>
    </otherContact>

  </user>
</rsp>
```

• events.Get:

http://30boxes.com/api/api.php?method=events.Get&apiKey={APIKEY}➥
&authorizedUserToken={AUTHTOKEN}&start=2007-01-01&end=2007-09-01

to which you will get something like this:

```
<?xml version="1.0" encoding="utf-8"?>
<rsp stat="ok">
  <eventList>
    <userId>40756</userId>
    <listStart>2007-01-01</listStart>
    <listEnd>2007-06-30</listEnd>
    <event>
      <id>1767437</id>
      <summary>YIRB Brain Jam: A CHI2007 Sampler</summary>
      <notes>[....]</notes>
      <start>2007-04-27 14:00:00</start>
      <end>2007-04-27 14:00:00</end>
      <lastUpdate>2007-04-11 15:08:58</lastUpdate>
      <allDayEvent>0</allDayEvent>
      <repeatType>no</repeatType>
      <repeatEndDate>0000-00-00</repeatEndDate>
      <repeatSkipDates/>
      <repeatICal/>
      <reminder>-1</reminder>
      <tags/>
      <externalUID>http://upcoming.org/event/172254/</externalUID>
      <privacy>shared</privacy>
```

```
            <invitation>
              <isInvitation>0</isInvitation>
            </invitation>
          </event>
     [....]
        </eventList>

     </rsp>
```

■**Note** The end parameter cannot be more than 180 days after start.

- events.GetDisplayList (to get an expanded and sorted list of events):

  http://30boxes.com/api/api.php?method=events.GetDisplayList&apiKey={APIKEY}➡
  &authorizedUserToken={AUTHTOKEN}&start=2007-01-01&end=2007-09-01

- todos.Get:

  http://30boxes.com/api/api.php?method=todos.Get&apiKey={APIKEY}&authorizedUser➡
  Token={AUTHTOKEN}

- todos.Add:

  http://30boxes.com/api/api.php?method=todos.Add&apiKey={APIKEY}&authorizedUser➡
  Token={AUTHTOKEN}&text=Eat+more+veggies&externalUID=123456x

- todos.Update:

  http://30boxes.com/api/api.php?method=todos.Update&apiKey={APIKEY}&authorized➡
  UserToken={AUTHTOKEN}&text=Eat+more+veggies+and+fruit&todoId=123110&externalUID=➡
  123456x

- todos.Delete:

  http://30boxes.com/api/api.php?method=todos.Delete&apiKey={APIKEY}&authorized➡
  UserToken={AUTHTOKEN}&text=Eat+more+veggies+and+fruit&todoId=123110

- events.AddByOneBox:

  http://30boxes.com/api/api.php?method=events.AddByOneBox&apiKey={APIKEY}➡
  &authorizedUserToken={AUTHTOKEN}&event=eat+some+sushi+tomorrow+at+7pm

---

■**Note** You can find a Python API wrapper for 30boxes.com at http://trentm.com/projects/
thirtyboxes/.

Event Aggregators

Google Calendar and 30boxes.com are examples of online calendars meant to allow individuals and small groups of people to coordinate their appointments. Complementing such calendars are event aggregators that gather and list events, many of which are public events. In the following sections, I'll cover two event aggregators that are programmable and hence mashable: Upcoming.yahoo.com and Eventful.com.

Upcoming.yahoo.com

The URL for Upcoming.yahoo.com is as follows:

```
http://upcoming.yahoo.com/
```

The URL for a specific event is as follows:

```
http://upcoming.yahoo.com/event/{event-id}/
```

For example, the following is the URL for CHI2007:

```
http://upcoming.yahoo.com/event/76140/
```

Feeds from Search Results

Upcoming.yahoo.com makes much of its data available through RSS 2.0 feeds. Let's consider an example. To look for events with the keyword Bach in the San Francisco Bay Area, you can use the following search:

```
http://upcoming.yahoo.com/search/?type=Events&rt=1&q=bach&loc=Berkeley%2C+California➡
%2C+United+States
```

In general, the URL for searching events is as follows:

```
http://upcoming.yahoo.com/search/?type=Events&rt=1&q={q}&loc={location}&sort={sort}
```

where you can set sort to w (to sort by popularity), r (by relevance), and p (by recently added).

The previous search gives you HTML. You can also get feeds out of the search results as either RSS 2.0 or iCalendar. The RSS 2.0 feed includes Dublin Core data, uses the xCal extension (http://en.wikipedia.org/wiki/XCal) to encode calendaring information, and includes latitude and longitude data encoded with the Compact W3C Basic Geo encoding (see Chapter 13 for details on this encoding):

```
http://upcoming.yahoo.com/syndicate/v2/search_all/?q=bach&loc=Berkeley%2C+California➡
%2C+United+States&rt=1
```

Take a look at a specific instance of an event:

```
<geo:lat>37.7774</geo:lat>
<geo:long>-122.4198</geo:long>
[....]
<dc:date>2007-03-18T17:59:58-07:00</dc:date>
<xCal:summary>San Francisco Symphony: Bach and Handel</xCal:summary>
<xCal:dtstart>2008-04-05T20:00:00Z</xCal:dtstart>
```

```
<xCal:dtend></xCal:dtend>
<xCal:location>http://upcoming.yahoo.com/venue/17246/</xCal:location>
<xCal:x-calconnect-venue>
 <xCal:x-calconnect-venue-id>http://upcoming.yahoo.com/venue/17246/
</xCal:x-calconnect-venue-id>
  <xCal:adr>
   <xCal:x-calconnect-venue-name>Davies Symphony Hall</xCal:x-calconnect-venue-➥
name>
   <xCal:x-calconnect-street>201 Van Ness Avenue</xCal:x-calconnect-street>
   <xCal:x-calconnect-city>San Francisco Bay Area</xCal:x-calconnect-city>
   <xCal:x-calconnect-region>California</xCal:x-calconnect-region>
   <xCal:x-calconnect-postalcode>94102</xCal:x-calconnect-postalcode>
   <xCal:x-calconnect-country>United States</xCal:x-calconnect-country>
  </xCal:adr>
  <xCal:url type='Venue Website'>http://upcoming.yahoo.com/venue/17246/
</xCal:url>
   <xCal:x-calconnect-tel></xCal:x-calconnect-tel>
  </xCal:x-calconnect-venue>
```

You can get an iCalendar version of the results, which you can subscribe to using an iCalendar-cognizant calendar (for example, Apple iCal, Google Calendar, or Microsoft Outlook 2007):

```
webcal://upcoming.yahoo.com/calendar/v2/search_all/?q=bach&loc=Berkeley%2C+➥
California%2C+United+States&rt=1
```

Note the use of the webcal URI scheme (http://en.wikipedia.org/wiki/Webcal). The webcal scheme tells the recipient to subscribe to the feed—to track updates—rather than just doing a one-time import of the iCalendar feed. (Note that you can replace webcal with http to get the contents of the iCalendar feed.)

```
http://upcoming.yahoo.com/calendar/v2/search_all/?q=bach&loc=Berkeley%2C+California%➥
2C+United+States&rt=1
```

What can you do with these feeds coming from Upcoming.yahoo.com? One example is to generate KML out of the RSS 2.0 feeds, which already contain geolocations for the events. In fact, you can use Yahoo! Pipes for this very task:

```
http://pipes.yahoo.com/pipes/pipe.info?_id=GlqEg8WA3BGZNw9ELO2fWQ
```

This pipe takes as input the parameters that can be used to generate an upcoming RSS 2.0 feed from Upcoming.yahoo.com (q, loc, and sort) and uses the Location Extractor operator to extract the geoRSS elements from the feed.

■**Note** You can extend the pipe to encompass the other search options at Upcoming.yahoo.com, such as date ranges or categories.

You can run the pipe for Bach events close to Berkeley, California, sorted by relevance:

```
http://pipes.yahoo.com/pipes/pipe.info?q=Bach&loc=Berkeley%2C+CA&sort=r&_cmd=Run+➥
Pipe&_id=GlqEg8WA3BGZNw9ELO2fWQ&_run=1
```

Note that running this pipe generates a Yahoo! map showing the events contained in the feed. In addition to the RSS 2.0 feed version here:

```
http://pipes.yahoo.com/pipes/pipe.run?_id=GlqEg8WA3BGZNw9ELO2fWQ&_render=rss&loc=➥
Berkeley%2C+CA&q=Bach&sort=r
```

which isn't that interesting (since Upcoming.yahoo.com already generates an RSS 2.0 feed), you can get a KML version of this feed (by changing the _render parameter to kml):

```
http://pipes.yahoo.com/pipes/pipe.run?_id=GlqEg8WA3BGZNw9ELO2fWQ&_render=kml&loc=➥
Berkeley%2C+CA&q=Bach&sort=r
```

From Chapter 13, you learned how to sort KML feeds on Google Maps:

```
http://maps.google.com/maps?q=http:%2F%2Fpipes.yahoo.com%2Fpipes%2Fpipe.run%3F_id%3➥
DGlqEg8WA3BGZNw9ELO2fWQ%26_render%3Dkml%26loc%3DBerkeley%252C%2BCA%26q%3DBach%26➥
sort%3Dr&ie=UTF8
```

Read-Only Parts of the API

Let's now turn to the Upcoming.yahoo.com API. You can find the documentation for the API here:

```
http://upcoming.yahoo.com/services/api/
```

You can generate a key to use for the API here:

```
http://upcoming.yahoo.com/services/api/keygen.php
```

The upcoming API is structured to be similar (but not identical) in detail to the Flickr REST API. The authentication is simpler and less sophisticated, but you'll see the method parameter and api_key (similar naming). The base URL for the API is as follows:

```
http://upcoming.yahooapis.com/services/rest/
```

Like the Flickr API, you need a method (event.search), an api_key, and other parameters for the given method, which are documented here:

```
http://upcoming.yahoo.com/services/api/event.search.php
```

There is a wide range of options (such as date range and precise location, in addition to paging parameters such as per_page and page). In this case, we're using the search_text and location parameters to put together an HTTP GET request:

```
http://upcoming.yahooapis.com/services/rest/?api_key={api_key}&method=event.search&➥
search_text=bach&location=Berkeley%@C+California
```

to which you get back a series of event elements:

```
<event id="166104" name="San Francisco Symphony: Bach and Handel"
      description="Christophers makes music of three centuries ago sound ➡
contemporary and utterly vital. Here, he conducts Baroque blockbusters, music of ➡
dazzling color and invention."
      start_date="2008-04-05" end_date="" start_time="20:00:00" end_time=""
      personal="0"
      selfpromotion="0" metro_id="2;1311;1403;1849;1934;2122;2289;2466;2638;2962"
      venue_id="17246"
      user_id="59509" category_id="1" date_posted="2007-03-18 10:59:58"
      watchlist_count="6"
      url="http://www.sfsymphony.org/templates/event_info.asp?nodeid=250&amp;➡
eventid=1188"
      distance="10.91" distance_units="miles" latitude="37.7774"
      longitude="-122.4198"
      geocoding_precision="address" geocoding_ambiguous="0"
      venue_name="Davies Symphony Hall"
      venue_address="201 Van Ness Avenue" venue_city="San Francisco Bay Area"
      venue_state_name="California" venue_state_code="ca" venue_state_id="5"
      venue_country_name="United States" venue_country_code="us"
      venue_country_id="1"
      venue_zip="94102"/>
```

Note what you get back. In addition to the "what" and "when" of the event, there is also specific geocoding. You can make a map (for example, converting this KML and displaying it on a map), which I showed earlier in the case of using the RSS 2.0 feed.

What else can do you with the API without authentication?

- You can use event.getInfo to retrieve information about public events given its event_id. For example, you can use the WWW2008 Conference (http://upcoming.yahoo.com/ event/205875) here:

```
http://upcoming.yahooapis.com/services/rest/?method=event.getInfo&api_key=➡
{api-key}&event_id=205875
```

to get the following:

```
<?xml version="1.0" encoding="UTF-8"?>
<rsp stat="ok" version="1.0">
  <event id="205875" name="WWW 2008 (17th International World Wide Web ➡
Conference)"
      tags="www,web,www2008,ydn"
      description="&quot;The World Wide Web Conference is a global event bringing ➡
together key researchers, innovators, decision-makers, technologists, ➡
businesses, and standards bodies working to shape the Web. Since its inception ➡
in 1994, the WWW conference has become the annual venue for international ➡
discussions and debate on the future evolution of the Web.&quot;"
```

```
        start_date="2008-04-21" end_date="2008-04-25" start_time="" end_time=""
        personal="0"
        selfpromotion="0" metro_id="420" venue_id="33275" user_id="18772"
        category_id="5"
        url="http://www2008.org/" date_posted="2007-06-12" latitude="" ➥
longitude=""
        geocoding_precision="" geocoding_ambiguous=""
        venue_name="Beijing International Conference Center"
        venue_address="No.8 Beichendong Road Chaoyang District" ➥
venue_city="Beijing"
        venue_state_name="Beijing" venue_state_code="bj" venue_state_id="171"
        venue_country_name="China"
        venue_country_code="cn" venue_country_id="44" venue_zip="" venue_url=""
        venue_phone="+86-10-64910248"/>
    </rsp>
```

- You can use `metro.getForLatLon` to retrieve a venue for a given latitude and longitude. Let's use the latitude and longitude for a building on the UC Berkeley campus in Berkeley, California:

```
37.869111,-122.260634
```

to formulate the following request:

```
http://upcoming.yahooapis.com/services/rest/?method=metro.getForLatLon&➥
api_key={api-key}&latitude=37.869111&longitude=-122.260634
```

which returns this:
```
<?xml version="1.0" encoding="UTF-8"?>
<rsp stat="ok" version="1.0">
  <metro id="2" name="San Francisco" code="sf" state_id="5"
state_name="California"
          state_code="ca"
          country_id="1" country_name="United States" country_code="us"/>
</rsp>
```

Parts of the API That Require Authentication

You will need to supply a callback URL for token-based authorization if you need that. How do you authenticate? The documentation is here:

```
http://upcoming.yahoo.com/services/api/token_auth.php
```

Getting the Token

The documentation tells you how to set up a callback URL for web-based applications. I consider this a simpler case in which you don't set any callback URL and manually read off a token. That is, load up this in your browser, and read the frob:

```
http://upcoming.yahoo.com/services/auth/?api_key={api-key}
```

Then get a token with an `auth.getToken` call:

```
http://upcoming.yahooapis.com/services/rest/?method=auth.getToken&api_key={api-key}&➥
frob={frob}
```

to which you will get the following:

```
<?xml version="1.0" encoding="UTF-8"?>
<rsp stat="ok" version="1.0">
<token token="[TOKEN]" user_id="[USER_ID]" user_username="[USERNAME]"
       user_name="[FULLNAME]" />
</rsp>
```

Adding an Event with the API

Let's use the API to add an event with the `event.add` method, which is documented here:

```
http://upcoming.yahoo.com/services/api/event.add.php
```

To add an event, issue an HTTP POST request with the following parameters:

- `api_key` (required)
- `token` (required)
- `name` (required)
- `venue_id` (numeric, required)
- `category_id` (numeric, required)
- `start_date` (YYYY-MM-DD, required)
- `end_date` (YYYY-MM-DD, optional)
- `start_time` (HH:MM:SS, optional)
- `end_time` (HH:MM:SS, optional)
- `description` (optional)
- `url` (optional)
- `personal` (1=visible to friends only or 0=public, optional, defaults to 0)
- `selfpromotion` (1=self-promotion or 0=normal, optional, defaults to 0)

For an example, I added the JCDL 2008 conference to Upcoming.yahoo.com:

```
http://www.jcdl2008.org/
```

The best way is to practice using the user interface of Upcoming.yahoo.com to help you pick out the venue ID and category ID:

```
http://upcoming.yahoo.com/event/add/
```

The location (found at `http://www.jcdl2008.org/location.html`) is the Omni William Penn Hotel in Pittsburgh, Pennsylvania. When you type the name of the hotel and its city into Upcoming.yahoo.com, it locates a venue. But how do you get the ID? You can use the API method `venue.search` (`http://upcoming.yahoo.com/services/api/venue.search.php`):

```
http://upcoming.yahooapis.com/services/rest/?api_key={api_key}&method=venue.search&➥
search_text=Omni+William+Penn+Hotel&location=Pittsburgh%@C+PA
```
to which you get the following:

```
<?xml version="1.0" encoding="UTF-8"?>
<rsp stat="ok" version="1.0">
  <venue id="56189" name="Omni William Penn Hotel" address="530 William Penn Place"
    city="Pittsburgh" state="Pennsylvania" zip="" country="United States"
    url="http://www.omnihotels.com/FindAHotel/PittsburghWilliamPenn.aspx"
    description=""
    user_id="120115" metro_id="77" private="0" distance="0.14"
    distance_units="miles"
    latitude="40.4406" longitude="-79.997" geocoding_precision="address"
    geocoding_ambiguous="0"
    state_code="pa" state_id="39" country_code="us" country_id="1"/>
</rsp>
```

The conclusion is that the venue ID is 56189.

The next question is, how do you get the category ID? You can use the `category.getList` method (`http://upcoming.yahoo.com/services/api/category.getList.php`):

```
http://upcoming.yahooapis.com/services/rest/?api_key={api_key}&method=category.getList
```

to get:

```
<?xml version="1.0" encoding="UTF-8"?>
<rsp stat="ok" version="1.0">
<category id="1" name="Music" description="Concerts, nightlife, raves" />
<category id="2" name="Performing/Visual Arts" description="Theatre, dance, opera, ➥
exhibitions" />
<category id="3" name="Media" description="Film, book readings" />
<category id="4" name="Social" description="Rallies, gatherings, user groups" />
<category id="5" name="Education" description="Lectures, workshops" />
<category id="6" name="Commercial" description="Conventions, expos, flea markets" />
<category id="7" name="Festivals" description="Big events, often multiple days" />
<category id="8" name="Sports" description="Sporting events, recreation" />
<category id="10" name="Other" description="Who knows?" />
<category id="11" name="Comedy" description="Stand-up, improv, comic theatre" />
<category id="12" name="Politics" description="Rallies, fundraisers, meetings" />
<category id="13" name="Family" description="Family/kid-oriented music, shows,
theatre" />
</rsp>
```

For this event, let's pick Education (category 5).

Finally, I grab the description from here:

```
http://www.jcdl2008.org/index.html
```

Since 2001, the Joint Conference on Digital Libraries has served as the major international forum focused on digital libraries and associated technical, practical, and social issues . . .

Four hundred attendees are expected for the five days of events including a day of cutting edge tutorials; 3 days of papers, panels, and keynotes; and a day of research workshops.

OK—let's piece together a `curl` invocation that will create a new event in Upcoming.yahoo.com. Here is a Python program to generate the `curl` command:

```python
import urllib

# parameters for creating the upcoming event
method = 'event.add'
api_key = '[API-KEY]'
token = '[TOKEN]'
name = 'Joint Conference on Digital Libraries (JCDL) 2008'
venue_id = '56189'
category_id = '5'   #education
start_date = '2008-06-15'
end_date = '2008-06-20'
description = """
[DESCRIPTION]
"""
url = 'http://www.jcdl2008.org/'
params = {'api_key': api_key, 'method':method, 'token':token, 'name':name, ➥
'venue_id':venue_id, 'category_id': category_id, ➥
          'start_date':start_date, 'end_date':end_date, 'description': description, ➥
          'url': url}

command = 'curl -v -X POST -d "%s" %s' % (urllib.urlencode(params), "http://upcoming.➥
yahooapis.com/services/rest/")
print command
```

The resulting `curl` command is as follows:

```
curl -v -X POST -d "venue_id=56189&name=Joint+Conference+on+Digital+Libraries+➥
%28JCDL%29+2008&end_date=2008-06-20&url=http%3A%2F%2Fwww.jcdl2008.org%2F&description➥
{description}&start_date=2008-06-15&token=[TOKEN]&api_key=[API-KEY]&method=event.add➥
&category_id=5" http://upcoming.yahooapis.com/services/rest/
```

Remember that [TOKEN] is the authentication token received from the auth.getToken call issued earlier. The resulting event in Upcoming.yahoo.com is as follows:

```
http://upcoming.yahoo.com/event/300826/
```

API Kits for Upcoming.yahoo.com

To find API kits for Upcoming.yahoo.com, you can start with the links here:

```
http://upcoming.yahoo.com/help/w/Language-specific_Libraries
```

Although there does not seem to be any publicly available PHP kits at this point, you can find one for Python here:

```
http://code.google.com/p/upcoming-python-api/
```

Since this project currently has no downloads, you get the source via Subversion:

```
svn checkout http://upcoming-python-api.googlecode.com/svn/trunk/ upcoming-python-api
```

The following code searches for events with the Bach keyword that are within five miles of Berkeley, California:

```python
UPCOMING_API_KEY = '[UPCOMING_API_KEY]'

#from upcoming_api import Upcoming
from upcoming_api import UpcomingCached
import string

#upcoming = Upcoming(UPCOMING_API_KEY)

upcoming = UpcomingCached(UPCOMING_API_KEY)
bach_events = upcoming.event.search(search_text='Bach', location="Berkeley, CA")
print "There are %s events." % (len(bach_events))
for event in bach_events:

    print "%s\t%s\t%s" % (event['id'], event['name'], event['description']),

    v = upcoming.venue.getInfo(venue_id=event['venue_id'])
    print "%s\t%s\t%s\t%s" % (v[0]['name'], v[0]['address'], v[0]['city'], ➥
v[0]['zip']),

    # metro_id are ;-delimited list.  Sometimes  the metro list is empty....
    try:
        m_ids = string.split(event['metro_id'],";")
    # deal with only the first metro on the list
        m = upcoming.metro.getInfo(metro_id=m_ids[0])
        print 'metro name: ', m[0]['name']
    except:
        print "no metro name"
```

Here is an additional line of Python to add an event to Upcoming.yahoo.com:

```python
new_event = upcoming.event.add(token=token,name=name,venue_id=venue_id, \
category_id=category_id, start_date=start_date,end_date=end_date, \
                description=description)
```

■Caution As of this writing, I had to update `upcoming_api.py` to make sure `UPCOMING_API` is set to `http://upcoming.yahooapis.com/services/rest/`.

Eventful.com

Eventful.com is another event aggregator that has an API. You can find the web site here:

`http://eventful.com/`

Its API is documented is here:

`http://api.eventful.com/`

The list of methods in the API is here:

`http://api.eventful.com/docs/`

To use the API, you need to request a key from here:

`http://api.eventful.com/keys/`

The base URL for RESTful calls is here:

`http://api.evdb.com/rest/{path for methods}`

For example:

`http://api.evdb.com/rest/events/search`

Searching for Events (Using Feeds)

Before we jump into the API, let's see how to look at the URL language to search for events in the user interface and to return feeds. You can search for `Bach` events within five miles of Berkeley, California, with this:

`http://eventful.com/events?page_size=50&sort_order=Date&within=5&units=mi&q=bach&l=`➡
`berkeley%2C+ca&t=Future&c=`

You can get these results as an RSS 2.0 feed:

`http://eventful.com/rss/events/?page_size=50&sort_order=Date&within=5&units=mi&q=`➡
`bach&l=berkeley%2C+ca&t=Future&c=`

or as an Atom 1.0 feed:

`http://eventful.com/atom/events/?page_size=50&sort_order=Date&within=5&units=mi&q=`➡
`bach&l=berkeley%2C+ca&t=Future&c=`

You can change this Atom feed into KML using Yahoo! Pipes the way we did so for Upcoming.yahoo.com. The Eventful.com feeds have latitude/longitude information embedded (specifically, in the GeoRSS GML encoding). For example:

```
<georss:where>
  <gml:Point>
    <gml:pos>37.72084 -122.476619</gml:pos>
  </gml:Point>
</georss:where>
```

You can run Yahoo! Pipes here:

```
http://pipes.yahoo.com/pipes/pipe.info?_id=lJPPcvWA3BGvrWbY6kjTQA
```

to generate a KML feed for Bach-related events in the Berkeley area:

```
http://pipes.yahoo.com/pipes/pipe.run?_id=lJPPcvWA3BGvrWbY6kjTQA&_render=kml&l=➥
Berkeley%2C+CA&page_size=50&q=Bach&t=Future&units=mi&within=5
```

Searching for Events (Using the API)

Let's first get an XML response from the /events/search method, which is documented here:

```
http://api.eventful.com/docs/events/search
http://api.eventful.com/rest/events/search?app_key={api-key}&keywords=Bach&location=➥
Berkeley%2C%20CA&within=5&units=5&page_size=50
```

to which you get event elements like this:

```
<event id="E0-001-005962514-3">
  <title>SF State Recital by Roger Woodward, piano faculty</title>
  <description> &lt;b&gt;Details:&lt;/b&gt;&lt;br&gt;Program: J.S. Bach: Well-➥
Tempered Clavier, Book I </description>
  <start_time>2007-10-23 20:00:00</start_time>
  <stop_time/>
  <tz_id/>
  <tz_olson_path/>
  <tz_country/>
  <tz_city/>
  <venue_id>V0-001-000550476-8</venue_id>
  <venue_name>San Francisco State University</venue_name>
  <venue_display>1</venue_display>
  <venue_address>1600 Holloway Avenue</venue_address>
  <city_name>San Francisco</city_name>
  <region_name>California</region_name>
  <region_abbr>CA</region_abbr>
  <postal_code>94132</postal_code>
  <country_name>United States</country_name>
  <country_abbr2>US</country_abbr2>
  <country_abbr>USA</country_abbr>
  <latitude>37.72084</latitude>
  <longitude>-122.476619</longitude>
  <geocode_type>EVDB Geocoder</geocode_type>
```

```
    <all_day>0</all_day>
    <recur_string/>
    <trackback_count>0</trackback_count>
    <calendar_count>0</calendar_count>
    <comment_count>0</comment_count>
    <link_count>1</link_count>
    <going_count>0</going_count>
    <watching_count>0</watching_count>
    <created>2007-09-02 00:19:50</created>
    <owner>evdb</owner>
    <modified>2007-09-02 04:07:16</modified>
    <performers/>
    <image/>
    <privacy>1</privacy>
    <calendars/>
    <groups/>
    <going/>
</event>
```

Interestingly enough, we can also get iCalendar and RSS directly from the API. To get iCalendar, you use the /events/ical method documented here:

```
http://api.eventful.com/docs/events/ical
```

To get the Bach keyword–related events within five miles of Berkeley as an iCalendar feed, use this:

```
http://api.eventful.com/rest/events/ical?app_key={api-key}&keywords=Bach&location=➥
Berkeley%2C%20CA&within=5&units=5&page_size=50
```

You can also change http to webcal and feed it to Google Calendar.

PHP API Kit for Eventful.com

You can find a list of API kits for Eventful.com here:

```
http://api.eventful.com/
```

For PHP, there are two choices. One is Services_Eventful, which we won't cover here, and the other is Services_EVDB (which seems to be compatible with PHP 4 and 5). You can find the code here:

```
http://api.eventful.com/libs/Services_EVDB
```

Let's say you want to extract this:

```
http://eventful.com/events/categories/technology?l=Berkeley%2C%20California%2C%20USA
```

The corresponding REST call is as follows:

```
http://api.evdb.com/rest/events/search?category=technology&location=Berkeley%2C%20➥
California%2C%20USA&within=25&page_size=5&app_key={api-key}
```

Note that the default is a 25-mile radius of the location. This shows how you can do this with the Services_EVDB PHP API kit:

```php
<?php
// http://api.eventful.com/libs/Services_EVDB

ini_set(
  'include_path',
    ini_get( 'include_path' ) . PATH_SEPARATOR . "/home/rdhyee/pear/lib/php" .
PATH_SEPARATOR . '/usr/local/lib/php'
    );

require 'Services/EVDB.php';

// Enter your application key here. (See http://api.evdb.com/keys/)
$app_key = '[APP_KEY]';

$evdb = &new Services_EVDB($app_key);

// Authentication is required for some API methods.
$user     = $_REQUEST['user'];
$password = $_REQUEST['password'];

if ($user and $password)
{
  $l = $evdb->login($user, $password);

  if ( PEAR::isError($l) )
  {
      print("Can't log in: " . $l->getMessage() . "\n");
  }
}

// All method calls other than login() go through call().
$args = array(
  'id' => $_REQUEST['id'],
);
$event = $evdb->call('events/get', $args);

if ( PEAR::isError($event) )
{
    print("An error occurred: " . $event->getMessage() . "\n");
    print_r( $evdb );
}

// The return value from a call is an XML_Unserializer data structure.
print_r( $event );
?>
```

To see this code in action on Eventful.com, the event number is E0-001-004433237-3:[26]

```
http://examples.mashupguide.net/ch15/evdb1.php?id=E0-001-004433237-3
```

Python API Kit for Eventful.com

You can find the documentation for `eventfulpy` here:

```
http://api.eventful.com/libs/python/
```

As of writing, the latest version is as follows:

```
http://api.eventful.com/libs/python/eventfulpy-0.3.tar.gz
```

See "Installing simplejson and httplib2 on Windows Python" in case you run into problems installing the dependencies for `eventfulpy`.

INSTALLING SIMPLEJSON AND HTTPLIB2 ON WINDOWS PYTHON

`eventfulpy` depends on two other libraries: `simplejson` (http://undefined.org/python/ #simple_json) and `httplib2` (http://bitworking.org/projects/httplib2/). When I installed `simplesjon` for Python 2.5 for Windows, I needed to do the following (I'm using the default directory for Python 2.5 on Windows: `C:\Python25`):

1. Install `setuptools` (http://pypi.python.org/pypi/setuptools). The easiest way is to run the `.exe` installer (for example, `setuptools-0.6c7.win32-py2.5.exe`).

2. Use Subversion `svn` to check out `simplejson` from http://svn.red-bean.com/bob/ simplejson/trunk/.

3. I installed `mingw32` (http://www.mingw.org/) because I didn't have Visual Studio installed.

4. Build the `simplejson` library with the following command:

   ```
   c:\python25\python.exe setup.py build -c mingw32 --force
   ```

5. Install the library by copying the resulting `build\lib.win32-2.5\simplejson` to `C:\Python25\ Lib\site-packages` (I manually copied the directory because I could not find a way to coax the standard installation command (`c:\python25\python.exe setup.py install`) into working.

   You can find an alternative approach here:

   ```
   http://maurus.net/weblog/2007/10/02/simplejson-17x-activestate-python-➥
   and-the-visual-studio-2003-compiler/
   ```

   I found installing `httplib2` to be more straightforward. For instance, you can download the latest distribution from http://code.google.com/p/httplib2/downloads/list and run `c:\python25\ python.exe setup.py install`.

The following code shows how to query for events and list the results:

```python
import eventful

api = eventful.API('[API-KEY]')

# If you need to log in:
api.login('[USER]','[PASSWORD]')

events = api.call('/events/search', q='Bach', l='Berkeley, CA', within='5', \
units='mi', time='future', page_size=50)
for event in events['events']['event']:
    print "%s at %s" % (event['title'], event['venue_name'])
```

Let's now write JCDL 2008 to Eventful.com. Note that like Upcoming.yahoo.com, Eventful.com also uses IDs for venues. The following code has a venue_search method to help locate venues and their corresponding IDs:

```python
# parameters for creating the upcoming event -- now I want to write it to eventful

name = 'Joint Conference on Digital Libraries (JCDL) 2008'
start_date = '2008-06-15'
end_date = '2008-06-20'
description = """
[DESCRIPTION]
"""
url = 'http://www.jcdl2008.org/'

def venue_search(keywords,location):
    """
    print out possibilities...
    """
    import eventful

    api = eventful.API('[API-KEY]')
    api.login('[USER]','[PASSWORD]')
    vs = api.call('/venues/search', keywords = keywords, location=location)
    for v in vs['venues']['venue']:
        print "%s\t%s\t%s" % (v['id'], v['name'], v['address'])

import eventful

api = eventful.API('[API-KEY]')
api.login('[USER]','[PASSWORD]')

#http://api.eventful.com/docs/events/new
tz_olsen_path = 'America/New_York'
all_day = '1'
privacy = 1
```

```
tags = ''
free = 0

# this is the eventful venue_id for the hotel.
eventful_venue_id = 'VO-001-000412401-5'

ev = api.call('/events/new', title=name, start_time=start_date, \
              stop_time=end_date, tz_olsen_path=tz_olsen_path, all_day=all_day, \
              description=description, privacy=privacy, venue_id=eventful_venue_id)

import pprint
pprint(ev)
```

With success, you get back an ID for the event (`http://eventful.com/events/EO-001-006801918-6`):

```
{u'id': u'EO-001-006801918-6',
 u'message': u'Add event complete',
 u'status': u'ok'}
```

Programming with iCalendar

Since iCalendar is an important data format, it's worth looking a bit more at how to manipulate it in PHP and Python.

■**Note** The hCalendar microformat is designed to express the same information as iCalendar but in a form that is embeddable in HTML and RSS. See Chapter 18 on microformats for how to use and create hCalendar.

Python and iCalendar

A good Python module to use is iCalendar:

`http://codespeak.net/icalendar/`

As of this writing, the latest version is 1.2. You download this code here:

`http://codespeak.net/icalendar/iCalendar-1.2.tgz`

To run a basic test of iCalendar interoperability, I created an event on Apple iCal and e-mailed it to myself. On my notebook, the filename is as follows:

`D:\Document\Docs\2007\05\iCal-20070508-082112.ics`

What's actually in the file?

```
BEGIN:VCALENDAR
VERSION:2.0
X-WR-CALNAME:open house at the Academy
```

```
PRODID:-//Apple Computer\, Inc//iCal 2.0//EN
CALSCALE:GREGORIAN
METHOD:PUBLISH
BEGIN:VTIMEZONE
TZID:US/Pacific
LAST-MODIFIED:20070508T152112Z
BEGIN:DAYLIGHT
DTSTART:20070311T100000
TZOFFSETTO:-0700
TZOFFSETFROM:+0000
TZNAME:PDT
END:DAYLIGHT
BEGIN:STANDARD
DTSTART:20071104T020000
TZOFFSETTO:-0800
TZOFFSETFROM:-0700
TZNAME:PST
END:STANDARD
END:VTIMEZONE
BEGIN:VEVENT
DTSTART;TZID=US/Pacific:20070510T190000
DTEND;TZID=US/Pacific:20070510T200000
SUMMARY:open house at the Academy
UID:AAE603F6-A5A1-4E11-91CF-E6B06649A756
ORGANIZER;CN="Raymond Yee":mailto:rdhyee@yahoo.com
SEQUENCE:6
DTSTAMP:20070508T152047Z
END:VEVENT
END:VCALENDAR
```

Now, I want to read it in using Python. Let's also consult the documentation to build a simple example:[27]

```
from icalendar import Calendar
fname = r'D:\Document\Docs\2007\05\iCal-20070508-082112.ics'
cal = Calendar.from_string(open(fname,'rb').read())
ev0 = cal.walk('vevent')[0]
print ev0.keys()
print "summary: ", str(ev0['SUMMARY'])
print "start:", str(ev0['DTSTART'])
# ev0['DTSTART'] is datetime.date() object
print "end:", str(ev0['DTEND'])
```

27. http://codespeak.net/icalendar/, http://codespeak.net/icalendar/example.html, http://codespeak. net/icalendar/small.html, and http://codespeak.net/icalendar/groupscheduled.html

If you run it, you get this:

```
['DTSTAMP', 'UID', 'SEQUENCE', 'SUMMARY', 'DTEND', 'DTSTART', 'ORGANIZER']
summary:  open house at the Academy
start: 20070510T190000
end: 20070510T200000
```

Another Python iCalendar library is vobject:

http://vobject.skyhouseconsulting.com/usage.html

The following code shows how to use vobject to parse the same iCalendar file:

```python
import vobject
fname = r'D:\Document\Docs\2007\05\iCal-20070508-082112.ics'
cal = vobject.readOne(open(fname,'rb').read())
event = cal.vevent
print event.sortChildKeys()
print "summary: ", event.getChildValue('summary')
print "start:", str(event.getChildValue('dtstart'))
# event.getChildValue('dtstart') is datetime.date() object
print "end:", str(event.getChildValue('dtend'))
```

PHP and iCalendar

You can download iCalcreator, a PHP library for parsing and creating iCalendar files, here:

http://www.kigkonsult.se/iCalcreator/index.php

The module is documented here:

http://www.kigkonsult.se/iCalcreator/docs/using.html

Here is some code using iCalcreator to read and parse the same iCalendar file from the previous section:

```php
<?php

require_once 'iCalcreator/iCalcreator.class.php';

  $filename = 'D:\Document\Docs\2007\05\iCal-20070508-082112.ics';

  $v = new vcalendar(); // initiate new CALENDAR
  $v->parse($filename);

  # get first vevent
  $comp = $v->getComponent("VEVENT");

  #print_r($comp);
  $summary_array = $comp->getProperty("summary", 1, TRUE);
  echo "summary: ", $summary_array["value"], "\n";
```

```
$dtstart_array = $comp->getProperty("dtstart", 1, TRUE);
$dtstart = $dtstart_array["value"];
$startDate = "{$dtstart["year"]}-{$dtstart["month"]}-{$dtstart["day"]}";
$startTime = "{$dtstart["hour"]}:{$dtstart["min"]}:{$dtstart["sec"]}";

$dtend_array = $comp->getProperty("dtend", 1, TRUE);
$dtend = $dtend_array["value"];
$endDate = "{$dtend["year"]}-{$dtend["month"]}-{$dtend["day"]}";
$endTime = "{$dtend["hour"]}:{$dtend["min"]}:{$dtend["sec"]}";

echo "start: ",  $startDate,"T",$startTime, "\n";
echo "end: ",  $endDate,"T",$endTime, "\n";

?>
```

The output of the code is as follows:

```
summary: open house at the Academy
start: 2007-05-10T19:00:00
end: 2007-05-10T20:00:00
```

I will use iCalcreator in the following section to convert iCalendar feeds into Google calendar entries.

Exporting an Events Calendar to iCalendar and Google Calendar

In this section, I'll show you how to use what you've learned so far to solve a specific problem. After you have used event aggregators such as Upcoming.yahoo.com and Eventful.com, you'll get used to the idea of having a single (or at least a small number) of places to see all your events. iCalendar-savvy calendars (such as Google Calendar, Apple iCal, and Microsoft Outlook 2007) have also become unifying interfaces by letting you subscribe to iCalendar feeds containing events that might be of interest to you. As extensive as Upcoming.yahoo.com, Eventful.com, and Google Calendar (which has been a marketplace of events by letting users author publicly available calendars) might be, there are still many sources of events that are not covered by such services. This section teaches you how to turn event-related information toward destinations where you might like to see them.

Specifically, I will work through the following example: converting events listed under the Critic's Choice section of UC Berkeley's online event calendar (http://events.berkeley.edu) into two different formats:

- An iCalendar feed

- A Google calendar

I use this example to demonstrate how to use Python and PHP libraries to parse and write iCalendar feeds and to write to a Google calendar. I've chosen the UC Berkeley event calendar because it already has calendaring information in a structured form (XML and iCalendar), but as of the time of writing, it's not quite in the configuration that I create here. You can generalize this example to the event calendars that you might be interested in, some with more structured information than others. Moreover, instead of writing to Google Calendar, you can use the techniques I showed earlier in the chapter to write the events to Upcoming.yahoo.com or Eventful.com.

The Source: UC Berkeley Event Calendars

The Critic's Choice section of the UC Berkeley event calendar highlights some of the many events that happen on the campus:

```
http://events.berkeley.edu/
```

As documented here:

```
http://events.berkeley.edu/documentation/user/rss.html
```

the calendar provides feeds in three formats: RSS 2.0, a live_export XML format, and iCalendar. Of particular interest is that every event in the calendar, which is referenced by an event ID (for example, 3950), is accessible in a number of representations:

- As HTML:

  ```
  http://events.berkeley.edu/?event_ID={event_ID}
  ```

- As RSS 2.0:

  ```
  http://events.berkeley.edu/index.php/rss/sn/pubaff/?event_ID={event_ID}
  ```

- As iCalendar:

  ```
  http://events.berkeley.edu/index.php/ical/event_ID/{event_ID}/.ics
  ```

- As live_export XML:
  ```
  http://events.berkeley.edu/index.php/live_export/sn/pubaff/?event_ID={event_ID}
  ```

You can get feeds for many parts of the event calendar (including feeds for events for today, this week, or this month), but there is currently no Critic's Choice iCalendar feed. Having such a feed would enable one to track Critic's Choice events in Google Calendar or Apple iCal. The Critic's Choice is, however, available as an RSS 2.0 feed here:

```
http://events.berkeley.edu/index.php/critics_choice_rss.html
```

The following two sections show you how to extract the event ID for each of the events listed as part of Critic's Choice, read the iCalendar instance for an event to create a synthesized iCalendar feed, and write those events to Google Calendar.

Creating an iCalendar Feed of Critic's Choice Using Python

The following code, written in Python, knits together the iCalendar entries for each of the Critic's Choice events into a single iCalendar feed through the following steps:

1. Parsing the list event_ID from here:

   ```
   http://events.berkeley.edu/index.php/critics_choice_rss.html
   ```

2. Reading the individual iCalendar entries and adding it to the one for the Critic's Choice

Note that this code treats iCalendar essentially as a black box. In the next section, we'll parse data from iCalendar and rewrite it in a format demanded of Google Calendar:

```
"""
generate iCalendar feed out of the UC Berkeley events calendar
"""

import sys
try:
    from xml.etree import ElementTree
except:
    from elementtree import ElementTree

import httplib2
client = httplib2.Http(".cache")

import vobject

# a function to get individual iCalendar feeds for each event.
# http://events.berkeley.edu/index.php/ical/event_ID/3950/.ics

def retrieve_ical(event_id):
    ical_url = "http://events.berkeley.edu/index.php/ical/event_ID/%s/.ics" % (event_id)
    response, body = client.request(ical_url)
    return body

# read the RSS 2.0 feed for the Critic's Choice

from elementtree import ElementTree

cc_RSS = "http://events.berkeley.edu/index.php/critics_choice_rss.html"
response, xml = client.request(cc_RSS)
doc = ElementTree.fromstring(xml)

from pprint import pprint
import urlparse

# create a blank iCalendar
ical = vobject.iCalendar()

for item in doc.findall('.//item'):
    # extract the anchor to get the elementID
    # http://events.berkeley.edu/index.php/critics_choice.html#2875
    ev_url = item.find('link').text
    # grab the anchor of the URL, which is the event_ID
```

```
        event_id = urlparse.urlparse(ev_url)[5]
        print event_id
        s = retrieve_ical(event_id)
        try:
            ev0 = vobject.readOne(s).vevent
            ical.add(ev0)
        except:
            print "problem in generating iCalendar for event # %s " % (event_id)


ical_fname = r'D:\Document\PersonalInfoRemixBook\examples\ch15\critics_choice.ics'
f = open(ical_fname, "wb")
f.write(ical.serialize())
f.close()

# upload my feed to the server
# http://examples.mashupguide.net/ch15/critics_choice.ics

import os
os.popen('scp2 critics_choice.ics ➡
"rdhyee@pepsi.dreamhost.com:/home/rdhyee/examples.mashupguide.net/ch15')
```

By automatically running this script every day, whenever the RSS for the Critic's Choice is regenerated, the resulting iCalendar feed will be kept up-to-date:

```
http://examples.mashupguide.net/ch15/critics_choice.ics
```

Writing the Events to Google Calendar

In this section, instead of generating an iCalendar feed directly, I will instead write the events to Google Calendar using the PHP Zend Calendar API library. I created a new calendar for this purpose, whose user ID is as follows:

```
n7irauk3nns30fuku1anh43j5s@group.calendar.google.com
```

Hence, the public calendar is viewable here:

```
http://www.google.com/calendar/embed?src=n7irauk3nns30fuku1anh43j5s@group.calendar.➡
google.com
```

The following code loops through the events listed in the Critic's Choice RSS feed, extracts all the corresponding iCalendar entries, and then writes those events to the Google Calendar. The code first clears out the old events in the calendar before writing new events.

Perhaps the trickiest part of this code is handling recurring events. The relevant documentation in the Google Calendar API on recurring events includes the following:

- ```
  http://code.google.com/apis/calendar/developers_guide_php.html#Creating➡
  Recurring
  ```

- ```
  http://code.google.com/apis/gdata/elements.html#gdRecurrence
  ```

The Google Calendar API expresses recurrence using the syntax and data model of recurring events in iCalendar, which you can learn about in the following sections of the iCalendar specification (section 4.3.10 on RECUR, section 4.8.5.1 on EXDATE [exception dates/times], and section 4.8.5.4 on the Recurrence Rule):

- http://www.w3.org/2002/12/cal/rfc2445#sec4.3.10

- http://www.w3.org/2002/12/cal/rfc2445#sec4.8.5.1

- http://www.w3.org/2002/12/cal/rfc2445#sec4.8.5.4

More to the point, the following code captures information about recurring events by using regular expressions to extract occurrences of the DTSTART, DTEND, RRULE, RDATE, EXDATE, and EXRULE statements to pass to the Google Calendar API as recurrence data. (Remember to substitute your own Google username and password and the user ID for a Google Calendar for which you have write permission.)

```php
<?php

/*
 *
 * ucb_critics_gcal.php
 */

require_once 'Zend/Loader.php';
Zend_Loader::loadClass('Zend_Gdata');
Zend_Loader::loadClass('Zend_Gdata_ClientLogin');
Zend_Loader::loadClass('Zend_Gdata_Calendar');

require_once 'iCalcreator/iCalcreator.class.php';

function getResource($url){
  $chandle = curl_init();
  curl_setopt($chandle, CURLOPT_URL, $url);
  curl_setopt($chandle, CURLOPT_RETURNTRANSFER, 1);
  $result = curl_exec($chandle);
  curl_close($chandle);

  return $result;
}

// UCB events calendar

# gets all relevant rules for the first VEVENT in $ical_string
function extract_recurrence($ical_string) {
```

```php
$vevent_rawstr = "/(?ims)BEGIN:VEVENT(.*)END:VEVENT/";
preg_match($vevent_rawstr, $ical_string, $matches);

$vevent_str = $matches[1];

# now look for DTSTART, DTEND, RRULE, RDATE, EXDATE, and EXRULE

$rep_tags = array('DTSTART', 'DTEND', 'RRULE', 'RDATE', 'EXDATE', 'EXRULE');

$recur_list = array();

foreach ($rep_tags as $rep) {

  $rep_regexp = "/({$rep}(.*))/i";
  if (preg_match_all($rep_regexp, $vevent_str, $rmatches)) {
    foreach ($rmatches[0] as $match) {
      $recur_list[]= $match;
    }
  }

} //foreach $rep

  return implode($recur_list,"\r\n");

}

function parse_UCB_Event($event_id) {

  $ical_url = "http://events.berkeley.edu/index.php/ical/event_ID/{$event_id}/.ics";
  $rsp = getResource($ical_url);

  # write out the file
  $tempfile = "temp.ics";
  $fh = fopen($tempfile,"wb");
  $numbytes = fwrite($fh, $rsp);
  fclose($fh);

  $v = new vcalendar(); // initiate new CALENDAR
  $v->parse($tempfile);

  # how to get to the prelude to the vevent? (timezone)

  #echo $v->getProperty("prodid");

  # get first vevent
  $comp = $v->getComponent("VEVENT");
```

```php
  #print_r($comp);

  $event = array();

  $event["summary"] = $comp->getProperty("summary");
  $event["description"] = $comp->getProperty("description");

# optional -- but once and only once if these elements are here:
# dtstart, description,summary, url

  $dtstart = $comp->getProperty("dtstart", 1, TRUE);
  $event["dtstart"] = $dtstart;

# assume that dtend is used and not duration

  $event["dtend"] = $comp->getProperty("dtend", 1, TRUE);

  $event["location"] = $comp->getProperty("location");
  $event["url"] = $comp->getProperty("url");

# check for recurrence -- RRULE, RDATE, EXDATE, EXRULE

  $recurrence = extract_recurrence($rsp);

  $event_data = array();
  $event_data['event'] = $event;
  $event_data['recurrence'] = $recurrence;
  return $event_data;

} // parse_calendar

function extract_eventIDs($xml)
{

 $ev_list = array();

 foreach ($xml->channel->item as $item) {

   $link = $item->link;
   $k = parse_url($link);
   $ev_list[] = $k['fragment'];
 }
 return $ev_list;
}

// Google Calendar facade
```

```php
function getClientLoginHttpClient($user, $pass)
{
  $service = Zend_Gdata_Calendar::AUTH_SERVICE_NAME;

  $client = Zend_Gdata_ClientLogin::getHttpClient($user, $pass, $service);
  return $client;
}

// code adapted from the Google documentation
// this posts to the DEFAULT calendar -- how do I change to post elsewhere?

function createGCalEvent ($client, $title, $desc, $where, $startDate = '2008-01-20',
    $startTime = '10:00:00',
    $endDate = '2008-01-20', $endTime = '11:00:00', $tzOffset = '-08',
    $recurrence=null, $calendar_uri=null)
{
  $gdataCal = new Zend_Gdata_Calendar($client);
  $newEvent = $gdataCal->newEventEntry();

  $newEvent->title = $gdataCal->newTitle($title);
  $newEvent->where = array($gdataCal->newWhere($where));
  $newEvent->content = $gdataCal->newContent("$desc");

# if $recurrence is not null then set recurrence -- else set the start and enddate:

  if ($recurrence) {
    $newEvent->recurrence = $gdataCal->newRecurrence($recurrence);
  } else {
    $when = $gdataCal->newWhen();
    $when->startTime = "{$startDate}T{$startTime}{$tzOffset}:00";
    $when->endTime = "{$endDate}T{$endTime}{$tzOffset}:00";
    $newEvent->when = array($when);
  } //if recurrence

// Upload the event to the calendar server
// A copy of the event as it is recorded on the server is returned

    $createdEvent = $gdataCal->insertEvent($newEvent,$calendar_uri);
    return $createdEvent;
}

function listEventsForCalendar($client,$calendar_uri=null) {

  $gdataCal = new Zend_Gdata_Calendar($client);
```

```php
    $eventFeed = $gdataCal->getCalendarEventFeed($calendar_uri);
    foreach ($eventFeed as $event) {
      echo $event->title->text, "\t", $event->id->text, "\n";
      foreach ($event->when as $when) {
        echo "Starts: " . $when->startTime . "\n";
      }
    }
    echo "\n";
}

function clearAllEventsForCalendar($client, $calendar_uri=null) {

  $gdataCal = new Zend_Gdata_Calendar($client);

  $eventFeed = $gdataCal->getCalendarEventFeed($calendar_uri);
  foreach ($eventFeed as $event) {
    $event->delete();
  }

}

// bridge between UCB events calendar and GCal

function postUCBEventToGCal($client,$event_id, $calendar_uri=null) {

  $event_data = parse_UCB_Event($event_id);

  $event = $event_data['event'];
  $recurrence = $event_data['recurrence'];

  #print_r($event);
  #echo $recurrence;

  $title = $event["summary"];
  $description = $event["description"];
  $where = $event["location"];

# there is a possible parameter that might have TZ info. Ignore for now.
  $dtstart = $event["dtstart"]["value"];
  $startDate = "{$dtstart["year"]}-{$dtstart["month"]}-{$dtstart["day"]}";
  $startTime = "{$dtstart["hour"]}:{$dtstart["min"]}:{$dtstart["sec"]}";

# there is a possible parameter that might have TZ info. Ignore for now.
  $dtend = $event["dtend"]["value"];
  $endDate = "{$dtend["year"]}-{$dtend["month"]}-{$dtend["day"]}";
  $endTime = "{$dtend["hour"]}:{$dtend["min"]}:{$dtend["sec"]}";
```

```
        # explicitly set for now instead of calculating.
        $tzOffset = '-07';

        # I might want to do something with the url
        $description .= "\n" . $event["url"];

        echo "Event: ", $title,$description, $where, $startDate, $startTime, $endDate,
            $endTime, $tzOffset, $recurrence, "\n";

        $new_event = createGCalEvent($client,$title,$description, $where, $startDate,
            $startTime, $endDate, $endTime, $tzOffset,$recurrence, $calendar_uri);

    }

    # credentials for Google calendar

    $USER = "[USER]";
    $PASSWORD = "[PASSWORD]";

    # the calendar to write to has a userID of
    # n7irauk3nns30fuku1anh43j5s@group.calendar.google.com
    # substitute the userID of your own calendar
    $userID = urlencode("[USERID]");
    $calendar_uri = "http://www.google.com/calendar/feeds/{$userID}/private/full";

    $client = getClientLoginHttpClient($USER, $PASSWORD);

    # get UCB events list

    $cc_RSS = "http://events.berkeley.edu/index.php/critics_choice_rss.html";
    $rsp = getResource($cc_RSS);

    # for now, read the cached file
    #$fname = "D:\Document\PersonalInfoRemixBook\examples\ch15\cc_RSS.xml";
    #$fh = fopen($fname, "r");

    #$rsp = fread($fh, filesize($fname));
    #fclose($fh);

    $xml = simplexml_load_string($rsp);
    $ev_list = extract_eventIDs($xml);

    echo "list of events to add:";
    print_r($ev_list);
```

```
# loop through events list

# limit the number of events to do
$maxevent = 200;
$count = 0;

# clear the existing calendar

echo "Deleting existing events....";
clearAllEventsForCalendar($client,$calendar_uri);

# Add the events
foreach ($ev_list as $event_id) {

  $count +=1;
  if ($count > $maxevent) {
    break;
  }
  echo "Adding event: {$event_id}", "\n";
  postUCBEventToGCal($client,$event_id,$calendar_uri);

}

# list the events on the calendar
listEventsForCalendar($client,$calendar_uri);
?>
```

Summary

Here are some of things you learned in this chapter:

- You spent a considerable amount of time studying Google Calendar because of its sophisticated API and use of feeds including Atom feeds and iCalendar.

- You learned how to access and manipulate the feeds in Google Calendar, either by directly issuing the relevant RESTful HTTP requests with curl or by using the PHP and Python API kits.

- You took a quick look at 30boxes.com as another example of a web-based calendar with an API.

- You then studied how to consume feeds and exercise the APIs of two event aggregators: Upcoming.yahoo.com and Eventful.com.

- You studied how to program with iCalendar in PHP and Python.

- Finally, you learned how to synthesize an iCalendar feed from other iCalendar entries and how to write iCalendar information to a Google Calendar.

These are some key points to note:

- Online calendars are becoming more popular; they are especially useful when they have APIs and feeds to help with data integration.

- Event aggregators are interesting complements in this space to the online calendars.

- iCalendar is an important data exchange standard. There are variant forms that play off of it: hCalendar and parts of the Google Atom format for calendars.

■ ■ ■

## CHAPTER 16

Using Online Storage Services

Amazon S3 and comparable services are intriguing players to recently enter the world of online storage. As we produce more digital content to share, we often need to store that content in a place accessible to others. Moreover, if you are building a service for others to use and need to have access to lots of storage, it's valuable to be able to scale that storage up quickly without lots of upfront capital investment in storage hardware.

Amazon S3 is the poster child in the arena of online storage—and hence is the primary focus of this chapter. I will also cover some other web sites that have similar offerings but with important twists. For instance, some of these services are meant to be used as backup services and not really for serving up digital objects for web applications.

Some of the online storage services have APIs, which makes them highly mashable. They include the following:

- Amazon S3 (http://aws.amazon.com/s3)

- Box.net (http://box.net/) with its API[1]

- MediaMax (http://www.mediamax.com/) with its API[2]

- Omnidrive (http://www.omnidrive.com/) and its API[3]

This chapter shows the basics of using the most well known of the online storage services: Amazon S3.

Introducing Amazon S3

Amazon S3 (the S3 stands for Simple Storage Service) is described in the following way:[4]

> *Amazon S3 provides a simple web services interface that can be used to store and retrieve any amount of data, at any time, from anywhere on the Web. It gives any developer access to the same highly scalable, reliable, fast, inexpensive data storage infrastructure that Amazon uses to run its own global network of web sites.*

---

1. http://enabled.box.net/

2. http://www.mediamax.com/webservices/

3. http://dev.omnidrive.com/HomePage

4. http://aws.amazon.com/s3, which redirects to http://www.amazon.com/gp/browse.html?node=16427261

There is no direct user interface for S3; it is meant as a technical infrastructure upon which developers can build services. The only interface to S3 provided by Amazon.com is a web services API. You can access S3 through its REST or SOAP interface directly or via third-party language-specific API kits that use the REST or SOAP interface. Using the API kits generally makes accessing S3 easier, provided they are well documented and cover the parts of the API that you care about. Sometimes they do not shield you from all the subtleties of the underlying API. For instance, to use the SOAP/WSDL interface to S3, you need to understand how to sign your calls, a topic I will cover briefly in this chapter.

In the following sections, I will guide you through how to get started with Amazon S3, outlining how to use the API and referring you to the API's detailed documentation as appropriate.

Rationale for S3

Why use Amazon S3? Here are some arguments for using S3:

- S3 is potentially cheaper than the alternative solutions. For instance, Don MacAskill, of SmugMug, a photo-hosting service akin to Flickr, estimated that SmugMug saved about $692,000 in 2006 by using S3 instead of buying and maintaining the equivalent amount of storage.[5] (Note that the comparisons might have changed with Amazon.com's new pricing model.[6])

- S3 promises high scalability, both in volume and in the rate of change of storage needs. You "pay as you go" and pay for what you use. That means you don't have to invest up front in buying the maximum amount of storage you think you will need. The utility model lowers the barrier of entry to the level that a relatively poor individual can afford to create a Web 2.0 application.

- Robustness is part of the picture since Amazon.com claims it runs its own infrastructure on S3, and therefore you can expect reliability similar to that of Amazon.com itself.[7]

For specific examples of how S3 is being used, see the following:

- `http://jeremy.zawodny.com/blog/archives/007641.html` for a list of backup services and tools that use S3

- `http://solutions.amazonwebservices.com/connect/kbcategory.jspa?categoryID=66` to see the solutions that developers have already built

Because online storage is accessed through the Internet, latency (and how it will affect your application) is an important factor to consider when looking at S3 and similar services.

---

5. `http://blogs.smugmug.com/don/files/ETech-SmugMug-Amazon-2007.pdf`

6. `http://blogs.smugmug.com/don/2007/05/01/amazon-s3-new-pricing-model/`

7. `http://www.amazon.com/S3-FAQs-AWS-home-page/b/ref=sc_fe_c_0_16427261_9?&node=16427271&no=16427261#as9`

Conceptual Structure of Amazon S3

To get started, read the core concepts documented here:

`http://docs.amazonwebservices.com/AmazonS3/2006-03-01/CoreConcepts.html`

At its heart, S3 is conceptually simple; it lets you store objects in *buckets*. An object is associated with a bucket via a key. There are authentication and authorization schemes associated with S3 to grant you control over access to the buckets and objects. You can associate some amount of metadata (in the form of key-value pairs) with objects.

The following are a few more important points:

- Since a bucket name is global across the S3 service (akin to a domain name), each developer account can have up to 100 buckets at any one time. Bucket names can contain only alphanumeric characters, underscores (_), periods (.), and hyphens (-). They must be between 3 and 255 characters long, and buckets with names containing uppercase characters are not accessible using the virtual hosting method.[8]

- Objects consist of object data and associated metadata. An object can hold up to 5 gigabytes of data.[9]

- A key is like a filename for an object and must be unique within a bucket. Its UTF-8 encoding must be at most 1,024 bytes long.

- You use prefixes and delimiters in keys to simulate a hierarchical (folder within folder-like) organization within buckets.[10] (Buckets cannot contain other buckets.)

- For both REST and SOAP requests to S3, the user metadata size associated with objects is limited to 2,000 bytes. They are structured as key-value pairs.[11]

- There is an authentication and authorization system in place. You can have fine-grained authorization, where you can associate permissions with specific users or with larger preset groups (the owner, everyone, or authenticated users). Permissions are read, write, or full control.[12]

- You can retrieve a `.torrent` file for any publicly available object by adding a `?torrent` query string parameter at the end of the REST GET request for the object.[13]

- There is virtual hosting of buckets that allows one to associate your own non-Amazon.com domain name with an S3 bucket.[14] For example, objects accessible at the following URL:

  `http://s3.amazonaws.com/{bucket}/{key}`

---

8. `http://docs.amazonwebservices.com/AmazonS3/2006-03-01/UsingBucket.html`

9. `http://docs.amazonwebservices.com/AmazonS3/2006-03-01/UsingObjects.html`

10. `http://docs.amazonwebservices.com/AmazonS3/2006-03-01/ListingKeysHierarchy.html`

11. `http://docs.amazonwebservices.com/AmazonS3/2006-03-01/UsingMetadata.html`

12. `http://docs.amazonwebservices.com/AmazonS3/2006-03-01/UsingAccessControl.html`

13. `http://docs.amazonwebservices.com/AmazonS3/2006-03-01/S3TorrentRetrieve.html`

14. `http://docs.amazonwebservices.com/AmazonS3/2006-03-01/VirtualHosting.html`

are also accessible at the following (provided that the bucket name has no uppercase characters):

```
http://{bucket}.s3.amazonaws.com/{key}
```

For example, the following:

```
http://s3.amazonaws.com/raymondyee/858Xtoc___.pdf
```

is accessible here:

```
http://raymondyee.s3.amazonaws.com/858Xtoc___.pdf
```

SIGNING UP FOR AMAZON AWS

You need an Amazon Web Services (AWS) key and secret to use S3. The home page for AWS is here:

```
http://aws.amazon.com
```

You can find the documentation for the e-commerce services part of AWS here:

```
http://www.amazon.com/gp/browse.html?node=12738641
```

You need to sign up for an AWS account to get access keys:

```
http://www.amazon.com/gp/aws/registration/registration-form.html
```

To get your keys if you are already a member, go here:

```
http://aws-➥
portal.amazon.com/gp/aws/developer/account/index.html/?ie=UTF8&action=access-key
```

After you get an access key ID and a secret access key, you can also use an X.509 certificate.

The Firefox S3 Extension Gets You Started with S3

As I have argued throughout the book, it's helpful to learn an application well before diving into its API. That S3 has no built-in user interface means you have to either program S3 yourself right from the start or use someone else's user interface. I recommend installing the S3 Firefox Explorer add-on to get a UI to not only manage your files on S3 but to also learn how S3 works. You can get the extension from here:

```
http://www.rjonna.com/ext/s3fox.php
```

The extension is a great learning tool for S3. Using it, for instance, you can quickly create a bucket and populate that bucket with an object. You can then test the code included in this chapter by reading the list of buckets and what is contained in them. Without a UI tool such as the Firefox extension, you would first have to get your code working to populate the buckets. Figure 16-1 shows the S3 Firefox Explorer add-on. The left panel is an explorer-like interface to your desktop. The right panel shows you your buckets and objects within the folders. You can edit the access control list (ACL) for each object. You can also copy the URL for an object.

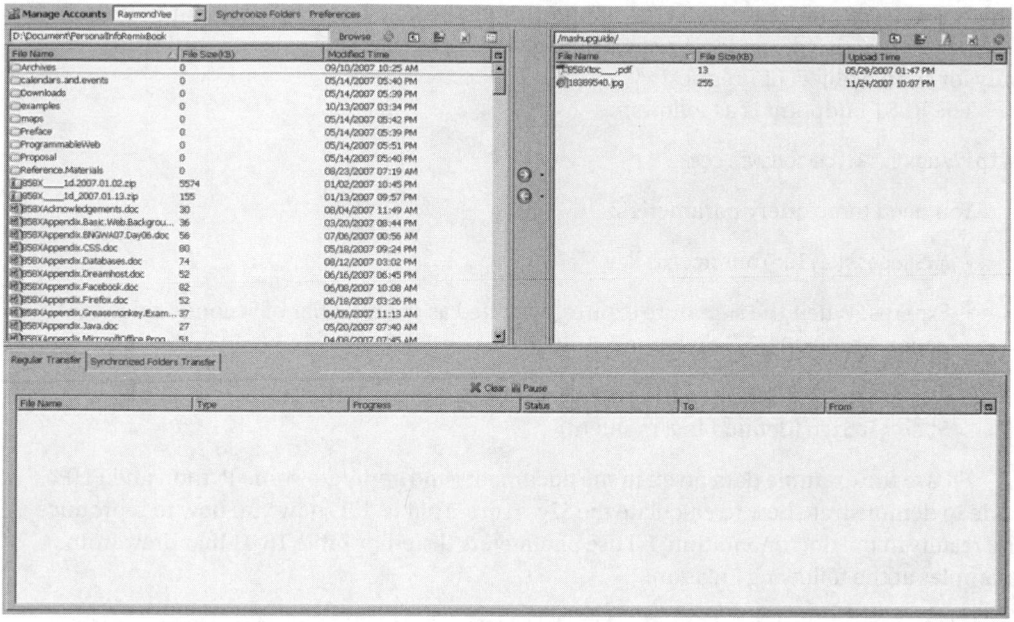

Figure 16-1. *S3 Firefox Explorer add-on*

Similarly, you might want to install S3Drive (http://www.s3drive.net/) on Microsoft Windows to have fairly seamless integration in Windows. The S3Drive service makes S3 look like a partition on a local hard drive.

Using the S3 REST Interface

The S3 REST interface is truly RESTful—you think in terms of resources, such as services (to get a list of all your buckets), buckets, and objects—and they have standard methods. See the following for a list of resources and methods:

http://docs.amazonwebservices.com/AmazonS3/2006-03-01/RESTAPI.html

Using the REST interface is a bit tricky because of the following:

- How authentication is handled, specifically, how the signature is calculated[15]

- The use of authorization control lists to handle authorization[16]

- How metadata is implemented

In this section, I will show one specific, relatively simple GET example to demonstrate how to use the REST interface. Let's first use the query string request authentication alternative,

---

15. http://docs.amazonwebservices.com/AmazonS3/2006-03-01/RESTAuthentication.html

16. http://docs.amazonwebservices.com/AmazonS3/2006-03-01/RESTAccessPolicy.html

which doesn't require the use of HTTP Authorization headers. As the documentation indicates, "The practice of signing a request and giving it to a third-party for execution is suitable only for simple object GET requests."

The REST endpoint is as follows:

```
http://host.s3.amazonaws.com
```

You need three query parameters:

- AWSAccessKeyId: Your access key

- Expires: When the signature expires, specified as the number of seconds since the epoch (00:00:00 UTC on January 1, 1970)

- Signature: The URL encoding of the Base64 encoding of the HMAC-SHA1 of StringToSign (defined in a moment)

I'll use the example data given in the documents and generate some Python and PHP code to demonstrate how to calculate the Signature. That is, I'll show you how to reproduce the results in the documentation. I'll use parameters (listed in Table 16-1) that draw from examples at the following location:

```
http://docs.amazonwebservices.com/AmazonS3/2006-03-01/RESTAuthentication.html
```

The parameters shown here would be used to access the object whose key is photos/puppy.jpg in the bucket named johnsmith. (Note that AWSAccessKeyId and AWSSecretAccessKey are not actually valid keys but are presented to illustrate the calculations.)

Table 16-1. *The Values Used in This Example Calculation for S3 Parameters*

Setting	Value
AWSAccessKeyId	OPN5J17HBGZHT7JJ3X82
AWSSecretAccessKey	uV3F3YluFJax1cknvbcGwgjvx4QpvB+1eU8dUj2o
Expires	1175139620
Host	johnsmith.s3.amazonaws.com
Key	photos/puppy.jpg
HTTP-Verb	GET
Content-MD5	
Content-Type	
CanonicalizedAmzHeaders	
CanonicalizedResource	/johnsmith/photos/puppy.jpg

The pseudo-code for calculating the signature is (quoting from the documentation) as follows:

```
StringToSign = HTTP-VERB + "\n" + Content-MD5 + "\n" + Content-Type + "\n" +
  Expires + "\n" + CanonicalizedAmzHeaders + CanonicalizedResource;
Signature = URL-Encode( Base64( HMAC-SHA1( UTF-8-Encoding-Of( StringToSign ) ) ));
```

We're told that the Signature based on the parameters in Table 16-1 should be rucSbHOyNEcP9oM2XNlouVI3BH4%3D. Let's figure out how we can reproduce this signature in Python and PHP.

First, here is the Python code to calculate the Signature:

```python
import sha, hmac, base64, urllib

AWSAccessKeyId = "0PN5J17HBGZHT7JJ3X82"
AWSSecretAccessKey = "uV3F3YluFJax1cknvbcGwgjvx4QpvB+leU8dUj2o"
Expires = 1175139620
HTTPVerb = "GET"
ContentMD5 = ""
ContentType = ""
CanonicalizedAmzHeaders = ""
CanonicalizedResource = "/johnsmith/photos/puppy.jpg"
string_to_sign = HTTPVerb + "\n" + ContentMD5 + "\n" + ContentType + "\n" + ➥
   str(Expires) + "\n" + CanonicalizedAmzHeaders + CanonicalizedResource
sig = base64.b64encode(➥
         hmac.new(AWSSecretAccessKey, string_to_sign, sha).digest())
print urllib.urlencode({'Signature':sig})
```

This produces the following:

```
Signature=rucSbHOyNEcP9oM2XNlouVI3BH4%3D
```

Here's some corresponding PHP code to calculate the Signature:

```php
<?php

# base64.encodestring
# The hex2b64 function is excerpted from the Amazon S3 PHP example library.
# http://developer.amazonwebservices.com/connect/entry.jspa?externalID=126

    function hex2b64($str) {
      $raw = '';
      for ($i=0; $i < strlen($str); $i+=2) {
        $raw .= chr(hexdec(substr($str, $i, 2)));
      }
      return base64_encode($raw);
    }

    require_once 'Crypt/HMAC.php';
    require_once 'HTTP/Request.php';

    $AWSAccessKeyId = "0PN5J17HBGZHT7JJ3X82";
    $AWSSecretAccessKey = "uV3F3YluFJax1cknvbcGwgjvx4QpvB+leU8dUj2o";
    $Expires = 1175139620;
    $HTTPVerb = "GET";
    $ContentMD5 = "";
```

```php
$ContentType = "";
$CanonicalizedAmzHeaders = "";
$CanonicalizedResource = "/johnsmith/photos/puppy.jpg";
$string_to_sign = $HTTPVerb . "\n" . $ContentMD5 . "\n" . $ContentType . "\n" .
  $Expires . "\n" . $CanonicalizedAmzHeaders . $CanonicalizedResource;

$hasher =& new Crypt_HMAC($AWSSecretAccessKey, "sha1");
$sig = hex2b64($hasher->hash($string_to_sign));
echo 'Signature=',urlencode($sig);

?>
```

Note that this PHP code depends on two PEAR libraries that need to be installed:

- Crypt_HMAC[17]

- HTTP_Request[18]

Unfortunately, after you get those libraries installed, I can't recommend using the S3 sample code on a remote host, because it requires sending the secret over the wire. Run it on your own secure machine.

Once you have calculated the Signature, you can package the corresponding HTTP GET request:

```
http://johnsmith.s3.amazonaws.com/photos/puppy.jpg?AWSAccessKeyId=0PN5J17HBGZHT7JJ3X➥
82&Signature=rucSbHOyNEcP9oM2XNlouVI3BH4%3D&Expires=1175139620
```

Listing Buckets Using the REST Interface

Now that you understand the basics behind signing an Amazon S3 request, I'll show you how to get a list of your S3 buckets. First I'll show the code, and then I'll offer an explanation:

```python
def listBuckets(AWSAccessKeyId,AWSSecretAccessKey):
    """
    use the REST interface to get the list of buckets --
    without the use the Authorization HTTP header
    """
    import sha, hmac, base64, urllib
    import time
    # give an hour for the request to expire (3600s)
    expires = int(time.time()) + 3600
    string_to_sign = "GET\n\n\n%s\n/" % (expires)
    sig = base64.b64encode(➥
      hmac.new(AWSSecretAccessKey, string_to_sign, sha).digest())
```

---

17. http://pear.php.net/package/Crypt_HMAC

18. http://pear.php.net/package/HTTP_Request

```
    request = "http://s3.amazonaws.com?AWSAccessKeyId=%s&Expires=%s&%s" % \
              (AWSAccessKeyId, expires, urllib.urlencode({'Signature':sig}))
    return request


if __name__ == "__main__":
    AWSAccessKeyId='[AWSAccessKeyID]'
    AWSSecretAccessKey = '[SecretAccessKey]'
    print listBuckets(AWSAccessKeyId,AWSSecretAccessKey)
```

This code generates a URL of the following form that returns a list of buckets:

```
http://s3.amazonaws.com?AWSAccessKeyId={AWSAccessKeyId}&Expires=1196114919➥
&Signature={Signature}
```

Note how we use some of the same parameters as in the previous example (AWSAccessKeyId, AWSSecretAccessKey, and Expires) and calculate the Signature with the same combination of SHA-1 hashing and Base64 encoding.

Using the SOAP Interface to S3

The following code sample illustrates how to use the SOAP interface to S3:

```
import sha, hmac, base64, urllib

# list buckets for Amazon s3

AWSAccessKeyId='[AWSAccessKeyID]'
AWSSecretAccessKey = '[AWSSecretAccessKey]'

from SOAPpy import WSDL

import sha

def calcSig(key,text):
    import hmac, base64
    sig = base64.b64encode(hmac.new(key, text, sha).digest())
    return sig

def ListMyBuckets(s):
    from time import gmtime,strftime
    method = 'ListAllMyBuckets'
    ts = strftime("%Y-%m-%dT%H:%M:%S.000Z", gmtime())
    text = 'AmazonS3' + method + ts
    sig = calcSig(AWSSecretAccessKey,text)
    print "ListMyBuckets: ts,text,sig->", ts, text, sig
    return s.ListAllMyBuckets(AWSAccessKeyId=AWSAccessKeyId, ➥
Timestamp=ts,Signature=sig)
```

```
def CreateBucket(s, bucketName):
    from time import gmtime,strftime
    method = 'CreateBucket'
    print 'method: ', method
    ts = strftime("%Y-%m-%dT%H:%M:%S.000Z", gmtime())
    text = 'AmazonS3' + method + ts
    sig = calcSig(AWSSecretAccessKey,text)
    print "CreateBuckets: ts,text,sig->", ts, text, sig
    return s.CreateBucket(Bucket=bucketName, AWSAccessKeyId=AWSAccessKeyId, ➥
Timestamp=ts,Signature=sig)

if __name__ == '__main__':
    s = WSDL.Proxy("http://s3.amazonaws.com/doc/2006-03-01/AmazonS3.wsdl")
    print ListMyBuckets(s)
    CreateBucket(s,"test20071126RY")
    print ListMyBuckets(s)
```

You can learn the following about S3 from this code:

- As with the REST interface, you need to have an Amazon.com AWS access key ID and secret access key, which you can get if you sign up for an account at AWS (see Chapter 7 or the "Signing Up for Amazon AWS" sidebar earlier in this chapter for more details).

- Although S3 is accessible by the REST and SOAP interfaces, this code uses SOAP and WSDL. The WSDL for the service at the time of writing is at http://s3.amazonaws.com/doc/2006-03-01/AmazonS3.wsdl; you can get the location of the latest WSDL URL at http://aws.amazon.com/s3.

- Two methods are used in this code sample: ListMyBuckets and CreateBuckets. You can get the list of all the methods at http://www.awszone.com/scratchpads/aws/s3.us/index.aws (the technical documentation is at http://developer.amazonwebservices.com/connect/kbcategory.jspa?categoryID=48, which leads to http://docs.amazonwebservices.com/AmazonS3/2006-03-01/).

- Note that one of the complicated aspects is to calculate a signature, something you learned to do in the previous section.

Amazon S3 API Kits

In the following sections, you'll look at some libraries to S3 written in PHP and Python.

PHP

The following API kits are available:

- php-aws[19]

- s3.class.zip at Neurofuzzy.net, which looks like a popular class implementation[20]

- edoceo's phps3tk[21]

In this section, we'll concentrate on how to use php-aws. You can access the source using SVN. In your web browser, you can download the library from here:

http://php-aws.googlecode.com/svn/trunk/class.s3.php

You can find documentation for the S3 class here:

http://code.google.com/p/php-aws/wiki/S3Class

The following blog entry introduces php-aws:

http://sitening.com/blog/2007/01/30/introducing-php-aws/

Note the following about this library:

- Its use of curl means it is built to handle larger files.

- Only the public read or private ACL is currently implemented.

- There is no implementation of user metadata for objects.

To get started with php-aws, follow these steps:

1. Download http://php-aws.googlecode.com/svn/trunk/class.s3.php to your favorite local PHP directory. (In my case, this is /home/rdhyee/phplib/php-aws/class.s3.php.)

2. Try the following sample code to get you started (this code first lists your S3 buckets and then creates a bucket by the name of mashupguidetest if it doesn't already exist):

```php
<?php
require_once("php-aws/class.s3.php");

$key = "[AWSAccessKeyID]";
$secret = "[SecretAccessKey]";

$s3 = new S3($key,$secret);
```

---

19. http://code.google.com/p/php-aws/ and specifically http://php-aws.googlecode.com/svn/trunk/class.s3.php

20. http://neurofuzzy.net/2006/08/26/amazon-s3-php-class-update/ and http://www.neurofuzzy.net/wp-content/2006/03/s3.class.zip

21. http://www.edoceo.com/creo/phps3tk/

```
// get list of buckets
$buckets = $s3->getBuckets();
print_r($buckets);

// if the bucket "mashupguidetest" doesn't exist, create it
$BNAME = "mashupguidetest";
if (! $s3->bucketExists($BNAME)) {
  $s3->createBucket($BNAME);
}

// get list of buckets again
$buckets = $s3->getBuckets();
print_r($buckets);
```

■**Note** For you to use `php-aws`, you need to have a command-line invokable instance of `curl` installed on your system. You might also need to set the `$_pathToCurl` parameter in `class.s3.php` so that `php-aws` can find `curl`.

Python

Some Python-based S3 libraries are as follows:

- boto[22]

- HanzoiArchive's S3 tools[23]

- BitBucket[24]

I recommend looking at `boto` as a good choice of a library. One of the best ways to learn how to use `boto` is to read the tutorial here:

`http://boto.googlecode.com/svn/trunk/doc/s3_tut.txt`

You can learn the basics of using `boto` by studying the next code sample, which does the following:

- It reads the list of your S3 buckets and displays the name, creation date, and XML representation of the bucket's ACL.

- It reads the list of objects contained in a specific bucket, along with the last modified time stamp and the object's metadata.

- It uploads a file to a bucket and reads back the metadata of the newly uploaded file.

---

22. `http://code.google.com/p/boto/`

23. `http://www.hanzoarchives.com/development-projects/s3-tools/`

24. `http://cheeseshop.python.org/pypi/BitBucket/0.4a`

```python
AWSAccessKeyId='[AWSAccessKeyId]'
AWSSecretAccessKey = '[AWSSecretAccessKey]'
FILENAME = 'D:\Document\PersonalInfoRemixBook\858Xtoc___.pdf'
BUCKET = 'mashupguidetest'

from boto.s3.connection import S3Connection

def upload_file(fname, bucket, key, acl='public-read', metadata=None):
    from boto.s3.key import Key

    fpic = Key(bucket)
    fpic.key = key
    #fpic.set_metadata('source','flickr')
    fpic.update_metadata(metadata)
    fpic.set_contents_from_filename(fname)
    fpic.set_acl(acl)
    return fpic

# set up a connection to S3

conn = S3Connection(AWSAccessKeyId, AWSSecretAccessKey)

# retrieve all the buckets
buckets = conn.get_all_buckets()
print "number of buckets:", len(buckets)

# print out the names, creation date, and the XML the represents the ACL
# of the bucket

for b in buckets:
    print "%s\t%s\t%s" % (b.name, b.creation_date, b.get_acl().acl.to_xml())

# get list of all files for the mashupguide bucket

print "keys in " + BUCKETmg_bucket = conn.get_bucket(BUCKET)
keys = mg_bucket.get_all_keys()
for key in keys:
    print "%s\t%s\t%s" % (key.name, key.last_modified, key.metadata)

# upload the table of contents to mashupguide bucket.

metadata = {'author':'Raymond Yee'}
upload_file(FILENAME,mg_bucket,'samplefile','public-read',metadata)

# read back the TOC
toc = mg_bucket.get_key('samplefile')
print toc.metadata
```

Summary

From reading this chapter, you should now know how to get started with the Amazon S3 API using PHP and Python. The APIs for other online storage systems are different but will have some conceptual similarity to S3.

## CHAPTER 17

Mashing Up Desktop and Web-Based Office Suites

I've long been excited about the mashability and reusability of office suite documents (for example, word processor documents, spreadsheets, and slide presentations), the potential of which has gone largely unexploited. There are many office suites, but in this chapter I'll concentrate on the latest versions of OpenOffice.org, often called OO.o (version 2.*x*), and Microsoft Office (2007 and 2003). Few people realize that both these applications not only have programming interfaces but also have XML-based file formats. In theory, office documents using the respective file formats (OpenDocument and Office Open XML) are easier to reuse and generate from scratch than older generations of documents using opaque binary formats. And as you have seen throughout the book, knowledge of data formats and APIs means having opportunities for mashups. For ages, people have been reverse engineering older Microsoft Office documents, whose formats were not publicly documented; however, recombining office suites has been made easier, though not effortless, by these new formats. In this chapter, I will also introduce you to the emerging space of web-based office suites, specifically ones that are programmable. I'll also briefly cover how to program the office suites.

This chapter does the following:

- Shows how to do some simple parsing of the OpenDocument format (ODF) and Office Open XML documents

- Shows how to create a simple document in both ODF and Open XML

- Demonstrates some simple scripting of OO.o and Microsoft Office

- Lays out what else is possible by manipulating the open document formats

- Shows how to program Google Spreadsheets and to mash it up with other APIs (such as Amazon E-Commerce Services)

Mashup Scenarios for Office Suites

Why would mashups of office suite documents be interesting? For one, word processing documents, spreadsheets, and even presentation files hold vast amounts of the information that we communicate to each other. Sometimes they are in narratives (such as documents), and sometimes they are in semistructured forms (such as spreadsheets). To reuse that information, it is sometimes a matter of reformatting a document into another format. Other times, it's about extracting valuable pieces; for instance, all the references in a word processor document might be extracted into a reference database. Furthermore, not only does knowledge of the file formats enable you to parse documents, but it allows you to generate documents.

Some use case scenarios for the programmatic creation and reuse of office documents include the following:

Reusing PowerPoint: Do you have collections of Microsoft PowerPoint presentations that draw from a common collection of digital assets (pictures and outlines) and complete slides? Can you build a system of personal information management so that PPT presentations are constructed as virtual assemblages of slides, dynamically associated with assets?

Writing once, publishing everywhere: I'm currently writing this manuscript in Microsoft Office 2007. I'd like to republish this book in (X)HTML, Docbook, PDF, and wiki markup. How would I repurpose the Microsoft Word manuscript into those formats?

Transforming data: You could create an educational website in which data is downloaded to spreadsheets, not only as static data elements but as dynamic simulations. There's plenty of data out there. Can you write programs to translate it into the dominant data analysis tool used by everyone, which is spreadsheets, whether it is on the desktop or in the cloud?

Getting instant PowerPoint presentations from Flickr: I'd like to download a Flickr set as a PowerPoint presentation. (This scenario seems to fit a world in which PowerPoint is the dominant presentation program. Even if Tufte hates it, a Flickr-to-PPT translator might make it easier to show those vacation pictures at your next company presentation.)

There are many other possibilities. This chapter teaches you what you need to know to start building such applications.

The World of Document Markup

This chapter focuses on XML-based document markup languages in two dominant groups of office suites: Microsoft Office 2007 and OpenOffice.org. There are plenty of other markup languages, which are covered well on Wikipedia:

- http://en.wikipedia.org/wiki/Document_markup_language

- http://en.wikipedia.org/wiki/List_of_document_markup_languages

- http://en.wikipedia.org/wiki/Comparison_of_document_markup_languages

The OpenDocument Format

ODF is "an open XML-based document file format for office applications to be used for documents containing text, spreadsheets, charts, and graphical elements," developed under the auspices of

OASIS.[1] ODF is also an ISO/IEC standard (ISO/IEC 206300:2006).[2] ODF is used most prominently in OpenOffice.org (http://www.openoffice.org/) and KOffice (http://www.koffice.org/), among other office suites. For a good overview of the file format, consult J. David Eisenberg's excellent book on ODF, called *OASIS OpenDocument Essentials*, which is available for download as a PDF (free of charge) or for purchase.[3]

The goal of this section is to introduce you to the issues of parsing and creating ODF files programmatically.

■**Note** For this section, I am assuming you have OpenOffice.org version 2.2 installed.

A good way to understand the essentials of the file format is to create a simple instance of an ODF file and then analyze it:

1. Fire up OpenOffice.org Writer, type **Hello World**, and save the file as helloworld.odt.[4]

2. Open the file in a ZIP utility (such as WinZip on the PC). One easy way to do so is to change the file extension from .odt to .zip so that the operating system will recognize it as a ZIP file. You will see that it's actually a ZIP-format file when you go to unzip it. (See the list of files in Figure 17-1.)

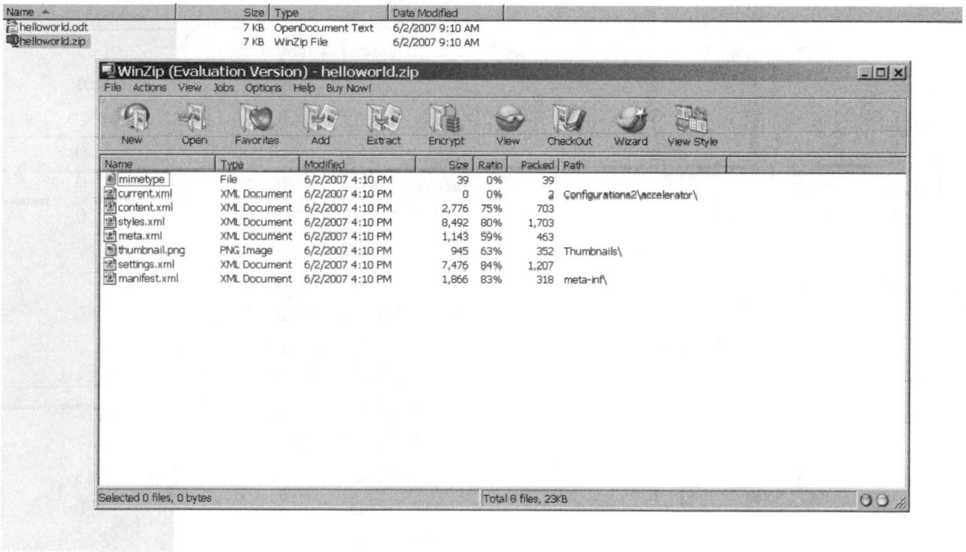

Figure 17-1. *Unzipping* helloworld.zip. *An OpenDocument file produced by OpenOffice.org is actually in the ZIP format.*

---

1. http://www.oasis-open.org/committees/office/

2. http://www.iso.org/iso/iso_catalogue/catalogue_tc/catalogue_detail.htm?csnumber=43485

3. http://books.evc-cit.info/OD_Essentials.pdf or
   http://develop.opendocumentfellowship.com/book/

4. http://examples.mashupguide.net/ch17/helloworld.odt

You'll see some of the files that can be part of an ODF file:

- `content.xml`

- `styles.xml`

- `meta.xml`

- `settings.xml`

- `META-INF/manifest.xml`

- `mimetype`

- `Configuration2/accelerator/`

- `Thumbnails/thumbnail.png`

You can also use your favorite programming language, such as Python or PHP, to generate a list of the files. The following is a Python example:

```python
import zipfile
z = zipfile.ZipFile(r'[path_to_your_file_here]')
z.printdir()
```

This generates the following:

File Name	Modified	Size
mimetype	2007-06-02 16:10:18	39
Configurations2/statusbar/	2007-06-02 16:10:18	0
Configurations2/accelerator/current.xml	2007-06-02 16:10:18	0
Configurations2/floater/	2007-06-02 16:10:18	0
Configurations2/popupmenu/	2007-06-02 16:10:18	0
Configurations2/progressbar/	2007-06-02 16:10:18	0
Configurations2/menubar/	2007-06-02 16:10:18	0
Configurations2/toolbar/	2007-06-02 16:10:18	0
Configurations2/images/Bitmaps/	2007-06-02 16:10:18	0
content.xml	2007-06-02 16:10:18	2776
styles.xml	2007-06-02 16:10:18	8492
meta.xml	2007-06-02 16:10:18	1143
Thumbnails/thumbnail.png	2007-06-02 16:10:18	945
settings.xml	2007-06-02 16:10:18	7476
META-INF/manifest.xml	2007-06-02 16:10:18	1866

You can get the equivalent functionality in PHP with the PHP `zip` library (see http://us2.php.net/zip):

```php
<?php

$zip = zip_open('[path_to_your_file]');
while ($entry = zip_read($zip)) {
  print zip_entry_name($entry) . "\t". zip_entry_filesize($entry). "\n";
```

```
}
zip_close($zip);
?>
```

This produces the following:

mimetype	39
Configurations2/statusbar/	0
Configurations2/accelerator/current.xml	0
Configurations2/floater/	0
Configurations2/popupmenu/	0
Configurations2/progressbar/	0
Configurations2/menubar/	0
Configurations2/toolbar/	0
Configurations2/images/Bitmaps/	0
content.xml	2776
styles.xml	8492
meta.xml	1143
Thumbnails/thumbnail.png	945
settings.xml	7476
META-INF/manifest.xml	1866

Generating a simple ODF file using OpenOffice.org gives you a basic file from which you can build. However, it's useful to boil the file down even further because even the simple ODF generated by OO.o contains features that make it difficult to see what's happening. Let's pare down the "Hello World" ODF document further.

There are at least two ways to figure out a minimalist instance of an ODF document. One is to consult the ODF specification, specifically the ODF schema, to generate a small instance. OO.o 2.2 uses the ODF 1.0 specification.[5] The specification contains a RELAX NG schema for ODF. RELAX NG (http://relaxng.org/) is a schema language for XML. That is, you can use RELAX NG to specify what elements and attributes can be used in ODF—and in what combination.

Schemas, stemming from the http://oasis-open.org page, include the following:

- The schema for office documents, "extracted from chapter 1 to 16 of the specification" —Version 1.0[6]

- "The normative schema for the manifest file used by the OpenDocument package format" —Version 1.0[7]

- "The strict schema for office documents that permits only meta information and formatting properties contained in this specification itself" —Version 1.0[8]

---

5. http://www.oasis-open.org/committees/tc_home.php?wg_abbrev=office

6. http://www.oasis-open.org/committees/download.php/12571/OpenDocument-schema-v1.0-os.rng

7. http://www.oasis-open.org/committees/download.php/12570/OpenDocument-manifest-schema-v1.0-os.rng

8. http://www.oasis-open.org/committees/download.php/12569/OpenDocument-strict-schema-v1.0-os.rng

Instead of taking this approach here, I will instead show you how to use OO.o and the online ODF Validator (http://opendocumentfellowship.com/validator). The basic approach is to use a bit of trial and error to generate an ODF file and add pieces while feeding it to the ODF Validator to see how far you can distill the file. Why should you care about minimal instances of ODF (and later OOXML) documents? ODF and OOXML are complicated markup formats. One of the best ways to figure out how to create formats is to use a tool such as OO.o or Microsoft Office to generate what you want, save the file, unzip the file, extract the section of the document you want, and plug that stuff into a minimalist document that you know is valid. That's why you're learning about boiling ODF down to its essence.

The ODF specification (and its RELAX NG schema) should tell you theoretically how to find a valid ODF instance—but in practice, you need to actually feed a given instance to the applications that are the destinations for the ODF documents. OpenOffice.org is currently the most important implementation of an office suite that interprets ODF, making it a good place to experiment.

J. David Eisenberg's excellent book on ODF, *OASIS OpenDocument Essentials*, provides an answer to the question of which files are actually required by OO.o:

> *The only files that are actually necessary are content.xml and the META-INF/manifest.xml file. If you create a file that contains word processor elements and zip it up and a manifest that points to that file, OpenOffice.org will be able to open it successfully. The result will be a plain text-only document with no styles. You won't have any of the meta-information about who created the file or when it was last edited, and the printer settings, view area, and zoom factor will be set to the OpenOffice.org defaults.*

Let's verify Eisenberg's assertion. Create an `.odt` file with the same `content.xml` as `helloworld.odt`, listed here:

```
<?xml version="1.0" encoding="UTF-8"?>
<office:document-content
  xmlns:office="urn:oasis:names:tc:opendocument:xmlns:office:1.0"
  xmlns:style="urn:oasis:names:tc:opendocument:xmlns:style:1.0"
  xmlns:text="urn:oasis:names:tc:opendocument:xmlns:text:1.0"
  xmlns:table="urn:oasis:names:tc:opendocument:xmlns:table:1.0"
  xmlns:draw="urn:oasis:names:tc:opendocument:xmlns:drawing:1.0"
  xmlns:fo="urn:oasis:names:tc:opendocument:xmlns:xsl-fo-compatible:1.0"
  xmlns:xlink="http://www.w3.org/1999/xlink"
  xmlns:dc="http://purl.org/dc/elements/1.1/"
  xmlns:meta="urn:oasis:names:tc:opendocument:xmlns:meta:1.0"
  xmlns:number="urn:oasis:names:tc:opendocument:xmlns:datastyle:1.0"
  xmlns:svg="urn:oasis:names:tc:opendocument:xmlns:svg-compatible:1.0"
  xmlns:chart="urn:oasis:names:tc:opendocument:xmlns:chart:1.0"
  xmlns:dr3d="urn:oasis:names:tc:opendocument:xmlns:dr3d:1.0"
  xmlns:math="http://www.w3.org/1998/Math/MathML"
  xmlns:form="urn:oasis:names:tc:opendocument:xmlns:form:1.0"
  xmlns:script="urn:oasis:names:tc:opendocument:xmlns:script:1.0"
  xmlns:ooo="http://openoffice.org/2004/office"
  xmlns:ooow="http://openoffice.org/2004/writer"
```

```
    xmlns:oooc="http://openoffice.org/2004/calc"
    xmlns:dom="http://www.w3.org/2001/xml-events"
    xmlns:xforms="http://www.w3.org/2002/xforms"
    xmlns:xsd="http://www.w3.org/2001/XMLSchema"
    xmlns:xsi="http://www.w3.org/2001/XMLSchema-instance" office:version="1.0">
    <office:scripts/>
    <office:font-face-decls>
      <style:font-face style:name="Tahoma1" svg:font-family="Tahoma"/>
      <style:font-face style:name="Times New Roman"
        svg:font-family="&apos;Times New Roman&apos;"
        style:font-family-generic="roman"
        style:font-pitch="variable"/>
      <style:font-face style:name="Arial" svg:font-family="Arial"
        style:font-family-generic="swiss"
        style:font-pitch="variable"/>
      <style:font-face style:name="Arial Unicode MS"
        svg:font-family="&apos;Arial Unicode MS&apos;"
        style:font-family-generic="system"
        style:font-pitch="variable"/>
      <style:font-face style:name="MS Mincho" svg:font-family="&apos;MS Mincho&apos;"
        style:font-family-generic="system" style:font-pitch="variable"/>
      <style:font-face style:name="Tahoma" svg:font-family="Tahoma"
        style:font-family-generic="system"
        style:font-pitch="variable"/>
    </office:font-face-decls>
    <office:automatic-styles/>
    <office:body>
      <office:text>
        <office:forms form:automatic-focus="false" form:apply-design-mode="false"/>
        <text:sequence-decls>
          <text:sequence-decl text:display-outline-level="0"
            text:name="Illustration"/>
          <text:sequence-decl text:display-outline-level="0" text:name="Table"/>
          <text:sequence-decl text:display-outline-level="0" text:name="Text"/>
          <text:sequence-decl text:display-outline-level="0" text:name="Drawing"/>
        </text:sequence-decls>
        <text:p text:style-name="Standard">Hello World!</text:p>
      </office:text>
    </office:body>
</office:document-content>
```

Now edit `META-INF/metadata.xml` to reference only `content.xml` and the `META-INF` directory:

```
<?xml version="1.0" encoding="UTF-8"?>
<manifest:manifest
    xmlns:manifest="urn:oasis:names:tc:opendocument:xmlns:manifest:1.0">
  <manifest:file-entry manifest:media-type="application/vnd.oasis.opendocument.text"
                       manifest:full-path="/"/>
```

```
<manifest:file-entry manifest:media-type="text/xml"
                      manifest:full-path="content.xml"/>
</manifest:manifest>
```

This leaves you with an `.odt` file that consists of only those two files.[9] You will find that such a file will load successfully in OpenOffice.org 2.2 and the OpenDocument Viewer[10]— giving credence to the assertion that, in OO.o 2.2 at least, you don't need any more than `content.xml` and `META-INF/manifest.xml`.

■**Note** You can download and install the OpenDocument Validator[11] or run the online version.[12]

Nonetheless, the OpenDocument Validator doesn't find the file to be valid; it produces the following error message:

```
1. warning
   does not contain a /mimetype file. This is a SHOULD in OpenDocument 1.0
2. error
   styles.xml is missing
3. error
   settings.xml is missing
4. error
   meta.xml is missing
```

Since the OpenDocument Validator dies on one of the Fellowship's test files,[13] you can see there are some unresolved problems with the validator or the test files produced by the OpenDocument Fellowship. Although there is nothing wrong with our minimalist file, it's a good idea to use a file that has all the major pieces in place.

If you insert skeletal `styles.xml`, `settings.xml`, and `meta.xml` files, you can convince the OpenDocument Validator to accept the resulting `.odt` file as a valid document. Furthermore, you can strip `content.xml` of extraneous declarations. (Strictly speaking, the namespace declarations are extraneous, but they are useful to have once you start plugging in chunks of ODF.) The resulting ODF text document is what you find here:

```
http://examples.mashupguide.net/ch17/helloworld_min_odt_2.odt
```

---

9. http://examples.mashupguide.net/ch17/helloworld_min_odt_1.odt

10. http://opendocumentfellowship.com/odfviewer

11. http://opendocumentfellowship.com/projects/odftools

12. http://opendocumentfellowship.com/validator

13. http://testsuite.opendocumentfellowship.com/testcases/General/DocumentStructure/
    SingleDocumentContents/testDoc/testDoc.odt via http://testsuite.opendocumentfellowship.com/
    testcases/General/DocumentStructure/SingleDocumentContents/TestCase.html

Here are the constituent files:

```
<!-- meta.xml -->

<?xml version="1.0" ?>
<office:document-meta office:version="1.0"
  xmlns:dc="http://purl.org/dc/elements/1.1/"
  xmlns:meta="urn:oasis:names:tc:opendocument:xmlns:meta:1.0"
  xmlns:office="urn:oasis:names:tc:opendocument:xmlns:office:1.0"
  xmlns:ooo="http://openoffice.org/2004/office"
  xmlns:xlink="http://www.w3.org/1999/xlink"/>

<!-- settings.xml -->
<?xml version="1.0" ?>
<office:document-settings office:version="1.0"
  xmlns:config="urn:oasis:names:tc:opendocument:xmlns:config:1.0"
  xmlns:office="urn:oasis:names:tc:opendocument:xmlns:office:1.0"
  xmlns:ooo="http://openoffice.org/2004/office"
  xmlns:xlink="http://www.w3.org/1999/xlink" />

<!-- styles.xml -->
<?xml version="1.0" ?>
<office:document-styles office:version="1.0"
  xmlns:chart="urn:oasis:names:tc:opendocument:xmlns:chart:1.0"
  xmlns:dc="http://purl.org/dc/elements/1.1/"
  xmlns:dom="http://www.w3.org/2001/xml-events"
  xmlns:dr3d="urn:oasis:names:tc:opendocument:xmlns:dr3d:1.0"
  xmlns:draw="urn:oasis:names:tc:opendocument:xmlns:drawing:1.0"
  xmlns:fo="urn:oasis:names:tc:opendocument:xmlns:xsl-fo-compatible:1.0"
  xmlns:form="urn:oasis:names:tc:opendocument:xmlns:form:1.0"
  xmlns:math="http://www.w3.org/1998/Math/MathML"
  xmlns:meta="urn:oasis:names:tc:opendocument:xmlns:meta:1.0"
  xmlns:number="urn:oasis:names:tc:opendocument:xmlns:datastyle:1.0"
  xmlns:office="urn:oasis:names:tc:opendocument:xmlns:office:1.0"
  xmlns:ooo="http://openoffice.org/2004/office"
  xmlns:oooc="http://openoffice.org/2004/calc"
  xmlns:ooow="http://openoffice.org/2004/writer"
  xmlns:script="urn:oasis:names:tc:opendocument:xmlns:script:1.0"
  xmlns:style="urn:oasis:names:tc:opendocument:xmlns:style:1.0"
  xmlns:svg="urn:oasis:names:tc:opendocument:xmlns:svg-compatible:1.0"
  xmlns:table="urn:oasis:names:tc:opendocument:xmlns:table:1.0"
  xmlns:text="urn:oasis:names:tc:opendocument:xmlns:text:1.0"
  xmlns:xlink="http://www.w3.org/1999/xlink" />

<!-- content.xml -->
<?xml version="1.0" ?>
<office:document-content office:version="1.0"
  xmlns:chart="urn:oasis:names:tc:opendocument:xmlns:chart:1.0"
```

```
    xmlns:dc="http://purl.org/dc/elements/1.1/"
    xmlns:dom="http://www.w3.org/2001/xml-events"
    xmlns:dr3d="urn:oasis:names:tc:opendocument:xmlns:dr3d:1.0"
    xmlns:draw="urn:oasis:names:tc:opendocument:xmlns:drawing:1.0"
    xmlns:fo="urn:oasis:names:tc:opendocument:xmlns:xsl-fo-compatible:1.0"
    xmlns:form="urn:oasis:names:tc:opendocument:xmlns:form:1.0"
    xmlns:math="http://www.w3.org/1998/Math/MathML"
    xmlns:meta="urn:oasis:names:tc:opendocument:xmlns:meta:1.0"
    xmlns:number="urn:oasis:names:tc:opendocument:xmlns:datastyle:1.0"
    xmlns:office="urn:oasis:names:tc:opendocument:xmlns:office:1.0"
    xmlns:ooo="http://openoffice.org/2004/office"
    xmlns:oooc="http://openoffice.org/2004/calc"
    xmlns:ooow="http://openoffice.org/2004/writer"
    xmlns:script="urn:oasis:names:tc:opendocument:xmlns:script:1.0"
    xmlns:style="urn:oasis:names:tc:opendocument:xmlns:style:1.0"
    xmlns:svg="urn:oasis:names:tc:opendocument:xmlns:svg-compatible:1.0"
    xmlns:table="urn:oasis:names:tc:opendocument:xmlns:table:1.0"
    xmlns:text="urn:oasis:names:tc:opendocument:xmlns:text:1.0"
    xmlns:xforms="http://www.w3.org/2002/xforms"
    xmlns:xlink="http://www.w3.org/1999/xlink"
    xmlns:xsd="http://www.w3.org/2001/XMLSchema"
    xmlns:xsi="http://www.w3.org/2001/XMLSchema-instance">
    <office:body>
      <office:text>
        <text:p>
          Hello World!
        </text:p>
      </office:text>
    </office:body>
</office:document-content>

<!-- manifest.xml -->
<?xml version="1.0" encoding="UTF-8"?>
<manifest:manifest
    xmlns:manifest="urn:oasis:names:tc:opendocument:xmlns:manifest:1.0">
  <manifest:file-entry manifest:media-type="application/vnd.oasis.opendocument.text"
                       manifest:full-path="/"/>
  <manifest:file-entry manifest:media-type="text/xml"
                       manifest:full-path="content.xml"/>
  <manifest:file-entry manifest:media-type="text/xml"
                       manifest:full-path="meta.xml"/>
```

```
<manifest:file-entry manifest:media-type="text/xml"
                     manifest:full-path="settings.xml"/>
<manifest:file-entry manifest:media-type="text/xml"
                     manifest:full-path="styles.xml"/>
</manifest:manifest>
```

You now have a *minimalist* and *valid* ODF document.

As an exercise to the reader, I'll leave it to you to generate minimal instances of the spreadsheet (.ods), presentation (.odp), graphics (.odg), and math (.odf) documents. In the rest of the chapter, I'll continue to focus on the text documents (.odt)—but what you learn from it applies to the other ODF formats as well.

Learning Basic ODF Tags

With a minimalist ODF text document in hand, let's look at how to generate a small example document that illustrates some of the basic features of ODF. Here we can consult Eisenberg once again on how to proceed:

> *Just start OpenOffice.org or KOffice, create a document that has the feature you want, unpack the file, and look for the XML that implements it. To get a better understanding of how things works, change the XML, repack the document, and reload it. Once you know how a feature works, don't hesitate to copy and paste the XML from the OpenDocument file into your program. In other words, cheat. It worked for me when I was writing this book, and it can work for you too!*

In this section, I'll walk you through how to create the ODF text document (see Figure 17-2) in steps here:

```
http://examples.mashupguide.net/ch17/odt_example_4.odt
```

You can study the parts of this document by downloading and unzipping it or by looking at the files here:

```
http://examples.mashupguide.net/ch17/odt_example_4/
```

Purpose (Heading 1)

The following sections illustrate various possibilities in ODF Text.

A simple series of paragraphs (Heading 2)

This section contains a series of paragraphs.

This is a second paragraph.

And a third paragraph.

A section with lists (Heading 2)

Elements to illustrate:

- hyperlinks
- italics and bold text
- lists (ordered and unordered)

How to figure out ODF

1. work out the content.xml tags
2. work styles into the mix
3. figure out how to apply what we learned to spreadsheets and presentations

The *URL* for Flickr is http://www.flickr.com. The **API page** is http://www.flickr.com/services/api/

A Table (Heading 1)

Website	Description	URL
Flickr	A social photo sharing site	http://www.flickr.com
Google Maps	An online map	http://maps.google.com

Footnotes (Heading 1)

This sentence has an accompanying footnote. Where does the text after a footnote go?

An Image

Figure 17-2. *The culminating ODF text document generated in this chapter*

I will show you how I took the approach advocated by Eisenberg to construct this document. I added a new element in an ODT, unzipped the file, found the corresponding XML fragment, took that fragment, and added it to the document I was building. I consciously stripped out any references to styles to focus first on content. And then I applied styles to achieve the effects I want. I will leave it to you to take this approach on spreadsheets and presentations; the ODF for those files formats have a similar framework as the text documents.

This example text contains some common elements:

- Headings of level 1 and 2
- Several paragraphs
- An ordered and unordered list
- Text that has some italics and bold and a font change
- A table
- An image

I'll show how to build this document in four steps to highlight what's involved in constructing a nontrivial ODF document:

1. Create an ODF text document without any styling of ODF elements.

2. Set the style of the paragraph text.

3. Format lists to distinguish between ordered and unordered lists.

4. Get bold, italics, font changes, and color changes into text spans.

Create an ODF Text Document Without Any Styling of ODF Elements

The first step is to create a document while purposefully eliminating any use of styling. This will let us focus on content-oriented tags, much like studying HTML first without CSS and then applying CSS. When studying ODF (and later Office Open XML), it's useful to keep in mind analogous constructs from HTML and CSS.

When you create an ODF text document with headers, paragraphs, lists, and the other features listed earlier and strip out the style, you get something like this:

```
http://examples.mashupguide.net/ch17/odt_example_1.odt
```

whose constituent files (once you unzip the document) are here:

```
http://examples.mashupguide.net/ch17/odt_example_1/
```

Not surprisingly, most of the action is in content.xml:

```
http://examples.mashupguide.net/ch17/odt_example_1/content.xml
```

Remember the overall structure of content.xml, a framework in which you can plug in the ODF tags representing various elements:

```
<?xml version="1.0" ?>
<!-- the namespace declarations of office:document-content are omitted -->
<office:document-content>
  <office:body>
    <office:text>
[INSERT CONTENT HERE]
    </office:text>
  </office:body>
</office:document-content>
```

Headers and Paragraphs

There are headers and paragraphs as in HTML—but in HTML, you have h1, h2, . . . , h6. With ODF, you use <text:h> with text:outline-level to indicate the level of the header. For paragraphs in ODF, you use the <text:p> element. Note the text: namespace:

```
urn:oasis:names:tc:opendocument:xmlns:text:1.0
```

Here's some ODF you can plug in to create two headers (one of level 1 and the other of level 2) along with a series of paragraphs:

```
<text:h text:outline-level="1">Purpose (Heading 1)</text:h>
<text:p>The following sections illustrate various possibilities in ODF Text.
</text:p>
<text:h text:outline-level="2">A simple series of paragraphs (Heading 2)</text:h>
<text:p>This section contains a series of paragraphs.</text:p>
<text:p>This is a second paragraph.</text:p>
<text:p>And a third paragraph.</text:p>
```

Lists

The following ODF markup creates two lists. The first one will ultimately be an unordered one, and the second one will be an ordered one. Unlike HTML in which you would use <ul> and <ol>, with ODF you get across the difference between an ordered and unordered list through styling alone, which we'll do in a moment. In the meantime, let's set up the two lists using <text:list> and <text:list-item>:

```
<text:h text:outline-level="2">A section with lists (Heading 2)</text:h>
<text:p>Elements to illustrate:</text:p>
<text:list>
  <text:list-item>
    <text:p>hyperlinks</text:p>
  </text:list-item>
  <text:list-item>
    <text:p>italics and bold text</text:p>
  </text:list-item>
  <text:list-item>
    <text:p>lists (ordered and unordered)</text:p>
  </text:list-item>
</text:list>
<text:p>How to figure out ODF</text:p>
<text:list>
  <text:list-item>
    <text:p>work out the content.xml tags</text:p>
  </text:list-item>
  <text:list-item>
    <text:p>work styles into the mix</text:p>
  </text:list-item>
  <text:list-item>
    <text:p>figure out how to apply what we learned to spreadsheets and
presentations</text:p>
  </text:list-item>
</text:list>
```

Using text:a and text:span to Bracket Text Styling

The following markup constructs a paragraph with embedded hyperlinks, indicated by `<text:a>` elements. You also want to eventually mark certain text areas as italics ("URL"), as bold ("API page"), and as Arial and red in color ("Flickr"). It turns out that doing so requires styling, which we'll do later. Here we partition out the regions to which styles can then be applied with `<text:span>`—akin to an HTML span.

```
<text:p>The <text:span>URL</text:span> for Flickr is
  <text:a xlink:type="simple"  xlink:href="http://www.flickr.com/">
    http://www.flickr.com
  </text:a>.
  <text:s/>The <text:span>API page</text:span> is
  <text:a  xlink:type="simple" xlink:href="http://www.flickr.com/services/api/">
    http://www.flickr.com/services/api/
  </text:a>
</text:p>
```

Table

The following markup creates a table with three columns and three rows. Note the use of `<table:table>`, `<table:table-row>`, and `<table:table-cell>` where the table namespace is `urn:oasis:names:tc:opendocument:xmlns:table:1.0`:

```
<text:h text:outline-level="1"> A Table (Heading 1)</text:h>
<table:table table:name="Table1">
  <table:table-column table:number-columns-repeated="3"/>
  <table:table-row>
    <table:table-cell office:value-type="string">
      <text:p>Website</text:p>
    </table:table-cell>
    <table:table-cell office:value-type="string">
      <text:p>Description</text:p>
    </table:table-cell>
    <table:table-cell office:value-type="string">
      <text:p>URL</text:p>
    </table:table-cell>
  </table:table-row>
  <table:table-row>
    <table:table-cell office:value-type="string">
      <text:p>Flickr</text:p>
    </table:table-cell>
    <table:table-cell office:value-type="string">
      <text:p>A social photo sharing site</text:p>
    </table:table-cell>
    <table:table-cell office:value-type="string">
      <text:p>
        <text:a xlink:type="simple" xlink:href="http://www.flickr.com/"
          >http://www.flickr.com</text:a>
```

```
      </text:p>
    </table:table-cell>
  </table:table-row>
  <table:table-row>
    <table:table-cell office:value-type="string">
      <text:p>Google Maps</text:p>
    </table:table-cell>
    <table:table-cell office:value-type="string">
      <text:p>An online map</text:p>
    </table:table-cell>
    <table:table-cell office:value-type="string">
      <text:p>
        <text:a xlink:type="simple" xlink:href="http://maps.google.com/"
          >http://maps.google.com</text:a>
      </text:p>
    </table:table-cell>
  </table:table-row>
</table:table>
```

Footnote

The following ODF shows how to embed a footnote through a `<text:note>` element, which contains `<text:note-citation>` , `<text:note-body>`, and `<text:note>` elements:

```
<text:h text:outline-level="1">Footnotes (Heading 1)</text:h>
<text:p>This sentence has an accompanying footnote.<text:note text:id="ftn0"
  text:note-class="footnote">
  <text:note-citation>1</text:note-citation>
  <text:note-body>
    <text:p text:style-name="Footnote">You are reading a footnote.</text:p>
  </text:note-body>
</text:note>
  <text:s text:c="2"/>Where does the text after a footnote go?
</text:p>
```

Embedded Image

The markup in this section embeds an image that I have shown before:

```
http://flickr.com/photos/raymondyee/18389540/
```

specifically the original size:

```
http://farm1.static.flickr.com/12/18389540_e37cc4d464_o.jpg
```

You download the image, rename it to `campanile_fog.jpg`, and insert it into the `Pictures` subdirectory of the ODF structure. (Remember that when you unzip an ODF text document, you can often find a `Pictures` subdirectory. That's where embedded images get placed.) Here's what you have to include in `content.xml`:

```
<text:h text:outline-level="1">An Image</text:h>
<text:p>
  <draw:frame draw:name="graphics1" text:anchor-type="paragraph"
    svg:width="5in" svg:height="6.6665in" draw:z-index="0">
    <draw:image xlink:href="Pictures/campanile_fog.jpg" xlink:type="simple"
      xlink:show="embed" xlink:actuate="onLoad"/>
  </draw:frame>
</text:p>
```

Note that you need to add the photo to the list of files in `META-INF/manifest.xml` (which keeps track of the files that are zipped up in an ODF text document). See the specific changes:[14]

```
<manifest:file-entry manifest:media-type="image/jpeg"
  manifest:full-path="Pictures/campanile_fog.jpg"/>
<manifest:file-entry manifest:media-type="" manifest:full-path="Pictures/"/>
```

Setting the Paragraph Text to text-body

Now that you have the content elements of the ODF text document in place, you can turn to applying styles. In this section, you'll focus first on styling the paragraphs. The default style for paragraphs in OpenOffice.org make it hard to tell when the paragraphs start and end. Let's apply the Text body style from OO.o to some paragraphs. You can do so in two steps: first define the relevant styles, and then apply the new styles to the relevant paragraphs.

To define the styles, you insert the following definition in `styles.xml`:[15]

```
<?xml version="1.0" ?>
<!-- the namespace declarations of office:document-styles are omitted -->
<office:document-styles office:version="1.0">
  <office:styles>
    <style:style style:name="Standard" style:family="paragraph" style:class="text"/>
    <style:style style:name="Text_20_body" style:display-name="Text body"
      style:family="paragraph"
      style:parent-style-name="Standard" style:class="text">
      <style:paragraph-properties fo:margin-top="0in" fo:margin-bottom="0.0835in"/>
    </style:style>
  </office:styles>
</office:document-styles>
```

Then you use `text:style-name` attribute to associate this style with a `<text:p>` in `content.xml` to the relevant paragraphs. For example:[16]

```
<text:p text:style-name="Text_20_body">The following sections illustrate various
possibilities in ODF Text.</text:p>
```

---

14. http://examples.mashupguide.net/ch17/odt_example_1/META-INF/manifest.xml

15. http://examples.mashupguide.net/ch17/odt_example_2/styles.xml

16. http://examples.mashupguide.net/ch17/odt_example_2/content.xml

You can see the resulting ODF text file here:

http://examples.mashupguide.net/ch17/odt_example_2.odt

whose constituent files are here:

http://examples.mashupguide.net/ch17/odt_example_2/

Formatting Lists to Distinguish Between Ordered and Unordered Lists

Let's now style the two lists. Recall that you couldn't make the first list unordered and the second ordered without using styling. Let's now do so by using <style:style> again—but this time embedded in an <office:automat-styles> element in content.xml.

```
<?xml version="1.0" ?>
<!-- the namespace declarations of office:document-content are omitted
<office:document-content>
  <office:automatic-styles>
[INSERT automatic-styles here]
  </office:automatic-styles>
  <office:body>
    <office:text>
[...]
    </office:text>
  </office:body>
</office:document-content>
```

specifically:

```
<office:automatic-styles>
  <style:style style:name="P1" style:family="paragraph"
    style:parent-style-name="Standard"
    style:list-style-name="L1"/>
  <style:style style:name="P6" style:family="paragraph"
    style:parent-style-name="Standard"
    style:list-style-name="L5"/>
  <text:list-style style:name="L1">
    <text:list-level-style-bullet text:level="1"
      text:style-name="Numbering_20_Symbols"
      style:num-suffix="." text:bullet-char="•">
      <style:list-level-properties text:space-before="0.25in"
        text:min-label-width="0.25in"/>
      <style:text-properties style:font-name="StarSymbol"/>
    </text:list-level-style-bullet>
[....]
  </text:list-style>
  <text:list-style style:name="L5">
    <text:list-level-style-number text:level="1"
      text:style-name="Numbering_20_Symbols"
```

```
        style:num-suffix="." style:num-format="1">
        <style:list-level-properties text:space-before="0.25in"
          text:min-label-width="0.25in"/>
    </text:list-level-style-number>
[....]
  </text:list-style>
</office:automatic-styles>
```

Note that the styling for levels beyond level 1 are deleted in this excerpt.

Once these styles are defined, you then use `text:style-name` attributes to associate the L1/ P1 and L5/P6 styles to the unordered and ordered lists, respectively:

```
<text:p>Elements to illustrate:</text:p>
<text:list text:style-name="L1">
  <text:list-item>
    <text:p text:style-name="P1">hyperlinks</text:p>
  </text:list-item>
  <text:list-item>
    <text:p text:style-name="P1">italics and bold text</text:p>
  </text:list-item>
  <text:list-item>
    <text:p text:style-name="P1">lists (ordered and unordered)</text:p>
  </text:list-item>
</text:list>
<text:p>How to figure out ODF</text:p>
<text:list text:style-name="L5">
  <text:list-item>
    <text:p text:style-name="P6">work out the content.xml tags</text:p>
  </text:list-item>
  <text:list-item>
    <text:p text:style-name="P6">work styles into the mix</text:p>
  </text:list-item>
```

Getting Bold, Italics, Font Changes, and Color Changes into Text Spans

The final changes to make are to define and apply the relevant styles to introduce a number of text effects (bold, italics, font changes, and color changes). Remember that you have the `<text:span>` in place already in `content.xml`. In `content.xml`, you need to do the following:

- Add an `<office:font-face-decls>` element containing a `<style:font-face>` that declares an Arial style.

- Create `<style:style>` elements named T1, T2, T5, respectively, to express the styles of the three `<text:span>` elements to which you are applying styling.

- Associate the T1, T2, and T5 styles with the `<text:span>` elements using `text:style-name` attributes.

Concretely, this means the following:[17]

```
<?xml version="1.0" ?>
<!-- the namespace declarations of office:document-content are omitted
<office:document-content office:version="1.0">
  <office:font-face-decls>
    <style:font-face style:name="Arial" svg:font-family="Arial"
      style:font-family-generic="swiss"
      style:font-pitch="variable"/>
  </office:font-face-decls>
  <office:automatic-styles>
[....]
    <style:style style:name="T1" style:family="text">
      <style:text-properties fo:font-style="italic" style:font-style-asian="italic"
        style:font-style-complex="italic"/>
    </style:style>
    <style:style style:name="T2" style:family="text">
      <style:text-properties fo:font-weight="bold" style:font-weight-asian="bold"
        style:font-weight-complex="bold"/>
    </style:style>
    <style:style style:name="T5" style:family="text">
      <style:text-properties fo:color="#ff0000" style:font-name="Arial"/>
    </style:style>
  </office:automatic-styles>
  <office:body>
    <office:text>
[...]
      <text:p>The <text:span text:style-name="T1">URL</text:span> for <text:span ➥
text:style-name="T5">Flickr</text:span> is <text:a xlink:type="simple"
        xlink:href="http://www.flickr.com/"
        >http://www.flickr.com</text:a>. <text:s/>
      The <text:span text:style-name="T2">API page</text:span> is <text:a
        xlink:type="simple" xlink:href="http://www.flickr.com/services/api/"
        >http://www.flickr.com/services/api/</text:a></text:p>
[....]
    </office:text>
  </office:body>
</office:document-content>
```

This series of changes brings you to the completed ODF text document here:

```
http://examples.mashupguide.net/ch17/odt_example_4.odt
```

There are obviously many other features in ODF that are not demonstrated here. But these examples should give you a good idea of how to learn about the other elements.

---

17. http://examples.mashupguide.net/ch17/odt_example_4/content.xml

API Kits for Working with ODF

In the previous sections, I showed the approach of working directly with the ODF specification and the validator and using trial and error to generate valid ODF files. In this section, you'll move up the abstraction ladder and look at using libraries/API kits/wrapper libraries that work with ODF. Such libraries can be a huge help if they are implemented well and reflect conscientious effort on the part of the authors to wrestle with some of the issues I discussed in the previous section.

You can find a good list of tools that support ODF here:

```
http://en.wikipedia.org/wiki/OpenDocument_software
```

You can find another good list here:

```
http://opendocumentfellowship.com/development/tools
```

In this chapter, I'll cover two API kits:

- I'll cover Odfpy (`http://opendocumentfellowship.com/projects/odfpy`). According to documentation for Odfpy: "Odfpy aims to be a complete API for OpenDocument in Python. Unlike other more convenient APIs, this one is essentially an abstraction layer just above the XML format. The main focus has been to prevent the programmer from creating invalid documents. It has checks that raise an exception if the programmer adds an invalid element, adds an attribute unknown to the grammar, forgets to add a required attribute or adds text to an element that doesn't allow it."

- I'll cover OpenDocumentPHP (`http://opendocumentphp.org/`), which is in the early stages of development.

In the next two subsections, I will show you how to use Odfpy and OpenDocumentPHP.

Odfpy

I'll first use Odfpy to generate a minimalist document and then to re-create the full-blown ODF text document from earlier in the chapter. To use it, follow the documentation here:

```
http://opendocumentfellowship.com/files/api-for-odfpy.odt
```

You can access the code via Subversion:

```
svn export http://opendocumentfellowship.com/repos/odfpy/trunk odfpy
```

To generate a "Hello World" document, use this:

```
from odf.opendocument import OpenDocumentText
from odf.text import P

textdoc = OpenDocumentText()
p = P(text="Hello World!")
textdoc.text.addElement(p)
textdoc.save("helloworld_odfpy.odt")
```

This code will generate `helloworld_odfpy.odt` with the following file structure:

File Name	Modified	Size
mimetype	2007-12-03 15:06:20	39
styles.xml	2007-12-03 15:06:20	403
content.xml	2007-12-03 15:06:20	472
meta.xml	2007-12-03 15:06:20	426
META-INF/manifest.xml	2007-12-03 15:06:20	691

But the generated instance doesn't validate (according to the ODF Validator), even though OO.o 2.2 has no problem reading the file. For many practical purposes, this may be OK, though it'd be nice to know that a document coming out of Odfpy is valid since that's the stated design goal of Odfpy.

Re-creating the Example ODF Text Document

Let's now use Odfpy to generate a more substantial document. The following code demonstrates how you can use Odfpy to re-create the full-blown ODF text document from earlier in the chapter. The code is a rather literal translation of the markup to the corresponding object model of Odfpy—and should give you a feel for how to use Odfpy.

```
# odfpy_gen_example.py

"""

  Description:  This program used odfpy to generate a simple ODF text document
  odfpy:  http://opendocumentfellowship.com/projects/odfpy
  documentation for odfpy:  http://opendocumentfellowship.com/files/api-for-➥
odfpy.odt

"""

from odf.opendocument import OpenDocumentText
from odf.style import Style, TextProperties, ParagraphProperties, ➥
ListLevelProperties, FontFace
from odf.text import P, H, A, S, List, ListItem, ListStyle, ListLevelStyleBullet, ➥
ListLevelStyleNumber, ListLevelStyleBullet, Span
from odf.text import Note, NoteBody, NoteCitation
from odf.office import FontFaceDecls
from odf.table import Table, TableColumn, TableRow, TableCell
from odf.draw import Frame, Image

# fname is the path for the output file
fname= '[PATH-FOR-OUTPUT-FILE]';
#fname='D:\Document\PersonalInfoRemixBook\examples\ch17\odfpy_gen_example.odt'

# instantiate an ODF text document (odt)
textdoc = OpenDocumentText()
```

```
# styles
"""
<style:style style:name="Standard" style:family="paragraph" style:class="text"/>
<style:style style:name="Text_20_body" style:display-name="Text body"
 style:family="paragraph"
 style:parent-style-name="Standard" style:class="text">
 <style:paragraph-properties fo:margin-top="0in" fo:margin-bottom="0.0835in"/>
</style:style>
"""

s = textdoc.styles

StandardStyle = Style(name="Standard", family="paragraph")
StandardStyle.addAttribute('class','text')
s.addElement(StandardStyle)

TextBodyStyle = Style(name="Text_20_body",family="paragraph", ➥
parentstylename='Standard', displayname="Text body")
TextBodyStyle.addAttribute('class','text')
TextBodyStyle.addElement(ParagraphProperties(margintop="0in", ➥
marginbottom="0.0835in"))
s.addElement(TextBodyStyle)

# font declarations
"""
 <office:font-face-decls>
    <style:font-face style:name="Arial" svg:font-family="Arial"
      style:font-family-generic="swiss"
      style:font-pitch="variable"/>
  </office:font-face-decls>
"""

textdoc.fontfacedecls.addElement((FontFace(name="Arial",fontfamily="Arial", ➥
fontfamilygeneric="swiss",fontpitch="variable")))

# Automatic Style

# P1
"""
<style:style style:name="P1" style:family="paragraph"
      style:parent-style-name="Standard"
      style:list-style-name="L1"/>
"""
P1style = Style(name="P1", family="paragraph", parentstylename="Standard", ➥
liststylename="L1")
textdoc.automaticstyles.addElement(P1style)
```

```
# L1
"""
<text:list-style style:name="L1">
  <text:list-level-style-bullet text:level="1"
    text:style-name="Numbering_20_Symbols"
    style:num-suffix="." text:bullet-char="•">
    <style:list-level-properties text:space-before="0.25in"
      text:min-label-width="0.25in"/>
    <style:text-properties style:font-name="StarSymbol"/>
  </text:list-level-style-bullet>
</text:list-style>
"""
L1style=ListStyle(name="L1")
# u'\u2022' is the bullet character (http://www.unicode.org/charts/PDF/U2000.pdf)
bullet1 = ListLevelStyleBullet(level="1", stylename="Numbering_20_Symbols", ➡
numsuffix=".", bulletchar=u'\u2022')
L1prop1 = ListLevelProperties(spacebefore="0.25in", minlabelwidth="0.25in")
bullet1.addElement(L1prop1)
L1style.addElement(bullet1)
textdoc.automaticstyles.addElement(L1style)

# P6
"""
  <style:style style:name="P6" style:family="paragraph"
      style:parent-style-name="Standard"
      style:list-style-name="L5"/>
"""

P6style = Style(name="P6", family="paragraph", parentstylename="Standard", ➡
liststylename="L5")
textdoc.automaticstyles.addElement(P6style)

# L5
"""
<text:list-style style:name="L5">
  <text:list-level-style-number text:level="1"
    text:style-name="Numbering_20_Symbols"
    style:num-suffix="." style:num-format="1">
    <style:list-level-properties text:space-before="0.25in"
      text:min-label-width="0.25in"/>
  </text:list-level-style-number>
</text:list-style>
"""

L5style=ListStyle(name="L5")
numstyle1 = ListLevelStyleNumber(level="1", stylename="Numbering_20_Symbols", ➡
numsuffix=".", numformat='1')
```

```
L5prop1 = ListLevelProperties(spacebefore="0.25in", minlabelwidth="0.25in")
numstyle1.addElement(L5prop1)
L5style.addElement(numstyle1)
textdoc.automaticstyles.addElement(L5style)

# T1
"""
    <style:style style:name="T1" style:family="text">
       <style:text-properties fo:font-style="italic" style:font-style-asian="italic"
          style:font-style-complex="italic"/>
    </style:style>
"""

T1style = Style(name="T1", family="text")
T1style.addElement(TextProperties(fontstyle="italic",fontstyleasian="italic",➡
fontstylecomplex="italic"))
textdoc.automaticstyles.addElement(T1style)

# T2
"""
 <style:style style:name="T2" style:family="text">
       <style:text-properties fo:font-weight="bold" style:font-weight-asian="bold"
          style:font-weight-complex="bold"/>
    </style:style>
"""

T2style = Style(name="T2", family="text")
T2style.addElement(TextProperties(fontweight="bold",fontweightasian="bold",➡
fontweightcomplex="bold"))
textdoc.automaticstyles.addElement(T2style)

# T5
"""
    <style:style style:name="T5" style:family="text">
       <style:text-properties fo:color="#ff0000" style:font-name="Arial"/>
    </style:style>
"""

T5style = Style(name="T5", family="text")
T5style.addElement(TextProperties(color="#ff0000",fontname="Arial"))
textdoc.automaticstyles.addElement(T5style)

# now construct what goes into <office:text>

h=H(outlinelevel=1, text='Purpose (Heading 1)')
textdoc.text.addElement(h)
p = P(text="The following sections illustrate various possibilities in ODF Text", ➡
stylename='Text_20_body')
textdoc.text.addElement(p)
```

```
textdoc.text.addElement(H(outlinelevel=2,text='A simple series of paragraphs ➡
(Heading 2)'))
textdoc.text.addElement(P(text="This section contains a series of paragraphs.", ➡
stylename='Text_20_body'))
textdoc.text.addElement(P(text="This is a second paragraph.", ➡
stylename='Text_20_body'))
textdoc.text.addElement(P(text="And a third paragraph.", stylename='Text_20_body'))

textdoc.text.addElement(H(outlinelevel=2,text='A section with lists (Heading 2)'))
textdoc.text.addElement(P(text="Elements to illustrate:"))

# add the first list (unordered list)
textList = List(stylename="L1")
item = ListItem()
item.addElement(P(text='hyperlinks', stylename="P1"))
textList.addElement(item)

item = ListItem()
item.addElement(P(text='italics and bold text', stylename="P1"))
textList.addElement(item)

item = ListItem()
item.addElement(P(text='lists (ordered and unordered)', stylename="P1"))
textList.addElement(item)

textdoc.text.addElement(textList)

# add the second (ordered) list

textdoc.text.addElement(P(text="How to figure out ODF"))

textList = List(stylename="L5")
#item = ListItem(startvalue=P(text='item 1'))
item = ListItem()
item.addElement(P(text='work out the content.xml tags', stylename="P5"))
textList.addElement(item)

item = ListItem()
item.addElement(P(text='work styles into the mix', stylename="P5"))
textList.addElement(item)

item = ListItem()
item.addElement(P(text='figure out how to apply what we learned to spreadsheets and ➡
presentations', stylename="P5"))
textList.addElement(item)

textdoc.text.addElement(textList)
```

```
# A paragraph with bold, italics, font change, and hyperlinks
"""
        <text:p>The <text:span text:style-name="T1">URL</text:span> for <text:span
            text:style-name="T5">Flickr</text:span> is <text:a xlink:type="simple"
            xlink:href="http://www.flickr.com/"
            >http://www.flickr.com</text:a>. <text:s/>The <text:span
            text:style-name="T2"
            >API page</text:span> is <text:a xlink:type="simple"
            xlink:href="http://www.flickr.com/services/api/"
          >http://www.flickr.com/services/api/</text:a></text:p>
"""
p = P(text='The ')
# italicized URL
s = Span(text='URL', stylename='T1')
p.addElement(s)
p.addText(' for ')
# Flickr in red and Arial font
p.addElement(Span(text='Flickr',stylename='T5'))
p.addText(' is ')
# link
link = A(type="simple",href="http://www.flickr.com", text="http://www.flickr.com")
p.addElement(link)
p.addText('.  The ')
# API page in bold
s = Span(text='API page', stylename='T2')
p.addElement(s)
p.addText(' is ')
link = A(type="simple",href="http://www.flickr.com/services/api", ➥
text="http://www.flickr.com/services/api")
p.addElement(link)

textdoc.text.addElement(p)

# add the table
"""
<table:table-column table:number-columns-repeated="3"/>
"""

textdoc.text.addElement(H(outlinelevel=1,text='A Table (Heading 1)'))

table = Table(name="Table 1")

table.addElement(TableColumn(numbercolumnsrepeated="3"))

# first row
tr = TableRow()
table.addElement(tr)
```

```
tc = TableCell(valuetype="string")
tc.addElement(P(text='Website'))
tr.addElement(tc)
tc = TableCell(valuetype="string")
tc.addElement(P(text='Description'))
tr.addElement(tc)
tc = TableCell(valuetype="string")
tc.addElement(P(text='URL'))
tr.addElement(tc)

# second row
tr = TableRow()
table.addElement(tr)
tc = TableCell(valuetype="string")
tc.addElement(P(text='Flickr'))
tr.addElement(tc)
tc = TableCell(valuetype="string")
tc.addElement(P(text='A social photo sharing site'))
tr.addElement(tc)
tc = TableCell(valuetype="string")

link = A(type="simple",href="http://www.flickr.com", text="http://www.flickr.com")
p = P()
p.addElement(link)
tc.addElement(p)

tr.addElement(tc)

# third row
tr = TableRow()
table.addElement(tr)
tc = TableCell(valuetype="string")
tc.addElement(P(text='Google Maps'))
tr.addElement(tc)
tc = TableCell(valuetype="string")
tc.addElement(P(text='An online map'))
tr.addElement(tc)
tc = TableCell(valuetype="string")

link = A(type="simple",href="http://maps.google.com", text="http://maps.google.com")
p = P()
p.addElement(link)
tc.addElement(p)
tr.addElement(tc)

textdoc.text.addElement(table)

# paragraph with footnote
```

```
"""
    <text:h text:outline-level="1">Footnotes (Heading 1)</text:h>
        <text:p>This sentence has an accompanying footnote.<text:note text:id="ftn0"
            text:note-class="footnote">
            <text:note-citation>1</text:note-citation>
            <text:note-body>
                <text:p text:style-name="Footnote">You are reading a footnote.</text:p>
            </text:note-body>
        </text:note>
        <text:s text:c="2"/>Where does the text after a footnote go?</text:p>
"""

textdoc.text.addElement(H(outlinelevel=1,text='Footnotes (Heading 1)'))
p = P()
textdoc.text.addElement(p)
p.addText("This sentence has an accompanying footnote.")
note = Note(id="ftn0", noteclass="footnote")
p.addElement(note)
note.addElement(NoteCitation(text='1'))
notebody = NoteBody()
note.addElement(notebody)
notebody.addElement(P(stylename="Footnote", text="You are reading a footnote."))
p.addElement(S(c=2))
p.addText("Where does the text after a footnote go?")

# Insert the photo

"""
    <text:h text:outline-level="1">An Image</text:h>
     <text:p>
       <draw:frame draw:name="graphics1" text:anchor-type="paragraph"
         svg:width="5in"
         svg:height="6.6665in" draw:z-index="0">
         <draw:image xlink:href="Pictures/campanile_fog.jpg" xlink:type="simple"
           xlink:show="embed"
           xlink:actuate="onLoad"/>
       </draw:frame>
     </text:p>
"""

textdoc.text.addElement(H(outlinelevel=1,text='An Image'))
p = P()
textdoc.text.addElement(p)
# add the image
# img_path is the local path of the image to include
img_path = '[PATH-FOR-IMAGE]';
#img_path = 'D:\Document\PersonalInfoRemixBook\examples\ch17\campanile_fog.jpg'
href = textdoc.addPicture(img_path)
```

```
f = Frame(name="graphics1", anchortype="paragraph", width="5in", height="6.6665in", ➡
zindex="0")
p.addElement(f)
img = Image(href=href, type="simple", show="embed", actuate="onLoad")
f.addElement(img)

# save the document
textdoc.save(fname)
```

You can examine the output from this code:

```
http://examples.mashupguide.net/ch17/odfpy_gen_example.odt
```

OpenDocumentPHP

OpenDocumentPHP (http://opendocumentphp.org/) is a PHP API kit for ODF in its early
stages of development.

In this section, I'll show how to use OpenDocumentPHP version 0.5.2, which you can get
from here:

```
http://downloads.sourceforge.net/opendocumentphp/OpenDocumentPHP-0.5.2.zip
```

Alternatively, you can install OpenDocumentPHP using PEAR:

```
http://opendocumentphp.org/index.php/home/11-new-pear-server-for-opendocumentphp
```

Some autogenerated documentation of the API is available here:

```
http://opendocumentphp.org/static/apidoc/svn/
```

Unzip the file in your PHP library area. To see a reasonably complicated example of what
you can do, consult the samples in OpenDocumentPHP/samples.

Here I will write a simple helloworld-generated document to demonstrate how to get
started with the library:

```
<?php
require_once 'OpenDocumentPHP/OpenDocumentText.php';
$text = new OpenDocumentText('D:\Document\PersonalInfoRemixBook\examples\ch17\➡
helloworld_opendocumentphp.odt');
$textbody = $text->getBody();
$paragraph = $textbody->nextParagraph();
$paragraph->append('Hello World!');
$text->close();
?>
```

■**Note** You need ZipArchive to be enabled in PHP to run OpenDocumentPHP. On Linux systems use the
--enable-zip option at compile time. On Windows systems, enable php_zip.dll inside php.ini.

The following is a more elaborate example using OpenDocumentPHP to generate a couple of headers and several paragraphs. The paragraphs are associated with a Text body style.

```php
<?php

require_once 'OpenDocumentPHP/OpenDocumentText.php';

$fullpath = 'D:\Document\PersonalInfoRemixBook\examples\ch17\odp_gen_example.odt';

/*
 * If file exists, remove it first.
 */
if (file_exists($fullpath)) {
    unlink($fullpath);
}

$text = new OpenDocumentText($fullpath);

# set some styles

/**

<style:style style:name="Standard" style:family="paragraph" style:class="text"/>
<style:style style:name="Text_20_body" style:display-name="Text body"
 style:family="paragraph"
 style:parent-style-name="Standard" style:class="text">
 <style:paragraph-properties fo:margin-top="0in" fo:margin-bottom="0.0835in"/>
</style:style>

**/

$Standard_Style = $text->getStyles()->getStyles()->getStyle();
$Standard_Style->setStyleName('Standard');
$Standard_Style->setFamily('paragraph');
$Standard_Style->setClass('text');

$textBody_Style = $text->getStyles()->getStyles()->getStyle();
$textBody_Style->setStyleName('Text_20_body');
$textBody_Style->setDisplayName('Text body');
$textBody_Style->setFamily('paragraph');
$textBody_Style->setClass('text');

$pp = $textBody_Style->getParagraphProperties();
$pp->setMarginTop('0in');
$pp->setMarginBottom('0.0835in');

# write the headers and paragraphs
```

```
$textbody = $text->getBody()->getTextFragment();

$heading = $textbody->nextHeading();
$heading->setHeadingLevel(1);
$heading->append('Purpose (Heading 1)');

$paragraph = $textbody->nextParagraph();
$paragraph->setStyleName('Text_20_body');
$paragraph->append('The following sections illustrate various possibilities in ODF
Text');

$heading = $textbody->nextHeading();
$heading->setHeadingLevel(2);
$heading->append('A simple series of paragraphs (Heading 2)');

$paragraph = $textbody->nextParagraph();
$paragraph->setStyleName('Text_20_body');
$paragraph->append('This section contains a series of paragraphs.');
$paragraph = $textbody->nextParagraph();
$paragraph->setStyleName('Text_20_body');
$paragraph->append('This is a second paragraph.');
$paragraph = $textbody->nextParagraph();
$paragraph->setStyleName('Text_20_body');
$paragraph->append('And a third paragraph.');

$text->close();

?>
```

You can examine the output from this script here:

```
http://examples.mashupguide.net/ch17/odp_gen_example.odt
```

Leveraging OO.o to Generate ODF

If you are willing and able to have OpenOffice.org installed on your computer, it is possible to use OO.o itself as a big library of sorts to parse and generate your ODF documents and to convert ODF to and from other formats. Libraries/tools that use this approach include the following:

- The JODConverter Java Library (http://www.artofsolving.com/opensource/jodconverter)

- OOoLib, Perl and Python libraries that use OO.o (http://sourceforge.net/projects/ooolib/)

On Win32-oriented systems, you can access OpenOffice.org via a COM interface. For instance, the following Python code running the win32all library will generate a new .odt document by scripting OO.o:

```
import win32com.client

objServiceManager = win32com.client.Dispatch("com.sun.star.ServiceManager")
objServiceManager._FlagAsMethod("CreateInstance")
```

```
objDesktop = objServiceManager.CreateInstance("com.sun.star.frame.Desktop")
objDesktop._FlagAsMethod("loadComponentFromURL")

args = []
objDocument = objDesktop.loadComponentFromURL("private:factory/swriter", "_blank",➡
0, args)
objDocument._FlagAsMethod("GetText")
objText = objDocument.GetText()
objText._FlagAsMethod("createTextCursor","insertString")
objCursor = objText.createTextCursor()
objText.insertString(objCursor, "The first line in the newly created text➡
document.\n", 0)
```

ECMA Office Open XML (OOXML)

Now we turn to a competing file format: Office Open XML. Wikpedia provides a good overview of the specification that underpins Microsoft Office 2007:

```
http://en.wikipedia.org/wiki/Office_Open_XML
```

The Office Open XML specification has been made into an ECMA standard (ECMA-376). You can find the specification here:

```
http://www.ecma-international.org/publications/standards/Ecma-376.htm
```

Note that the standard is 6,000 pages—in case you want to read it. ECMA provides an overview white paper:

```
http://www.ecma-international.org/news/TC45_current_work/OpenXML%20White%20Paper.pdf
```

Getting hard, easy-to-digest information on OOXML is challenging. I recommend the following, more colloquial overviews that you might find useful:

- The "5 Cool Things You Must Know About the New Office 2007 File Formats" article might prove helpful (`http://www.devx.com/MicrosoftISV/Article/30907/2046`).

- `http://openxmldeveloper.org/default.aspx` has some useful tutorials on the subject.

When working with Office Open XML, it's good to heed the following warning: "Open XML is a new standard. So new, in fact, that the schemas are still being edited and haven't been published by ECMA yet. And there are no books out on Open XML development, although that will surely change in the next year."[18]

The Office Open XML format has a predecessor in the Microsoft Office 2003 XML format. In the book *Office 2003 XML* (O'Reilly Media, 2004), the following was given as a minimalist Office 2003 XML document:[19]

---

18. `http://openxmldeveloper.org/articles/LearningOnline.aspx` (accessed on June 5, 2007)

19. `http://examples.mashupguide.net/ch17/helloworld_onedoc_2003.xml`

```
<?xml version="1.0"?>
<?mso-application progid="Word.Document"?>
<w:wordDocument
  xmlns:w="http://schemas.microsoft.com/office/word/2003/wordml">
  <w:body>
    <w:p>
      <w:r>
        <w:t>Hello, World!</w:t>
      </w:r>
    </w:p>
  </w:body>
</w:wordDocument>
```

This document is actually readable by Microsoft Office 2007, though in "compatibility mode." Can you get a valid document by using the Microsoft Office 2003 document and updating the namespace of the document? That is, can you just update the namespace for w?

```
xmlns:w="http://schemas.openxmlformats.org/wordprocessingml/2006/main"
```

You therefore have the following:

```
<?xml version="1.0"?>
<?mso-application progid="Word.Document"?>
<w:wordDocument
  xmlns:w="http://schemas.openxmlformats.org/wordprocessingml/2006/main">
  <w:body>
    <w:p>
      <w:r>
        <w:t>Hello, World!</w:t>
      </w:r>
    </w:p>
  </w:body>
</w:wordDocument>
```

Unfortunately this document as an Office Open XML instance to Microsoft Office 2007 causes an error. You can certainly keep pushing in this direction by looking through the specification and schema. However, a more promising lead right now is to see what file gets written out by a simple little C# script aimed at generating a simple .docx file:

```
http://blogs.msdn.com/dmahugh/archive/2006/06/27/649007.aspx
```

I downloaded the Microsoft Visual Studio C# Express Edition to run the script and made a small change to update the namespace from this:

```
http://schemas.openxmlformats.org/wordprocessingml/2006/3/main
```

to this:

```
http://schemas.openxmlformats.org/wordprocessingml/2006/main
```

With that change, you can generate a simple Office Open XML document file (http:// examples.mashupguide.net/ch17/helloworld_simple.1.docx) that is acceptable by Microsoft

Office 2007. (This doesn't prove that the file is valid but only that you are on the right track in terms of generating OOXML.)

Unzipping and studying the file gives you insight into what goes into a minimalist instance of OOXML. The list of files is as follows:

File Name	Modified	Size
word/document.xml	2007-06-04 16:43:44	246
[Content_Types].xml	2007-06-04 16:43:44	346
_rels/.rels	2007-06-04 16:43:44	285

Let's look at the individual files. The first is the document.xml file in the word directory, which holds the content of the document and corresponds most closely to content.xml in ODF.

```xml
<?xml version="1.0" encoding="utf-8"?>
<w:document
    xmlns:w="http://schemas.openxmlformats.org/wordprocessingml/2006/main">
  <w:body>
    <w:p>
      <w:r>
        <w:t>Hello World!</w:t>
      </w:r>
    </w:p>
  </w:body>
</w:document>
```

The .rels file in the rels directory contains information about relationships among the various files that make up the package of files (a bit like the METAINF/meta.xml file in ODF):

```xml
<?xml version="1.0" ?>
<Relationships xmlns="http://schemas.openxmlformats.org/package/2006/relationships">
  <Relationship Id="rId1" Target="/word/document.xml"
                Type="http://schemas.openxmlformats.org/officeDocument/2006/➥
relationships/officeDocument"/>
</Relationships>
```

The final file in the package is [Content_Types].xml:

```xml
<?xml version="1.0" ?>
<Types xmlns="http://schemas.openxmlformats.org/package/2006/content-types">
  <Default ContentType="application/vnd.openxmlformats-officedocument.➥
wordprocessingml.document.main+xml" Extension="xml"/>
  <Default ContentType="application/vnd.openxmlformats-package.relationships+xml"
           Extension="rels"/>
</Types>
```

These files should give you a feel of what's in OOXML. To learn more, take a look at the following resources:

- The "Ecma Office Open XML Format Guide" is an official high-level conceptual/marketing overview of OOXML.

* `http://openxmldeveloper.org/articles/directory.aspx` lists tutorial articles that are gathered by the OOXML community.

- `http://openxmldeveloper.org/articles/OpenXMLsamples.aspx` has sample OOXML documents.

- `http://msdn2.microsoft.com/en-us/library/bb187361.aspx` gives the object model of Microsoft Office 2007.

- `http://en.wikipedia.org/wiki/User:Flemingr/Microsoft_Office_2003_XML_formats` documents the older Office 2003 XML format, which has some family resemblance to OOXML—though an unclear one to me.

- Brian Jones of Microsoft has written some clear tutorials on generating spreadsheets in OOXML: `http://blogs.msdn.com/brian_jones/archive/2007/05/29/simple-spreadsheetml-file-part-3-formatting.aspx`.

Viewers/Validators for OOXML

A big point of OOXML is being able to read and generate documents that are readable in the latest versions of Microsoft Office without having to directly manipulate the object models of Microsoft Office. Yet, it's always helpful to have tools that view and validate OOXML documents—other than Microsoft Office 2007 itself. Some promising tools are as follows:

- Open XML Package Explorer, which lets you browse and edit Open XML packages and validate against the ECMA final schemas (`http://www.codeplex.com/PackageExplorer`).

- If you are using Microsoft Office XP and 2003, you can download a Microsoft Office compatibility pack for the Word, Excel, and PowerPoint 2007 file formats to read and write OOXML.[20] This will also enable you to use the free Microsoft Office Word Viewer 2003 and Microsoft Office Excel Viewer 2003 to view Word 2007 and Excel 2007 files.[21]

Comparing ODF and OOXML

I will not get into surveying the complicated and often-heated comparisons made between ODF and OOXML other than to refer you to the following articles, which in turn provide more references:

- `http://en.wikipedia.org/wiki/Comparison_of_OpenDocument_and_Office_Open_XML_formats` compares formats.

- `http://weblog.infoworld.com/realitycheck/archives/2007/05/odf_vs_openxml.html` gives a flavor of the conflation of political, economical, PR, and technical issues.

---

20. `http://www.microsoft.com/downloads/details.aspx?FamilyId=941b3470-3ae9-4aee-8f43-c6bb74cd1466&displaylang=en`

21. `http://support.microsoft.com/kb/925180`

Online Office Suites

Web-based offices suites are emerging in addition to the traditional desktop office suites and their respective file formats. Prominent examples of such applications include the Zoho Office Suite (http://zoho.com/) and Google Docs and Spreadsheets (http://docs.google.com/). There are others, of course. You can see a list of online spreadsheets, for instance, here:

http://en.wikipedia.org/wiki/List_of_online_spreadsheets

I will focus on using a programmable online spreadsheet, specifically Google Spreadsheets, in this section. Google Spreadsheets has an API (which we will use in a mashup later in the chapter):

http://code.google.com/apis/spreadsheets/overview.html

Usage Scenarios for Programmable Online Spreadsheets

What might one want to do with an online spreadsheet? Here are a few examples I brainstormed:

- Tracking one's weight, finances, or time and sharing that information with your family and friends—or not.

- Having bots calculate data that they put into your spreadsheets that you can then analyze. For instance, if you wanted to track your stock portfolio, you could use the StrikeIron fee-based real-time stock quote service to calculate the value of your portfolio. (You might think twice before storing that portfolio information online, but this is feasible in principle.)

- Build an application to track and disseminate grades.

- Manage a wedding database.

- Build a project management tool that you can update and read with the API.

- Back up a list of your del.icio.us bookmarks in a spreadsheet form.

- Track your library books.

- Build online charts (see http://imagine-it.org/google/spreadsheets/makechart.htm).

There are many other applications. Consider StrikeIron SOA Express for Excel (http://www.strikeiron.com/tools/tools_soaexpress.aspx) as a source of hints about what people might do with the Google Spreadsheets API; that is, start to think of Google Spreadsheets as Excel in the cloud, but account for its lack of some of Excel's current internal extensibility such as macros. (There is no equivalent to Google Mapplets for the spreadsheets or VBA macros—yet.)

The application I will demonstrate in detail is copying my Amazon.com wishlist and prices to a spreadsheet to more easily take that information with me (say to a real-life bookstore or library).

Google Spreadsheets API

Let's figure out how to use the Google Spreadsheets API, focusing specifically on PHP and Python wrapper libraries. You can also directly manipulate the feed protocol:

```
http://code.google.com/apis/spreadsheets/developers_guide_protocol.html
```

There are also a number of API kits available for Google Spreadsheets. I will first demonstrate how to use the Python API kit by creating a mashup involving the Amazon.com web services. I'll then show you a simple example of using the Zend PHP API kit to read the spreadsheets generated in the mashup.

Python API Kit

Google provides a Python GData library and sample code to access the Google spreadsheet. You can either download specific releases (from `http://code.google.com/p/gdata-python-client/downloads/list`) or access the SVN repository:

```
svn checkout http://gdata-python-client.googlecode.com/svn/trunk/➥
gdata-python-client
```

Note the dependencies on other libraries, especially ElementTree, which was not part of the standard Python libraries until version 2.5.[22]

I highly recommend reading the documentation on the Google site specific to the Python library:

```
http://code.google.com/apis/spreadsheets/developers_guide_python.html
```

Once you have the Python GData library installed, you can try some code samples, using the Python interpreter, to teach yourself how it works. First here are the obligatory imports:

```
import gdata.spreadsheet.service
```

Let's then declare some convenience functions and variables:

```
GoogleUser = "[your Google email address]"
GooglePW = "[your password]"
```

Define the following convenience function:

```
def GSheetService(user,pwd):
    gd_client = gdata.spreadsheet.service.SpreadsheetsService()
    gd_client.email = user
    gd_client.password = pwd
    gd_client.source = 'amazonWishListToGSheet.py'
    gd_client.ProgrammaticLogin()

    return gd_client
```

---

22. http://code.google.com/p/gdata-python-client/wiki/DependencyModules

Instantiate a Google data client for your spreadsheet:

```
gs = GSheetService(GoogleUser,GooglePW)
sheets = gs.GetSpreadsheetsFeed()
```

To get a list of the spreadsheets, their titles, and their IDs, use this:

```
print map(lambda e: e.title.text +➥
" : "  + e.id.text.rsplit('/', 1)[1],sheets.entry)
```

This yields something like the following (which is based on my own spreadsheets):

```
['My Amazon WishList : o06341737111865728099.3585145106901556666', 'Udell Mini-
Symposium May 1, 2007 : o06341737111865728099.1877210150658854761', 'weight.journal
: o06341737111865728099.6289501454054682788', 'Plan : o10640374522570553588.
5762564240835257179']
```

Note the key for the spreadsheet "My Amazon WishList." The spreadsheet that the code I write here will be reading from and writing to is as follows:

```
o06341737111865728099.3585145106901556666
```

You will need to create your own Google spreadsheets to work with since you won't be able to write to mine. Note the ID of your spreadsheet, which you will use here.

In the browser, if I'm logged in as the owner of the spreadsheet, I can access this:

```
http://spreadsheets.google.com/feeds/spreadsheets/private/full/{GSheetID}
```

For example:

```
http://spreadsheets.google.com/feeds/spreadsheets/private/full/o06341737111186572809➥
.3585145106901556666
```

Otherwise, I get a 404 error. Now I need to get the ID of the one *worksheet* in the "My Amazon Wishlist" *spreadsheet*. First use this:

```
gs.GetWorksheetsFeed(key="[GSheetID]").entry[0].id.text
```

For example, I use this:

```
gs.GetWorksheetsFeed(key="o06341737111865728099.3585145106901556666").entry[0].➥
id.text
```

to return the URL whose last segment is a worksheet ID—that is, a URL of the following form:

```
http://spreadsheets.google.com/feeds/worksheets/{GSheetID}/private/full/➥
{worksheetID}
```

For example:

```
http://spreadsheets.google.com/feeds/worksheets/o06341737111865728099.35851451069015➥
56666/private/full/od6
```

(in which case the worksheet ID is od6).

Now you can get the worksheet ID:

```
gs.GetWorksheetsFeed(key="[GSheetID]").entry[0].id.text.rsplit('/', 1)[1]
```

For example:

```
gs.GetWorksheetsFeed(key="o06341737111865728099.3585145106901556666").entry[0].➡
id.text.rsplit('/', 1)[1]
```

There are two ways to get at the data in a worksheet—either in a list-based way that gets you rows or in a cell-based way that gets you a range of cells. I will show the list-based approach here, which depends on the assumption that the first row is the header row.

For testing purposes, I created a spreadsheet with the header row and one line of data that I entered, as shown in Table 17-1.

Table 17-1. *The Sample Spreadsheet*

ASIN	DetailPageURL	Title	Author	Date Added	Price	Quantity Desired
1590598385	http://www.amazon.com/gp/product/1590598385/	*Smart and Gets Things Done: Joel Spolsky's Concise Guide to Finding the Best Technical Talent* (Hardcover)	Joel Spolsky	6/5/2007	13.25	1

The following returns a feed for the rows (there's only one):

```
lfeed = gs.GetListFeed(key="[GSheetID]",wksht_id="[worksheetID]")
```

For example:

```
lfeed =➡
gs.GetListFeed(key="o06341737111865728099.3585145106901556666",wksht_id="od6")
```

You can see the content of the row with the following:

```
lfeed.entry[0].content.text
```

This results in the following:

```
'ASIN: 1590598385, DetailPageURL:
http://www.amazon.com/gp/product/1590598385/ref=wl_it_dp/103-8266902-5986239?
ie=UTF8&coliid=I1AOWT8LH796DN&colid=1U5EXVPVS3WP5, Author: Joel Spolsky, Date Added:
6/5/2007, Price: 13.25, Quantity Desired: 1'
```

The following holds the data that has been mapped from namespace-extended elements in the entry (see http://code.google.com/apis/spreadsheets/developers_guide_protocol. html#listFeedExample):

```
lfeed.entry[0].custom
```

Let's see this in action:

```
map(lambda e: (e[0],e[1].text), lfeed.entry[0].custom.items())
```

Running this returns the following:

```
[('asin', '1590598385'), ('dateadded', '6/5/2007'), ('detailpageurl',
'http://www.amazon.com/gp/product/1590598385/ref=wl_it_dp/103-8266902-5986239?
ie=UTF8&coliid=I1AOWT8LH796DN&colid=1U5EXVPVS3WP5'), ('author', 'Joel
Spolsky'), ('quantitydesired', '1'), ('price', '13.25'), ('title', "Smart and Gets
Things Done: Joel Spolsky's Concise Guide to Finding the Best Technical Talent
(Hardcover) ")]
```

Now let's look at adding another row of data. Let's see whether you can just duplicate the row by creating a dictionary of the first row and stick it into the second row:

```
h = {}
for (key,value) in lfeed.entry[0].custom.iteritems():
  h[key] = value.text
```

h now is as follows:

```
{'asin': '1590598385', 'dateadded': '6/5/2007', 'detailpageurl':
'http://www.amazon.com/gp/product/1590598385/ref=wl_it_dp/103-8266902-5986239?
ie=UTF8&coliid=I1AOWT8LH796DN&colid=1U5EXVPVS3WP5', 'author': 'Joel
Spolsky', 'quantitydesired': '1', 'price': '13.25', 'title': "Smart and Gets Things
Done: Joel Spolsky's Concise Guide to Finding the Best Technical Talent (Hardcover)
"}
```

To add the new row, use this:

```
gs.InsertRow(row_data=h,key="[GSheetID]",wksht_id="[worksheetID]")
```

For example:

```
gs.InsertRow(row_data=h,key="o06341737111865728099.3585145106901556666",➥
wksht_id="od6")
```

To clear the second row you just added, you need to get an update lfeed that reflects the current state of the spreadsheet/worksheet and then issue a delete command:

```
lfeed = gs.GetListFeed(key="[GSheetID]",
wksht_id="[worksheetID]")
gs.DeleteRow(lfeed.entry[1])
```

■Note The Google Spreadsheets API is under active development and is still in the process of maturation.

Mashup: Amazon Wishlist and Google Spreadsheets Mashup

To demonstrate how to use Google Spreadsheets for a simple mashup, I will show you how to write code that will transfer the contents of an Amazon.com wishlist to a Google Spreadsheets spreadsheet. Why do that? I use my wishlist to keep track of books and other stuff that I find interesting. If the wishlist belonged to someone else, I might want to download it into a spreadsheet to make it easier to generate a hard-copy shopping list I could use.

Accessing the Wishlist Through the Amazon.com ECS Web Service

First, a word about how you can use Awszone.com to help you formulate the right Amazon.com ECS query to get the information you want to find. I figured out that I wanted to use the ListLookup query by using this:

```
http://www.awszone.com/scratchpads/aws/ecs.us/ListLookup.aws
```

Furthermore, I am using a ListType=WishList and the ListID=1U5EXVPVS3WP5. The URL for web interface to an Amazon.com wishlist is this:

```
http://www.amazon.com/gp/registry/wishlist/{ListID}/
```

Substituting your own AccessKeyId, you can get information about the list as a whole:

```
http://ecs.amazonaws.com/onca/xml?Service=AWSECommerceService&Version=2007-05-14&➥
AWSAccessKeyId=[YourAccessKeyID]&Operation=ListLookup&ListType=WishList&➥
ListId=1U5EXVPVS3WP5http://ecs.amazonaws.com/onca/xml?Service=AWSECommerceService&➥
Version=2007-10-29&AWSAccessKeyId=[YourAccessKeyID]&Operation=ListLookup&ListType=➥
WishList&ListId=1U5EXVPVS3WP5
```

To get a page of the individual items, use the following URL:

```
http://ecs.amazonaws.com/onca/xml?Service=AWSECommerceService&Version=2007-10-29&➥
AWSAccessKeyId=[YourAccessKeyID]&Operation=ListLookup&ListType=WishList&ListId=1U5➥
EXVPVS3WP5&ResponseGroup=ListItems,Medium&ProductPage=2
```

Python Code to Mash Up Amazon.com and Google Spreadsheets

Now you can stitch all of this together with the following code, called amazonWishListtoGSheet.py. (Remember to substitute your own parameters into this code.)

```
"""
an example to copy over a public Amazon wishlist to a Google Spreadsheet
owned by the user based on code at
http://code.google.com/apis/spreadsheets/developers_guide_python.html
"""

GoogleUser = "[GoogleUSER]"
GooglePW = "[GooglePASSWORD]"
GSheet_KEY = "[GSheetID]"
# GSheet_KEY = "o06341737111865728099.3585145106901556666"
GWrkSh_ID = "[worksheetID]"
#GWrkSh_ID = "od6"
```

```
AMAZON_LIST_ID = "[LIST_ID_FOR_WISHLIST]"
# AMAZON_LIST_ID = "1U5EXVPVS3WP5"
AMAZON_ACCESS_KEY_ID = "[AMAZON_KEY]"

from xml.dom import minidom

import gdata.spreadsheet.service

def getText(nodelist):
    """
    convenience function to return all the text in an array of nodes
    """
    rc = ""
    for node in nodelist:
        if node.nodeType == node.TEXT_NODE:
            rc = rc + node.data
    return rc

# a sample row for testing the insertion of a row into the spreadsheet➥
GS_Example_Row = {'asin': '1590598385', 'dateadded': '6/5/2007', 'detailpageurl':➥
'http://www.amazon.com/gp/product/1590598385/ref=wl_it_dp/103-8266902-5986239?➥
ie=UTF8&coliid=I1AOWT8LH796DN&colid=1U5EXVPVS3WP5', 'author': 'Joel Spolsky',➥
'quantitydesired': '1', 'price': '13.25', 'title': "Smart and Gets Things Done: Joel➥
Spolsky's Concise Guide to Finding the Best Technical Talent (Hardcover) "}

GS_HEADER = ['ASIN', 'DetailPageURL', 'Title', 'Author', 'Date Added', 'Price',➥
'Quantity Desired']

GS_KEYS = ['asin', 'detailpageurl', 'title', 'author', 'dateadded', 'price',➥
'quantitydesired']

class GSheetForAmazonList:
    def __init__(self,user=GoogleUser,pwd=GooglePW):
        gd_client = gdata.spreadsheet.service.SpreadsheetsService()
        gd_client.email = user
        gd_client.password = pwd
        gd_client.source = 'amazonListToGsheet.py'
        gd_client.ProgrammaticLogin()
        self.gd_client = gd_client
    def setKey(self,key):
        self.key = key
    def setWkshtId(self,wksht_id):
        self.wksht_id = wksht_id
    def listSpreadsheets(self):
        """
        return a list with information about the spreadsheets available to the user
        """
        sheets = self.gd_client.GetSpreadsheetsFeed()
```

```python
            return map(lambda e: (e.title.text , e.id.text.rsplit('/', 1)[1]), ➥
sheets.entry)
    def listWorkSheets(self):
        wks = self.gd_client.GetWorksheetsFeed(key=self.key)
        return map(lambda e: (e.title.text , e.id.text.rsplit('/', 1)[1]),wks.entry)
    def getRows(self):
        return self.gd_client.GetListFeed(key=self.key,wksht_id=self.wksht_id).entry
    def insertRow(self,row_data):
        return
self.gd_client.InsertRow(row_data,key=self.key,wksht_id=self.wksht_id)
    def deleteRow(self,entry):
        return self.gd_client.DeleteRow(entry)
    def deleteAllRows(self):
        entrylist = self.getRows()
        i = 0
        for entry in entrylist:
            self.deleteRow(entry)
            i += 1
            print "deleted row ", i


class amazonWishList:

# we can use Python and WSDL
# http://webservices.amazon.com/AWSECommerceService/AWSECommerceService.wsdl?

# I've been wondering how to introspect using WSDL -- Mark Pilgrim has some answers:
# http://www.diveintopython.org/soap_web_services/introspection.html
# well -- the introspection of the input parameters doesn't seem to yield the useful
# stuff. I was hoping for more info

    def __init__(self,listID=AMAZON_LIST_ID,amazonAccessKeyId=AMAZON_ACCESS_KEY_ID):
        self.listID = listID
        self.amazonAccessKeyId = amazonAccessKeyId
        self.getListInfo()

    def getListInfo(self):

        aws_url = "http://ecs.amazonaws.com/onca/xml?Service=AWSECommerceService&➥
Version=2007-10-29&AWSAccessKeyId=%s&Operation=ListLookup&ListType=WishList&ListId➥
=%s" % (self.amazonAccessKeyId, self.listID)
        import urllib
        f = urllib.urlopen(aws_url)
        dom = minidom.parse(f)
        self.title = getText(dom.getElementsByTagName('ListName')[0].childNodes)
        self.listLength = int(getText(dom.getElementsByTagName('TotalItems')[0].➥
childNodes))
        self.TotalPages = int(getText(dom.getElementsByTagName('TotalPages')[0].➥
childNodes))
```

```
        return(self.title, self.listLength, self.TotalPages)

    def ListItems(self):
        """
        a generator for the items on the Amazon list
        """

        import itertools
        for pageNum in xrange(1,self.TotalPages):
            aws_url = "http://ecs.amazonaws.com/onca/xml?Service=AWSECommerce➥
Service&Version=2007-10-29&AWSAccessKeyId=%s&Operation=ListLookup&ListType=Wish➥
List&ListId=%s&ResponseGroup=ListItems,Medium&ProductPage=%s" % (self.amazon➥
AccessKeyId,self.listID,pageNum)
            import urllib
            f = urllib.urlopen(aws_url)
            dom = minidom.parse(f)
            f.close()
            items = dom.getElementsByTagName('ListItem')
            for c in xrange(0,10):
                yield items[c]

    def parseListItem(self,item):
        from string import join
        from decimal import Decimal

        itemDict = {}

        itemDict['asin'] = getText(item.getElementsByTagName('ASIN')[0].childNodes)
        itemDict['dateadded'] = getText(item.getElementsByTagName('DateAdded')[0].➥
childNodes)
        itemDict['detailpageurl'] = getText(item.getElementsByTagName(➥
'DetailPageURL')[0].childNodes)

        # join the text of all the author nodes, if they exist
        authorNodes = item.getElementsByTagName('Author')
        # blank not allowed
        itemDict['author'] = join(map(lambda e: getText(e.childNodes), ➥
authorNodes), ", ") or ' '

        itemDict['quantitydesired'] = getText(item.getElementsByTagName(➥
'QuantityDesired')[0].childNodes)

        titleNodes = item.getElementsByTagName('Title')
        # blank title not allowed
        itemDict['title'] = join(map(lambda e: getText(e.childNodes), ➥
titleNodes), ", ") or ' '
```

```
        # to fix -- not all things have a LowestNewPrice
        itemDict['price'] = str(Decimal(getText(item.getElementsByTagName(➥
'LowestNewPrice')[0].getElementsByTagName('Amount')[0].childNodes))/100) or ' '

        return itemDict

def main():

    gs = GSheetForAmazonList(user=GoogleUser,pwd=GooglePW)
    gs.setKey(GSheet_KEY)
    gs.setWkshtId(GWrkSh_ID)

    aWishList = amazonWishList(listID=AMAZON_LIST_ID,amazonAccessKeyId=➥
AMAZON_ACCESS_KEY_ID)
    items = aWishList.ListItems()
    print "deleting all rows..."
    gs.deleteAllRows()
    for item in items:
        try:
            h = aWishList.parseListItem(item)
            print h['asin']
        except Exception, e:
            print "Error %s parsing %s" % (e, item.toprettyxml("  "))
        try:
            gs.insertRow(h)
        except Exception, e:
            print "Error %s inserting %s" % (e, h['asin'])

if __name__ == '__main__':
    main()
```

Here are some things to note about this code:

- The GSheetForAmazonList class provides convenience methods for the Google GData library.

- The error handling is essential since not all wishlist items necessarily have all the pieces of data requested. It's important for the code to keep moving even if data is missing.

- At least in the Python GData interface to Google Spreadsheets, you can't insert blank cells.

- amazonWishList.ListItems is a Python generator, which creates an iterator to parcel out the Amazon items one at a time. See http://www.ibm.com/developerworks/library/ l-pycon.html?t=gr,lnxw16=PyIntro for a tutorial on Python generators.

- You can speed up the operation of this code through batch operations (http://code. google.com/apis/gdata/batch.html), which are currently supported in the GData interface and in the Java API kit (but not Python).

Zend PHP API Kit for Google Spreadsheets

In this section, I'll show you how to use the PHP API kit for Google Spreadsheets to read the contents of the Google Spreadsheets that we'll generate In the previous mashup. You can download the Zend Framework from here:

```
http://framework.zend.com/
```

and read about how to use the Zend Framework to access Google Spreadsheet here:

```
http://framework.zend.com/manual/en/zend.gdata.spreadsheets.html
```

and here:

```
http://code.google.com/apis/spreadsheets/developers_guide_php.html
```

The following code first lists your spreadsheets and then the rows and named columns of the spreadsheet containing items from your Amazon.com wishlist:

```php
<?php

# user and password for google spreadsheet
$user = "[GoogleUSER]";
$pass = "[GooglePASSWORD]";

# set parameters for your version of "My Amazon WishList" Google Spreadsheet
$GSheetID = "[GSheetID]";
$worksheetID="[worksheetID]";
#$GSheetID = "oO6341737111865728099.3585145106901556666";
#$worksheetID="od6";

# list entries from a spreadsheet

require_once('Zend/Loader.php');
Zend_Loader::loadClass('Zend_Gdata');
Zend_Loader::loadClass('Zend_Gdata_ClientLogin');
Zend_Loader::loadClass('Zend_Gdata_Spreadsheets');
Zend_Loader::loadClass('Zend_Http_Client');

$service = Zend_Gdata_Spreadsheets::AUTH_SERVICE_NAME;
$client = Zend_Gdata_ClientLogin::getHttpClient($user, $pass, $service);
$spreadsheetService = new Zend_Gdata_Spreadsheets($client);

#  the following printFeed shows how to parse various types of feeds
#  coming from Google Spreadsheets API
#  function is extracted from
#  http://code.google.com/apis/spreadsheets/developers_guide_php.html

function printFeed($feed)
{
  $i = 0;
```

```php
    foreach($feed->entries as $entry) {
      if ($entry instanceof Zend_Gdata_Spreadsheets_CellEntry) {
        print $entry->title->text .' '. $entry->content->text . "\n";
      } else if ($entry instanceof Zend_Gdata_Spreadsheets_ListEntry) {
        print $i .' '. $entry->title->text .' '. $entry->content->text . "\n";
      } else {
        print $i .' '. $entry->title->text . "\n";
      }
      $i++;
    }
}

# figuring out how to print rows

function printWorksheetFeed($feed)
{
  $i = 2;  # the first row of content is row 2
  foreach($feed->entries as $row) {
    print "Row " . $i .' '. $row->title->text . "\t";
    $i++;
    $rowData = $row->getCustom();
    foreach($rowData as $customEntry) {
      print $customEntry->getColumnName() . " = " . $customEntry->getText(). "\t";
    }
    print "\n";
  }
}

# first print a list of your Google Spreadsheets

$feed = $spreadsheetService->getSpreadsheetFeed();
printFeed($feed);

# Print the content of a specific Spreadsheet/Worksheet
# set a query to return a worksheet and print the contents of the worksheet

$query = new Zend_Gdata_Spreadsheets_ListQuery();
$query->setSpreadsheetKey($GSheetID);
$query->setWorksheetId($worksheetID);
$listFeed = $spreadsheetService->getListFeed($query);
printWorksheetFeed($listFeed);

?>
```

A Final Variation: Amazon Wishlist to Microsoft Excel via COM

With code to access the Amazon.com wishlist in hand, you can use COM programming to
generate an Excel spreadsheet with the same information. To learn more about the details
about how to do so, consult Chapter 12 of *Python Programming on Win32*.[23]

```python
from amazonListToGSheet import GS_HEADER, amazonWishList, AMAZON_LIST_ID, ➡
AMAZON_ACCESS_KEY_ID, GS_KEYS
from win32com.client import Dispatch

# fire up the Excel application
xlApp = Dispatch("Excel.Application")
xlApp.Visible = 1
xlApp.Workbooks.Add()

# write the headers
col = 1

def insertRow(sheet,row,data,keys):
    col = 1
    for k in keys:
        sheet.Cells(row,col).Value = data[k]
        col += 1

for h in GS_HEADER:
    xlApp.ActiveSheet.Cells(1,col).Value = h
    col +=1
# now loop through the amazon wishlist

aWishList =
amazonWishList(listID=AMAZON_LIST_ID,amazonAccessKeyId=AMAZON_ACCESS_KEY_ID)
items = aWishList.ListItems()

row = 2
for item in items:
    try:
        p = aWishList.parseListItem(item)
        print p['asin']
    except Exception, e:
        print "Error %s parsing %s" % (e, item.toprettyxml("  "))
    try:
        insertRow(xlApp.ActiveSheet,row,p,GS_KEYS)
        row += 1
    except Exception, e:
        print "Error %s inserting %s" % (e, p['asin'])
```

---

23. http://www.oreilly.com/catalog/pythonwin32/chapter/ch12.html

Zoho APIs

Zoho (http://zoho.com) has been generating a good amount of attention for its online office suite, which is the most comprehensive one available right now.[24] Among its offerings are Zoho Writer (a word processor), Zoho Sheet (a spreadsheet), and Zoho Show.

There are currently APIs for Writer, Sheet, and Show:

http://writer.zoho.com/public/help/zohoapi/fullpage

Currently, the APIs do not talk deeply to pieces of documents. There are storage APIs that let you upload and download documents. To access pieces, you have to use the techniques shown in the rest of this chapter to parse and write documents (for instance: http://writer.zoho.com/public/help/userView.AddWorkbook/noband). I suspect that API calls to access parts of documents will follow at some point in the future.

Summary

This chapter focused on two aspects of desktop and web-based office suites. First, you examined two major XML-based document formats: OpenDocument format (used in such applications as OpenOffice.org) and Open Office XML (used by Microsoft Office 2007). Then, you studied how to figure out how to generate some basic ODF text documents (through writing ODF directly and through using API kits) and how to generate a rudimentary OOXML document. You can apply the techniques shown here to deepen your understanding of ODF and Office Open XML.

Second, you studied a major instance of a programmable online office application: Google Spreadsheets. You studied how to use the Python API kit to create a Google spreadsheet from an Amazon.com wishlist using the APIs of their respective services. You also looked briefly at how to use the PHP API kit.

---

24. http://www.technologyreview.com/Biztech/18816/ provides a useful analysis of the Zoho vs. Google Docs battle and how they compare.

■ ■ ■

Using Microformats and RDFa As Embeddable Data Formats

The central problem that we will study in this chapter is how to embed information in web pages in a way that is easy to understand by both humans and computer programs. The solution that we will consider in depth is *microformats*, little chunks of structured data that are seamlessly embedded in web pages. (X)HTML is designed primarily to produce a human user interface (via a web browser). However, by carefully following certain conventions (ones that constitute microformats), you can produce (X)HTML out of which data can be unambiguously extracted. The consequence is that it is relatively easy to write computer programs to parse microformats so that the data can be reused in other contexts—giving rise to plenty of mashup possibilities. Moreover, having data embedded right in the context of a user interface is helpful. A user can decide what to do with this data (how to "operate" on a given piece of data) while in the context of normal browsing.

Now, the previous paragraph is a bit abstract. What I will do in this chapter is walk you through some concrete examples describing microformats in general. We will use Operator, a Firefox extension, to help parse and view microformats and to create scripts that enable users to take specific actions in response to microformats. Specifically, we will do the following:

- Study specific examples of microformats

- Look at how to use the Firefox add-on Operator to jump-start your study of microformats

- Look at programmatic approaches to consuming and creating microformats

- Compare microformats to leading alternatives such as RDFa as a way to embed data in human-readable contexts.

Using Operator to Learn About Microformats

Installing the Operator add-on in Firefox and seeing it in action is a good way to learn about microformats. You can download it from here:

```
https://addons.mozilla.org/en-US/firefox/addon/4106
```

As of writing, the latest stable version is 0.8, the one I will use and describe in this chapter. (Note that there is also a 0.9 beta version.[1])

When using Operator, you should have on hand the closest thing to official documentation for the extension:

```
http://www.kaply.com/weblog/operator/
```

Now let's see what Operator can do for you once it is installed. Let's look at Operator in action by loading a page from Upcoming.yahoo.com (the event aggregation site you learned about in Chapter 15):

```
http://upcoming.yahoo.com/event/144855
```

Figure 18-1 shows what happens in the Operator toolbar. I've chosen this page to show you an example of microformats in use "in the wild." (Later in this chapter, I'll show you an example HTML page I created to show examples of microformats.)

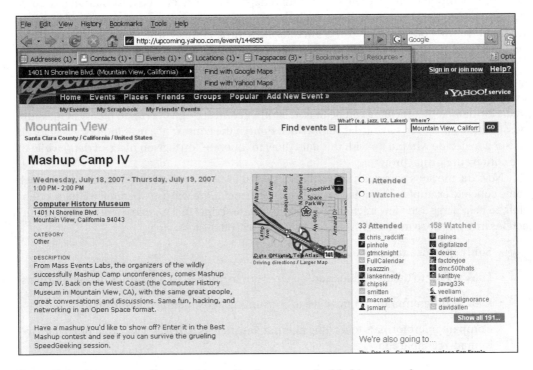

Figure 18-1. *Operator toolbar showing microformats embedded in a page from Upcoming.yahoo.com. Actions available for the location microformat are shown boxed. (Reproduced with permission of Yahoo! Inc. ® 2007 by Yahoo! Inc. YAHOO! and the YAHOO! logo are trademarks of Yahoo! Inc.)*

---

1. See the blog entry announcing 0.9b (http://www.kaply.com/weblog/2007/12/03/operator-09-beta-available/). You can download the latest develop version of Operator from http://www.kaply.com/operator/operator.xpi.

You will notice in the Operator toolbar a list of data formats recognized by Operator, along with the number of instances of each format. By default, these formats (listed by their descriptive and formal names) are as follows:

- Addresses (adr)

- Contacts (hCard)

- Events (hCalendar)

- Location (geo)

- Tagspaces (tag or rel-tag)[2]

- Bookmarks (xFolk)

- Resources (RDF)

By default, the Operator toolbar uses the descriptive names. You can instead display the formal names of the data formats in the Operator toolbar (by doing to the General tab and unchecking Use Descriptive Names under Data Formats). Toggling that option allows you to correlate the formal and descriptive names of the data formats.

I will cover the individual data formats in detail later in the chapter. Continuing with the example from Upcoming.yahoo.com, note that Operator indicates the presence of instances for the following formats: adr, hCard, hCalendar, geo, and tag. What do these microformats have to do with the event in question (Mashup Camp IV)? The UI for Upcoming.yahoo.com gives you many options to package information about the event:

- You can send it to a number of calendars.

- You can download the event information in the iCalendar format.

- You can use the Upcoming.yahoo.com API (as explained in Chapter 15) to extract the event information from Upcoming.yahoo.com.

For instance, examine the event in iCalendar format, which you can access from http://upcoming.yahoo.com/calendar/v2/event/144855:

```
BEGIN:VCALENDAR
VERSION:2.0
X-WR-CALNAME:Upcoming Event: Mashup Camp IV
PRODID:-//Upcoming.org/Upcoming ICS//EN
CALSCALE:GREGORIAN
METHOD:PUBLISH
BEGIN:VEVENT
DTSTART:20070718T130000
DTEND:20070718T140000
RRULE:FREQ=DAILY;INTERVAL=1;UNTIL=20070720T000000
TRANSP:TRANSPARENT
SUMMARY:Mashup Camp IV
```

---

2. The format called tag in Operator is known as rel-tag on http://microformats.org.

```
DESCRIPTION: [Full details at http://upcoming.yahoo.com/event/144855/ ] From Mass
Events Labs\, the organizers of the wildly successfully Mashup Camp unconferences\,
comes Mashup Camp IV.  Back on the West Coast (the Computer History Museum in
Mountain View\, CA)\, with the same great people\,  great conversations and
discussions.  Same fun\, hacking\, and networking in an Open Space format.
        Have a mashup you'd like to show off?  Enter it in the Best Mashup contest and
see if you can survive the grueling SpeedGeeking session.  Event submitted by
Eventful.com on behalf of chris_radcliff .
URL;VALUE=URI:http://upcoming.yahoo.com/event/144855/
UID:http://upcoming.yahoo.com/event/144855/
DTSTAMP:20070125T124529
LAST-UPDATED:20070125T124529
CATEGORIES:Other
ORGANIZER;CN=chris_radcliff:X-ADDR:http://upcoming.yahoo.com/user/19139/
LOCATION;VENUE-UID="http://upcoming.yahoo.com/venue/259/":Computer History Museum @
1401 N Shoreline Blvd.\, Mountain View\, California 94043 US
END:VEVENT
BEGIN:VVENUE
X-VVENUE-INFO:http://evdb.com/docs/ical-venue/draft-norris-ical-venue.html
NAME:Computer History Museum
ADDRESS:1401 N Shoreline Blvd.
CITY:Mountain View
REGION;X-ABBREV=ca:California
COUNTRY;X-ABBREV=us:United States
POSTALCODE:94043
GEO:37.4149;-122.078
URL;X-LABEL=Venue Info:http://www.computerhistory.org/
END:VVENUE
END:VCALENDAR
```

As the Operator toolbar indicates, the event information is also embedded in the (X)HTML source at the following location as a series of microformats:

```
http://upcoming.yahoo.com/event/144855
```

Let's take a look at each of these example microformats in turn. I'll give a more formal discussion of each one in the following sections.

■**Tip** You can use Operator to help in this exercise by checking the Debug Mode option (on the General tab) in Operator so that you have access to the Debug action for each microformat instance. The Debug action lists the (X)HTML source fragment containing the microformat instance.

---

adr (Addresses)

From the web page, you can read the address for the event: 1401 N Shoreline Blvd., Mountain View, California, 94043. Operator picks out the address as an instance of the adr data format, with the corresponding (X)HTML source fragment:

```
<div class="address adr">
  <span class="street-address">1401 N Shoreline Blvd.</span><br />
  <span class="locality">Mountain View</span>,
  <span class="region">California</span> <span class="postal-code">94043</span>
</div>
```

Note the use of the `<div>` tag to wrap the address and class attributes to separate and name the parts of the address. This (X)HTML fragment meets two goals simultaneously: it displays an address naturally and appropriately for a human reader of the web page, and it uses (X)HTML elements and attributes to enable programs (such as Operator) to reliably parse an address from the (X)HTML. You will see this design goal of satisfying human and computer readers repeated among all the microformats.

With the `adr` microformat parsed out, you as a user can then apply an *action* to the address. Operator has by default two actions (in addition to Debug) that you can apply to an address: Find with Google Maps and Find with Yahoo! Maps. Selecting the first action, for instance, loads the following into the browser:

```
http://maps.google.com/maps?q=1401%20N%20Shoreline%20Blvd.,%20California,%20Mountain➥
%20View,%2094043
```

This action, in effect, enables Operator to perform a mashup of Upcoming.yahoo.com and Google Maps—and more generally, any web site that has `adr` microformat data with Google Maps. Note also how Operator enables the user to invoke this action in the context of web browsing. Firefox with Operator joins a web site with an `adr` microformat to Google Maps—and not a third-party web application.

Operator allows you to add other actions. Later in the chapter, I will show you how to add other user scripts to Operator and to write a basic user script to geocode addresses.

hCard (Contacts)

The `hCard` data format is meant to represent a person or organization, specifically contact information for the entity. The (X)HTML source for the embedded `hCard` microformat is as follows:

```
<div class="venue location vcard">
  <span class="fn org">
    <a href="/venue/259/">Computer History Museum</a>
  </span>
  <br />
  <div class="address adr">
    <span class="street-address">1401 N Shoreline Blvd.</span><br />
    <span class="locality">Mountain View</span>,
    <span class="region">California</span>
    <span class="postal-code">94043</span>
  </div>
  <span class="geo" style="display: none">
    <span class="latitude">37.4149</span>,
    <span class="longitude">-122.078</span>
  </span>
</div>
```

You might be wondering why you will see vcard (instead of hcard) as a class attribute. The reason is that hCard is derived from the vCard standard. You can compare the vCard data that Operator creates for this page to the (X)HTML source to see the similarities:

```
BEGIN:VCARD
PRODID:-//kaply.com//Operator 0.8//EN
SOURCE:http://upcoming.yahoo.com/event/144855
NAME:Mashup Camp IV at Computer History Museum (Wednesday, July 18, 2007) - Upcoming
VERSION:3.0
N:;;;;
ORG;CHARSET=UTF-8:Computer History Museum
FN;CHARSET=UTF-8:Computer History Museum
UID:
ADR;CHARSET=UTF-8:;;1401 N Shoreline Blvd.;Mountain View;California;94043;
GEO:37.4149;-122.078
END:VCARD
```

Among the default actions in Operator for hCard is Add to Yahoo! Contacts, which, when invoked for this page, loads the following URL into the browser:

```
http://address.yahoo.com/?fn=Computer%20History%20Museum&co=Computer%20History%20Mus➥
eum&ha1=1401%20N%20Shoreline%20Blvd.&hc=Mountain%20View&hs=California&hz=94043&A=C
```

hCalendar (Events)

The hCalendar microformat represents events and is roughly speaking the iCalendar format transformed into a microformat. (See Chapter 15 for a discussion of iCalendar.) The (X)HTML source for the hCalendar microformat is a large fragment that I will not quote here. To find it, you can use Operator or look at the source and find a <div> element that begins with this:

```
<div id="calendarContainer" class="vcalendar"> <!-- Begin vCalendar -->
```

and ends lines later with this:

```
</div> <!-- End vCalendar -->
```

The pieces of (X)HTML in between contain event data, such as this:

```
<abbr class="dtstart" title="20070718T130000">Wednesday, July 18, 2007
</abbr>
```

and the following:

```
<abbr class="dtend" title="20070719T140000">
```

As in the case of hCard, you might wonder why the hCalendar format would use class="vcalendar" and not class="hcalendar". vCalendar was the precursor to iCalendar, a fact that is reflected in the iCalendar standard (which if you look at the iCalendar for the Upcoming.yahoo.com event listed earlier), you have the following structure:

```
BEGIN:VCALENDAR
[...]
DTSTART:20070718T130000
DTEND:20070718T140000
[...]
END:VCALENDAR
```

Among the default actions associated with hCalendar are ones to send the event data to Google Calendar, Yahoo! Calendar, and 30boxes.com. Compare how you moved event data with APIs in Chapter 15 with this approach of extracting microformat data and sending that data to other services via an HTTP GET request.

geo (Locations)

The geo data format represents a geospatial location, specifically a latitude and longitude. The (X)HTML source for the geo instance is as follows:

```
<span class="geo" style="display: none">
  <span class="latitude">37.4149</span>,
  <span class="longitude">-122.078</span>
</span>
```

With Operator, you can map this location to Google Maps and Yahoo! Maps, or you can export it as KML.

tag (Tagspaces)

Upcoming.yahoo.com supports the tagging of individual events. For instance, among the tags for the example event is mashup. You can find this tag marked up using the tag microformat in the (X)HTML source. For example:

```
<a href="/tag/mashup/" rel="tag" class="category">mashup</a>
```

You'll see from the following discussion that the combination of rel=tag in an <a> element is indicative of a tag microformat and that the last path component of the URL (that is, mashup) is the text of the tag. By default, there are actions in Operator to look this tag up in such web sites as del.icio.us, Flickr, Upcoming.yahoo.com, and YouTube.

Definitions and Design Goals of Microformats

This is the current official definition of microformats from http://microformats.org/:

> *Designed for humans first and machines second, microformats are a set of simple, open data formats built upon existing and widely adopted standards.*

Many other definitions of microformats have been proposed, some of which I find more illuminating. This is the definition on the Microformats.org site:[3]

Microformats can be defined as: simple conventions for embedding semantic markup for a specific problem domain in human-readable (X)HTML/XML documents, Atom/RSS feeds, and "plain" XML that normalize existing content usage patterns using brief, descriptive class names often based on existing interoperable standards to enable decentralized development of resources, tools, and services.

Out of this definition, I would emphasize the following points:

- Human-readable (X)HTML/XML documents, Atom/RSS feeds, and "plain" XML

- Using brief, descriptive class names

It's important to know about the intentional limitations built into microformats before criticizing them. From the list of things that microformats are *not* at http://microformats.org/about/, I will highlight a few. Microformats are not the following:

- Infinitely extensible and open-ended

- A panacea for all taxonomies, ontologies, and other such abstractions

Keep those limitations in mind when we compare microformats to specifications such as RDFa, which are aimed to be highly generalizable.

Because microformats involve both design philosophies and concrete formats (which you can use whether or not you subscribe to the microformats design philosophy), it's easy to just ignore the philosophy. So if you want to just use the work of the microformats community, is this philosophy relevant? Probably—since there are a lot of design decisions that are hard to understand without knowing that philosophy.

Finally, with so many other ways to already get event data, what does having the microformat contribute to the mix? Well, there are at least two advantages:

- For user-centered contexts, programs that have the (X)HTML source already—for instance, a web browser such as Firefox and its associated machinery (browser extensions, Greasemonkey scripts, and so on)—can reliably extract the event data and then present options to the user about what to do with that data. (The Operator Firefox add-on instantiates this idea.)

- Spiders and other screen-scrapers can also extract the information reliably—without the usual heuristical guessing—to build aggregated databases of events across web pages. That's what sites such as Technorati are doing.

In both cases, there is no need to make an extra call to the API to get this desired information about the event.

---

3. http://microformats.org/wiki/what-are-microformats retrieved as http://microformats.org/wiki?title=what-are-microformats&direction=next&oldid=21422.

Microformats Design Patterns

Microformats are meant to be embeddable in (X)HTML—so anywhere you can put (X)HTML, you should be able to stick in microformats—including RSS and Atom feeds.

The best way to start with microformats is to look at some specific examples while keeping an eye out for some general design patterns that are behind microformats; see http://microformats.org/wiki/design-patterns. That is, what are some tried-and-true ways to insert data into HTML?

rel-design-pattern

rel-design-pattern uses values in a rel attribute to indicate the meaning of a link.[4] You already saw an example with the tag or rel-tag microformat:

```
<a href="/tag/mashup/" rel="tag" class="category">mashup</a>
```

In addition to rel-tag, you'll learn about rel-license, a data format that also uses rel-design-pattern.

The rev attribute is also used in this design pattern. In case you're not up on what rev is supposed to mean (don't feel bad if you don't—I didn't before reading about microformats), read the FAQ (http://microformats.org/wiki/rev#Then_what_does_.22rev.22_mean.3F):

> *'rev' is the precise opposite (or 'reverse') of the 'rel' attribute. E.g. a* rev="help" *link indicates that the current document is 'help' for the resource indicated by the href.*

MULTIPLE VALUES IN ATTRIBUTES

You can stick multiple values in an attribute by separating the individual values by whitespace. The following is how you associate an HTML element with multiple classes. This is also standard usage for other attributes such as rel and rev.

```
http://www.w3.org/TR/html401/struct/links.html#adef-rel
http://www.w3.org/TR/html401/struct/links.html#adef-rev
```

class-design-pattern

This design pattern[5] involves selecting an appropriate (X)HTML element and the class attribute to hold a whitespace-separated list of semantic class names (http://microformats.org/wiki/semantic-class-names). The <span> and <div> elements can be used in the absence of other appropriate (X)HTML elements to demarcate content.

---

4. http://microformats.org/wiki/rel-design-pattern

5. http://microformats.org/wiki/class-design-pattern

As you have already seen from the earlier examples, the adr, hCard, geo, and hCalendar formats use class-design-pattern. For instance:

```
<div class="address adr">
  <span class="street-address">1401 N Shoreline Blvd.</span><br />
  <span class="locality">Mountain View</span>,
  <span class="region">California</span> <span class="postal-code">94043</span>
</div>
```

and for example:

```
<span class="geo" style="display: none">
  <span class="latitude">37.4149</span>,
  <span class="longitude">-122.078</span>
</span>
```

When you come to selecting class names, you should note the ones that are already in use to avoid reinventing the wheel and causing namespace collisions: http://microformats.org/wiki/existing-classes.

abbr-design-pattern

This pattern[6] uses the <abbr> HTML tag to wrap text with a machine-readable version of that information, which is stored in the title attribute of the <abbr> element. This pattern is most commonly used to encode the date and time in datetime-design-pattern (http://microformats.org/wiki/datetime-design-pattern):

```
<abbr class="dtstart" title="20080310T1700-08">
  March 10, 2008 at 5 PM
</abbr>
```

There are some concerns about the accessibility of such constructions (http://microformats.org/wiki/datetime-design-pattern#Accessibility_issues). Here is a recommended alternative:

```
<span class="dtstart" title="20080310T1700-08">
  March 10, 2008 at 5 PM, Pacific Standard Time
</span>
```

include-pattern

This pattern[7] is for including data from one microformat into another microformat from the same page. A major reason for this pattern is to avoid redundancy. It's used in the proposed hResume, hReview, and hAtom microformats. For example, I can reuse the content contained in the following hCard:

---

6. http://microformats.org/wiki/abbr-design-pattern

7. http://microformats.org/wiki/include-pattern

```
<span class="vcard">
 <span class="fn n" id="ryee-hcard">
  <span class="given-name">Raymond</span> <span class="family-name">Yee</span>
 </span>
</span>
```

in a second hCard:

```
<span class="vcard">
 <a href="#ryee-hcard" class="include" title="Raymond Yee"></a>
 <span class="org">UC Berkeley</span>
 <span class="title">Alumnus</span>
</span>
```

Note the use of id="ryee-hcard" in the first hCard instance and href="#ryee-hcard" to tie the two hCard instances, as well as class="include" in the <a> element in the hCard instance that reuses data from the other instance.

Examples of Microformats

In this section, I will show more examples of a number of microformats. (You can find a list of microformats at http://microformats.org/wiki/Main_Page.) I have gathered the examples in this section into one page:

http://examples.mashupguide.net/ch18/sample_microformats.html

Try Operator on this URL to have it parse the various microformats. Some of the following data formats are not supported natively by Operator, but you might be able to find extra user scripts that add such support. (See "Installing User Scripts to Operator" for a how-to.)

INSTALLING USER SCRIPTS TO OPERATOR

To install user scripts in Operator, download a script to your local drive. Then go to the User Scripts tab in Operator Options. Next, hit the New button, and enter the path of the script on your drive. You can go to the Data formats tab to load any new formats (using the New button) and to the Actions tab to make actions visible on the Operator tab.

Make sure to restart Firefox for the scripts to take effect.

You can find more details at http://www.kaply.com/weblog/operator/.

A good place to find Operator user scripts is http://www.kaply.com/weblog/operator-user-scripts/.

---

rel-license

rel-license (http://microformats.org/wiki/rel-license) is for specifying a license to be associated with the embedding page. For instance, when you go to the Creative Commons site (http://creativecommons.org/license) to select a license, you will be given some HTML that uses the `rel-license` microformat to indicate a license. For instance, if you select the defaults, you will get something like this:[8]

```
<a rel="license" href="http://creativecommons.org/licenses/by/3.0/">
<img alt="Creative Commons License" style="border-width:0"
    src="http://i.creativecommons.org/l/by/3.0/88x31.png" />
</a>
<br />This work is licensed under a
<a rel="license" href="http://creativecommons.org/licenses/by/3.0/">
Creative Commons Attribution 3.0 License</a>.
```

As noted, `rel-license` uses `rel-design-pattern` (that is, it uses the `rel` attribute in an `<a>` element).

rel-tag

The `rel-tag` microformat (`http://microformats.org/wiki/rel-tag`) is used to relate a tag (as in a folksonomic tag; see Chapter 4) to a URL. You use it by implementing `rel-design-pattern`, specifically, by adding `tag` to the list of values in the `rel` attribute. The last path segment of the URL in the `href` attribute is then considered the value of the tag, and the URL value of `href` points to a collection of items having the same tag.

Consider the following example generated by WordPress for the Google Maps category for `http://blog.mashupguide.net`:

```
<a rel="tag" title="View all posts in Google Maps"
   href="http://blog.mashupguide.net/category/google-maps/">Google Maps</a>
```

In this case, `google-maps` is the tag (the last path segment of the URL in the `href` attribute), and `http://blog.mashupguide.net/category/google-maps/` points to the blog entries that have been tagged with the tag `google-maps`.

xfn

`xfn` (`http://www.gmpg.org/xfn/`), which stands for XHTML Friends Network and also uses `rel-design-pattern`, is used to denote personal relationships between the author of a web page and the people associated with the linked page. The easiest way is to get started is to fill out the XFN Creator (`http://gmpg.org/xfn/creator`).

I'll now present two examples. The first is for my wife's weblog:

```
<a href="http://laurashefler.net/blog"
   rel="friend met colleague coresident spouse muse sweetheart">Laura Shefler</a>
```

The second is for Tim Berners-Lee's web page. In this case, he is a contact since I don't know him personally:

```
<a href="http://www.w3.org/People/Berners-Lee/" rel="contact">Tim Berners-Lee</a>
```

---

8. `http://creativecommons.org/license/results-one?q_1=2&q_1=1&field_commercial=yes&field_derivatives=yes&field_jurisdiction=&field_format=&lang=en&language=en&n_questions=3`

xFolk

xFolk (http://microformats.org/wiki/xfolk) is used to publish a bookmark (like the bookmarks you see in social bookmarking sites, covered in Chapter 14). That is, you can use xFolk to tie a URL to a description and tags. (I imagine that the name xFolk is meant to suggest folksonomies since you can use it to tag URLs.)

xFolk uses class-design-pattern (with class="xfolkentry"). In the following example, the URL of the bookmark is http://www.w3.org/People/Berners-Lee, the description is The inventor of the WWW, and the tag associated with the bookmark is WWW:

```
<div class="xfolkentry">
  <a class="taggedlink" href="http://www.w3.org/People/Berners-Lee/">Tim Berners-Lee
  </a>: <span class="description">The inventor of the WWW</span>
  <a rel="tag" href="http://technorati.com/tag/WWW"></a>
</div>
```

Note the use of the xfolkentry, taggedlink, and description class names.

With Operator, you can try the "Bookmark with del.icio.us" action, which sends the bookmark to del.icio.us through the following URL:

```
https://secure.del.icio.us/login?url=http%3A%2F%2Fwww.w3.org%2FPeople%2FBerners-Lee%➥
2F&title=Tim%20Berners-Lee&notes=The%20inventer%20of%20the%20WWW&v=4
```

geo

geo (http://microformats.org/wiki/geo) is used to denote the latitude and longitude of the resource tied to the embedding web page. Using http://microformats.org/wiki/geo-cheatsheet, you can figure out how to use class-design-pattern and use the geo, latitude, and longitude class names to write an example such as the following:

```
<div class="geo">Tim Berners-Lee's location is:
  <span class="latitude">42.3633690</span>,
  <span class="longitude">-71.091796</span>.
</div>
```

Given all the attention we paid to mapping geotagged photos in Flickr, I should mention that Flickr uses the geo microformat to denote the location of geotagged photos. For instance, if you load this:

```
http://flickr.com/photos/raymondyee/18389540/
```

into Firefox, you can use Operator to extract the geo instance:

```
<span class="geo" style="display: none">
  <span class="latitude">37.4149</span>,
  <span class="longitude">-122.078</span>
</span>
```

Then you can invoke one of the default actions (for example, Find with Google Maps) to plot the location of the photo at this location:

```
http://maps.google.com/maps?ll=37.8721,-122.257704&q=37.8721,-122.257704
```

hCard and adr

hCard (http://microformats.org/wiki/hcard) is used to represent such entities as people, organizations, companies, and places. An easy way to get started with hCard is to use the hCard Creator at http://microformats.org/code/hcard/creator.

Let's create an hCard for Tim Berners-Lee, the inventor of the Web, drawing on his web page at http://www.w3.org/People/Berners-Lee/ to come up with the following:

```
<div id="hcard-Tim-Berners-Lee" class="vcard">
  <a class="url fn" href="http://www.w3.org/People/Berners-Lee/">Tim Berners-Lee</a>
  <div class="org">World Wide Web Consortium</div>
  <a class="email" href="mailto:timbl@w3.org">timbl@w3.org</a>
  <div class="adr">
    <div class="street-address">77 Massachusetts Ave. (MIT Room 32-G524)</div>
    <span class="locality">Cambridge</span>
    ,
    <span class="region">MA</span>
    ,
    <span class="postal-code">02139</span>

    <span class="country-name">USA</span>

  </div>
  <div class="tel">+1 (617) 253 5702</div>
  <p style="font-size:smaller;">This <a href="http://microformats.org/wiki/hcard">
hCard</a> created with the <a href="http://microformats.org/code/hcard/creator">
hCard creator</a>.
  </p>
</div>
```

You'll notice that inside the hCard microformat is the adr microformat (http://microformats.org/wiki/adr). adr is a mapping of vCard:

> *This specification introduces the adr microformat, which is a 1:1 representation of the aforementioned adr property from the vCard standard, by simply reusing the adr property and sub-properties as-is from the hCard microformat.*

There is support in adr for the following properties, which show up in adr as (X)HTML attributes according to class-design-pattern:

- post-office-box
- extended-address
- street-address
- locality
- region

- postal-code

- country-name

hCalendar

hCalendar (http://microformats.org/wiki/hcalendar) is a microformat-based iCalendar used to represent calendar information. To quickly create an instance, use the hCalendar Creator (http://microformats.org/code/hcalendar/creator), or consult the hCalendar cheat sheet (http://microformats.org/wiki/hcalendar-cheatsheet). Let's create an hCalendar for the WWW 2008 conference (http://www2008.org/):

```
<div class="vevent"
    id="hcalendar-WWW-2008-17th-International-World-Wide-Web-Conference">
  <a class="url" href="http://www2008.org/">
    <abbr class="dtstart" title="20080421">April 21th</abbr> &mdash;
    <abbr class="dtend" title="20080426">25th, 2008</abbr>
    <span class="summary">
      WWW 2008 (17th International World Wide Web Conference)
    </span>&mdash; at
    <span class="location">Beijing International Convention Center, </span>
  </a>
  <div class="description">"The World Wide Web Conference is a global event bringing
together key researchers, innovators, decision-makers, technologists, businesses,
and standards bodies working to shape the Web. Since its inception in 1994, the WWW
conference has become the annual venue for international discussions and debate on
the future evolution of the Web."</div>
  <p style="font-size: smaller;">This
    <a href="http://microformats.org/wiki/hcalendar">hCalendar event</a>
brought to you by the
    <a href="http://microformats.org/code/hcalendar/creator">hCalendar Creator</a>.
  </p>
</div>
```

Other Microformats

Here are some other noteworthy microformats:

- xoxo (http://microformats.org/wiki/xoxo) represents hierarchical outlines (that is, nested lists).

- vote-links (http://microformats.org/wiki/vote-links) indicates whether a link represents a vote-for, vote-abstain, or vote-against the link.

- hReview (http://microformats.org/wiki/hreview) represents reviews of URLs.

- hResume (http://microformats.org/wiki/hresume) represents resumes.

Microformats in Practice

You can learn a lot about microformats by studying how they are actually being used on the Web. Some implementations include the following:

- The use of adr, hCard, hCalendar, tag, and geo by Upcoming.yahoo.com and Eventful.com

- The use of adr and hCard at Yahoo! Local

- The use of hCard and adr on Technorati

I suggest using the list of implementations of microformats in the wild (http://microformats.org/wiki/examples-in-the-wild), which includes lists for geo, hCalendar, hCard, hReview, and include-pattern. Go to the listed sites, and use Operator to pick out the microformats.

Programming with Microformats

For simple microformats, including the ones that depend on rel-design-pattern, it should be simple enough to write your own code to parse data from and write data to the appropriate rel and rev attributes. It takes a lot more work to handcraft parsers for complicated microformats such as hCard and hCalendar because there are many possible properties.

There are no schemas for microformats, only specifications written for direct human interpretation, which makes difficult any autogeneration of high-quality language-specific parsers from the specifications.[9]

A challenge in working with microformats is the lack of validators. Norm Walsh argues that W3C Schema and Relax-NG will not work for the purpose of expressing the syntax of microformats as schemas, though Schematron might be up for the task.[10] You can use XMDP, a schema (of sorts) geared to easy human consumption, to get partway to generating validators, argues Brian Suda, at least for some simple formats.[11]

Hence, you will need to look for some handcrafted language-specific libraries to handle microformats. Start by looking at http://microformats.org/wiki/implementations.

Language-Specific Libraries

Here are some language-specific libraries:

- mofo (http://mofo.rubyforge.org/) is a new Ruby library that has support for a variety of microformats including hCard, hCalendar, and xfn.

- uformats (http://rubyforge.org/projects/uformats/) is another Ruby library that has support for hReview, hCard, hCalendar, rel-tag, rel-license, and include-pattern.

---

9. http://smackman.com/2006/06/01/an-old-idea/ and http://lists.w3.org/Archives/Public/public-rdf-in-xhtml-tf/2006Jun/0011.html.

10. See http://norman.walsh.name/2006/04/13/validatingMicroformats for more about validating microformats. Erik van der Vlist adds to this analysis at http://eric.van-der-vlist.com/blog/2277_Validating_microformats.item.

11. http://norman.walsh.name/2005/09/05/microformats#comment0008

- For PHP 5, consider using hKit (http://allinthehead.com/hkit/), which has support for hCard.

- Probably the best library out there is Microformats.js, which is the heart of the Operator add-on.[12]

There are interesting things to do with Operator, both for what it can do today and for how it might be a harbinger of things to come in Firefox 3 (which might have native support for microformats).[13] Operator makes a great sandbox for experimenting with microformats. Here are some things to try:

- Download and install user-scripts to add new actions and new microformats (http://www.kaply.com/weblog/operator-user-scripts/).

- Try your hand at writing new actions or support for new microformats by studying existing scripts and the documentation.[14]

- Study the code for Operator to pick up on the subtleties that go into working code using microformats.[15]

Writing an Operator Script

In this section, I'll lead you through the process of creating a simple user script for Operator. Start by looking through the best documentation for understanding Operator scripts:

http://www.kaply.com/weblog/operator-user-scripts/

There you will find a tutorial for writing a script that lets users find the closest Domino's Pizza to a given instance of an address (adr):

http://www.kaply.com/weblog/operator-user-scripts/creating-a-microformat-action-user-script-basic/

In this section, I will walk you through the steps to create a script that performs a similar function. Instead of converting an adr instance into a URL to the Domino's Pizza web site, our script will geocode the address by creating a URL to http://geocoder.us. Since our script is similar to that of the tutorial, we will follow a two-step strategy:

1. Install the tutorial script to understand how it works.

2. Convert the script to one that geocodes the adr instance.

---

12. http://svn.mozilla.org/labs/operator/chrome/operator/content/Microformats/Microformats.js

13. http://www.readwriteweb.com/archives/mozilla_does_microformats_firefox3.php

14. http://www.kaply.com/weblog/2007/04/24/operator-action-architecture/ and
    http://www.kaply.com/weblog/2007/04/18/microformat-objects-in-javascript/

15. http://svn.mozilla.org/labs/operator/

Studying the Tutorial Script

You will find the tutorial script here:

```
http://www.kaply.com/weblog/wp-content/uploads/2007/07/dominos.js
```

It's possible that after this book is published, there might be a newer version of the referenced user scripts. You can check here: `http://www.kaply.com/weblog/operator-user-scripts/`.
Install it and restart your web browser. If you run the action on this:

```
http://upcoming.yahoo.com/event/144855
```

your browser will conduct a search for the closest Domino's Pizza stores to 1401 N Shoreline
Blvd in Mountain View, CA:

```
http://www.dominos.com/apps/storelocator-EN.jsp?street=1401%20N%20Shoreline%20Blvd.&➥
cityStateZip=California,%20Mountain%20View%2094043
```

Let's now study the script to understand how it works:

```
var dominos = {
  description: "Find the nearest Domino's Pizza",
  shortDescription: "Domino's",
  scope: {
    semantic: {
      "adr" : "adr"
    }
  },
  doAction: function(semanticObject, semanticObjectType) {
    var url;
    if (semanticObjectType == "adr") {
      var adr = semanticObject;
      url = "http://www.dominos.com/apps/storelocator-EN.jsp?";
      if (adr["street-address"]) {
        url += "street=";
        url += adr["street-address"].join(", ");
      }
      if ((adr.region) || (adr.locality) || (adr["postal-code"])) {
        url += "&cityStateZip=";
      }
      if (adr.region) {
        url += adr.region;
        url += ", ";
      }
      if (adr.locality) {
        url += adr.locality;
        url += " ";
      }
      if (adr["postal-code"]) {
        url += adr["postal-code"];
      }
```

```
    }
    return url;
  }
};
```

SemanticActions.add("dominos", dominos);

There are several elements to notice about this script as you think about how to adapt it:

- The dominos JavaScript object defines an action. An action consists of four properties: description, shortDescription, scope, and doAction.

- You should change the name of the JavaScript object, its description, and its shortDescription to fit the purpose of the new script.

- The scope property is used to tie an action to a specific data format. The following:

```
scope: {
    semantic: {
      "adr" : "adr"
    }
```

means any adr instance. You can limit the scope to only adr instances with the property locality with this:

```
scope: {
    semantic: {
      "adr" : "locality"
    }
```

or to a certain URL:

```
 scope: {
  url: "http://www.flickr.com"
  }
```

- Associated with the doAction property is a function that actually creates the URL for Domino's Pizza by concatenating the various pieces of the adr instance. To adapt this function, you need to understand the URL structure of http://geocoder.us, the service we will use to geocode the address.

- Note that the simplest type of action of an Operator script is to return a URL, which the browser then loads. (You can learn how to get Operator actions to perform other operations by reading the advanced tutorials at http://www.kaply.com/weblog/operator-user-scripts/.)

Writing a Geocoding Script

As you learned in Chapter 13, there are a variety of sites to use to geocode an address in the United States. One service is Geocoder.us. You can geocode an address here:

```
http://geocoder.us/demo.cgi?address={address}
```

For example:

```
http://geocoder.us/demo.cgi?address=1600+Pennsylvania+Ave%2C+Washington+DC
```

Taking the URL template for Geocoder.us into account, you can adapt the script to come up with something like the following:

```
// based on http://www.kaply.com/weblog/wp-content/uploads/2007/07/dominos.js

var geocoder_us = {
  description: "Geocode with geocoder_us",
  shortDescription: "geocoder_us",
  scope: {
    semantic: {
      "adr" : "adr"
    }
  },
  doAction: function(semanticObject, semanticObjectType) {
    var url;
    if (semanticObjectType == "adr") {
      var adr = semanticObject;
      url = "http://geocoder.us/demo.cgi?address=";
      if (adr["street-address"]) {
        url += adr["street-address"].join(", ");
        url += ", ";
      }
      if (adr.locality) {
        url += adr.locality;
        url += ", ";
      }
      if (adr.region) {
        url += adr.region;
        url += ", ";
      }
      if (adr["postal-code"]) {
        url += adr["postal-code"];
      }
    }
    return url;
  }
};

SemanticActions.add("geocoder_us", geocoder_us);
```

The resulting URL for Mashup Camp IV on Upcoming.yahoo.com is as follows:

```
http://geocoder.us/demo.cgi?address=1401%20N%20Shoreline%20Blvd.,%20Mountain%20View,➡
%20California,%2094043
```

Resources (RDFa): A Promising Complement to Microformats

There's a lot of hype around RDF and the semantic Web, but the core concept of the Resource Description Framework (RDF) is simple:

- An RDF document is just a series of statements about resources in a subject-predicate-object (triplet) form. In other words, they are statements where a resource (R) has a property (P) of a value (V)—a triplet (R,P,V). For example: (`"Raymond Yee"`, `"has age of "`, `40`).

- RDF vocabularies define ways to talk about such things as types of resources and terms for properties. For example, a genealogical vocabulary would define properties such as "is mother of" and "is sister of."

- Once we have these types of RPVs around, we can add to the mix various logical propositions. If V > 30 of an RPV with P=`"has age of"`, then (`R, "has to trust status", No`). In other words, a computer program should be able to deduce that Raymond Yee should not be trusted since he is older than 30, since one must not trust anyone older than 30.

Tim Bray's "What is RDF?" (`http://www.xml.com/pub/a/2001/01/24/rdf.html`) was the first essay I read in my attempts to understand RDF. It's still very good. However, I think that the triplets idea was still unclear to me after reading the essay. (And I don't blame Tim Bray for that since the idea is clearly in the essay.) So, you should follow up Bray's essay with reading something like Aaron Schwartz's "RDF Primer Primer" (`http://notabug.com/2002/rdfprimer/`). The two complement each other.

You can express RDF triplets in many ways, including the standard RDF/XML syntax (`http://www.w3.org/TR/rdf-syntax-grammar/`). Since we have been discussing how microformats embed machine-understandable data in (X)HTML, we'll now look at RDFa (`http://rdfa.info/about/`), described in the following way:

> With RDFa, you can easily include extra "structure" in your HTML to indicate a calendar event, contact information, a document license, etc. . . . RDFa is about total publisher control: you choose which attributes to use, which to reuse from other sites, and how to evolve, over time, the meaning of these attributes.

Here is a sample RDFa assertion, in which the *resource* (a book with ISBN of 9781590598580) has a *property* (namely, the Dublin Core title) whose *value* is `Pro Web 2.0 Mashups: Remixing Data and Web Services`:[16]

```
<span xmlns:dc="http://purl.org/dc/elements/1.1/" about="isbn:9781590598580"
    property="dc:title">Pro Web 2.0 Mashups: Remixing Data and Web Services</span>
```

---

16. `http://examples.mashupguide.net/ch18/sample_rdf.html`

I think that microformats and RDFa will both have a place on the Web. Microformats already have some good uptake and are grounded in today's real-world problems. They are focused on very specific applications. RDFa provides a mechanism for making more general assertions about pieces of data.

Reference for Further Study

The following are useful resources for more on microformats:

- The microformat book at `http://microformatique.com/book/`

- Micah Dubinko's "What Are Microformats?"[17]

- Uche Ogbuji's "Microformats in Context"[18]

Summary

You can use microformats and RDFa to embed data into the human-readable contexts of (X)HTML. In this chapter, you looked at instances of microformats that you can find "in the wild" (such as on Upcoming.yahoo.com) and ones that you can craft as simple examples, and you learned about how you can use microformats to embed data (such as contact information, addresses, geolocations, bookmarks, tags, and licenses) into (X)HTML. Microformats tend to follow certain common design patterns (that is, use class attributes or use the rel attribute) and are adapted from existing standards (such as iCalendar and vCard).

In this chapter, you learned how to use the Operator Firefox extension to work with microformats, including extracting them from web pages and invoking actions on them. You saw how these Operator actions enact simple mashups that move data from any web site with embedded microformats to another web site.

---

17. `http://www.xml.com/pub/a/2005/03/23/deviant.html`

18. `http://www.xml.com/pub/a/2006/04/26/microformats-grddl-rdfa-nvdl.html`

■ ■ ■

Integrating Search

No one needs to be reminded that search engines are at the heart of the current web infra-structure. Not surprisingly, it's useful to be able to integrate search functionality and search results into mashups. If a mashup is integrated with search engines via their APIs, users of the mashups can more easily find and reuse that digital content.

This chapter shows how to use the Google, Yahoo!, and Live.com search APIs, as well as configuring searchable web sites for access as a search plug-in in Firefox 2.0 or Internet Explorer 7 using OpenSearch. This chapter will also examine briefly how to use the Google Desktop Search API.

Google Ajax Search

Google was one of the first major search companies to provide an API: the Google SOAP API. Since December 2006, no new developer keys have been issued because Google is directing users to its newer Ajax Search API, which we will now study.

The Google Ajax Search API (`http://code.google.com/apis/ajaxsearch/`) gives you a search widget that you can embed in your web site. You can access functionality for searching the Web, doing local searches (tied to maps), and doing video searches. The widget displays a search box and takes care of displaying search results in an HTML element that you designate.

Like Google Maps, you have to sign up for a key that is tied to a specific directory; you can do that here:

`http://code.google.com/apis/ajaxsearch/signup.html`

Paste the "Hello, World" code into your page, and load it.[1] The "Hello, World" code shows you how to create a basic search box and display the results.

Manipulating Search Results

Let's adapt the basic code to let a user search a particular search source (the web search) and save a result. This is done by creating a callback (`KeepHandler`) with the `setOnKeepCallback` method. You'll also see some code to access the attributes of the result.[2]

---

1. `http://examples.mashupguide.net/ch19/google.ajax.1.html`
2. `http://examples.mashupguide.net/ch19/google.ajax.2.html`

```
<!DOCTYPE html PUBLIC "-//W3C//DTD XHTML 1.0 Strict//EN"
"http://www.w3.org/TR/xhtml1/DTD/xhtml1-strict.dtd">
<html xmlns="http://www.w3.org/1999/xhtml">
  <head>
    <meta http-equiv="content-type" content="text/html; charset=utf-8"/>
    <title>google.ajax.2.html</title>
    <link href="http://www.google.com/uds/css/gsearch.css" type="text/css"
        rel="stylesheet"/>
    <script src="http://www.google.com/uds/api?file=uds.js&amp;v=1.0&amp;key=[KEY]"
          type="text/javascript"></script>
    <script type="text/javascript">
    //<![CDATA[

    function KeepHandler(result) {
      // clone the result html node
      var node = result.html.cloneNode(true);

      // attach it
      var savedResults = document.getElementById("saved_results");
      savedResults.appendChild(node);

      // extract some info from the result to show to get at the individual
      // attributes.
      // see http://code.google.com/apis/ajaxsearch/documentation/reference.html
      var title = result.title;
      var unformattedtitle = result.titleNoFormatting;
      var content = result.content;
      var unescapedUrl = result.unescapedUrl;
      alert("Saving " + unformattedtitle + " " + unescapedUrl + " " + content);
    }


    function OnLoad() {
      // Create a search control
      var searchControl = new GSearchControl();

      // attach a handler for saving search results
      searchControl.setOnKeepCallback(this, KeepHandler);

      // expose the control to manipulation by the JavaScript shell and Firebug.
      window.searchControl = searchControl

      // Add in the web searcher
      searchControl.addSearcher(new GwebSearch());

      // Tell the searcher to draw itself and tell it where to attach
      searchControl.draw(document.getElementById("search_control"));
```

```
    // Execute an initial search
    searchControl.execute("flower");
  }
  GSearch.setOnLoadCallback(OnLoad);

  //]]>
  </script>
</head>
<body>
  <div id="search_control"></div>
  <div id="saved_div"><span>Saved Search Results:</span>
  <div id="saved_results"></div></div>
</body>
</html>
```

There's obviously more you can do with the Google Ajax Search API, such as styling the search widget. Consult the documentation to learn how. Here are some noteworthy extras:

- Adding local search to a Google map: `http://www.google.com/uds/solutions/localsearch/index.html`

- Searching outside the widget context to do raw searching: `http://www.google.com/uds/samples/apidocs/raw-searchers.html`

Indeed, you can learn plenty of things for your specific applications from the sample code:

`http://code.google.com/apis/ajaxsearch/samples.html`

For those of you who are looking for a way of using Google search without creating an HTML interface, take a look specifically at the following:

`http://www.google.com/uds/samples/apidocs/raw-searchers.html`

This sample gets the closest to giving you back the raw search functionality that the SOAP interface has, although you still need to use JavaScript and embed that search in a web page on the public Web.

Yahoo! Search

The Yahoo! Search API (`http://developer.yahoo.com/search/`) is a RESTful one. I'll now show how to use the Yahoo! Search API.

You need an application ID, which you get from here:

`https://developer.yahoo.com/wsregapp/index.php`

You can see your registered apps here:

`https://developer.yahoo.com/wsregapp/index.php?view`

Yahoo! has an authentication system called BBAuth:

`http://developer.yahoo.com/auth/`

In the authentication system, there is a single sign-on option. For this example, I signed up for the ability to do single sign-on, for which I needed to state an application endpoint:

```
http://examples.mashupguide.net/ch07/yahoo.php
```

Once you have registered your application, you can get an application ID and a shared secret.

Now, let's do a web search that doesn't require any authentication. Consulting the documentation (`http://developer.yahoo.com/search/web/`) and specifically the classic web search documentation (`http://developer.yahoo.com/search/web/V1/webSearch.html`), you can see a sample query:

```
http://search.yahooapis.com/WebSearchService/V1/webSearch?appid=YahooDemo&➥
query=madonna&results=2
```

If you substitute your own API key and search for `flower`, you'll come up with the following query:

```
http://search.yahooapis.com/WebSearchService/V1/webSearch?appid=[YourAppID]&➥
query=flower&results=1
```

An excerpt of the search results follows:

```
<Result>
  <Title>1-800-FLOWERS.COM - Official Site</Title>
  <Summary>1-800-Flowers delivers flowers and floral arrangements, gift baskets,➥
    gourmet treats, or other presents for anniversaries, birthdays, and special➥
    occasions. Order online, over the phone, or by visiting a store location.
  </Summary>
  <Url>http://www.1800flowers.com/</Url> <ClickUrl>http://uk.wrs.yahoo.com/_ylt=➥
A0Je5VZ47HdGmOQAzhvdmMwF;_ylu=X3oDMTB2cXVjNTM5BGNvbG8DdwRsA1dTMQRwb3MDMQRzZWMDc3IEdn➥
RpZAM-/SIG=19qu9j9dq/EXP=1182350840/**http%3A//rdrw1.yahoo.com/click%3
    Fu=http%3A//clickserve.cc-dt.com/link/click%253Flid%253D41000000011562437%26
    y=04765B7ED3D00A0BB4%26i=482%26c=37687%26q=02%255ESSHPM%255BL7ysphzm6%26
    e=utf-8%26r=0%26d=wow~WBSV-en-us%26n=LP94K1LESHRKDFP3%26s=3%26t=%26m=4677EC78%26
    x=057E49A7F20A924F7B2C30A7101C217A96</ClickUrl>
  <DisplayUrl>www.1800flowers.com/</DisplayUrl>
  <ModificationDate>1181631600</ModificationDate>
  <MimeType>text/html</MimeType>
</Result>
```

The parameters for this RESTful interface are documented here:

```
http://developer.yahoo.com/search/web/V1/webSearch.html
```

I find it interesting that there is a published W3C XML Schema published for the response:

```
http://search.yahooapis.com/WebSearchService/V1/WebSearchResponse.xsd
```

There are also API Kits for Yahoo! Search; you may find one for your favorite language. They are BSD-licensed:

```
http://developer.yahoo.com/download/
```

Yahoo! Images

The documentation for Yahoo!'s image search is at the following location:

`http://developer.yahoo.com/search/image/V1/imageSearch.html`

Note the sample search:

`http://search.yahooapis.com/ImageSearchService/V1/imageSearch?appid=YahooDemo&` ➡
`query=Corvette&results=2`

You can substitute your own key and search term. For example, you can use this:

`http://search.yahooapis.com/ImageSearchService/V1/imageSearch?appid=[YourAppId]&` ➡
`query=flower&results=2`

and receive an XML response similar to the following:

```
<?xml version="1.0" encoding="UTF-8"?>
<ResultSet xmlns:xsi="http://www.w3.org/2001/XMLSchema-instance"
  xmlns="urn:yahoo:srchmi"
  xsi:schemaLocation="urn:yahoo:srchmi http://api.search.yahoo.com/➡
ImageSearchService/V1/ImageSearchResponse.xsd"
  totalResultsAvailable="5446610" totalResultsReturned="2" firstResultPosition="1">
  <Result>
    <Title>Flower.jpg</Title>
    <Summary>Flower.jpg</Summary>
    <Url>http://home.mchsi.com/~gentle501/images/Flower.jpg</Url>
    <ClickUrl>http://home.mchsi.com/~gentle501/images/Flower.jpg</ClickUrl>
    <RefererUrl>http://home.mchsi.com/~gentle501/pages/Flower.html</RefererUrl>
    <FileSize>104755</FileSize>
    <FileFormat>jpeg</FileFormat>
    <Height>800</Height>
    <Width>771</Width>
    <Thumbnail>
      <Url>http://sp1.mm-a7.yimg.com/image/3966820083</Url>
      <Height>155</Height>
      <Width>149</Width>
    </Thumbnail>
  </Result>
  <Result>
    <Title>dca_sunshine_flower.jpg</Title>
    <Summary>Sunshine Flower Sunday, 14 Nov 2004 | Disneyland , Flora A flower taken➡
at Disney's California Adventure. Nikon D100 | 50mm f/1.4 D | 50mm | 1/250 sec |➡
f/2.5 | ISO 200 | 26 Jun 2004</Summary>
    <Url>http://www.disneymike.com/photoblog/dca_sunshine_flower.jpg</Url>

    <ClickUrl>http://www.disneymike.com/photoblog/dca_sunshine_flower.jpg</ClickUrl>

    <RefererUrl>http://www.disneymike.com/photoblog/archives/2004/11/sunshine_flower➡
.html</RefererUrl>
```

```
    <FileSize>311603</FileSize>
    <FileFormat>jpeg</FileFormat>
    <Height>635</Height>
    <Width>700</Width>
    <Thumbnail>
      <Url>http://sp1.mm-a4.yimg.com/image/2928630219</Url>
      <Height>136</Height>
      <Width>150</Width>
    </Thumbnail>
  </Result>
</ResultSet>
```

Yahoo! Local Search has a similar architecture:

```
http://developer.yahoo.com/search/local/V2/localSearch.html
```

Microsoft Live.com Search

Microsoft's Live Search APIs (`http://msdn2.microsoft.com/en-us/library/bb251794.aspx`) are SOAP-based. The WSDL for version 1.1 is as follows:

```
http://soap.search.msn.com/webservices.asmx?wsdl
```

The Getting Started Guide is located here:

```
http://dev.live.com/blogs/livesearch/archive/2006/03/23/27.aspx
```

You need to set up an API ID (or get an existing one) to use the service; you can do this at the following location:

```
http://search.msn.com/developer
```

If you have access to Microsoft Visual Studio, I recommend trying the code samples:

```
http://msdn2.microsoft.com/en-us/library/bb251815.aspx
```

There are Express editions of Microsoft Visual Studio that are available for a free download:

```
http://www.microsoft.com/express/
```

■**Note** In theory, because of the WSDL interface, you should be able to use Live.com in non-Microsoft environments. In practice, you will find it much easier to use Microsoft tools because the documentation and the samples are geared to those tools. To use other tools, I still refer to Microsoft tools to help me understand the important parameters.

The search parameters for the Live Search API are more complicated than those for the Google SOAP search because the former uses complex, nested types. As I described in Chapter 7, there are a variety of ways to invoke WSDL-described SOAP calls. Some generate language-specific bindings. The one I find the easiest to understand is the approach taken by such tools as the

WSDL/SOAP tools in XML Spy and oXygen: feed them the WSDL, and they determine the SOAP connection endpoint, the SOAPaction, and a template for the body. That combination of parameters allows you to call the method without resorting directly to any SOAP libraries.

■Note XML Spy and oXygen are not free, although you can try them for 30 days free of charge. I don't know of any freeware (except perhaps Eclipse) that makes it quite so easy to work with WSDL and SOAP.

The search parameters are confusing, and it is not at all clear which parameters are mandatory without studying the WSDL directly; it's also not clear what the valid parameters would be. For instance, I needed to study the following:

`http://msdn2.microsoft.com/en-us/library/bb266177.aspx`

to get help with the `CultureInfo` field to figure out that an acceptable value is en-US for American English.

Feeding the Live.com WSDL to XML Spy, you will get the following:

- Connection endpoint: `http://soap.search.msn.com:80/webservices.asmx`

- SOAPaction HTTP header: `http://schemas.microsoft.com/MSNSearch/2005/09/fex/Search`

- The following template for a SOAP request:

```
<SOAP-ENV:Envelope xmlns:SOAP-ENV="http://schemas.xmlsoap.org/soap/envelope/"
xmlns:SOAP-ENC="http://schemas.xmlsoap.org/soap/encoding/"
xmlns:xsi="http://www.w3.org/2001/XMLSchema-instance"
xmlns:xsd="http://www.w3.org/2001/XMLSchema">
  <SOAP-ENV:Body>
    <m:Search xmlns:m="http://schemas.microsoft.com/MSNSearch/2005/09/fex">
      <m:Request>
        <m:AppID>String</m:AppID>
        <m:Query>String</m:Query>
        <m:CultureInfo>String</m:CultureInfo>
        <m:SafeSearch>Moderate</m:SafeSearch>
        <m:Flags>None</m:Flags>
        <m:Location>
          <m:Latitude>3.14159265358979E0</m:Latitude>
          <m:Longitude>3.14159265358979E0</m:Longitude>
          <m:Radius>3.14159265358979E0</m:Radius>
        </m:Location>
        <m:Requests>
          <m:SourceRequest>
            <m:Source>Web</m:Source>
            <m:Offset>0</m:Offset>
            <m:Count>0</m:Count>
            <m:FileType>String</m:FileType>
            <m:SortBy>Default</m:SortBy>
            <m:ResultFields>All</m:ResultFields>
```

```
      <m:SearchTagFilters>
        <m:string>String</m:string>
      </m:SearchTagFilters>
    </m:SourceRequest>
  </m:Requests>
</m:Request>
</m:Search>
</SOAP-ENV:Body>
</SOAP-ENV:Envelope>
```

If you just enter a key and a search term, no search results will come back. To figure out which parameters in the SOAP request are required and the range of possible values, start by reading this:

`http://msdn2.microsoft.com/en-us/library/bb266182.aspx`

which distinguishes between the following required parameters:

- AppID: Your application key
- CultureInfo: Language and regional information that must be chosen from a list of possible values[3] (for example, en-US)
- Query: Your search term
- Requests: A list of SourceRequest values drawn from a set of possible values[4] (for example, Web, Ads, Image)

and the following optional parameters:

- Flags: One of None, DisableHostCollapsing, DisableSpellCheckForSpecialWords, or MarkQueryWord (None is the default value)
- Location: The latitude, longitude, and optional search radius for the search
- SafeSearch: One of Strict, Moderate, or Off (Moderate is the default value)

Here's a sample SOAP request that searches the Web for flower in the American English context:

```
<SOAP-ENV:Envelope xmlns:SOAP-ENV="http://schemas.xmlsoap.org/soap/envelope/"
xmlns:SOAP-ENC="http://schemas.xmlsoap.org/soap/encoding/"
xmlns:xsi="http://www.w3.org/2001/XMLSchema-instance"
xmlns:xsd="http://www.w3.org/2001/XMLSchema">
  <SOAP-ENV:Body>
    <m:Search xmlns:m="http://schemas.microsoft.com/MSNSearch/2005/09/fex">
      <m:Request>
        <m:AppID>[YOURKEY]</m:AppID>
```

---

3. `http://msdn2.microsoft.com/en-us/library/bb266177.aspx`

4. `http://msdn2.microsoft.com/en-us/library/bb266167.aspx`

```
      <m:Query>flower</m:Query>
      <m:CultureInfo>en-US</m:CultureInfo>
      <m:SafeSearch>Moderate</m:SafeSearch>
      <m:Flags>None</m:Flags>
      <m:Requests>
        <m:SourceRequest>
          <m:Source>Web</m:Source>
        </m:SourceRequest>
      </m:Requests>
    </m:Request>
   </m:Search>
 </SOAP-ENV:Body>
</SOAP-ENV:Envelope>
```

This shows how to do this with curl:

```
curl -H 'SOAPAction: "http://schemas.microsoft.com/MSNSearch/2005/09/fex/Search"'➥
-d '<SOAP-ENV:Envelope xmlns:SOAP-ENV="http://schemas.xmlsoap.org/soap/envelope/"➥
xmlns:SOAP-ENC="http://schemas.xmlsoap.org/soap/encoding/"➥
xmlns:xsi="http://www.w3.org/2001/XMLSchema-instance"➥
xmlns:xsd="http://www.w3.org/2001/XMLSchema"><SOAP-ENV:Body> <m:Search➥
xmlns:m="http://schemas.microsoft.com/MSNSearch/2005/09/fex"><m:Request><m:AppID>➥
[YOURKEY]</m:AppID> <m:Query>flower</m:Query><m:CultureInfo>en-US</m:CultureInfo>➥
<m:SafeSearch>Moderate</m:SafeSearch> <m:Flags>None</m:Flags><m:Requests>➥
<m:SourceRequest> <m:Source>Web</m:Source> </m:SourceRequest> </m:Requests>➥
</m:Request></m:Search></SOAP-ENV:Body></SOAP-ENV:Envelope>'
http://soap.search.msn.com:80/webservices.asmx
```

This will return a SOAP message with search results:

```
<?xml version="1.0" encoding="utf-8" ?>
<soapenv:Envelope xmlns:soapenv="http://schemas.xmlsoap.org/soap/envelope/"
  xmlns:xsd="http://www.w3.org/2001/XMLSchema"
  xmlns:xsi="http://www.w3.org/2001/XMLSchema-instance">
  <soapenv:Body>
    <SearchResponse xmlns="http://schemas.microsoft.com/MSNSearch/2005/09/fex">
      <Response>
        <Responses>
          <SourceResponse>
            <Source>Web</Source>
            <Offset>0</Offset>
            <Total>192000000</Total>
            <Results>
              <Result>
                <Title>Flowers, Roses, Plants, Gift Baskets - 1-800-FLOWERS.COM -
Your ... </Title>
                <Description>Florist and gift retailer and franchisor with more than➥
100 stores nationwide offering online purchasing of arrangements, plants, gift➥
baskets, confections and gourmet foods ... </Description>
```

```
                <Url>http://www.1800flowers.com/</Url>
            </Result>
            <Result>
                <Title>Flowers, plants, roses, &amp; gifts. Flower delivery with➡
fewer handlers ... </Title>
                <Description>Flowers, roses, plants and gift delivery. Order flowers➡
from ProFlowers once, and you&apos;ll never use flower delivery from florists➡
again</Description>
                <Url>http://www.proflowers.com/</Url>
            </Result>
[...]
            </Results>
          </SourceResponse>
        </Responses>
      </Response>
    </SearchResponse>
  </soapenv:Body>
</soapenv:Envelope>
```

OpenSearch

The A9 search engine (http://a9.com) created the OpenSearch protocol (http://www.
opensearch.org/Home) as a "collection of simple formats for the sharing of search results."

Many web sites have their own search boxes; many are also capable of creating RSS and
Atom feeds. OpenSearch is a set of extensions that can wrap existing search functionality, lever-
aging the feeds to create lightweight search APIs. The most prominent clients for OpenSearch
are the search plug-ins for Firefox 2 and Internet Explorer 7.

Let's get more concrete. One of the easiest ways to learn how to create a search plug-in is to
use the search plug-in generator at the Mozilla Mycroft project (http://mycroft.mozdev.org/
submitos.html).

Here I use http://blog.mashupguide.net as an example site for which I want to generate
a search plug-in. I go to the blog to type in a term (for example, **Yahoo**) to search on and see
what URLs come back:

http://blog.mashupguide.net/?s=Yahoo&searchsubmit=Find

I can then replace Yahoo with {searchTerms} to generate the search URL for the plug-in
generator:

http://blog.mashupguide.net/?s={searchTerms}&searchsubmit=Find

You are given the option to register your search plug-in. One of the great features of
the search plug-in wizard is its generation of OpenSearch documents. Here's the one for the
Mashupguide.net plug-in (http://mycroft.mozdev.org/installos.php/17890/orangeremix.xml):

```
<?xml version="1.0" encoding="UTF-8"?>
<OpenSearchDescription xmlns="http://a9.com/-/spec/opensearch/1.1/"
xmlns:moz="http://www.mozilla.org/2006/browser/search/">
  <!-- Created on Sun, 17 Jun 2007 17:08:21 GMT -->
```

```
<ShortName>MashupGuide.net</ShortName>
<Description>Search for info about mashups</Description>
<Url type="text/html" method="get"
template="http://blog.mashupguide.net/?s={searchTerms}&amp;searchsubmit=Find"/>
<Image width="16" height="16">
  http://mycroft.mozdev.org/updateos.php/id0/orangeremix.png
</Image>
<Developer>Raymond Yee</Developer>
<InputEncoding>UTF-8</InputEncoding>
<moz:SearchForm>http://blog.mashupguide.net/</moz:SearchForm>
<moz:UpdateUrl>
  http://mycroft.mozdev.org/updateos.php/id0/orangeremix.xml
</moz:UpdateUrl>
<moz:IconUpdateUrl>
  http://mycroft.mozdev.org/updateos.php/id0/orangeremix.png
</moz:IconUpdateUrl>
<moz:UpdateInterval>7</moz:UpdateInterval>
</OpenSearchDescription>
```

With the OpenSearch XML document in hand, you can then embed some JavaScript to let a user install the plug-in. The relevant method is `window.external.AddSearchProvider()`, which you find documented here:

- `http://msdn2.microsoft.com/en-us/library/Aa744112.aspx` (for Internet Explorer 7)

- `http://developer.mozilla.org/en/docs/Adding_search_engines_from_web_pages` (for Firefox)

You can get a list of search engine plug-ins here:

- `https://addons.mozilla.org/en-US/firefox/browse/type:4` (a popular list linked to from within the Firefox Manage Search Engine List widget)

- `http://mycroft.mozdev.org/dlstats.html` (the top downloads)

Note a caveat from `http://mycroft.mozdev.org/contribute.html`:

While the implementation of Sherlock [the legacy Apple search tool] in Mozilla-based browsers only supported GET requests, the introduction of OpenSearch has also allowed POST requests to be used but unfortunately this is not currently supported in IE7.

You can use the following WordPress plug-in to generate a search plug-in:

`http://inner.geek.nz/projects/wordpress-plugins/mycroft-search-plugin-generator/`

There is another half to the OpenSearch specification. If the search results that come out of the search engine are in RSS 2.0 or Atom 1.0 format, wrapped with special elements documented here:

`http://www.opensearch.org/Specifications/OpenSearch/1.1#OpenSearch_response_elements`

then the search results can be consumed and presented by search clients that support the OpenSearch protocol:

`http://www.opensearch.org/Community/OpenSearch_search_clients`

and by programming libraries that can use it:

`http://www.opensearch.org/Community/OpenSearch_software`

In other words, you can get lightweight APIs for these sources and build metasearch systems from them. In the specific case of WordPress search results, you can make WordPress into a full OpenSearch source using a WordPress plug-in, such as the following:

`http://williamsburger.com/wb/archives/opensearch-v-1-1`

Google Desktop HTTP/XML Gateway

If you find the Google Desktop useful, you might be glad to know that you can access results programmatically via an HTTP/XML gateway, documented at the following location:

`http://desktop.google.com/dev/queryapi.html#httpxml`

■**Note** There is also a COM-based interface in Windows, located at `http://desktop.google.com/dev/queryapi.html#registering`. The XML gateway works on Mac OS X in Google Desktop Mac 1.0.3+. The API is currently unsupported for the Linux version of Google Desktop.

On Windows, you get the query URL from the registry key using this:

`HKEY_CURRENT_USER\Software\Google\Google Desktop\API\search_url`

The query URL will be of the following form:

`http://127.0.0.1:4664/search&s={SECRETKEY}?q=`

You can get XML out by tacking on &format=xml. A sample query is as follows:

`http://127.0.0.1:4664/search&s={SECRETKEY}?q=bach`

This query returns the following (excerpted here):

```
<results count="447">

  <result>
    <category>web</category>
    <doc_id>247278</doc_id>
    <event_id>277975</event_id>

    <title>
      Eventful - Mountain View Events - Mashup Camp IV at Computer History Museum
```

```
    </title>
    <url>http://eventful.com/events/E0-001-002642665-0</url>
    <flags>259</flags>
    <time>128263024673430000</time>
 −
    <snippet>
    Add to Reddit Add to calendar Eventful calendar Add to Calendar: <b>Bach</b>
in San Francisco metro area Berkeley, California, USA My Events Add to
    </snippet>
 −
    <thumbnail>
      /thumbnail?id=6%5F76xk4cxwsgMBAAAA&s=KLp8LKWLzFxwQ25pvDi42EHVfTk
    </thumbnail>
 −
    <icon>
      /icon?id=http%3A%2F%2Feventful%2Ecom%2F&s=YtdjKx9s9jRBxC11CW7vm377nN0
    </icon>
 −
    <cache_url>
      http://127.0.0.1:4664/redir?url=http%3A%2F%2F127%2E0%2E0%2E1%3A4664%2Fcache%3➥
Fevent%5Fid%3D277975%26schema%5Fid%3D2%26q%3Dbach%26s%3DuSIdPgul9xWiUyUybC6Ko3XA2cI➥
&src=1&schema=2&s=uADtUWTU45Sf6jKTCjeexKOwxjY
    </cache_url>
  </result>
```

Summary

In this chapter, you learned the basics of using APIs for Google Ajax Search, Yahoo! Search, Yahoo! Image Search, and Microsoft Live.com for searching content on the Web. You looked at how you can use OpenSearch to wrap existing search functionality so that it can be accessed in search bars for web browsers. Finally, I presented an example of an API for desktop search by outlining the Google Desktop HTTP/XML gateway.

Creative Commons Legal Code

Attribution-NonCommercial-ShareAlike 2.5

Reprinted from `http://creativecommons.org/licenses/by-nc-sa/2.5/legalcode`

CREATIVE COMMONS CORPORATION IS NOT A LAW FIRM AND DOES NOT PROVIDE LEGAL SERVICES. DISTRIBUTION OF THIS LICENSE DOES NOT CREATE AN ATTORNEY-CLIENT RELATIONSHIP. CREATIVE COMMONS PROVIDES THIS INFORMATION ON AN "AS-IS" BASIS. CREATIVE COMMONS MAKES NO WARRANTIES REGARDING THE INFORMATION PROVIDED, AND DISCLAIMS LIABILITY FOR DAMAGES RESULTING FROM ITS USE.

License

THE WORK (AS DEFINED BELOW) IS PROVIDED UNDER THE TERMS OF THIS CREATIVE COMMONS PUBLIC LICENSE ("CCPL" OR "LICENSE"). THE WORK IS PROTECTED BY COPYRIGHT AND/OR OTHER APPLICABLE LAW. ANY USE OF THE WORK OTHER THAN AS AUTHORIZED UNDER THIS LICENSE OR COPYRIGHT LAW IS PROHIBITED.

BY EXERCISING ANY RIGHTS TO THE WORK PROVIDED HERE, YOU ACCEPT AND AGREE TO BE BOUND BY THE TERMS OF THIS LICENSE. THE LICENSOR GRANTS YOU THE RIGHTS CONTAINED HERE IN CONSIDERATION OF YOUR ACCEPTANCE OF SUCH TERMS AND CONDITIONS.

1. **Definitions**

   a. **"Collective Work"** means a work, such as a periodical issue, anthology or encyclopedia, in which the Work in its entirety in unmodified form, along with a number of other contributions, constituting separate and independent works in themselves, are assembled into a collective whole. A work that constitutes a Collective Work will not be considered a Derivative Work (as defined below) for the purposes of this License.

b. **"Derivative Work"** means a work based upon the Work or upon the Work and other pre-existing works, such as a translation, musical arrangement, dramatization, fictionalization, motion picture version, sound recording, art reproduction, abridgment, condensation, or any other form in which the Work may be recast, transformed, or adapted, except that a work that constitutes a Collective Work will not be considered a Derivative Work for the purpose of this License. For the avoidance of doubt, where the Work is a musical composition or sound recording, the synchronization of the Work in timed-relation with a moving image ("synching") will be considered a Derivative Work for the purpose of this License.

c. **"Licensor"** means the individual or entity that offers the Work under the terms of this License.

d. **"Original Author"** means the individual or entity who created the Work.

e. **"Work"** means the copyrightable work of authorship offered under the terms of this License.

f. **"You"** means an individual or entity exercising rights under this License who has not previously violated the terms of this License with respect to the Work, or who has received express permission from the Licensor to exercise rights under this License despite a previous violation.

g. **"License Elements"** means the following high-level license attributes as selected by Licensor and indicated in the title of this License: Attribution, Noncommercial, ShareAlike.

2. **Fair Use Rights.** Nothing in this license is intended to reduce, limit, or restrict any rights arising from fair use, first sale or other limitations on the exclusive rights of the copyright owner under copyright law or other applicable laws.

3. **License Grant.** Subject to the terms and conditions of this License, Licensor hereby grants You a worldwide, royalty-free, non-exclusive, perpetual (for the duration of the applicable copyright) license to exercise the rights in the Work as stated below:

a. to reproduce the Work, to incorporate the Work into one or more Collective Works, and to reproduce the Work as incorporated in the Collective Works;

b. to create and reproduce Derivative Works;

c. to distribute copies or phonorecords of, display publicly, perform publicly, and perform publicly by means of a digital audio transmission the Work including as incorporated in Collective Works;

d. to distribute copies or phonorecords of, display publicly, perform publicly, and perform publicly by means of a digital audio transmission Derivative Works;

The above rights may be exercised in all media and formats whether now known or hereafter devised. The above rights include the right to make such modifications as are technically necessary to exercise the rights in other media and formats. All rights not expressly granted by Licensor are hereby reserved, including but not limited to the rights set forthin Sections 4(e) and 4(f).

4. Restrictions. The license granted in Section 3 above is expresslymade subject to and limited by the following restrictions:

a. You may distribute, publicly display, publicly perform, or publicly digitally perform the Work only under the terms of this License, and You must include a copy of, or the Uniform Resource Identifier for, this License with every copy or phonorecord of the Work You distribute, publicly display, publicly perform, or publicly digitally perform. You may not offer or impose any terms on the Work that alter or restrict the terms of this License or the recipients' exercise of the rights granted hereunder. You may not sublicense the Work. You must keep intact all notices that refer to this License and to the disclaimer of warranties. You may not distribute, publicly display, publicly perform, or publicly digitally perform the Work with any technological measures that control access or use of the Work in a manner inconsistent with the terms of this License Agreement. The above applies to the Work as incorporated in a Collective Work, but this does not require the Collective Work apart from the Work itself to be made subject to the terms of this License. If You create a Collective Work, upon notice from any Licensor You must, to the extent practicable, remove from the Collective Work any credit as required by clause 4(d), as requested. If You create a Derivative Work, upon notice from any Licensor You must, to the extent practicable, remove from the Derivative Work any credit as required by clause 4(d), as requested.

b. You may distribute, publicly display, publicly perform, or publicly digitally perform a Derivative Work only under the terms of this License, a later version of this License with the same License Elements as this License, or a Creative Commons iCommons license that contains the same License Elements as this License (e.g. Attribution-NonCommercial-ShareAlike 2.5 Japan). You must include a copy of, or the Uniform Resource Identifier for, this License or other license specified in the previous sentence with every copy or phonorecord of each Derivative Work You distribute, publicly display, publicly perform, or publicly digitally perform. You may not offer or impose any terms on the Derivative Works that alter or restrict the terms of this License or the recipients' exercise of the rights granted hereunder, and You must keep intact all notices that refer to this License and to the disclaimer of warranties. You may not distribute, publicly display, publicly perform, or publicly digitally perform the Derivative Work with any technological measures that control access or use of the Work in a manner inconsistent with the terms of this License Agreement. The above applies to the Derivative Work as incorporated in a Collective Work, but this does not require the Collective Work apart from the Derivative Work itself to be made subject to the terms of this License.

c. You may not exercise any of the rights granted to You in Section 3 above in any manner that is primarily intended for or directed toward commercial advantage or private monetary compensation. The exchange of the Work for other copyrighted works by means of digital file-sharing or otherwise shall not be considered to be intended for or directed toward commercial advantage or private monetary compensation, provided there is no payment of any monetary compensation in connection with the exchange of copyrighted works.

d. If you distribute, publicly display, publicly perform, or publicly digitally perform the Work or any Derivative Works or Collective Works, You must keep intact all copyright notices for the Work and provide, reasonable to the medium or means You are utilizing: (i) the name of the Original Author (or pseudonym, if applicable) if supplied, and/or (ii) if the Original Author and/or Licensor designate another party or parties (e.g. a sponsor institute, publishing entity, journal) for attribution in Licensor's copyright notice, terms of service or by other reasonable means, the name of such party or parties; the title of the Work if supplied; to the extent reasonably practicable, the Uniform Resource Identifier, if any, that Licensor specifies to be associated with the Work, unless such URI does not refer to the copyright notice or licensing information for the Work; and in the case of a Derivative Work, a credit identifying the use of the Work in the Derivative Work (e.g., "French translation of the Work by Original Author," or "Screenplay based on original Work by Original Author"). Such credit may be implemented in any reasonable manner; provided, however, that in the case of a Derivative Work or Collective Work, at a minimum such credit will appear where any other comparable authorship credit appears and in a manner at least as prominent as such other comparable authorship credit.

e. For the avoidance of doubt, where the Work is a musical composition:

i. **Performance Royalties Under Blanket Licenses**. Licensor reserves the exclusive right to collect, whether individually or via a performance rights society (e.g. ASCAP, BMI, SESAC), royalties for the public performance or public digital performance (e.g. webcast) of the Work if that performance is primarily intended for or directed toward commercial advantage or private monetary compensation.

ii. **Mechanical Rights and Statutory Royalties**. Licensor reserves the exclusive right to collect, whether individually or via a music rights agency or designated agent (e.g. Harry Fox Agency), royalties for any phonorecord You create from the Work ("cover version") and distribute, subject to the compulsory license created by 17 USC Section 115 of the US Copyright Act (or the equivalent in other jurisdictions), if Your distribution of such cover version is primarily intended for or directed toward commercial advantage or private monetary compensation.

f. **Webcasting Rights and Statutory Royalties**. For the avoidance of doubt, where the Work is a sound recording, Licensor reserves the exclusive right to collect, whether individually or via a performance-rights society (e.g. SoundExchange), royalties for the public digital performance (e.g. webcast) of the Work, subject to the compulsory license created by 17 USC Section 114 of the US Copyright Act (or the equivalent in other jurisdictions), if Your public digital performance is primarily intended for or directed toward commercial advantage or private monetary compensation.

5. **Representations, Warranties and Disclaimer**

UNLESS OTHERWISE MUTUALLY AGREED TO BY THE PARTIES IN WRITING, LICENSOR OFFERS THE WORK AS-IS AND MAKES NO REPRESENTATIONS OR WARRANTIES OF ANY KIND CONCERNING THE WORK, EXPRESS, IMPLIED, STATUTORY OR OTHERWISE, INCLUDING, WITHOUT LIMITATION, WARRANTIES OF TITLE, MERCHANTIBILITY, FITNESS FOR A PARTICULAR PURPOSE, NONINFRINGEMENT, OR THE ABSENCE OF LATENT OR OTHER DEFECTS, ACCURACY, OR THE PRESENCE OF ABSENCE OF

ERRORS, WHETHER OR NOT DISCOVERABLE. SOME JURISDICTIONS DO NOT ALLOW THE EXCLUSION OF IMPLIED WARRANTIES, SO SUCH EXCLUSION MAY NOT APPLY TO YOU.

6. **Limitation on Liability.** EXCEPT TO THE EXTENT REQUIRED BY APPLICABLE LAW, IN NO EVENT WILL LICENSOR BE LIABLE TO YOU ON ANY LEGAL THEORY FOR ANY SPECIAL, INCIDENTAL, CONSEQUENTIAL, PUNITIVE OR EXEMPLARY DAMAGES ARISING OUT OF THIS LICENSE OR THE USE OF THE WORK, EVEN IF LICENSOR HAS BEEN ADVISED OF THE POSSIBILITY OF SUCH DAMAGES.

7. **Termination**

   a. This License and the rights granted hereunder will terminate automatically upon any breach by You of the terms of this License. Individuals or entities who have received Derivative Works or Collective Works from You under this License, however, will not have their licenses terminated provided such individuals or entities remain in full compliance with those licenses. Sections 1, 2, 5, 6, 7, and 8 will survive any termination of this License.

   b. Subject to the above terms and conditions, the license granted here is perpetual (for the duration of the applicable copyright in the Work). Notwithstanding the above, Licensor reserves the right to release the Work under different license terms or to stop distributing the Work at any time; provided, however that any such election will not serve to withdraw this License (or any other license that has been, or is required to be, granted under the terms of this License), and this License will continue in full force and effect unless terminated as stated above.

8. **Miscellaneous**

   a. Each time You distribute or publicly digitally perform the Work or a Collective Work, the Licensor offers to the recipient a license to the Work on the same terms and conditions as the license granted to You under this License.

   b. Each time You distribute or publicly digitally perform a Derivative Work, Licensor offers to the recipient a license to the original Work on the same terms and conditions as the license granted to You under this License.

   c. If any provision of this License is invalid or unenforceable under applicable law, it shall not affect the validity or enforceability of the remainder of the terms of this License, and without further action by the parties to this agreement, such provision shall be reformed to the minimum extent necessary to make such provision valid and enforceable.

   d. No term or provision of this License shall be deemed waived and no breach consented to unless such waiver or consent shall be in writing and signed by the party to be charged with such waiver or consent.

   e. This License constitutes the entire agreement between the parties with respect to the Work licensed here. There are no understandings, agreements or representations with respect to the Work not specified here. Licensor shall not be bound by any additional provisions that may appear in any communication from You. This License may not be modified without the mutual written agreement of the Licensor and You.

Creative Commons is not a party to this License, and makes no warranty whatsoever in connection with the Work. Creative Commons will not be liable to You or any party on any legal theory for any damages whatsoever, including without limitation any general, special, incidental or consequential damages arising in connection to this license. Notwithstanding the foregoing two (2) sentences, if Creative Commons has expressly identified itself as the Licensor hereunder, it shall have all rights and obligations of Licensor.

Except for the limited purpose of indicating to the public that the Work is licensed under the CCPL, neither party will use the trademark "Creative Commons" or any related trademark or logo of Creative Commons without the prior written consent of Creative Commons. Any permitted use will be in compliance with Creative Commons' then-current trademark usage guidelines, as may be published on its website or otherwise made available upon request from time to time.

Creative Commons may be contacted at `http://creativecommons.org/`.

Index

Special Characters

You Need the Companion eBook

Your purchase of this book entitles you to buy the companion PDF-version eBook for only $10. Take the weightless companion with you anywhere.

We believe this Apress title will prove so indispensable that you'll want to carry it with you everywhere, which is why we are offering the companion eBook (in PDF format) for $10 to customers who purchase this book now. Convenient and fully searchable, the PDF version of any content-rich, page-heavy Apress book makes a valuable addition to your programming library. You can easily find and copy code—or perform examples by quickly toggling between instructions and the application. Even simultaneously tackling a donut, diet soda, and complex code becomes simplified with hands-free eBooks!

Once you purchase your book, getting the $10 companion eBook is simple:

❶ Visit **www.apress.com/promo/tendollars/**.

❷ Complete a basic registration form to receive a randomly generated question about this title.

❸ Answer the question correctly in 60 seconds, and you will receive a promotional code to redeem for the $10.00 eBook.

2855 TELEGRAPH AVENUE │ SUITE 600 │ BERKELEY, CA 94705

Offer valid through 8/25/08.